CONTROL AND DYNAMIC SYSTEMS

*Advances in Theory
and Applications*

Volume 52

CONTRIBUTORS TO THIS VOLUME

HAIM BARUH
HONG C. CHEN
V. H. L. CHENG
G. A. CLAPP
GIAN LUCA GHIRINGHELLI
JOSEPH P. GIESING
JEAN GROSSIN
MARC R. ILGEN
MASSIMILIANO LANZ
C. T. LEONDES
MATTI J. LOIKKANEN
ANTHONY E. MAJOROS
PAOLO MANTEGAZZA
PETER S. MAYBECK
P. K. A. MENON
TIMOTHY R. MOES
MARCELLO R. NAPOLITANO
SERGIO RICCI
GREGORY D. SIKES
JASON L. SPEYER
ROBERT L. SWAIM
D. D. SWORDER
GEORGE T. J. TZONG
ELAINE A. WAGNER
STEPHEN A. WHITMORE

CONTROL AND
DYNAMIC SYSTEMS

ADVANCES IN THEORY
AND APPLICATIONS

Edited by

C. T. LEONDES

School of Engineering and Applied Science
University of California, Los Angeles
Los Angeles, California
and
Department of Electrical Engineering
and Computer Science
University of California, San Diego
La Jolla, California

VOLUME 52: INTEGRATED TECHNOLOGY METHODS
AND APPLICATIONS IN AEROSPACE
SYSTEMS DESIGN

ACADEMIC PRESS, INC.
Harcourt Brace Jovanovich, Publishers
San Diego   New York   Boston
London   Sydney   Tokyo   Toronto

ACADEMIC PRESS RAPID MANUSCRIPT REPRODUCTION

Academic Press, Inc.
1250 Sixth Avenue, San Diego, California 92101-4311

United Kingdom Edition published by
Academic Press Limited
24–28 Oval Road, London NW1 7DX

Library of Congress Catalog Number: 64-8027

International Standard Book Number: 0-12-012752-0

PRINTED IN THE UNITED STATES OF AMERICA
92 93 94 95 96 97   BB   9 8 7 6 5 4 3 2 1

CONTENTS

CONTRIBUTORS

Numbers in parentheses indicate the pages on which the authors' contributions begin.

Haim Baruh (359), *Department of Mechanical and Aerospace Engineering, Rutgers University, New Brunswick, New Jersey 08903*

Hong C. Chen (117), *Douglas Aircraft Company, McDonnell Douglas Corporation, Long Beach, California 90846*

V. H. L. Cheng (391), *NASA Ames Research Center, Moffett Field, California 94035*

G. A. Clapp (513), *Department of Communications, Naval Oceans Systems Center, San Diego, California 92152*

Gian Luca Ghiringhelli (57), *Dipartimento de Ingegneria Aerospaziale, Politecnico di Milano, 20133 Milano, Italy*

Joseph P. Giesing (1), *Douglas Aircraft Company, McDonnell Douglas Corporation, Long Beach, California 90846*

Jean Grossin (435), *AEROSPATIALE, Aircraft Division, 31060 Toulouse Cedex 03, France*

Marc R. Ilgen (229), *The Aerospace Corporation, El Segundo, California 90009*

Massimiliano Lanz (57), *Dipartimento de Ingegneria Aerospaziale, Politecnico di Milano, 20133 Milano, Italy*

C. T. Leondes (229, 453), *Department of Electrical Engineering, University of Washington, Seattle, Washington 98122, and Department of Electrical Engineering and Computer Science, University of California, San Diego, La Jolla, California 92093*

Matti J. Loikkanen (1), *Douglas Aircraft Company, McDonnell Douglas Corporation, Long Beach, California 90846*

Anthony E. Majoros (117), *Douglas Aircraft Company, McDonnell Douglas Corporation, Long Beach, California 90846*

Paolo Mantegazza (57), *Dipartimento de Ingegneria Aerospaziale, Politecnico di Milano, 20133 Milano, Italy*

Peter S. Maybeck (291), *Department of Electrical Engineering, Air Force Institute of Technology/ENG, Wright-Patterson AFB, Ohio 45433*

P. K. A. Menon (391), *Optimal Synthesis, Palo Alto, California 94303*

Timothy R. Moes (453), *NASA Ames Research Center, Dryden Flight Research Facility, Edwards, California 93523*

Marcello R. Napolitano (155), *Department of Mechanical and Aerospace Engineering, West Virginia University, Morgantown, West Virginia 26505*

Sergio Ricci (57), *Dipartimento de Ingegneria Aerospaziale, Politecnico di Milano, 20133 Milano, Italy*

Gregory D. Sikes (1), *Douglas Aircraft Company, McDonnell Douglas Corporation, Long Beach, California 90846*

Jason L. Speyer (229), *School of Engineering and Applied Science, University of California, Los Angeles, Los Angeles, California 90024*

Robert L. Swaim (155), *School of Mechanical and Aerospace Engineering, Oklahoma State University, Stillwater, Oklahoma 74078*

D. D. Sworder (513), *Department of AMES, University of California, San Diego, La Jolla, California 92093*

George T. J. Tzong (1), *Douglas Aircraft Company, McDonnell Douglas Corporation, Long Beach, California 90846*

Elaine A. Wagner (321), *General Dynamics, Fort Worth, Texas 76101*

Stephen A. Whitmore (453), *NASA Ames Research Center, Dryden Flight Research Facility, Edwards, California 93523*

PREFACE

The modern era of aviation systems began with the end of World War II and accelerated further with the introduction of jet propulsion in military and commercial aircraft. The launch of *Sputnik* marked the beginning of the space age and all the many remarkable achievements that followed thereafter. As a result, the term aerospace systems, to include both aeronautical and space systems, was introduced.

The past decade has seen the strong rise of another trend, namely, the fuller systems integration of the various technologies utilized in aerospace systems, including propulsion, structures, flight control, avionics, man–machine interfaces, etc. These system integration techniques and their applications will continue to grow and expand in increasingly effective ways in future aerospace systems. The implications are many, including increased reliability, safety, efficiency, cost effectiveness, and expanded systems capabilities. As a result, this is a particularly appropriate time to treat the issue of aerospace systems integration techniques in this international series. Thus, this volume is devoted to the most timely theme of "Integrated Technology Methods and Applications in Aerospace Systems Design."

The first contribution to this volume is "Integrated Technologies in Aircraft Design Optimization," by George T. J. Tzong, Gregory D. Sikes, Matti J. Loikkanen, and Joseph P. Giesing. It presents techniques for the automation and integration of the different analysis and design disciplines and associated computer programs so that aircraft structural design can be completed by the utilization of a unified, multidisciplinary design system with only one analysis model. It is a most appropriate contribution with which to begin this volume.

The next contribution is "Active Flutter Suppression Techniques in Aircraft Wings," by Gian Luca Ghiringhelli, Massimiliano Lanz, Paolo Mantegazza, and Sergio Ricci. It introduces techniques for the suppression of aircraft wing flutter through the utilization of active control techniques which, in turn, result in aircraft weight saving and improved aircraft structural efficiency.

The next contribution is "Techniques in the Design of Aircraft for Maintainability," by Anthony E. Majoros and Hong C. Chen. It provides techniques for facilitating the maintenance of aircraft as a result of the early and deliberate attention during the design phase to aircraft characteristics that simplify maintenance.

The next contribution is "New Techniques for Aircraft Flight Control Reconfiguration," by Marcello R. Napolitano and Robert L. Swaim. In the event of damage or failure of an aircraft flight control system or control surface, the human operator may not be able to react quickly enough to deal with this situation. This contribution presents techniques for automatic aircraft flight control reconfiguration in order to deal instantly with aircraft damage or failure.

The next contribution is "Robust Approximate Optimal Guidance Strategies for Aeroassisted Plane Change Missions: A Game Theoretic Approach," by Marc R. Ilgen, Jason L. Speyer, and C. T. Leondes. It provides techniques for the development of effective guidance strategies in an uncertain environment, such as would occur in interplanetary exploration such as a Mars landing vehicle.

The next contribution is "Application of Multiple Model Adaptive Algorithms to Reconfigurable Flight Control," by Peter S. Maybeck. It introduces techniques for the development of aircraft flight control systems with reconfiguration capabilities based on detection and isolation of failures of sensors and/or activators and then employing controller algorithms that have been specifically designed for the current failure mode status.

The next contribution is "Techniques for On-Board Automatic Aid and Advisory for Pilots of Control Impaired Aircraft," by Elaine A. Wagner. It discusses techniques with respect to the significant role that expert systems can play in the case of control impaired aircraft.

The next contribution is "Placement of Sensors and Actuators in Structural Control," by Haim Baruh. It presents techniques for the determination of how many sensors and actuators should be used to implement control action and where these sensors, actuators, and their backups should be placed with respect to aerospace vehicle systems structural dynamics.

The next contribution is "Minimum-Exposure Near-Terrain Flight Trajectories," by P. K. A. Menon and V. H. L. Cheng. It introduces techniques for the development of optimal trajectories for rotorcraft penetrating unfriendly environments utilizing NOE (nap-of-the-earth) flight trajectories in order to achieve survivability.

The next contribution is "Technology Integration in Advanced Commercial Aircraft Cockpits and Operational Systems," by Jean Grossin. It presents a retrospective of, the status of, and trends in technology integration in commercial aircraft cockpits and operational systems while illustrating the great significance and power of technology integration in modern commercial aircraft.

The next contribution is "Development of a Pneumatic High-Angle-of-Attack Flush Airdata Sensing (HI-FADS) System," by Stephen A. Whitmore,

Timothy R. Moes, and C. T. Leondes. It provides techniques for noninvasive air data measurement systems that will be of significance in future flight control systems.

The final contribution to this volume is "Command, Control and Communications: The Human Role in Military C^3 Systems," by G. A. Clapp and D. D. Sworder. It illustrates some of the modeling issues that arise in C^3 systems and examines aspects of C^3 communication networks and the human decision-makers that underlie the effectiveness of C^3 systems.

This volume rather clearly manifests the significance and power of integrated technology methods and applications in aerospace systems design. The coauthors are all to be commended for their splendid contributions to this volume, which will provide a significant reference source for workers on the international scene for years to come.

Integrated Technologies in
Aircraft Design Optimization

George T.J. Tzong
Gregory D. Sikes
Matti J. Loikkanen
Joseph P. Giesing

Douglas Aircraft Company
McDonnell Douglas Corporation
Long Beach, California 90846

I. INTRODUCTION

Aircraft structural design and related product development is a complicated process which requires interaction among various design disciplines including static strength, flutter, dynamics, loads, aeroservoelasticity, etc. Currently, this interaction is taken into account in "series", in which each discipline receives its required data from previous groups and supplies its results as input to subsequent groups. Several iterations through all disciplines are required to converge the design since all disciplines influence one another. Frequently, the quality and accuracy of the results from the diverse disciplines are compromised because of the inconsistent modelling practices and insufficient communication between the groups. Furthermore, as many iterations are required, a tremendous amount of labor and time is involved. In order to improve this process and to reduce the design cycle time, different analysis and design disciplines and associated computer programs should be integrated and automated so that the aircraft structural design can be completed using a unified, multidisciplinary design system with only one analysis model.

Considering the recent advances in computational methods and computer hardware and recognizing the shortcomings in the present design process, the development of an aeroelastic design optimization program, ADOP, has been undertaken at the Douglas Aircraft Company of the McDonnell Douglas Corporation. ADOP is being developed for efficient static, dynamic, and aeroelastic optimization of large, finite element, aircraft structural models. The program optimizes the models to achieve a minimum weight while simultaneously satisfying all structural performance requirements. ADOP incorporates recent advances in areas such as finite element formulation, equation solving, dynamic modes and flutter. It is a self-contained computer system and does not rely on any existing structural analysis software [1,2]. The program is modularized by discipline and logical tasks. The modules are then linked together through a master control program and data base system [3]. Current modules include finite element bulk data translation, matrix abstraction computations, global matrix assembly and equation solving, large order eigenvalue and eigenvector extraction, fully stressed design, flutter analysis, dynamic transient response, design sensitivity calculation, design variable linking, and multidisciplinary optimization. Case control logic is established to guide analysis and design flow and access appropriate discipline modules. Also, the ADOP system is readily expandable to accommodate new developments in other structural related areas such as risk and reliability analysis.

Presently, multidisciplinary design in ADOP optimizes aircraft structural models subject to stress, displacement, modal frequency and flutter constraints. Static strength optimization ensures that the stresses are below the allowable values and the structural stiffness meets the deformation requirements subject to the design loads. Fully stressed design resizes each finite element using the ratio between actual and allowable stresses. The resulting model is then used in the more rigorous numerical optimization. Frequency constraints prevent the structural vibration modes from falling into a specific range of frequencies.

Aeroelasticity and loads are important factors for the aircraft structural design. Because of the strong interaction between structural stiffness and loads, the optimized weight solution cannot be achieved without considering this interaction. Control surface effectiveness is also an essential aeroelastic design constraint that must be included.

Flutter analysis of a transport aircraft is conventionally performed using simple beam-stick models. A three dimensional finite element model for static analysis is converted into a beam model by representing the wing and fuselage cross sections by the cross-section properties (EI and GJ) of an equivalent beam. This conversion usually results in a stiffer structure than the original finite element model. Moreover, the relationship between the finite elements and the associated EI and GJ are not always clearly defined. This leads to complications in the design sensitivity calculation and optimization. It is more straightforward to use the three dimensional finite element model for all the strength, dynamic modal and flutter design and analysis. The change in any element dimension is therefore directly reflected in the flutter speed, frequency and structural stresses. In ADOP all design sensitivities are analytically computed to reduce the possibility for numerical errors and also to increase computational efficiency.

An efficient data management system is obviously required to transfer a large amount of data between disciplines. Currently, a typical transport aircraft is represented with up to 50,000 degrees of freedom (DOF) at the advanced design level and in excess of 500,000 DOF in the production phase. The system therefore has to allow for the manipulation of very large arrays associated with large structural models, and should be very general and able to cope with the increasing demands on computing capacity. A data base management system ADACS (ADOP disk and core system) [3], is developed. ADACS uses a dynamic memory and file allocation scheme to store and retrieve data. Arrays are accessed by name and qualifier. The computer central memory is partitioned into named arrays and dynamically managed by ADACS.

An ADOP control language (ACL) [4] is developed to access discipline modules, perform matrix operations, and establish logical looping and branching. The language provides flexibility in design and analysis in such a way that users can select necessary discipline modules for their needs. Graphical data display is preferred over manual searches through thousands of pages of hard copy print-out. A graphical interface program is implemented to perform intermediate and post processing associated with the analysis and design optimization.

This chapter summarizes the technologies of multidisciplinary design optimization of aircraft structures currently included or being implemented in ADOP. These technologies, including numerical optimization, design variable linking, static strength, aeroelastic loads, modal analysis, dynamic transient response and flutter analysis, are described in separate sections. Numerical examples are provided along with individual sections. Conclusions regarding the application of the multidisciplinary design program and remarks on the future development are also presented.

II. NUMERICAL OPTIMIZATION

Aircraft design optimization is in fact a constrained minimization problem. Structural design variables are determined so as to minimize the aircraft weight

$$F(\underset{\sim}{D}) \tag{1}$$

subject to the performance and sizing constraints

$$G_j(\underset{\sim}{D}) \leq 0 \qquad j = 1, ..., M$$
$$D_I^L \leq D_I \leq D_I^U \qquad I = 1, ..., N \tag{2}$$

where F is the structural weight or objective function; G_j is the jth performance constraint; and D_I is the Ith design variable. D_I^L and D_I^U are the lower and upper bounds of D_I.

In the design optimization both the objective and constraint functions change with respect to the structural design. The weight design sensitivities (i.e. the change of weight to the change of design variables) are constant in a sizing problem and are simply proportional to the panel areas or the stringer lengths. The constraint design sensitivities are much more involved and are described in the following sections.

In the optimization process, a numerical search is performed to locate the new design in a multi-dimensional design space spanned by all structural design variables and dictated by the design variable bounds. Many linear or nonlinear optimization methods could be used. However, the selection of an appropriate method depends on the nature of the problem and the overall cost of the numerical search. For a large finite-element model, it is very expensive to compute higher (than the first) order design sensitivities. For example, the computation of the second order design sensitivity of frequency requires the decomposition of a modified stiffness matrix [5] for every single design variable. ADOP employs the method of modified feasible directions [6]. This method determines a new design along a search direction dictated by the objective and constraint function gradients and the side constraints. The new design is selected by obtaining a minimum weight with the least constraint violations. More details about the ADOP optimization are described in Section IX, A.

III. DESIGN VARIABLE LINKING

A finite element structural model is well suited for the design process, since finite elements are defined by size parameters such as thickness of plate and membrane elements, cross-section area of bar elements, or mass value and location of lumped mass elements. The influences of finite elements on the performance must be known when a particular constraint needs to be satisfied. However, it is unnecessary to retain each element size as an independent design variable. Also, the number of design variables is limited by the available computer resources. The number can be reduced by using a simple relationship of size properties in structures. For example, a long rod with a linearly varying cross-section area can be defined by the values at both ends; elements anywhere in the rod have cross-section areas defined as a linear combination of the two end areas. Similarly, in a panel region with a linearly varied thickness along the sides the four corner thicknesses can be used as independent design variables, and they in turn define the thickness of every panel element. This relationship, called "design variable linking" [7], is primarily based on the manufacturing constraints and users' design experience.

The finite elements, that can be represented by a few design variables and a shape function, are grouped together and their sizes are expressed as

$$\underline{t} = \underline{R}\,\underline{D} \qquad\qquad (3)$$

in which $\underline{t}$ is the element size vector, $\underline{R}$ is the ratio between $\underline{t}$ and the independent design variables $\underline{D}$. Additionally, the entries in the vector $\underline{t}$ are the basic sizes of elements such as the width and height of a rectangular beam cross section or the global orientation of a composite panel, which then define the element section properties, e.g. the areas and moments of inertia (A, I and J) of beams. Using Eq. (3) the number of independent design variables can be reduced to a reasonable level in the optimization process. The finite elements serve as a liaison between the design variables and constraint functions. The design sensitivities of disciplines with respect to independent design variables are then computed using the chain rule for derivatives as follows

$$\frac{\partial G_j}{\partial D_I} = \sum_{k=1}^{N} \frac{\partial G_j}{\partial t_k}\,\frac{\partial t_k}{\partial D_I} \qquad\qquad (4)$$

in which N is the number of elements associated with the design variable D_I.

A comprehensive design variable linking scheme is incorporated in ADOP. Ten different beam cross sections such as T, Z, I, etc., bending plates, offset lumped masses, membranes, shear panels and rods are resizable. In addition, fixed and free design variables for the same group are allowed so that, for instance, panels can maintain a minimum thickness while any additional thickness will be adjusted for best design. Constant, linear and bi-linear shape functions are presently used to define element size variation. A graphics program (described in Section X, C) is available to help users define the design variable groups. Users can view the finite element model and based on their experience define the design groups and the best linking for each group.

IV. STATIC STRENGTH

A. FINITE ELEMENT LIBRARY

Presently there are fourteen finite element types in ADOP to allow full modelling capability of complex aircraft structures. These are: 2-node axial bar, 2-node beam, 4-node quadrilateral plane stress element, 2-node spring, 8-node solid element, lumped mass element, 4-node quadrilateral shell, 3-node triangular shell, 3-node triangular plane stress element, quadrilateral shear panel, 4-node composite quadrilateral shell, 3-node composite triangular shell, and 3- and 4-node composite in-plane elements. Rigid connection elements, a general element (GENEL) and multiple point constraints (MPC) are also implemented to enhance the modelling capability. The stiffness and mass matrices are computed for all element types for unit size parameter (except the composites) such as thickness of membranes and area and moments of inertia of beams and stored in a disk file. In each design and analysis cycle, the matrices are retrieved and "scaled" by the real element size parameters before they are assembled into the global matrices or used in the design sensitivity calculation. Thus, they can be reused in each iteration with new design variables.

The beam and axial bar elements are the conventional types with two nodes and constant cross-section. Design variables for the bending beams can be the real dimensions of the cross-section, e.g. the flange thickness and height of a J-shaped beam, or more general the cross-section area and moments of inertia. Spring elements are provided for modelling convenience of special aircraft components like flap hinges, and the spring stiffness coefficients can be designed. The mass element, as the name implies, does not have stiffness associated with it; its design variables are the scalar mass value and offset from a node. It is needed to simulate the weight of non-structural components like rivets and heavy and relatively rigid structural components such as engines and landing gears.

The 3-node membrane and shell elements have constant thickness and homogeneous orthotropic material properties. The finite element formulation for the triangular elements is the classical displacement type with extra "bubble" functions [8] to improve the accuracy. Both the in-plane and bending 4-node quadrilateral finite elements are based on the stress hybrid formulation where two interpolation functions are used to compute the element matrices. Displacement interpolation is defined on the element boundary and stress interpolation is used inside the element [9]. Then, minimizing the potential (or Hellinger-Reissner) energy functional yields accurate finite element matrices. The isoparametric shape functions are used for the in-plane displacement interpolation and the cubic "beam" functions for the transverse and rotational displacements. There must be five in-plane stress functions and nine moment (generalized stress) functions in the transverse direction to ensure a full rank element stiffness matrix and the best overall performance. The 8-node solid element is implemented to model solid objects, but can not be resized in the optimization process. Like the quadrilaterals, the solid element uses the hybrid formulation.

The complications of the hybrid formulation are contained at the element level. The nodal degrees of freedom, material definition, etc., are the same as for any other finite element; therefore, the hybrid elements can be freely assembled with other element types.

There are four laminated composite element types in ADOP: 3-node and 4-node membrane elements and 3-node and 4-node bending type elements. The classical lamination theory is used throughout; the Kirchhoff-Love hypothesis stipulates that the stresses and strains perpendicular to the plate remain zero, the plane sections remain plane and the transverse shear strains are neglected. Since the aircraft composite structures are "thin", these assumptions are reasonable. Each ply can be independently oriented from the others. Membrane type elements must have a symmetric laminate stacking sequence, but otherwise there are no restrictions on the ply orientation or thickness. The stacking can be completely general for the bending elements and to comply with any constraints dictated by manufacturing process. Finite element nodal points are defined on a "reference surface" from which the offset of each ply is measured. Like their homogeneous counterparts, the 3-node elements use the displacement interpolation and the 4-node elements are based on the stress hybrid formulation. The membrane and bending actions are coupled. In-plane and out-of-plane interpolations are defined simultaneously and tied together via the six by six material constitutive matrix.

Element stress-displacement transformation matrices are also computed for unit size parameters like other element matrices. The hybrid formulation does not present any difficulties in the stress calculation: the matrix is just the shape function array evaluated at a given point and premultiplied by the material modulus matrix, it can be used for other purposes involving initial strain.

The element mass matrices for ADOP elements are computed from the displacement interpolation. Either the consistent or the "diagonal" mass matrix can be chosen.

B. STATIC ANALYSIS

The static analysis equation is written as

$$\underline{K}\underset{\sim}{u} = \underset{\sim}{p} \tag{5}$$

where $\underline{K}$ is the global stiffness matrix, $\underset{\sim}{u}$ is the displacement vector, and $\underset{\sim}{p}$ is the load vector.

The finite element stresses are computed as

$$\underset{\sim}{\sigma} = \underline{S}\underset{\sim}{u} \tag{6}$$

in which σ is the element stress vector, and $\underline{S}$ is the stress-displacement transformation matrix.

The stiffness matrix of large finite element models requires a large amount of disk and central memory; and the demand is rapidly increasing due to larger production models created for new and advanced aircraft. Because a lot of entries in the matrix are zeros and remain unchanged during solution, an envelope storage format [10] is employed by storing entries of each stiffness matrix column between the first nonzero entry and the diagonal term. Additionally, a nodal numbering technique [11] based on the wavefront method [12] is used to minimize the envelope size of the stiffness matrix. This technique symbolically performs the wavefront solution and leads to a nearly minimum size. Although, the matrix size has been minimized, it is still impossible to fit a large aircraft finite element model into the computer central memory. A blocking scheme is used to partition the large matrix into small blocks, each of which fits into half of the available central memory.

Singularities may be introduced to the model by use of rank deficient finite elements, i.e. thin plate-shells and membranes, or beam elements but with zero moments of inertia. A diagnostic routine is installed to automatically detect and conditionally remove any singularities due to missing stiffness. If a slightly curved surface is made of flat elements, spurious local vibration modes may be present. A criterion is included to restrain the out-of-plane, nearly singular DOF.

In ADOP, different loading conditions -- point, pressure, thermal, inertia, and any combination -- are included for analysis. The point loads can be from the integration of aerodynamic pressure, which are aeroelastic, i.e. a function of structural deformation. More details about the loads are given in Section V.

C. FULLY STRESSED DESIGN

ADOP uses the "fully stressed design" technique (FSD) to resize finite elements and obtain a nearly optimum solution for static strength before entering numerical optimization. This will reduces the number of iterations in the optimization. The process assumes that in the optimum structure each element is subject to the allowable stress under at least one applied load condition. The element sizes are each "scaled" by the ratio of the actual element stress to the allowable stress as

$$t_i^{(k+1)} = t_i^{(k)} \frac{\sigma_i^{(k)}}{\sigma_i^{\text{all}}} \tag{7}$$

where $t_i^{(k)}$ is the *ith* element size after *kth* FSD iteration, $\sigma_i^{(k)}$ is the corresponding stress, and σ_i^{all} is the element allowable stress.

The new element size is computed for all the applied load conditions, checked against maximum and minimum size limits, and the maximum permitted size is taken. If the structure is "statically determinant", subject to only one load condition, and has constant allowable stresses, the process will converge to the exact optimum in one iteration. However, in most cases several iterations are required for convergence because the load paths through structures change between iterations. There is no guarantee that the solution from fully stressed design will converge, but the result serves as a good start towards the optimum. Furthermore, the required number of iterations is not directly related to the problem's dimension, although it may depend on the degree of redundancy, model configuration and loadings. Three to six cycles usually suffice to bring the design to near optimum. The improved model from fully stressed design is then converted into independent design variables and used in the more rigorous numerical optimization.

The global matrix assembly, solution and the stress computations have to be performed in each FSD iteration and the structural weight is computed to monitor the progress. The process is usually stopped after a specified number of iterations.

The stress criteria in both fully stressed design and strength optimization include von Mises-Hill, principal stress, and maximum shear stress. Local panel buckling [13] and two-bay crack criteria [14] are also accounted for. All possible buckling conditions including skin buckling between stringers, overall stringer buckling, stringer crippling, and the torsional stability of a skin-stringer combination are checked. Buckling stress allowables are computed using either the Euler-Engesser equation or Johnson's parabola [15]. The two-bay crack stress criterion requires that the structural integrity be maintained even if the center stringer and skin of two bays are broken. The crack must be arrested by the stringers at both ends of the two bays.

The stress used in buckling design is defined in a presumed buckling direction. The two-bay crack criterion checks the tensile stress of the stringers and that parallel to the stringers in the adjacent skin panels. Different criteria also dictate the location of stress points. In a shell element the outer fiber stresses are checked against material and two-bay crack allowables. The in-plane stress (or the average stress across the thickness) is used for panel buckling design. After every FSD or optimization iteration, the panel buckling and two-bay crack stress allowables are updated according to the new element sizes.

In the fully stressed design each element is sized independently based on its stress state. This gives a discontinuity in the skin thickness and stringer areas, which would be difficult to manufacture. Because the design variable linking is used with FSD and because the linking is a better representation of the manufacturing requirements, the finite element sizes need to be converted into independent design variables. The least squares method is used to "smooth" the zig-zaging between element sizes. Due to the weighted averaging of least squares, this smoothing usually generates a design which is below the margin of safety [16]. However, the numerical optimization will consequently modify the design to comply with all performance requirements.

D. STATIC DESIGN SENSITIVITY

Both the stress and displacement constraints are used in the optimization. The stresses of finite elements are checked against specified allowable stresses depending on the element locations. For example, elements on the upper surface of a wing would be subject to compressive stress and possible buckling and those on the lower surface are in tension and have to satisfy the two-bay crack stress criteria. Structural deformations such as wing tip deflection or rotation may also be restrained. The stress and displacement constraints can be written as

$$G_s = \frac{\sigma}{\sigma_0} - 1 \le 0$$

$$G_u = \frac{u}{u_0} - 1 \le 0$$

(8)

in which σ can be the normalized von Mises equivalent stress or stress in a particular direction, depending on the stress criterion; u can be a displacement or rotation; and σ_0 and u_0 are the stress allowable and constrained displacement, respectively.

The displacement design sensitivities are computed using the direct gradient method as

$$K \frac{\partial u}{\partial D_I} = \frac{\partial p}{\partial D_I} - \frac{\partial K}{\partial D_I} u$$

(9)

where $\frac{\partial u}{\partial D_I}$ and $\frac{\partial p}{\partial D_I}$ are the displacement and load sensitivity vectors, respectively. The load design sensitivities are only present for loads associated with structural sizes such as thermal, inertia and static aeroelastic loads. $\frac{\partial K}{\partial D_I}$ is the design sensitivity of stiffness matrix, which is very sparse and only the entries associated with D_I are nonzero. In ADOP, $\frac{\partial K}{\partial D_I} u$ is performed element by element and directly added to $\frac{\partial p}{\partial D_I}$ to avoid the assembly of $\frac{\partial K}{\partial D_I}$ which would be very inefficient and requires a large amount of computer core and disk storage.

The stress design sensitivity is obtained from the displacement design sensitivity and the sensitivity of the stress-displacement transformation matrix as

$$\frac{\partial \underset{\sim}{\sigma}}{\partial D_I} = \frac{\partial \underline{S}}{\partial D_I} \underset{\sim}{u} + \underline{S} \frac{\partial \underset{\sim}{u}}{\partial D_I} \qquad (10)$$

in which $\dfrac{\partial \underset{\sim}{\sigma}}{\partial D_I}$ is the design sensitivity of the element stress vector, and $\dfrac{\partial \underline{S}}{\partial D_I}$ is the sensitivity of the transformation matrix.

The normalized equivalent stress in the von Mises criterion and its design sensitivity are expressed as

$$\sigma = \sqrt{\left(\frac{\sigma_x}{S_1}\right)^2 + \left(\frac{\sigma_y}{S_2}\right)^2 - \frac{\sigma_x \sigma_y}{S_1 S_2} + \left(\frac{\tau_{xy}}{S_{12}}\right)^2} \qquad (11)$$

and

$$\begin{aligned}
\frac{\partial \sigma}{\partial D_I} = \frac{1}{2\sigma}\Bigg[&\left(\frac{2\sigma_x}{S_1^2} - \frac{\sigma_y}{S_1 S_2}\right)\frac{\partial \sigma_x}{\partial D_I} \\
&+ \left(\frac{2\sigma_y}{S_2^2} - \frac{\sigma_x}{S_1 S_2}\right)\frac{\partial \sigma_y}{\partial D_I} + \frac{2\tau_{xy}}{S_{12}^2}\frac{\partial \tau_{xy}}{\partial D_I}\Bigg]
\end{aligned} \qquad (12)$$

where σ_x, σ_y and τ_{xy} are the element normal and shear stresses; and S_1, S_2 and S_{12} are their corresponding stress allowables.

V. AEROELASTIC LOADS

In the past, the role of loads and aeroelasticity has not been fully recognized in the design optimization process, thus neglecting additional, potential savings in design cycle time and weight. The following sections outline the loads and aeroelasticity in the design process. Emphasis will be given to subsonic transport wings whose structure strongly interacts with the loads and aerodynamics.

A. LOADS PROCESS AND OPTIMIZATION

The loads process may require the analysis of thousands of cases, including steady maneuvers, abrupt maneuvers, gusts, landing taxi conditions, flaps in different positions, various fuel and payload levels and combinations of these at every aircraft operating velocity, altitude and load factor condition. The number of cases is then reduced to approximately one hundred before the stress analysis. The final critical load cases (about 50) are identified in conjunction with the stress analysis.

The loads process must be iterative since the structure strongly influences the loads. A typical iteration starts with an assumed stiffness and weight distribution. The "aeroelastic" loads are then estimated based on these structural data. These loads are used to resize the structure and thus modify the stiffness and weight. New loads are recalculated based on the updated stiffness and mass and this cycle is repeated until convergence. This process is very labor and time intensive although it is usually conducted with a simplified structural beam model. The interaction between structure and loads, however, can be estimated more accurately and consistently with the three dimensional finite element model, so that the chordwise deformation of the wing is also considered.

Consider a subsonic transport wing undergoing a steady 2.5-g maneuver at a given velocity and altitude. The aircraft angle of attack is increased over its 1-g cruise value and trimmed by the elevator. The wing deforms from its cruise shape under the increasing load. Specifically the tip bends upward and, because the wing is swept backwards, induces a negative angle-of-attack in the streamwise direction in the outer wing. Also, the torsional deformation of the structure causes a counteracting positive angle-of-attack at the tip. The negative angle-of attack due to wing bending is generally larger than the positive angle-of-attack due to torsion. The wing therefore discharges some of the lift at the wing tip. Because of this aeroelastic loss of lift, the aircraft must be retrimmed to a higher angle-of-attack to maintain the 2.5-g lift condition. This will shift the spanwise center of pressure inboard and significantly reduce the bending moments along the wing span.

The viscous effects due to these elastic changes are also significant. A large transport can develop 8 to 10 degrees of negative tip twist which then changes the flow pattern from separated to attached flow with an attendant change in loads. The changes in loading due to changes in the flow regime can be as large as those due to twist itself.

Another important structural interaction with loads is the "jig shape" design. The jig, i.e. unloaded wing shape, must be recalculated each time the structural stiffness or weight is updated. For performance reasons, the span loading across the wing at the cruise condition must be as specified. This requires a specific twist configuration. This cruise condition twist cannot be used for aeroelastic load calculations; instead the jig twist shape is needed. This must be calculated by subtracting the increment in elastic twist, from the unloaded to cruise condition, from the cruise twist. Elastic twist is a function of stiffness and thus a function of the structural sizing. In essence, the jig shape which influences loads at all conditions, including the critical design conditions, depends upon the structural sizing and the cruise twist. All these effects have to be considered in the design optimization.

Since the aeroelastic loads are a function of structural stiffness, the possibility of reducing loads in the optimization by tailoring the stiffness distribution exists. Again, consider the steady 2.5-g maneuver of the subsonic transport. As the outer wing bending stiffness is reduced, from its baseline values, during the optimization the negative elastic tip twist increases under wing loading. Similarly, as the outer wing torsional stiffness is increased, the positive elastic twist decreases. The net result of these two changes is an increase in elastic negative wing tip twist, thus a reduction in the outer wing loading and bending moment -- and ultimately the weight.

The load sensitivities have to be used in the optimization to reduce the structural weight by load reduction. The sensitivities include the effects of the elastic deflections, modified aircraft trim and jig shape changes accompanying these deflections. These sensitivities are used to augment the displacement and stress sensitivities in Eqs. (9) and (10). The weight reduction, obtained by reducing loads, may be in the same order of magnitude as that obtained by direct optimization.

B. STATIC AEROELASTIC CONSTRAINTS

Static aeroelastic constraints are included in the structural optimization by requiring a specified control surface effectiveness (or reversal speed) and wing deflection (or divergence). For instance, the aileron of a transport aircraft must be effective enough (producing enough rolling moment) to trim a half degree of tip twist from each wing ($+0.5$ right wing, -0.5 left wing is a standard manufacturing rigging tolerance) using less than 5 degree of aileron. (Certain banking requirements may exist for a fighter aircraft which necessitates a specific aeroelastic effectiveness for the ailerons.)

A description of how elasticity influences control surface effectiveness is now given. When the aileron of a high aspect ratio aft swept wing is deflected it creates lift at its location; usually near the wing tip. This lift produces elastic up bending and nose-down twisting in addition to the desired rolling moment. Both the bending and twisting create an effective negative streamwise twist or angle-of-attack near the tip. This, in turn, reduces some of the lift created there and thus reduces the rolling moment. In other words, elasticity reduces the effectiveness of the ailerons. This reduction increases as the aircraft velocity (dynamic pressure) increases until eventually the effective rolling moment produced by the ailerons vanishes. This is termed reversal.

The aileron effectiveness and reversal speed are a function of structural wing stiffness; the stiffer the wing the more effective is the aileron and the higher the reversal speed. In some cases it is desirable to maintain a given aileron effectiveness by stiffening the structure. One measure of aileron effectiveness, $E/R = C_{l_{\delta_a}}^E / C_{l_{\delta_a}}^R$, is the ratio of aileron rolling moment for the elastic wing to that of the rigid wing. The ratio, or even the elastic rolling moment itself $C_{l_{\delta_a}}^E$, can be used as a static aeroelastic constraint in the structural optimization process. Actually any other aeroelastic coefficient that is appropriate or required can be used as a constraint, however, care must be exercised because large weight penalties can be incurred. For instance, if the rolling moment is specified during optimization and the aileron is undersized, the structure will be forced to compensate by increasing stiffness (and thus weight). This is very inefficient since the ratio

E/R approaches unity asymptotically as the stiffness becomes infinity. This results in large stiffness increase for small gain on E/R.

Reversal speed (i.e. aileron effectiveness, E/R, is zero) can be specified in lieu of aileron effectiveness. This speed is a function of stiffness and can be restrained in the optimization; but, one must be careful not to constrain the design with an unrealistically high reversal speed.

Wing deflection can be a constraint for swept back wings but generally it is of more concern for unswept or swept forward wings. Divergence is also more critical for other than swept back wings. For swept forward wings, divergence speed usually replaces flutter speed as the critical aeroelastic constraint. The divergence mechanism is caused by increasing the effective twist or angle-of-attack in the outer wing due to elastic bending and torsion. This increase amplifies the loading on the wing: the more flexible the wing the greater is the amplification. Also, the higher the speed (dynamic pressure) the greater is the amplification until the wing becomes unstable. Obviously divergence speed must lie outside the flight regime, and therefore, a constraint on divergence speed must be included in the design optimization process for both unswept and swept back wings.

Finally, the integration of loads, aeroelasticity and structural sizing is needed to reduce the design cycle time, weight and expense. Presently, ADOP is being developed toward this goal so that the optimization between structure, aeroelasticity and loads will be automated.

VI. MODAL ANALYSIS

An accurate and efficient modal analysis is essential to various dynamic evaluations of structures. In the past, a structure was either represented by a simple model with a few hundred DOFs or by a model whose size was significantly reduced using dynamic reduction techniques [1]. Today, analysis of large unreduced structural models is possible with powerful computers and advanced computing techniques, allowing accurate representations of dynamic behavior of structures and greatly reducing time and labor involved in defining and interpreting the simplified dynamic models.

ADOP incorporates two large-order modal analysis methods, the block Lanczos method [17,18,19] and accelerated subspace iteration [20,21]. Both methods are designed to directly extract eigenvalues and eigenvectors of large structural models.

A. SUBSPACE ITERATION AND LANCZOS METHOD

The subspace iteration uses a small subspace (in ADOP, eight vectors are used) and continuously updates the subspace to match the invariant one spanned by all the required eigenvectors. During the iteration procedure, converged eigenvectors are removed from the subspace and the iteration continues for the remaining eigenvectors. To accelerate the convergence, numerical techniques such as stiffness shifting and overrelaxation are incorporated.

The governing equation for modal analysis with stiffness shifting can be written as

$$(\underline{K} - \mu \underline{M}) \, \underline{\phi} \;=\; (\lambda - \mu) \, \underline{M} \underline{\phi} \tag{13}$$

where $\underline{K}$ and $\underline{M}$ are the stiffness and mass matrices of the structure, respectively; λ is the eigenvalue of the system; $\underline{\phi}$ is the corresponding eigenvector; and μ is the shift point.

Starting with an arbitrary subspace, $\underline{X}_1$, the subspace iteration algorithm in ADOP is written as follows:

(1) For $k = 1, 2, \ldots$, iterate from the kth subspace to the $(k + 1)$th subspace by solving

$$(\underline{K} - \mu \underline{M}) \, \overline{\underline{X}}_{k+1} \;=\; \underline{M} \, \underline{X}_k \tag{14}$$

where $\underline{X}_k$ is the matrix of vectors of the kth subspace, and $\overline{\underline{X}}_{k+1}$ is the matrix of intermediate vectors to be computed.

(2) Solve the eigenvalue problem of a projected system.

$$\underline{K}^*_{k+1} \, \overline{\underline{Q}}_{k+1} = \underline{M}^*_{k+1} \, \overline{\underline{Q}}_{k+1} \, \underline{\Omega}_{k+1} \qquad (15)$$

in which $\underline{K}^*_{k+1} = \overline{\underline{X}}^T_{k+1} \, (\underline{K} - \mu\underline{M}) \, \overline{\underline{X}}_{k+1}$ and $\underline{M}^*_{k+1} = \overline{\underline{X}}^T_{k+1} \, \underline{M} \, \overline{\underline{X}}_{k+1}$ are projectors of the stiffness and mass matrices; and $\overline{\underline{Q}}_{k+1}$ and $\underline{\Omega}_{k+1}$ are matrices of the eigenvectors and eigenvalues of the projected system.

(3) The new subspace is then updated as

$$\underline{X}_{k+1} = \underline{X}_k + (\overline{\underline{X}}_{k+1} \, \overline{\underline{Q}}_{k+1} - \underline{X}_k)\underline{\alpha} \qquad (16)$$

where $\underline{\alpha}$ is a diagonal matrix containing the overrelaxation factors. The factors are determined by the convergence rate of subspace vectors toward the corresponding eigenvectors [20].

Numerical error is a major problem in the accelerated subspace iteration. Due to the finite precision of computers, the converged eigenvectors close to the shift point may return to the subspace and disturb the search for subsequent eigenvectors. Gram-Schmidt orthogonalization could be used in every iteration to avoid the problem, but would be too expensive for large models. A simple numerical error correction scheme [21] was developed to monitor the return of converged eigenvectors to the subspace and perform the Gram-Schmidt orthogonalization against only selected eigenvectors in selected iterations.

In the Lanczos method a different kind of subspace is formed. The method generates new vectors and expands the "Lanczos subspace" step-by-step until the invariant subspace spanned by the required eigenvectors is enclosed. The block Lanczos method, which generates a small set of vectors in every step, is adopted in ADOP. The block size can be one vector, which represents the simple Lanczos method, or several vectors depending on the multiplicity of eigenvalues in the problem.

Starting with a set of random vectors $\underline{Q}_0$, the governing equation of the block Lanczos method is, for all steps $j = 1, 2, 3, ...,$

$$\underline{Q}_{j+1}\underline{\beta}_{j+1}^{T} = (\underline{K} - \mu\underline{M})^{-1}\underline{M}\underline{Q}_j - \underline{Q}_j\underline{\alpha}_j - \underline{Q}_{j-1}\underline{\beta}_j \qquad (17)$$

where $\underline{Q}_{j+1}$, dimensioned n by s, is the matrix of Lanczos vectors of the $(j+1)th$ step, n is the dimension of the finite element model and s is the number of vectors in a Lanczos block. In addition, $\underline{Q}_j$ is orthonormal with respect to the mass matrix ($\underline{Q}_i^T \underline{M} \underline{Q}_i = \underline{I} \delta_{ij}$ in which δ_{ij} is the Kronecker delta and $\underline{I}$ is the identity matrix). The coefficient matrices $\underline{\alpha}_j$ and $\underline{\beta}_j$, dimensioned s by s, are

$$\begin{aligned}
\underline{\alpha}_j &= (\underline{M}\,\underline{Q}_j)^T (\underline{K} - \mu\underline{M})^{-1} (\underline{M}\,\underline{Q}_j) \\
\underline{\beta}_j &= (\underline{M}\,\underline{Q}_{j-1})^T (\underline{K} - \mu\underline{M})^{-1} (\underline{M}\,\underline{Q}_j)
\end{aligned} \qquad (18)$$

where $\underline{\beta}_j$ is a lower triangular matrix.

Premultiplying Eq. (13) by $((\underline{K} - \mu\underline{M})^{-1}\underline{M}\underline{V})^T$, the eigenvalue problem is reduced to

$$\underline{T}\underline{y} = \frac{1}{(\lambda - \mu)}\,\underline{y} \qquad (19)$$

where $\underline{V} = \{ \underline{Q}_1, \underline{Q}_2, \underline{Q}_3, ..., \underline{Q}_j \}$ is the subspace spanned by all Lanczos vectors up to the jth step. Matrix $\underline{T} = (\underline{M}\,\underline{V})^T (\underline{K} - \mu\underline{M})^{-1} \underline{M}\,\underline{V}$ is symmetric and banded with the bandwidth of the Lanczos block size. $\underline{y}$ contains the multiplication factors for all Lanczos vectors and is obtained using inverse iteration. An eigenvector is then computed as $\underline{\phi} = \underline{V}\underline{y}$.

Similar to the accelerated subspace iteration, there are numerical problems associated with the Lanczos method: the return of converged eigenvectors and the duplication of Lanczos vectors. They exist because the generated Lanczos vectors contain the components of all eigenvectors and also the components of all Lanczos vectors. The components are amplified in every step, causing the numerical problems. To avoid an expensive full Gram-Schmidt orthogonalization (applied to each new Lanczos vector against all preceding vectors and all converged eigenvectors), two schemes are adopted. A selective orthogonalization scheme [18], which eliminates the returned eigenvectors, monitors the error growth and performs orthogonalization against only the eigenvectors corresponding to an unacceptable error term. A partial orthogonalization scheme [22] is designed to monitor the error growth in Lanczos vectors. Orthogonalization is then performed against a selected range of preceding Lanczos vectors to avoid the loss of orthogonality between the vectors.

In general, the block Lanczos method converges faster than the accelerated subspace iteration [19]. Its superiority, however, is diminished if frequent numerical error corrections are required. (In the subspace iteration the error treatment is more straightforward and less expensive.)

Several options exist in the ADOP modal analysis module for user requirements and to reduce computation: (1) The rigid body modes can be calculated independently by balancing the inertia force from the corresponding motion. (2) Users can request the lowest structural vibration modes or modes in a range of frequencies of interest. (3) Variable subspace and Lanczos block sizes can be chosen. A default size of eight vectors is used in the subspace iteration. The Lanczos block size can be from one to 15 vectors with a default size of seven. (4) If additional modes are required, the user can restart the modal analysis, assuming all related disk files for stiffness and mass matrices and eigenvectors from the previous run are saved. The module will automatically shift the stiffness matrix close to the first expected eigenvalue in the new run. (5) Either the consistent or diagonal mass matrices can be selected.

The full modal analysis methods require better modelling practices than the dynamic reduction methods. As mentioned in Section III, B, models with rank deficient elements may result in low frequency local modes which should be removed from dynamic and flutter analyses. ADOP automatically diagnoses and restrains the singular degrees of freedom. However, it cannot always resolve all singularities since many of them come from modelling errors. User training is the best remedy for these problems.

B. MODAL DESIGN SENSITIVITY

The frequency constraints allow engineers to restrain the structural vibration modes from falling into a specified range of frequencies. The constraints and the constraint gradients can be written as

$$
G_U = \frac{\lambda_i}{(2\pi f_{up})^2} - 1 \quad \text{and} \quad G_L = 1 - \frac{\lambda_i}{(2\pi f_{low})^2} \tag{20}
$$

and

$$
\frac{\partial G_U}{\partial D_I} = \frac{1}{(2\pi f_{up})^2} \frac{\partial \lambda_i}{\partial D_I} \quad \text{and} \quad \frac{\partial G_L}{\partial D_I} = \frac{-1}{(2\pi f_{low})^2} \frac{\partial \lambda_i}{\partial D_I} \tag{21}
$$

in which f_{up} and f_{low} are the upper and lower bounds of the frequency and G_U and G_L are their corresponding constraints. The eigenvalue λ_i can be restrained by either bound or both of them. $\dfrac{\partial G_U}{\partial D_I}$ and $\dfrac{\partial G_L}{\partial D_I}$ are the constraint gradients for upper and lower bounds, respectively; and $\dfrac{\partial \lambda_i}{\partial D_I}$ is the eigenvalue design sensitivity.

After the modes are computed, the eigenvalue design sensitivities [5] can be computed by differentiating Eq. (13) with a zero shift and premultiplying the resulting equation by the transpose of the eigenvectors. For eigenvalue λ_i with multiplicity m the design sensitivities are expressed as

$$
\left(\Phi_m^T \frac{\partial K}{\partial D_I} \Phi_m - \lambda_i \Phi_m^T \frac{\partial M}{\partial D_I} \Phi_m \right) \Gamma = \Gamma \frac{\partial \Lambda}{\partial D_I} \tag{22}
$$

where $\dfrac{\partial K}{\partial D_L}$ and $\dfrac{\partial M}{\partial D_I}$ are the design sensitivities of the global stiffness and mass matrices, respectively; and $\dfrac{\partial \Lambda}{\partial D_I}$ is a diagonal matrix with diagonal terms equal to the design sensitivities of the eigenvalue λ_i. Φ_m are the vibration modes and Γ are the eigenvectors of Eq. (22).

The frequency constraints can also be used in the system identification of dynamic characteristics of structures. A detailed finite element model does not guarantee an accurate representation of a structure. With this technique, being implemented in ADOP, the finite element design variables can be adjusted to match the analysis results to ground vibration test data. In this case the objective function would be the absolute difference between measured and computed results.

C. Numerical Examples

Two numerical examples are presented here to illustrate the modal analysis module. The first is a large transport model, as shown in Fig. 1, and has a detailed, three dimensional finite element wing and a beam representation of the fuselage and tail. It contains 9636 finite elements, 3027 nodal points and 9854 degrees of freedom. These elements include membranes, shear panels, rods, springs, bars, lumped masses and GENEL's. The wing alone has 9580 elements and 2854 nodal points. The engine and pylon are modeled by a lumped mass and a GENEL element, respectively. The first 25 modes were computed using the block Lanczos method and the eighth mode, second wing bending plus torsion, is shown in Fig. 2.

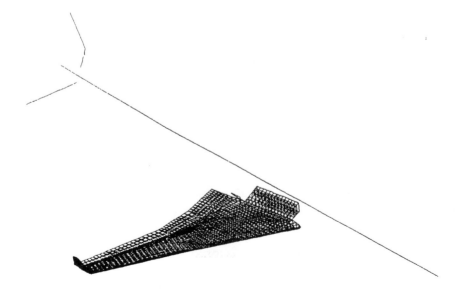

Fig. 1. Finite Element Model of a Large Transport Aircraft

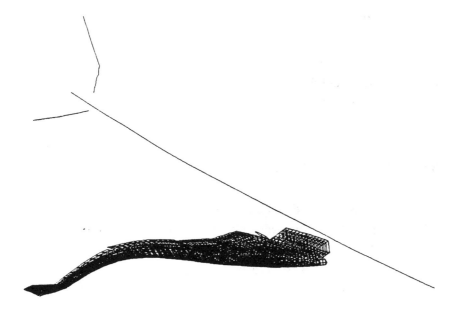

Fig. 2. Eighth Mode Shape of the Transport

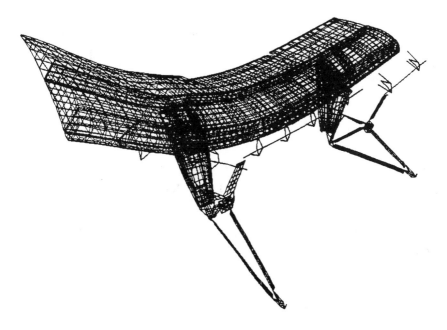

Fig. 3. First Bending Mode Shape of a Transport Flap Model

A 35,557 DOF transport aircraft inboard flap model is used as the second example. This model, including 12278 finite elements and 6411 nodal points, was solved for the first 20 modes using both the block Lanczos method and the accelerated subspace iteration. The results compared reasonably well with MSC/NASTRAN. Figure 3 illustrates the first flap bending mode shape.

VII. DYNAMIC TRANSIENT RESPONSE

Two independent time-domain transient response procedures are available in ADOP: Newmark-Beta and mode superposition [23,24]. Newmark-Beta is a direct integration method commonly used in evaluating the dynamic response of structures. The procedure is an implicit integration where the global equations of motion (below) are solved step-by-step in time.

$$\underline{M}\,\ddot{u} + \underline{C}\,\dot{u} + \underline{K}\,\underline{u} = \underline{p}(t) \tag{23}$$

in which $\underline{C}$ is the overall structural damping matrix primarily from the material viscosity and joint friction, $\ddot{u}$, $\dot{u}$ are the structural acceleration and velocity vectors, and $\underline{p}(t)$ is the time dependent load vector.

The advantages of this method are that it is unconditionally stable and also suitable for nonlinear dynamic analysis. The current scheme for Newmark-Beta integration in ADOP can handle matrices in both discrete and generalized (modal) coordinates. The matrices can be in the form of envelope, general (square), banded, or diagonal. The Wilson-θ scheme [23,24], a variation of the Newmark-Beta method, is also available to the user.

The mode superposition method, i.e. $\underline{u} = \sum_{i=1}^{n} \phi_i Y_i$, is ideal for linear structural systems. The basis of this approach is that the original set of equilibrium equations, in geometric coordinates, can be transformed to a reduced set of n uncoupled equations in generalized coordinates.

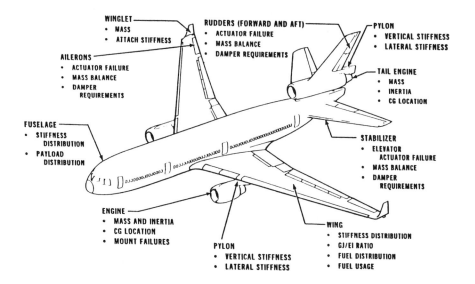

Fig. 5.   Flutter Design Parameters

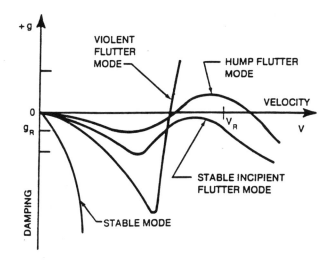

Fig. 6.   Mode Types in Flutter V-g Diagram

The ADOP flutter module is developed to perform (1) flutter analysis with a direct search for the flutter velocity and the matched air density, and (2) calculation of flutter design sensitivity for velocity and frequency. If the flutter performance is deficient, a new design will be determined using the design sensitivities to satisfy the flutter constraints with a minimum increase in weight.

A. ANALYSIS METHODS

Both the k and p-k flutter analysis methods are available in ADOP. The k-method flutter equation is written as

$$[\,\overline{K} - \lambda_m(\overline{M} + \overline{A})\,]\,U_m = 0 \qquad (25)$$

where $\overline{K}$ and $\overline{M}$ are the generalized, or modal, stiffness and mass matrices, respectively. Hysteretic damping can be incorporated in $\overline{K}$ using a modal damping ratio. λ_m and U_m are the complex eigenvalue and eigenvector of the aeroelastic system, respectively, and $\lambda_m = \omega_m^2/(1 + ig_m)$, where g_m is the damping of the system, ω_m is the circular frequency, and $i = \sqrt{-1}$ is the so-called imaginary unit. $\overline{A}$ is the generalized aerodynamic influence coefficient matrix, which is obtained by pre- and postmultiplying the discrete aerodynamic influence coefficient matrix by the splined mode shapes from the structural nodal points to the aerodynamic grid points. Two surface splining methods, the Harder spline [25] and a beam spline, and a motion axis linear splining method are adapted from Reference 26.

The above equation is usually solved step-by-step along the reduced velocity, $1/k$, axis. A flutter point, defined by modes with zero damping ratio, is obtained by interpolating the damping of the same mode between two $1/k$ values. However, this procedure is troublesome since the magnitudes of modal damping may switch from one step to another and the reduced velocity step size is not always sufficiently small to track the switching of modes. A direct numerical search for the flutter point using the information from a nearby reduced velocity is therefore better.

The ADOP flutter analysis module directly computes the flutter velocity and frequency using the Laguerre method [27,28]. The approximate locations of flutter roots are first identified in the step-by-step solution and only one root is allowed between two consecutive reduced frequencies. If more than one root is present, the step size will be automatically refined for that particular step until the roots are distinguished. The step size is then recovered for the subsequent calculation. The numerical search is performed using the derivatives of damping [29] as

$$(1/k)_{new} = (1/k)_{old} \pm \frac{g}{\sqrt{(g_{,1/k})^2 - g\, g_{,1/k1/k}}} \tag{26}$$

where $g_{,1/k}$ and $g_{,1/k1/k}$ are the first and second derivatives of damping with respect to reduced velocity, respectively. If there is more than one root, deflation is applied to avoid repeated detection of the same root. After the reduced frequency k is determined, the flutter velocity can be obtained as

$$V = \frac{\omega_m b}{k} \tag{27}$$

where b is a half of the reference chord length.

The governing equation of the p-k flutter analysis method is

$$\left[\overline{M} \frac{V^2}{c^2} p^2 + \overline{D} \frac{V}{c} p + \overline{K} - \frac{\rho_0 V^2}{2\xi^2} \overline{A} \right] U_m = 0 \tag{28a}$$

or

$$Q\, U_m = 0 \tag{28b}$$

in which $\underline{D}$ is the generalized viscous damping matrix, $p = k\,(g/2 + i)$, V is the true air speed (flutter speed), $\xi = \sqrt{\rho_0/\rho}$ is the air density ratio and ρ_0 is the air density at sea level. The modal damping ratio, g, computed by the p-k method is very close to the real damping of the aeroelastic system, but in the k-method this is only true when the damping is zero.

The flutter search is similar to that in the k-method and is initially carried out by stepping along the velocity axis, solving the complex eigenvalues for each velocity and identifying the approximate locations of flutter points. The eigenvalue solution of Eq. (28a) is performed with Muller's method [28,30] in a determinant search procedure with a rough initial estimate of roots. The flutter points are then found by

$$(V)_{new} = (V)_{old} \pm \frac{g}{\sqrt{(g_{,V})^2 - g\,g_{,VV}}} \tag{29}$$

where $g_{,V}$ and $g_{,VV}$ are the first and second derivatives of damping with respect to velocity, respectively.

The numerical search procedure requires that the aerodynamic influence coefficient matrix be a continuous function of the reduced frequency k. However, only the matrices of discrete k values are computed by an aerodynamic program. The continuous function is obtained by using a standard cubic spline through all discrete reduced frequencies for each entry in the aerodynamic influence matrix. The matrix of an intermediate reduced frequency is then obtained from the interpolation. The real and imaginary parts of the matrices are splined separately. Additionally, the magnitude of the imaginary part used in the splining is $\dfrac{A^I(k)}{k}$ rather than $A^I(k)$, since the former quantity is a much smoother function of reduced frequency than the latter. The derivatives of the aerodynamic matrix are simply formed from the derivatives of the spline function for each entry in the matrix.

It is appropriate to introduce an allowable damping g_G in the aeroelastic system to ensure a margin of safety for flutter. This prevents critical conditions such as a hump mode with a small negative damping from getting into the range of aircraft operating velocities. The small damping may result in high loads and structural fatigue. The allowable damping can be treated as a hysteretic structural damping in the k-method or as a direct safety damping in the p-k method. Now the critical roots in the p-k method are the crossing points between modal damping curves and the velocity axis at the damping ratio equal to g_G.

A search for the matched air density to match the airspeed to the lowest flutter velocity is necessary for establishing the flight envelope for flutter associated with the structure. The search is conducted after the flutter velocity associated with an initial air density is found. The numerical procedure is similar to that for the flutter velocity (Eq. 29).

B. FLUTTER DESIGN SENSITIVITY

In the ADOP flutter optimization a constraint is applied by imposing an acceptable flutter speed V_R as

$$G = 1 - \frac{V}{V_R} \tag{30}$$

If the constraint is not satisfied, the structural finite elements have to be resized to increase the flutter speed to meet the design requirement. The flutter sensitivity, necessary to determine the new design, is obtained by differentiating Eq. (27) with respect to design variable D_I as

$$\frac{\partial V}{\partial D_I} = \frac{b}{k_m} \frac{\partial \omega_m}{\partial D_I} - \frac{\omega_m b}{k_m^2} \frac{\partial k_m}{\partial D_I} \tag{31}$$

in which $\frac{\partial \omega_m}{\partial D_I}$ and $\frac{\partial k_m}{\partial D_I}$ are the design sensitivities of frequency and reduced frequency at flutter, respectively. In the k-method the two design sensitivities are computed by differentiating Eq. (25) and premultplying the resulting equation by the left eigenvector of Eq. (25). They are expressed as

$$\frac{\partial k}{\partial D_I} = -\frac{Im\left(\mu_I - \frac{s_I}{\omega_m^2}\right)}{Im(\bar{\alpha}_k)} \qquad (32)$$

and

$$\frac{\partial \omega_m}{\partial D_I} = -\frac{\omega_m^3}{2}\left[\frac{\partial k}{\partial D_I} Re(\bar{\alpha}_k) + Re\left(\mu_I - \frac{s_I}{\omega_m^2}\right)\right] \qquad (33)$$

where $s_I = \underline{V}_m^T \dfrac{\partial \overline{K}}{\partial D_I} \underline{U}_m$, $\mu_I = \underline{V}_m^T \dfrac{\partial \overline{M}}{\partial D_I} \underline{U}_m$ and $\bar{\alpha}_k = \underline{V}_m^T \dfrac{\partial \overline{A}}{\partial k} \underline{U}_m$; and $Re(.)$ and $Im(.)$ are the real and imaginary parts of the enclosed quantity. $\underline{V}_m^T$ is the left eigenvector. $\dfrac{\partial \overline{K}}{\partial D_I}$ and $\dfrac{\partial \overline{M}}{\partial D_I}$ are the design sensitivities of the generalized stiffness and mass matrices, respectively.

The calculation of $\dfrac{\partial \overline{K}}{\partial D_I}$ and $\dfrac{\partial \overline{M}}{\partial D_I}$ are performed element by element accounting for the design variable linking. Since the element stiffness and mass matrices are normalized to a size parameter, e.g. the thickness of a plate element, the generalized stiffness and mass matrices can also be normalized by pre- and post-multiplying the normalized element matrices by the matrix of structural vibration modes. The design sensitivity of the generalized stiffness or mass is then obtained by summing the products of the associated normalized, generalized element matrices and the design sensitivity of the size parameter as follows:

$$\frac{\partial \overline{K}}{\partial D_I} = \sum_{i=1}^{N} \frac{\partial x_i}{\partial D_I} \overline{K}_{x_i} \quad \text{and} \quad \frac{\partial \overline{M}}{\partial D_I} = \sum_{i=1}^{N} \frac{\partial x_i}{\partial D_I} \overline{M}_{x_i} \qquad (34)$$

where x_i is a size parameter of the *ith* element and is a function of design variable D_I. N is the total number of elements associated with the design variable in the model. $\overline{K}_{x_i}$ and $\overline{M}_{x_i}$ are the normalized, generalized element stiffness and mass matrices, respectively. The above computation is very efficient for homogeneous finite elements such as membranes, shear panels and rods, since $\dfrac{\partial x_i}{\partial D_I}$ is a constant. If the vibration modes from the previous iteration are used in the new iteration to reduce computation, the design sensitivities of the generalized matrices for membranes, shear panels and rods remain unchanged and the new generalized matrices can be easily obtained by summing up the product of the design sensitivities and D_I for all design variables.

In the p-k method $\dfrac{\partial \omega_m}{\partial D_I}$ and $\dfrac{\partial k_m}{\partial D_I}$ can be computed by differentiating Eq. (28a) with respect to the design variable D_I as

$$
\begin{aligned}
&\left[\left(\frac{g_G}{2} + i \right)^2 \left\{ \omega_m^2 \, \frac{\partial \overline{M}}{\partial D_I} + 2\omega_m \, \frac{\partial \omega_m}{\partial D_I} \, \overline{M} \right\} \right. \\
&+ \left(\frac{g_G}{2} + i \right) \left\{ \frac{\partial \overline{D}}{\partial D_I} \, \omega_m + \frac{\partial \omega_m}{\partial D_I} \, \overline{D} \right\} + \frac{\partial \overline{K}}{\partial D_I} - \frac{\rho_0}{2\xi^2} \\
&\left. \left\{ 2V \frac{\partial V}{\partial D_I} \, \overline{A} + \overline{A}_{,k} \frac{\partial k_m}{\partial D_I} \, V^2 \right\} \right] U_m + Q \, \frac{\partial U_m}{\partial D_I} = 0
\end{aligned}
\tag{35}
$$

where $\overline{A}_{,k} = \dfrac{\partial \overline{A}}{\partial k} \big|_{k=k_m}$. The generalized aerodynamic matrix is an implicit function of the design variables through the reduced frequency k. $\dfrac{\partial U_m}{\partial D_I}$ is the design sensitivity of the right eigenvector.

Premultiplying Eq. (35) by the corresponding left eigenvector V_m^T and denoting

$$
\begin{aligned}
\mu &= V_m^T \, \overline{M} \, U_m \\
d &= V_m^T \, \overline{D} \, U_m \\
\bar{\alpha} &= V_m^T \, \overline{A}(k_m) \, U_m \\
d_I &= V_m^T \, \frac{\partial \overline{D}}{\partial D_I} \, U_m
\end{aligned}
\tag{36}
$$

leads to

$$
\left(\frac{g_G}{2} + i \right) \left[2 \left(\frac{g_G}{2} + i \right) \omega_m \mu + d \right] \frac{\partial \omega_m}{\partial D_I} \quad - \frac{\rho_0}{2 \xi^2} \left(\bar{\alpha}_k V^2 \frac{\partial k_m}{\partial D_I} \right)
$$

$$
\left(-2V \bar{\alpha} \frac{\partial V}{\partial D_I} \right) + \left(\frac{g_G}{2} + i \right)^2 \omega_m^2 \mu_I + \left(\frac{g_G}{2} + i \right) \omega_m d_I + s_I = 0 \tag{37}
$$

The above equation can be simplified as

$$
\bar{a} \frac{\partial \omega_m}{\partial D_I} + \bar{b} \frac{\partial k_m}{\partial D_I} + \bar{e} \frac{\partial V}{\partial D_I} + \bar{f} = 0 \tag{38}
$$

Since $\dfrac{\partial \omega_m}{\partial D_I}$, $\dfrac{\partial k_m}{\partial D_I}$ and $\dfrac{\partial V}{\partial D_I}$ are all real numbers, Eq. (38) can be separated into two equations, one for the real part and the other for the imaginary part, as

$$
Re(\bar{a}) \frac{\partial \omega_m}{\partial D_I} + Re(\bar{b}) \frac{\partial k_m}{\partial D_I} + Re(\bar{e}) \frac{\partial V}{\partial D_I} + Re(\bar{f}) = 0
$$

$$
Im(\bar{a}) \frac{\partial \omega_m}{\partial D_I} + Im(\bar{b}) \frac{\partial k_m}{\partial D_I} + Im(\bar{e}) \frac{\partial V}{\partial D_I} + Im(\bar{f}) = 0 \tag{39}
$$

In conjunction with Eq. (31), the above equations can be solved. $\dfrac{\partial \omega_m}{\partial D_I}$, $\dfrac{\partial k_m}{\partial D_I}$ and $\dfrac{\partial V}{\partial D_I}$ are then substituted into the optimization search procedure. It is noted that the coefficients $\bar{a}, \bar{b}$ and $\bar{e}$ in the above equations are constant. Only the coefficient $\bar{f}$ needs to be evaluated for each design variable.

In general, there are multiple flutter roots in an aeroelastic system; however, only the lowest one is meaningful. A typical flutter V-g diagram is shown in Fig. 7, which has ten roots. In the optimization procedure, a good prediction of flutter speed for the next iteration is essential to the numerical search. However, for complex aeroelastic systems it is common that between the old and new designs a higher flutter root switches with lowest one and yields a wrong flutter speed in the approximate solution. To avoid this problem all flutter roots in a particular range of velocities are restrained to be above the design speed.

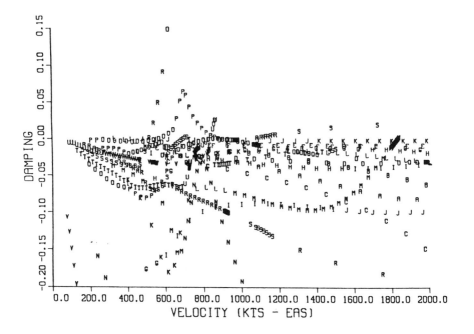

Fig. 7. V-g Diagram of a Complex Aircraft

Table I. A Flutter Comparison

Model	Young's modulus	Flutter speed, fps	Flutter frequency	Natural frequencies
Wind Tunnel[b]	—	495 (M = 0.45) (0.0%)	120	36, 210, 242
Beam-Stick model	—	509 (+ 2.83%)	134	—
NASTRAN[b] HA75E[a,c]	8.86E + 6[d]	483 (− 2.42%)	113	34.7, 210, 255
ADOP[b]	10.2E + 6[e]	495.42 (+ 0.08%)	120.03	34.4, 210, 262

[a]Ref. *MSC/NASTRAN Handbook for Aeroelastic Analysis*, Vol. II, Nov. 1987, pp. 6.2–107.
[b]Aluminum alloy, measured material density = 0.097464 lb/in.^{3}
[c]Using NASTRAN KE method of flutter analysis.
[d]Young's modulus ratioed to match measured and NASTRAN-calculated natural frequency.
[e]Young's modulus ratioed to match measured and ADOP-calculated natural frequency.

C. NUMERICAL EXAMPLES

A simple flat-plate wing with fifteen degrees of sweepback is used to demonstrate the flutter analysis in ADOP [31]. The wing was tested in a wind tunnel for subsonic flutter at Mach Number of $m = 0.45$. The subsonic aerodynamic influence coefficient matrices were computed by the Doublet Lattice Method [32,33]. A comparison of results from ADOP, MSC/NASTRAN and the wind tunnel test is shown in Table I.

IX. MULTIDISCIPLINARY OPTIMIZATION

A. OPTIMIZATION STRATEGY

ADOP uses a multidisciplinary design optimization strategy to minimize the structural weight while simultaneously satisfying stress, displacement, frequency and flutter constraints. Because of the symmetry of aircraft geometry, only half of the structure needs to be modeled. However, the model has to be used to evaluate and design for all maneuvering conditions. This can be achieved by properly restraining the structure; for instance, symmetrically and anti-symmetrically restraining the centerline of a structure can simulate different motions of aircraft. ADOP allows for different boundary conditions of the same structure along with multiple load cases, payload conditions and flight conditions. The strategy is that static strength, dynamic modal and flutter analyses and their design sensitivity calculations are performed analytically between major iterations with the updated structure. The active and violated constraints [6] from all analyses along with their design sensitivities are then collected for optimization. Including all active and violated constraints in the optimization procedure can be prohibitively expensive; therefore, in each design iteration only a subset of these constraints is selected. The constraints are evenly distributed among all design variable groups. Results from all boundary, payload and flight conditions and load cases are checked and highly inactive (feasible) conditions are neglected in the next iteration to reduce computation.

The method of modified feasible directions in the optimization code DOT [34] is used. This method first determines a search direction in the design space from the objective function gradient, the gradients of the active and violated constraints and the design variable side constraints. For each change in search direction, a complete reanalysis of all involved disciplines is performed as the related design sensitivities will change. Once the direction is defined, a one-dimensional search is performed to determine the optimum travel distance in the design space. Each distance evaluation requires computing the new objective and constraint values. The cost of a complete analysis in every step is too expensive; instead, an approximate analysis (described in the next section) is performed. The optimum travel distance is selected based on the minimum objective value and least constraint violations. The design variables are then updated and a new iteration starts.

Convergence is achieved by satisfying the Kuhn-Tucker criteria [6] or if the relative or absolute change in the objective function stays below a specified value in a given number of iterations.

B. APPROXIMATE ANALYSIS

In the ADOP optimization procedure, the structural constraints including stress, displacement, frequency and flutter speed have to be re-evaluated in every one-dimensional numerical search. To avoid the costly exact analysis, an approximate technique comprised of the first order Taylor series expansion and the inverse of the design variables [6] is used. (The flutter approximation is slightly different with the velocity computed by Eq. (27) using an approximate reduced frequency k and circular frequency ω.)

The approximation of the *jth* constraint with an inverse design variable defined as $x_l = 1/D_l^{\mu}$ is expressed as

$$G_j = G_j^0 + \sum^L \frac{\partial G_j}{\partial x_I} \Delta x_I$$

$$= G_j^0 + \sum^L \frac{\partial G_j}{\partial D_I} \frac{D_I}{M} \left[1 - \left(\frac{D_I}{D_I + \Delta D_I} \right)^M \right] \qquad (40)$$

where G^0 is the constraint before approximation, L is the number of independent design variables associated with the constraint, ΔD_I is the increment of Ith design variable, and M is equal to one for axial and membrane type elements and three for bending plates.

The approach has good accuracy. For a highly nonlinear response like flutter, it generally predicts results with less than a three percent error. Another approximation scheme, especially good for frequency constraint evaluation, is introduced in Reference 35. Numerical search in optimization requires all constraints to be evaluated. Using the above approximation, constraints can be computed rapidly for a number of maneuvering and payload conditions, permitting simultaneous design optimization for all cases.

C. NUMERICAL EXAMPLES

Two numerical examples are presented using the stress and flutter constraints. The first is a simple wing, shown in Fig. 8, with membrane elements for all skins, spars and rib panels and rod elements for stringers. Both the upper and lower skins are divided into six design panels with constant thickness. Each rib is designated as a design group. The stringers on the upper and lower skins are divided into three groups in the spanwise direction and two groups in the chordwise direction with a constant area for each group. The front and rear spars are separated into six groups. An 800 lbs lumped mass, not available for design, is rigidly connected to the trailing edge of the wing to make the model flutter at 449 knots. The upper skin panels and stringers are designed using the buckling stress criterion, and the lower skin panels are subject to the two-bay crack stress criterion. The total number of design variables is 37.

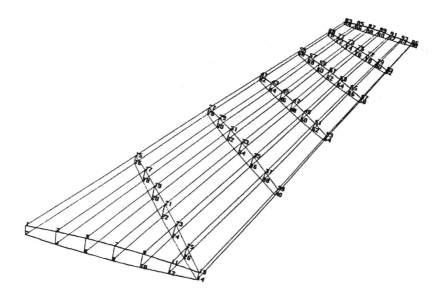

Fig. 8. Finite Element Model of a Small Wing

In the flutter analysis a free-free model should be used to account for the influence of rigid-body modes. The static analysis can not accept a singular model unless the loads applied to the structure are balanced. Therefore, two boundary conditions were used in the analysis: a free-free model symmetrically restrained at the wing root for flutter optimization and a cantilevered wing for stress optimization. A total of 13,500 lbs of point loads were applied normal to the wing at the wing tip. In this example only one flight condition (Mach Number of $m = 0.8$) was used to demonstrate ADOP and the constrained flutter speed was designated at 484 knots.

Two cases were chosen to study the influence of FSD on the optimization results. The first one (labeled "FSD" in Figs. 9 and 10) was started using three fully stressed design iterations and the second (labeled "No FSD") using the original model. Ten optimization iterations were performed. Figures 9 and 10 show the structural weight and flutter speed versus iteration in both cases, in which the first three iterations refer to FSD. At the beginning, the flutter constraint was critical, and therefore,

stiffness and weight was redistributed during the first two iterations. In the
second case the flutter constraint was maintained active until the tenth iteration. A flutter speed much higher than the design speed indicates that
there is no flutter condition in the subsonic range.

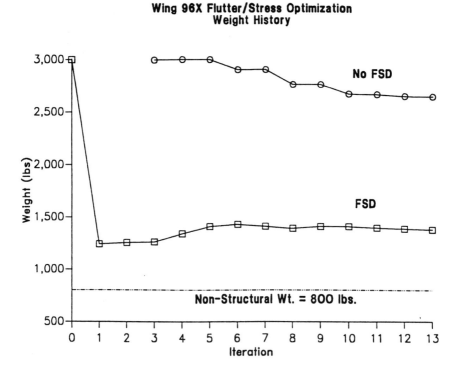

Fig. 9. Weight-Iteration History of the Small Wing

In the first case ("FSD") the fully stressed design (with smoothing)
significantly reduced the structural weight but made approximately half of
the elements over-stressed. To satisfy the violated stress constraints, skin
thickness and stringer areas and therefore structural weight were increased.
In the same case the flutter requirements were satisfied after the fifth iteration; only the stress constraints dominated the design change but again
resulted in an active flutter constraint after Iteration 9. Although the total
weight was only changed slightly between iterations, the flutter speed varied
notably. This is due to shifting of structural stiffness and weight.

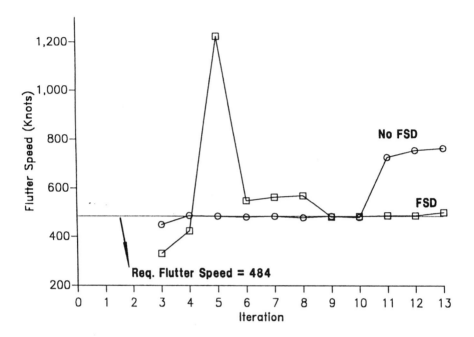

Wing 96X Flutter/Stress Optimization
Flutter Speed History

Fig. 10. Flutter Speed versus Iteration of the Small Wing

The first case ("FSD") ended up with a much lighter structure than the second. The main difference was that the rib panel thicknesses were not substantially reduced by the optimizer in the second case even though low stresses were observed. They were, however, decreased to minimum gauge by the fully stressed design prior to the numerical optimization. The first case also yielded smaller stringer areas. This demonstrates that it is advantageous to use fully stressed design to start the optimization process even though it introduces an infeasible starting design.

The panel buckling stress allowables (function of structural sizes) on the upper skin, ranging from 28,000 psi at the wing root to 18,000 psi at the wing tip, were substantially lower than their material counterparts (55,000 psi). The reason for the difference is that the panel stringer configurations

were not selected carefully here. The two-bay crack stress allowables were
in the range of 40,000 to 45,000 psi.

The second example is the large transport aircraft shown in Fig. 1.
The wing resizing effort through numerical optimization considered only
the skin panels and attached stringers in the wing box. Each of the upper
and lower skins is divided into ten design groups. The stringers attached to
a skin group are defined as another group. The panel thickness and stringer
areas are linearly tapered in both chord and spanwise directions. The
number of design variables is reduced to 160.

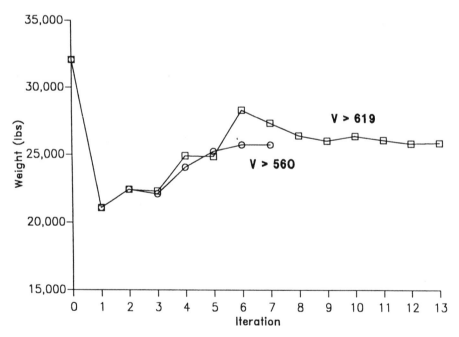

Fig. 11. Weight-Iteration History of a Transport Aircraft

Similar to the first example, two boundary conditions were used in the
analysis: a free-free symmetric model for flutter optimization and a

cantilevered model for stress optimization. Only the symmetric and empty fuel condition and one flight case (Mach Number of $m = 0.87$) were used. A 2.5 g rigid maneuver load was applied to the structure. The first 25 modes including three rigid-body modes and the aerodynamic influence coefficients of 16 reduced frequencies ranging from 0.01 to 1.5 were computed for the flutter analysis.

Transport Flutter/Stress Optimization
Flutter Speed History

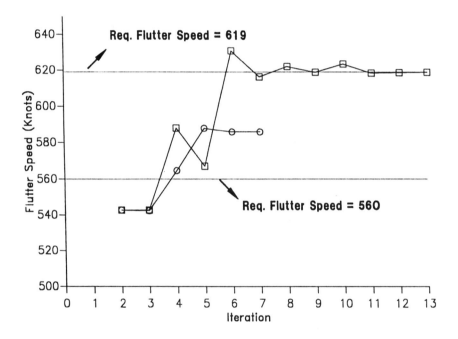

Fig. 12. Flutter Speed versus Iteration of the Transport

Two fully stressed design iterations were performed prior to the numerical optimization. Similar to the first example, the structure became over-stressed. The optimizer then increased skin and stringer sizes to meet the stress requirements. Figures 11 and 12 show the weight and flutter speed versus iteration. Two constrained flutter speeds 560 knots and 619 knots, both higher than the initial flutter speed, were separately tested. The first two iterations, not showing flutter speed, refer to the fully stressed design. The 560-knot case yielded a design with the 586-knot flutter speed and was controlled by stress in the last three iterations. The second case (619 knots) was flutter critical (flutter speed settled on the constrained speed) and required more iterations to converge. The weight increase between Iterations 5 and 6 for the second case corresponds to a jump in the flutter speed. However, the structural stiffness and weight were then re-distributed in subsequent iterations to minimize the flutter penalty. The two final designs, although converging toward the same weight, have different structural stiffness and mass distributions, and the results show over 20 percent reduction in structural weight from the original design.

Although, two different constrained flutter speeds were used, it is shown that ADOP successfully designed a flutter-free structure and reduced the weight. Also, the entire analysis requires less than 4 CPU hours using an IBM 3090 without vectorizaiton. This represented substantial savings in both time and man-power compared with the conventional design process conducted between the stress and flutter groups.

X. AUXILIARY SOFTWARE SYSTEMS

A. DISK AND CORE MANAGEMENT SYSTEM

The ADOP Disk and Core Management System (ADACS) is a central input/output and memory manager. The features described below allow very large models to be handled. A region of virtual memory is dynamically allocated at run time as a work area, resulting in a substantially smaller load module and avoiding recompilation of the source code when more memory is required. The work area is managed by a set of routines which partition it into named arrays. Arrays are referenced at the user level through ACL (see below) or by the programmer through the memory management routines. A catalog of the work area contents and attributes is stored in a set of COMMON blocks for central access. Each array may be divided into subarrays. This feature is particularly useful when it is desired to write only a portion of an array to file; for example, when shifting converged eigenvectors from the array of approximations to file, and replacing them with new vectors. ADACS dynamically allocates files used in ADOP, sparing the user from operating system details. Each file has an associated name and a catalog describing its contents and attributes. Arrays are easily located through a catalog search which is far more efficient than a search of the file records.

Sequential and direct-access file formats are available through ADACS. Sequential files are beneficial when the contents are accessed in a sequential fashion and do not require large numbers of data retrievals. Direct-access files are efficient when the contents are frequently accessed and overwritten. Since IBM direct-access files and the ADOP catalogs associated with sequential and direct-access files are of fixed dimension, a provision was made for automatic allocation of "continuation" files. Each continuation file is related to the original file via a linklist, and subsequent file use automatically accesses the continuation files.

B. ADOP CONTROL LANGUAGE (ACL)

An advanced control language cannot be an interpretive language in which each instruction is read and executed before the next one is processed. The drawback is that semantic errors are detected only at run time, so that after correction the entire program must be rerun. In contrast, ACL is a high-level, compiler-based language [4]. The compiler is composed of a parser and lexical analyzer. The entire instruction set is compiled and checked for semantic and logic errors and variable type inconsistencies. Once error free, the "object code" is then used to govern program execution.

The syntax of ACL is similar to FORTRAN and includes in-line procedures, logical looping and branching, standard arithmetic operators and direct matrix operators. The default data entity is the real array. Like in FORTRAN, ADOP analysis and function modules are accessed with a CALL statement. Each of the modules generates related arrays which are stored on file and may be used by other analysis modules or accessed by the user through ACL. Arrays may also be input via ACL as direct matrix input (DMI).

An ACL example is shown in Fig. 13, in which logical looping and branching, file input/output and the use of an analysis module are demonstrated. In the example the analysis module SOLVE is used to find a set of displacements, given a stiffness matrix and a load vector.

```
IMPLICIT REAL GENERAL MATRIX (A-H, O-Z)
INTEGER I,II,IMAX,ICOUNT
LABEL LAB1,LAB2
REAL PIVOT,XMAXT
""
IMAX = 12
II = IMAX**2-IMAX/3
DO I = 1,II
    IF((I.EQ.3) .OR. (I.EQ.4)) THEN GOTO LAB1
    ICOUNT = ICOUNT + 1
    IF(ICOUNT.GT.9) THEN GOTO LAB2
    XMAXT = XMAXT * A
    LAB1:ENDDO
""
PIVOT = 1.E-6
""
" ***** OPEN STIFFNESS, LOAD
AND DISPLACEMENT FILES ***** "
""
OPEN STIFFDSK(TYPE = INPUT, &
DSN = 'USERID.STIFF.DATA')
OPEN LOADDSK(TYPE = INPUT, &
DSN = 'USERID.LOAD.DATA')
OPEN DISPDSK(TYPE = OUTPUT, &
DSN = 'USERID.DISP.DATA')
""
" ***** READ STIFFNESS MATRIX AND
LOAD VECTOR FROM FILES ***** "
""
READ (STIFFDSK) STIFF
READ (LOADDSK) RLOAD
DISP = SOLVE(STIFF, RLOAD, PIVOT)
WRITE (DISPDSK) DISP
PRINT DISP
END
```

Fig. 13. An ACL Example

C. INTERACTIVE GRAPHICS

ADOP is a self-contained design and analysis system. However, the system does not include a finite element modelling program, since there are a number of highly developed commercial modelling programs available. Currently, two operational modules capable of translating NASTRAN or CASD (Computer Aided Structural Design) bulk data files to ADOP format are implemented. (CASD is the McDonnell Douglas in-house structural analysis system.) NASTRAN or CASD bulk data files are generated by the in-house modelling program CGSA (Computer Graphics Structural Analysis) and PATRAN is commonly used to generate NASTRAN models.

In ADOP interactive graphics is developed as an aid to the optimization process. The program is written in C language and is developed on a Silicon Graphics work station. Coding of the graphics module is greatly simplified by use of the comprehensive SG firmware library of graphics functions, but at the cost of machine dependency. The workstations are linked to the mainframe for file transfers to and from the main ADOP system. It is also possible to run ADOP on work stations, so that the analysis results can be accessed and displayed through a "window" to allow the user to either continue or stop the job.

The primary functions of the graphics module are:

(1) Display of the finite element model, animated mode shapes and static deformations to allow visual checking for modelling errors and inconsistencies.

(2) Definition of mass and weights data. Weights data are translated from the advanced design model to the detailed finite element model and redefined as distributed or concentrated masses.

(3) Color contour displays of stresses, deformations, design sensitivities, load conditions and design variables.

(4) Graphical splining display. This feature allows the user to verify that the splining of mode shapes between the structural and aerodynamic models is accurate.

(5) Generation of data points for the aerodynamic model (program N5KDRAW).

(6) Grouping of finite elements with design variable linking for numerical optimization.

XI. CONCLUSIONS

This chapter demonstrates the technologies implemented in the aeroelastic design optimization program (ADOP), which is developed to design large finite element aircraft structural models subject to strength, dynamic modal and flutter constraints. It is shown that a good design optimization tool can significantly reduce the design cycle time and labor required in the conventional design process. Also, the structural stiffness and weight can be more accurately distributed to meet the aeroelastic performance requirements. More important through, the program integrates key engineering disciplines in the design optimization process and automatically generates a good design for all design phases.

As a large design optimization program reaches production status, various other user requirements may emerge. Improvements and technical advances are necessary. Presently, the to-be-implemented list of technologies includes design of composite structures complying with manufacturing constraints, state space flutter analysis with active controls, sub-optimization of panel cross-sections, and load and aeroelastic optimization. Additionally, the structural optimization is merely a small part of a global design optimization system, which should integrate the structural disciplines with other engineering aspects such as manufacturing, maintainability, life-cycle costs, mission cost-effectiveness. Therefore, the design of future aircraft will become an automated optimization process starting from flight mission definition through advanced and detailed design to manufacturing readiness, with the resulting design being the most efficient, maintainable and cost-effective.

XII. ACKNOWLEDGEMENTS

The authors wish to thank American Institute of Aeronautics and Astronautics for permission to use References 3 and 16 for this chapter. Thanks are also due to the Douglas management for their generous support.

XIII. REFERENCES

1. R. H. MacNeal, *The NASTRAN Theoretical Manual*, NASA SP-221 (03), March, 1976.

2. D. J. Neill, E. H. Johnson and R. Canfield, "ASTROS - A Multidisciplinary Automated Structural Design Tool," *Journal of Aircraft*, Vol. 27, December, 1990, pp. 1021-1027.

3. A. J. Dodd, K. E. Kadrinka, M. J. Loikkanen, B. A. Rommel, G. D. Sikes, R. C. Strong and T. J. Tzong, "Aeroelastic Design Optimization Program," *Journal of Aircraft*, Vol. 27, December, 1990, pp. 1028-1036.

4. D. L. Herendeen and G. D. Sikes, "ADOP Executive System - Programmers' Manual," Universal Analytics, Inc., Playa del Rey, California, Report UAI-TR88-0003, 1989.

5. R. L. Dailey, "Eigenvector Derivatives with Repeated Eigenvalues," *AIAA Journal*, Vol. 27, April, 1989, pp. 486-491.

6. G. N. Vanderplaats, *Numerical Optimization Techniques for*

Engineering Design, McGraw-Hill Series in Mechanical Engineering, McGraw-Hill, 1984.

7. R. M. Pickett, M. F. Rubinstein and R. B. and Nelson, "Automated Structural Synthesis Using a Reduced Number of Design Coordinates," *AIAA/ASME/SAE   14th Structures, Structural   Dynamics and Materials Conference*, Williamsburg, Virginia, March, 1973.

8. T. H. H. Pian and D. P. Chen, "Alternative Ways for Formulation of Hybrid   Stress   Elements,"   *International Journal for   Numerical Methods in Engineering*, Vol. 18, 1982, pp. 1679-1684.

9. M. J. Loikkanen, "A 4-Node Thin Hybrid Plate Finite Element," *Engineering Computations*, United Kingdom, Vol. 2, No. 2, 1985, pp. 151-154.

10. A. George and J. W. Liu, *Computer Solution of Large Sparse Positive Definite Systems*, Prentice-Hall, Inc., New Jersey, 1981.

11. M. Hoit and E. L. Wilson, "An Equation Numbering Algorithm Based on a Minimum Front Criteria," *Computers and Structures*, Vol. 16, No. 1-4, Pergamon Press Ltd., Great Britain, 1983, pp. 225-239.

12. B. Irons and S. Ahmad, *Techniques of Finite Elements*, Ellis Horwood, Chichester, England, 1980.

13. B. E. Schofield, "Computer-Aided Design of Skin-Stiffened Compression Panels," *AIAA/ASME 8th Structures, Structural Dynamics and Materials Conference*, Palm Springs, California, March, 1967.

14. T. Swift, "The Effects of Fastener Flexibility and Stiffener Geometry on the Stress Intensity in Stiffened Cracked Sheet," *Prospects of Fracture Mechanics*, Leydon, Netherlands: Noordhoff International, 1974.

15. R. M. Rivello, *Theory and Analysis Flight Structures*, McGraw-Hill, 1969.

16. T. J. Tzong, G. D. Sikes and M. J. Loikkanen, "Multidisciplinary Design Optimization of a Large Transport Aircraft Wing," *AIAA Aerospace Design Conference*, Paper No. 92-1002, Irvine, California, February, 1992.

17. C. Lanczos, "An Iteration Method for the Solution of the Eigenvalue Problem of Linear Differential and Integral Operators," *Journal Research of the Numerical Bureau of Standards*, Vol. 45, October, 1950, pp. 255-282.

18. B. N. Parlett and D. S. Scott, "The Lanczos Algorithm with Selective Orthogonalization," *Mathematics of Computation*, Vol. 33, 1979, pp. 217-238.

19. T. J. Tzong, G. D. Sikes and A. J. Dodd, "Large Order Modal Analysis Module in the Aeroelastic Design Optimization Program (ADOP)," *MSC 1991 World Users Conference*, Vol. II, Paper No. 36, Universal City, California, March, 1991.

20. K. J. Bathe and S. Ramaswamy, "An Accelerated Subspace Iteration Method," *Computer Methods in Applied Mechanics and Engineering*, North-Holland Publishing Company, Vol. 23, 1980, pp. 313-331.

21. T. J. Tzong, G. D. Sikes and M. J. Loikkanen, "Large Order Modal Analysis Techniques in the Aeroelastic Design Optimization Program (ADOP)," SAE Technical Paper Series No.   892323, *Aerospace Technology Conference and Exposition*, Anaheim, California, September, 1989.

22. H. D. Simon, "The Lanczos Algorithm for Solving Symmetric Linear Systems," *Ph.D. Dissertation*, University of California, Berkeley, June 1982.

23. R. W. Clough and J. Penzien, *Dynamics of Structures*, McGraw-Hill, New York, 1975.

24. K. J. Bathe and E. L. Wilson, *Numerical Methods in Finite Element Analysis*, Prentice-Hall, Inc., New Jersey, 1976.

25. R. L. Harder and R. N. Desmarais, "Interpolation Using Surface Splines," *Journal of Aircraft*, Vol. 9, February, 1972, pp. 189-191.

26. R. I. Kroll and M. Y. Hirayama, "Modal Interpolation Program L 215 (INTERP)," Vol. 1, NASA CR 2847, Boeing Commercial Airplane Company, 1979.

27. K. G. Bhatia, "An Automated Method for Determining the Flutter Velocity and the Matched Point," *Journal of Aircraft*, Vol. 11, January, 1974, pp. 21-27.

28. S. D. Conte and C. de Boor, *Elementary Numerical Analysis*, Second Edition, McGraw-Hill, 1965.

29. C. S. Rudisill and K. G. Bhatia, "Second Derivatives of the Flutter Velocity and the Optimization of Aircraft Structures," *AIAA Journal*, Vol. 10, December, 1972, pp. 1569-1572.

30. J. Markowitz and G. Isakson, "FASTOP-3: A Strength, Deflection and Flutter Optimization Program for Metallic and Composite Structures," Vols. I and II, AFFDL-TR-78-50, May, 1978.

31. *MSC/NASTRAN Handbook for Aeroelastic Analysis*, Version 65, Vol. 1, MacNeal-Schwendler Corp., Los Angeles, California, November, 1987, pp. 2.6-1 - 2.6-8.

32. E. Albano and W. P. Rodden, "A Double-Lattice Method for Calculating Lift Distribution on Oscillating Surfaces in Subsonic Flows," *AIAA Journal*, Vol. 7, February, 1969, pp. 279-285.

33. T. P. Kalman and J. P. Giesing, "Subsonic Steady and Oscillatory Aerodynamics for Multiple Interfering Wings and Bodies," *Journal of Aircraft*, Vol. 26, October, 1972, pp. 693-702.

34. *DOT USERS MANUAL*, Version 2.00, VMA Engineering Inc., Santa Barbara, California, February, 1989.

35. R. A. Canfield, "An Approximation Function for Frequency Constrained Structural Optimization," *Second NASA/Air Force Symposium on Recent Advances in Multidisciplinary Analysis and Optimization*, Hampton, Virginia, September, 1988.

ACTIVE FLUTTER SUPPRESSION TECHNIQUES
IN AIRCRAFT WINGS

Gian Luca Ghiringhelli
Massimiliano Lanz
Paolo Mantegazza
Sergio Ricci

Dipartimento di Ingegneria Aerospaziale
Politecnico di Milano
Via C.Golgi 40
20133 MILANO - Italy

I. INTRODUCTION

The suppression of flutter by using active control systems has achieved a high degree of maturity, and the advantages it can offer, in terms of weight saving and improved overall structural efficiency, are now well known. The above statement is proved by the large body of available literature and by the numerous verifications carried out to demonstrate different design methods and implementations, on commercial and combat aircraft, wind tunnel and flying test models [1-14]. A further proof of the maturity of the subject is given by the appearance of specific items related to aeroelastic stability and interaction of systems and structure in JAR and FAR regulations and of papers explicitly addressing these requirements [15]. We will not attempt a comprehensive review of the subject and of the related literature, but the references that will be cited in this work will be enough to open a long chain of further references that should satisfy even the most interested of the readers.

A fast skimming of the subject shows that several methods are available to design an Active Flutter Suppression System (AFSS). A rough classification can be made by grouping these methods under two main categories.

The first category includes general purpose design techniques, based either on classical or modern control theory, and it is the most adopted one. The application of classical control theory, e.g. frequency response and root locus, which is primarily based on designing in the frequency domain, is well suited to the usual flutter modeling techniques but is somewhat awkward to be applied in the multi input-output applications typical of AFSSs. Nonetheless, when it is used in a well implemented computer aided design procedure, it can be very successful in producing robust designs and the many trials often required can be useful in building a strong physical understanding of the system [16,17]. Modern control design methods in the state space are more suited to large order multi input-output mathematical models of AFSSs and many of the techniques available within this framework have been successfully employed [18-31], so that it is difficult to ascertain the superiority of any of them over the others. It must be remarked that the use of state space formulations in aeroservoelasticity suffers from the need of augmenting the order of the model to recast the aerodynamic transfer matrices into state space. The fictitious aerodynamics states thus introduced are unmeasurable and very sensitive to the approximations implied in the aerodynamic formulations adopted. Moreover they depend on flight conditions, so any compensation determined by taking them into account is also strongly influenced by the aerodynamics and it can be difficult to insure robustness in the control laws so designed. Different forms of robustness recovery have been used, e.g singular value analysis of the return difference matrices and loop transfer recovery through process noise addition [32-41]. Often, for an effective application of these techniques and in search of low order compensators, model reduction techniques must be applied, either a priori to reduce the order of the system or, after the design, to reduce the order of otherwise complex compensators. Nevertheless AFSSs designed by modern control methods are relatively complex, can be sensitive to sensor types and locations and can be difficult to test and tune in flight. This is especially true if a gain scheduling policy is required to cover different operating conditions, since there is no way to insure a smooth continuous variation of the controller structure and parameters. To cope with some of the previously cited drawbacks different design methods, including multi model formulations and constraints on singular values of the return difference matrices, have been adopted [42-45].

The second group of design techniques develops an AFSS with a controller structure determined by emphasizing the basic physical understanding of the aeroelastic system. Notable examples of this approach are the Aerodynamic Energy and the Identical Location of Accelerometer and Force (ILAF) concepts [3,46,47]. The aerodynamic energy based methods can be useful for preliminary designs or feasibility studies but they do not seem capable of taking into account refined design conditions in which it is necessary to include compensators, sensors and actuators dynamics into the mathematical model [48]. The ILAF concept cleverly tries to mimic grounded passive dampers through aerodynamic forces generated by control surfaces thus achieving a robust energy dissipation irrespective of the flight condition and/or configuration [3].

A possible solution to many of the problems presented in the previous brief review could be the adoption of adaptive controllers and some attempts have been carried out in this direction [49]. However since an AFSS is a multi variable system with high frequency content and working under rapidly varying operating conditions, it is still difficult, despite the increased power of on board computers, to envisage and realize adequate adaptive techniques for it.

So far we have addressed the final and most fashionable of the steps to be undertaken to design an AFSS. It must however be remarked that, whatever controller robustness can be achieved, it is important to start the final design phase on the base of a good mathematical model of the open loop aeroservoelastic system. The determination of such a model is the most lengthy and costly part of the whole process. Even if it is based on a long tradition and well established flutter analysis procedures, mainly in relation to structure and aerodynamic modeling, it should be understood that aeroelastic analysts are nonetheless well aware of the limitations of their techniques. So a cautious attitude and deep physical understanding of the problem is often needed. A point of utmost importance is the determination of the unsteady aerodynamic forces related to control surfaces especially when AFSSs are to be operated in transonic flight regimes [50]. Also the choice of sensor types and locations as well as the positioning and configuration of control surfaces, often constrained to be shared with other control functions, deserves due attention [24,53-55]. A further important point is the correct modeling of the actuators and of their coupling to the structure. The possibility of integrating the design of the actuators into the design of the AFSS should not be excluded if this can bring a further break through in satisfying the assigned requirements in an optimal way. In fact even if in this work aerodynamic forces are assumed as the only mean to control the motion of the structure, the newly born concept of intelligent structural components could lead to new concepts and solutions for the design of future AFSSs [51,52].

This work will take into account most of the modeling facets of an aeroservoelastic system including aerodynamics, coupling of the aeroelastic system to arbitrary actuators and design of AFSSs with methods that can include the determination of sensors/actuators locations and combine the design of structurally constrained active controllers with passive structural components. The latter point will be developed in a more detailed way in a paragraph that introduces the reader to an important subset of interdisciplinary optimization to hopefully demonstrate the improvements that can be obtained by a truly integrated design of the structure and AFSS.

II. AERODYNAMIC MODEL

The generalized unsteady aerodynamic forces $\{fa\}$ needed for aeroelastic analyses are generally available in the domain of the Laplace transform variable $s = \delta + j\omega$. They can be viewed as the sum of a term related to structural motions, $\{fam\}$, and a term related to gusts and/or turbulence, $\{fag\}$, depend on the Mach number $\mathcal{M}$, and can be written

$$\{fa(s,\mathcal{M})\} = \{fam(s,\mathcal{M})\} + \{fag(s,\mathcal{M})\} =$$

$$= q[Ham(p,\mathcal{M})]\{qs(s)\} + q/V[Hag(p,\mathcal{M})]\{vg(s)\} \qquad (1)$$

where [Ham] and [Hag] are respectively the aerodynamic transfer matrices related to the unsteady boundary conditions imposed by the motion of the structure and control surfaces $\{qs\}$ and by discrete gusts and/or turbulence discretized by $\{vg\}$, q is the dynamic pressure, $p = sc/V$ is the complex reduced frequency, c is an aerodynamic reference length and V is the free stream velocity. The above equation generally implies a linearized inviscid flow for which the matrices [Ham] and [Hag] are evaluated numerically by using well developed harmonic potential formulations [56]. When the flow is strongly non linear, e.g transonic, there is no unique linearization and it is necessary to calculate the different steady state solutions of interest around which the linearization must be carried out. Analytically linearized formulations for transonic flows have been developed in integral equation methods for harmonic motions [57-60]. Due to the availability of more general purpose unsteady flow solvers for computational fluid dynamics (CFD) applications, the linearization process is often carried out numerically by imposing small structural motions and gusts. The aerodynamic transfer functions can then be obtained directly by imposing harmonic motions, either in the frequency [61] or time domain [62], or, more effectively, through the determination of indicial responses [63,64]. The determination of the aerodynamic transfer matrices is a costly undertaking in any case so, when a linearized harmonic formulation is used, they are generally known only at a small set of reduced frequencies $k = \omega c/V$, i.e for $p = jk$, ranging from zero to a relatively low value k_{max}. In such a case and in view of the identification of the transfer matrices for arbitrary p it can be useful to expand their knowledge to a larger set of reduced frequencies by a suitable causal inter-extrapolation, based on dispersion relations, of the type presented in [65,66]. Generally no expansion is needed for a numerical linearization based on unsteady CFD formulations in the time domain combined with the determination of the indicial responses, as a fairly large set of transfer matrices can be obtained at a cost that is negligible with respect to that required to determine the indicial responses themselves.

The identification of a suitable analytical model of the generalized aerodynamic forces for the whole domain p, that can be easily transformed to a finite state time invariant linear system, is a must in aeroservoelasticity especially if active control systems have to be designed by using multi variable time domain techniques. It should nonetheless be remarked that finite state aerodynamic models were developed well before the advent of aeroservoelasticity as a more rational way to set flutter problems in a standard eigenvalue form and to allow the real time simulation of aeroelastic response problems on analog computers [67-69]. It is also important to recall that for inviscid flows these models are only an acceptable approximation of the real behavior [70,71].

A finite state approximation of [Ham] and [Hag] can be written in the reduced frequency domain p as

$$[Ham] = [Am0] + [Am1]p + [Am2]p^2 + [Cm](p[I] - [Am])^{-1}[Bm] \qquad (2a)$$

$$[Hag] = [Ag0] + [Cg](p[I] - [Ag])^{-1}[Bg] \qquad (2b)$$

with [Am] and [Ag] being stable matrices, i.e having eigenvalues with a real part less than zero. If $\{xam\}$ and $\{xag\}$ are suitable vectors of aerodynamic states the time domain counterpart of Eqs. (1)-(2) is given by

$$\{\dot{x}am\} = (V/c)[Am]\{xam\} + (V/c)[Bm]\{qs\} \qquad (3a)$$

$$\{fam\} = q[Am0]\{qs\} + q(c/V)[Am1]\{\dot{q}s\} + q(c/V)^2[Am2]\{\ddot{q}s\} +$$
$$+ q[Cm]\{xam\} \qquad (3b)$$

$$\{\dot{x}ag\} = (V/c)[Ag]\{xag\} + V/c[Bg]\{vg\} \qquad (4a)$$

$$\{fag\} = q/V[Ag0]\{vg\} + q/V[Cg]\{xag\} \qquad (4b)$$

Limiting, for the moment, our analysis only to Eqs. (2a),(3a)-(3b), it should be noted that $\{xam\}$ is representative of the hundreds to even hundreds of thousands of aerodynamic unknowns of the discretized aerodynamic solution while [Am0], [Am1] and [Am2] are related to the physical simplification adopted in the aerodynamic calculations. In fact the polynomial part of Eq. (2a) up to p, i.e. [Am0] and [Am1], involves a direct transmission of the variation of the boundary conditions to the loading that can exist only for perfectly inviscid flows. The quadratic term in p, i.e. [Am2], is the so called apparent mass that should exist only for $\mathcal{M} = 0$ [67]. So [Am0], [Am1], [Am2] determine the high frequency behavior of $\{fam\}$ and are hardly related to the relatively low reduced frequency knowledge of [Ham] often available. In practice Eqs. (2) can only be justified and accepted as a reduced order approximation of the true dynamics of the aerodynamics to the minimum number of aerodynamic states that can correctly model [Ham] in the frequency range of practical interest for the analysis at hand. From a structural analyst point of view these aerodynamic states play the same role of the normal vibration modes in structural dynamics. Thus the polynomial part can be assumed as derived from a low frequency residualization, see appendix A, of the dynamics of the aerodynamics up to the second order of the structural input $\{q_s\}$, i.e $\{\ddot{q}_s\}$. This will not cause an increase in the order of the aeroservoelastic equations, as $\{\ddot{q}_s\}$ is already present in the inertia terms of the structural part. These aerodynamic states cannot be related to any physical quantity and will hardly appear directly in any response measurement of aeroservoelastic interest.

Many methods have been developed for the direct determination of the smallest possible order of $\{x_{am}\}$ giving an acceptable approximation of [Ham], [71-75], and the direct determination of a form of the type of Eqs. (2) has been termed minimum-state aerodynamic model [75]. The determination of such a model is similar to the identification of linear systems parameters from experimental data and it is a difficult task if undertaken from scratch because of the non uniqueness and strong nonlinearity implied in the term containing [Cm], [Am] and [Bm] while constraining [Am] to be stable. We will then present an alternative approach that reduces a precise initial Padé approximation to a minimum state by again adopting the residualization procedure of appendix A.

A Padé approximation of [Ham], of order n, can be written either as a right

$$[\text{Ham}] = \left(\sum_{i=0}^{n+2} [N_i]p^i \right) \left(p^n + \sum_{i=0}^{n-1} [D_i]p^i \right)^{-1} \qquad (5a)$$

or as a left

$$[\text{Ham}] = \left(p^n + \sum_{i=0}^{n-1} [D_i]p^i \right)^{-1} \left(\sum_{i=0}^{n+2} [N_i]p^i \right) \qquad (5b)$$

product of matrix polynomials and inverse matrix polynomials. Through a polynomial division Eqs. (5a),(5b) can be rewritten either as

$$[\text{Ham}] = [A_{m0}] + [A_{m1}]p + [A_{m2}]p^2 + \left(\sum_{i=0}^{n-1}[R_i]p^i \right) \left(p^n + \sum_{i=0}^{n-1}[D_i]p^i \right)^{-1} \qquad (6a)$$

or as

$$[\text{Ham}] = [A_{m0}] + [A_{m1}]p + [A_{m2}]p^2 + \left(p^n + \sum_{i=0}^{n-1}[D_i]p^i \right)^{-1} \left(\sum_{i=0}^{n-1}[R_i]p^i \right) \qquad (6b)$$

Equation (6a) can be put in the form of Eq. (2a) by setting

$$[C_m]^T = \begin{bmatrix} [R_0]^T \\ [R_1]^T \\ \vdots \\ [R_{n-2}]^T \\ [R_{n-1}]^T \end{bmatrix} \quad [B_m] = \begin{bmatrix} [0] \\ [0] \\ \vdots \\ [0] \\ [I] \end{bmatrix} \quad [A_m] = \begin{bmatrix} [0] & [I] & \dots & [0] \\ [0] & [0] & \dots & [0] \\ \vdots & \vdots & & \vdots \\ [0] & [0] & \dots & [I] \\ -[D_0] & -[D_1] & \dots & -[D_{n-1}] \end{bmatrix} \qquad (7a)$$

while Eq. (6b) leads to

$$[Cm]^T = \begin{bmatrix} [I] \\ [0] \\ \vdots \\ [0] \\ [0] \end{bmatrix} \quad [Bm] = \begin{bmatrix} [R_{n-1}] \\ [R_{n-2}] \\ \vdots \\ [R_1] \\ [R_0] \end{bmatrix} \quad [Am] = \begin{bmatrix} -[D_{n-1}] & [I] & .. & [0] \\ -[D_{n-2}] & [0] & .. & [0] \\ \vdots & \vdots & : & \vdots \\ -[D_1] & [0] & .. & [I] \\ -[D_0] & [0] & .. & [0] \end{bmatrix} \tag{7b}$$

The Padé matrix polynomials, i.e. the [N]s and [D]s, can be determined by a linear least square fit and a detailed presentation of the method for a right Padé approximation is given below.

Equation (5a) is rewritten as

$$p^n[Ham] = \sum_{i=0}^{n+2} [N_i]p^i - [Ham]\sum_{i=0}^{n-1} [D_i]p^i \tag{8}$$

We then impose that Eq. (8) is satisfied in such a way that [Ham] is correctly approximated with its first derivative with respect to p for $p = 0$. The derivative is evaluated numerically, possibly by using the same inter-extrapolation procedure adopted to expand the few available raw matrices [Ham] [65,66]. It is a real matrix corresponding to the slope of the imaginary part of [Ham] at $p = 0$. This constraint enforces an approximation that is equivalent to guaranteeing that for a small p the aerodynamics is approximated in the same way as if aerodynamic derivatives were used. It could be possible to enforce an even higher order approximation but this is not done to avoid the numerical evaluation of second order derivatives at a singular point [70,71]. The previous constraints are equivalent to enforcing the satisfaction of the following

$$[N_0] = [Ham(0)][D_0] \tag{9}$$

$$[N_1] = [Ham(0)][D_1] + [Ham'(0)][D_0] \tag{10}$$

with $'$ indicating the derivative with respect to p. Taking into account the previous equations we rewrite Eq. (8)

$$1/W(k)(\sum_{i=2}^{n+2} p^i[N_i] - \sum_{i=2}^{n-1} p^i[Ham][D_i] +$$
$$+ p([Ham(0)] - [Ham])[D_1] + \tag{11}$$
$$+ ([Ham(0)] + p[Ham'(0)] - [Ham])[D_0] - p^n[Ham]) = 0$$

in which $W(k)$ is a weighting function introduced to decrease the possible bias toward the polynomial terms of Eq. (6a) at high reduced frequencies.

Often a simple power of k well suits the scope, its choice is however not critical as we are just determining a preliminary approximation. Equation (11) is imposed on the discrete set of known [Ham]s and gives rise to an overdetermined system of linear equations that is solved in a least square sense by a recursive formula leading directly to the solution without the need of building the coefficient and right hand side matrices of Eq. (11) [76]. A similar procedure can be applied to the left Padé approximation. It is only necessary to consider the transpose of Eqs. (9)-(11) so that the matrices [N]s and [D]s are determined by rows instead of by columns. In both cases a finite state modeling of the type of Eq. (2a) is obtained by using Eqs. (7).

The procedure is very fast and can be repeated for different orders of left and right approximations till an acceptable fit is met. It is possible to obtain very good results but a stable state matrix is not insured by this approach. It is generally observed that the higher the order of the approximation the better is the fit, but also many unstable eigenvalues are generated. The procedure of appendix A is then applied again and the best Padé approximation obtained is reduced to a set of minimum states equal to the number of eigenvalues having real part less than an assigned negative value and with modulus less than another assigned value of the order of $|k_{max}|$. In this way the final fitting can start from a good initial approximation of the matrices of Eqs. (2). It is recalled that the reduced [Am] matrix thus obtained is in an upper Schur form. So, before carrying out the final part of the identification of the minimum-state model, any two by two block around the main diagonal is transformed to the first companion form [77] by a similarity transformation, and [Cm] and [Bm] are modified accordingly. This is needed to make the number of elements determining the eigenvalues of [Am] equal to the order of the matrix itself so that the optimum fitting of its eigenvalues we are going to describe is made unique. The final refined approximation is then carried out on the following formulation

$$[Ham] = [Am2]p^2 + [Cm]([Am]^{-1} - [Am]^{-2} - (p[I] - [Am])^{-1})[Bm] \qquad (12)$$

$$[Am0] = [Ham(0)] - [Cm][Am]^{-1}[Bm] \qquad (13)$$

$$[Am1] = [H\acute{a}m(0)] + [Cm][Am]^{-2}[Bm] \qquad (14)$$

which again insures a correct approximation, up to the first order, for a small p. Equation (12) and its transposed are again solved in a linear least square sense for [Am2], [Bm] and [Am2], [Cm] in turn, till no improvement is obtained. It can be noted that if [Am2] and [Bm] are calculated first only [Am] and [Cm] must be given a starting value so that the residualization need not to be carried out after the reduction of

Eqs. (7) to Eqs. (A5). The matrices [Am2], [Bm] and [Cm] are then kept fixed and the, now unique, terms determining the eigenvalues of [Am], always maintained in Schur form, are changed to minimize the overall least square error summed over all the terms of the aerodynamic transfer matrix, under the constraint of keeping it stable, without necessarily enforcing purely real eigenvalues. This procedure is non linear but involves a reduced number of unknowns, even for large order systems, and is carried out by Gauss-Newton iterations [78]. The whole process is repeated till convergence to an acceptable error. Often no iteration on the eigenvalues is needed as very good results are obtained after carrying out only the first part of the procedure.

For sake of conciseness, only the minimum state approximation of [Ham] has been presented, as its extension to [Hag] can be easily carried out along the same pattern. In this case only the right Padé form should be used, as the left one will generate a uselessly large initial system with a number of states related to the structural degrees of freedom and not to the number of gusts input. Furthermore the residualization of the eigenvalues not retained in the approximation must be taken only to the first order to satisfy Eqs. (4) without including derivatives of the gust with respect to time into the output. This implies also that the summation over the matrices [N] of Eq. (5a) is carried out only up to n so that the corresponding finite state approximation of Eq. (6) contains no linear and quadratic terms in p.

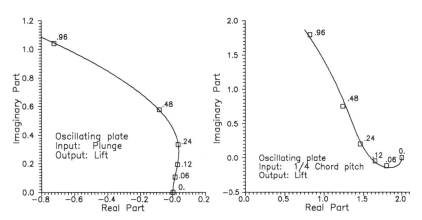

Fig. 1 - Fit of lift transfer functions for an oscillating plate in incompressible flow: □ known from Theodersen theory.

Fig. 1 shows some results that can be obtained by this approach when it is applied to the two dimensional flat plate Theodorsen formulation for incompressible flow [67]. The displayed results are obtained with two states residualized from a six states initial approximation and perfected through the final procedure previously described without any non linear iteration to improve the eigenvalues.

Finally Fig. 2 demonstrates the very good approximation afforded by three states, obtained after reduction of fifteen initial states, for some terms of the five by five aerodynamic transfer matrix related to a wing model to be used later in the design of an AFSS.

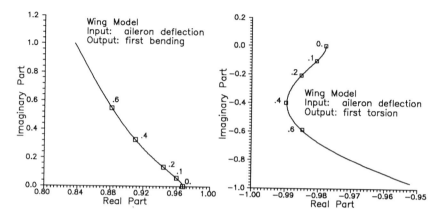

Fig. 2 - Fit of some aerodynamic transfer functions for an oscillating wing model: □ known from doublet lattice with body sources and interference bodies.

III. CLASSICAL AEROSERVOELASTIC EQUATIONS

Aeroelastic response equations are traditionally developed directly in the Laplace transform domain s. The dynamics of the structure, including control surfaces, is described by a relatively small number of free coordinates $\{q_s\}$, mostly related to the amplitude of a set of free vibration and/or static modes appropriately chosen to correctly model the dynamics of the system. Often $\{q_s\}$ includes a discrete set of physical degrees of freedom to simplify the modeling and design task, a notable instance of this practice being the explicit inclusion of the rotation of aerodynamic control surfaces in $\{q_s\}$. The equation of motion of the structure can be written

$$([M_s]s^2 + [D_s]s + [K_s] - q[\text{Ham}(p, \mathcal{M})])\{q_s(s)\} =$$

$$[F_{sa}]\{f_{sa}(s)\} + q/V[\text{Hag}(p, \mathcal{M})]\{v_g(s)\} + [F_{sd}]\{d(s)\} \tag{15}$$

where $[M_s]$, $[D_s]$, $[K_s]$ are the structural mass, damping and stiffness matrices, $\{f_{sa}\}$ is the vector of generalized forces applied to the structure by the actuators, $\{d\}$ is the vector of generic external generalized forces and/or disturbances, [Fsa] and [Fsd] are the modal force distribution matrices related to {fsa} and {d}. A peculiar feature of this approach is the maintenance of the aerodynamic transfer matrices in their implicit form, i.e. without defining a specific dynamic model for them, with Eqs. (2) used only for their interpolation.

The dynamics of the actuators connected to the structure is given by the following relation

$$[W_a(s)]\{q_a(s)\} + [W_s(s)]\{q_s(s)\} = [W_f(s)]\{f_{sa}(s)\} + [W_u(s)]\{u(s)\} \qquad (16)$$

where [Wa], [Ws], [Wf] and [Wu] are polynomial matrices in s, the vector {qa} is related to the internal dynamics of the actuators and {u} is their input control vector. This equation is derived from an initial modeling of the actuators alone given by

$$[Z_a(s)]\{q_c(s)\} = [Z_f(s)]\{f_{as}(s)\} + [W_u(s)]\{u(s)\} \qquad (17)$$

where {qc} contains all the generalized actuators degrees of freedom, [Za] and [Zf] are polynomial matrices in s and {fas} represents the generalized forces applied to the actuator by the structure. Introducing the kinematic compatibility equation between the actuators and the structure and the action-reaction relation for the forces exchanged between the structure and the actuators, i.e.

$$[U_a]\{q_c\} = [U_s]\{q_s\} \qquad (18a)$$

$$[F_a]\{f_{as}\} = [F_s]\{f_{sa}\} \qquad (18b)$$

partitioning the vector of actuators degrees of freedom in an independent part, {qa}, and dependent part, {qd}, i.e.: $\{q_c\}^T = [\{q_a\}^T \mid \{q_d\}^T]$, we can rewrite Eqs. (18) as

$$\{q_d\} = [T_{qa}]\{q_a\} + [T_{qs}]\{q_s\} \qquad (19a)$$

$$\{f_{as}\} = [T_f]\{f_{sa}\} \qquad (19b)$$

so that after substituting Eqs. (19) into Eq. (17), partitioned according to Eq. (19a), we obtain Eq. (16).

The actuators involved in AFSSs are mostly electrohydraulic even if, in some particular cases, it is possible to envisage the use of electric motors. They are usually controlled as position servos driving aerodynamic control surfaces. Control forces can also be included in {u} and this would imply a direct hinge moment control that is likely to be adoptable for control surfaces used only for flutter suppression. A certain amount of position servoing is nonetheless always needed to avoid drift so that a pure hinge moment control can be rarely applied. In order to arrive to the dynamic equations of the servoed structure it is necessary to eliminate {fsa} between Eq. (15) and Eq. (16). In view of the implicit calculation of the aerodynamic forces it is possible to avoid the introduction of matrices with rational functions in s if {fsa} is calculated by partitioning Eq. (15) by rows into two set of equations that allow to write

$$([M_{s1}]s^2 + [D_{s1}]s + [K_{s1}] - q[Ham1])\{q_s(s)\} =$$
$$[F_{sa1}]\{f_{sa}(s)\} + q/V[Hag1]\{v_g(s)\} + [F_{sd1}]\{d(s)\} \qquad (20a)$$

$$\{f_{sa}(s)\} = [F_{sa2}]^{-1}(([M_{s2}]s^2 + [D_{s2}]s + [K_{s2}] - q[Ham2])\{q_s(s)\} +$$
$$- q/V[Hag2]\{v_g(s)\} - [F_{sd2}]\{d(s)\}) \qquad (20b)$$

After substitution of Eq. (20b) into Eqs. (16),(20a) we obtain the following equations

$$([\overline{M}_s]s^2 + [\overline{D}_s]s + [\overline{K}_s] - q[\overline{H}am(p,\mathscr{M})])\{q_s(s)\} =$$
$$q/V[\overline{H}ag(p,\mathscr{M})]\{v_g(s)\} + [\overline{F}d]\{d(s)\} \qquad (21a)$$

$$([\overline{W}_s(s)]-q[\overline{W}am(s,p,\mathscr{M})])\{q_s(s)\} + [W_a(s)]\{q_a\} = q/V[\overline{W}ag(s,p,\mathscr{M})]\{v_g(s)\} +$$
$$+ [W_u(s)]\{u(s)\} + [\overline{W}d(s)]\{d(s)\} \qquad (21b)$$

where

$$[\overline{H}am]=[Ham1]-[F_{sa1}][F_{sa2}]^{-1}[Ham2] \qquad [\overline{H}ag]=[Hag1]-[F_{sa1}][F_{sa2}]^{-1}[Hag2]$$

$$[\overline{M}_s]=[M_{s1}]-[F_{sa1}][F_{sa2}]^{-1}[M_{s2}] \qquad [\overline{F}d]=[F_{sd1}]-[F_{sa1}][F_{sa2}]^{-1}[F_{sd2}]$$

$$[\overline{D}_s]=[D_{s1}]-[F_{sa1}][F_{sa2}]^{-1}[D_{s2}] \qquad [\overline{W}am]=-[W_f][F_{sa2}]^{-1}[Ham2]$$

$$[\overline{K}_s]=[K_{s1}]-[F_{sa1}][F_{sa2}]^{-1}[K_{s2}] \qquad [\overline{W}ag]=-[W_f][F_{sa2}]^{-1}[Hag2]$$

$$[\overline{W}_s]=[W_s]-[W_f][F_{sa2}]^{-1}(s^2[M_{s2}]+s[D_{s2}]+[K_{s2}]) \qquad [\overline{W}d]=-[W_f][F_{sa2}]^{-1}[F_{sd2}]$$

The appearance of terms depending simultaneously on s and p is used to remark that they combine aerodynamic matrices kept in implicit form and matrix polynomials in s. Equations (21) can be finally written as

$$([T(s)] - q[Ka(s,p,\mathscr{M})])\{q(s)\} =$$
$$[Fu(s)]\{u(s)\} + q/V[Kg(s,p,\mathscr{M})]\{v_g(s)\} + [Fd(s)]\{d(s)\} \qquad (22)$$

where

$$\{q\}^T = [\{q_s\}^T \mid \{q_a\}^T]$$

$$[T(s)] = \left[\begin{array}{c|c} [\overline{M}_s]s^2 + [\overline{D}_s]s + [\overline{K}_s] & 0 \\ \hline [\overline{W}_s(s)] & [W_a(s)] \end{array}\right]$$

$$[K_g] = \left[\begin{array}{c} [\overline{H}_{ag}] \\ \hline [\overline{W}_{ag}] \end{array}\right] \quad [F_u] = \left[\begin{array}{c} 0 \\ \hline [W_u] \end{array}\right] \quad [K_a] = \left[\begin{array}{c|c} [\overline{H}_{am}] & 0 \\ \hline [\overline{W}_{am}] & 0 \end{array}\right] \quad [F_d] = \left[\begin{array}{c} [\overline{F}_d] \\ \hline [\overline{W}_d] \end{array}\right]$$

The modeling approach just presented is here termed classical as it evolves from the ground of the most traditional aeroelastic analysis methods [56]. If the control surfaces rotations are explicitly included in $\{q_s\}$ Eqs. (21),(22) are even simpler as $[F_{sa1}] = 0$. Moreover if servo positioned actuators of adequate power and bandwidth are used, it is common practice to further simplify the formulation by discarding the aerodynamic and external force terms of Eq. (20b). That is tantamount to assuming $\{f_{sa}\}$ negligible in Eq. (16) and to adding a simple correction of the inertia term of the actuators to account for the control surface inertia. Then Eq. (22) can be obtained directly by simply appending Eq. (16) to Eq. (21a). In this way the modeling is simplified and experimentally determined actuators transfer functions, i.e. Eq. (17) with $\{f_{as}\} = 0$, can be readily used without the need of taking into account the compliance of the actuator to external forces applied to it. Equation (20b) can then be used to determine $\{f_{sa}\}$ and to verify whether the actuators are capable or not of producing the required generalized forces. A further advantage of this simplified modeling is achieved if the polynomial matrices of Eq. (17), and then also those of Eq. (16), are of second order in s at most. This is always possible by defining appropriate fictitious actuators degrees of freedom and leads to a quadratic expression for $[T(s)]$, i.e.

$$[T(s)] = [M]s^2 + [D]s + [K]$$

so that the actuators can be easily included in already existing general purpose aeroelastic analysis programs [79]. It is clear that the previous [M], [D] and [K] matrices can no more be interpreted as the usual structural matrices. The adoption of this practice is not always acceptable especially in the development of new designs or in the analysis of critical cases in which the actuators operate at frequencies close to the limit of their bandwidth. That, beside introducing a substantial lag, makes their response strongly affected by the loads applied to them. It should also be remarked that, because of the implicit treatment of the aerodynamic terms, specialized ad hoc techniques are required to solve response and stability problems related to Eq. (22) [56,79].

The modeling of the system is completed by defining a set of output $\{y\}$, related to both measurements and performances, that can be written

$$\{y(s)\} = [M_q(s)]\{q(s)\} + [M_u]\{u(s)\} + [M_g]\{v_g(s)\} + [M_d]\{d(s)\} \tag{23}$$

with $[M]$ being appropriate matrices and $[M_q]$ being a polynomial matrix with terms up to s^2, if acceleration measurements and inertia forces are to be taken into account.

IV. MODERN AEROSERVOELASTIC EQUATIONS

To allow the adoption of the most general multi input-output modern control design methods we must develop a state space model of the aeroservoelastic system. This simply requires that both the structure and the actuators are set, from the very beginning, as systems of first order time invariant differential equations to which the same coupling procedure previously presented is applied. To this end, defining the vector of aerostructural states $\{x_{ae}\}^T = [\{q_s\}^T \mid \{\dot{q}_s\}^T \mid \{x_{am}\}^T \mid \{x_{ag}\}^T]$, Eqs. (3),(4), (15) are rewritten as

$$[V_{ae}]\{\dot{x}_{ae}\} = [A_{ae}]\{x_{ae}\} + [B_{sa}]\{f_{sa}\} + [B_{sd}]\{d\} + [B_{sg}]\{v_g\} \tag{24}$$

Calling

$$[M_{ae}] = [M_s] - q(c/V)^2[Am2]$$
$$[D_{ae}] = [D_s] - q(c/V)[Am1]$$
$$[K_{ae}] = [K_s] - q[Am0]$$

the different terms of Eq. (24) are given by the followings

$$[V_{ae}] = \begin{bmatrix} [I] & [0] & [0] & [0] \\ [0] & [M_{ae}] & [0] & [0] \\ [0] & [0] & [I] & [0] \\ [0] & [0] & [0] & [I] \end{bmatrix} \quad [B_{sa}] = \begin{bmatrix} [0] \\ [F_{sa}] \\ [0] \\ [0] \end{bmatrix} \quad [B_{sg}] = \begin{bmatrix} [0] \\ q/V[Ag0] \\ [0] \\ V/c[Bg] \end{bmatrix} \tag{25a}$$

$$[A_{ae}] = \begin{bmatrix} [0] & [I] & [0] & [0] \\ -[K_{ae}] & -[D_{ae}] & q[Cm] & q/V[Cg] \\ V/c[Bm] & [0] & V/c[Am] & [0] \\ [0] & [0] & [0] & V/c[Ag] \end{bmatrix} \quad [B_{sd}] = \begin{bmatrix} [0] \\ [F_{sd}] \\ [0] \\ [0] \end{bmatrix} \tag{25b}$$

The actuators dynamics, either directly or through an appropriate realization of their transfer functions [77], i.e. Eq. (17), can be transformed to a state space equation and written

$$[Va]\{\dot{z}c\} = [Aa]\{zc\} + [Bas]\{fas\} + [Bau]\{u\} \qquad (26)$$

The connection of the actuators to the aeroelastic system described in the previous paragraph is quite different from the standard procedures of connecting different dynamic systems by having the output of one becoming the input to another [80]. To apply the correct approach we must rewrite the kinematic compatibility equation corresponding to Eq. (18) as

$$[Za]\{zc\} = [Xae]\{xae\} \qquad (27)$$

while the action-reaction force relation, i.e. Eq. (19), remains unchanged. To connect Eq. (26) to Eq. (24) under the constraints of Eqs. (19),(27) we take the following partition $\{zc\}^T = [\{zd\}^T \,|\, \{za\}^T]$ after which Eq. (27) gives

$$\{zd\} = [Tza]\{za\} + [Txae]\{xae\} \qquad (28)$$

Substituting Eq. (19b) and Eq. (28) and its derivative with respect to time into Eq. (26), whose columns are also partitioned according to Eq. (28), we obtain

$$[\overline{V}a]\{\dot{z}a\}+[\overline{V}ae]\{\dot{x}ae\} = [\overline{A}a]\{za\}+[\overline{A}ae]\{xae\}+[\overline{B}as]\{fsa\}+[Bau]\{u\} \qquad (29)$$

The matrix [Bsa] has the rank of the order of {fsa} so it is possible to partition Eq. (24) by rows thus obtaining the following equations

$$[Vae1]\{\dot{x}ae\} = [Aae1]\{xae\} + [Bsa1]\{fsa\} + [Bsd1]\{d\} + [Bsg1]\{vg\} \qquad (30)$$

$$\{fsa\} = [Bsa2]^{-1}([Vae2]\{\dot{x}ae\} - [Aae2]\{xae\} - [Bsd2]\{d\} - [Bsg2]\{vg\}) \qquad (31)$$

Substituting Eq. (31) into Eqs. (29),(30) and appending the resulting equations to each other we have the final aeroservoelastic system in the form

$$[\overline{V}]\{\dot{w}\} = [\overline{A}]\{w\} + [\overline{B}u]\{u\} + [\overline{B}d]\{d\} + [\overline{B}g]\{vg\} \qquad (32)$$

with

$$\{w\}^T = [\{xae\}^T |\{za\}^T]$$

$$[\overline{V}] = \begin{bmatrix} [Vae1]-[B\,s\,a1][Bsa2]^{-1}[Vae2] & 0 \\ [\overline{V}ae] - [\overline{B}as][Bsa2]^{-1}[Vae2] & [\overline{V}a] \end{bmatrix}$$

$$[\overline{A}] = \begin{bmatrix} [A_{ae1}]-[B_{sa1}][B_{sa2}]^{-1}[A_{ae2}] & 0 \\ [\overline{A}_{ae}] - [\overline{B}_{as}][B_{sa2}]^{-1}[A_{ae2}] & [\overline{A}_a] \end{bmatrix}$$

$$[\overline{B}_u] = \begin{bmatrix} 0 \\ [B_{au}] \end{bmatrix} \qquad [\overline{B}_d] = \begin{bmatrix} [B_{sd1}]- [B_{sa1}][B_{sa2}]^{-1}[B_{sd2}] \\ [\overline{B}_{as}][B_{sa2}]^{-1}[B_{sd2}] \end{bmatrix}$$

$$[\overline{B}_g] = \begin{bmatrix} [B_{sg1}]-[B_{sa1}][B_{sa2}]^{-1}[B_{sg2}] \\ [\overline{B}_{as}][B_{sa2}]^{-1}[B_{sg2}] \end{bmatrix}$$

The same simplification explained in the classical formulation can be used to obtain a relation equivalent to Eq. (32) if the actuators are connected to the structure by simply appending Eq. (29), with $\{f_{sa}\} = 0$, to Eq. (30), with $\{f_{sa}\}$ given by Eq. (31). This procedure deserves the same comments previously made.

The matrix $[\overline{V}]$ must be full rank if the constraints Eqs. (19),(27) are correctly assigned. It is nonetheless possible to end with a singular $[\overline{V}]$ if either Eq. (26) or Eq. (24) include relations defining kinematic states already defined in the other. However if a set of consistent equations is contained in Eq. (32) it must be possible to partition it into the two following equations

$$[\overline{V}_{11}]\{\dot{w}_1\} + [\overline{V}_{12}]\{\dot{w}_2\} =$$

$$[\overline{A}_{11}]\{w_1\} + [\overline{A}_{12}]\{w_2\} + [\overline{B}_{u1}]\{u\} + [\overline{B}_{d1}]\{d\} + [\overline{B}_{g1}]\{v_g\} \qquad (33a)$$

$$[\overline{V}_{21}]\{\dot{w}_1\} + [\overline{V}_{22}]\{\dot{w}_2\} =$$

$$[\overline{A}_{21}]\{w_1\} + [\overline{A}_{22}]\{w_2\} + [\overline{B}_{u2}]\{u\} + [\overline{B}_{d2}]\{d\} + [\overline{B}_{g2}]\{v_g\} \qquad (33b)$$

with Eq. (33a) corresponding to the set of independent and consistent equations, and with $[V_{11}]$ being a full rank matrix. We can then evaluate $\{\dot{w}_1\}$ from Eq. (33a) and after substituting it into Eq. (33b) we must verify that

$$([\overline{B}_{g2}] - [\overline{V}_{21}][\overline{V}_{11}]^{-1}[\overline{B}_{g1}]) = 0$$

$$([\overline{B}_{u2}] - [\overline{V}_{21}][\overline{V}_{11}]^{-1}[\overline{B}_{u1}]) = 0$$

$$([\overline{B}_{d2}] - [\overline{V}_{21}][\overline{V}_{11}]^{-1}[\overline{B}_{d1}]) = 0$$

to avoid having $\{u\}$, $\{d\}$, $\{v_g\}$ constraining the definition of purely kinematic states, which is physically impossible. Then, since

$$([\overline{V}_{22}] - [\overline{V}_{21}][\overline{V}_{11}]^{-1}[\overline{V}_{12}]) = 0$$

because of the singularity of $[\overline{V}]$, Eq. (33) contains the hidden constraint

$$\{w_2\} = [W]\{w_1\} \tag{34}$$

with

$$[W] = -([\overline{V}_{21}][\overline{V}_{11}]^{-1}[\overline{A}_{12}]-[\overline{A}_{22}])^{-1}([\overline{V}_{21}][\overline{V}_{11}]^{-1}[\overline{A}_{11}]-[\overline{A}_{21}])$$

Substituting Eq. (34) and its derivative with respect to time into Eq. (33a), after defining $\{x\} = \{w_1\}$, we end by recovering the consistent and very final equation

$$[V]\{\dot{x}\} = [A]\{x\} + [B_u]\{u\} + [B_d]\{d\} + [B_g]\{v_g\} \tag{35}$$

This formulation of the aeroservoelastic equations is then termed modern [81].
To complete the modeling the following output relation, equivalent to Eq. (23), is defined

$$\{y\} = [C_x]\{x\} + [C_{\dot{x}}]\{\dot{x}\} + [C_u]\{u\} + [C_g]\{v_g\} + [C_d]\{d\} \tag{36}$$

As already noted the modern formulation can lead to relatively large mathematical models that are difficult to be used and eventually produce controllers of unacceptable dimension so that methods to reduce the order of dynamic systems can be very useful in the design of AFSSs. These methods should work both on stable and unstable systems and general purpose [34] and specialized formulations [82] can be found in the literature. The method described in appendix A can also be useful if possible unstable eigenvalues are included in the retained part. It is noted that such a reduction method, based on stability and frequency content, could not be the most effective one. Nonetheless it is physically appealing and intuitive and can be more than enough if AFSSs can be designed by assigning simple controllers from the very beginning so that a model reduction is needed only to speed up the computation and not to simplify the control system.

V.   A PREMISE TO CLOSING THE LOOP

From the comments made in the introduction we will assume that much is to be gained if it is possible to design relatively simple, and possibly decentralized, AFSSs that can satisfy the design requirements while taking into account model uncertainties, different operating conditions, gain

scheduling and failed sensors and/or actuators. In this way the fine tuning
and validation in flight would be easier because of the more intuitive
physical properties that can be associated to controller parameters and
less design iterations, along with the detailed post design simulations,
would be required. In this perspective an actively controlled aircraft can
be synthesized by the functional blocks of Fig. 3. The AFSS is there
presented as a minor stabilizing loop around which all the other major
functional capabilities of active controls, e.g. Control and Stability
Augmentation Systems (CSAS), Load Alleviation and Modal Suppression
(LAMS), are built.

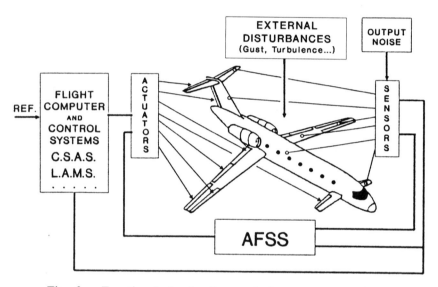

Fig. 3 - Functional sketch of an actively controlled aircraft.

This framework allows a separate design of the AFSS without much care of
other control loops and make it easier to satisfy the simplicity
constraints imposed on its controller structure. The approach can be
justified by the different frequency ranges on which the controllers
operate, since flutter related frequencies are often higher and relatively
well separated from those of the rigid body degrees of freedom that
determine the aircraft flight path and orientation. This can no more be
true for aircraft with very high flexibility, unconventional configuration
[83] or adopting load alleviation systems as in such cases the AFSS is
bound to interact with rigid body motions. Nonetheless, even in these
cases, it can be acceptable to adopt a separate loop for flutter
stabilization since its possible adverse effects on other requirements can
be corrected with appropriate compensations in the outer loops. A complete
decentralization of the flutter control is however rarely feasible since

often the control surfaces, and possibly some sensors, must be shared with the outer control loops. Nonetheless this approach allows to simplify the design, implementation, test and tuning of the AFSS in flight and will be followed here.

VI. CLOSING THE LOOP IN THE MODERN FORMULATION

No general theory is yet available that allows to design a stabilizing, structurally constrained controller capable of achieving adequate performances to satisfy a given set of design specifications while maintaining robustness against modeled and unmodeled uncertainties. So, if it is believed possible to assign the structure of the AFSS in the hope of making it simpler without sacrificing its effectiveness, the designer must resort to a numerical approach. In this view we will present a formulation based on the minimization of a quadratic performance function that is well suited to the modern formulation and can treat most of the active design problems implied in Fig. 3, i.e not only those related to the minor flutter stabilization loop to be treated here. As we have seen, the modern formulation allows to model the aeroservoelastic system according to Eqs. (35),(36). We will rewrite Eq. (35) as

$$[V(\{\gamma\})]\{\dot{x}\} = [A(\{\gamma\})]\{x\} + [Bu(\{\gamma\})]\{u\} + [Bd]\{d\} \qquad (37)$$

in which, for sake of conciseness, all the external disturbances are represented by $\{d\}$. The outputs, divided into two groups related to measurements and performances, are extended to include the possible presence of a reference command vector $\{r\}$ and rewritten

$$\{m\} = [M\dot{x}(\{\gamma\})]\{\dot{x}\} + [Mx(\{\gamma\})]\{x\} + [Md]\{d\} + [Mr]\{r\} \qquad (38a)$$

$$\{y\} = [R\dot{x}]\{\dot{x}\} + [Rx]\{x\} + [Ru]\{u\} + [Rd]\{d\} + [Rr]\{r\} \qquad (38b)$$

where the vector $\{m\}$ and $\{y\}$ are respectively the available measures and the response performances of interest. It should be noted that $\{u\}$ no more appears in Eq. (38a) as it is redundant in view of the presence of $\{\dot{x}\}$. In fact $\{u\}$ can be obtained from any suitable subset or linear combination of the equations of Eq. (37) , e.g.

$$\{u\} = ([Bu]^T[Bu])^{-1}[Bu]^T([V]\{\dot{x}\} - [A]\{x\} - [Bd]\{d\}) \qquad (39)$$

which when substituted into Eq. (36) gives Eq. (38a). It is clearly also possible to eliminate $\{\dot{x}\}$ while maintaining $\{u\}$. This will not be done since it would complicate the numerical procedure related to the design methods that we are going to describe. We note that some matrices of the previous equations are assumed dependent on a set of generic parameters $\{\gamma\}$ which can be available for passive design. In particular the parameters related to $[Bu]$ and to the matrices $[Mx]$ and $[Mx]$ allow to assume actuators and sensors locations as design variables.

To complete the design method we have to establish the types of external excitation we want to take into account. We will assume that performance specifications can be related to the imposition of initial conditions $\{x_o\}$, step disturbances $\{d\}$ and constant desired reference conditions $\{r\}$ or to any output that can be obtained by exciting a suitable asymptotically stable dynamic system with them. In the latter case we have just to append the chosen dynamics to Eq. (37). As we will see this choice can include steady state specifications in the performance index and it is then believed capable of modeling a variety of design conditions, including load alleviation to practical maneuvers, larger than the usual choice of modeling $\{d\}$ as a white noise [44,45,84]. In practice a combination of the two will be the best choice, as it allows a wider modeling of operating conditions, but such a mixed formulation will not be pursued here to avoid a too lengthy presentation [85,86]. The design is then carried out by minimizing the following

$$
J = E\left(\int_0^\infty \left((\{y\}-\{\overline{y}\})^T [Qy](\{y\}-\{\overline{y}\}) + (\{u\}-\{\overline{u}\})^T [Qu](\{u\}-\{\overline{u}\}) + \right.\right.
$$

$$
\left.\left. \{\dot{u}\}^T [Q\dot{u}]\{\dot{u}\})\exp(-2\alpha t)dt + \{\overline{y}\}^T [Q\overline{y}]\{\overline{y}\}\right)\right) \tag{40}
$$

where the overlined terms indicate the steady state value of the corresponding quantities and E is the expected value with respect to all the possible uncorrelated $\{x_o\}$, $\{d\}$ and $\{r\}$ having null mean and assigned covariances $[X_o]$, $[D]$ and $[R]$ i.e.:

$$
E(\{x_o\}\{x_o\}^T) = [X_o] \qquad E(\{d\}\{d\}^T) = [D] \qquad E(\{r\}\{r\}^T) = [R]
$$

The weighting matrices $[Qy]$, $[Q\overline{y}]$, $[Q\dot{u}]$ are positive semidefinite and $[Qu]$ is positive definite. The parameter α is a penalty parameter guaranteeing that no eigenvalue of the optimized system will have a real part less than α and is very useful in achieving stability for initially unstable systems [42]. The design variables can be the parameters of $\{\gamma\}$ and the gain matrix $[Kf]$ of the following feedback law

$$
\{u\} = [Kf]\{m\} \tag{41}
$$

The structure of $[Kf]$ can be freely assigned by the designer, on the base of his understanding of the system, to simplify the controller without sacrificing performances. Compensator dynamics, of assigned structure, can either be included into Eq. (37), i.e. in $\{\gamma\}$, or into $[Kf]$ by expanding

[Bu], {u} and {x} to include compensator input and state. In any case the compensator state will be fully available in the measurement {m}. It can be seen that derivative control can be designed directly, if derivatives of the state can be measured, and that the performance index, i.e. Eq. (40), allows to take into account transient, steady state responses and control rate limitations. Thus response specifications and constraints on control activity could be related directly to Eq. (40) with an appropriate choice of the matrices [Q]. Moreover the matrices [Q] affect the robustness of the obtainable controller. In order to avoid sacrificing the intuitive appeal of the weighting matrices in a trade off against robustness specifications, we choose to design a single instance of {γ} and [Kf] by minimizing a weighted sum of equations (40)

$$J_{tot} = \sum_{i=1}^{m} \beta_i \, J_i \qquad (42)$$

where the summation is extended to a given set of m models of the aeroelastic system. This allows to take into account varying operating conditions and components failures, thus introducing robustness against major modeled uncertainties. Furthermore the possible need of a scheduling policy to improve performances against known varying operating conditions is included in the definition of [Kf] by making it dependent on an appropriate set of scheduling parameters {τ}, e.g $\mathscr{M}$, q, and writing

$$[K_f] = \sum_{i=1}^{n} S_i(\{\tau\}) \, [k_i] \qquad (43)$$

where the S_is are assigned base scheduling functions. Even if the multi model approach with the structured scheduling of Eq. (43) is appropriate to enhance robustness and allows to avoid many of the after design simulations needed to finely tune the controller, the choice of too many models can make the approach impracticable. So it is necessary to back up the procedure with a general robustification method capable to take into account imprecise and unstructured model knowledge in a less detailed way. In relation to robustness with respect to stability, unstructured uncertainties can be accounted for by singular value analyses of the input and output return difference matrices [37,38]. They have been a subject of much research and their use is often the back bone of many general purpose design procedures [32-41]. Unfortunately in these methods there is no way to take into account possible constraints on the structure of the controller, while no problem is posed to including constraints on the allowed singular values in a numerical approach, whatever is the controller structure.

It has been shown that phase and gain margins against independent multiplicative uncertainties, either at the input or at the output, acting simultaneously on all loops, can be conservatively related to the minimum singular value of the return difference matrices [37,38]. Adequate margins can then be obtained if the overall minimum singular value is greater than a minimum desired value. In view of the conservativeness of the criteria relatively low minimum singular values can be accepted especially if they are complementing design methods already enforcing robustness, as in the case of a multi model design. In our notation the input and output return difference matrices are respectively

$$[\Sigma_i] = [I] - [K_f]([M_{\dot{x}}]j\omega + [M])(j\omega[V] - [A])^{-1}[B_u] \qquad (44a)$$

$$[\Sigma_o] = [I] - ([M_{\dot{x}}]j\omega + [M])(j\omega[V] - [A])^{-1}[B_u][K_f] \qquad (44b)$$

It must be noted that the presence of derivatives of the state in Eqs. (44), which is equivalent to a direct linking of the input to the output, should not be allowed, since gain and phase margins related to minimum singular values are proved on the assumption that $[\Sigma_i]$ and $[\Sigma_o]$ tend to $[I]$ as ω tend to infinite [37,38]. The problem can be solved by assuming Eq. (38b) as a low frequency approximation of large bandwidth sensors of the state derivatives. Thus in a more detailed model, including sensors dynamics, the derivatives will appear at the output as sensors states whose transfer functions decay at least with ω at high frequencies so that any direct feedthrough from the input to the output will be eliminated making $[\Sigma_i]$ and $[\Sigma_o]$ tend to $[I]$. Equations (44) can then be used as acceptable approximations in the sense that they do not substantially change the singular values in the frequency range in which model uncertainties are of interest.

Finally we impose some constraints on the eigenvalues of the closed loop system in order to force them in an acceptable domain in the left s plane so that the design task becomes: determine $\{\gamma\}$ and $[k_i]$ to

$$\min \, J_{tot}(\{\gamma\},[k_i]) \qquad (45)$$

with each model possibly subjected to any of the following constraints:

$$\sigma_{min}([\Sigma_i(\omega)]) \leq \sigma(\omega)^* \qquad \sigma_{min}([\Sigma_o(\omega)]) \leq \sigma(\omega)^* \qquad (46a)$$

to guarantee robustness against unmodeled uncertainties;

$$\delta \leq \delta^* \qquad \omega^*_{min} \leq \omega \leq \omega^*_{max} \qquad (\delta/\omega) \leq (\delta/\omega)^* \qquad (46b)$$

to maintain the eigenvalues in acceptable domains; while the design parameters can be imposed the following:

$$[k_i^*]_{min} \leq [k_i] \leq [k_i^*]_{max} \qquad \{\gamma^*\}_{min} \leq \{\gamma\} \leq \{\gamma^*\}_{max} \qquad (46c)$$

to satisfy possible implementation constraints and all the starred quantities are assigned by the designer.

Even if the above statement of the design procedure encompasses a wide variety of design conditions and specifications, some care is required for its use, as a blind imposition of constraints on a multi model design can easily lead to a void design space. Moreover there is no way to define the conditions under which a given controller can satisfy the desired constraints. So a step by step approach should be applied in which models and/or constraints are gradually added in view of the continuous refinement of the design. For stabilizing an unstable system a good approach is to enforce an implicit model following to approximately obtain a desired eigenstructure [87]. As it will be shown in the example, the possibility of taking state derivatives into Eq. (38b) makes this approach quite easy. The formulae required to carry out the minimization task are given in appendix B. It is noted that the design procedure just described requires an asymptotically stable system and this is a major drawback since the method will not work when the initial guess for $\{\gamma\}$ and $[k_i]$ do not stabilize the system. This is a crucial point as it implies that the design must begin with an already known, even if not optimal, AFSS. This problem, common to all procedure of this type, has no guaranteed solution and can be practically solved in many ways [42-45]. It should be remarked that this is just the general problem of producing an initial feasible solution for a constrained minimization problem and most of the codes generally available for this task can tackle it with the formulation most suitable for the algorithms used in a specific implementation [44,45]. Nonetheless we will recall here a penalty approach that is specifically designed for the problem we are facing. It is based on a sequence of unconstrained minimization performed using α as a penalty parameter in order to stabilize the system over a given set of models [42]. The procedure goes as follows:
- assign α to make the shifted system stable (see Eq. (B1a));
- perform an unconstrained optimization. This will improve the stability of the system as the performance index is positive and gets higher as stability decreases;
- repeat the procedure till a stable system is obtained.

If this procedure fails either an unsuitable controller structure has been assigned or too many models with conflicting behavior have been taken into account and the design set up should be changed. If the models are related to continuously varying operating conditions a scheduled control can be adopted to widen the design space. Nonetheless if we want to enforce specific constraints on the singular values, design variables and on the eigenvalues we must eventually rely on the capability of the chosen optimization technique to enforce feasibility for initial unfeasible designs [78,88-90]. It is finally remarked that an equivalent formulation can be carried out for discrete linear systems to design controllers that can be directly implemented on a digital computer [91].

VII. CLOSING THE LOOP IN THE CLASSICAL FORMULATION

The design of an AFSS having a constrained structure with a classical aeroservoelastic formulation is in principle much the same as in the modern formulation. Substantially different are instead the numerical methods used for the solution of the analysis and response problems related to the design task because of the implicit treatment of the aerodynamic terms [56]. For a stable aeroservoelastic systems it would not be difficult to translate Eq. (40), or any equivalent approach for random disturbances, into the frequency domain. Nonetheless restraining our interest to the mere AFSS we substitute Eq. (45) with the more simple

$$J = 1/2\{a\}^T[W]\{a\} \tag{47}$$

in which $\{a\}$ is a vector containing all the design parameters, i.e $\{\gamma\}$ and $[k_i]$s, and $[W]$ is a positive diagonal weighting matrix adopted for scaling purposes and to limit actuators activity by maintaining small $[k_i]$s. The multi model and side constraints, i.e Eqs. (46), are instead maintained unaltered. The closed loop equation to be solved to take into account the constraints on the eigenvalues, i.e Eq. (22), is rewritten as

$$[Z(\{a\},s)]\{q\} = ([T(\{\gamma\},s)]-q[K_a(s,p,\mathcal{M})] +$$

$$- [F_u(\{\gamma\},s)][K_f][M_q(s,\{\gamma\})])\{q(s)\} = 0 \tag{48}$$

while the corresponding return difference matrices are

$$[\Sigma_i] = [I] - [K_f][M_q(j\omega)]([T(j\omega)] - q[K_a(j\omega,jk,\mathcal{M})])^{-1} [F_u(j\omega)] \tag{49a}$$

$$[\Sigma_o] = [I] - [M_q(j\omega)]([T(j\omega)] - q[K_a(j\omega,jk,\mathcal{M})])^{-1} [F_u(j\omega)][K_f] \tag{49b}$$

Apart from the different objective function, all the comments made in the previous paragraph for the design in the modern formulation could be repeated here. However the implicit treatment of the aerodynamics deserve some further comments. At first it is noted that the the minimum singular values of Eqs. (49) are the same as those of Eqs. (44) even if the aerodynamics is treated implicitly. In fact Eqs. (49) are equivalent to Eqs. (44) as far as the same aerodynamic approximation, the same measurements and the same input are used. Also the cost of performing the transfer functions calculations would not be much different [81].

A second and most important point is the solution of implicit eigenvalue problems of the type of Eq. (48). Here it is important to recall that classical flutter analyses are performed on the tacit assumption that eigenvalues hidden in the implicit treatment of the aerodynamics never become unstable, so that only those related to the servo elastic part need to be calculated. These are known for $V = 0$, as in this case Eq. (48) is a polynomial matrix in s and can be easily translated into a standard eigenvalue equation. So the problem of following their variation for changing flight conditions must be solved with an ad hoc procedure. Many ways have been devised to solve this problem and we will briefly recall the one we prefer, since this establishes also the basis for the determination of a starting design for the optimization. To this end we recast Eq. (48) by making explicit its dependence upon the asymptotic speed V and write

$$[Z(s,V)]\{q\} = 0 \qquad\qquad (50a)$$

$$1/2\{q\}^T\{q\} = {}^{\text{\tiny 1}} \qquad\qquad (50b)$$

Equations (50), in which Eq. (50b) is added to impose a solution with $\{q\}$ different from zero, are a set of nonlinear equations with unknown $\{q\}$ and s. If Eqs. (50) are differentiated with respect to V they lead to the following system of differential equations

$$[Z(s,V)]d\{q\}/dV + (\partial/\partial s[Z(s,V)]\{q\})ds/dV = 0 \qquad\qquad (51a)$$

$$\{q\}^T d\{q\}/dV = 0 \qquad\qquad (51b)$$

and the solution of Eqs. (50) is reduced to the integration of the above with initial conditions, known for $V = 0$, corresponding to the different eigensolutions we want to track. Equations (50,51) can be combined in a very effective predictor corrector scheme whose details can be found in [92]. Often no finite state approximation of the aerodynamics is needed and the well known p-k approximation can be used [93,94]. The method can fail at bifurcation points, e.g. when two complex conjugate solutions meet the real axis to split into two real eigenvalues. In that case Eqs. (51) become singular and we can use a state model to recover the split branches to be followed. The effectiveness of the approach can be very high as only the few eigensolutions that make active the eigenconstraints must be determined. Moreover the sensitivities required for the numerical optimization are easily integrated into the above formulation so that the effectiveness of the method in relation to an optimization is further improved [95,96].

We finally come to the determination of a feasible starting point for the optimization. The problem is quite similar to the one already encountered in the modern approach but since no special penalty formulation can be devised we have to rely on the capability of the chosen optimization algorithm to produce an initial feasible design. Of some help can be the eigenvalue assignment procedure of [97] that, beside being useful in view of satisfying Eq. (46b), can be used also as a stand alone design

method. It is again based on Eqs. (50) except that now they are written for
an assigned si^* at a given flight condition V^*

$$[Z(\{a\},si^*,V^*)]\{q_i\} = 0 \tag{52a}$$

$$1/2\{q_i\}^T\{q_i\} = 0 \tag{52b}$$

Equations (52) are still a nonlinear system of equations but now their
unknowns are $\{q_i\}$ and either one or two components of $\{a\}$, according to si^*
being real or complex. The procedure can be extended to include the
assignment of any component of $\{q_i\}$ provided that for every assigned
component an equal number of free terms of $\{a\}$ is available. We can then
impose as many Eqs. (52) as allowed by the order of $\{a\}$. The assignment
need not be made for all the eigenvalues at a single flight condition, but
corresponding eigenvalues can be assigned for different V^* letting the
others move freely if they do not become unstable. To cope with the
possibility of imposing a number of eigenvalues which is less than that
required by the order of $\{a\}$ we define a set of Lagrange multipliers
$\{\lambda_i\},\mu_i$ and write the following

$$\mathscr{L}=1/2\{a\}^T[W]\{a\} +\sum_{i=1}^{n}(\{\lambda_i\}^T[Z(\{a\},si^*,V^*)]\{q_i\} + \mu_i(1/2\{q_i\}^T\{q_i\}-1)) \tag{53}$$

The minimization of the above equation with respect to $\{a\},\{q_i\},\{\lambda_i\}$ and μ_i
leads to a set of nonlinear equations that can be solved in a continuation
form on an assigned path that leads from known eigenvalues to the desired
ones. The continued solution can be implemented in a very effective
predictor corrector method whose details are given in [97]. The interested
reader could also refer to [98] for an extension of the method to the
design of compensators in the form of aeroelastic observers and to [12] for
an experimental verification of this design technique. While the procedure
can stabilize an aeroelastic system for different flight conditions, a
feasible design for the constraints of Eq. (46b) cannot be guaranteed. So
tedious trials on different flight conditions and chosen assigned
eigenvalues are often required to push the starting point as close as
possible to the satisfaction of Eq. (46b). As in the application of
classical control methods [16,17], this work can be worth the cost as it
adds to the physical understanding of the systems and often leads to a good
initial approximation that can make the obtainment of a fully feasible
solution easier.

VIII. SOME APPLICATIONS

An exhaustive exemplification, capable of showing all the flexibility allowed by the previously described procedures, will far exceed the space allowed to this work. So we limit ourself to a small number of cases, all consistently related to the design of an AFSS for the wing model of Fig. 4.

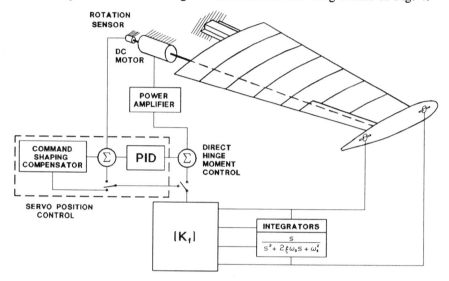

Fig. 4 - AFSS for a wing model.

The main structure of the wing is a composite longeron to which unconnected wing profiled sectors, a wing tip and an outboard trailing edge aileron are attached [12]. The dynamic behavior of the structure is modeled by the first two bending and torsional modes. The higher two, not significantly involved in the flutter, are used only for modeling precision and as a safeguard against possible control and measurement spillovers. The aileron motion is described by the corresponding rotational degree of freedom. The unsteady aerodynamic forces are obtained by a doublet lattice formulation combined with body sources and aerodynamic interference elements to model the wing tip. The aeroelastic modeling is carried out by using MSC/NASTRAN.

The minimum state model of the five by five aerodynamic transfer matrices leads to a three state approximation and some sample results related to this phase have been previously shown. The finite state modeling of the aerodynamics will not be used for the interpolation of the aerodynamic transfer functions required in the classical formulation, which will instead adopt a standard $p\text{-}k$ approximation with spline interpolation without causality constraints. The aileron is controlled through a DC motor driven by a current amplifier that guarantees a current control with a bandwidth more than a decade higher than the highest frequency of the aeroelastic system so that its dynamics is fast enough to be discarded. The motor is then servoed either in torque or in position so that the actuator dynamics can be written

$$Js^2\theta = \left(g \, \frac{z_2 \, s^2 + z_1 \, s + 1}{p_2 \, s^2 + p_1 \, s + 1} \right)(\theta - \theta_c) + T_c + T_{as} \qquad (54)$$

with J being the moment of inertia of the motor rotor, θ and θ_c the aileron rotation and command, T_c the control torque, T_{as} the couple transmitted to the motor by the aileron. The rational function in s is a PID compensation whose poles and zeros are in the left s plane and g is the loop gain. Friction and other torque disturbances are neglected. Equation (54) can be put in the form of Eq. (17) in many ways. A possibility is to define an internal degree of freedom ϕ to give the following matrices

$$[Z_a] = \begin{bmatrix} J & -z_2 \, g \\ 0 & p_2 \end{bmatrix} s^2 + \begin{bmatrix} 0 & -z_1 \, g \\ 0 & p_1 \end{bmatrix} s + \begin{bmatrix} 0 & -g \\ -1 & 1 \end{bmatrix}$$

$$(55)$$

$$[W_u] = \begin{bmatrix} 0 & 1 \\ -1 & 0 \end{bmatrix} \qquad [Z_f] = \begin{bmatrix} 1 \\ 0 \end{bmatrix} \qquad \{q_c\} = \begin{Bmatrix} \theta \\ \phi \end{Bmatrix} \qquad \{u\} = \begin{Bmatrix} \theta_c \\ T_c \end{Bmatrix}$$

The state equation corresponding to Eq. (26) can be obtained directly from the first companion form of Eq. (55) and is given by

$$[V_a] = \begin{bmatrix} 1 & 0 & 0 & 0 \\ 0 & 1 & 0 & 0 \\ 0 & 0 & J & -z_2 \, g \\ 0 & 0 & 0 & p_2 \end{bmatrix} \qquad [A_a] = - \begin{bmatrix} 0 & 0 & 1 & 0 \\ 0 & 0 & 0 & 1 \\ 0 & -g & 0 & -z_1 \, g \\ -1 & 1 & 0 & p_1 \end{bmatrix}$$

$$(56)$$

$$[B_{au}] = \begin{bmatrix} 0 & 0 \\ 0 & 0 \\ 0 & 1 \\ -1 & 0 \end{bmatrix} \qquad [B_{as}] = \begin{bmatrix} 0 \\ 0 \\ 1 \\ 0 \end{bmatrix} \qquad \{z_a\} = \begin{Bmatrix} \theta \\ \phi \\ \dot{\theta} \\ \dot{\phi} \end{Bmatrix}$$

or derived from the second companion form [77] of the fourth order differential equation corresponding to Eq. (54) and is given by

$$[V_z] = \begin{bmatrix} J \; p_2 & 0 & 0 & 0 \\ 0 & 1 & 0 & 0 \\ 0 & 0 & 1 & 0 \\ 0 & 0 & 0 & 1 \end{bmatrix} \qquad [A_z] = - \begin{bmatrix} J \; p_1 & 1 & 0 & 0 \\ J - z_2 g & 0 & 1 & 0 \\ -z_1 g & 0 & 0 & 1 \\ -g & 0 & 0 & 0 \end{bmatrix}$$

$$[B_{au}] = \begin{bmatrix} 0 & 0 \\ -z_2 g & p_2 \\ -z_1 g & p_1 \\ -g & 1 \end{bmatrix} \qquad [B_{as}] = \begin{bmatrix} 0 \\ p_2 \\ p_1 \\ 1 \end{bmatrix} \qquad \{z_a\} = \begin{Bmatrix} \theta \\ \phi_1 \\ \phi_2 \\ \phi_3 \end{Bmatrix}$$

(57)

ϕ_i being internal states. Applying the connection procedures we end up with six second order equations for the classical formulation and fifteen state equations for the modern one. In both cases the input available for control purpose are θ_c and T_c which allow to compare active flutter suppression through direct hinge moment control against position servoing. When hinge moment control is adopted the position servo is kept active with $\theta_c = 0$ to avoid drift. The behavior of the wing in open loop is shown in the V-g plot of Fig. 5.

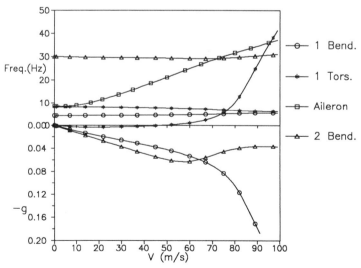

Fig. 5 - Wing model open loop V-g plot

It must be remarked that the aeroelastic eigensolutions calculated by the modern approach are undistinguishable from those given by a classical formulation adopting the p-k approximation. This will be true also for all the eigensolutions related to active control that will be shown in this paper so we will not specify how the different V-g plots are calculated in the different cases. Figure 5 shows only the two fluttering modes and part of the other modes, as long as they remain within the scale of the figure.

It can be seen that the wing flutter is mainly a classical binary bending-torsion flutter. It is remarked that the mode having an increasing frequency, close to the first torsional frequency at low speeds, is related to the dominant pole of the aileron position servo. The flutter branch of the V-g plots shows a very small damping within the stable range of speeds. This is due partly to having neglected any structural damping and partly to the high rearward unbalancing of the wing tip center of gravity purposely chosen to worsen the flutter behavior. Also the closeness of the servo bandwidth to that of an important structural mode is kept to emphasize possible servo structural coupling problems. Thus it is believed that, despite its simplicity, the model is representative of a realistic application. We then aim at the design of a flutter controller that, with a unique control law, should extend the flutter free speed domain by 50% with a sizable increase of the damping within the whole extended flight envelope.

In this view we attempt to suppress the flutter by using only a couple of accelerometers placed at the wing tip. The accelerometer signals plus the speeds obtained by their integration with two equal band pass filters, i.e by passing the acceleration through the following transfer function

$$v(s) = \frac{s}{s^2 + 2\xi\omega_o s + \omega_o^2} \tag{58}$$

are used in a direct feedback control.

Equation (58), with ω_o equal to one third of the lowest structural frequency and ξ equal to .1, behaves like $1/s$ in the frequency range of the structural modes and avoids possible drifts due to low frequency biases in the measured accelerations. The above compensation adds two second order equations to the classical model and four state to the modern one so that we end with a total of eight and nineteen equations respectively and four gains to be designed in both cases. In all the designs that we are now going to carry out in the state space we chose as performance response the following equation

$$\{y\} = \{\dot{x}\} - [Am]\{x\} \tag{59}$$

to attempt a shaping of the eigenvalues of the controlled wing by an implicit model following technique. The model state matrix [Am] is chosen at each design speed in such a way to maintain the eigenvectors and the already acceptable eigenvalues of the uncontrolled wing while assigning those that are unacceptable. Thus only the fluttering eigenvalue is modified by keeping its imaginary part unchanged while assigning a desired value to its real part. The identity matrix is then taken as the weight matrix for {y} and the weights of the unique control and of its speed are defined by the inverses of the squares of their maximum admissible values. The system is perturbed with $[X_0] = [I]$, $[D] = [R] = 0$. Different design stabilizing the wing at a single flight speed with a direct hinge moment control and guaranteeing a minimum singular value of the return difference matrices of .8 can be easily obtained.   However, despite the supposedly high phase and gain margins assured by such a singular value, the wing is always highly unstable outside the design points. We then resort to a seven models design at the speeds of 10-20-30-40-50-60-70 m/s. The stabilization is carried out again through a penalty shift and the matrices $[A_m]$ are chosen at each speed according to the previously described procedure. Three consecutive shifts were required to find the four gains needed to simultaneously stabilize all models. The minimum singular value thus obtained, without imposing any constraint, was .32. Then three cycles of constrained optimization with a feasible direction method [90] were performed and succeeded in gradually pushing the minimum singular value to .6. The resulting final design is shown in the V-g plot of Fig. 6 which demonstrates that the flutter free domain is well beyond the required 50% increase and the improvement in damping is really significant.

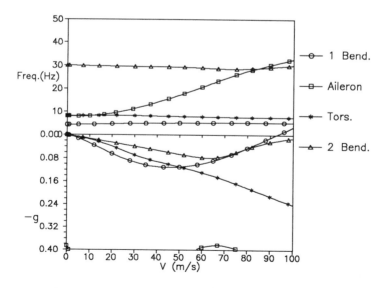

Fig. 6 - Wing model closed loop V-g plot with direct hinge moment controldesigned with the modern formulation.

It can then be seen that the adoption of a multi model approach gives a significant increase of the robustness against structured uncertainties related to dynamic pressure variations and also against possible unstructured uncertainties. Thus, despite the constraints imposed on the compensator structure, the simplicity of the direct feedback controller and the small number of gains, a very satisfactory result has been obtained. The modern design procedure is applied again by adopting a position control of the aileron. Going through the same phases it is again found that single flight point stabilizations fail to stabilize the wing at points different from those used for the design. The multi model approach is instead successful as shown in Fig. 7.

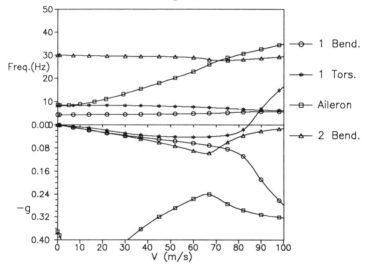

Fig. 7 - Wing model closed loop V-g plot with servo-position control designed with the modern formulation.

Nonetheless, despite several trials, it has been impossible to obtain a minimum singular value greater than .35 and the overall damping of the controlled wing is well below that obtained through direct hinge moment control. This is blamed on the limited bandwidth of the actuator, as a trial design, carried out on a wing with a servo having a 50% larger bandwidth, demonstrated capable of performances better than those related to the direct hinge moment control. This clearly demonstrates the importance of an adequate servo bandwidth but the obtainment of a bandwidth improvement can be hindered by technological constraints so that it can be simpler to try an appropriate compensation. A common technique to achieve this is to put a command shaping on θ_c to cancel undesired dynamics of the actuators. From Eq. (54) it can be seen that the transfer function from any command $\theta_c = \beta$ to the aileron can be written

$$\theta = \frac{z_2 s^2 + z_1 s + 1}{(q_2 s^2 + q_1 s + 1)(r_2 s^2 + r_2 s + 1)} \beta \tag{60}$$

Since the PID transfer function is minimum phase, β can be related to the command θ_c through the following command shaping compensation

$$\beta = \frac{q_2 s^2 + q_1 s + 1}{z_2 s^2 + z_1 s + 1} \theta_c \tag{61}$$

with the numerator corresponding to the slowest couple of poles of Eq. (60). We can then write

$$\theta = \frac{1}{r_2 s^2 + r_1 s + 1} \theta_c \tag{62}$$

so that the actuator behaves like a faster second order system. In practice it is clearly not possible to achieve a perfect cancellation but a substantial improvement of performances can however be expected and the uncertainties introduced by the imprecise cancellation should be well absorbed by a robust AFSS. The obtained results are displayed in the V-g plot of Fig. 8.

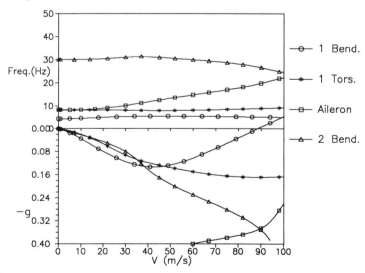

Fig. 8 - Wing model closed loop V-g with servo-position control + command shaping compensation designed with the modern formulation.

It can be seen that the performances are very good and the compensation is highly effective as demonstrated by the minimum singular value of .6 that it has been again possible to obtain. We have thus shown that different simple designs can be capable of suppressing the flutter guaranteeing good robustness both against structured uncertainties related to varying dynamic pressure and against generic model errors.

It would be possible to obtain similar results within the realm of the classical formulation. However, to avoid repeating the same examples, we will demonstrate the use the classical formulation by a refinement of the latter design. This consists in maintaining the structure of the compensator, i.e. the integrators and command shaping compensation, while taking their parameters, i.e poles and zeros, into the design. Then we explore the possibility of avoiding redundant sensors without any safety loss and try to obtain an AFSS that is capable of maintaining the wing stable also with a failed accelerometer. A relaxed requirement is however set in that case by accepting a restricted flutter free domain corresponding to the flight envelope, i.e with a flutter speed 20% below the maximum flutter speed obtainable with unfailed sensors. In this way any single accelerometer failure will produce only the loss of the expected flutter safety margin but will maintain a large part of the operating conditions flutter free and well damped. The above assumptions are set just to demonstrate the capabilities of the classical approach by simulating a plausible design objective taking into account robustness against sensor failures.

The design is based on the optimization of Eq. (47) with the constraints of Eq. (46c), to shape acceptable damping factors at different flight speeds, and Eq. (46d) to avoid implementation problems and unacceptable poles and zeros, e.g. too high in frequencies and/or in the right s plane. A first tentative design taking into account twenty one models corresponding to the seven flight speed previously used and including a condition with unfailed sensors and two condition with a single accelerometer failure was unsuccessful.

Instead two independent designs with fourteen models related to the unfailed system and with separated sensors failures show that the requirements can be satisfied only with a failed leading edge accelerometer. A failure of the trailing edge accelerometer cannot be stabilized with a single controller operating also with both accelerometers and this indicates the need of a redundant trailing edge sensor.

The results obtainable with a single control law are presented in Fig. 9, for the AFSS with no failure, and in Fig. 10, for the failed leading edge accelerometer, with the constraints on the allowed damping factor explicitly shown.

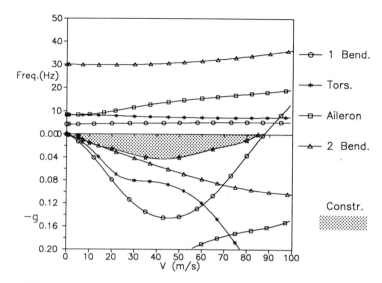

Fig. 9 - Wing model closed loop V-g plot with servo-position control + command shaping compensation designed with the classical formulation and supporting a failure in the leading edge accelerometer.

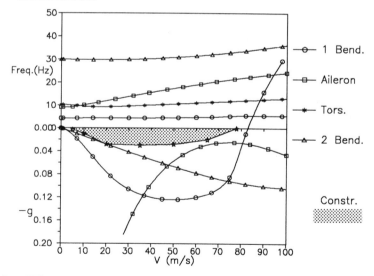

Fig. 10 - Wing model closed loop V-g plot with servo-position control + command shaping compensation designed with the classical formulation with failed leading edge accelerometer.

No constraint was imposed on the minimum acceptable singular value of the return difference matrices. Nonetheless a verification analysis showed a minimum singular value of .38, indicating that the partially fail safe controller thus obtained is acceptably robust also against possible further unmodeled uncertainties. It is remarked that the above results have been obtained by using the classical formulation as implemented in an integrated design procedure that will be presented in the following part of the work. The effectiveness of a single trailing edge accelerometer can be explained by noting that the reduced frequencies, around and beyond the flutter speed, are relatively low so that the aerodynamic forces generated by the aileron are almost instantaneously related to the aileron rotation command. Then, since the accelerometer is roughly collocated with the aileron, we are somewhat emulating the ILAF concept, and passive damping and inertia forces are generated. In fact the gains related to velocity and acceleration are of opposite signs so that if a passive damping is produced by the former a negative inertia force is generated by the latter. That is equivalent to taking away some mass from the wing trailing edge thus advancing the center of gravity upstream, which is known to be beneficial for a bending-torsion flutter.

IX. INTEGRATED DESIGN OF STRUCTURES AND
ACTIVE FLUTTER SUPPRESSION SYSTEMS

In the previous sections of this chapter several methods to design AFSSs have been presented. All these methods take the structure as assigned while designing the active control system. Instead the methods specific to this work allow the integration of passive and active design even if the examples previously shown were related only to the active part of an AFSS. In this way we have missed the possibility of coupling the advantages determined by the active control technology to those offered by passive structural modifications. While this is adequate to design an AFSS for an already existing wing, i.e. one that cannot be subjected to relevant structural modifications, it appears too restrictive in the preliminary design of new structural solutions, especially if the adoption of a modern optimization procedure can be the only mean to satisfy enhanced design requirements and highly demanding performance criteria [88,89]. Structural optimization methods generate the best solution, in terms of minimum structural weight or in term of a specified optimal performance index, by iteratively modifying the structure to satisfy the imposed constraints.

Mainly adopted during the preliminary design phase, structural optimization procedures are capable to determine the best solution in presence of several and different requirements, e.g.:
- static responses, e.g. stresses and/or displacements, buckling loads
- dynamic responses, e.g. frequency and/or modal displacements
- aeroelastic responses, e.g. divergence, flutter speed, control efficiency.

Since the solution of different and multiple kinds of structural analysis problems is required, the term *"structural synthesis"* in place of *"structural optimization"* is the most appropriate.

A general structural synthesis problem can be formulated as:

$$\min \ OBJ(a_i)$$
$$\text{subject to } G_j(a_i) \le 0$$
$$i=1...N; \quad J=1...M$$

where OBJ is the objective function, representing a general structural performance index [108,110], a_i are the design variables, i.e. panels thicknesses, stringers areas, fibers orientations in elements of composite material, and G_j are the constraint functions that must be satisfied at the optimal design. Presently most of the structural synthesis algorithms adopt the same computational scheme which is based on three phases [88]:

a) problem formulation;
b) computation of structural responses and their derivatives with respect to the design variables;
c) generation of an approximate explicit optimization problem and minimization of the objective function in the approximate domain.

Active controls offer new opportunities to the designer but require a modification of this well established approach to the structural synthesis problem. In fact the preliminary design can lead to better solutions if it is able to provide an integrated servo-structural design, i.e. carrying out different solutions capable to guarantee the obtainment of the assigned requirements, based both on active and passive control techniques. It is then important to define a procedure of servo-structural synthesis in which the objective function could include a structural performance index, such as the structural weight, and a control performance index, in which the design variables would be mixed servo-structural, i.e. sizes of structural elements (thicknesses, cross section areas, etc.) and control parameters (gains, actuator and/or sensor positions, compensation parameters, etc...) [99-101].

This result is not simple to obtain because while several well established, but disjoint, techniques exist both for structural optimization and control design, efficient methodologies for an integrated servo-structural design are not so well developed yet.

The difficulty to express in a common analytical form both the analysis and the optimization phases for structural and control problems represents in fact one of the difficulties in the extension of a classical structural synthesis algorithm to servo-structural optimization.

Three seem the more attractive approaches to this problem: sequential [102,103], integrated (simultaneous) [104-109] and multi level [110,111].

To evaluate the effectiveness of the integrated approach, several researches have been developed at the Aerospace Department of the

Politecnico di Milano, which have lead to a general purpose code, named *AIDIA* [112], based on the following features:

- A multi-configuration problem formulation allowing to simultaneously consider completely different and independent servo-structural models and/or operating conditions coupled only by a set of common design parameters.
- A weighted multi-criteria minimization in which the objective and the constraint functions can be chosen in each optimization step among different response and performance indices.
- Several analysis and sensitivity modules for the computation of servo-structural responses and performance criteria such as: displacement, stresses, buckling loads, flutter, different static and dynamic aeroservoelastic responses.
- An integrated servo-structural design formulation in which the optimization phase is performed using structural and control variables simultaneously.

A. DESCRIPTION OF *AIDIA*

AIDIA (*A*ircraft *I*ntegrated *D*esign – *I*ngegneria *A*erospaziale) is a numerical procedure allowing to solve several and different optimization problems aiming in particular at preliminary design phases in which not excessively detailed models are needed. *AIDIA* adopts reduced order models that can be obtained through appropriate interfaces to different external structural and aerodynamic modules, presently MSC/NASTRAN, to avoid the development of new basic analysis programs capable of treating very fine parent approximations. A scheme of the procedure is represented in Fig.11.

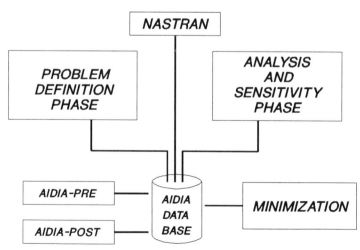

Fig. 11 - *AIDIA* overview

The optimization approach used in *AIDIA* is mainly based on two approximation levels: a modal approach both for static and dynamic problems and an approximate analytic minimization problem based on convex linearization.

The basic assumption in the modal approach is that the true displacement of the structure can be represented as a linear combination of a limited set of mode shapes of unknown amplitude. In the *AIDIA* approach the elementary mode shapes are, for dynamic and static problems respectively, natural and static mode shapes and static and perturbation mode shapes. The latter modes are the structural displacements corresponding to real loadings and their derivatives with respect to design parameters [113]. This choice generally allows the solution of very complex optimization problems by one or two cycles of external analyses on detailed models.

An approximate optimization problem is then generated by the so called "convex linearization" of the servo-structural response functions [114,115] except for those that are known in analytical form, e.g. structural weight and/or gains norm.

Any problem is formulated in three distinct phases. The first is the *Definition* phase, in which the type of analysis and the optimization required for any model are defined. The second is the *Analysis* phase, in which the structural and control responses and sensitivities are computed for each configuration. Finally it comes the *Optimization* phase in which the results of the analysis and sensitivity phases are gathered to generate an analytical approximate problem on which the minimization of the chosen objective function is carried out and the design variables updated.

The versatility of the procedure is enhanced by the possibility of maintaining the designer in the loop to monitor and interact with the different phases, up to the definition phase, allowing him to choose interactively among the different computational strategies and the different kinds of servo-structural problems to be solved at each iteration. The different phases are briefly illustrated below.

1. PROBLEM DEFINITION

In *AIDIA* configurations or models assume a fundamental role. Any model is composed by all the modal data describing the aeroservoelastic system, the specific analysis requested by the problem associated to it and all the information that allow this analysis to be performed. In particular any model includes the definition of the set of design parameters selected from the overall design space that are specific to it, the structural and/or control responses and the functional relations that are briefly detailed in the following.

The available design parameters used in an optimization problem are:

section properties, thickness of isotropic plates including bending behavior, thickness and fiber orientation of layers of plane stress composite plates, positions of balancing or tuning masses and the gains of active control systems including compensator parameters. It is possible to link the structural parameters to reduce the dimension of the design space.

2. ANALYSIS PHASE

During this phase all the structural-control responses are calculated, the classical formulation being adopted for those related to aeroservoelasticity. The computed responses can be the following:
- stresses in any structural element
- physical displacements at discrete points
- natural frequencies and modes shapes
- aeroelastic eigensolutions and responses to external excitations including random gusts
- divergence speed
- control effectiveness including inversion
- corrections of stability derivatives due to structural deformation.

To improve the capabilities to consider several and complex design requirements some analytical expression are introduced, named functional relations, which establish an arbitrary relation among different design parameters and/or responses. Using functional relations it is possible to guarantee :
- an assigned safety margins both on isotropic or composite structural elements (Von Mises or Tsai criteria);
- a particular deformation of the overall structure ;
- an acceptable damping and frequency domains within the flight envelope allowing to define a limit flutter condition, avoid unacceptable damping humps and define desired frequency separations both between modes and with respect to zero.

3. OPTIMIZATION PHASE

One of the most useful techniques actually adopted in the optimization algorithms to generate the approximate problem is the so called "convex linearization". The convex linearization is applied to the servo-structural responses and functional relations except for those that are known in analytical form, i.e. structural weight or gains norm. This approximation leads to a linear Taylor expansion expressed in direct or reciprocal variables, depending on the positive or negative sign of the first derivatives with respect to any design variable:

$$G(a)=G(a_0)+\sum_{1}^{NI}\left(-a_0^2\frac{\partial G}{\partial a_i}\right)_{a_0}\left(\frac{1}{a_i}-\frac{1}{a_0}\right)+\sum_{1}^{ND}\left(\frac{\partial G}{\partial a_i}\right)_{a_0}\left(a_i-a_0\right)$$

NI = number of variables with gradient < 0

ND = number of variables with gradient > 0

This approximation is generally conservative and allows the use of relatively large move limits on the design variables. All the responses and gradients are computed analytically and this represent the most expensive operation in the optimization process. The minimization is carried out on the approximate problem by a feasible directions method, i.e. CONMIN [90].

After the minimization of the reduced order multi-model problem, a complete "exact" analysis is performed by looping back to large order models and external analysis programs and, if the results do not match those of the low orders models, the previous two steps are repeated till a satisfactory match is obtained.

During the optimization phase it is possible to choose any of the responses and/or functional relations established in the definition phase either as objective or constraint function. It is worth noting that problems, that often cannot be considered in the most common structural optimizations such as min-max problems, can be routinely faced by *AIDIA*. This can be very useful in forcing a feasible design or to alleviate particularly critical constraints , e.g. the minimization of the maximum stress in certain part of the structure.

The minimization is the only point in the global optimization process in which all design variables, structural and control responses and the functional relations are simultaneously considered. In fact in *AIDIA* until the optimization phase, all the models describe independent design problems that can be characterized by a completely different structural and/or control model, design parameters and flight conditions. Generally the structural design variables common to different models have the same values since they are associated to the same structural elements. On the contrary the control variables can assume different values for different and independent models. In fact since the control variables are not associated to an invariant geometrical property of the structure they can be reconfigured depending on the flight condition and so the adoption of several control models to design an active control system can reflect a possible gain scheduling policy. On the other hand maintaining the same gains for different models can reflect the search of robust controllers and/or insensitivity to sensors and actuators failures or both.

B. EXAMPLE

A demonstration of the use of AIDIA in designing a control system alone
has been previously presented. That and other applications [116] are
important as they prove the possibility of using for this task a
methodology stemming from the structural design ground.

However to demonstrate the validity of the integrated servo-structural
optimization an example is reported in which an all metal swept wing is
optimized to satisfy static and flutter requirements in presence of an
active flutter control system. Some difficulties can arise in setting up an
integrated servo-structural optimization due to the large number of
potential design variables and to preliminary decisions that must be
assumed before starting the optimization. For example we must choose the
controller structure, i.e. compensator dynamics, the number and location of
sensors and actuators, and the optimization problem, i.e. the constraints,
the objective function and how to include control performances into the
objective function. Due to the lack of similar integrated examples no
comparison can be made and we can simply try to develop a reasonable
application.

Fig.12 shows the structural layout with the aileron control surface and
two accelerometers located at the wing tip.

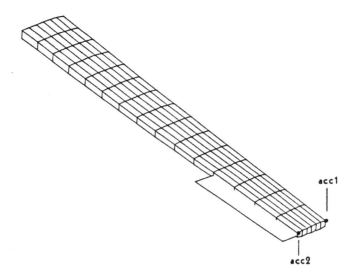

Fig. 12 - Finite element mesh of the considered swept wing

A direct feedback of accelerations and integrated velocities of the
type already used in the previous applications is adopted and an objective

function composed by the structural weight and a control gain norm, with homogeneous weight coefficients, have been chosen for the optimization. Fig. 13 shows the initial V-g plot obtained through MSC/NASTRAN and reports also the imposed damping curves.

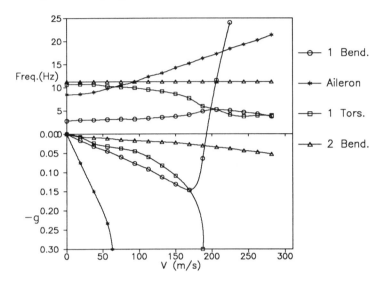

Fig. 13 - Swept wing initial V-g plot

Two different constraint curves are considered: the first is applied to the flutter mode to increase its flutter speed and the aeroelastic damping; the second is applied to guard against instabilities of higher frequency modes.

To verify the adequacy of the integrated approach the computation has been completed in two subsequent steps. In the first step only the structural design variables were modified till a minimum weight was obtained at the tenth iteration. This solution can be representative of the optimum design achievable by passive means only. Then a second integrated step, considering both structural and control design variables, was undertaken till a possible new optimum. Figs.14-16 present the total structural weight versus iteration number and the final V-g plots.

From Fig.14 it can be seen that a substantial improvement is caused by the integrated design and the possible benefits of integration, in terms of weight saving, seem to be much more consistent.

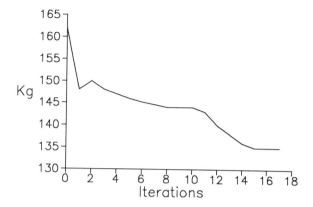

Fig. 14 - Structural weight versus the iteration number

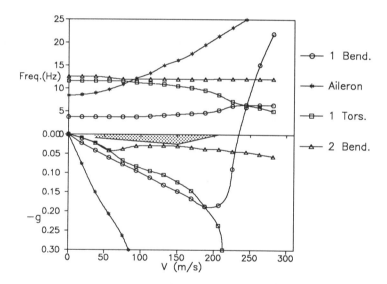

Fig. 15 - Swept wing final *V-g* plot

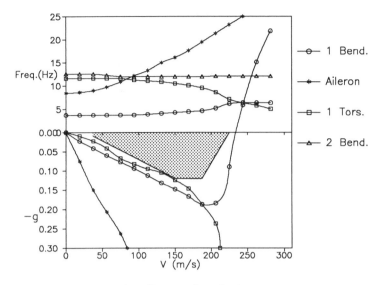

Fig. 16 - Swept wing final V-g plot

X.   CONCLUDING REMARKS

This work, either directly or through the references, should have given a fairly comprehensive illustration of the different facets and tools required to design an AFSS. The aerodynamic and open loop modeling of aeroservoelastic systems have been extensively treated and established in a general form both for the classical and modern formulation. A correct coupling of the actuators to the structure has been emphasized to make clear the possible limitations of more traditional and simplified approaches. The choice between the two formulations is generally made mostly on the base of the designer's personal experience and tradition. So their pros and cons have, and will not, be discussed. Nonetheless it should be remarked that the modern approach, by reducing an aeroservoelastic system to just a linear system, can share all the improvements and experiences in design and analysis afforded by a community of researchers and practitioners far larger than that of the aeroelastic analysts alone. This could create a commonalty of tools and language that will be a good asset anyway and will spur many aeroelasticians to jump on the bandwagon of the modern approach without regretting too much the possible advantages of the classical formulation. This is even truer when one comes to the controller design of an AFSS, as it can be inferred from the cited references.

The present work has however emphasized the possibility of adopting design methods that, irrespective of the aeroservoelastic formulation adopted, allow the designer to integrate active and passive control, include sensors/actuators locations as design parameters, assign a simplified controller structure and directly take into account a large variety of specifications, e.g. robustness against structured and unstructured uncertainties, gain scheduling, eigenstructure assignments, sensors and/or actuators failures. This can lead to the obtainment of AFSSs requiring less redundancies to insure safety and that can be simpler to implement, test and finely tune in flight. It should be however remarked that these capabilities cannot be used blindly as it is up to the designer's experience and physical understanding of the system to avoid struggling for clogged solutions because of too many and conflicting requirements. Even if the design framework thus established takes into account integrated active and passive design, its capabilities can be exploited only in a more comprehensive software of the type presented in the last paragraph. That is just a sample of the subject of integrated multi disciplinary design, a field of much interest both for research and application purposes, for which extensions that include aerodynamic shape and performances can already be found in the literature.

It is important to remark that the AFSS methodologies presented here can require a very high computer power to produce results in a snap. However the simple but realistic examples presented have been solved, almost in a snap, on a PC 386 personal computer. Thus the computational power is not believed to be a problem as the multi model approaches presented in this work are well suited to exploit the capabilities of present and future generation parallel computers. In fact the expensive analyses and sensitivities calculations can be carried out in perfect parallelism on each of the processing unit available without any special requirement or software sophistication. Thus, provided a processing unit is available for each model, the computing time is not increased. In the realms of multi model AFSSs and integrated interdisciplinary design massively parallel computations can be equivalent to massively multi models design and the solution time and cost should not be a problem at all.

APPENDIX A

This appendix presents a method to reduce the order of a linear system on the base of its frequency content by maintaining the whole dynamics of a chosen subspace of the state while recovering the remaining part through a residualization procedure. The method is equivalent to a modal residualization but avoids the calculation of eigenvectors which can be troublesome for systems with coincident or closely spaced eigenvalues.
A generic linear time invariant system

$$\{\dot{x}\} = [A]\{x\} + [B]\{u\} \qquad (A1)$$

$$\{y\} = [C]\{x\} + [D]\{u\} \tag{A2}$$

can be easily transformed to Schur form, i.e

$$\{\dot{w}\} = [F]\{w\} + [G]\{u\} \tag{A3}$$

with [F] being an upper quasi triangular matrix with diagonal terms corresponding to the real eigenvalues of [A] and two by two diagonal blocks around the main diagonal corresponding to the complex conjugate eigenvalues of [A]. The similarity transformation required is written

$$\{x\} = [W]\{w\} \tag{A4}$$

and can be determined numerically by using the QR method [117]. Moreover it is possible to order the eigenvalues and the two by two blocks in any desired way along the diagonal of [F] [118]. So we can write Eqs. (A2),(A3) as

$$\{\dot{w}_1\} = [F_{11}]\{w_1\} + [F_{12}]\{w_2\} + [G_1]\{u\} \tag{A5a}$$

$$\{\dot{w}_2\} = \qquad\qquad [F_{22}]\{w_2\} + [G_2]\{u\} \tag{A5b}$$

$$\{y\} = [H_1]\{w_1\} + [H_2]\{w_2\} + [D]\{u\} \tag{A5c}$$

with Eq. (A5a) containing the desired subspace dynamics and having no eigenvalue in common with Eq. (A5b). By applying to Eqs. (A5) a further transformation of the type

$$\begin{aligned} \{w_1\} &= \{z_1\} + [Z]\{z_2\} \\ \{w_2\} &= \{z_2\} \end{aligned} \tag{A6}$$

with [Z] being the solution of the following Sylvester-Lyapunov linear matrix equation

$$[F_{11}][Z] - [Z][F_{22}] + [F_{12}] = 0 \tag{A7}$$

we obtain

$$\{\dot{z}_1\} = [F_{11}]\{z_1\} + ([G_1] - [Z][G_2])\{u\} \tag{A8a}$$

$$\{\dot{z}_2\} = [F_{22}]\{z_2\} + [G_2]\{u\} \tag{A8b}$$

$$\{y\} = [H_1]\{z_1\} + ([H_1][Z]+[H_2])\{z_2\} + [D]\{u\} \tag{A8c}$$

in which the dynamics of the states $\{z_1\}$ and $\{z_2\}$ are coupled only by the output equation. The solution of Eq. (A7) is assured to exist and be unique since [F11] and [F22] have no common eigenvalue [119]. We will then call nth order residualization of Eqs. (A8) the evaluation of $\{z2\}$ with the following

$$\{z2\} = -\sum_{i=0}^{n} [F22]^{-(i+1)}[G2]\{u^{(i)}\} \tag{A9}$$

which is obtained by assuming that all the derivatives with respect to time of $\{z2\}$ beyond n are null. The output equation can then be written

$$\{y\} = [H1]\{z1\} + ([D]-([H2] + [H1][Z])([F22]^{-1}[G2])\{u\} -$$
$$\sum_{i=1}^{n} ([H2] + [H1][Z])[F22]^{-(i+1)}[G2]\{u^{(i)}\} \tag{A10}$$

Since $\{u\}$ must satisfy Eqs. (A8a) and $([G1]-[Z][G2])$ has rank equal to the dimension of $\{u\}$ it is always possible to obtain

$$\{u\} = [T1]\{\dot{z}1\} + [T2]\{z1\} \tag{A11}$$

so that Eq. (A10) can also be written

$$\{y\} = \sum_{i=0}^{n+1} [Di]\{z1^{(i)}\} \tag{A12}$$

where the [Di]s matrices are obtained after substituting Eq. (A11) and its derivatives with respect to time into Eq. (A10).

The possibility of adopting improper dynamic systems of the types implied by Eqs. (A10),(A12), as well as their meaning, usefulness and appropriate order, is strongly dependent on the physico-mathematical modeling situation at hand. It is noted that if the desired subspace is chosen on the base of its frequency content, e.g. with [F22] having faster and separated eigenvalues with respect to [F11], the above residualization is tantamount to assuming that the dynamics of $\{z2\}$, which is related to the transfer function $([H1][Z] + [H2])(s[I] - [F22]^{-1})[G2]$, is analytic around $s = 0$ and its interaction with the dynamics of $\{z1\}$ can be approximated by a Taylor series of order n in s.

APPENDIX B

This appendix presents the basic formulae needed to evaluate Eq. (40) and its gradients, i.e the basic ingredients required for its numerical optimization, since they are peculiar to the formulation presented and not widely available, even if simple enough to be worked out anew. No further details are instead given for the calculations related to eigenvalues, return difference matrices, singular values and their related derivatives, since these are either standard or well known and documented methods [33,76,81,117,119-121].

In relation to Eqs. (37),(38),(40),(41) defining the following matrices

$$[E] = [V] - [B_u][K_f][M_{\dot{x}}] \tag{B1a}$$

$$[F] = [A] - \alpha[V] + [B_u][K_f][M_x] \tag{B1b}$$

$$[G] = [B_d] + [B_u][K_f][M_d] \tag{B1c}$$

$$[H] = [B_u][K_f][M_r] \tag{B1d}$$

$$[N] = [E]^{-1}[F] \tag{B1e}$$

$$[K] = [K_f][M_x] + [K_f][M_{\dot{x}}][N] \tag{B1f}$$

$$[R] = [R_x] + [R_{\dot{x}}][N] + [R_u][[K] \tag{B1g}$$

$$[W] = [R]^T[Q_y][R] + [K]^T[Q_u][K] + [N]^T[K]^T[Q_{\dot{u}}][K][N] \tag{B1h}$$

$$[R_1] = [R_x] + [R_u][K_f][M_x] \tag{B1i}$$

$$[R_2] = [R_d] + [R_u][K_f][M_d] \tag{B1j}$$

$$[R_3] = [R_r] + [R_u][K_f][M_r] \tag{B1k}$$

we can write Eq. (40) as

$$J = tr(\; [P]([X_e]+[X_0]) + [X_e][R_1]^T[Q_{\bar{y}}][R_1] + 2[X_d][R_2]^T[Q_{\bar{y}}][R_1] +$$

$$+ \; 2[X_r][R_3]^T[Q_{\bar{y}}][R_1] + [D][R_2]^T[Q_{\bar{y}}][R_2] + [R][R_3]^T[Q_{\bar{y}}][R_3]) \tag{B2}$$

$tr[\;\;]$ being the trace of a matrix; $[P]$, $[X_e] = E(\{\bar{x}\}\{\bar{x}\}^T)$, $[X_d] = E(\{\bar{x}\}\{d\}^T)$ and $[X_r] = E(\{\bar{x}\}\{r\}^T)$ are the solutions of the following equations

$$[N]^T[P] + [P][N] = -[W] \tag{B3a}$$

$$[F][X_e][F]^T = [H][R][H]^T + [G][D][G]^T \tag{B3b}$$

$$[F][X_d] = -[G][D] \tag{B3c}$$

$$[F][X_r] = -[H][R] \tag{B3d}$$

The numerical optimization of Eq. (42), which becomes now a sum of equations (B2), requires the gradients, with respect to any coefficient γ_i of $\{\gamma\}$ and/or $k_{i,k}$ of the gain matrices $[k_i]$, of each model. They are indicated with a $<'>$, meaning either $\partial/\partial k_{i,k}$ or $\partial/\partial \gamma_i$ according to the design parameter to be taken into account, and are given by

$$J' = tr(\ [U_0][V_0] + [U_1][V_1] + 2[U_2][V_2] + 2[U_3][V_3] +$$
$$[X_e]([R_1]^T[Q_{\bar{y}}][R_1])' + 2[X_d]([R_2]^T[Q_{\bar{y}}][R_1])' +$$
$$2[X_r]([R_3]^T[Q_{\bar{y}}][R_1])' + [D]([R_2]^T[Q_{\bar{y}}][R_2])' +$$
$$[R]([R_3]^T[Q_{\bar{y}}][R_3])'\ ) \tag{B4}$$

where the matrices $[U_0]$, $[U_1]$, $[U_2]$ and $[U_3]$ are the solutions of the followings

$$[N][U_0] + [U_0][N]^T = -\ ([X_e] + [X_0]) \tag{B5a}$$
$$[F]^T[U_1][F] = [P] + [R_1]^T[Q_{\bar{y}}][R_1] \tag{B5b}$$
$$[U_2][F] = [R_2]^T[Q_{\bar{y}}][R_1] \tag{B5c}$$
$$[U_3][F] = [R_3]^T[Q_{\bar{y}}][R_1] \tag{B5d}$$

and $[V_0]$, $[V_1]$, $[V_2]$ and $[V_3]$ are defined by

$$[V_0] = [W]' + [P][N]' + [N]'^T[P]^T \tag{B6a}$$
$$[V_1] = [H]'[R][H]^T + [H][R][H]'^T + [G]'[D][G]^T + [G][D][G]'^T + \tag{B6b}$$
$$-\ [F]'[X_e][F]^T - [F][X_e][F]'^T$$
$$[V_2] = -[G]'[D] - [F]'[X_d] \tag{B6c}$$
$$[V_3] = -[H]'[R] - [F]'[X_r] \tag{B6d}$$

The derivatives that appear in the above equations are easily computed as the structure of the matrices is assigned. Note that Eqs. (B5a)-(B5d) are the adjoint of Eqs. (B3a)-(B3d). The Schur transformation required to solve the two Lyapunov Eqs. (B3a),(B5a) can be carried out only once [118,122,123] and also Eqs. (B3b)-(B3d),(B5b)-(B5d) can be solved by using a single factorization of [F]. Then an appropriate constrained or unconstrained optimization technique can be used depending on the presence or less of the constraint equations, i.e Eqs. (46).

XI. REFERENCES

1. H. Ashley, "Flutter Suppression Within Reach", *Aerospace America*, Vol. 26, No. 8, 1988, pp. 14-16.

2. M.A. Ostgaard and F.R. Swortzel, "CCVs Active Control Technology Creating New Military Aircraft Design Potential", *Aeronautics & Astronautics*, Vol. 15, No. 2, 1977, pp. 42-51.

3. H.J. Wikes and E.E. Kordes, "Analytical and Flight Tests of a Modal

Suppression System on the XB-70 Airplane", AGARD CP-40, 1970.

4. K.L. Roger, G.E. Hodges and L.R. Felt, "Active Flutter Suppression - A Flight Test Demonstration", *Journal of Aircraft*, Vol. 12, No. 6, 1975, pp. 551-556.

5. T.E. Noll and L.J. Huttsell, "Wing Store Active Flutter Suppression - Correlation of Analysis and Wind Tunnel Data", *Journal of Aircraft*, Vol. 16, No. 7, 1979, pp. 491-497.

6. T.E. Noll, L.J. Huttsell and D.E. Cooley, "Wing/Store Flutter Suppression Investigation", *Journal of Aircraft*, Vol. 18, No. 11, 1981, pp. 969-975.

7. H. Hoenlinger, "Active Flutter Suppression of an Airplane with Wing Mounted External Stores", AGARD CP-228, 1977.

8. R.P. Peloubet, R.L. Haller and R.M. Bolding, "F-16 Flutter Suppression System Investigation Feasibility Study and Wind Tunnel Test", *Journal of Aircraft*, Vol. 19, No. 2, 1982, pp. 169-179.

9. R.P. Peloubet, R.L. Haller and R.M. Bolding, "Recent Developments in the F-16 Flutter Suppression with Active Control Program", *Journal of Aircraft*, Vol. 21, No. 9, 1984, pp. 716-721.

10. R.F. O'Connel and A.F. Messina, "Development of an Active Flutter Margin Augmentation System for a Commercial Transport", *Journal of Guidance and Control*, Vol. 3, No. 4, 1980, pp. 352-360.

11. H. Foersching (Editor), "Active Control Application for Flutter Suppression and Gust Load Alleviation", *Group for Aeronautical Research and Technology in Europe*, TP-022.

12. G.L. Ghiringhelli, M. Lanz and P. Mantegazza, "Active Flutter Suppression for a Wing Model", *Journal of Aircraft*, Vol. 27, No. 3, 1990, pp. 334-341.

13. L.T. Redd, J. Gillman, D.E. Cooley and F.D. Stewart, "A Wind Tunnel Investigation of a B-52 Model Flutter Suppression System", *Journal of Aircraft*, Vol. 11, No. 11, 1974, pp. 659-663.

14. H. Matsushita, Y. Miyazawa, T. Ueda and S. Suzuki, "Multi-Surface Control Law Synthesis and Wind Tunnel Test Verification of Active Flutter Suppression for a Transport-Type Wing", *Proceedings of the European Forum on Aeroelasticity and Structural Dynamics*, DGLR-1989.

15. W. Dehmel and K. Koenig, "Damping Augmentation Functions of a Civil Aircraft", *Proceedings of the European Forum on Aeroelasticity and Structural Dynamics*, DGLR-1991.

16. D.K. Schmidt and T.K. Chen, "Frequency Domain Synthesis of a Robust Flutter Suppression Control Law", *Journal Guidance, Control and*

Dynamics, Vol. 9, No. 3, 1986, pp. 346-351.

17. T.E. Noll, F.E. Eastep and R.A. Calico, "Prevention of Forward Swept Wing Aeroelastic Instabilities with Active Control", *Proceedings of the 14th International Council of the Aeronautical Sciences*, 1984, pp. 439-448.

18. H.H.E. Leipholz (Editor), *Structural Control*, North-Holland Publishing Co., Amsterdam, 1980.

19. A.V. Balakrishnan, "Active Control of Airfoils in Unsteady Aerodynamics", *Applied Mathematics and Optimization*, Vol. 8, No. 5, 1985, pp. 605-611.

20. J.R. Newsom, "Control Law Synthesis for Active Flutter Suppression Using Optimal Control Theory", *Journal of Guidance and Control*, Vol. 2, No. 5, 1979, pp. 388-394.

21. J.R. Newsom, A.S. Potozky and I. Abel, "Design of a Flutter Suppression System for an Experimental Drone Aircraft", *Journal of Aircraft*, Vol. 22, No. 5, 1985, pp. 380-386.

22. G.S. Alag and J.J. Burken, "Eigensystem Synthesis for Active Flutter Suppression on an Oblique-Wing Aircraft", *Journal of Guidance, Control, and Dynamics*, Vol. 10, no. 6, 1987, pp. 535-539.

23. I. Abel, B. Perry III, and H.N. Murrow, "Two Synthesis Techniques Applied to Flutter Suppression on a Flight Research Wing", *Journal of Guidance and Control*, Vol. 1, No. 5, 1978, pp. 340-346.

24. J.K. Mahesh, C.R. Stone, W.L. Garrard and H.J. Dunn, "Control Law Synthesis for Flutter Suppression Using Linear Quadratic Gaussian Theory", *Journal of Guidance and Control*, Vol. 4, No. 4, 1981, pp. 415-422.

25. W.L. Garrard and B.S. Liebst, "Active Flutter Suppression Using Eigenvalue and Linear Quadratic Design Techniques", *Journal of Guidance, Control, and Dynamics*, Vol. 8, No. 3, 1985, pp. 304-311.

26. B.S. Liebst, W.L. Garrard and W.M. Adams, "Design of an Active Flutter Suppression System", *Journal of Guidance, Control, and Dynamics*, Vol. 9, No. 1, 1986, pp. 64-71.

27. B.S. Liebst, W.L. Garrard and J.A. Farm, "Design of a Multivariable Flutter Suppression/Gust Load Alleviation System", *Journal of Guidance, Control, and Dynamics*, Vol. 11, No. 3, 1988, pp. 220-229.

28. W.L. Garrard, J.K. Mahesh, C.R. Stone and H.J. Dunn, "Robust Kalman Filter Design for Active Flutter Suppression Systems", *Journal of Guidance and Control*, Vol. 5, No. 4, 1982, pp. 412-414.

29. D.K. Schmidt, T.A. Weisshaar and M.G. Gilbert, "Quadratic Synthesis of

Integrated Active Controls for an Aeroelastic Forward-Swept-Wing Aircraft", *Journal of Guidance, Control, and Dynamics*, Vol. 7, No. 2, 1984, pp.190-196.

30. R.R. Chipman, A.M. Zislin and C. Waters, "Control of Aeroelastic Divergence", *Journal of Aircraft*, Vol. 20, No. 12, 1983, pp. 1007-1013.

31. M. Takahashi and G.L. Slater, "Design of a Flutter Mode Controller Using Positive Real Feedback", *Journal of Guidance, Control, and Dynamics*, Vol. 9, No. 3, 1986, pp. 339-345.

32. P. Dorato, *Robust Control*, IEEE Press, 1987.

33. Many Authors, " Multivariable Analysis and Design Techniques", AGARD LS-117, 1981.

34. R.Y. Chiang and M.G. Safonov, "Robust-Control Toolbox", The MathWorks Inc., 1988.

35. G.J. Balas, J.C. Doyle, K. Glover, A. Packard and R. Smith, "μ Analysis and Synthesis Toolbox", The MathWorks Inc., 1991.

36. J.C. Doyle and G. Stein, "Robustness with Observers", IEEE Transaction on Automatic Control, Vol. AC-26, No. 1, 1981, pp. 4-16.

37. A.N. Lehtomaki, N.R. Sandel and M. Athans, "Robustness Results in Linear Quadratic Gaussian Based Multivariable Control Design", *IEEE Transaction on Automatic Control*, Vol. AC-26, No. 1, 1981, pp. 75-92.

38. V. Mukhopadhyay, "Stability Robustness Improvement Using Constrained Optimization Techniques", *Journal of Guidance, Control and Dynamics*, Vol. 10, No. 2, 1987, pp. 172-177.

39. J.C. Doyle and G. Stein, "Multivariable Feedback Design: Concepts for a Classical/Modern Synthesis", *IEEE Transaction on Automatic Control*, Vol. AC-26, No. 1, 1981, pp. 4-16.

40. M.G. Safonov, A.J. Laub and G.L. Hartmann, "Feedback Properties of Multivariable Systems, the Role and Use of the Return Difference Matrix", *IEEE Transaction on Automatic Control*, Vol. AC-26, No. 1, 1981, pp. 47-65.

41. P.R. Apkarian, "Structured Stability Robustness Improvement by Eigenspace Techniques: A Hybrid Methodology", *Journal of Guidance, Control and Dynamics*, Vol. 12, No. 2, 1989, pp. 162-168.

42. P. Mantegazza, "A Technique to Design Structurally Constrained Stabilizing Control Systems For Actively Controlled Aircraft", *l'Aerotecnica Missile e Spazio*, Vol. 63, No. 3/4, 1984, pp. 315-317.

43. V. Mukhopadhyay, J.R. Newsom and I. Abel, "Reduced-Order Optimal

Feedback Control Law Synthesis for Flutter Suppression", *Journal of Guidance and Control*, Vol. 5, No. 4, 1982, pp. 389-395.

44. V. Mukhopadhyay, B. Perry III, and T.E. Noll, "Flutter Suppression Control Law Synthesis for the Active Flexible Wing Model", *Proceedings of the European Forum on Aeroelasticity and Structural Dynamics*, DGLR-1989.

45. Y. Miyazawa and E.H. Dowell, "Robust Control System Design with Multiple Model Approach and Its Application to Active Flutter Control", *AIAA Guidance, Navigation and Control Conference*, AIAA 89-3578-CP 1989.

46. E. Nissim, "Flutter Suppression Using Active Controls Based on the Concept of Aerodynamic Energy", NASA TN-D-6199, 1971.

47. E. Nissim and I. Lottati, "Active Control for Flutter Suppression and Gust Alleviation in Supersonic Aircraft", *Journal of Guidance and Control*, Vol. 3, No. 7, 1980, pp. 345-351.

48. A.F. Klein, "The Synthesis of an Active Flutter Suppression Law Based on an Energy Criterion", *Aeronautical Quarterly*, Vol. 34 N.4, 1983, pp. 260-281.

49. C.H. Perisho, W.E. Triplett and W.J. Mykytow, "Design Considerations for an Active Suppression System for Fighter Wing/Store Flutter", AGARD-CP-175, 1975.

50. J.T. Batina and T.Y. Yang, "Application of Transonic Codes to Aeroelastic Modeling of Airfoils Including Active Controls", *Journal of Aircraft*, Vol. 21, 1984, pp. 623-630.

51. E.F. Crawley and K.B. Lazarus, "Induced Strain Actuation of Isotropic and Anisotropic Plates", *AIAA Journal*, Vol. 29, No. 6, 1991, pp. 944-951.

52. K.B. Lazarus and E.F. Crawley, "Static Aeroelastic Control Using Strain Actuated Adaptive Structures", *Proceedings of the First Joint U.S./Japan Conference on Adaptive Structures*, Technomic, Lancaster, 1991.

53. B.S. Liebst, "Accelerometer Placement in Active Flutter Suppression Systems", *Journal of Guidance, Control, and Dynamics*, Vol. 10, No. 5, 1987, pp. 441-446.

54. T.L. Johnson and J.G. Lin, "Optimal Control-Surface Locations for Flexible Aircraft", *IEEE Transaction on Automatic Control*, Vol. AC-26, No. 4, 1971, pp. 320-331.

55. E. Nissim and J.J. Burken, "Control Surface Spanwise Placement in Active Flutter Suppression Systems", NASA TP-2873, 1988.

56. M. Lanz and P. Mantegazza, "Numerical Methods for Predicting the Aeroelastic Stability and Response of Flexible Airplanes", *l'Aerotecnica Missili e Spazio*, Vol. 63, No. 2, 1984, pp. 105-118.

57. M.H.L. Hounjet, "A Field Panel/Finite Difference Method for the Potential Unsteady Transonic Flow", *AIAA Journal*, Vol. 23, No. 4, 1985, pp. 537-545.

58. L. Morino and K. Tseng, "Nonlinear Green's Function Method for Unsteady Transonic Flows", *AIAA Progress in Aeronautics and Astronautics*, Vol. 81, 1982, pp. 565-603.

59. D. Nixon, "Prediction of Aeroelastic and Unsteady Aerodynamic Phenomena in Transonic Flows", Von Karman Insitute LS-1981-4, 1981.

60. E.H. Dowell, "Unsteady Transonic Aerodynamics and Aeroelasticity", in "Recent Advances in Aerodynamics", Krothapelli A. and Smith C.A. Editors, Springer-Verlag, 1986.

61. E.F. Ehlers, "A Finite Difference Method for the Solution of the Transonic Flow Around Harmonically Oscillating Wings", NASA CR-2257, 1974.

62. T.Y. Yang, P. Guruswamy, A.G. Striz and J.J. Olsen, "Flutter Analysis of a NACA 64A006 Airfoil in Small Disturbance Transonic Flow", *Journal of Aircraft*, Vol. 17, No. 4, 1980, pp. 225-232.

63. W.F. Ballhaus and P.M. Goorjian, "Computation of Unsteady Transonic Flows by the Indicial Method", *AIAA Journal*, Vol. 16, No. 2, 1978, pp. 117-124.

64. C. Bagnari, "Un Metodo per il Calcolo del Flutter in Campo Transonico", *Thesis*, Dipartimento di Ingegneria Aerospaziale, Politecnico di Milano, 1991.

65. P. Mantegazza, "Interpolation and Extrapolation of Transfer Functions", *l'Aerotecnica Missili e Spazio*, Vol. 59, No. 1, 1980, pp. 69-75.

66. G.L. Ghiringhelli and P. Mantegazza, "Identification of Aerodynamic Transfer Functions", to be published.

67. R.L. Bisplingoff, H. Ashley and R.L. Halfman, *Aeroelasticity*, Addison-Wesley, 1955.

68. J.R. Richardson, "A More Realistic Method for Routine Flutter Calculations", *Proceedings of AIAA Symposium on Structural Dynamics and Aeroelasticity*, 1965, pp. 10-17.

69. S. Fifer, *Analogue Computation. Theory, Techniques and Applications*, Vol. 4, Mc Graw-Hill, 1961.

70. R.D. Milne, *Asymptotic Solutions of Linear Integro-Differential Equations*, A.R.C. R. & M. 3548, 1966.

71. J.W. Edwards, "Unsteady Aerodynamic Modeling and Active Aeroelastic Control", NASA CR-148019, 1977.

72. K.L. Rogers, "Airplane Math Modeling Methods for Active Control Design", *Structural Aspects of Active Control*, AGARD CP-228, 1977.

73. R. Vepa, "Finite State Modeling of Aeroelastic Systems", NASA CR-2779, 1977.

74. H.J. Dunn, "An Analytical Technique for Approximating Unsteady Aerodynamics in the Time Domain", NASA TP-1738, 1980.

75. M. Karpel, "Design for Active and Passive Flutter Suppression and Gust Alleviation, NASA CR-3482, 1981.

76. J.J. Dongarra, C.B. Moler, J.R. Bunch and G.W. Stewart, *LINPACK User's Guide*, SIAM, 1979.

77. B. Friedland, *Control System Design. An Introduction to State-Space Methods*, McGraw-Hill, 1987.

78. P.E. Gill, W. Murray and M.H. Wright, *Practical Optimization*, Academic Press, 1981.

79. MSC NASTRAN, *Handbook for Aeroelastic Analysis*, Vol. 1-2, The MacNeal-Schwendler Corporation, 1987.

80. J.W. Edwards, "A Fortran Program for the Analysis of Linear Continuous and Sampled-Data Systems", NASA TM-56038, 1976.

81. M. Lanz and P. Mantegazza, "Modern Methods for the Analysis of the Dynamic Response of Aeroelastic Systems", *l'Aerotecnica Missili e Spazio*, Vol. 64, No. 3, 1985, pp. 170-176.

82. M. Karpel, "Reduced-Order Aeroelastic Models via Dynamic Residualization", *Journal of Aircraft*, Vol. 27, No. 5, 1990, pp. 449-455.

83. M. Rimer, R. Chipman and R. Mercadante, "Divergence/Flutter Suppression System for a Forward Swept-Wing Configuration with Wing-Mounted Stores", *Journal of Aircraft*, Vol. 21, No. 8, 1984, pp. 631-638.

84. H. Kwakernaak and R. Sivan, *Linear Optimal Control*, Wiley-Interscience, 1972.

85. F. Rizzani, "Controllo Attivo di Veicoli Aerospaziali", *Thesis*, Dipartimento di Ingegneria Aerospaziale, Politecnico di Milano, 1991.

86. R. Crotti, "Un Metodo di Progetto di Sistemi di Controllo Attivo per

l'Alleviazione dei Carichi da Raffica Continua e Discreta", *Thesis*, Dipartimento di Ingegneria Aerospaziale, Politecnico di Milano, 1986.

87. F. Bernelli Zazzera, M. Lanz and P. Mantegazza, "Eigenstructure Assignement by Structurally Constrained Suboptimal Control Laws", *Proceedings of the 11th AIDAA Congress*, 1991.

88. R.T. Haftka, M.P. Kamat, *Elements of structural optimization*, Martinus Nijhoff Publishers 1985.

89. A.J. Morris, *Foundations of Structural Optimization: A Unified Approach* , Jhon Wiley & Sons, 1982.

90. G.N. Vanderplaats, "CONMIN a Fortran Program for Constrained Minimization", NASA TM X 62282 1973.

91. F. Bernelli Zazzera, P. Mantegazza and F. Ongaro, "A Method to Design Structurally Constrained Discrete Suboptimal Control Laws for Actively Controlled Aircraft", *l'Aerotecnica Missili e Spazio*, Vol. 67, No. 1-4, 1988, pp.18-25.

92. C. Cardani and P. Mantegazza, "Continuation and Direct Solution of the Flutter Equation", *Computers and Structures*, Vol. 8, 1978, pp. 185-192.

93. A.J. Lawrence and P. Jackson, "Comparison of Different Methods of Assessing the Free Oscillatory Characteristics of Aeroelastic Systems", Technical Report of Aeronautical Research Committee CP-1084, 1968.

94. H.J. Hassig, "An Approximate True Damping Solution of the Flutter Equation by Determinant Iteration", *Journal of Aircraft*, Vol. 8, No. 11, 1971, pp. 885-889.

95. C. Cardani and P. Mantegazza, "Calculation of Eigenvalue and Eigenvector Derivatives for Algebraic, Flutter and Divergence Eigenproblems", *AIAA Journal*, Vol. 17, No. 4, 1979, pp. 408-415.

96. G. Bindolino and P. Mantegazza, "Aeroelastic Derivatives as a Sensitivity Analysis of Nonlinear Equations", *AIAA Journal*, Vol. 25, No. 8, 1987, pp. 1145-1146.

97. M. Lanz and P. Mantegazza, "An Improved Method for the Design of Flutter Suppression System by Eigenvalue Assignment", *l'Aerotecnica Missili e Spazio*, Vol. 60, 1981, pp. 92-97.

98. M. Lanz and P. Mantegazza, "Design of Compensated Flutter Suppression Systems", *Proceedings of the 13th International Council of the Aeronautical Sciences*, 1982, pp. 270-280.

99. Many Authors, "Impact of Active Control Technology on Airplane Design"

AGARD CP 157, 1974.

100. Many Authors, "Structural Aspects of Active Controls" *AGARD UP 228*. *AGARD CP 384*, 1974.

101. Many Authors, "Active Control Systems - Review, Evaluation and Projections", AGARD CP 384, 1984.

102. N.S. Khot, H. Oz, R.V. Granghi, F.E. Eastep and V.B. Venkayya, "Optimal Structural Design with Control Gain Norm Constraint", *AIAA Journal*, Vol. 26, No. 5, 1988, pp. 604-611.

103. N.S. Khot, "Structure/Control Optimization to Improve the Dynamic Response of Space Structures", *Computational Mechanics*, Vol.3, No. 3 1988, pp. 179-187.

104. J. Onoda and R.T. Haftka, "An Approach to Structure/Control Simultaneous Optimization for Large Flexible Spacecraft", *AIAA Journal* Vol.25, No. 8, 1987, pp. 1133-1138.

105. T.A. Zeiler and T.A. Weisshaar, "Integrated Aeroservoelastic Tailoring of Lifting Surfaces", *Journal of Aircraft*, Vol.25, No. 1, 1988, pp. 76-83.

106. V.B. Venkayya and V.A. Tischler, "Frequency Control and its Effect on the Dynamic Response of Flexible Structures", *AIAA Journal*, Vol.23, No. 11, 1985, pp. 1768-1774.

107. R.V. Lust and L.A. Schmit, "Control Augmented Structural Synthesis", *AIAA Journal*, Vol.26, No. 1, 1988, pp. 86-95.

108. D.F. Miller and J. Shim, "Gradient Based Combined Structural and Control Optimization", *Journal of Guidance, Control, and Dynamics*, Vol. 10, No. 3, 1987, pp. 291-298.

109. K.K. Gupta, M.J. Brenner and L.S. Voelker, "Integrated Aeroservoelastic Analysis Capability with X-29A Comparisons", *Journal of Aircraft*, Vol. 26, No. 1, 1989, pp. 84-90.

110. T.Y. Kam and M.D. Lai, "Multilevel Optimal Design of Laminated Composite Plate Structures", *Computer and Structures*, Vol. 31, No. 2, 1989, pp. 197-205.

111. J.S. Sobieski, B.B. James and A.R. Dovi, "Structural Optimization by Multilevel Decomposition", *AIAA Journal*, Vol. 23, No. 11, 1985, pp. 1775-1782.

112. G. Bindolino, M. Lanz, P. Mantegazza and S. Ricci, "Integrated Structural Optimization in the Preliminary Aircraft Design", *Proceedings of the 17th International Council of the Aeronautical Sciences*, 1990, pp. 1366-1378.

113. A.K. Noor and H.E. Lowder, "Approximate Techniques of Structural Reanalysis", *Computer & Structures*, Vol.4, 1974, pp. 801-812.

114. J.H. Starnes and R.T. Haftka, "Preliminary Design of Composite Wings for Buckling, Strenght, and Displacement Constraints", *Journal of Aircraft*, Vol. 16, No. 8, 1979, pp. 564-570.

115. C. Fleury, "A Unified Approach to Structural Weight Minimization", *Computer Methods in Appl. Mech. and Eng.*, Vol. 20, 1979, pp. 17-25.

116 P. Mantegazza and S. Ricci, "Stuctural Optimization for the Design of Active Flutter Suppression Systems", to be published.

117. B.T. Smith, J.M. Boyle, J.J. Dongarra, B.S. Garbow, I. Ikebe, V.C. Klema and C.B. Moler, *Matrix Eigensystem Routines. EISPACK Guide, Lecture Notes in Computer Science*, Springer-Verlag, 1976.

118. G.E. Stewart, "ALGORITHM 506 - HQR3 and EXCHNG : Fortran Subroutines for Calculating and Ordering the Eigenvalues of a Real Upper Hessemberg Matrix", *ACM Transactions on Mathematical Software*, Vol. 2, No. 3, 1976, pp.820-826.

119. R.H. Bartels and G.W. Stewart, "ALGORITHM 432 - Solution of the Matrix Equation [A][X] + [X][B] = [C]", *Commun. ACM*, Vol. 15, No. 9, 1972, pp.820-826.

120. J.H. Wilkinson, *The Algebraic Eigenvalue Problem*, 1978. Oxford University Press, 1965.

121. V. Mukhopadhyay and J.R. Newsom, "A Multiloop System Stability Margin Study Using Matrix Singular Values", *Journal of Guidance, Control, and Dynamics*, Vol. 7, No. 5, 1984, pp. 582-587.

122. C.A. Harvey and R.E. Pope, "Insensitive Control Technology Development", NASA-CR-2947, 1978.

123. D.L. Kleinman and P. Krishna Rao, "Extensions to the Bartels-Stewart Algorithm for Linear Matrix Equations", *IEEE Transactions on Automatic Control*, Vol. AC-23, 1978, pp.85-87.

ACKNOWLEDGMENTS

The authors wish to thank their friend and colleague G.Bindolino for his cooperation in preparing and running the examples related to classical and integrated design and for his constructive criticism and help during the writing of this work.

TECHNIQUES IN THE DESIGN OF AIRCRAFT FOR MAINTAINABILITY

ANTHONY E. MAJOROS
HONG C. CHEN
Human Factors Technology
Douglas Aircraft Company
Long Beach, California

"Yet I do seriously, and upon good grounds, affirm it possible to make a Flying Chariot, in which a man may sit, and give such a motion unto it, as shall convey him."

Bishop John Wilkins
(1638) [1]

"Most operators think an airplane flies because that's what the system is aerodynamically designed to do. In reality, it is the maintenance people who throw them up in the morning and catch them when they come down broken later that day — only to work into the night to get ready for the next mission in the morning."

Lt. Gen. Leo Marquez,
USAF (1985) [1]

I   INTRODUCTION

The general's comment above is only partly tongue in cheek. The great dependence of aircraft on maintenance and the liability represented by aircraft that cannot be flown because of needed maintenance impress most people in military and commercial aircraft operations. Faster, easier maintenance translates into increased aircraft availability, so efforts to improve and streamline maintenance processes probably go back as far as the first requirement for repetitive servicing, repair, or inspection. The most important factor in the relative ease of aircraft maintenance today is generally considered to be the early and deliberate attention during design to aircraft characteristics that simplify

---

[1] These two quotations are significant for those interested in aircraft maintenance so I have had them at hand for some years; unfortunately, I am unable to report where they can be found. AEM

CONTROL AND DYNAMIC SYSTEMS, VOL. 52

maintenance. With effective design for maintainability (DFM), equipment downtime can be reduced at many points within the typical repair cycle, as suggested in Figure 1 [1].

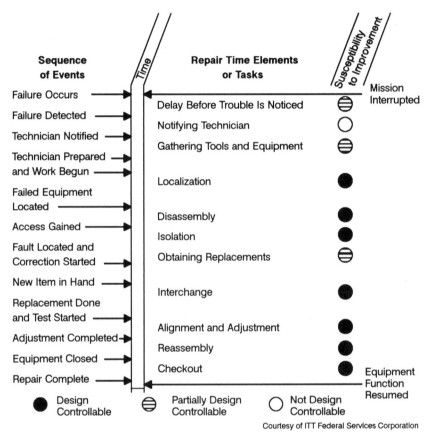

Figure 1. Typical Maintenance Cycle

I.A   Goal of Design for Maintainability

Designing for ease of maintenance serves two fundamental objectives. The first objective, as suggested by the quotations, is high availability — a condition in which equipment is in flying condition when it is needed. Only an aircraft that is available can perform a mission for a military operator or generate revenue for a commercial operator. Availability is a function of both equipment reliability and maintainability. The basic form is given by

$$A = R/(R + M) \tag{1}$$

where R is a reliability term (hours between failure) and M is a maintainability term (hours to repair). Availability can be used as a measure of system effectiveness, but the term is modified to reflect different meanings. In this chapter, we are most concerned with inherent availability, which is the probability that a system will be ready for use in an ideal environment, with interruption only for unscheduled maintenance. Another term, operational availability, refers to system status in an operational environment where training, delay, spares, maintenance policy, and related factors — normally not in the designer's control — influence system functioning.

Although we are oriented to inherent availability, another distinction pointed out by at least one source [2] should be mentioned. In this view, availability applies to systems required to operate continuously around-the-clock, such as a generator in a power station that is in constant demand and only stops for repair at failure. It is the probability that a system is available at an arbitrary time once it has been started. On the other hand, operational readiness is a term that applies to systems that are required to operate during a specific period of time after which repairs, if necessary, can be made to ready the system for the next mission. It is the probability that a system will start operating when a demand arrives to perform a mission. Thus, operational readiness is an appropriate label for aircraft effectiveness, because aircraft systems have idle time between missions in which maintenance can be performed. Our immediate concerns are not affected by this important distinction.

The second objective in designing for ease of maintenance is low cost of product ownership. Cost of ownership due to maintenance difficulties includes a host of problems for operators, such as special tools and support equipment, training, crew size, spares, and technical media. For commercial operators during the 1980s, direct maintenance costs (time and material expended exclusively on the item being maintained) increased faster than total operating costs: from 15.8 percent of operating costs in 1980 to 24 percent in 1988 [3].

Successful DFM can, and with increasing frequency does, greatly affect program success. Supportability factors worth up to 30 percent of total selection points have characterized recent competitions [4, p. 221]. DFM figured importantly in the competition for the Air Force Advanced Tactical Fighter (ATF). For the ATF, a reduced radar cross section increased electronics-dependent capability, and composite airframe demanded the earliest design consideration for maintenance solutions [5]. Ultimately, the winning team predicted its F-22 would cost 35 percent less to operate and maintain than the F-15 [6]. Furthermore, in the recent competition to design and build a new U.S. Army light helicopter, Army officials indicated that the winning design's easy maintenance for soldiers in the field was a deciding factor [7,8].

Numerous large removable panels allow generous access to the aircraft interior and easy-to-operate mechanisms ensure quick ground servicing [9].

Increases in availability have often come about through reliability improvements, perhaps because equipment and materials characteristics are more familiar to design engineers than the characteristics of technicians, mechanics, troubleshooters, and inspectors. However, a phenomenon of which safety experts have been aware for years may be affecting this approach to availability. The effect is that as aircraft increase in reliability, the proportion of human involvement in mishaps does not decrease [10, p. I-1]. Over time, the "inability" of humans to perform beyond a given level tends to increase the importance of human error in accidents relative to the importance of equipment reliability [11, p. 266].

This realization has created an audience for the argument that the industry sometimes faces diminishing returns on investments for greater reliability. In operations, research in cockpit resource management (CRM) symbolizes increased attention to human involvement in flight safety [12]. On the equipment side, increased attention to maintainability may be an analogous indicator of industry's shifting view of investment in R&M. For example, one writer noted the following regarding avionics:

> "Often...it eventually is realized that the price of achieving (very high) reliability goals is too high. Either the price is an unacceptable compromise in performance or an intolerably long schedule for development and maturation of new technologies and specific equipments. In the world of combat avionics, we often end up trading reduced reliability goals for additional performance and earlier availability. Following such trades, maintainability almost always becomes a significant need" [13, p. 1].

I.B   Definition of Maintainability

According to MIL-STD-721C, *Definitions of Terms for Reliability and Maintainability*, maintainability is "the measure of the ability of an item to be retained in, or restored to, specified condition when maintenance is performed by personnel having specified skill levels, using prescribed procedures and resources, at each prescribed level of maintenance and repair" [14]. A slightly different but familiar definition describes maintainability as the probability that a failed item can be repaired in a specified amount of time using a specified set of resources [15, p. 26]. For aircraft, this characteristic may be expressed in at least two probabilities [16]: (1) that an aircraft will be retained in, or restored to, a specified condition within a given period of time, when maintenance is performed in accordance with prescribed procedures and resources; or (2) that the maintenance cost for an aircraft will not exceed X dollars per designated period of time, when the aircraft is operated and maintained in accordance with prescribed procedures. These probabilities are generally increased by deliberate and methodical application during product development of techniques that promote design for ease of maintenance. In practice, however, probabilities of successful maintenance actions or costs are less frequently discussed for aircraft systems than are estimates of more direct measures such as mean hours to repair an aircraft system. Additionally, contracts may specify maintainability as a ratio of direct maintenance burden to flying hours, such as direct maintenance man-hours per flying hour (DMMH/FH). In this case, all anticipated maintainer hours for all systems over a time period are divided by the anticipated flying hours for the same time period. This measure varies widely — from about 20 to 60 DMMH/FH — and only makes sense when aircraft with similar missions and capabilities are compared.

The Air Force indicates that the preferred approach to stating operational requirements for maintenance is in terms of the aircraft mission profile rather than in terms of availability, mean time to repair, and/or DMMH/FH [17, p. 32]. The parameters for stating operational maintainability requirements in terms of aircraft mission profile are:

- Mission profile and environment

- Mission-essential functions

- Performance over time

- Restoral time for mission-essential functions

- Direct maintenance manpower

We agree. The advantage of mission profile descriptions, whether for military or commercial projects, is that designers have more realistic information about the expected maintenance environment and are more likely to design to a true application rather than a maintainability number. In fact, the above parameters should be made easily available to designers and analysts, possibly at a workstation to be described later. Of course, units of measurement and figures of merit are still necessary; in the ideal design situation, selected figures of merit are directly related to mission profile.

II DESIGNING FOR MAINTAINABILITY

Maintainability covers a wide spectrum and interacts with a variety of other engineering domains. The scope of topics shown in Figure 2 [18] suggests the many avenues along which maintainability design is achieved.

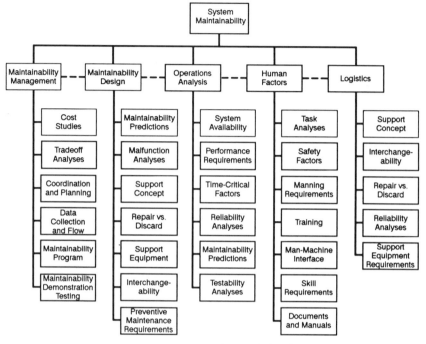

Courtesy of U.S. Air Force Aeronautical Systems Division

Figure 2. The Maintainability Sphere of Influence

Many commercial and government sources treat these activities in detail [18-23]. Such a broad range implies that useful techniques could be examined at great length, but in the space we have here, we are able to focus only on a few topics — establishing maintainability requirements, maintainability design processes, and design controls.

II.A   Establishing Maintainability Requirements

This activity determines how much time and money and what type of tools, equipment, and personnel skills will be necessary to service, repair, and inspect the aircraft. The best quantitative measures of maintainability are selected in this activity, and trade studies are performed to determine cost-effective combinations of factors influencing maintainability. A knowledge of the aircraft operational objective or mission is prerequisite to selecting numerical maintainability requirements. A military airlifter capable of landing in austere fields will generate different maintainability requirements from those of a commercial transport. For the airlifter, support equipment and special tools would be severely limited, and time available for field maintenance would be compressed. For the transport, more choices in support equipment and tools are possible; dispatch time is likely to be every bit as compressed as a military operation, but regular periods of downtime will be available.

II.A.1   Trade Studies

Trade studies or tradeoffs are logistics analyses that compare a piece of equipment's characteristics, cost factors, or operating parameters for the purpose of determining the least costly alternative for the desired effectiveness. For example, consider an existing air-conditioning pack that offers a mean time between failure (MTBF) of 10,000 hours and a mean time to repair of 8.5 hours. The inherent availability is 0.9992, and is plotted in Figure 3. A new design is sought with an availability of at least 0.9995. The area of possible trade between reliability and maintainability is the striped region in Figure 3. Any combination of reliability and maintainability falling in the tradeoff region meets the new availability requirement. A more limiting specification could be stated, such as an MTBF of at least 12,000 hours and an MTTR not to exceed 6 hours. The tradeoff area with such a specification is the cross-stripped area of the figure. Trades on other dimensions are common, including repair versus discard, the planned site (level) of repair of an item, cost versus expected life, make or buy, and level of automation. Blanchard [23] provides an excellent discussion of trade studies.

II. A. 2   Determining Opportunities for Improving Maintainability

Maintainability engineering must begin an allocation process in advance of detail design, particularly in an era of compressed design time. Maintainability allocation is the translation of system maintainability objectives into detailed maintainability requirements for system components. This topic is treated again later, but here we are concerned with preliminary expectations about the maintenance time requirements for various systems. When the general composition of equipment is known, but before actual design features are known, maintenance time can be initially allocated according to system or equipment complexity (indicated by failure rate), the more complex equipment receiving the greater allocation [22]. However, additional insight into this preliminary failure rate-based allocation is available by searching aircraft systems for tasks that can be simplified. Two points regarding this search can be noted. First, while maintainability is a characteristic of virtually all parts of an aircraft, it may be that the greatest opportunity for reducing aircraft maintenance costs is through innovations in line maintenance, specifically fault isolation, on-aircraft repair, remove and replace procedures, and inspection. Design improvements in engine and component overhaul have resulted in wide and effective standardization [24, pp. 7-9], and it is likely that further advances for maintainability in these areas would not be as cost-effective as advances in line maintenance.

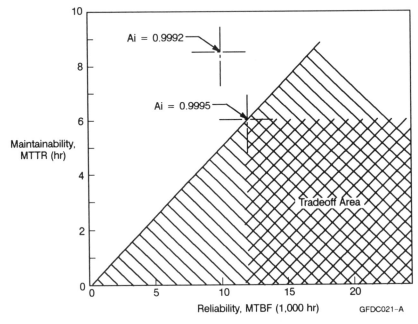

Figure 3. Reliability – Maintainability Tradeoff With Specified Level of Availability

Second, an examination of the distributions of maintenance task times for tasks in existing systems similar to those proposed for a new aircraft can reveal tasks that require an excessive amount of time relative to those tasks that are typical for the system. There are, of course, a variety of reasons for these "extreme scores" in distributions, but it is also true that subsidiary subtasks are often associated with the extreme scores. These subtasks are such activities as solving access absurdities, isolating faults through convoluted procedures, removing good components to reach faulty ones, on-aircraft calibrating of equipment, and securing fasteners with safety wire. These subtasks and many others are candidates for removal through design simplification.

Line maintenance for most systems produces task time distributions where a significant proportion of tasks in a system take much more time than typical tasks in the system. The usual shape of these distributions is skewed to the right; they are most frequently modeled with the lognormal distribution. Observers suggest that lognormality is due to complexity, as well as to the presence of extremely time-consuming tasks. It may be that fault location and correction processes in line maintenance involve activities related to classification, such as classifying symptoms, responding to test signals, and selecting procedures, and since the principles of human search and classification obey the assumptions leading to lognormal distributions, task times for line maintenance are also usually lognormally distributed [19, pp. 8-13 to 8-17]. Additional observations are that systems with predominantly complex tasks [23, pp. 36-37], systems that require tasks with subtasks of unequal frequency and duration [20, p. 2-11], or systems that require tasks that vary greatly or have a mean greater than 1 hour with many subtasks [25, pp. 1-12 to 1-14] will produce task time distributions skewed to the right. Towne et al., [26, p. 5] note that distributions of system maintenance task times are actually made bimodal by a small proportion of tasks that require an excessively long time for completion.

Therefore, it is probably fair to conclude that systems with generally complicated tasks *or* systems with some tasks that are complicated (compared to typical tasks in the system) and protracted by time-consuming subsidiary tasks will produce lognormal task-time distributions. In fact, the writers of MIL-HDBK-472 *Maintainability Prediction* suggested, at least for avionics and electromechanical systems, that design has a greater influence on the occurrence of subsidiary task elements than on the time for their accomplishment [25]. In other words, once design has committed to safety wire, poor fault isolation, on-aircraft calibration, and so on, there is little that can be done to reduce the time these subtasks will take. We can infer that if equipment design requires maintenance tasks with relatively many steps, that design may offer more opportunities to improve maintainability than equipment requiring maintenance tasks with relatively few steps. This suggestion is entirely consistent with the current Air Force urging to simplify and modularize [17].

A simple statistical method exists for quantifying the likelihood of tasks taking more time than typical tasks in a system. If typical tasks are those defined as requiring the most commonly occurring time for completion, the likelihood can be determined by finding the area in a system's lognormal distribution beyond the mode. Any lognormally distributed variable X with parameters μ and σ^2 can be transformed into a normally distributed one with a mean of μ and variance σ^2 by finding the natural logarithm of each X value. The mode of a lognormal distribution is calculated by $M_o = \exp(\mu - \sigma^2)$; this value can be transformed just like any other into a normally distributed equivalent and then converted into a standardized score (difference between mode and mean divided by the standard deviation). The proportion of X values above the lognormal mode is then available from a table of areas under the normal curve (normal distribution table). Actually, because of the nature of lognormal distributions, the negative square root of the lognormal parameter σ^2 is equal to the z score representation of the lognormal mode — after it has been transformed into its normal equivalent. So one can go directly to normal distribution tables with $-\sigma$, treating it as z, and find the probability of its occurrence. The likelihood that task times will be greater than z is equal to the area greater than z from a normal distribution table. For example, for a lognormal distribution with parameters 8 and 4, the z score representing the mode is -2 (the negative square root of 4); a normal distribution table indicates that 98 percent of task times occur above this value.

Use of the normalized transformation is handy for another reason: design requirements in the lognormal (ln) case may be in the form of a median maintenance time (Md) and an upper limit of some value (M_{max}) not to be exceeded with at least a given probability [$P(M_{max})$]. The median and maximum values with a given probability define the parameters μ and σ of the lognormal distribution. The mean is μ = ln Md, and the standard deviation is given by

$$\sigma = \frac{[\ln(M_{max}/Md)]}{Z_P} \qquad (2)$$

where Z_P is the value of the standard normal variable Z at $P(M_{max})$ from normal distribution tables. For example, when $P(M_{max})$ = 0.95, then Z_P = 1.65. Assume for example that the specification calls for Md = 20 minutes, M_{max} = 60 minutes, and $P(M_{max})$ = 0.95. Then ln(60/20) = ln 3 or 1.10; since Z_P = 1.65, the standard deviation is 1.10/1.65 or 0.67 logminutes; and μ = ln 20 or 3.00 logminutes [19, p. 8-21].

II.B   Maintainability Design Processes

These processes translate system maintainability goals into specific design features. Specifically, they involve allocating maintainability objectives to subsystems and components, selecting and applying design alternatives, and predicting maintainability. We will discuss the first two topics.

II.B.1   Maintainability Allocation

The above discussion on allocation was focused on locating opportunities for DFM attention. Here we describe a general approach for determining necessary improvements in component maintainability when the components do not at first yield the desired level of maintainability. The first step in allocation is to organize a system as a set of functionally independent components, in both a block diagram and a table. This organization is very helpful in accounting for all elements of a system, locating system elements that are candidates for DFM improvement, and understanding how DFM in one element might allow relaxation of maintainability goals for another element. The blocks and table entries should reflect each component's level of maintenance. For example, an assembly whose repair is accomplished by removing the next larger component would not be shown as a separate block. Next, add to each table entry the reliability (MTBF), failure rate (1/MTBF), and maintainability (MTTR) figures of merit that will define the availability expected for the component.

Figure 4 shows a cockpit temperature control in block diagram and table format. The system operates by changing the mix of warm bleed air and cold air made available through ducting to the cockpit. Power for this system comes from a power bus, through a circuit breaker, and to a power supply integrated with the control amplifier. Of these power-related elements, only the control amplifier is shown in Figure 4. (The temperature control is a small system and, as might be expected, computerized maintainability engineering programs are available to handle the bookkeeping encountered in large systems.)

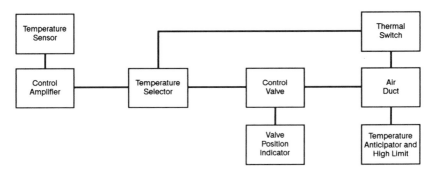

Component	MTBF (hr)	1/MTBF	MTTR (hr)
A. Temperature Sensor	12,000	0.000083	2
B. Control Amplifier	6,000	0.000166	1
C. Temperature Anticipator and High Limit	3,200	0.000313	1
D. Temperature Selector	7,000	0.000143	1
E. Control Valve	2,500	0.0004	4
F. Valve Position Indicator	2,500	0.0004	1
G. Thermal Switch	7,000	0.000143	1
H. Air Duct	24,000	0.000042	6

Figure 4. Functional Block Diagram and Table R and M Values for a Cockpit Temperature Control System

Names of the components and their reliability, failure rate, and maintainability are shown below the block diagram (all values invented for our example). Values of this nature are available from predictive methods [25, 18] or from experience with similar components.

Overall system maintainability can be determined by

$$MT\hat{T}R_s = \frac{\sum\limits_{i=1}^{n} \lambda_i \, MT\hat{T}R_i}{\sum\limits_{i=1}^{n} \lambda_i} \tag{3}$$

where

$MT\hat{T}R_s$ = predicted system MTTR

λ_i = failure rate of the ith component

$MT\hat{T}R_i$ = predicted mean corrective maintenance downtime for system repair when the ith component fails

An example with an imaginary two-component system:

	λ	MTTR
A	0.000002	4 hours
B	0.0001	1 hour

$$MT\hat{T}R_s = \frac{0.000002(4) + 0.0001(1)}{0.000002 + 0.0001} = 1.059 \text{ hours}$$

For the cockpit temperature control, the system mean time to repair is 1.88 hours, with one failure expected in the system every 592 hours. If we specified 1.5 hours, the as-is condition is excessive. To correct, we use

$$\overline{MTTR_i} = \frac{MT\hat{T}R_i \, MTTR_o}{MT\hat{T}R_s} \tag{4}$$

for each block in the diagram, where

$\overline{MTTR_i}$ = allocated mean corrective maintenance downtime for the system when the ith component fails

$MT\hat{T}R_i$ = predicted mean corrective maintenance downtime for system repair when the ith component fails

$MTTR_o$ = system objective in terms of mean corrective maintenance time

$MT\hat{T}R_s$ = predicted value of system mean corrective maintenance time

For example, the imaginary two-component system is specified with a maintainability of 0.5 hour. For the two components,

$$\overline{MTTR}_A = \frac{4(0.5)}{1.059} = 1.89$$

$$\overline{MTTR}_B = \frac{1(0.5)}{1.059} = 0.47$$

Then, to verify, Eq. (3) can be repeated:

$$M\hat{T}TR_s = \frac{0.000002(1.89) + 0.0001(0.47)}{0.000002 + 0.0001} = 0.499 \text{ hours}$$

II.B.2   Selection and Application of Design Alternatives

The objective of design selection is to reconcile the predicted maintainability with the allocated value, but attempting that match for each component is far too restrictive. Instead, the system allocation is the target; innovation and improvement for DFM of one or a few components can sometimes be enough to reach the objectives for the entire system. In the cockpit temperature control, a new access concept to the control valve might reduce downtime enough that the system meets its allocated level. Other methods include changes in modularization, improved visibility, special tools, crew size, and so on. Trade studies may be necessary to select the best alternative.

The selection of design alternatives is certainly near the core of DFM. Such a selection assumes that design/build teams have produced candidates that are open for critique and defense. A variety of simulation and prediction techniques are available to help evaluate candidates, such as PC-based discrete-event and continuous-process simulation, certain cost/availability/fault isolation models, and, as suggested above, maintainability prediction packages. Fresh insight from customers and maintainers is also useful in this process. We will discuss three topics relevant to the selection of design alternatives in this section: computer-aided design (CAD) techniques, checklists, and design for testability.

II.B.2.a   CAD Techniques with Human Models — The use of CAD-drawn models of people to examine human interaction with structure and equipment is an emerging technique that is proving helpful in evaluating structural design and installation alternatives. These "human models" are used for electronically examining maintenance access, visual obscuration of components, and related variables during those stages when design itself exists only in electronic form. Additionally, the variety of human sizes and populations available in electronic form and the speed with which they can be

interposed in drawings enable some analyses to be performed that would be essentially impossible with actual equipment and actual people.

Human models are computer-drawn forms that are expressions of anthropometric and biomechanical equations. Normally, the software for their generation will reside in a central computer that executes a CAD drafting package or in a stand-alone workstation. Human model software is available commercially and through the Air Force [27, p. 25]. Some companies have developed their own packages. Although no model has every desirable feature, some of the features in current human models include multiple populations, accurate joint centers and joint angle limits, initial posture libraries, rapid posture adjustment, detailed hands, animation, detection of movement interference, vision, strength, apparel, and protective gear.

Usually, a human model analysis is undertaken because designers and/or maintainability engineers suspect that humans will not be able to fit into, reach, or see some place critical to a maintenance task. For example, Figure 5 presents a computer human form generated with the Douglas Human Modeling System (DHMS) [28] and interposed with an electronic drawing of an inert gas bottle and surrounding structure. The bottle is one of several located below the cargo floor of a military transport, and the question behind this analysis is whether a large man will have enough space overhead and between the sidewalls to manipulate tools and remove bottles for inspection or replacement. (In practice, surfaced models are preferred, but wire-frame drawings of humans are shown here because they are more interpretable in black and white reproduction.)

The use of human models in designing for ease of maintenance was presented earlier [29], but the following scenario, built around the bottle removal task, highlights the process. After detemining that a question of sufficient space exists, critical segments of the expected maintenance "choreography" are located. A study of the bottle removal task reveals that releasing a bottle's upper fastener is a clearance-critical task segment, so that segment is selected for model development.

Next, preliminary equipment/human model combinations are created. Details of the maintainer's expected movements, fastener type and necessary tool, and expected support surface for the maintainer are obtained and often prove sufficient to suggest how the human model will be interposed with the structure model. For the bottle removal question, a model of a 95th percentile (by stature) Air Force male mechanic is chosen because clearance is the concern. The structure file is called and attachment points for the human model (places in the structure where a human anatomical landmark will be connected and from which human orientation will be determined) are created.

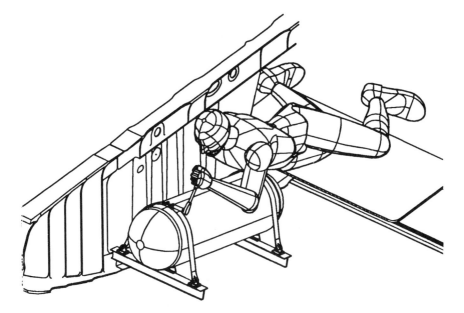

Figure 5. Human Model Representation of Removal of Gas Bottle

Reasonable postures are attempted after the human is attached until one (or more) appears to depict the essence of the critical segment. Animation files are created if human or equipment motion is crucial to understanding the design (e.g., movement of the arm using a ratchet wrench or movement of the gas bottle after fasteners are released).

Next, geometric and analytic capabilities resident in the drawing package or associated with the human model software can be called to garner information about the task and the design. For instance, important clearances for use of a ratchet wrench in the bottle removal task were calculated using the geometric capabilities of the host computer. The clearances could be added to the file and could appear in a close-up view of the fastener area. If the design alternative raised questions about human strength limitations we would want to perform strength analyses; if questions of reach existed, reach envelopes would be constructed, and so on. In this example, we conclude that no necessary movements for releasing the upper fastener are prevented by the proposed design. In more complicated analyses, the images produced with human models may provide the analyst with insight to form judgments that are not possible without visualization of equipment/human interaction.

Two interesting visual problems underlie Figure 6. By way of background, a Supplemental Inspection Document from the FAA required visual inspection of structure in the vertical stabilizer of a transport aircraft. If the inspector lies on his/her back (on the horizontal stabilizer where it bisects the tail cone), his/her head movement is limited. So one of the questions asks whether inspection as shown in the figure is possible. Since head movement is limited, the model's head position is set at several plausible, but not equally comfortable, positions and the inspector's would-be fields of view (foveal vision) with reasonable eye movement are determined. The fields of view are mapped on the aircraft structure and shown as different shadings in Figure 6. From this mapping, we see that with the proposed method of inspection, only a small portion of structure is available to foveal vision with the inspector's head and eyes in comfortable positions.

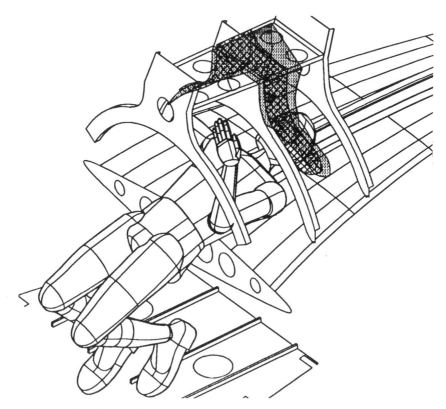

Figure 6. Human Model Representation of Structure Inspection With CAD Plots of Field of View

Figure 7 reveals the second problem. Some of the structure is too close to the eyes for people of average sight to accommodate; that is, they would not be able to focus on some of the structure to be inspected. Simple point-to-point distance determination indicates which parts fall below the minimum focal range. Because such a small portion of the important structure is available to

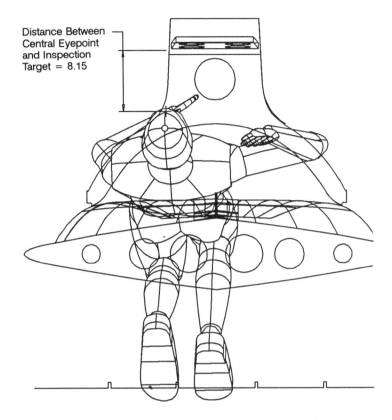

Distance Between
Central Eyepoint
and Inspection
Target = 8.15

**Figure 7. Representation of Inspection Reveals Distance Between
Structure and Inspector's Eyes**

foveal vision or within adequate focal range, we conclude that this inspection
concept is inadequate.

These examples might suggest that human model analyses are rather
abrupt procedures, but they may require many hours. Ironically, preparation
of structure models for use with human models is usually the most time-
consuming step, rather than the use of human models per se. The following
steps are taken in building equipment/human models for examining designs
and tasks [29]:

• Identify task to be simulated and maintenance approach.

• Select representative populations, percentiles, and apparel.

• State the question to be answered by the model.

- Identify critical segments in the task.

- Describe the task segment in joint configuration terms.

- Create or acquire the CAD files of relevant aircraft structure.

- Combine drawings of structure and human model.

- Perform analyses and interpret the model.

- Report results of analyses and interpretation.

II.B.2.b   CAD Techniques With Working Envelopes — A CAD technique related to human models is the representation of space needed for the movement of hands, tools, and components during a maintenance task. The representation can be called a working envelope [30]. The technique addresses a growing problem: with each new generation of aircraft, structure becomes more crowded. Currently, nearly any space is eyed keenly by hydraulics, electrical, environmental, fuel, mechanical, or other disciplines as potential "real estate" for components or lines of some kind. Not infrequently, the dense packing of equipment leaves some line-replaceable unit (LRU) virtually inaccessible or accessible only to a tool but not adequate for handling the LRU and maneuvering it out of its installation location.

In prior efforts on this problem, investigators photographed subjects' hands against grid-marked backgrounds as they engaged in simple tasks with hand tools [31, 32, 33]. Generally, these studies revealed that maintenance time for tasks involving reach through access openings was strongly affected by the space available for movement, but investigators' attention — of necessity at the time — was directed to relatively symmetrical envelopes.

Working envelopes that are not symmetrical are more realistic and are difficult to define mathematically, such as the ones shown in Figures 8 and 9. The envelope in Figure 8 depicts the space necessary to reach an LRU through an access hole in the horizontal stabilizer of a wide-body transport. The irregular shape from the access hole to the target in Figure 8 is a motion envelope made up of the maximum excursions of a human hand on repeated reaches to the target. The envelope in Figure 9 depicts the space necessary to reach through ribs in a composite rudder assembly for repair purposes. In both figures, the envelopes represent space that must not be obstructed with hardware or components so that the target locations can be reached.

These envelopes are constructed with instrumentation that records hand position in three-dimensional space over time, using the following steps:

- Identify design alternatives to be investigated.

- Build structure files in CAD of the area under study.

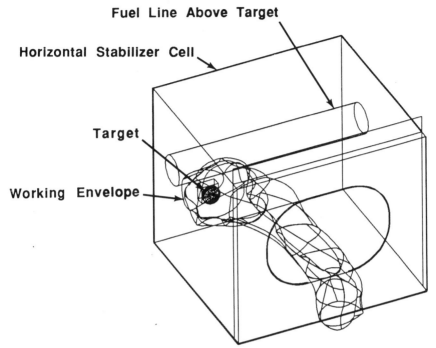

Fuel Line Above Target

Horizontal Stabilizer Cell

Target

Working Envelope

Figure 8. Working Envelope for Access to Component in a Horizontal Stabilizer

- Build a physical design fixture (e.g., using foam board) of the area under study.

- Instrument a human subject's hand and obtain three-dimensional coordinate points during simulation of the maintenance task on a physical design fixture.

- Transfer coordinate points to the CAD system and establish the maximum surface of those points.

- Place surfaced volume in electronic drawings and analyze component placement alternatives.

II.B.2.c   Design Features and Checklists — Clearly, equipment that is easy to maintain has features that make it so. Hundreds of design attributes tending to make equipment easy to maintain have been listed in a variety of sources. As a whole, these sources form a large collection of ideas and discoveries about how to design things so they are easier to fix when they fail. Of course, not all features are appropriate for all aircraft: the aircraft mission usually affects the variety of options available to improve maintainability. A few design items and examples of their application (the examples are not intended

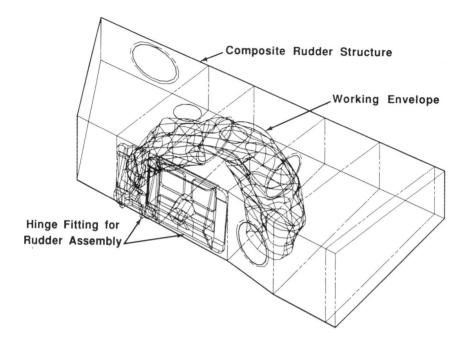

Figure 9. Working Envelope for Access Into Rudder for Repair of Composite Material

to mean that the referenced source was the origin of the maintainability idea) are presented below.

- Locate each unit in the equipment in such a way that no other unit or piece of equipment has to be removed to get to the unit [19, (p. 5-39]. Example: The Army's new RAH-66 Comanche helicopter uses a box beam frame that relieves the skin of load. The design allows most of the skin to be removed as panels; LRUs are spread out no more than one deep just below the panels.

- Provide a hinged windscreen (canopy) [34]. Example: The hinged F-5A canopy is easy to replace and provides access to the back of the instrument panel.

- Design assemblies, subassemblies, and parts to be interchangeable within and between equipment [35]. Example: The new Air Force F-22 will carry four or five common avionics modules: each can perform the functions of certain others, so there is no need to stock spares of 25 or so uniquely functioning modules.

- Items that are frequently pulled out of their installed positions for checking should be mounted on rollout racks, slides, or hinges [36]. Example:

With its nose cone swung open, the F/A-18's APG-65 radar runs out on rails for easy access to modules.

- Locate access openings at convenient working positions [37]. Example: The Marine Corps AV8B is fitted with 190 access doors; 118 can be opened from the ground without a workstand.

- Access provisions must be compatible with the frequency of maintenance [23]. Example: The folding wing design of the Boeing 777 places certain wing folding hydraulic components outside the lofted surface of the wing into a faired pod for easy maintenance access.

Hundreds of other items are listed in the references cited above and in related sources. Designers, maintainability engineers, and human factors specialists can study these lists to learn the fundamental characteristics that tend to reduce aircraft maintenance time.

Reviewing sources of DFM information makes it clear that checklists are surprisingly popular products of the maintainability community. Their popularity merits some discussion. The checklists can be faulted because they lack application information and are often too general for actual design problems, but there is no doubt about the importance of the design criteria they list. Maintainability criteria in checklist format are statistically related to maintenance time [38]. Furthermore, checklists compile more details and descriptions of good design than engineers can typically recall [39, p. 225], and they lend themselves to communication among designers. Nevertheless, a question exists about their effectiveness as a design technique. It is their use in integrated design that the following discussion examines.

In general, checklists are listings of procedures, items, or characteristics arranged so that some type of task, count, or identification is accomplished as the user progresses through the list. A checklist implies that, when an item is checked in the order listed, attention can be released from the checked item and directed to the next item on the list.

In practice, checklists can be attached to drawings during reviews, can be used to "rate" a design, or used in conjunction with maintainability prediction, even though these uses somewhat symbolize late review of a design after its features are fairly well solidified. Earlier in design cycles, maintainability engineers may use a checklist to define an initial maintainability concept, or design engineers may translate checklist items into design features. In concurrent engineering, comprehensive checklists containing desired human engineering and DFM characteristics that express customers' interests could be products of design/build teams.

The usual checklist found in published sources may contain only a few items or hundreds of items loosely organized into gross categories such as connectors, displays, and so on. An example of a typical checklist item is found in the *Air Force Systems Command Checklist of General Design Criteria* [40], which contains a checklist for maintainability. The item reads, "Locate test points used in checking close to the controls or displays that are used in the checking procedure." Like items in most checklists, this may refer to any of several vehicles or systems in any vehicle. The ambiguous nature of the items allows checklists to be used with a great variety of equipment types, but in doing so, requires more knowledge and interpretation on the part of the analyst.

Despite the problem with vague items, the ability of checklists to guide behavior (e.g., evaluate or estimate or bring about design adherence to ease of maintenance) is usually accepted as self-evident. Their advantages, say, over prose or statements of abstract goals, appear to be so obvious that questions of their effectiveness have only occasionally been raised (e.g., [41]). However, it is clear that not all types of checklists are intended to guide behavior of equal difficulty, and it is probably true that simple behavior is more easily guided by checklists than is complex behavior. For example, among untrained people, verifying the contents of a shipping crate with a packing list would surely be easier than inspecting parts for defects using a checklist having the same number of items. Verifying a container's contents would only require that pieces be identified by part number or some other method, but parts inspection requires complicated evaluations.

Planning or evaluating designs for maintainability is very near or at the extreme of cognitive complexity among tasks for which checklists have been written. Even with extensive training and experience, it is very difficult to envision all the equipment/human interactions occurring in maintenance because of variance in human capabilities, variance in maintenance tasks, and the complex influence of the environment (e.g., cold weather) on maintenance workload. Table 1 presents a possible scheme by which to compare features and the relative ease of using various types of checklists. Most DFM checklists require the user to evaluate, to judge quality or value, and to visualize use of equipment with or without certain features. As in judging art, the task does not reduce to a "do this, do that" process, and the user's actual evaluation task is scarcely implied by the "packing list" structure of most DFM checklists. In fact, while checklisted DFM criteria are statistically related to actual maintainability, there is unfortunately little evidence that checklists help analysts conceive effective DFM or locate maintainability problems. Indeed, the fact that common problems continue to appear in design could certainly cause one to wonder why checklists are so popular.

Features such as the organization of items in a list may influence the effectiveness of checklists intended to guide complex cognitive processes. Goldberg

Table 1
Types and Features of Checklists

Feature	Type of List						
	Evaluation Forms, DFM Checklists	Identifiers (Categorize Elements)	Trouble-Shooting Guides	Medical History Forms	"Checkoff" Inventories	Procedures Manuals	Manifests and Packing List
	Increasing Ease of Use →						
One-on-One Correspondence Between Elements of List and Referent						●	●
More Elements or Conditions In List Than In Referent	●	●	●	●	●		
User Must Locate or Verify a Condition	●	●		●	●		●
User Must Perform a Task			●			●	
Characteristics of the Referent Are Named or Identified In the List	●	●	●	●			
Referent Is Named or Identified In List		●	●		●	●	●

and Gibson [42] found that a logically organized checklist produced more accurate circuit board inspection than unorganized checklists. Perhaps most important for DFM is the simple tenet of tailoring a checklist specifically to the equipment being designed [43, p. 395]. The tailoring can be in ways that coincide with checklist users' mental representation or image of how elements are connected into a functioning whole. Actually, Goldberg and Gibson believed that superior performance was obtained with their logically organized checklist because its organization agreed with users' mental representation of circuit board defects.

A recent checklist of human engineering requirements [44] is an example of a list we would expect to successfully influence design. First, it was tailored — in this case for a T-lug bomb rack. Second, it was organized so that sections coincided with functions of, and support concepts for, a bomb rack, as Table 2 indicates.

II.B.2.d   Design for Testability — Fault isolation, diagnosis, or trouble-shooting is often a time-consuming, frustrating operation for maintainers and an expensive one for operators. Indeed, most corrective maintenance time is spent on fault isolation. Furthermore, fault isolation is not necessarily accu-rate: even with a well-equipped operator and skilled maintenance personnel, up to 50 percent of avionics removals can be wasted efforts — removals of good modules that were suspected of being faulty. Adding to this situation, remov-als can induce problems such as loose pins in connections that later become maddeningly difficult to track down.

Table 2
Sections of a Checklist Tailored for a T-Lug Bomb Rack

Section	Number of Checklist Items
Cartridge Retainers	3
Hook Engagement and Latching	1
Manual Store Release	15
Hook Safety Interlock	6
Interlock Operation	5
Interlock Labeling	15
Unscheduled Organizational and Intermediate Maintenance	9
Personnel Skill Level for Depot Maintenance	3
Characteristics for Lifting, Carrying, and Transporting	9
Error Proofing	7
Accessibility	17
Connectors	11
Operation and Human Capabilities	1
Cables	9
General Labeling	14
Component Labeling	5

Identifying the faulty component in a degraded or failed system is obviously related to repair or correct removal and replacement. When testing is easy (checking status at test points and following diagnostic logic), maintainers will probably try to pinpoint a faulty module before removal rather than skip over the fault isolation step and simply begin removing any and all suspect modules — a practice called "shotgunning." When testing is easy *and* effective, maintainers will probably pinpoint and remove only the truly faulty module. A commercial transport operator's experience with a lateral control problem illustrates the tendency of technicians to "short-circuit" a rational fault isolation approach [45]. Pilots reported that aileron surfaces did not respond normally to control wheel input, regardless of the wheel used. Maintenance too quickly concluded that the cause was a dual mechanical fuse failure, and, as is often the case with human problem solving, went on to expend considerable time trying to locate the nonexistent failed fuses and the cause of their failure. Eventually, a system expert was called in and found the source to be sticking tension regulators — a problem solved by cleaning and lubricating the devices.

It is not easy to anticipate all that can go wrong for the troubleshooter. Several reasons why designing for effective fault isolation is so challenging are presented below.

- Fault isolation reasoning during design may be less pressured than fault isolation reasoning during maintenance in a hanger or on a flight line.

- Built-in test (BIT) may be unreliable due to hardware or software problems.

- Conventional measures of aircraft availability may mask faults [13].

- Fault isolation instructions may be difficult to acquire, to use in the field, or to comprehend.

- Test and qualification of BIT in a laboratory by inserting known faults is conservative and may create an unrealistic prediction of performance.

- Test tolerances must become tighter as measurement is applied to successively higher level assemblies or applied up the ladder of repair organizations. If organizational level test tolerances are tighter than those of the shop, equipment is likely to retest okay (RTOK) when pulled because of nonconformance.

- Pilots may rely more on their senses than quantitative measurement and incorrectly cite faults in equipment, driving up the false alarm rate.

Designing for fault isolation is part of the discipline called testability. Testability in design allows the status of an item to be determined and faults to be isolated [15, p. 43]. Government contractor requirements for a testability program are found in MIL-STD-2165, *Testability Program for Electronic Systems and Equipments* [46]. Requirements for built-in test, test points, and indicators are found in MIL-STD-2084(AS), *General Requirements for Maintainability of Avionic and Electronic Systems and Equipment* [47].

For at least 20 years, the trend in aircraft design for testability has been toward technologies that reveal faults, most notably BIT. For example, one supplier's central air data computer permits interrogation of its own performance. It will log two failures per flight for five flights in the flight regime above 10,000 feet and greater than 120 knots. To interrogate, the maintainer disengages the computer by pulling a circuit breaker, selects a failure warning mode on the front of the unit, then presses a push-to-test button. A pattern of "failure history" lights indicates the internal faults, if any. The meaning of the possible light patterns is explained by a placard on the front of the unit; the unit is replaced if failures are indicated. Other fault-revealing technology includes sensors and indicators (e.g., stress, composite damage) that may not be associated with BIT. Increasingly, interrogation, fault isolation test, and system data collection (e.g., for trend analysis) are brought together in a single maintenance computer.

Testability design emerges from two fundamental sources: failure/criticality analyses and the equipment's support and maintenance concepts.

The analyses are often concerned with failure of some unit with an expected life less than that of the airframe, propagation of effects through the system, and symptoms or implications of the failure throughout the system. Failure/ criticality analyses and maintenance concepts interact; components with relatively short lives and those that are more critical are candidates for line rather than depot replacement. Ultimately, testability takes the form of a set of decisions about the type of fault detection, the points where fault detection and isolation can be implemented, and the proportion of faults in each item that are detectable by a proposed design approach. For example, (1) frequent failure items should have the means for easy confirmation of failure; (2) "discard at failure" items will require only their output indication, but no test points; (3) organizational-level maintenance limited to removal and replacement of failed components may be supported by BIT identifying faults at the assembly level, although locating faults *within* assemblies by BIT would be excessive in this case.

The proven technique in design for testability is to break a system down into functional elements (often this step is accomplished earlier in preliminary design and/or maintainability allocation) in order to locate inputs and outputs and to develop logic troubleshooting flow diagrams to determine the information needed to judge an element (part, subassembly, assembly, subsystem — depending on the maintenance concept) either good or bad. The basic idea is illustrated in Figure 10 [18], which presents common flow patterns in electronic systems, although the principles are applicable to energy flow in any system. In Panel A, three test points, in addition to the output indication, are necessary to determine which of four elements is faulty. In B, failure indication may depend on the position of the switch at the time of failure: four test points are needed for isolation. In C, elements depend on each other for proper operation: the switch is necessary to determine the status of elements in more than one circuit condition.

Functional partitioning or segmenting divides a system into subsystems with distinct purposes. The step reveals (in simple cases) the logical points where a test must be made to verify input and/or output. Accurate partitioning also helps to improve the resolution, reduce the time necessary for fault isolation, and diminish the effects of multiple faults.

Logic troubleshooting flow diagrams are block and arrow charts that state the sequence of tests needed to trace a fault down to one element. Consider Panel A of Figure 10: If the output indication is faulty, test the output of Element 1. If Element 1 output is bad, replace or repair Element 1 and recheck the output indication. If Element 1 output is okay, test Element 2 output, and so on. The origin of these diagrams is the (1) review of FMEA data to determine likely failures and the propagation of a fault's effects through a

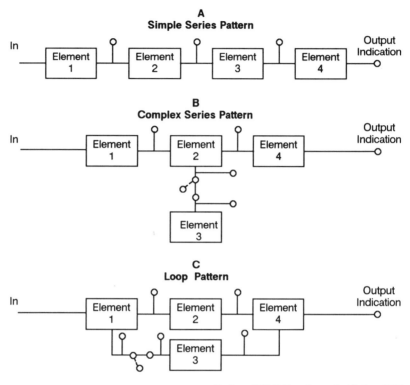

Courtesy of U.S. Air Force Aeronautical Systems Division

Figure 10. Data-Flow Patterns Encountered in Electronic Systems

system, (2) listing of symptoms associated with faults, (3) logical determination of test sequences that lead efficiently to failed components in order of their failure likelihood, and (4) selection of troubleshooting approaches in terms of time and resources (e.g., crew size and tools) to arrive at the one offering the lowest life-cycle cost.

Of course, the process described above is complicated for large systems. Many aircraft systems are simply too complicated for any person to foresee all possible states, and the resulting problems in testability extend to fielded equipment. One writer likened troubleshooting of modern avionics to "a hog looking at a wristwatch" [48, p. 303], meaning that system complexity can overwhelm the man. To apply troubleshooting logic to large systems, techniques are needed to model many functions within systems and show the interrelationship among functions.

One set of tools that helps in addressing complexity is the class of CAD tools specifically intended for testability design of complex electronic systems. These testability analysis tools are aimed at the circuit card assembly level of analysis and may include libraries of devices and their behavior. The best of the tools will yield a testability figure of merit for the system, will indicate where to break feedback loops to improve testability, and will provide information on addition/elimination of test nodes and on the level of uncertainty in fault isolation [49]. Some will produce test strategies and troubleshooting logic trees. The use of these packages and their output are relatively structured, and they successfully manage electronic system complexity.

Another set of tools are computer-aided engineering products. These include behavioral models, computer-aided software engineering (CASE) packages, and computer-aided engineering (CAE) tools designed for system simulation and analysis. These could be effectively used for testability design where systems incorporate a variety of components in addition to electronics. For example, when subcontractors supply various sections of an aircraft, airframers and systems integration contractors normally undertake the interface chore of designing a testability approach that is appropriate to multiple systems.

System simulators, as the CASE and CAE tools and behavioral models might be called, have been developed to reduce the time expended in cycles of specification, software/hardware prototyping, testing, and redesign traditionally encountered in system development. The tools enable the user to rapidly represent system structure, develop functioning models of interrelationships within a system, express control algorithms as performance parameters, and observe the effects of inputs and changes in state over time. Models of very complex systems can be constructed; one simulator package allows nearly 50 inputs and outputs on each one of scores of "icons" (which can represent functions or components). The model builder selects or writes the mathematical or logical conditions that characterize each input.

System simulators are more advanced and accurate in some areas (e.g., software) than in others (e.g., fluid power), but for those aspects of system design that can be faithfully modeled, the simulators may offer advantages from the standpoint of the testability engineer. These advantages include:

- Verification of complex system states and dynamics.

- Easy insertion of faults and observation of the propagation of the faults' effects.

- Earlier identification of a system's hierarchical structure — important for selecting maintenance concepts.

- Fast adjustment and refinement of design.

- Experimentation with fault isolation strategies.

- Fast access to the system design if it is shared on a network.

- Testability design concurrent with the evolution of system design.

Figure 11 presents a Northrop behavioral model of the leading edge flap control system of a "generic" fighter [50]. The model shown was created with RAPIDS II, a program mainly intended for developing maintenance instruction [51], but which is an excellent example of a behavioral model that can be applied to testability design. Operation of controls such as the flap switch, conditions such as hydraulic pressurization, and effects such as angle of attack (AOA) will combine to produce appropriate flap response in the model. The model shown is actually a top-level simulation: functions such as "Hyd Sys 2," "CPU," or flap mechanisms could be modeled in great detail with all their behavior rules if their failure rate justified the testability design; if not, perhaps only control outputs would be shown.

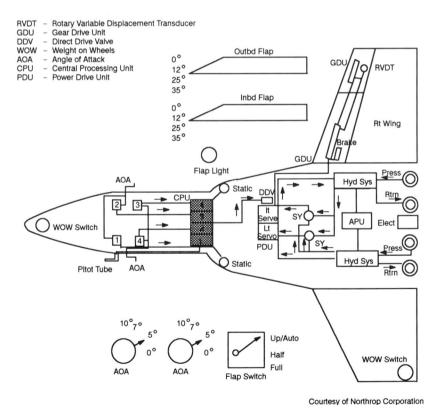

RVDT – Rotary Variable Displacement Transducer
GDU – Gear Drive Unit
DDV – Direct Drive Valve
WOW – Weight on Wheels
AOA – Angle of Attack
CPU – Central Processing Unit
PDU – Power Drive Unit

Courtesy of Northrop Corporation

Figure 11. Leading Edge Flap Control System Simulation

The human decision-making involved in creating a simulation with RAPIDS II can be applied to testability. The following steps reveal the advantages of system simulators to design for testability.

- Develop a general overview of the system through discussion with system experts or by studying existing descriptions.

- Locate system status indicators and controls or create "dummys" to reveal and control status in critical states. Determine the value of indicators and controls for system status checking.

- Write rules representing the transitions in system functions that produce changes in indicators. Rules may be high fidelity (e.g., control algorithms) for critical or low-reliability functions or mere input/output links for non-critical or high-reliability functions. Repeat the second and third steps for all system functions.

- As the model is built up, test the behavior of functions to find flaws in the model. Insert faults and determine symptoms.

- Combine functions, verify that computer representation runs as intended, and continue to insert faults. Locate complex effects such as cascading faults and effects that propagate "upstream" in the system.

- Where possible, model functions as they will be grouped in hardware.

- Observe the signals from functions (or components); identify normal and abnormal ranges and determine their value for fault isolation.

- Create dummy test instruments and "wire" them into the system to determine their value to fault isolation.

- Develop troubleshooting logic trees based on findings from system simulation; perform trials with troubleshooting logic.

- Validate model behavior with assistance from system experts.

II.C   Design Controls

Design controls are formal policies, plans, and procedures set up to ensure that design intent is achieved and conventional engineering requirements are accomplished. Maintainability policies, plans, and procedures are described in a program plan. When the plan is authorized by engineering management, it becomes the guide and rule for maintainability activities.

II.C.1   Program Plan

The remaining comments in this section concern the program plan and the use of data from various groups in designing for maintainability.

MIL-STD-470A, *Maintainability Program for Systems and Equipment* [52], presents the requirements for conducting a maintainability program for government contracts. The essential elements, some of which are discussed in this chapter, are shown below. The contents of the program plan are broken out in the first item.

- Program Plan
    - Work to be accomplished
    - Time phasing
    - Responsibilities of organizational elements
    - Lines of communication between prime and others
    - Review points
    - Techniques to be used for maintainability allocation, analysis, and prediction
    - Interfaces between maintainability and related functions (e.g., reliability, human factors)
- Maintainability analysis
- Maintenance inputs
- Design criteria
- Trade studies
- Prediction
- Vendor controls
- Systems integration
- Design review
- Data system
- Maintainability demonstration
- Status reporting

Commercial programs should also have a program plan. If major assemblies are subcontracted, the supplier should be asked to write a plan that is satisfactory to the customer. Depending on the needs of the customer, various types of guidance for writing a plan may be found in MIL-STD-470A; MIL-H-46855B, *Human Engineering Requirements for Military Systems, Equipment, and Facilities* [53]; *AFSC Design Handbook 1-9 Maintainability* [18]; or a model prepared by the customer.

II.C.2   Networked Data

The lines of communication section of this program plan describes how data will be shared among involved parties. Needs for information sharing and the current intense interest in concurrent engineering imply an importance of proximity so that engineers of different disciplines can collaborate on design. However, trends in aircraft design and manufacturing are leading to greater dispersion of functions across companies and countries. For designs to emerge characterized by ease of maintenance, maintainability engineers must advocate essential requirements, tradeoffs, and innovations across a variety of functions that are geographically dispersed. Methods of advocating and exchanging information are every bit as crucial to maintainability as breakthough innovations and maintenance concepts.

Many companies are linking design workstations, terminals, and personal computers in increasingly sophisticated networks. These networks can enable individuals at different sites to have access to design as it evolves. For example, one workstation can act as a master with other workstations slaved to it for the purpose of simultaneous review of design. Voice communication or on-line entries into review and comment "pages" by maintainability, manufacturing, or other parts of a design/build team become part of the collective insight brought into a design as a result of networking. Networking and related topics are widely discussed [54, 55, 56].

Figure 12 presents a concept for the use of networked data at a workstation for DFM analysis and planning for maintenance. In this concept, examination of existing information (e.g., current status of a design) is primarily accomplished on a graphics computer, and the generation of new information (e.g., evaluation of maintainability or task planning) is accomplished on a graphics and a personal computer. Characteristics of the data are given below (paragraph numbers are matched to block numbers in Figure 12).

1. Geometry — User creates structure files and transfers them to/from an electronic development fixture (EDF). The EDF enables designers and analysts to perform traditional fit/interference studies and indicates the association between drawings (drawing tree). Geometry from suppliers is also part of the EDF; necessary drawing practices are specified to suppliers so that their files are compatible. If necessary, passwords limit who may change files.

2. Design Assistance — User may obtain checklists, design and drawing standards, a parts library, and lessons learned.

3. Component Recognition — Analytic models such as human fit/function and kinematics can be called from an analysis methods collection and

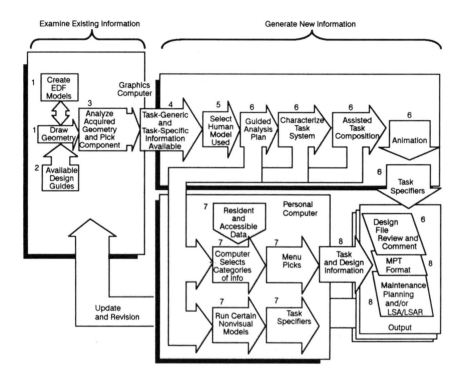

Figure 12. Workstation Functions for DFM Analysis

applied to the geometry. Components such as LRUs that were earlier added to files are marked as objects for computer recognition so that a pick of the component calls up a description of the features enabling the item to meet maintainability requirements. Sources of this information are maintainability analysis entries associated with the component.

4. Maintenance Task Information — Most important information is a list of maintenance procedures associated with a component (expected remove and replace sequence, time, anticipated difficulties, skill demands) or structure (expected inspection sequence). Source is logistics support analysis (LSA) data bases.

5. Compatibility of Design With Human Use — To learn more about the tasks associated with equipment, user may examine interaction of human model with components or structure. Algorithms to construct human image or parameters of human behavior are resident in the workstation. Selection "disconnects" structure data file from EDF.

6. Composing Models of Maintenance Tasks — Sample tasks and strategies available from the computer guide the user in describing expected

tasks, performing analyses to evaluate maintainability, and producing predictions about maintenance (task specifiers). If user is not authorized to change drawings, he or she can modify the "disconnected" version and identify it as part of a design file review and comment that is sent back to the EDF.

7. Performance Data Bases and Models — The workstation is networked to occupational and human performance data bases. Guided searches reveal information about predicted tasks. Maintenance workload, error prediction, and other nongraphic models are primed by earlier description of tasks.

8. Logistics Support Information — Information about maintenance performance is sent to manpower/personnel/ training and logistics support analysis record (LSAR) functions for completing LSAR tasks and data records; design insight resulting from application of workstation output to LSAR functions is rapidly associated with design through review and comment capabilities.

III SUMMARY

Maintainability of aircraft is achieved through deliberate attention during design to human capacities of mechanics, inspectors, and technicians. The stakes in DFM are high enough that less than outstanding maintainability can defeat a program or significantly increase aircraft operating expense. Traditional and emerging techniques are available for designing and evaluating the attributes of equipment by which it will meet preestablished maintainability goals. Use of DFM techniques and design/build teams by which attention to DFM can be concentrated increases the chances of designing aircraft that can be cost effectively maintained.

ACKNOWLEDGMENT

The authors are grateful for John Garrett and Susan Taylor's expert preparation of CAD drawings in this chapter. We are also grateful for the support of the Human Factors Technology group and the Advanced Supportability Technology business unit of Douglas Aircraft Company during the writing of this chapter.

IV REFERENCES

1. *Maintainability Design Criteria Handbook for Designers of Shipboard Electronic Equipment*, Federal Electric Corporation, Paramus, NJ, 1962.

2. *AFSC Design Handbook 1-2: General Design Factors* (Design Note 3B2, Para. 2), Air Force Systems Command, Wright-Patterson AFB, Ohio, 1986.

3. *Aircraft Maintenance: Potential Shortages in National Aircraft Repair Capacity* (GAO/RCED-91-14), Government Accounting Office, Washington, DC, 1990.

4. J. Stracener (Ed.), *Reliability, Maintainability and Supportability Guidebook,* Society of Automotive Engineers, Warrendale, PA, 1990.

5. B. W. Henderson, "Design and Planning Make High-Tech F-22 Easy to Maintain and Support," *Aviation Week and Space Technology,* Vol. 135, No. 2, pp. 50-51, 1991.

6. W. B. Scott, "Lockheed F-22 Design Balances Stealth, Agility and Speed," *Aviation Week and Space Technology,* Vol. 134, No. 17, pp. 22-23, 1991.

7. D. F. Bond, "Cost, Supportability Key to Boeing Sikorsky LH Award," *Aviation Week and Space Technology,* Vol. 134, No. 15, pp. 18-19, 1991.

8. "Boeing-Sikorsky Team Wins Helicopter Design," *Design News,* p. 6, May 6, 1991.

9. S. W. Kandebo, "Boeing Sikorsky LH Technologies Will Increase Army Combat Capability," *Aviation Week and Space Technology,* Vol. 134, No. 15, pp. 20-22, 1991.

10. *The National Plan for Aviation Human Factors (Draft), Vol. I,* U.S. Department of Transportation, Federal Aviation Administration, Washington, DC, 1990.

11. D. C. Nagel, "Human Error in Aviation Operations," in *Human Factors in Aviation,* pp. 263-303, (E. L. Wiener and D. C. Nagel, eds.), Academic Press, San Diego, CA, 1988.

12. H. C. Foushee, "Development of a National Plan for Addressing Future Aviation Human Factors Needs," in *Proc. of Human Error Avoidance Techniques Conference,* Herndon, VA, Sept. 18-19, SAE Publication No. P-229, 1989.

13. J. Gebman, "Avionics Maintainability — More Important Than Reliability," presented at AIAA/AHS/ASEE Aircraft Design, Systems and Operations Conference, Seattle, WA, July 31 - August 2, AIAA Paper No. 89-2096, 1989.

14. *MIL-STD-721C, Definitions of Terms for Reliability and Maintainability,* Department of Defense, Washington, DC, 1981.

15. J. V. Jones, *Engineering Design: Reliability, Maintainability and Testability,* Tab Books, Blue Ridge Summit, PA, 1988.

16. R. Smiljanic, *Reliability and Maintainability Plan (Commercial Aircraft Programs),* Report No. MDC-JXXX, McDonnell Douglas Corporation, Long Beach, CA, 1986.

17. *USAF R&M 2000 Process*, Office of the Special Assistant for Reliability and Maintainability, HQ USAF/LE-RD, Dayton, OH, 1987.

18. *AFSC Design Handbook 1-9: Maintainability*, Air Force Systems Command, Andrews AFB, DC, 1978.

19. *AMCP 706-133, Engineering Design Handbook: Maintainability Engineering Theory and Practice*, U.S. Army Materiel Command, Alexandria, VA, 1976.

20. *NAVAIR 01-1A-33, Maintainability Engineering Handbook*, Naval Air Systems Command, Washington, DC, 1977.

21. C. E. Cunningham and W. Cox, *Applied Maintainability Engineering*, Wiley, New York, 1972.

22. B. S. Blanchard, Jr. and E. E. Lowery, *Maintainability: Principles and Practices*, McGraw-Hill, New York, 1969.

23. B. S. Blanchard, *Logistics Engineering and Management*, Prentice-Hall, Englewood Cliffs, 1986.

24. "Repair Station Capacity to 2000," *Aircraft Maintenance International Yearbook*, Camrus Airport Publishers, Sutton, Surrey, England, 1991.

25. *MIL-STD-472, Maintainability Prediction*, Washington, DC, Naval Air Systems Command, Washington, DC, 1966.

26. D. M. Towne, M. R. Fehling, and N. A. Bond, *Design for the Maintainer: Projecting Maintenance Performance from Design Characteristics*, Tech Report 1, Office of Naval Research, Contract No. N00014-80-C-0493, Arlington, VA, 1981.

27. M. S. Bogner, M. Kibbe, R. Laine, and G. Hewitt, *Directory of Design Support Methods*, Department of the Army, MANPRINT Directorate, Washington, DC, 1990.

28. W. B. Scott, "Computer Simulations Place Models of Humans in Realistic Scenarios," *Aviation Week and Space Technology*, Vol. 134, No. 25, pp. 64-65, 1991.

29. A. E. Majoros, "Aircraft Design for Maintainability," *Journal of Aircraft*, Vol. 28, No. 3, pp. 187-192, 1991.

30. S. Taylor and A. Majoros, "The Data Glove Applied to Maintainability," presented at the meeting of the Annual Human Factors Society Los Angeles Chapter Symposium, Huntington Beach, CA, Nov., 1990.

31. J. W. Altman, A. C. Marchese, and B. W. Marchiando, *Guide to Design of Mechanical Equipment for Maintainability*, ASD Report 61-381, U.S. Air Force Aeronautical Systems Division, Wright-Patterson AFB, OH, 1961.

32. P. Baker, J. M. McKendry, and G. Grant, *Anthropometry of One-Handed Maintenance Actions*, Report No. NAVTRADEVCEN 330-1-3, U. S. Naval Training Device Center, Port Washington, NY, 1960.

33. W. N. Kama, *Volumetric Workspace Study, Part 1: Optimum Workspace Configuration for Using Various Screwdrivers*, Technical Documentary Report No. AMRL-TDR-63-68(1), Air Force Systems Command, Wright-Patterson AFB, OH, 1963.

34. D. D. Gregor, J. A. Bado, J. R. Jarvis, D. L. Peterson, C. N. Saldin, and N. S. Walker, *Comparative Evaluation of the Maintainability Features of the F-4C and F-5A Aircraft*, Vol I, Contract No. N00123-70-C-1999, AD880545, Naval Air Systems Command, Washington, DC, 1971.

35. *AFSC Design Handbook 1-X: Checklist of General Design Criteria, Design Note 3B7-4*, U.S. Air Force Aeronautical Systems Division, Wright-Patterson AFB, OH, 1987.

36. *MIL-STD-1472C, Military Standard: Human Engineering Design Criteria for Military Systems, Equipment and Facilities*, Department of Defense, Washington, DC, 1981.

37. *Human Factors Test and Evaluation Manual, Vol. III: Methods and Procedures*, Pacific Missile Test Center, Point Mugu, CA, 1976.

38. B. M. Crawford and J. W. Altman, "Designing for Maintainability," in *Human Engineering Guide to Equipment Design, Rev. Ed* (H. P. Van Cott and R. G. Kinkade, eds.), Washington, DC, Joint Army-Navy-Air Force Steering Committee, pp. 585-631, 1972.

39. D. P. Miller and A. D. Swain, "Human Error and Human Reliability," in *Handbook of Human Factors* (G. Salvendy, ed.), Wiley, New York, NY, pp. 219-250, 1987.

40. *AFSC Design Handbook DH 1-X, Checklist of General Design Criteria, 2nd Ed, Design Note 3B7*, U.S. Air Force Systems Command, Wright-Patterson AFB, OH, 1987.

41. D. E. Kieras, "The Psychology of Technical Devices and Technical Discourse," in *Artificial Intelligence in Maintenance* (J. J. Richardson, ed.), Noyes, Park Ridge, NJ, pp. 232-259, 1985.

42. J. H. Goldberg and D. C. Gibson, "The Effects of Training Method and Type of Checklist Upon Visual Inspection Accuracy," *Trends in Ergonomics/Human Factors III* (W. Karwowski, ed.), North-Holland, Amsterdam, pp. 359-368, 1986.

43. J. H. Burgess, *Designing for Humans: The Human Factor in Engineering*, Petrocelli, Princeton, NJ, 1986.

44. J. P. Dwyer and C. A. Nelson, *Human Engineering Requirements Checklist — T-Lug Bomb Rack*, Report No. MDC K4429, McDonnell Douglas Corporation, Long Beach, CA, 1989.

45. F. L. Behringer, "A Systematic Approach to System Troubleshooting," *Douglas Service Magazine*, 2nd Quarter, pp. 23-25, 1986.

46. *MIL-STD-2165, Testability Program for Electronic Systems and Equipments*, Department of Defense, Washington, DC, 1985.

47. *MIL-STD-2084(AS), Military Standard — General Requirements for Maintainability of Avionic and Electronic Systems and Equipment*, Department of Defense, Washington, DC, 1982.

48. J. Davison, "Expert Systems in Maintenance Diagnostics for Self-Repair of Digital Flight Control Systems," in *Artificial Intelligence in Maintenance* (J. J. Richardson ed.), Noyes, Park Ridge, NJ, pp. 294-305, 1985.

49. S. Natarajan and B. K. Herman, *Comparison of Testability Analysis Tools for USAF, Final Report*, Air Force Office of Scientific Research, Contract No. F49620-88-C-0053/ SB5881-0378, Booling AFB, Washington, DC, 1991.

50. B. A. Babbitt, *RAPIDS II: Lessons Learned*, Report No. 91-55, Northrop Corporation, Hawthorne, CA, 1991.

51. D. M. Towne and A. Munro, "Simulation-Based Instruction of Technical Skills," *Human Factors*, Vol. 33, No. 3, pp. 325-341, 1991.

52. *MIL-STD-470A, Maintainability Program for Systems and Equipment*, Department of Defense, Washington, DC, 1983.

53. *MIL-H-46855B, Human Engineering Requirements for Military Systems, Equipment and Facilities*, Department of Defense, Washington, DC, 1984.

54. "Concurrent Engineering," *Computer-Aided Engineering*, Vol. 10, No. 10, pp. 38-94, Oct. 1991.

55. "Communications, Computers, and Networks," *Scientific American*, Vol. 265, No. 3, pp. 62-164, Sept. 1991.

56. "Concurrent Engineering," *IEEE Spectrum*, Vol. 28, No. 7, pp. 22-37, July 1991.

NEW TECHNIQUES FOR AIRCRAFT FLIGHT
CONTROL RECONFIGURATION

Marcello R. Napolitano
Department of Mechanical and Aerospace Engineering
West Virginia University, Morgantown WV 26505

Robert L. Swaim
School of Mechanical and Aerospace Engineering
Oklahoma State University, Stillwater OK 74078

I. INTRODUCTION

Due to the ever-rising costs of new military aircraft and, consequently, to their relatively low procurements, a growing importance has been given in the last few years to the design of a flight control system with a reconfiguration capability. This would occur following battle damage and/or generic failure of a component of the flight control system, i.e., a malfunction of sensors or actuators or even a damaged aerodynamic control surface. Often, the accident investigations report that there was a way in which the disaster could have been avoided if the proper actions had been taken in a timely fashion. However, the length of time when valid effective actions to save the aircraft could be taken is just a few seconds. Given the understandable panic during those moments, a pilot may not find the solution in time.

The dynamics of an aircraft system in a given region of the flight envelope can be linearized and its motion can be described by the discrete state variable equations

$$X(k+1) = A\ X(k) + B\ U(k) + L\ W(k)$$

$$Z(k) = C\ X(k) + V(k)$$

where $X(k)$ and $U(k)$ are the state variable and the control vectors respectively; $W(k)$ and $V(k)$ are the system noise vector and the sensor noise vector respectively. Note that for our purposes these equations describe the closed-loop dynamics of the aircraft.

A sensor failure implies a wrong information in the vector $Z(k)$; this condition does not involve any change in the values of the coefficients of the A and B matrices. Such an event can be critically dangerous when the information from the sensor is used by the flight control system to generate a control sequence. However in modern flight control systems the comparison monitoring of sensors is a commonly implemented procedure and it is reasonable to expect that the faulty sensor would be quickly isolated. An actuator failure for a control surface implies a stuck fixed value of an element of the control vector $U(k)$, but again, there will be no changes in the values of the coefficients of the A and B matrices.

In the following of this chapter we will consider what is believed to be the worst possible scenario, i.e., a battle damage on a control surface involving a stuck actuator along with a missing part of the control surface. This is a realistic condition for a typical air-to-ground maneuver of an aircraft subjected to ground fire or even for an air-to-air combat situation. From a mathematical point of view such condition implies drastic changes of the values of the coefficients of the A and B matrices, in addition to a fixed value for the element of the control vector $U(k)$ relative to the damaged control surface [1-3]. However the approaches which will be later introduced can be applied, without any loss of generality, to the more common sensor failure and actuator failure problems.

Note that this classification of failures does not include unsolvable problems, e.g., wings falling off, where the aircraft cannot be saved. Following the battle damage and/or the generic failure, the flight control task is to utilize whatever control resources remain in order to regain control of the aircraft, to prevent further damage by excessive air loads, and to give the crew enough time to assess the options.

In order to implement a reconfiguration strategy we may introduce a variety of control surfaces (speed brakes, wing flaps, differential dihedral canards, spoilers, rudder below fuselage) and thrust control mechanisms (differential thrust, thrust vectoring, canted engines). The selection of the control mechanisms to be used in a reconfiguration is a function of several factors, e.g., control effectiveness, increased aircraft complexity and costs, weight penalties, increased aerodynamic drag due to the increased wetted area with the application depending on aircraft type.

The following quantities from operative sensors along with a fully operational flight computer are assumed to be available for reconfiguration purposes [1-3,5] :

- Aircraft angular velocity and linear velocity in the three body axes.

- Aircraft attitude and angle of attack.

It would also be desirable to have information on the actuator position for each control surface.

The task of battle damage and/or generic failure accommodation can be broken down into the following main tasks:

1 - EXECUTIVE CONTROL task, which provides essentially synchronization of the remaining tasks.

2 - FAILURE DETECTION and IDENTIFICATION task, which controls the aircraft behavior, detects significant abnormalities and searches the cause or a set of probable causes.

3 - DAMAGED MODEL ESTIMATION task, which generates a mathematical model of the aircraft dynamics considered to reflect changes due to the damage.

4 - RECONFIGURATION LAW DESIGN task, which, finally, determines what actions should be taken in order to recover the damaged aircraft, by using alternative control surfaces or thrust control mechanisms.

5 - FEEDBACK STRUCTURE REDESIGN task, which calculates a new set of feedback gains, in order to retain stability and desirable handling qualities even after the damage.

Figure 1 shows a simplified 'step-by-step' overview of the problem [1-4]. Eventually another task to be introduced is a PILOT ADVISORY function. While the computers of the flight control system are reconfiguring the aircraft, it would be desirable for the pilot to be able to have a cockpit display indicate which control surface has been damaged, what the flight control system is trying to achieve, and what actions, if possible under current conditions, could eventually benefit the overall reconfiguration.

This chapter is organized as follows : Section II describes an alternative approach to the Failure Detection and Identification (F.D.I.) task based on Neural Network theory; Section III introduces a Multiple Model Kalman Filter approach for the correct estimation of the mathematical model of the damaged aircraft provided that a successful F.D.I. was previously performed; Section IV introduces a two instants delay matching technique [1-3,39] for the on-line calculation of the compensating deflections from alternative control surfaces or mechanisms which would make the damaged aircraft system behave as closely as possible to the nominal system under normal circumstances; Section V instead suggests a particular eigenstructure assignment technique for the redesign of the feedback structure with the goal of restoring desirable or at least acceptable handling qualities, and to remove the damage induced coupling between the longitudinal and the lateral-directional dynamics; Section VI summarizes the chapter with conclusions and recommendations.

II. FAILURE DETECTION AND IDENTIFICATION

Failure Detection and Identification is a widely investigated problem in the design of modern sophisticated flight control systems [6-18]. From the time sequence of Fig. 1, the F.D.I. task can be considered to be just a step (although the first and, for this reason, most crucial step) of the overall flight control reconfiguration problem.

Generally speaking, F.D.I. implies a constant monitoring of the measurable output variables of the aircraft system. At nominal

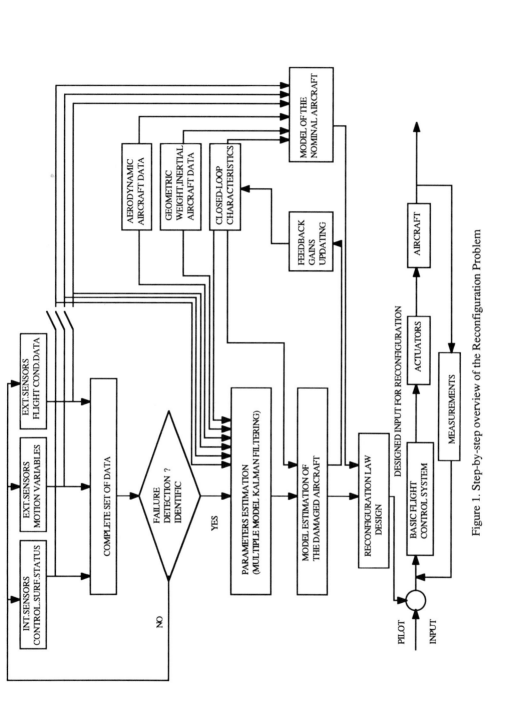

Figure 1. Step-by-step overview of the Reconfiguration Problem

conditions these variables follow some known patterns within a certain degree of uncertainty due to system disturbance (such as atmospheric turbulence) and sensor measurement noises. However, when failures of any component of the flight control system occur, the observable output variables deviate from their nominal somewhat predictable trajectories [10]. Most F.D.I. techniques are based on spotting these deviations of the output variables from predictable trajectories. It is clear that this approach implies a knowledge by the flight control system of these predictable or somewhat reasonable trajectories of the system at each possible operating conditions.

In the selection of a F.D.I. technique the following points have to be considered :

- Nature of the failure (type and severity).

- Degree of observability of the effects of the failure within the measurements.

- Length of time required to accumulate enough data to reveal the occurrence of the failure with the presence of system disturbances (for example atmospheric turbulence) and sensor noise (including enemy jamming).

- Degree of distinguishability from similar failures for unambiguous F.D.I.

For the purposes of detecting and identifying a damage on a control surface with a missing part, it should be recalled that such failure is quite severe, very "observable" from sensors measurements, and usually very distinguishable, especially in the cases of a damage on a primary control surfaces. The problem of the sensor redundancy is not addressed, and a comparison monitoring of the sensors measuring the same motion parameter is assumed to be effective. The reference bibliography [6-18] presents an excellent review of the most common F.D.I. techniques. An analytical description of these techniques is beyond the goal of this discussion; a partial list can be given by

- Generalized Likelihood Ratio (G.L.R.).

- Sequential Probability Likelihood Ratio Test (S.P.R.T.).

- Generalized Likelihood Test/Maximum Likelihood Detector

(G.L.T./M.L.D.).

- Multiple Model (M.M.).

Among these techniques the last two seem to present the smallest number of problems for practical implementations. However, typical problems associated with the application of these techniques are

- Applicable only to linear time-invariant systems.
- Demonstrated only for low-order systems.
- Demonstrated only when system model is identical to Kalman Filter model, even if, due to constraints on computational speed and power, only reduced-order Kalman Filters are practically implemented.
- Demonstrated only for large signal-to-noise ratios.
- Impossibility of accounting for correlations in the estimates.

The goal of this section is to introduce an alternative approach to these techniques with the goal of avoiding their common problems. Most of these problems are due to the fact the flight control system uses on-line calculated or pre-calculated system models to generate a finite knowledge of predicted trajectories, sometimes at the expense of a great computational burden. These models are usually linear and time-invariant with gaussian modeled system and sensor noises. It is clear that the success of the F.D.I. is not guaranteed when some of these key assumptions are violated with the signal-to-noise ratio playing a key rule.

An approach for achieving higher degrees of success for the F.D.I. is the introduction of a more general technique, valid for linear and non-linear dynamic systems, of any size and order, with state and sensor noises, and where a knowledge of the system dynamics can be developed on-line without an excessive computational cost. This can be possible through the introduction of modern Neural Network theory [19-22].

Neural Network (N.N.), also referred to as Artificial Neural Network (A.N.N.), is a reemerging technology. There is a vast quantity of literature dating back to the 1940s regarding N.N. theory and various applications. However, it is only since the mid 1980's that there has been an increasing number of Neural Network engineering applications, mostly in the fields of image processing and speech processing for robotics applications. A possible milestone has been the introduction of the Back-Propagation algorithm [20] in 1985. However, to date, there have been a relatively limited number of applications of N.N. for the design of flight control systems, although increasing interest has been generated very recently [26-33]. Particularly, a certain number of investigations have suggested the use of N.N. for parameter estimation [26-28] and for controller design [29-32]. The suggested use of a N.N. in this discussion is quite different, and is essentially that of an on-line state estimator [23-24]. In this sense it may be said that the Neural Network is a powerful alternative to classic state estimation structures such as Leunberger Observers and Kalman Filters (full or reduced order) [25]. For these structures the state estimation is obtained in such a way that they 'have to learn' about the dynamics of the system that they are estimating at each time step starting from ground zero. In contrast, a key feature of a Neural Network used for state estimation is that it will 'learn' about the dynamics of the system during a training section made of several training cycles, with training data coming from either previous computer numerical simulations or from actual real-time data. During the training the design of the Neural Network is actually being performed. After each training cycle the N.N. will know a little more about the dynamics of the system. Mathematically this will mean that the estimation error will be decreased with each cycle. The training section can be considered completed when a selected parameter related to the estimation error becomes smaller than a small acceptable margin. A typical choice for such parameter is

$$\text{ERRTOT}(k) = 1/2 \sum_{i=1}^{n} (X_i(k) - \hat{X}_i(k/k-1))^2 \qquad (10)$$

where 'n' is the number of states to be estimated.

Once the training session has been completed the N.N. 'has learned' the dynamics of the system and it is able to estimate each state at each time step. Among the other remarkable features of a N.N. there is the ability of learning the dynamics of a non-linear system as well as the dynamics of a linear system. The main difference is that non-linear dynamic systems require a longer 'training'. The output of the N.N. would be the correct estimates of all the states of the system; also, note that there is no need for assuming the initial conditions of the system. It may be concluded that a N.N. has several potential advantages with respect to classic estimation structure. A solid background of the theoretical principles on which the functioning of a N.N. is based is provided in [19-22].

A basic architecture of a N.N. is shown in Figure 2 [23-24]. Such a N.N. may be a state estimation structure for a dynamic system with 4 states of which only 2 can actually be measured. A N.N. must contain at least 3 layers :

1 Input layer

1 Hidden layer

1 Output layer

Note that it may contain more than 1 hidden layer. Each cell shown in Fig.2 is called a Processing Element (P.E.) or sometimes called a neuron from which the name N.N. descends. While the number of P.E.s for the input and output layers depends respectively on the number of available measurements and on the number of states to be estimated, the number of P.E.s in the hidden layer(s) can be arbitrary. In an attempt to classify the architecture shown in Fig.2 we can say that it is a feed-forward type of structure with inter-layer connections, which means that each P.E. sends its output to P.E.s in higher layers and receives its input from lower layers. It is intuitive that an alternative to this type of structure is a feedback type of N.N. in which each P.E. may send its output to P.E.s in both higher and lower layers and/or recursively, i.e., back to the same P.E. [21]. Additionally we may have intra-layer connections, i.e., connections between P.E.s of the same layer, besides inter-layer connections. In the structure shown in Fig.2 the output of each P.E. is calculated as a manipulation of the weighted sum of the output of all the P.E.s of the lower layer (with the option of adding a threshold parameter) through an activation function 'f' which must be non-decreasing and

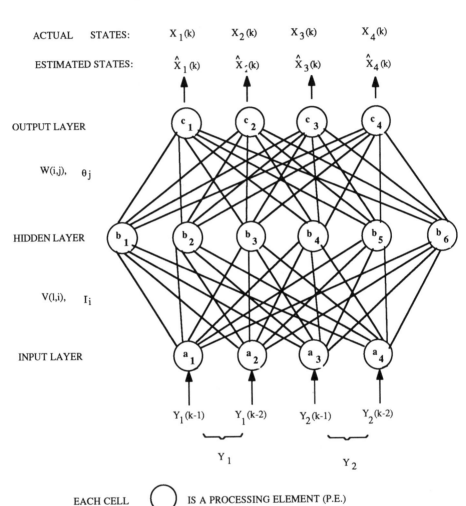

Figure 2   General architecture of a Neural Network

differentiable. A typically used activation function is the sigmoid function :

$$f(x) = (1 + e^{-x})^{-1} \qquad (11)$$

For example the output of a P.E. of the hidden layer is given by

$$H_i = f (\sum_{l=1}^{m} v(l,i) \ I_l + \theta_i) \qquad for \ i=1,....,k \qquad (12)$$

The set of weights V(I,H) and W(H,O) are calculated during the training session with the goal of minimizing the previously introduced parameter ERRTOT (Eq. 10). The process of minimizing such parameter is the learning process. Such a process can be generally classified in two types : supervised and unsupervised learning [21]. A supervised learning is a process that incorporates an external teacher (either numerical simulation data or experimental data), information when to turn off the learning, and performance error information. An unsupervised learning is a process that self-organizes the learning without external data and relies upon only local information and internal control. In the following of this section we will refer to a N.N. of feed forward type with inter-layer connections, trained with a supervised learning process. The design of the N.N. structure, i.e., the determination of the sets of weighting coefficients (V(I,H),W(H,O)) and relative thresholds, will be performed using the Back-Propagation algorithm , which is essentially a gradient-based optimization method [20-22]. Note that if there are a number 'C' of hidden layers, then 'C+1' sets of weighting coefficients and relative thresholds must be calculated.

II. A. THE BACK-PROPAGATION ALGORITHM

The Back-Propagation method applies to a N.N. operating in discrete time with 3 types of layers : input, output and hidden layers [20-22]. Generally, it is possible to have several hidden layers, recurrent intra-layer connections between the P.E.s. However, for the purpose of introducing such a method, a 3 layer structure with inter-layer connections as shown in Fig.2 will be used. The method

performs the input to output mapping by minimizing a cost function.
The task is accomplished by making weight connection adjustments
according to the error between the computed and desired output values
of the P.E.s of the output layer. The algorithm proceeds as in the
following description, based on the architecture introduced in Fig.2.
The values of the P.E.s will be given by

I_1 for the P.E.s of the input layer, with $l=1,...,m$;

H_i for the P.E.s of the hidden layer, with $i=1,...,k$;

O_j for the P.E.s of the output layer, with $j=1,...,n$.

STEP 1

Initial random values between $(-1,+1)$ are assigned to the sets of
weight coefficients $V(I,H)$, $W(H,O)$ and to the thresholds for the
hidden layer $(\Theta's)$ and output layer $(\Gamma's)$.

At each training cycle the following is done :

STEP 2

Determine H_i using Eq. (12),

$$H_i = f \left(\sum_{l=1}^{m} v(l,i) \, I_l + \theta_i \right) \qquad \text{for } i=1,....,k \qquad (12)$$

where 'f' is the sigmoid activation function and H_i is the output of
the i-th P.E. of the hidden layer.

STEP 3

Determine O_j using

$$O_j = f \left(\sum_{i=1}^{k} w(i,j) \, H_i + \Gamma_j \right) \qquad \text{for } j=1,....,n \qquad (13)$$

where O_j is the output of the j-th P.E. of the output layer.

STEP 4

Compute the error between the computed and desired values of the P.E.s
of the output layer using

$$D_j = O_j (1 - O_j) \, (O_j^* - O_j) \qquad \text{for } j=1,....,n \qquad (14)$$

where O_j^* is the desired value for the j-th P.E. of the output layer at
that particular instant of time.

STEP 5

Determine the error relative to each P.E. of the hidden layer using

$$E_i = H_i (1 - H_i) \sum_{j=1}^{n} w(i,j) D_j \quad \text{for } i=1,\ldots,k \quad (15)$$

STEP 6

Adjust the weights W(H,O) for the next training cycle using

$$\Delta w(i,j) = \alpha \, H_i D_j \quad \text{for } i=1,..,k \; ; \; \text{for } j=1,..,n \quad (16)$$

where α is a positive constant related to the learning rate to be selected between 0 and 1.

STEP 7

Adjust the thresholds (Γ's) of the P.E.s of the output layer for the next training cycle using

$$\Delta\Gamma_j = \alpha \, D_j \quad \text{for } j=1,\ldots,n \quad (17)$$

STEP 8

Adjust the weights V(I,H) for the next training cycle using

$$\Delta v(l,i) = \beta \, I_l E_i \quad \text{for } l=1,..,m \; ; \; \text{for } i=1,..,k \quad (18)$$

where β is a positive constant related to the learning rate to be selected between 0 and 1.

STEP 9

Adjust the thresholds (Θ's) of the P.E.s of the hidden layer for the next training cycle using

$$\Delta\theta_i = \beta \, E_i \quad \text{for } i=1,\ldots,k \quad (19)$$

The process described by STEP 2 to STEP 9 will be repeated for each training cycle until D_j, with $j=1,\ldots,n$ at each time step of the dynamic simulation will be smaller than a desired low value.

The Back-Propagation method is by far the most widely used method for the design of the structure of the feed-forward type of N.N. with supervised learning. It should be pointed out that the main drawbacks of this algorithm are long training times and the possibility for the solution to stop progressing when a local minimum of the function ERRTOT occurs. This has not been the case in this application, most likely because of the relatively small order of the model of the aircraft system.

II. B. IMPLEMENTATION OF A NEURAL NETWORK FOR F.D.I.

In the previous part of this section the concept of using a N.N., designed with the Back-Propagation algorithm, has been introduced. At this point it will be explained how the N.N. could be an excellent tool for F.D.I.. Given that an high performance military aircraft is essentially a non-linear time varying dynamic system, the main idea is to have a permanent on-going on-line training for a N.N. in the flight computer. Data from the different sensors located for the measurements of state variables $(\alpha, q, VEL, \theta, \beta, p, r, \phi$ with the option of adding $a_z, a_y)$ from time 'k-1' down to time 'k-p' are at each time step given as input to a N.N. in order to predict the same state variables at time 'k'; these estimates are then compared with the actual measured value of the state variable coming from the sensors at time 'k'. The difference between the actual and the estimated values of the state variables is used by the Back-Propagation algorithm to calculate adjustments of the weights and thresholds of the N.N. so as to decrease the estimation error at the next time step. If the process is repeated iteratively, smaller and smaller values of the parameter ERRTOT should result. Note that this is essentially an on-line in-flight training with the N.N. being a portion of the software of the flight control system. Given that the learning process is always on-going, if the aircraft moves from one region to another region of its flight envelope in terms of Altitude vs. Mach, the N.N. will quickly be redesigned through the Back-Propagation algorithm and the new dynamics will be learned after a certain delay, function of the learning rates of Eqs. 16-19.

Let us suppose now that the aircraft is flying at a given condition of its flight envelope and let us assume that at a certain point a battle damage occurs on a primary control surface, e.g., the elevator. It is clear that following the damage the aircraft will experience one or more of the following [1-5,39] :

- Altered trim conditions.

- Changed aerodynamic forces and moments.

- Changed control effectiveness.

This implies that the state vector of the measurements at the instant immediately following the damage will be very different from the state estimates provided by the N.N.. If the parameter ERRTOT becomes bigger than a given threshold (to account for false alarms, such as the ones induced by atmospheric turbulence or noise corrupted sensors data) then this will be an effective tool for failure detection.

II. C. AERODYNAMIC MODELING OF THE EFFECTS OF A DAMAGE AND/OR GENERIC FAILURE ON A CONTROL SURFACE

The process described in the previous section has been numerically simulated using the aerodynamic, geometric, inertial data and a given flight condition of .an advanced training aircraft ([34], App. C, Aircraft C) shown in Fig.3 [5, Source AIAA].

For the purpose of this simulation it was assumed that a damage had occurred on the left elevator of the aircraft implying a damaged elevator with a stuck actuator. In order to be able to simulate numerically the F.D.I. process in a realistic fashion it was necessary to model the aerodynamic effects of a damage on a control surface. It is important to recall that a damaged primary control surface, especially one located at a certain distance form the center of gravity, can imply severe deterioration of the aircraft handling qualities in terms of dampings and natural frequencies along with an unavoidable coupling between the longitudinal and lateral-directional dynamics. Therefore, for an accurate aerodynamic simulation of the damage, different values of the elements of the state and control matrices A and B had to be introduced, because the damage implies a stuck value of the deflection of the left elevator and an instantaneous change of the matrices A_{NOM}, B_{NOM} to A_{DAM}, B_{DAM} where the subscripts 'NOM' and 'DAM' indicate nominal and damaged conditions respectively. Next, an approach for the aerodynamic modeling of the damage will be introduced [1-3].

The aerodynamic characteristics of a surface are expressed in terms of normal force, axial force and moment around some fixed points or axes. A damage on a control surface, which involves a missing part of it, implies changes in the aerodynamic characteristics of the

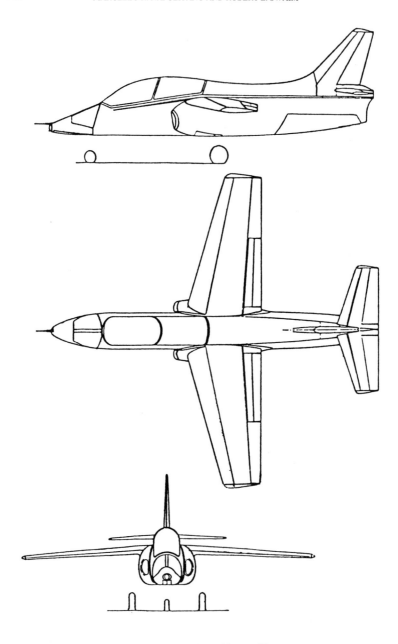

Figure 3.   Advanced Training Aircraft
            (SIAI-Marchetti, S211 - SIAI , ITALY)

surface. In order to evaluate these changes the following aerodynamic assumption can be made: the main control surfaces (typically ailerons, elevator and rudder) and their deflections do not cause appreciable aerodynamic drag. The aerodynamic moments of a control surface around various axes are proportional, through the geometric parameters of the aircraft, to the normal forces exerted on the surfaces. With axial forces assumed being negligible, and the control aerodynamic moments being functions of the normal forces, the changed aircraft dynamics following damage is due essentially to instantaneous changes of the damaged surface normal force coefficients. These coefficients are then used for the calculation of the corresponding dimensionless stability and control derivatives.

It would be very useful to implement a set of closed-form expressions of the dimensionless aerodynamic stability and control derivatives as functions of the normal force coefficient of the control surface ($C_{N_\delta} = C_{L_\delta}$) considered to be damaged; for example

$$C_{m_\alpha} = C_{m_\alpha}(C_{L_\delta}), \quad C_{L_\alpha} = C_{L_\alpha}(C_{L_\delta}), \quad \ldots\ldots$$
$$C_{\ell_\beta} = C_{\ell_\beta}(C_{L_\delta}), \quad C_{n_\beta} = C_{n_\beta}(C_{L_\delta}), \quad \ldots\ldots \qquad (20)$$

While efficient analytical closed-form expressions for aerodynamic stability derivatives as functions of the normal coefficients of the control surfaces for conventional subsonic airplanes may be calculated, an accurate wind-tunnel investigation and relative data correlation would be needed for unconventional supersonic aircraft. For example purposes, a relatively conventional aircraft at subsonic conditions has been considered.

Considering a damage to the left elevator, the following stability derivatives would be affected by changes in the values of $C_{L_{\delta E}}$

$$C_{L_\alpha}, \quad C_{m_\alpha}, \quad C_{L_{\dot\alpha}}, \quad C_{m_{\dot\alpha}}, \quad C_{L_q}, \quad C_{m_q}.$$

Furthermore, there will be an induced rolling moment. It has been shown in [1] that closed-form expression of these stability

derivatives at nominal conditions as function of $C_{L_{\delta E}}$ can be
calculated in the form

$$C_{L_\alpha} = k_{11} + k_{12} \, C_{L_{\delta E}} \qquad (21a)$$

$$C_{m_\alpha} = k_{21} + k_{22} \, C_{L_{\delta E}} \qquad (21b)$$

$$C_{L_{\dot\alpha}} = k_{31} + k_{32} \, C_{L_{\delta E}} \qquad (21c)$$

$$C_{m_{\dot\alpha}} = k_{41} + k_{42} \, C_{L_{\delta E}} \qquad (21d)$$

$$C_{L_q} = k_{51} + k_{52} \, C_{L_{\delta E}} \qquad (21e)$$

$$C_{m_q} = k_{61} + k_{62} \, C_{L_{\delta E}} \qquad (21f)$$

The values of the 'k$_{ij}$' constants can be calculated using [35-36]. At
this point, assuming the occurrence of a damage on the left elevator
with a missing part of it, we have

$$C_{L_{\delta E}} = C_{L_{\delta ER}} + C_{L_{\delta EL}} \qquad (22)$$

$$d\text{-}C_{L_{\delta E}} = C_{L_{\delta ER}} + d\text{-}C_{L_{\delta EL}} \qquad (23)$$

with $d\text{-}C_{L_{\delta EL}} < C_{L_{\delta EL}}$ and $d\text{-}C_{L_{\delta E}} < C_{L_{\delta E}}$
where 'd-' indicates the value of the parameter after the damage.
The following expressions for the dimensionless stability derivatives
at damaged conditions will then be obtained

$$d\text{-}C_{L_\alpha} = k_{11} + k_{12} \, d\text{-}C_{L_{\delta E}} \qquad (24a)$$

$$d\text{-}C_{m_\alpha} = k_{21} + k_{22} \, d\text{-}C_{L_{\delta E}} \qquad (24b)$$

$$d\text{-}C_{L_{\dot\alpha}} = k_{31} + k_{32} \, d\text{-}C_{L_{\delta E}} \qquad (24c)$$

$$d\text{-}C_{m_{\dot{\alpha}}} = k_{41} + k_{42} \ d\text{-}C_{L_{\delta E}} \tag{24d}$$

$$d\text{-}C_{L_q} = k_{51} + k_{52} \ d\text{-}C_{L_{\delta E}} \tag{24e}$$

$$d\text{-}C_{m_q} = k_{61} + k_{62} \ d\text{-}C_{L_{\delta E}} \tag{24f}$$

Furthermore, there will be damaged induced rolling moment

$$\text{DAMAGED INDUCED} = \pm \ \{ \ C_{L_{\delta EL}} \ Y_{\delta EL} \ / \ (b/2) \ \} \tag{25}$$
ROLL.MOMENT COEF.

where $Y_{\delta EL}$ represents the arm of the damaged half elevator.

It has been assumed that the left elevator has been damaged with a reduction of 50% of its effectiveness such that

$$d\text{-}C_{L_{\delta EL}} = C_{L_{\delta EL}} \ / \ 2 \tag{26}$$

The flight conditions, the aircraft geometric data and the dimensionless values of the stability derivatives at nominal and at damaged conditions are shown in Table I [5, Source AIAA] along with the values of the coefficients K_{ij}s at the given flight conditions. Once these dimensionless stability derivatives are introduced the associated dimensional stability derivatives [34] are calculated, and then the determination of the matrices A and B of Eq.1 for both nominal and damaged conditions is performed using the standard modeling procedures. For the particular aircraft it resulted that the open-loop dynamic characteristics at nominal conditions in terms of natural frequencies and damping coefficients were acceptable; if this were not the case a state feedback control system would need to be designed in order to have a more realistic numerical simulation. The presence of atmospheric turbulence was simulated by introducing white noise disturbances with the procedure described in [37]. The numerical simulation of the Failure Detection and Identification using the Neural Network approach can now be attempted using the dynamic models of the aircraft at damaged and nominal conditions. It is assumed that the aircraft system described by Eq. 1 has
8 state variables : $\alpha, q, u, \theta, \beta, p, r, \phi$

TABLE I

Flight Conditions, Geometric and Aerodynamic Characteristics for and Advanced Trainer Jet ([36], App.C, Aircraft C).

Cruise altitude	:	25,000	ft
Air density	:	0.0001066	$slug/ft^3$
Speed	:	610	ft/sec
Mach	:	0.6	
Center of gravity	:	0.25 MAC	
Initial attitude	:	0.0	deg
Wing area	:	136	ft^2
Wing span	:	26.3	ft
Wing MAC	:	5.4	ft
Weight	:	4,000	lbs
I_{xx}	:	800	$slug\ ft^2$
I_{yy}	:	4,800	$slug\ ft^2$
I_{zz}	:	5,200	$slug\ ft^2$
I_{xz}	:	200	$slug\ ft^2$

STEADY STATE COEFFICIENTS

$C_{L_1} = 0.15, C_{D_1} = 0.022, C_{T_{X1}} = 0.022, C_{m_1} = 0.0, C_{m_{T1}} = 0.0$

NOMINAL AERODYNAMIC DERIVATIVES

$C_{m_u} = 0.0, C_{L_u} = 0.0, C_{D_u} = 0.0, C_{l_\beta} = -0.11, C_{n_\beta} = 0.17, C_{y_\beta} = -1.00$

$C_{m_\alpha} = -.24, C_{L_\alpha} = 5.5, C_{D_\alpha} = .12, C_{l_p} = -0.39, C_{n_p} = 0.09, C_{y_p} = -0.14$

$C_{m_{\dot\alpha}} = -9.6, C_{L_{\dot\alpha}} = 4.2, C_{T_{Xu}} = 0.0, C_{l_r} = 0.280, C_{n_r} = -.26, C_{y_r} = 0.610$

$C_{m_q} = -17.7, C_{L_q} = 10.0, C_{D_q} = 0.0, C_{l_{\delta A}} = 0.100, C_{n_{\delta A}} = -0.003, C_{y_{\delta A}} = 0.0$

$C_{m_{Tu}} = 0.0, C_{L_{\delta E}} = 0.38, C_{D_{\delta E}} = 0.0, C_{l_{\delta R}} = 0.050, C_{n_{\delta R}} = -0.120, C_{y_{\delta R}} = 0.280$

$C_{m_{\delta E}} = -0.88$

AERODYNAMIC DERIVATIVES AFTER THE DAMAGE ON THE LEFT ELEVATOR

$d\text{-}C_{L_\alpha} = 5.3765$, $d\text{-}C_{L_{\dot\alpha}} = 3.834$, $d\text{-}C_{L_q}$

$d\text{-}C_{m_\alpha} = 0.0992$, $d\text{-}C_{m_{\dot\alpha}} = -8.594$, $d\text{-}C_{m_q} = -17.7$

$d\text{-}C_{L_{\delta E}} = 0.285$, $d\text{-}C_{L_{\delta EL}} = 0.095$, $d\text{-}C_{L_{\delta ER}} = C_{L_{\delta ER}} = 0.19$;

$K_{11} = 5.006$, $K_{12} = 1.3$, $K_{21} = 1.118$, $K_{22} = -3.575$, $K_{31} = 2.737$, $K_{32} = 3.85$

$K_{41} = -5.576$, $K_{42} = -10.588$, $K_{51} = 5.82$, $K_{52} = 11.0$, $K_{61} = -6.205$, $K_{62} = -30.25$

6 control inputs : $\delta_{EL}, \delta_{ER}, \delta_{AL}, \delta_{AR}, \delta_{R}, \delta_{THROTTLE}$
2 disturbances : α_{GUST} , β_{GUST}.

II.D. NUMERICAL SIMULATION OF THE F.D.I.

A MATLAB software simulating the F.D.I. was assembled. The
aircraft dynamics was simulated using the discretized equations of the
motion (Eqs. 1,2); it was assumed that all the states were available
for measurements (as described in the previous sections), such that
the matrix C is an identity matrix. A typical multiple step elevator
input maneuver was considered for this dynamic simulation conducted
with a time step of 0.01 sec..

The values of the parameters for each sensor of the states from
time instant '(k-1)' down to '(k-p)' were given as input to a Neural
Network (N.N.) with 1 hidden layer which is continuously training
on-line. In this simulation the value of 5 was used for the parameter
'p'. Also, a moderately low value of the learning rate (0.2) was
assigned in the Back-Propagation algorithm in order to avoid
oscillations of the ERRTOT parameter and to guarantee a steady
learning of the aircraft dynamics by the N.N.. Also, the hidden layer
of the N.N. is assumed to have 10 processing elements (P.E.s) in order
to avoid an overly complex structure. At each instant 'k' the values
of the sensors are compared with the estimates of the N.N. whose input
are the sensors data from instant 'k-1' down to 'k-p'; the estimation
error is then used by the Back-Propagation algorithm to update the
values of the weights and thresholds for the next time step and so on.
The numerical simulation of the F.D.I. proceeds as in the following.

The motion of the aircraft at the nominal configuration starts at
time instant 'k=1' without the on-line state estimation. At time
instant 'k=kinit' the N.N. is turned on and, after a certain
transient, should be able to estimate accurately the aircraft
dynamics. Note that in order to avoid false alarms, it will be
desirable to automatically disengage the F.D.I. every time a pilot
voluntarily changes the aerodynamic configuration, as it is the case
for variable wing geometry or for the dropping of empty fuel tanks or

war loads. At a certain time instant, 'k=kfail', the damage takes place
on the left elevator, implying an instantaneous change of the matrices
A_{NOM}, B_{NOM} to the new matrices A_{DAM} and B_{DAM} with a fixed value of
δ_{EL}, either to maximum or minimum deflection or at the position at the
instant of the damage. In this case, in order to test the F.D.I. with
relatively small failures, the fixed position at the instant of the
damage has been used. The aircraft dynamics has now changed but it
will take few instants of time for the N.N. to learn the new dynamics.
However, during this delay, the estimation error of the N.N., ERRTOT,
which becomes bigger than a selected threshold, could be a quick
indication that a failure has indeed occurred. The magnitude of such
threshold can be object of discussion; it is desirable to keep low the
level of false alarms (due for example to simple atmospheric
turbulence) and still be able to very quickly detect significant
abnormalities. The robustness of this approach for state estimation
within an highly perturbed environment has not yet been fully
investigated and needs further research.

The Failure Detection process can be closely followed in Figs.
4,5,6 [5, Source AIAA] which show the time histories for α, q, p
respectively. In these figures it can be noticed that the N.N., turned
on at time=0.1 sec. ('kinit'=10), quickly provides an accurate state
estimation of the dynamic variables, considering the atmospheric
turbulence acting on the aircraft. At the bottom of each figure the
associated multiple-step elevator maneuver is shown. The simulation
proceeds at nominal conditions until t=4 sec. ('kfail'=400) when the
damage occurs. Notice that the effects of the damage are felt in two
successive phases. In fact, immediately after the damage, that is from
t=4.0 sec. to t=4.5 sec., the left elevator is fixed at -4 DEG. but
the pilot still has the right elevator at -4 DEG. During this time the
differences between the estimated values and the actual values of
α, q, p are due only to the transition of the A,B matrices from
A_{NOM}, B_{NOM} to A_{DAM}, B_{DAM}. In a second phase, that is form t=4.5 sec. to
the end of the simulation at t=5 sec., the effects of the damage due
to the fixed position of the left elevator at -4 DEG, while the pilot

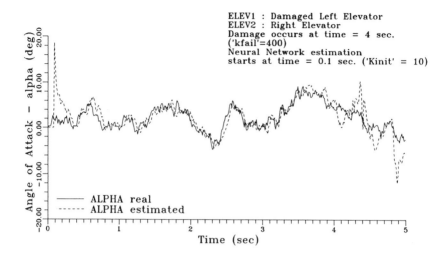

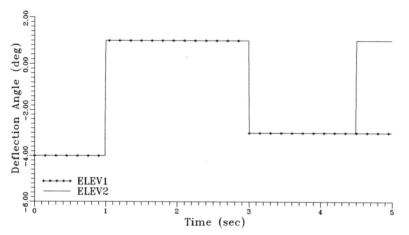

Figure 4   Angle of Attack   vs. Time for a Multiple Step
             Elevators Maneuver

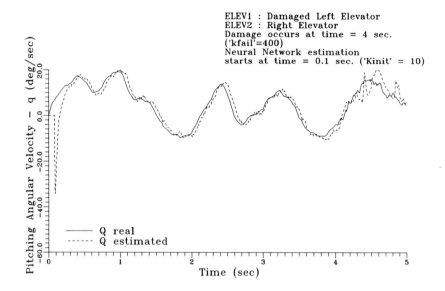

ELEV1 : Damaged Left Elevator
ELEV2 : Right Elevator
Damage occurs at time = 4 sec.
('kfail'=400)
Neural Network estimation
starts at time = 0.1 sec. ('Kinit' = 10)

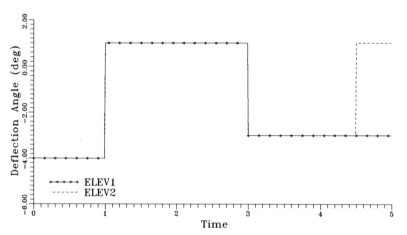

Figure 5   Pitching Angular Velocity vs. Time for a Multiple Step
             Elevators Maneuver

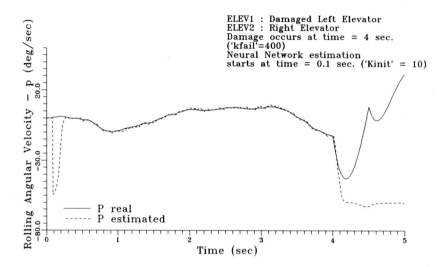

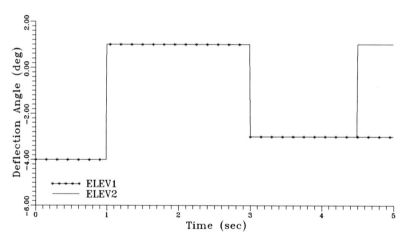

Figure 6   Rolling Angular Velocity vs. Time for a Multiple Step
Elevators Maneuver

moves the 'healthy' right elevator to +1 DEG. are felt, along with the changed dynamic characteristics. This can be noticed very clearly, especially in Fig. 6 refering to the rolling angular velocity p. The non zero values of p for zero input of the ailerons are due to the atmospheric turbulence. Fig. 7 [5, Source AIAA] shows the trends vs. time of some parameters related to the state estimation with the Neural Network. The top part of Fig. 7 shows the parameter ERRTOT, described in Eq. 10, vs. time. As it may be expected, such estimation error, which is large immediately after the Neural Network is turned on at t=0.1 sec. ('kinit'=100), quickly decreases with time, implying that the N.N. has learned the dynamics of the aircraft, even in the presence of atmospheric turbulence. However, as soon as the damage takes place, the parameter ERRTOT drastically increases, meaning that a damage has indeed occurred. The double effect of the damage may also be seen in this figure. Eventually, if given enough time to learn the new dynamics, the N.N. will return to provide accurate estimates. It is hoped that during that time, once the Failure Detection and Identification has been successfully accomplished, the Flight Control System will attempt to regain control of the damaged aircraft. The bottom part of Fig. 7 shows the trend with the time of the parameters DVTOT and DWTOT which are essentially the squared sum of the weights adjustments Δw and Δv calculated using Eqs. (16) and (18). They also decrease with the time until the damage takes place and then they take on an oscillatory behavior because of the double effect of the damage previously explained.

Up to this point, by analyzing the parameter ERRTOT the Failure Detection has been accomplished. However, it is also desirable to be able "to interpret" the sensors data in the shortest time possible with the goal of identifying the location of the damage. An approach to the Failure Identification could be given by an analysis of the cross-correlation functions between some key state variables. For example, we know that ordinarily the values of the pitch rate and the roll rate are not correlated (if the values of the angular rates are not high enough to generate gyroscopic effects). However, we also know

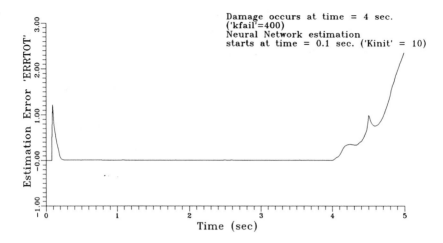

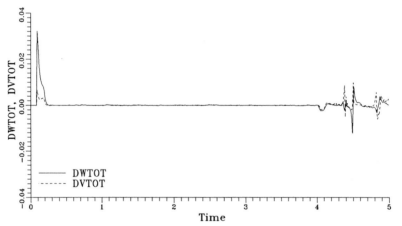

Figure 7   Neural Network Estimation Parameters vs. Time

that following the damage on the left elevator a certain rolling moment will take place along with the primary effect of a steady pitch rate, depending on the value of the stuck position of the damaged elevator. In other words there will be a certain cross-correlation between the pitch rate, q, and the roll rate, p, which in turn is coupled with the yaw rate r. For the same reason, in the case of a rudder damage , there will be a certain correlation between the yaw rate, r, and the roll rate, p. Similarly, a damage on one of the ailerons will imply a certain cross-correlation between p,q and r.

By definition, given two generic random processes Y(k) and X(k), the cross-correlation function [19,38] is defined as :

$$R_{yx}(n) = E [Y(k) X(k+n)] \tag{27}$$

where 'E' is the expectation operator. Note that the cross-correlation function will have (2n) points. In order to use this concept for damage identification purposes, not knowing when the damage is going to occur, different cross-correlation functions, e.g., example R_{PQ}, R_{PR} and R_{QR}, should be calculated at each time instant 'k' and stored in temporary self-flushing memory locations of the flight computer for a time window of size 'm'. In other words, the flight control system should have always available at each time 'k' the cross-correlation functions $R_{PQ}(j)$, $R_{PR}(j)$ and $R_{QR}(j)$ with 'j' varying from 'k-m' to 'k'. If no abnormal flight conditions due to the damage are detected the flight computer will continue on calculating these cross-correlation functions and storing them in temporary memory locations. If a failure is detected (that is, ERRTOT > THRESH.$_{F.D.}$) the flight computer will then proceed to analyze the cross-correlation functions data. Particularly the sums of the absolute values of each of the cross-correlation functions (R_{PQ},R_{PR},R_{QR}) need to be calculated on-line at each time instant from 'k-m' to 'k'; if it is observed that the values of these sums are increasing, then the damaged control surface may be identified using the relative cross-correlation function. In the case of a damage on the left elevator , for 'k >

kfail', and (ERRTOT > THRESH.$_{F.D.}$), there results

$$sum(abs(elem.R_{PQ}))) \ (k-1) \ -$$
$$sum(abs(elem.R_{PQ}))) \ (k-2) \ > \ THRES._{F.I.(PQ:ELEV.)} \qquad (28)$$

If damage occurs on the rudder, the same will be true for the cross-correlation function R_{QR}. Reservations on the validity of this approach exist for the identification of a damage on the ailerons because of the 'mild' induced pitching moment due to the reduced distance of the ailerons from the center of gravity for conventional geometries (unless the damaged aileron becomes stuck at the maximum or minimum deflection). However, along with a small cross-correlation between p and q, there will be in this case a strong correlation between p and r.

A suitable decision process is shown in Fig.8 [5, Source AIAA]. The selection of the values of all the THRESHOLDS can be performed within a flight simulator or with a dynamic simulation program. These values will have to be trade-offs between the desire for a quick detectability and identifiability of the damage and the desire to keep low the false alarm rate. Note that comparative studies must be performed with the same size of the window, the same number of points for each cross-correlation function, and with the same computer sampling time. It should be pointed out that different values of the thresholds associated with the same cross-correlation function are required depending on which surface has been damaged.

The block diagram of the overall F.D.I. process is shown in Fig.9 [5, Source AIAA]. The sum of the absolute values of the elements of the cross-correlation functions (R_{PQ},R_{PR},R_{QR}) are shown in Fig. 10 [5, Source AIAA] for a time window of size 'm=200' between 'kfail-(m/2)' and 'kfail+(m/2)' with '2n=200' points for each cross-correlation function. It can be noticed that, starting from 'k=kfail', there is a sharp increase in the sum of the absolute values of all three cross-correlation functions, due to the coupling between the rolling and the yawing angular velocity.

if ERRTOT *(k)* > THRES.$_{\text{F.D.}}$ *then*

    if { *sum(abs(elem.*R_{PQ}*)))* *(k-1)* $-$

        sum(abs(elem.R_{PQ}*)))* *(k-2)* > THRES.$_{\text{F.I.(PQ:ELEV.)}}$ *}* *then*

    DAMAGE ON THE ELEVATOR

    end

    elseif { *sum(abs(elem.*R_{PR}*)))* *(k-1)* $-$

        sum(abs(elem.R_{PR}*)))* *(k-2)* > THRES.$_{\text{F.I.(PR:RUDDER.)}}$ *}* *then*

    DAMAGE ON THE RUDDER

    end

    elseif { *sum(abs(elem.*R_{PR}*)))* *(k-1)* $-$

        sum(abs(elem.R_{PR}*)))* *(k-2)* > THRES.$_{\text{F.I.(PR:AILER.)}}$ *}*

                        and

    { *sum(abs(elem.*R_{PQ}*)))* *(k-1)* $-$

        sum(abs(elem.R_{PQ}*)))* *(k-2)* > THRES.$_{\text{F.I.(PQ:AILER.)}}$ *}* *then*

    DAMAGE ON THE AILERONS

    end

    else

    FALSE ALARM

    end

end

        Figure 8.   Rules for the Failure Detection
                     and Identification Process

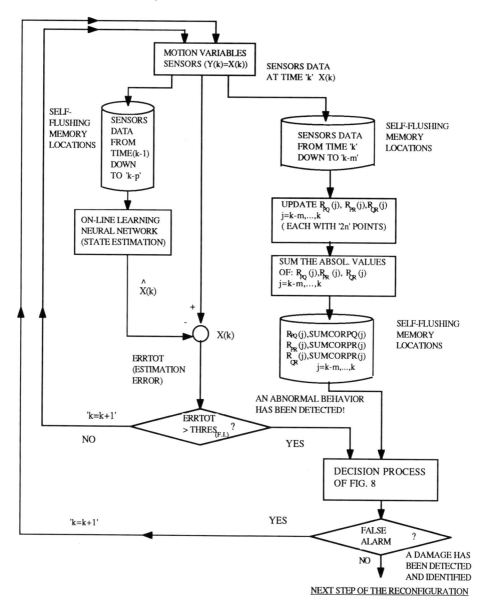

Figure 9: Block Diagram of the Failure Detection
and Identification Process

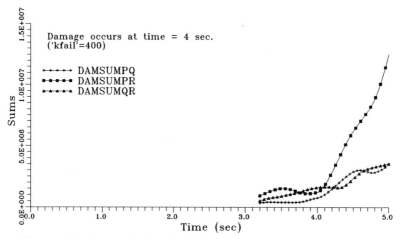

Figure 10   Sum of the Absolute Values of the Cross−Correletion
            Functions

Once the Failure Detection and Identification process has been satisfactorily performed, the next step would be to proceed in the overall flight control reconfiguration process shown in Fig.1. Simultaneously, given that the instants immediately following damage are moments of concern and sometimes panic even for a well trained pilot, it will be desirable to briefly inform the pilot about the location and the type of the damage with an emergency message displayed on the main CRT of the cockpit, as shown in Fig. 11 [5, Source AIAA].

As concluding statements for this section, it may be said that a Neural Network, implemented in the flight computer software and trained on-line in-flight using motion variables sensors data, has shown to be an effective state estimator. Its flexibility in quickly learning the dynamics of the aircraft system along with its capability to filter out system noises make it an attractive alternative to classic estimation structures such as Kalman Filters and Observers, of both full and reduced order. From a computational point of view, given the simple nature of the mathematical operations (mostly additions and multiplications) involved in the training, its implementation in a flight computer should be very simple compared with the implementation of a large bank of Kalman Filters, which is frequently attempted in modern high performance flight computers. Special care should be taken in calculating and storing the cross-correlation functions R_{QR}, R_{PR} and R_{PQ} in temporary memory locations at each time step. However, even this task should not constitute a major computational burden.

The practical operation of the F.D.I. with high frequency and high intensity system noises must be evaluated. Also the efficiency of the N.N. as on-line state estimator considering the full non-linear dynamics of the aircraft remains to be evaluated, even if in the [19-22] applications of N.N. to simple non-linear systems are shown to be extremely effective with only the drawback of longer training times. Further investigations are also needed for the integration of this F.D.I. technique with the remaining tasks of the flight control

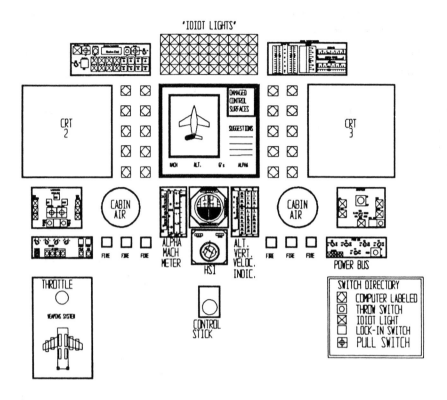

Figure 11. Pilot Advisory Function Following
            Failure Detection and Identification

reconfiguration problem with the approaches described in the following sections [1-4]. However, the results furnished by this simple but realistic simulation are very promising. The relative simplicity of the algorithms and the efficiency of the method may be the key factors for a successful practical implementation of this approach.

III. MODEL ESTIMATION OF THE DAMAGED AIRCRAFT

As stated previously, the objective of the flight control reconfiguration is to identify and to control an aircraft system with changed dynamics. Once the F.D.I. has been successfully accomplished, a more efficient approach to the estimation of the model describing the changed dynamics can be implemented if there is some knowledge of how the dynamics may change following a control surface damage. This is true regardless of the approach used for the control scheme for the damaged system.

For the numerical simulation of the F.D.I. section II.C. has described a realistic aerodynamic modeling of the effects of control surface damage and/or generic failure. Particularly, it has been pointed out [1-3] that a set of closed-form expressions (Eq.20) of the dimensionless aerodynamic stability and control derivatives as functions of the normal force coefficient can be developed for each control surface, as shown in Eq. 21. These closed-form expressions can be calculated numerically for conventional subsonic airplanes and by wind tunnel investigations for supersonic configurations. Once obtained, a set of these expressions for each control surface can be stored in the flight computer memory. ready to be used for on-line model estimation purposes. At this point it can be recalled that a damage on a control surface implies a change or, more specifically a decrease, in the value of the normal force coefficient. Therefore, provided that the F.D.I. is able to indicate which control surface has been damaged, we can discretize the value of the normal force coefficient of the damaged control surface in a number N of intervals spanning, for example, the value of the normal force coefficient from 0 (i=1) to the nominal undamaged value (i=N). Eqs.(1-2) will then become

$$X_i(k+1) = A_i \, X_i(k) \; + \; B_i \, U(k) \; + \; L_i \, W(k) \qquad (29)$$
$$Z_i(k) = C \, X_i(k) \; + \; V(k) \qquad\qquad \text{with } i = 1,\dots,N \qquad (30)$$

The estimation task is to determine which one of the N models correctly characterizes the system. Denote by H_j the event that model 'j' is the most exact system characterization; let 'H' be a random variable that takes on the discrete values $H_1, H_2, \ldots H_n$ and let $Y(k)$ be defined as

$$Y(k) = \{U(0), U(1), \ldots U(k-1); Z(1), Z(2), \ldots, Z(k)\}$$

Then we can define :

$$P_i(k) = P[\ H = H_i\ /\ Y(k)\ ] \qquad (31)$$

which is the probability that model 'i' is the correct system characterization, given measurements $Y(k)$. The algorithm proceeds as follows:

STEP 1

A Kalman filter is developed for each of the N system models, and N filtered estimates of the system states X_i are obtained.

STEP 2

The filter residuals are calculated by using :

$$r_i(k+1) = Z(k+1) - C\ \hat{X}_i(k+1/K) \qquad (32)$$

STEP 3

The Bayesian probabilities are updated using :

$$P_i(k+1) = \frac{\beta_i\ e^{-\frac{1}{2}[\ r_i^T(k+1)\ S_i^{-1}\ r_i(k+1)\ ]}\ P_i(k)}{\displaystyle\sum_{j=1}^{N} \beta_j\ e^{-\frac{1}{2}[\ r_j^T(k+1)\ S_j^{-1}\ r_j(k+1)\ ]}\ P_j(k)} \qquad (33)$$

where S_i is the covariance matrix for residuals r_i (calculated from the Kalman filter equations for each model) and

$$\beta_j = (2\pi)^{-l/2}\ \det[S_j]^{-1/2}$$

where l is the dimension of the vector $Z(k)$.

Summarizing, a bank of Kalman Filters has been built and by analyzing the residuals of the different N estimates the probabilities that each model is the correct characterization of the true damaged aircraft system are calculated. A convergence of one of the probabilities to a value close to 1 will indicate that a reasonably correct mathematical model has been found.

This approach for the estimation of the model of the damaged aircraft has been tested with data from a dynamic simulation of the same aircraft model introduced in Section II (Fig. 3) with relative data in TABLE I. Again, the damage is assumed on the left elevator with a loss of almost 50% of its effectiveness. The damage is modeled aerodynamically using Eqs. (23-24). Although it was previously assumed that a set of functioning sensors for each motion variable is available, the approach has been tested with $l=6 < n=8$, that is

$$ Z = [\ \alpha \ , \ q \ , \ U \ , \ \beta \ , \ p \ , \ r \ ]^T $$

If all the sensors are available, i.e., if all the motion variables can be measured, the estimation should be even better. For the purposes of introducing this approach for the damaged model estimation, the considered aircraft exhibits satisfactory handling qualities under normal undamaged conditions. Therefore, no stability augmentation system (SAS) has been considered. Also no control configured vehicle (CCV) function (e.g., gust and load alleviation systems, ride quality control system, flight envelope limiting system) is considered on the aircraft.

For this dynamic simulation the corresponding nominal input is shown in Fig. 12 [3, Source AIAA]. Note that the left elevator has been damaged and it remains fixed at -5 deg deflection.

By discretizing the value of the normal force coefficient of the damaged control surface in a set of N values, the corresponding sets of 'N' A and B matrices are constructed by the algorithm. In the control matrix B only the elements of the column corresponding to the left elevator change. The parameter N plays an important role. For high values of N, corresponding to a high modeling accuracy, excessively long convergence times are expected for the probability corresponding to the model that more closely describes the damaged system [1]. The reverse occurs for small values of N, which imply shorter convergence times [1]. For the present analysis N = 12 has been used, corresponding to a desirable modeling accuracy. With such a number of on-line constructed models, when considering damaged dynamics numerically described by a model somewhere between model #5 and model #6, but closer to model #6, the probability corresponding to model #6 converges to 1, as shown in Fig. 13 [3, Source AIAA] in a short amount of time (about 2 sec. with a time increment of 0.01 sec.).

Since this algorithm has to be implemented on line for an accurate selection of a value for N, the computational speed of the airborne computer must also be considered. The role played by the various parameters for the selection of N is qualitatively shown in Fig. 14 [3, Source AIAA].

The advantage of this approach is its relative simplicity since is take advantage of the particular way that the elements of the matrices A and B may change following a damage on a control surface.

An analysis of the robustness of the damaged model estimation process has been performed [1]. The result is that the Kalman filters structure is shown to be a remarkably robust environment to discrepancies between Q and Q_M (where Q is the covariance of the atmospheric turbulence acting on the aircraft dynamics and Q_M is the covariance of the atmospheric turbulence as modeled in the Kalman filters structure) and for real life correlated atmospheric turbulence incorrectly modeled in the Kalman filters structure as white noise. In terms of the robustness of the multiple model Kalman filtering approach to the nonlinearity of the real system, the issue is whether the Kalman filter tracking error corresponding to the linearized model closest to the true nonlinear system is markedly smaller than the errors from filters based on more distant models. This will also depend on how far apart the different linearized models are [12]. An analysis of how the introduced method performs at nonlinear conditions has not been performed because nonlinear aerodynamic characteristics

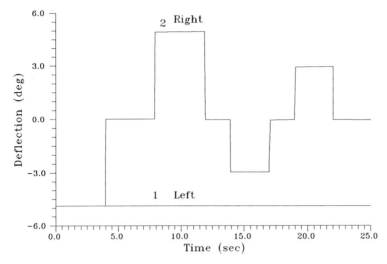

Figure 12   Nominal Elevetors Deflections

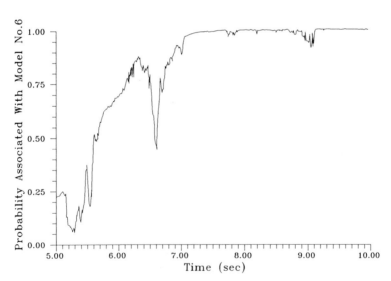

Figure 13   Probability Convergence to the
             Closest Model (N=12)

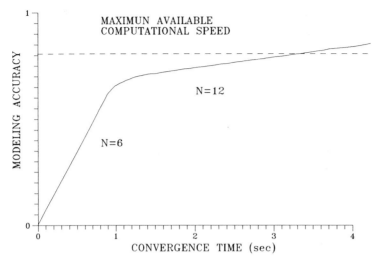

Figure 14   Parameters of the Selection
of the Number of Models N

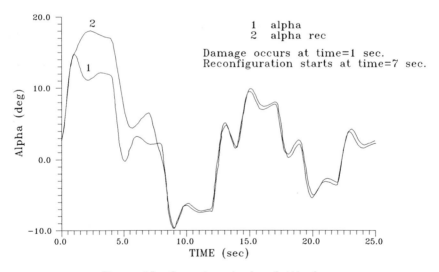

Figure 15   Case 1 — Angle of Attack

describing flow separation at high angles of attack were not
available. A full study of the nonlinearity problem should be
considered only when the complete closed-loop dynamics (with all the
SAS and CCV functions implemented on the aircraft) are considered.

As the final result of the application of this Multiple Model
Kalman Filtering approach, the flight computer will have a reasonably
accurate mathematical model describing the dynamics of the damaged
aircraft. A possible limitation of this approach is the available
computational power and speed of the airborne computers; however, it
is reasonable to expect that the constant improvements in the
performance of the flight computers will overcome this problem. The
next goal will be to calculate a set of compensating deflections from
other control surfaces.

IV. A RECONFIGURATION ALGORITHM
In this section a particular algorithm is proposed for the control
system reconfiguration, i.e., the determination of the compensating
inputs required for the other control surfaces. This methodology was
introduced in [39]. For the purpose of presenting such an approach,
consider a second-order linear controllable system. In the continuous
time state variables form

$$\dot{x}_1 = x_2 \tag{34}$$
$$\dot{x}_2 = a_1 x_2 + a_2 x_1 + a_3 u \tag{35}$$

where u is the control variable required to be bounded; a_1, a_2, and a_3
are constant coefficients.

The goal is to determine a method of computing u that will make
the system defined by Eqs. (34) and (35) behave like the ideal system
described in the same state variables form by

$$\dot{y}_1 = y_2 \tag{36}$$
$$\dot{y}_2 = b_1 y_2 + b_2 y_2 + b_3 u_m \tag{37}$$

where u_m is the control variable, which is also required to be bounded; b_1, b_2, and b_3, are constant coefficients.

By integrating Eq. (35) between the time t=nh and t=(n+1)h, assuming that u has a value u(n) over this interval, we will have

$$x_2(n+1) - x_2(n) = C_1 + C_2 u(n) \qquad (38)$$

where $x_2(n)$ and $u(n)$ are used to denote $x_2(nh)$ and $u(nh)$ and C_1 and C_2 are given by

$$C_1 = a_1 \int_{nh}^{(n+1)h} x_2(t)dt + a_2 \int_{nh}^{(n+1)h} x_1(t)dt \qquad (39)$$

$$C_2 = a_3 h \qquad (40)$$

The desired change in x_2 over the time interval is defined as V(n). If the actual change must be the same as the desired change, from Eq. (38)

$$u(n) = (V(n) - C_1) / C_2 \qquad (41)$$

Once we determine C_1 and C_2, the control required to make the actual change in x_2 equal to the desired change can be provided by Eq. (41). Note that the two terms in C_1 will generally not be constant, and they will depend on the varying values of x_1 and x_2. If, however, we assume that x_1 and x_2 are almost constant over a small group of intervals, then C_1 and C_2 both will be approximately constant over the same group of intervals. Therefore, by applying Eq. (38) on these preceding intervals, we have

$$x_2(n) - x_2(n-1) = C_1 + C_2 u(n-1) \qquad (42)$$

$$x_2(n-1) - x_2(n-2) = C_1 + C_2 u(n-2) \qquad (43)$$

At the beginning of the n-th interval, where u(n) is to be computed, all the terms in Eqs. (42) and (43) will be known from measurements (or from computer simulations), except C_1 and C_2. These can be determined by elimination between the two equations

$$C_1 = \frac{u(n-2)\ [x_2(n)-x_2(n-1)] - u(n-1)\ [\dot{x}_2(n-1)-\dot{x}_2(n-2)]}{u(n-2) - u(n-1)} \qquad (44)$$

$$C_2 = \frac{2\ x_2(n-1) - x_2(n-2) - x_2(n)}{u(n-2) - u(n-1)} \qquad (45)$$

The last parameter needed to be calculated is the desired change $V(n)$. For example, with the system responding to a constant step input of magnitude M, then the desired change in x_2 over the nth interval is taken as

$$V(n) = h\ [b_1 x_2(n) + b_2 x_1(n) + b_3 M] \qquad (46)$$

Substituting this value of $V(n)$ into Eq. (41), together with the values of C_1 and C_2 previously calculated, a control algorithm is achieved which will make the real system behave as the ideal one would at the same point under normal circumstances. By accomplishing this in succeeding time intervals, the real system will be reconfigured. The introduced methodology looks surprisingly simple and, at the same time, efficient. However, there are two problems that need to be kept in mind:

(1) - the resulting value of $u(n)$ might not be bounded. On the other hand, there are minimum and maximum angular deflections for the control surfaces. Given that the considered mathematical models are deterministic and, therefore, not affected by noise, this situation occurs when the reconfiguration algorithm is applied too late. In this case, there is not enough control authority to reconfigure the aircraft. Also, this may occur when the aircraft dynamics become unstable following the damage.

(2) - $u(n)$ might be too close to $u(n-1)$, and numerical problems may arise from the computation of $u(n+1)$. This is because there are small denominators in Eqs. (44) and (45). This is typical of a flat input situation. To overcome this problem, in the body of the algorithm, after checking $[u(n-2)-u(n-1)]$, a minimum fixed quantity is assumed if this difference is zero.

Before going into the details of the application of the method to flight control reconfiguration, some further considerations need to be made. This can be essentially classified as a "model following" problem, where the model of the nominal aircraft can be constructed on line by using aerodynamic, inertial and geometric characteristics stored in the flight computer together with SAS or CCV functions and the flight data coming from the operational sensors. The dynamic model of the real damaged aircraft is also constructed on line by the airborne computer using the previously introduced multiple model Kalman filtering approach. The algorithm manipulates these deterministic models regardless of whether they represent closed-loop or open-loop dynamics.

Note that using such an approach, the model estimation task and the control task are totally separated. The damaged aircraft model used by the reconfiguration algorithm is deterministic. The noise-sensitivity problem has been faced previously in the model estimation task. By recalling Eqs. (42-46), note that this is a two sample delay matching technique. It is potentially able to handle nonlinear mathematical models as long as there is an aerodynamic data bank which includes nonlinear characteristics. In fact, Eqs. (41-20) are valid for a nonlinear mathematical model [39].

The technique introduced for a simple single-input, second-order system has been used for the example multi-input aircraft system. In order to test the behavior of the control reconfiguration algorithm only, it is assumed that the damaged model has already been estimated and that the damaged aircraft dynamics is exactly described by one of the N models of the multiple model Kalman filters. This is a reasonable assumption if a sufficiently high number (N) of models is implemented (N = 10-15). For a realistic simulation, the following possibilities for a damaged control surface must be considered:
(1) a control surface that remains fixed at a particular position.
(2) a control surface that jams to the maximum or minimum angular deflection.

In order to be able to implement a reconfiguration strategy, the basic aircraft shown in Fig. 3 with the data of TABLE I is modified

with the introduction of two additional longitudinal control surfaces,
i.e. a pair of canards. Therefore, the aircraft is assumed to have
nine independent control surfaces: right and left elevators, right and
left ailerons (with limit at ± 25 deg), right and left spoilers (with
limit at ± 45 deg), right and left canards and a rudder(with limit at
± 30 deg).

A key factor for a successful application of this reconfiguration
technique consists of being able to implement on line a very small
value of the reconfiguration step h, introduced in Eq. (39), i.e. at
each interval of time that the reconfiguration method is applied. Such
a value is a function of the modeling accuracy, reconfiguration
algorithm complexity, and available computational power of the
airborne computer.

Given that a linearized set of equations represents the best
compromise between modeling accuracy and low computational time for
modeling a six degree-of-freedom aircraft, the next goal is to
minimize the reconfiguration algorithm complexity. To do so it is
noticed that, because of the nature of the aircraft dynamics, such a
system is a completely state controllable system. From a mathematical
point of view, this implies that

$$\text{rank } W_c = \text{rank } [B, AB, .., A^{n-1}B] = n \qquad (47)$$

This also means that it would be sufficient to find the control inputs
that reconfigure some of the states to be sure that all the states are
reconfigured. A typical choice would be to reconfigure p,q and r, the
aircraft angular velocities.

Once the amount of control needed for the reconfiguration of a
state is calculated using Eq. (41), the next step is to efficiently
distribute (from an aerodynamic point of view) this control power
among all the available healthy independent control surfaces. The
approach that has been implemented is that each control surface
contributes to the reconfiguration with an amount proportional to its
control derivative.

For example, the right elevator will contribute to the

reconfiguration of the q state, following damage to the left elevator, with an amount :

$$W_{er} = \frac{C_{m\delta er}}{|C_{m\delta er}| + |C_{m\delta al}| + |C_{m\delta ar}| + |C_{m\delta cl}| + |C_{m\delta cr}|} \tag{48}$$

Such an approach will avoid the saturation of a particular control surface used for the reconfiguration, leaving some angular deflection margins to be used in the following flight maneuvers by the pilot or by the flight control system.

The previously introduced control techniques have been numerically simulated with the damage on the left elevator. Two different cases have been considered, both with damage taking place at time = 1 sec.

Case 1 (Figs. 15-17 [5, Source AIAA]) is relative to a situation where damage to the left elevator implies a reduction of about one-half of its control effectiveness, because of some missing surface area, with the deflection fixed at the position at the instant of the damage, that is, -5 deg. The task of the damaged surface is distributed, using the previously introduced criteria (Eq. (48)), among the remaining half elevator, the right and left spoilers, and the right and left canards.

The enclosed graphs show that the introduced algorithm, which takes over 6 sec after the damage occurs (after the failure detection and identification are obtained and the damaged model estimation is accomplished as previously discussed), achieves in a very short amount of time an accurate reconfiguration for the angle of attack and the pitching angular velocity, and properly counteracts the rolling moment induced by the damaged half elevator.

Note that from Fig. 15 we can see that the stability characteristics of the aircraft have changed following the damage to the left elevator. This brings up the issue that the damage may decrease the longitudinal stability, and we can even reach the point where the aircraft becomes unstable after the damage. In this extreme case, time is really a key factor because if the reconfiguration algorithm is applied too late and the unstable dynamic trend is

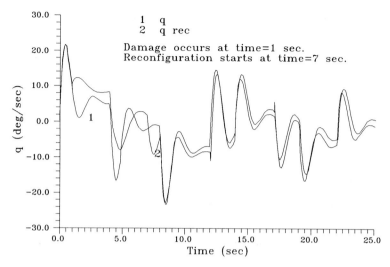

Figure 16   Case 1 – Pitch Angular Velocity

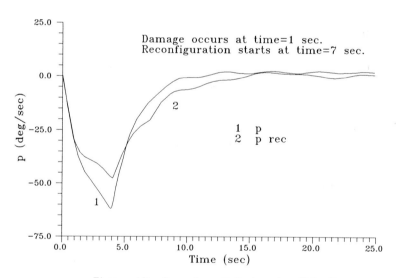

Figure 17   Case 1 – Roll Angular Velocity

already well developed, there may not be enough control authority to bring back the aircraft to perform with the desired dynamic characteristics because the aircraft may have already gone into some unrecoverable flight conditions.

Case 2 (Figs. 18-19 [3, Source AIAA]) is relative to a similar situation. The only difference is that following the damage, the left elevator jams to the minimum angular deflection, that is, -25 deg. Note that this is a very severe condition. Even in this case, an acceptable reconfiguration is achieved for the angle of attack and for the rolling angular velocity. Note that the induced rolling moment is, in this case, a non negligible side effect. However, the magnitudes of the parameters plotted in Figs. 18-19 leads us to some considerations. In fact, such magnitudes are surely outside the limits of the assumption of linear dynamics and aerodynamics. Recall that we have considered an open-loop aircraft, without any form of SAS or CCV functions implemented in the flight control system. In real life, these closed-loop systems would actuate multiple control surfaces (excluding of course the one that has been damaged), even if not for reconfiguration purposes, that would keep the values of p,q,r, and all other state variables at lower magnitudes than the ones shown in Fig. 18-19. It is important to point out that other main factors for the reconfiguration success are the maximum angular velocity of the actuators and the maximum number of impulses that can be sent to such actuators in a time unit. This brings up the problem that the advantages of a reconfiguration technique can be experienced only if the remaining actuators implemented are sufficiently strong and fast acting.

Concluding, a simple reconfirmation algorithm has been introduced for the determination of a set of compensating deflections for the remaining control surfaces to accommodate the damage on a primary control surface. The next step of the overall reconfiguration process shown in Figure 1 is the redesign of the feedback gains of the control laws.

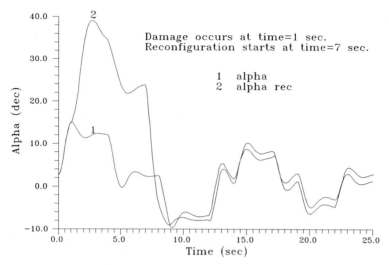

Figure 18   Case 2 – Angle of Attack

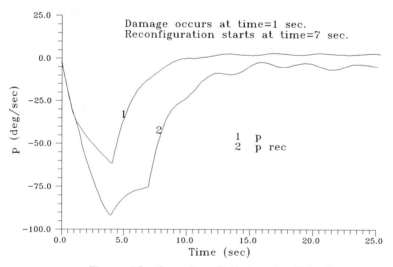

Figure 19   Case 2 – Roll Angular Velocity

V. REDESIGN OF THE FEEDBACK GAINS OF THE CONTROL LAW

In this section a particular Eigenspace Assignment technique is proposed for the redesign of the feedback structure. From a flight management point of view it is clear that the feedback structure should be redesigned in order to account for the changed dynamics of the system, due to the damage and/or the generic failure. In fact, it should be considered that following a damage to any control surface (with or without a missing part of it) the aircraft is subjected to a coupling between the longitudinal and the lateral directional dynamics. The magnitude of the coupling for damage on the main longitudinal control surfaces (elevators, canards, symmetrically deployed outboard spoilers) is larger than the magnitude for lateral directional control surface (rudder, ailerons) damage. This is caused by the lower aerodynamic forces exerted by the lateral directional control surfaces and the smaller moment arms of these forces with respect to the aircraft center of gravity.

Also, it is clear that a damage on a control surface deteriorates the handling qualities of the aircraft in terms of natural frequencies, damping and time constants of the longitudinal and lateral directional modes.

The feedback gains should be recalculated with the goal of retaining desirable handling qualities and removing the damage induced dynamic coupling. This should be accomplished for that particular flight condition where the flight control reconfiguration is taking place and for all the regions of the aircraft flight envelope.

V. A. EIGENSTRUCTURE ASSIGNMENT FOR CONTROL
OF A MULTI-INPUT SYSTEM

For the design of a feedback structure for a linear (or linearized) time-invariant multi-input system, two different approaches can be followed :

1 - Linear Quadratic Optimal Control method [25].

2 - Eigenstructure Assignment technique (a more general definition for

the pole assignment approach) [51-56].

The first approach is very commonly applied to multivariable control systems in order to design controllers which achieve desired characteristics minimizing a certain performance index. Within the L.Q. control strategy we may have an implicit or an explicit model-following approach. The main differences between these two techniques are that with the implicit method it is possible to place closed-loop poles or eigenvalues (which is important for some particular problems), while with the explicit method such a feature is not possible. However, a common problem associated with the implicit method is that it may require excessive control activity.

This section will emphasize the importance of eigenspace techniques and their suitability for practical implementation in order to solve particular flight control problems. Generally speaking, eigenspace techniques use feedback control to place closed loop eigenvalues and shape closed loop eigenvectors to achieve performance specifications. In recent years, applications of these techniques have been attempting to achieve decoupling between rigid and elastic modes [54] and suppress flutter phenomena of an oblique wing aircraft [52].

An Eigenstructure Assignment approach is proposed to redesign the feedback structure with the goals of restoring desirable handling qualities and removing dynamic coupling. In the single-input case a unique feedback matrix is required to obtain desired eigenvalues. With each eigenvalue there is an associated eigenvector which is also unique. However, for a multi-input system there are an infinite number of feedback matrices which can assign specified eigenvalues. With each feedback matrix there is a new set of associated eigenvectors. Since the eigenvectors also affect the time response, it is important to assign both the eigenvalues and the associated eigenvectors [51-56]. Therefore, there are a number of degrees of freedom given by free parameters. It may be attempted to use these extra degrees of freedom to obtain the most desirable dynamic response. In this case the eigenstructure assignment problem reduces to an optimization problem [1,4,51-56].

Given a multi-input aircraft system, the control input vector at time instant k, U(k), can be expressed as

$$U(k) = U_F(k) + U_P(k) \tag{49}$$

where $U_F(k)$ indicates control inputs used by the state feedback and $U_P(k)$ indicates pilot deflection inputs. Note that $U_P(k)$ and $U_F(k)$ may have some common elements. The generic discrete-time state variable form without the atmospheric turbulence can be given by

$$X(k+1) = A \, X(k) \; + \; B \, U(k) \tag{50}$$

The A matrix is relative to the open-loop dynamics. Using the state feedback approach

$$U_F(k) = K \, X(k) \tag{51}$$

where K is a matrix of feedback gains. By using Eq.(49), Eq.(50) becomes

$$X(k+1) = [\, A + B_F \, K \,] \, X(k) + B_P \, U_P(k) =$$
$$= A_{C.L.} \, X(k) + B_P \, U_P(k) \tag{52}$$

where B_F and B_P are relative to $U_F(k)$ and $U_P(k)$ respectively.

For a n-th order observable and controllable system, with m control inputs and ℓ measurements available for direct output feedback, MAX(m,ℓ) eigenvalues and MIN(m,ℓ) of the associated eigenvectors can be assigned.

An approach to this problem would be to assign, together with the desired eigenvalues, a set of desirable eigenvectors which reflects uncoupling between the modes associated with the given eigenvalues. In other words, it would be desirable to assign a set of desirable eigenvectors which reflects the original nominal undamaged decoupled dynamics. Note that m < 1; therefore , if it is desired to specify more than m eigenvectors, the best achievable result can be some least-squares fit to the desired eigenvectors. Assume that $\ell = n$, where all the states, measured by appropriate sensors, are directly available for feedback purposes. Therefore

$$Z(k) = M \, X(k) \qquad\qquad (53)$$

where M is an (n x n) identity matrix.

In order to determine K, note that the augmented closed-loop system eigenvalues (Γ_i) and eigenvectors (Ω_i) are related by the following relation

$$(A + B_F \, K \, M) \, \Omega_i = \Gamma_i \, \Omega_i \qquad \text{for } i=1,\ldots,n=\ell \qquad (54)$$

A set of m-dimensional vectors W_i is introduced

$$W_i = K \, M \, \Omega_i \qquad \text{for } i=1,\ldots,n=\ell \qquad (55)$$

Given that m < n, the best achievable eigenvectors for each of the ℓ = n modes will be obtained by minimizing the following modes' cost function :

$$J_i = 1/2 \, (\Omega_{ai} - \Omega_{di})^{*T} \, Q_i \, (\Omega_{ai} - \Omega_{di}) \qquad \text{for } i=1,\ldots,n=\ell \qquad (56)$$

where Ω_{ai} = achievable eigenvector associated with Γ_i;

$\qquad \Omega_{di}$ = desired eigenvector associated with Γ_i;

$\qquad Q_i$ = i-th (n x n) symmetric positive semi-definite weighting

$\qquad\qquad$ matrix for the eigenvectors;

$\qquad$ *T indicates conjugate transpose.

Such a cost function represents the error between the achievable eigenvectors and some desired eigenvectors, weighted by the matrix Q_i. It can be shown that the W_i that minimizes J_i is given by

$$W_i^{*T} = \Omega_{Di}^{*T} Q_i L_i [L_i^{*T} Q_i L_i]^{-1} \qquad \text{for } i=1,\ldots,n=\ell \qquad (57)$$

where $L_i = (\Gamma_i I_n - A)^{-1} B_F$.

Note that in order for the inverse of Eq.(9) to exist

$$\text{Rank } [Q_i] > \text{Rank } [B_F] \qquad\qquad (58)$$

Also such an approach can be extended for synthesizing reduced order feedback control laws, depending on the dimension ℓ of vector $Z(k)$. Once W_i is found, the relation that allows the achievable eigenvectors to be calculated is given by

$$(\Gamma_i I_n - A)\, \Omega_{ai} = B_F W_i \qquad \text{for } i=1,\ldots,n=\ell \tag{59}$$

which gives

$$\Omega_{ai} = (\Gamma_i I_n - A)^{-1} B_F W_i \qquad \text{for } i=1,\ldots,n=\ell \tag{60}$$

Finally, the control gain matrix is given by

$$K = W\,[\,M\,V\,]^{-1} \tag{61}$$

where W = matrix of concatenated W_i vectors = $[\,W_1,\ldots,W_1\,]$;

V = matrix of concatenated achievable Ω_{ai} eigenvectors =

$\quad = [\,\Omega_{a1},\ldots,\Omega_{a1}\,]$.

V. B. APPLICATION OF THE EIGENSTRUCTURE ASSIGNMENT TO THE REDESIGN OF THE FEEDBACK GAINS FOR A DAMAGED AIRCRAFT

The introduced method for the redesign of the feedback structure of the stability augmentation system has been numerically simulated. For this study the aerodynamic data and the flight conditions of a typical fighter aircraft ([36], App.C, Aircraft E) has been used; in order to implement a reconfiguration strategy, a pair of canards has been fictitiously introduced. The considered flight conditions are high subsonic cruise speed (Mach = 0.8) at an altitude of 35,000 ft. Of course, the feedback structure redesign must be performed for all the regions of the flight envelope. Without any loss of generality the previously introduced study can be performed in the continuous time given that the handling qualities requirements are known mostly in the s-domain.

The open-loop continuous-time state matrix A and the control matrices B_F and B_P at undamaged conditions are shown in TABLE II [4, Source AIAA]. In order to show the results of the application of the introduced method three steps have been followed :

STEP 1 - At the introduced flight conditions the design of the feedback structure is performed for the undamaged aircraft with the

TABLE II

OPEN-LOOP CONTINUOUS TIME STATE MATRIX A AT NOMINAL CONDITIONS.

```
-0.5091   1.0000  -0.0001   0.0000   0.0000   0.0000   0.0000   0.0000
-7.6691  -0.7111  -0.0026   0.0000   0.0000   0.0000   0.0000   0.0000
27.1241   0.0000  -0.0038  -31.175   0.0000   0.0000   0.0000   0.0000
 0.0000   1.0000   0.0000   0.0000   0.0000   0.0000   0.0000   0.0000
 0.0000   0.0000   0.0000   0.0000  -0.0952   0.0000  -1.0000   0.0367
 0.0000   0.0000   0.0000   0.0000  -19.004  -1.2144   0.3849   0.0000
 0.0000   0.0000   0.0000   0.0000   5.5422  -0.0065  -0.2532   0.0000
 0.0000   0.0000   0.0000   0.0000   0.0000   0.0000   1.0000   0.0000
```

CONTINUOUS TIME CONTROL MATRIX B AT NOMINAL CONDITIONS

```
-0.0280  -0.0280  -0.0280  -0.0280  -0.0210  -0.0210   0.0000   0.0000
-5.6390  -5.6390   6.8199   6.8199  -2.9152  -2.9152   0.0000   0.0000
 0.0000   0.0000   0.0000   0.0000   0.0000   0.0000   0.0000   0.0000
 0.0000   0.0000   0.0000   0.0000   0.0000   0.0000   0.0000   0.0000
 0.0000   0.0000   0.0000   0.0000   0.0000   0.0000  -0.0022   0.0070
12.0380  -12.038   13.132  -13.132   24.623  -24.623   1.3839   1.7057
-0.2593   0.2593  -0.2829   0.2829  -0.5305   0.5305  -0.2491  -2.7469
 0.0000   0.0000   0.0000   0.0000   0.0000   0.0000   0.0000   0.0000
```

CONTINUOUS TIME CONTROL MATRIX B$_F$ AT NOMINAL CONDITIONS

```
 -0.0560   0.0000
-11.2780   0.0000
  0.0000   0.0000
  0.0000   0.0000
  0.0000   0.0070
  0.0000   1.7057
  0.0000  -2.7469
  0.0000   0.0000
```

$$X^T = \{ \alpha , q , u , \theta , \beta , p , r , \phi \} ;$$

$$U^T = \{ \delta_{SL} , \delta_{SR} , \delta_{CL} , \delta_{CR} , \delta_{SP.L} , \delta_{SP.R} , \delta_A , \delta_R \} ;$$

$$U^T_F = \{ \delta_{S(L+R)} , \delta_R \} ;$$

TABLE III

INITIAL OPEN-LOOP EIGENVALUES FOR THE NOMINAL AIRCRAFT

$-0.6106 \pm i\ 2.7685$	(Short Period)
-0.0486	(Phugoid - 1)
0.0458	(Phugoid - 2)
$-0.1134 \pm i\ 2.3788$	(Dutch Roll)
-1.3229	(Rolling)
-0.0131	(Spiral)

DESIRED CLOSED-LOOP EIGENVALUES FOR THE NOMINAL AIRCRAFT

$-1.1510 \pm i\ 2.8598$	(Short Period)
$-0.0003 \pm i\ 0.0870$	(Phugoid)
$-0.0700 \pm i\ 1.6859$	(Dutch Roll)
-1.0000	(Rolling)
-0.0080	(Spiral)

CLOSED-LOOP CONTINUOUS TIME STATE MATRIX A AT NOMINAL CONDITIONS

```
-0.5152  0.9947 -0.0001  0.0014  0.0000  0.0000  0.0000  0.0000
-8.9047 -1.7836  0.0031  0.2724  0.0000  0.0000  0.0000  0.0000
27.1241  0.0000 -0.0038 -31.175  0.0000  0.0000  0.0000  0.0000
 0.0000  1.0000  0.0000  0.0000  0.0000  0.0000  0.0000  0.0000
 0.0000  0.0000  0.0000  0.0000 -0.0893 -0.0003 -1.0012  0.0367
 0.0000  0.0000  0.0000  0.0000 -17.556 -1.2848  0.0873  0.0071
 0.0000  0.0000  0.0000  0.0000  3.2099  0.1069  0.2261 -0.0115
 0.0000  0.0000  0.0000  0.0000  0.0000  0.0000  1.0000  0.0000
```

GAIN MATRIX K ASSOCIATED WITH U_F AT NOMINAL CONDITIONS

```
-0.1096 -0.0951  0.0005  0.0242  0.0000  0.0000  0.0000  0.0000
 0.0000  0.0000  0.0000  0.0000 -0.8491  0.0413  0.1745 -0.0042
```

TABLE IV

OPEN-LOOP CONTINUOUS TIME STATE MATRIX A AT DAMAGED CONDITIONS

```
-0.5041   1.0000  -0.0001   0.0000   0.0000   0.0000   0.0000   0.0000
-5.1072  -0.6438  -0.0026   0.0000   0.0000   0.0000   0.0000   0.0000
27.1214   0.0000  -0.0038 -31.175    0.0000   0.0000   0.0000   0.0000
 0.0000   1.0000   0.0000   0.0000   0.0000   0.0000   0.0000   0.0000
 0.0000   0.0000   0.0000   0.0000  -0.0952   0.0000  -1.0000   0.0367
 0.0000   0.0000   0.0000   0.0000 -19.004   -1.2144   0.3849   0.0000
 0.0000   0.0000   0.0000   0.0000   5.5422  -0.0065  -0.2532   0.0000
 0.0000   0.0000   0.0000   0.0000   0.0000   0.0000   1.0000   0.0000
```

CONTINUOUS TIME CONTROL MATRIX B AT DAMAGED CONDITIONS

```
-0.0070  -0.0280  -0.0280  -0.0280  -0.0210  -0.0210   0.0000   0.0000
-1.4094  -5.6390   6.8199   6.8199  -2.9152  -2.9152   0.0000   0.0000
 0.0000   0.0000   0.0000   0.0000   0.0000   0.0000   0.0000   0.0000
 0.0000   0.0000   0.0000   0.0000   0.0000   0.0000   0.0000   0.0000
 0.0000   0.0000   0.0000   0.0000   0.0000   0.0000  -0.0022   0.0070
 3.0095 -12.038   13.132  -13.132   24.623  -24.623    1.3839   1.7057
-0.0648   0.2593  -0.2829   0.2829  -0.5305   0.5305  -0.2491  -2.7469
 0.0000   0.0000   0.0000   0.0000   0.0000   0.0000   0.0000   0.0000
```

CONTINUOUS TIME COMTROL MATRIX B$_F$ AT DAMAGED CONDITIONS.

```
-0.0350   0.0000
-7.0484   0.0000
 0.0000   0.0000
 0.0000   0.0000
 0.0000   0.0070
-9.0285   1.7057
 0.1945  -2.7469
 0.0000   0.0000
```

$$X^T = \{\ \alpha\ ,\ q\ ,\ u\ ,\ \theta\ ,\ \beta\ ,\ p\ ,\ r\ ,\ \phi\ \}\ ;$$

$$U^T = \{\ \delta_{SL}\ ,\ \delta_{SR}\ ,\ \delta_{CL}\ ,\ \delta_{CR}\ ,\ \delta_{SP.L}\ ,\ \delta_{SP.R}\ ,\ \delta_A\ ,\ \delta_R\ \}\ ;$$

$$U_F^T = \{\ \delta_{S(L+R)}\ ,\ \delta_R\ \}\ ;$$

data taken from [36]. The basic aircraft shows unacceptable longitudinal handling qualities (low damped short period and a degenerated phugoid with an unstable real root); the lateral-directional handling qualities also need some minor improvements, in terms of rolling characteristics and dutch roll natural frequency. The eigenvalues of the basic undamaged aircraft associated with the continuous time state matrix are given in TABLE III [4, Source AIAA]. Also in TABLE III the desired eigenvalues for the undamaged, nominal aircraft for the continuous time domain are given.

At nominal undamaged conditions the left and right horizontal tail surfaces are deployed symmetrically; only the stabilizers and the rudder control inputs must be introduced in this design. Note that the design of the feedback structure at undamaged nominal conditions can be performed separately for the longitudinal and the lateral-directional dynamics since there is no damage induced dynamic coupling which can arise through elements of the B matrix in the closed loop state matrix. TABLE III shows the associated gain matrix K and the resulting closed-loop state matrix A , which has all the eigenvalues located in the desired positions, which implies desirable handling qualities.

STEP 2 - At the introduced flight conditions the damage has occurred. It is assumed that such damage implies a partial destruction of the left stabilizer with the control surface locked at the position at the instant of the damage as in the previous sections. The determination of the mathematical model following the damage proceeds as described in section II.C.. The open-loop continuous time state matrix A at damaged conditions is shown in TABLE IV [4, Source AIAA]. Note that at this point both stabilizers, along with the rudder, are still used in the feedback structure, with the left stabilizer being locked following the damage.

As expected the damage on the left stabilizer has implied a coupling between longitudinal and lateral directional dynamics. This can be seen in the elements of the closed-loop continuous time matrix

A shown in TABLE V [4, Source AIAA], where the gain matrix K is the one originally calculated for undamaged conditions. Such coupling can also be seen in the values of the associated eigenvectors and eigenvalues, as shown in TABLE V.

STEP 3 - The redesign of the feedback structure is finally attempted using the introduced method. The desired eigenvalues and eigenvectors need to be assigned. The selection of the desired eigenvalues has already been shown. For the selection of the desired set of eigenvectors the following considerations may be made.

The eigenvectors associated with the short period mode are chosen such that the variation in forward velocity is zero, with angle of attack being the predominant state, and pitch rate and pitch angle being of secondary importance. The eigenvectors associated with the phugoid mode are chosen such that the variation in angle of attack is zero; the phugoid motion should mainly imply variations in the forward velocity, with the pitch rate and pitch angle arbitrarily chosen. The eigenvectors associated with the dutch roll mode are chosen such that all the lateral-directional variables of motion are involved in the mode. On the contrary, the eigenvector associated with the rolling mode is chosen such that only the roll angle Φ and the associated angular velocity p are the predominant variables in this mode. Finally, the eigenvector associated with the spiral mode is chosen such that the angular velocity r is the predominant variable in this mode. Assuming that all the dynamic modes are equally important, all the Q matrices were selected to be identity matrices. The desired set of eigenvectors is shown in TABLE VI [4, Source AIAA].

The next point is to select which control surface to implement in the feedback structure. As we have previously stated, the aircraft is assumed to have independent control surfaces. Clearly, following a damage on a stabilizer, the most effective remaining longitudinal control surfaces would be the remaining 'healthy' stabilizer along with the pair of canards. Also the rudder must be used in order to have some control authority over the lateral-directional dynamics. With the selected desired eigenvalues and eigenvectors and with the

TABLE V

CLOSED-LOOP CONTINUOUS TIME STATE MATRIX A AT DAMAGED CONDITIONS WITH THE ORIGINAL GAIN MATRIX K OF TABLE II

```
-0.5079   0.9967  -0.0001   0.0008   0.0000   0.0000   0.0000   0.0000
-5.8794  -1.3141   0.0010   0.1702   0.0000   0.0000   0.0000   0.0000
27.1985   0.0000  -0.0038 -31.175   0.0000   0.0000   0.0000   0.0000
 0.0000   1.0000   0.0000   0.0000   0.0000   0.0000   0.0000   0.0000
 0.0000   0.0000   0.0000   0.0000  -0.0893  -0.0003  -1.0012   0.0367
-0.9891  -0.8586   0.0046   0.2181 -17.556  -1.2848   0.0873   0.0071
 0.0213   0.0185  -0.0001  -0.0047   3.2099   0.1069   0.2261  -0.0115
 0.0000   0.0000   0.0000   0.0000   0.0000   0.0000   1.0000   0.0000
```

EIGENVALUES ASSOCIATED WITH THE CLOSED-LOOP CONTINUOS TIME STATE MATRIX A AT DAMAGED CONDITIONS

```
-0.9153 ± i 2.3515    (Short Period)
 0.0024 ± i 0.0701    (Phugoid)      -----> UNSTABLE MODE
-0.0700 ± i 1.6859    (Dutch Roll)
-1.0000               (Rolling)
-0.0080               (Spiral)
```

EIGENVECTORS ASSOCIATED WITH THE CLOSED-LOOP CONTINUOS TIME STATE MATRIX A AT DAMAGED CONDITIONS

(Short Period)	(Phugoid)	(Dutch Roll)
0.0032 ± i 0.0696	0.0001 ± i 0.0001	0.0000 ± i 0.0000
0.1629 ± i 0.0361	0.0001 ± i 0.0001	0.0000 ± i 0.0000
0.8610 ± i 0.4650	0.8000 ± i 0.5970	0.0000 ± i 0.0000
-0.0101 ± i 0.0653	-0.0015 ± i 0.0016	0.0000 ± i 0.0000
0.0010 ± i 0.0003	-0.0001 ± i 0.0000	-0.0995 ± i 0.0120
0.0008 ± i 0.0678	0.0032 ± i 0.0027	0.5763 ± i 0.6178
0.0010 ± i 0.0031	-0.0013 ± i 0.0017	-0.0323 ± i 0.1560
0.0249 ± i 0.0101	-0.0367 ± i 0.0470	-0.3800 ± i 0.3261

(Rolling)	(Spiral)
0.0000	0.0000
0.0000	0.0000
0.0000	0.0000
0.0000	0.0000
0.0119	-0.0012
-0.7066	0.0080
0.0370	-0.0366
0.7066	-0.9993

$$X^T = \{ \alpha , q , u , \theta , \beta , p , r , \phi \} ;$$

TABLE VI

SELECTED DESIRED EIGENVECTORS

(Short Period)		(Phugoid)		(Dutch Roll)		(Rolling)	(Spiral)
1.0000	1.0000	0.0000	0.0000	0.0000	0.0000	0.0000	0.0000
0.8000	0.8000	0.2000	0.2000	0.0000	0.0000	0.0000	0.0000
0.0000	0.0000	1.0000	1.0000	0.0000	0.0000	0.0000	0.0000
0.8000	0.8000	0.2000	0.2000	0.0000	0.0000	0.0000	0.0000
0.0000	0.0000	0.0000	0.0000	1.0000	1.0000	0.0000	0.0000
0.0000	0.0000	0.0000	0.0000	1.0000	1.0000	1.0000	0.0000
0.0000	0.0000	0.0000	0.0000	1.0000	1.0000	0.0000	1.0000
0.0000	0.0000	0.0000	0.0000	1.0000	1.0000	1.0000	0.0000

$$X^T = \{\ \alpha\ ,\ q\ ,\ u\ ,\ \theta\ ,\ \beta\ ,\ p\ ,\ r\ ,\ \phi\ \}\ ;$$

new control feedback matrix B_F shown in TABLE VII [4, Source AIAA], the redesign of the feedback structure has been attempted with the introduced approach implemented in a user-defined MATLAB function.

The new closed-loop continuous time state matrix A (which has the desired eigenvalues) and the associated gain matrix K are shown in TABLE VI. The set of eigenvectors achieved with the redesign of the feedback structure is also shown in TABLE VIII [4, Source AIAA]. These eigenvectors are not immediately comparable with the desired ones, shown in TABLE VI, because of the phase shift. However, the normalized magnitudes of each element of the desired and achieved eigenvector matrices are shown in TABLE IX [4, Source AIAA]. The normalized magnitudes have the maximum values placed corresponding to the desired state variables.

In fact the angle of attack is the predominant state variable in the short period mode, with the pitch rate and pitch angle having a smaller importance, and the importance of the forward velocity being practically neglectable. Similarly, the forward velocity is the predominant state in the phugoid mode, with only a small importance of the angle of attack state. For the dutch roll mode some contribution from all the lateral-directional variables of motion is observed, as expected, while the rolling mode is dominated by the rolling rate and roll angle, as it should be. The only mode where the biggest contribution does not result from the expected state is the spiral mode. However, the eigenvalues are appropriately located. In addition there is no coupling with the longitudinal dynamics; therefore, the matter is not of particular concern. No attempt has been made in this study to control the phase relationships between the desired eigenvectors since for reconfiguration purposes the goals are only to remove dynamic coupling and to restore desirable handling qualities. [54-55] introduce a way of choosing particular relationships between the desired eigenvector elements, through a modification of Eqs. (56-57), such that

$$J_i = 1/2 \ (\Omega_{a_i} - \Omega_{d_i})^{*T} Q_i (\Omega_{a_i} - \Omega_{d_i}) + 1/2 \sum_{j=1}^{k} (v_j \Omega_{a_L})^{*} \alpha_j (v_j \Omega_{a_i}) \qquad (62)$$

TABLE VII

CONTINUOUS TIME CONTROL MATRIX B_F AT DAMAGED CONDITIONS FOR THE REDESIGN OF THE FEEDBACK STRUCTURE

-0.0280	-0.0280	-0.0280	0.0000
-5.6390	6.8199	6.8199	0.0000
0.0000	0.0000	0.0000	0.0000
0.0000	0.0000	0.0000	0.0000
0.0000	0.0000	0.0000	0.0070
-12.0380	13.132	-13.1320	1.7057
0.2593	-0.2829	0.2829	-2.7469
0.0000	0.0000	0.0000	0.0000

$$U_F^T = \{ \delta_{SR}, \delta_{CL}, \delta_{CR}, \delta_R \} \;;$$

CLOSED-LOOP CONTINUOUS TIME STATE MATRIX A AT DAMAGED CONDITIONS WITH THE REDESIGNED GAIN MATRIX K

0.0297	-6.5250	0.0014	0.0222	0.0000	0.0000	0.0000	0.0000
1.4744	-2.3285	-0.0047	0.0549	0.0000	0.0000	0.0000	0.0000
27.1985	0.0000	-0.0038	-31.175	0.0000	0.0000	0.0000	0.0000
0.0000	1.0000	0.0000	0.0000	0.0000	0.0000	0.0000	0.0000
0.0000	0.0000	0.0000	0.0000	-0.0821	-0.0060	-0.9942	0.0306
0.0000	0.0000	0.0000	0.0000	-0.0410	1.3611	-3.7794	2.4367
0.0000	0.0000	0.0000	0.0000	0.0502	2.2753	-2.4270	2.3051
0.0000	0.0000	0.0000	0.0000	0.0000	0.0000	1.0000	0.0000

REDESIGNED GAIN MATRIX K ASSOCIATED WITH U_F

-0.1096	1.4725	-0.0003	-0.0044	0.0000	0.0000	0.0000	0.0000
-0.0908	1.2824	-0.0003	-0.0038	0.0060	0.0015	-0.0021	0.0015
0.0097	-0.0674	0.0000	0.0002	-0.0060	-0.0015	0.0021	-0.0015
0.0000	0.0000	0.0000	0.0000	0.0188	-0.0086	0.0084	-0.0087

TABLE VIII

ACHIEVED EIGENVECTORS WITH THE REDESIGN

OF THE FEEDBACK STRUCTURE

```
          (Short period)                          (Phugoid)
 0.0144+i 0.7211;0.7211+i 0.0144 ; -0.1720+i 0.1383;0.2206+i 0.0054
-0.3135+i 0.1364;0.1364-i 0.3135 ; -0.0135+i 0.0063;0.0145-i 0.0032
 0.0033+i 0.0110;0.0110+i 0.0033 ; -48.127+i 38.163;61.413+i 1.0734
-0.0031-i 0.1109;-0.111-i 0.0031 ; -0.0714-i 0.1557;-0.038-i 0.1670
 0.0000        ;0.0000          ;0.0000         ;0.0000
 0.0000        ;0.0000          ;0.0000         ;0.0000
 0.0000        ;0.0000          ;0.0000         ;0.0000
 0.0000        ;0.0000          ;0.0000         ;0.0000
```

```
          (Dutch Roll)              (Rolling)        (Spiral)
 0.0000        ;0.0000          ;0.0000        ;0.0000
 0.0000        ;0.0000          ;0.0000        ;0.0000
 0.0000        ;0.0000          ;0.0000        ;0.0000
 0.0000        ;0.0000          ;0.0000        ;0.0000
-0.2848-i 0.0627;0.2643+i 0.1233 ;-0.0081      ;2.9888
-0.4438-i 0.3343;0.5556+i 0.0041 ;-0.4472      ;0.0025
 0.1188-i 0.4880;0.2021-i 0.4598 ;0.0090       ;-0.2323
 0.2089-i 0.2546;-0.011- i 0.3291;0.4472       ;-0.3113
```

$$X^T = \{ \alpha , q , u , \theta , \beta , p , r , \phi \} ;$$

ACHIEVED CLOSED-LOOP EIGENVALUES FOR THE DAMAGED AIRCRAFT
WITH THE REDESIGN OF THE FEEDBACK STRUCTURE

```
-1.1510 ± i 2.8598    (Short Period)
-0.0003 ± i 0.0870    (Phugoid)
-0.0700 ± i 1.6859    (Dutch Roll)
-1.0000               (Rolling)
-0.0080               (Spiral)
```

TABLE IX

COMPARISON BETWEEN THE NORMALIZED MAGNITUDES OF THE
ACHIEVED EIGENVECTORS AND THE SELECTED EIGENVECTORS

(ACHIEVED EIGENVECTORS)

(Short Period)		(Phugoid)		(Dutch Roll)		(Rolling)	(Spiral)
1.0000	1.0000	0.0036	0.0036	0.0000	0.0000	0.0000	0.0000
0.4740	0.4740	0.0002	0.0002	0.0000	0.0000	0.0000	0.0000
0.0160	0.0160	1.0000	1.0000	0.0000	0.0000	0.0000	0.0000
0.1538	0.1538	0.0028	0.0028	0.0000	0.0000	0.0000	0.0000
0.0000	0.0000	0.0000	0.0000	0.5248	0.5248	0.0180	1.0000
0.0000	0.0000	0.0000	0.0000	1.0000	1.0000	1.0000	0.0008
0.0000	0.0000	0.0000	0.0000	0.9040	0.9040	0.0202	0.0777
0.0000	0.0000	0.0000	0.0000	0.5926	0.5926	1.0000	0.1042

(DESIRED EIGENVECTORS)

(Short Period)		(Phugoid)		(Dutch Roll)		(Rolling)	(Spiral)
1.0000	1.0000	0.0000	0.0000	0.0000	0.0000	0.0000	0.0000
0.8000	0.8000	0.2000	0.2000	0.0000	0.0000	0.0000	0.0000
0.0000	0.0000	1.0000	1.0000	0.0000	0.0000	0.0000	0.0000
0.8000	0.8000	0.2000	0.2000	0.0000	0.0000	0.0000	0.0000
0.0000	0.0000	0.0000	0.0000	1.0000	1.0000	0.0000	0.0000
0.0000	0.0000	0.0000	0.0000	1.0000	1.0000	1.0000	0.0000
0.0000	0.0000	0.0000	0.0000	1.0000	1.0000	0.0000	1.0000
0.0000	0.0000	0.0000	0.0000	1.0000	1.0000	1.0000	0.0000

$$X^T = \{ \alpha , q , u , \theta , \beta , p , r , \phi \} ;$$

$$W_i^{*T} = \Omega_{Di}^{*T} Q_i L_i \{L_i^{*T}[Q_i + \sum_{j=1}^{k} (v_j^* \alpha_j v_j)] L_i\}^{-1} \qquad (63)$$

where v_j = desired directional orthogonal to Ω_{ai}, if any.

α_j = scalar weighting;

$*$ denotes conjugate transpose.

The second terms of the right side of Eqs. (62-63) reflect the condition to have the achieved eigenvector orthogonal to some direction v_j. Such further shaping of the eigenvectors' structure has been considered unnecessary in an emergency situation such as battle damage and/or generic failure in a control surface.

A particular Eignestructure Assignment technique for the redesign of the feedback gains for a damaged aircraft has been introduced. This is the last step of the overall reconfiguration process shown in Fig. 1. There are some problems that can eventually arise with this approach when eigenstructure assignment is coupled with state estimation in the case when not all the states are available for feedback. Particularly, the effect of the state estimation on the transient response due to pilot input is of some concern. It was shown that the closed-loop system transient response due to pilot input is independent of the state estimator dynamics [54]. However, the estimator gains and also the states to be measured should be selected such that they do not generate unstable eigenvalues of the controller dynamics.

VI. CONCLUSIONS AND RECOMMENDATIONS

In this chapter original approaches for all phases of the overall flight control reconfiguration problem shown in Figure 1 have been introduced. First, in Section II, the implementation of a Neural network for Failure Detection and Identification has been suggested. In Section III, a Multiple Modal Kalman Filtering technique has been proposed for the correct determination of the mathematical model of the damaged aircraft, provided that a F.D.I. has been successfully accomplished. Next, in Section IV, a very simple algorithm has been proposed for the calculation of the deflection for the other control surfaces to compensate for the damage. Finally, in Section V, an eigenstructure assignment technique has been proposed for the recalculation of the feedback gains of the flight control system with the goal of restoring desirable, or at least acceptable, handling qualities and to remove the unavoidable damage-induced coupling between the longitudinal and the lateral-directional dynamics.

All these techniques are relatively simple and very suitable for software implementation in the flight control computer. Some reservations do exist because of the required computational power and speed for the Multiple Model Kalman Filtering approach especially for high values of the number of model N (N > 8-10). However, it is reasonable to expect that this potential problem will be solved with the introduction of more and more powerful flight computers, as it has been the trend in recent years.

All these techniques require further investigation. The full integration between these techniques and, more importantly, the integration of these techniques with the preexisting control laws of the Control Configured Vehicle (C.C.V.) functions of the flight control system have yet to be evaluated. However, the relative simplicity and the efficiency of the algorithms may be the key factors for a successful practical implementation of these approaches in a software designed to be an extremely valuable aid for the pilot in the crucial task of maintaining optimum aircraft control after damage occurs.

VII. REFERENCES

1 - Napolitano, M.R., "*A New Approach to the Flight Control System Reconfiguration Following a Battle Damage and/or a Generic Failure on a Control Surface*", Ph.D. Thesis, School of Mechanical and Aerospace Engineering, Oklahoma State University, December 1989.

2 - Napolitano, M.R., Swaim, R.L. and Goodner, C.E. (1989) "An Aircraft Flight Control Reconfiguration Algorithm", 1989 *NAECON-IEEE Conference*, Dayton, OH. (1989)

3 - Napolitano, M.R., Swaim, R. L., "New Technique for Aircraft Flight Control Reconfiguration", *AIAA Journal of Guidance, Navigation and Control*, Vol. 14, Number 1, pp. 184-190 (1991)

4 - Napolitano, M.R., Swaim, R.L., "Redesign of the Feedback Structure Following a Battle Damage and/or a Failure on a Control Surface by Eigenstructure Assignment", *Proceedings of the AIAA Guidance, Navigation and Control Conference*, AIAA Paper 91-2626, New Orleans, LA (1991)

5 - Napolitano, M.R., Chen, C.I., "Application of a Neural Network for Failure Detection and identification in Reconfigurable Flight Control Systems", submitted for review to the *AIAA Journal of Guidance, Navigation and Control*, December 1991

6 - Kerr, T., "Real-Time Failure Detection: A Non-Linear Optimization Problem That Yields a Two-Ellipsoid Overlap Test", *Journal of Optimization Theory and Applications*, Vol. 22, No.4, pp.509-535 (1977)

7 - Kerr, T., "Failure Detection Aids for Human Operator Decisions in a Precision Inertial Navigation System Complex", *Proceedings of the Symposium on Applications of Decision Theory to Problems of Diagnosis and Repair*, Fairborn, OH, pp.98-127 (1976)

8 - Kerr, T., "Statistical Analysis of a Two Ellipsoid Overlap Test for Real-Time Failure Detection", *IEEE Transactions on Automatic Control*, Vol. AC-25, No.4, pp.762-773 (1980)

9 - Kerr, T., "False Alarm and Correct Detection Probabilities Over a Time Interval for Restricted Classes of Failure Detection Algorithms",

IEEE Transactions on Information Theory, Vol. IT-20, No.4, pp.619-631, July 1982 10 - Willsky, A.S., "A Survey of Several Failure Detection Methods", *Automatica*, pp. 601-611 (1976).

11 - Willsky, A.S., Jones, H.L., "A Generalized Likelihood Ratio Approach to the Detection and Estimation of Jumps in Linear Systems", *IEEE Transactions on Automatic Control*, Vol. AC-21, pp.108-112 (1976)

12 - Willsky, A.S., "Failure Detection in Dynamic Systems", *Agard LS*-109, Neuilly sur Seine, FRANCE, (1980)

13 - Handelman, D.A., Stengel, R.F., "A Theory for Fault Tolerant Flight Control Combining Expert System and Analytical Redundancy Concepts", *Proceedings of the Guidance and Control Conference*, AIAA Paper 86-2092, Williamsburg, VA (1986)

14 - Montoya, R., Howeel, W., Bundick, W., Ostroff, A., Hueschen, R., Belcastro, C., "Restructurable Controls", *NASA CP*-2277, Hampton, VA, (1982).

15 - Friedland, B., "Maximum Likelihood Failure Detection of Aircraft Flight Control Sensors", *AIAA Journal of Guidance, Control and Dynamics*, Vol. 5, No.5, (1982)

16 - Chow, E., Willsky, A., "Analytical Redundancy and the Design of Robust Failure Detection Systems", *IEEE Transactions on Automatic Control*, Vol. AC-29, No. 7, (1984)

17 - "Fault Tolerance Design and Redundancy Management Technique" (Multiple Authors), *AGARD-LS*-109, Neuilly sur Seine, FRANCE, (1980)

18 - Massoumnia, M.A., Verghese, G.C., Willsky, A.S., "Failure Detection and Identification", *IEEE Transactions on Automatic Control*, Vol. AC-34, No. 3, (1989)

19 - Widrow, B., Stearns, S. "*Adaptive Signal Processing*", MIT Press, Cambridge, Ma, (1986)

20 - Rumelhart, D., McClelland, J. "*Parallel Distributed Processing*", MIT Press, Cambridge, Ma, (1986)

21 - Simpson, P.K. "*Artificial Neural Systems*", Pergamon Press Inc., Fairview Park, NY, (1990)

22 - Nielsen, R.B. "*Neurocomputing*", Addison-Wesley Pub. Co., Reading, Ma, (1990)

23 - Napolitano, M.R., Nutter R., Ching, I.C. "Numerical Investigation of the Application of a Neural Observer for State Estimation Purposes in the Active Control of Structural Vibrations for a Cantilevered Beam", accepted for publication in the *IOP International Journal on Smart Materials and Structures*, First issue : March 1992.

24 - Napolitano, M.R., Nutter R., Ching, I.C. "Application of a Neural Network to the Active Control of Structural Vibrations", *Proceedings of the ACTIVE MATERIALS AND ADAPTIVE STRUCTURES CONFERENCE*, Arlington, Va, (1991)

25 - Ogata,K. "Discrete-Time Control Systems", Prentice-Hall Inc., Englewood Cliffs, NJ, (1987)

26 - Parlos, A.G., Atiya, A.F., Sunkel, J.W., "Parameter Estimation in Space Systems Using Recurrent Neural Networks", *Proceedings of the AIAA Guidance, Navigation and Control Conference*, AIAA Paper 91-2716, New Orleans, LA, (1991)

27 - Lam, Q.M., Foster, L., "Parameter Estimation Using an Optimized Learning Network", *Proceedings of the AIAA Guidance, Navigation and Control Conference*, AIAA Paper 91-2774, New Orleans, LA, (1991)

28 - Lam, Q.M., Chipman, R., Sunkel, J., "Mass Property Identification : A Comparison Study Between Extended Kalman Filter and Neuro-Filter Approaches", *Proceedings of the AIAA Guidance, Navigation and Control Conference*, AIAA Paper 91-2664, New Orleans, LA, (1991)

29 - Aldridge, J., "Terminology and Concepts of Control and Fuzzy Logic", *Proceedings of the AIAA Guidance, Navigation and Control Conference*, AIAA Paper 91-2798, New Orleans, LA, (1991)

30 - Baker, W.L., Farrell, J.A., "Learning Augmented Flight Control for High Performance Aircraft", *Proceedings of the AIAA Guidance, Navigation and Control Conference*, AIAA Paper 91-2836, New Orleans, LA, (1991)

31 - Troudet, T., Garg, S., Merrill, W.C., "Neural Network Application to Aircraft Control System Design", *Proceedings of the AIAA Guidance, Navigation and Control Conference*, AIAA Paper 91-2715, New Orleans, LA, (1991)

32 - Ha, C.M., "Neural Network Approach to AIAA Aircraft Control

Design Challenge", *Proceedings of the AIAA Guidance, Navigation and Control Conference*, AIAA Paper 91-2672, New Orleans, LA, (1991)

33 - "Artificial Neural Network Approaches in Guidance and Control" (Multiple Authors), *AGARD-LS-179*, Neuilly sur Seine, FRANCE, (1991)

34 - Roskam, J., *"Flight Dynamics of Rigid and Elastic Airplanes - Part I"*, Roskam Aviation and Engineering Corporation, (1982)

35 - Hoak, D.E., Ellison, D.E. et al, *"USAF Stability and Control Datcom"*, Flight Control Division, Air Force Flight Dynamics Laboratory, Wright-Patterson Air Force Base, OH, (1960)

36 - Roskam, J., *"Methods for Estimating Stability and Control Derivatives of Conventional Subsonic Airplanes"*, Roskam Aviation and Engineering Corporation, (1973)

37 - Athans, M. et al, "The Stochastic Control of the F-8C Aircraft Using a Multiple Model Adaptive Control (MMAC) Method - Part I : Equilibrium Flight", *IEEE Transactions on Automatic Control*, Vol. AC-22, No. 5, pp. 767-780, (1977)

38 - Newland, D.E. *"Random Vibrations and Spectral Analysis"*, Longman Group, (1984)

39 - Robinson, A.C., "Totally Robust Control - A New Concept for Design of Flight Control Systems", *Proceedings of the AIAA Guidance and Control Conference*, AIAA Paper 85-1974, Snowmass, CO, (1985)

40 - J. J. D'Azzo, and R. A. Eslinger, "Multivariable Control Law Design for the AFTI/F-16 with a Failed Control Surface," *Proceedings of the National Aerospace and Electronics Conference*, IEEE, New York, pp. 453-456, (1985)

41 - J. S. Eterno, and J. L. Weiss, "Reconfigurable Multivariable Control Law for a Commercial Airplane Using a Direct Digital Output Feedback Design," NASA-TM-85759, (1985)

42 - M. T. Hagan, and C. E. Goodner, "Aircraft Model-Follower Design; Phase V," School of Electrical and Computer Engineering, Oklahoma State Univ., Stillwater, OK (prepared for Boeing Military Airplane Co., Wichita, KS), (1988)

43 - I. Horowitz, P. B. Arnold, and C. H. Houpis, "YF-16 - CCV Flight Control System Reconfiguration Design Using Quantitative Feedback

Theory," *Proceedings of the National Aerospace and Electronics Conference*, IEEE, New York, pp. 578-585, (1985)

44 - D. P. Looze, J. L. Weiss, J. S. Eterno, and N. M. Barrett, "An Automatic Redesign Approach for Restructurable Control Systems," *Proceedings of the National Aerospace and Electronics Conference*, IEEE, New York, pp. 570-576, (1985)

45 - R. C. Montgomery, and A. K. Caglayan, "Failure Accommodation in Digital Flight Control Systems by Bayesian Decision Theory," *Journal of Aircraft*, Vol. 13, No. 2, pp. 69-75, (1976)

46 - R. S. Rattan, "Evaluation of a Control Mixer Concept for Reconfiguration of Flight Control System," *Proceeding of the National Aerospace and Electronics Conference,* IEEE , New York, pp. 560-569, (1985)

47 - S. J. Raza, and J. T. Silverthorn, "Use of the Pseudo-Inverse for Design of a Reconfigurable Flight Control System," *Proceedings of the AIAA Guidance, Navigation and Control Conference*, AIAA Paper 85-1900, Snowmass, CO, (1985)

48 - J.L. Weiss, D. P. Looze, and J. S. Eterno, "Simulation Results of Automatic Restructurable Flight Control System Concept," *Proceedings of the AIAA Guidance, Navigation and Control Conference*, AIAA Paper 86-2032, Williamsburg, VA, (1986)

49 - "Multivariable Control Systems," Wright-Patterson AFB, OH, AFWAL TR-83-3093, (1983)

50 - "Reconfiguration Strategies for Aircraft with Flight Control System Subjected to Actuator Failure/Surface Damage," Wright-Patterson AFB, OH, AFWAL TR-86-3110, (1987)

51 - Moore, B.C., "On the Flexibility Offered by State Feedback in Multivariable Systems Beyond Closed Loop Eigenvalue Assignment", *IEEE Transactions on Automatic Control*, Vol. AC-21, (1976)

52 - Garrard, W. and Liebst, B., "Active Flutter Suppression Using Eigenspace and Linear Quadratic Design Techniques", AIAA Paper 83-2222, *Proceedings of the Guidance and Control Conference*, Gatlinburg, TN, (1983)

53 - Schmidt, D.K. and Foxgrover, J.A., "Multivariable Control

Synthesis Approaches to Meet Handling Qualities Objectives", AIAA Paper 84-1831, *Proceeding of the Guidance and Control Conference*, Seattle, WA, (1984)

54 - Schmidt, D.K. and Davidson, J.B., "Flight Control Law Synthesis for an Elastic Vehicle by Eigenspace Assignmant", AIAA Paper 85-1898, *Proceedings of the Guidance and Control Conference*, Snowmass, CO, (1985)

55 - Srinathkuar, S., "Eigenvalue/Eigenvector Assignment Using Output Feedback", *IEEE Transactions on Automatic Control*, Vol. AC-23, No. 1, (1978)

56 - Cunningham, T.B., "Eigenspace Selection Procedures for Closed Loop Response Shaping with Modal Control", *Proceedings of the IEEE Conference on Decision and Control*, Albuquerque, NM, (1980)

Robust Approximate Optimal Guidance Strategies for Aeroassisted Plane Change Missions: A Game Theoretic Approach

Marc R. Ilgen
The Aerospace Corporation
El Segundo, California
Jason L. Speyer
School of Engineering and Applied Science
University of California
Los Angeles, California
Cornelius T. Leondes
Department of Electrical Engineering
University of Washington
Seattle, Washington

I. Introduction

The design of explicit, optimal or near optimal guidance laws for aerospace vehicles remains a challenging task. Since the vehicle equations of motion are nonlinear for most situations of practical interest, the optimization process generally results in a nonlinear two point boundary value problem that has thus far defied analytical solution for all but the simplest of cases and has proven to be difficult (and time consuming) to solve even numerically. The additional requirement that the guidance law must be robust to system uncertainties complicates the solution process even further. The computational complexity of the exact optimal solution coupled with the limitations of present day computing capability makes the real time computation of this solution to be thus far an unrealized dream.

The complexity of the optimal formulation has led to the development of a number of approximation techniques that seek to obtain analytical or semianalytical solutions while retaining as many properties of the optimal solution as possible. Of these techniques, the regular perturbation technique shows particular promise. Past studies have shown the usefulness of this technique in Linear Quadratic (LQ) problems [1][2][3][4], while more recent work has extended the technique to nonlinear problems using both the calculus of variations approach [5][6] and the Hamilton-Jacobi-Bellman approach [7][8]. The particular problems studied included launch vehicle guidance and aeroassisted plane change guidance. Unfortunately, the issue of robustness to parameter uncertainties was not addressed by these studies.

In [9] stochastic optimal control methods were used to address robustness with respect to atmospheric density for the aeroassisted plane change problem. This work was based on a regular perturbation series expansion of the stochastic Hamilton-Jacobi-Bellman equation, and the resulting guidance law minimized the expected value of the specified cost function. However, a more useful solution for many guidance problems is the guidance law that minimizes a cost function in the presence of worst-case values of the system uncertainties. The use of such a guidance law guarantees a certain minimal level of vehicle performance rather than indicating what the average performance over a number of missions is likely to be. This formulation converts the optimization problem to a problem in the field of differential games [10].

The contribution of the present study is to extend the calculus of variations regular perturbation methodology to the solution of a class of differential game problems and to apply this methodology to the development of robust approximate optimal guidance laws for aeroassisted plane change missions. The class of differential game problems examined arises from the treatment of system parameter uncertainties as deterministic control variables controlled by Nature as an intelligent adversary. When the parameter uncertainties are introduced using the concept of ficticious internal feedback loops [11], the optimal solutions to the resulting formulation are sought from the class of solutions satisfying first and second order necessary conditions for a game theoretic saddle point [12]. The solution to the zeroth order problem (the problem resulting from setting a small parameter ϵ to zero in the equations of motion) is found analytically while first and higher order corrections are found from a set of numerical quadratures and the solution to a set of linear algebraic equations. The required calculations are quite modest in number and can easily be performed in real time.

The calculus of variations approach was chosen in favor of the Hamilton-Jacobi-Bellman approach since the latter approach was recently studied for a similar class of optimal control problems [7][8][9]. This choice can also be justified by the fact that, while both methods are ultimately equivalent, the calculus of variations approach is somewhat less awkward to implement and is more often used in the literature to solve problems of practical interest than is the Hamilton-Jacobi-Bellman approach.

The remainder of this chapter is divided into two major parts. Section II presents the derivation of the calculus-of-variations regular perturbation solution methodology applied to a class of differential game problems admitting saddle point solutions. A summary of the algorithms used to obtain solutions to any order in ϵ is presented at the end of the section. Finally, Section III applies this solution methodology to the aeroassisted plane change problem for a hypothetical vehicle and analyzes guidance law performance resulting from implementing zeroth order and first order corrected algorithms as feedback guidance laws.

II. Regular Perturbations in Differential Games

A. Problem Statement

The equations of motion for a class of differential game problems that can be solved using regularly perturbation methodology can be written in the form

$$\dot{x} = f(x, u, w) + \epsilon g(x) \tag{1}$$
$$x(t = 0) = a \tag{2}$$

Here x is the state, u and w are the control vectors of Players 1 and 2, and t is the independent variable. The independent variable in most dynamic optimization problems is time, although for some problems it becomes convenient to use a different independent variable. The actual independent variable used in a particular problem has no bearing on the applicability of the solution methods to be presented, so for purposes of simplicity, the independent variable will henceforth be referred to as time. The functions f and g are continuous and at least twice differentiable in $\Re^n$. The function f is a function of the controls u and w as well as the state x, while g is a function only of the state x. Finally, f is assumed separable in u and w.

The boundary conditions on the state x are given at time $t = 0$. The final time T is free and is determined by the satisfaction of a set of terminal constraints, as discussed below. Denote the current time by t_i, where t_i is in the range $0 \le t_i \le T$. The guidance law operates closed loop by regularly recalculating the optimal controls from the current state and time to the final state and time. Therefore, for the very first guidance law calculation cycle, the boundary conditions $x(t = 0) = a$ are used. For all subsequent guidance law calculation cycles along the trajectory, the current value for the state $x(t_i)$ at the current time t_i is used in place of the boundary conditions (2). Since the right hand side of (1) does not depend explicitly on the time, a shifted time $\bar{t}$ and shifted final time $\bar{T}$ can be defined by

$$\bar{t} = t - t_i \tag{3}$$
$$\bar{T} = T - t_i \tag{4}$$

At each guidance law calculation cycle, the optimization problem is then solved from the current time $\bar{t} = 0$ to the final time $\bar{t} = \bar{T}$. In other words, the boundary conditions for the optimization problem are always the current values for the state, and the current value of the independent variable in the optimization problem can always be set to zero without loss of generality. Denoting the current value for the state by α, the boundary conditions on x can be written explicitly as

$$x(\bar{t} = 0) = \alpha \tag{5}$$

For purposes of notational simplicity, we drop the overbar on the independent variable and final time in all subsequent analysis and simply denote these by t and T respectively.

The performance of the guidance law is measured by the cost function J defined as

$$J = \int_0^T L(u, w)dt + \Phi(x(T)) \tag{6}$$

where $L(u, w)$ is a separable function of u and w chosen to penalize large values of either control. While L can in general be a function of x as well as u and w, the dependence of L on x complicates the process of obtaining an analytical zeroth order solution to the perturbation equations derived in the following section. In this study it is therefore assumed that L depends only on the controls u and w.

The objective of the optimization problem is to determine the controls u and w that yield the saddle point for the problem

$$J_{opt} = \min_{u \in \mathcal{U}} \max_{w \in \mathcal{W}} J \tag{7}$$

subject to the terminal constraints

$$\Psi(x(T)) = 0 \tag{8}$$

Here $\mathcal{U}$ and $\mathcal{W}$ are the allowable control sets for the control vectors u and w. Since u and w are sought in the class of feedback strategies, the sets $\mathcal{U}$ and $\mathcal{W}$ contain bounded measureable functions of the state vector.

In the calculus-of-variations approach to determining the solution, Lagrange multipliers $p(t)$ and ν are used to append the system dynamics (1) and the terminal constraints (8) to the cost function (6) resulting in

$$J = \int_0^T L(u, w) + p^T(f + \epsilon g - \dot{x})dt + \Phi(x(T)) + \nu^T \Psi(x(T)) \tag{9}$$

Variations of J can then be taken to yield

$$\begin{aligned}
\delta J = &\int_0^T \left[\left(\dot{p}^T + \frac{\partial \mathcal{H}}{\partial x} \right) \delta x + \mathcal{H}_u \delta u + \mathcal{H}_w \delta w \right] dt + \\
&\left(\Phi_x(x(T)) + \nu^T \Psi_x(x(T)) - p^T(T) \right) \delta x(T) + \Psi^T(x(T))\delta\nu + \\
&\mathcal{H}(x(T), u(T), w(T), p(T))\delta T + \mathcal{O}(2)
\end{aligned} \tag{10}$$

where the Hamiltonian function $\mathcal{H}$ is defined as

$$\mathcal{H} = L(u, w) + p^T(f + \epsilon g) \tag{11}$$

and $\mathcal{O}(2)$ refers to terms of order 2 or higher. The necessary conditions for control vectors u^* and w^* to yield a saddle point are found by requiring δJ to vanish, yielding

$$\dot{p} = -\left(\frac{\partial \mathcal{H}}{\partial x}\right)^T \tag{12}$$

$$\frac{\partial \mathcal{H}}{\partial u} = 0 \tag{13}$$

$$\frac{\partial \mathcal{H}}{\partial w} = 0 \tag{14}$$

$$p(T) = \left(\Phi_x(x(T)) + \nu^T \Psi_x(x(T))\right)^T \tag{15}$$

$$\Psi(x(T)) = 0 \tag{16}$$

$$\mathcal{H}(x(T), u(T), w(T), p(T)) = 0 \tag{17}$$

If the controls u and w are subject to constraints of the form

$$c(u) \leq 0 \tag{18}$$

$$d(w) \leq 0 \tag{19}$$

and some number n_u (n_w) of the constraints on u (w) are currently active, then the necessary conditions (12), (15)-(17) are unchanged and the necessary conditions (13)-(14) become

$$\mathcal{H}(x, u^*, w, p) = \min_{u \in \mathcal{U}} \mathcal{H}(x, u, w, p) \tag{20}$$

$$\mathcal{H}(x, u, w^*, p) = \max_{w \in \mathcal{W}} \mathcal{H}(x, u, w, p) \tag{21}$$

In order to clarify the subsequent analysis, the strong local optimal conditions (20) and (21) are replaced by the weak local optimal conditions

$$\frac{\partial \mathcal{H}}{\partial u} + \lambda^T \frac{\partial c}{\partial u} = 0 \tag{22}$$

$$\frac{\partial \mathcal{H}}{\partial w} + \sigma^T \frac{\partial d}{\partial w} = 0 \tag{23}$$

where λ and σ are additional Lagrange multiplier vectors of length n_u and n_w determined from the set of equations (18)-(23).

While the necessary conditions (12)-(23) appear to be straightforward extensions of the necessary conditions for one sided optimal control problems, it is important to note that the controls u^* and w^* found from (22) and (23) must satisfy additional conditions in order to qualify as saddle point control functions. The first condition is that the min and max operations implied by (22) and (23) must be interchangeable. In other words

$$\min_{u \in \mathcal{U}} \max_{w \in \mathcal{W}} \mathcal{H}(x, u, w, p) = \max_{w \in \mathcal{W}} \min_{u \in \mathcal{U}} \mathcal{H}(x, u, w, p) \qquad (24)$$

Since $\mathcal{H}$ is assumed to be separable in u and w, this condition is satisfied automatically. A more stringent condition is that the controls u^* and w^* must satisfy the saddle point inequality

$$J(u^*, w) \le J(u^*, w^*) \le J(u, w^*) \qquad (25)$$

In other words, u^* and w^* must actually minimax the cost function. If the condition (25) is satisfied, then $J(u^*, w^*)$ can be evaluated from (6) and the game is said to have value. The value function $V(x, t)$ is then defined as the value of the cost function J evaluated from an arbitrary point x along the optimal trajectory x^*. Under the assumption that the value function $V(x, t)$ exists and is continuously differentiable, the existence of controls that satisfy (24) and allow the game to terminate in finite time also implies that (25) is satisfied, i.e. that these controls form a saddle point solution [10]. Unfortunately, in many game problems a continuously differentiable value function does not exist, and straightforward application of the necessary conditions for optimality yields control functions that do not satisfy (25). Furthermore, it is extremely difficult to determine a priori whether or not a continuously differentiable $V(x, t)$ exists for all but the simplest of game problems (such as LQ problems).

   In the present study, these difficulties are circumvented by assuming a priori that a value function exists for the particular differential game problem to be solved. This assumption should be satisfied for game problems in which one player's control has a much greater effect on the dynamics than the other player's control does, as is generally the case for game problems resulting from the robust reformulation of one sided optimal control problems. While it is still somewhat mathematically unsatisfying to assume away many of the difficulties encountered in proving the existence of a game theoretic saddle point, it should be noted that most successful applications of differential game theoretic methods to general nonlinear problems have proceeded under precisely the same assumptions[10][12].

B. Regular Perturbation Solution Methodology

   For a general nonlinear system, the task of determining the optimal controls u^* and w^* exactly is quite formidable since it requires the solution of a nonlinear two point boundary value problem. Many numerical methods (nonlinear programming with collocation [13], multiple shooting [14], quasilinearization [15], differential dynamic programming [16], etc.) can be utilized to solve for optimal trajectories, but these methods are often too computationally intensive and time consuming to be implemented in real time using present day flight computer architectures. For systems of the form (1), the method of regular perturbations can often be used successfully to determine these controls approximately. The equations to be solved are expanded in a power series in the small parameter ϵ, and an approximate (zeroth order) solution is obtained by solving the equations for $\epsilon = 0$. The key to this method is that the zeroth order problem can be solved in closed form. The parameter ϵ is then reintroduced into the set of equations, and terms of like powers of ϵ are equated to yield a set of differential equations to be solved for each higher order correction term. The homogeneous part of the linear differential equations are related only to the zeroth order solution for all the correction terms. The equations for correction terms of order k are driven by terms of order $k - 1$ or lower but are also linear in terms of order k. The advantage of this method lies in the fact that sets of inhomogeneous linear differential equations are usually much easier to solve than a single set of nonlinear differential equations. In fact, it will be shown that the solution to these equations can be obtained through quadrature integration.

1. Derivation of State and Costate Equations

For the systems considered in this study, the method of regular perturbations procedes formally as follows. The state vector x, the control vectors u and w, and the costate vector p are expanded in powers of ϵ as

$$x = x_0 + \epsilon x_1 + \epsilon^2 x_2 + ... \tag{26}$$

$$u = u_0 + \epsilon u_1 + \epsilon^2 u_2 + ... \tag{27}$$

$$w = w_0 + \epsilon w_1 + \epsilon^2 w_2 + ... \tag{28}$$

$$p = p_0 + \epsilon p_1 + \epsilon^2 p_2 + ... \tag{29}$$

Assume that the functions f, g, and L can all be expanded in power series in x, u, and w as follows:

$$
\begin{aligned}
f(x, u, w) = {} & \bar{f} + \bar{f}_x(x - x_0) + \bar{f}_u(u - u_0) + \bar{f}_w(w - w_0) + \\
& \frac{1}{2}(x - x_0)^T \bar{f}_{xx}(x - x_0) + (x - x_0)^T \bar{f}_{xu}(u - u_0) + \\
& (x - x_0)^T \bar{f}_{xw}(w - w_0) + \frac{1}{2}(u - u_0)^T \bar{f}_{uu}(u - u_0) + \\
& \frac{1}{2}(w - w_0)^T \bar{f}_{ww}(w - w_0) + ...
\end{aligned}
\tag{30}
$$

$$g(x) = \bar{g} + \bar{g}_x(x - x_0) + \frac{1}{2}(x - x_0)^T \bar{g}_{xx}(x - x_0) + ... \tag{31}$$

$$L(u, w) = \bar{L} + \bar{L}_u(u - u_0) + \bar{L}_w(w - w_0) + \frac{1}{2}(u - u_0)^T \bar{L}_{uu}(u - u_0) +$$

$$\frac{1}{2}(w - w_0)^T \bar{L}_{ww}(w - w_0) + ... \qquad (32)$$

where the bar over f, g, and L signifies that the function is evaluated at $x = x_0$, $u = u_0$, and $w = w_0$. Note that the derivative functions $\bar{f}_{xx}$, $\bar{f}_{xu}$, $\bar{g}_{xx}$, etc. are actually tensors, even though formal tensor notation is not used here. The proper method for evaluating the terms involving these tensors becomes self evident when the evaluation is attempted. As an example, the term $(x - x_0)^T \bar{f}_{xu}(u - u_0)$ is a vector γ of dimension n (the number of states) where each component γ_i, $1 \le i \le n$ is given by

$$\gamma_i = \sum_{j=1}^{n} \sum_{k=1}^{m} \frac{\partial^2 f_i}{\partial x_j \partial u_k}(x_j - x_{0j})(u_k - u_{0k}) \qquad (33)$$

Here m and n are the dimensions of the control and state vectors, the subscripts k and j refer to components of these vectors, and the partial derivative is evaluated at $x = x_0$ and $u = u_0$.

Since the Hamiltonian $\mathcal{H}$ depends on the functions L, f, g as well as on the Lagrange multiplier function p, $\mathcal{H}$ can also be expanded as:

$$\mathcal{H}(x, u, w, p) = \bar{L} + \bar{L}_u(u - u_0) + \frac{1}{2}(u - u_0)^T \bar{L}_{uu}(u - u_0) +$$

$$\bar{L}_w(w - w_0) + \frac{1}{2}(w - w_0)^T \bar{L}_{ww}(w - w_0) +$$

$$\left[(p_0 + \epsilon p_1 + \epsilon^2 p_2 + ...)^T \cdot \right.$$

$$\left(\bar{f} + \bar{f}_x(x - x_0) + \bar{f}_u(u - u_0) + \bar{f}_w(w - w_0) + \right.$$

$$\frac{1}{2}(x - x_0)^T \bar{f}_{xx}(x - x_0) + (x - x_0)^T \bar{f}_{xu}(u - u_0) +$$

$$(x - x_0)^T \bar{f}_{xw}(w - w_0) + \frac{1}{2}(u - u_0)^T \bar{f}_{uu}(u - u_0) +$$

$$\frac{1}{2}(w - w_0)^T \bar{f}_{ww}(w - w_0) + ... + \epsilon \bar{g} +$$

$$\left. \epsilon \bar{g}_x(x - x_0) + \epsilon \frac{1}{2}(x - x_0)^T \bar{g}_{xx}(x - x_0) + ... \right) \right] \qquad (34)$$

Substituting the expressions (26)-(29) into (30)-(32) and grouping like powers of ϵ yields

$$f(x, u, w) = \bar{f} + \epsilon \left(\bar{f}_x x_1 + \bar{f}_u u_1 + \bar{f}_w w_1 \right) +$$

$$\epsilon^2 \left(\bar{f}_x x_2 + \bar{f}_u u_2 + \bar{f}_w w_2 + \frac{1}{2} x_1^T \bar{f}_{xx} x_1 + x_1^T \bar{f}_{xu} u_1 + \right.$$

$$x_1^T \bar{f}_{xw} w_1 + \frac{1}{2} u_1^T \bar{f}_{uu} u_1 + \frac{1}{2} w_1^T \bar{f}_{ww} w_1 \Big) + ... \tag{35}$$

$$g(x) = \bar{g} + \epsilon \bar{g}_x x_1 + \epsilon^2 \left(\bar{g}_x x_2 + \frac{1}{2} x_1^T \bar{g}_{xx} x_1 \right) + ... \tag{36}$$

$$L(u,w) = \bar{L} + \epsilon \left(\bar{L}_u u_1 + \bar{L}_w w_1 \right) + \epsilon^2 \Big(\bar{L}_u u_2 + \bar{L}_w w_2 +$$
$$\frac{1}{2} u_1^T \bar{L}_{uu} u_1 + \frac{1}{2} w_1^T \bar{L}_{ww} w_1 \Big) + ... \tag{37}$$

It is evident that the functions f, g, and L can be expressed in a power series in ϵ such that

$$f = f_0 + \epsilon f_1 + \epsilon^2 f_2 + ... \tag{38}$$
$$g = g_0 + \epsilon g_1 + \epsilon^2 g_2 + ... \tag{39}$$
$$L = L_0 + \epsilon L_1 + \epsilon^2 L_2 + ... \tag{40}$$

where

$$f_0 = \bar{f} \tag{41}$$
$$f_1 = \bar{f}_x x_1 + \bar{f}_u u_1 + \bar{f}_w w_1 \tag{42}$$
$$f_2 = \bar{f}_x x_2 + \bar{f}_u u_2 + \bar{f}_w w_2 + \frac{1}{2} x_1^T \bar{f}_{xx} x_1 +$$
$$x_1^T \bar{f}_{xu} u_1 + x_1^T \bar{f}_{xw} w_1 + \frac{1}{2} u_1^T \bar{f}_{uu} u_1 + \frac{1}{2} w_1^T \bar{f}_{ww} w_1 \tag{43}$$
$$g_0 = \bar{g} \tag{44}$$
$$g_1 = \bar{g}_x x_1 \tag{45}$$
$$g_2 = \bar{g}_x x_2 + \frac{1}{2} x_1^T \bar{g}_{xx} x_1 \tag{46}$$
$$L_0 = \bar{L} \tag{47}$$
$$L_1 = \bar{L}_u u_1 + \bar{L}_w w_1 \tag{48}$$
$$L_2 = \bar{L}_u u_2 + \bar{L}_w w_2 + \frac{1}{2} u_1^T \bar{L}_{uu} u_1 + \frac{1}{2} w_1^T \bar{L}_{ww} w_1 \tag{49}$$

The expansions for f and g can be used in the state equations to yield

$$\dot{x}_0 + \epsilon \dot{x}_1 + \epsilon^2 \dot{x}_2 + ... = f_0 + \epsilon (f_1 + g_0) + \epsilon^2 (f_2 + g_1) + ... \tag{50}$$

Equating powers of ϵ and substituting in the relations (41)-(46) yields the following system of state equations:

$$\dot{x}_0 = \bar{f} \tag{51}$$
$$\dot{x}_1 = \bar{f}_x x_1 + \bar{f}_u u_1 + \bar{f}_w w_1 + \bar{g} \tag{52}$$
$$\dot{x}_2 = \bar{f}_x x_2 + \bar{f}_u u_2 + \bar{f}_w w_2 + \bar{g}_x x_1 +$$

$$\frac{1}{2}x_1^T \bar{f}_{xx} x_1 + x_1^T \bar{f}_{xu} u_1 + x_1^T \bar{f}_{xw} w_1 +$$
$$\frac{1}{2}u_1^T \bar{f}_{uu} u_1 + \frac{1}{2}w_1^T \bar{f}_{ww} w_1 \tag{53}$$

$$\vdots$$

The boundary conditions can be taken as

$$x_0(0) = \alpha \tag{54}$$
$$x_i(0) = 0 \ \forall i \geq 1 \tag{55}$$

where expressions (5) and (26) have been used.

The expressions (38)-(49) can also be substituted into the expression (34) for the Hamiltonian, yielding

$$\begin{aligned}
\mathcal{H} =& \ \bar{\mathcal{H}} + \epsilon \left(\bar{\mathcal{H}}_x x_1 + \bar{\mathcal{H}}_u u_1 + \bar{\mathcal{H}}_w w_1 + f_0^T p_1 + p_0^T g_0 \right) + \\
& \epsilon^2 \left(\bar{\mathcal{H}}_x x_2 + \bar{\mathcal{H}}_u u_2 + \bar{\mathcal{H}}_w w_2 + f_0^T p_2 + f_1^T p_1 + p_1^T g_0 + \right. \\
& p_0^T g_1 + \frac{1}{2}x_1^T \bar{\mathcal{H}}_{xx} x_1 + x_1^T \bar{\mathcal{H}}_{xu} u_1 + x_1^T \bar{\mathcal{H}}_{xw} w_1 + \\
& \left. \frac{1}{2}u_1^T \bar{\mathcal{H}}_{uu} u_1 + \frac{1}{2}w_1^T \bar{\mathcal{H}}_{ww} w_1 \right)
\end{aligned} \tag{56}$$

where $\bar{\mathcal{H}}$ is the Hamiltonian evaluated at $\epsilon = 0$. Thus

$$\bar{\mathcal{H}} = L_0 + p_0^T f_0 \tag{57}$$

Again, f_i and g_i are given explicitly by (41)-(46). Taking the derivative of (56) with respect to x and substituting in the relationships (41)-(46) yields

$$\begin{aligned}
\mathcal{H}_x =& \ \bar{\mathcal{H}}_x + \epsilon \left(x_1^T \bar{\mathcal{H}}_{xx} + u_1^T \bar{\mathcal{H}}_{ux} + w_1^T \bar{\mathcal{H}}_{wx} + p_1^T \bar{f}_x + p_0^T \bar{g}_x \right) + \\
& \epsilon^2 \left[x_2^T \bar{\mathcal{H}}_{xx} + u_2^T \bar{\mathcal{H}}_{ux} + w_2^T \bar{\mathcal{H}}_{wx} + p_2^T \bar{f}_x + \right. \\
& p_1^T \left(\bar{f}_{xx} x_1 + \bar{f}_{xu} u_1 + \bar{f}_{xw} w_1 \right) + p_1^T \bar{g}_x + p_0^T \bar{g}_{xx} x_1 + \\
& \frac{1}{2}x_1^T \bar{\mathcal{H}}_{xxx} x_1 + x_1^T \bar{\mathcal{H}}_{xxu} u_1 + x_1^T \bar{\mathcal{H}}_{xxw} w_1 + \\
& \left. \frac{1}{2}u_1^T \bar{\mathcal{H}}_{uxu} u_1 + \frac{1}{2}w_1^T \bar{\mathcal{H}}_{wxw} w_1 \right]
\end{aligned} \tag{58}$$

Expression (58) can be used in the necessary condition (12) for the multiplier p. Equating like powers of ϵ yields

$$\dot{p}_0 = -\bar{\mathcal{H}}_x^T \tag{59}$$
$$\dot{p}_1 = - \left(\bar{\mathcal{H}}_{xx} x_1 + \bar{\mathcal{H}}_{xu} u_1 + \bar{\mathcal{H}}_{xw} w_1 + \bar{f}_x^T p_1 + \bar{g}_x^T p_0 \right) \tag{60}$$

$$
\dot{p}_2 = -\left[\bar{\mathcal{H}}_{xx}x_2 + \bar{\mathcal{H}}_{xu}u_2 + \bar{\mathcal{H}}_{xw}w_2 + \bar{f}_x^T p_2 + \right.
$$

$$
\left(x_1^T \bar{f}_{xx}^T + u_1^T \bar{f}_{xu}^T + w_1^T \bar{f}_{xw}^T\right) p_1 + \bar{g}_x^T p_1 + x_1^T \bar{g}_{xx}^T p_0 +
$$

$$
\left(\frac{1}{2}x_1^T \bar{\mathcal{H}}_{xxx}x_1 + x_1^T \bar{\mathcal{H}}_{xxu}u_1 + x_1^T \bar{\mathcal{H}}_{xxw}w_1 + \right.
$$

$$
\left.\left.\frac{1}{2}u_1^T \bar{\mathcal{H}}_{uxu}u_1 + \frac{1}{2}w_1^T \bar{\mathcal{H}}_{wxw}w_1\right)^T\right] \tag{61}
$$

$$\vdots$$

Expressions (51)-(53) and (59)-(61) represent coupled differential equations for determining the perturbation series approximation to the optimal state vector x^* and the optimal costate vector p^* in terms of the perturbation series coefficients for x^*, p^*, u^*, and w^*. In order to complete the solution, two further steps are required. First, relationships for u^* and w^* in terms of x^* and p^* must be found so that the expressions (51)-(53) and (59)-(61) can be written in terms of x^* and p^* only. Finally, the boundary conditions (15) for $p(T)$ depend on the unknown quantities ν and T, and the expressions (16)-(17) must be used to determine these quantities. Once these two steps are completed, the problem can be solved to each order in ϵ by solving a set of coupled differential equations with known boundary conditions. If an analytical solution for the zeroth order equations (which may be nonlinear) can be found, the solutions to higher orders in ϵ can be found by solving coupled sets of linear inhomogeneous differential equations with known boundary conditions. The solution for $x^*(t = 0)$ and $p^*(t = 0)$ up to any order in ϵ yields the perturbation series approximation to $u^*(t = 0)$ up to that order in ϵ. This is the quantity of real interest for guidance law purposes, since this is the amount of control the vehicle will apply at the current time.

The required relationships for u^* and w^* as functions of x^* and p^* can be easily found from the optimality conditions (13)-(14) or (18)-(23). To simplify the notation in the subsequent analysis, we drop the superscript "*" on the optimal control, state, and costate histories. The reader should note that all subsequent references to u, w, x, and p refer to the saddle point optimal values for these quantities. Furthermore, in order to keep the derivation as general as possible, assume that some subset of the constraints on u and w are indeed active along the zeroth order trajectory and that they remain active in the presence of small perturbations in x, p, u, and w. This assumption requires that the Lagrange multiplier vectors λ and σ be perturbed according to

$$
\lambda = \lambda_0 + \epsilon\lambda_1 + \epsilon^2\lambda_2 + \dots \tag{62}
$$

$$\sigma = \sigma_0 + \epsilon\sigma_1 + \epsilon^2\sigma_2 + ... \tag{63}$$

Using the expression (56) for the Hamiltonian and setting terms multiplying each power of ϵ to zero yields

$$\bar{\mathcal{H}}_u + \lambda_0^T \bar{c}_u = 0 \tag{64}$$

$$\bar{\mathcal{H}}_w + \sigma_0^T \bar{d}_w = 0 \tag{65}$$

$$\bar{\mathcal{H}}_{ux}x_1 + \bar{\mathcal{H}}_{uu}u_1 + \lambda_0\bar{c}_{uu}u_1 + \bar{c}_u^T\lambda_1 + \bar{f}_u^T p_1 = 0 \tag{66}$$

$$\bar{\mathcal{H}}_{wx}x_1 + \bar{\mathcal{H}}_{ww}w_1 + \sigma_0\bar{d}_{ww}w_1 + \bar{d}_w^T\sigma_1 + \bar{f}_w^T p_1 = 0 \tag{67}$$

$$\bar{\mathcal{H}}_{ux}x_2 + \bar{\mathcal{H}}_{uu}u_2 + \lambda_0\bar{c}_{uu}u_2 + \lambda_1\bar{c}_{uu}u_1 + \bar{c}_u^T\lambda_2 +$$

$$\bar{f}_u^T p_2 + (f_{ux}x_1 + f_{uu}u_1)^T p_1 + \frac{1}{2}x_1^T\bar{\mathcal{H}}_{xux}x_1 +$$

$$x_1^T\bar{\mathcal{H}}_{xuu}u_1 + \frac{1}{2}u_1^T\bar{\mathcal{H}}_{uuu}u_1 + \lambda_0\frac{1}{2}u_1^T\bar{c}_{uuu}u_1 = 0 \tag{68}$$

$$\bar{\mathcal{H}}_{wx}x_2 + \bar{\mathcal{H}}_{ww}w_2 + \sigma_0\bar{d}_{ww}w_2 + \sigma_1\bar{d}_{ww}w_1 + \bar{d}_w^T\sigma_2 +$$

$$\bar{f}_w^T p_2 + (f_{wx}x_1 + f_{ww}w_1)^T p_1 + \frac{1}{2}x_1^T\bar{\mathcal{H}}_{xwx}x_1 +$$

$$x_1^T\bar{\mathcal{H}}_{xww}w_1 + \frac{1}{2}w_1^T\bar{\mathcal{H}}_{www}w_1 + \sigma_0\frac{1}{2}w_1^T\bar{d}_{www}w_1 = 0 \tag{69}$$

For perturbations in u and w, the contraint relationships become

$$\bar{c} = 0 \tag{70}$$

$$\bar{d} = 0 \tag{71}$$

$$\bar{c}_u u_1 = 0 \tag{72}$$

$$\bar{d}_w w_1 = 0 \tag{73}$$

$$\bar{c}_u u_2 + \frac{1}{2}u_1^T c_{uu}u_1 = 0 \tag{74}$$

$$\bar{d}_w w_2 + \frac{1}{2}w_1^T d_{ww}w_1 = 0 \tag{75}$$

The zeroth order optimality relationships (64)-(65) and (70)-(71) can be used to obtain u_0 and w_0 as functions of x_0 and p_0. Assuming that these expressions can be solved explicitly for u_0 and w_0, the first order controls u_1 and w_1 and second order controls u_2 and w_2 can be determined from (66)-(67), (72)-(73), (68)-(69), and (74)-(75). The explicit expressions for u_1 and w_1 are derived below, and explicit expressions for the second order controls u_2 and w_2 are presented in [17]. Higher order control terms can be derived in a similiar manner, although the algebra required becomes quite tedious.

We now derive expressions first order controls u_1 and w_1. Assuming that $\bar{\mathcal{H}}_{uu} + \lambda_0 \bar{c}_{uu}$ and $\bar{\mathcal{H}}_{ww} + \sigma_0 \bar{d}_{ww}$ are nonsingular, the expressions (66) and (67) can be solved for u_1 and w_1 to yield

$$u_1 = -\left(\bar{\mathcal{H}}_{uu} + \lambda_0 \bar{c}_{uu}\right)^{-1} \left(\bar{c}_u^T \lambda_1 + \bar{\mathcal{H}}_{ux} x_1 + \bar{f}_u^T p_1\right) \tag{76}$$

$$w_1 = -\left(\bar{\mathcal{H}}_{ww} + \sigma_0 \bar{d}_{ww}\right)^{-1} \left(\bar{d}_w^T \sigma_1 + \bar{\mathcal{H}}_{wx} x_1 + \bar{f}_w^T p_1\right) \tag{77}$$

Multiplying both sides of (76) by $\bar{c}_u$ and both sides of (77) by $\bar{d}_w$ and using (72)-(73) yields

$$\lambda_1 = -\left[\bar{c}_u \left(\bar{\mathcal{H}}_{uu} + \lambda_0 \bar{c}_{uu}\right)^{-1} \bar{c}_u^T\right]^{-1} \bar{c}_u \left(\bar{\mathcal{H}}_{uu} + \lambda_0 \bar{c}_{uu}\right)^{-1} \cdot$$
$$\left(\bar{\mathcal{H}}_{ux} x_1 + \bar{f}_u^T p_1\right) \tag{78}$$

$$\sigma_1 = -\left[\bar{d}_w \left(\bar{\mathcal{H}}_{ww} + \sigma_0 \bar{d}_{ww}\right)^{-1} \bar{d}_w^T\right]^{-1} \bar{d}_w \left(\bar{\mathcal{H}}_{ww} + \sigma_0 \bar{d}_{ww}\right)^{-1} \cdot$$
$$\left(\bar{\mathcal{H}}_{wx} x_1 + \bar{f}_w^T p_1\right) \tag{79}$$

Finally, these expressions can be substituted into the expressions (76)-(77) to give

$$u_1 = -\left(\bar{\mathcal{H}}_{uu} + \lambda_0 \bar{c}_{uu}\right)^{-1} \left\{I_{n_u} - \bar{c}_u^T \left[\bar{c}_u \left(\bar{\mathcal{H}}_{uu} + \lambda_0 \bar{c}_{uu}\right)^{-1} \bar{c}_u^T\right]^{-1} \cdot \right.$$
$$\left. \bar{c}_u \left(\bar{\mathcal{H}}_{uu} + \lambda_0 \bar{c}_{uu}\right)^{-1}\right\} \left(\bar{\mathcal{H}}_{ux} x_1 + \bar{f}_u^T p_1\right) \tag{80}$$

$$w_1 = -\left(\bar{\mathcal{H}}_{ww} + \sigma_0 \bar{d}_{ww}\right)^{-1} \left\{I_{n_w} - \bar{d}_w^T \left[\bar{d}_w \left(\bar{\mathcal{H}}_{ww} + \sigma_0 \bar{d}_{ww}\right)^{-1} \bar{d}_w^T\right]^{-1} \cdot \right.$$
$$\left. \bar{d}_w \left(\bar{\mathcal{H}}_{ww} + \sigma_0 \bar{d}_{ww}\right)^{-1}\right\} \left(\bar{\mathcal{H}}_{wx} x_1 + \bar{f}_w^T p_1\right) \tag{81}$$

Here I_{n_u} and I_{n_w} are the identity matrices of rank n_u and n_w respectively. Now define the matrices β and η as

$$\beta = I_{n_u} - \bar{c}_u^T \left[\bar{c}_u \left(\bar{\mathcal{H}}_{uu} + \lambda_0 \bar{c}_{uu}\right)^{-1} \bar{c}_u^T\right]^{-1} \bar{c}_u \cdot$$
$$\left(\bar{\mathcal{H}}_{uu} + \lambda_0 \bar{c}_{uu}\right)^{-1} \tag{82}$$

$$\eta = I_{n_w} - \bar{d}_w^T \left[\bar{d}_w \left(\bar{\mathcal{H}}_{ww} + \sigma_0 \bar{d}_{ww}\right)^{-1} \bar{d}_w^T\right]^{-1} \bar{d}_w \cdot$$
$$\left(\bar{\mathcal{H}}_{ww} + \sigma_0 \bar{d}_{ww}\right)^{-1} \tag{83}$$

Then (80)-(81) can be written in compact form as

$$u_1 = -\left(\bar{\mathcal{H}}_{uu} + \lambda_0 \bar{c}_{uu}\right)^{-1} \beta \left(\bar{\mathcal{H}}_{ux} x_1 + \bar{f}_u^T p_1\right) \tag{84}$$

$$w_1 = -\left(\bar{\mathcal{H}}_{ww} + \sigma_0 \bar{d}_{ww}\right)^{-1} \eta \left(\bar{\mathcal{H}}_{wx} x_1 + \bar{f}_w^T p_1\right) \tag{85}$$

Expressions (84) and (85) are expressions for u_1 and w_1 in terms of x_1, p_1, and derivatives of the Hamiltonian evaluated along the zeroth order trajectory. These expressions can be substituted into expressions (52) and (60) to yield the following coupled set of differential equations

$$\dot{x}_1 = \bar{A}x_1 - \bar{B}p_1 + \bar{g} \tag{86}$$

$$\dot{p}_1 = -\bar{C}x_1 - \bar{A}^T p_1 - \bar{g}_x^T p_0 \tag{87}$$

where

$$\begin{aligned}\bar{A} &= \bar{f}_x - \bar{f}_u \left(\bar{\mathcal{H}}_{uu} + \lambda_0 \bar{c}_{uu}\right)^{-1} \beta \bar{\mathcal{H}}_{ux} - \\ &\quad \bar{f}_w \left(\bar{\mathcal{H}}_{ww} + \sigma_0 \bar{d}_{ww}\right)^{-1} \eta \bar{\mathcal{H}}_{wx}\end{aligned} \tag{88}$$

$$\bar{B} = \bar{f}_u \left(\bar{\mathcal{H}}_{uu} + \lambda_0 \bar{c}_{uu}\right)^{-1} \beta \bar{f}_u^T + \bar{f}_w \left(\bar{\mathcal{H}}_{ww} + \sigma_0 \bar{d}_{ww}\right)^{-1} \eta \bar{f}_w^T \tag{89}$$

$$\begin{aligned}\bar{C} &= \bar{\mathcal{H}}_{xx} - \bar{\mathcal{H}}_{ux}^T \left(\bar{\mathcal{H}}_{uu} + \lambda_0 \bar{c}_{uu}\right)^{-1} \beta \bar{\mathcal{H}}_{ux} - \\ &\quad \bar{\mathcal{H}}_{wx}^T \left(\bar{\mathcal{H}}_{ww} + \sigma_0 \bar{d}_{ww}\right)^{-1} \eta \bar{\mathcal{H}}_{wx}\end{aligned}$$

$$\tag{90}$$

If (86) and (87) can be solved to find x_1 and p_1 at time $t = 0$ (the current time), then (84) and (85) can be used to find the first order controls to be applied at the current time.

The important thing to realize about equations (86) and (87) is that they are coupled linear inhomogeneous equations in the first order states x_1 and first order costates p_1. All the coefficients $\bar{A}$, $\bar{B}$, and $\bar{C}$ and all the forcing functions $\bar{g}$ and $\bar{g}_x^T p_0$ are evaluated along the zeroth order trajectory x_0 found using the zeroth order controls u_0 and w_0. The fact that this set of equations is linear in x_1 and p_1 greatly simplifies the process of solution.

The optimality conditions for the second and higher order controls u_i and w_i can be rewritten to express these controls as linear functions of the x_i and p_i in a manner similar to the derivation of (76) and (77) for the first order controls. Furthermore, the higher order state and costate equations are linear in x_i, p_i, u_i and w_i, so it can be easily shown that for any order $i \geq 1$ the following equations determine x_i and p_i

$$\dot{x}_i = \bar{A}x_i - \bar{B}p_i + D_i \tag{91}$$

$$\dot{p}_i = -\bar{C}x_i - \bar{A}^T p_i + E_i \tag{92}$$

where D_i and E_i are functions of the states, costates, and controls of orders $1, 2, ..., i-1$. In other words, the solution to the zeroth order equations and the solution to the perturbation equations of order up to $i - 1$ become driving terms for the coupled linear differential equations used to solve for the states and costates of order i.

The method used to solve the perturbation equations (86)-(87) and (91)-(92) is based on obtaining an analytical expression for the state transition matrix. It will be shown that if the state transition matrix for the set of equations (91)-(92) can be determined analytically, the higher order corrections to the state, costate, and control vectors can be found through quadrature. This method requires only moderate computational capability and is quite suitable for on-board guidance implementation.

Before this solution methodolgy can be applied, however, the boundary conditions for the states and costates must be obtained. The initial conditions on x_i are simply

$$x_i(t = 0) = 0 \tag{93}$$

for all $i \geq 1$, since the zeroth order equations are solved using the boundary condition

$$x_0(t = 0) = \alpha \tag{94}$$

However, the terminal boundary conditions relating $x_i(T)$ and $p_i(T)$ are somewhat more difficult to obtain. The derivation of these boundary conditions is presented in the following section.

2. Terminal Boundary Conditions

The terminal boundary conditions are obtained by first expressing the terminal conditions (15), the terminal constraint conditions (16), and the terminal condition on the Hamiltonian (17) in terms of perturbation series expansions for x, p, the terminal Lagrange multipliers ν, and the final time T. We begin by expanding ν and T according to

$$T = T_0 + \epsilon T_1 + \epsilon^2 T_2 + ... \tag{95}$$
$$\nu = \nu_0 + \epsilon \nu_1 + \epsilon^2 \nu_2 + ... \tag{96}$$

Since T_0 is known from the zeroth order solution, the approach to obtaining terminal boundary conditions is to transform the boundary conditions at time T to boundary conditions at the known time T_0. This process will also provide sufficient information for the determination of the higher order correction terms T_i and ν_i. In many respect, this process is quite similar to the process used to obtain terminal boundary conditions for the second variation problem [18].

The terminal penalty and terminal constraints can be expanded in power series about $x_0(T_0)$ yielding

$$\Phi(x(T)) = \bar{\Phi} + \bar{\Phi}_x(x(T) - x_0(T_0)) +$$
$$\frac{1}{2}(x(T) - x_0(T_0))^T \bar{\Phi}_{xx}(x(T) - x(T_0)) + ... \tag{97}$$
$$\Psi(x(T)) = \bar{\Psi} + \bar{\Psi}_x(x(T) - x_0(T_0)) +$$
$$\frac{1}{2}(x(T) - x_0(T_0))^T \bar{\Psi}_{xx}(x(T) - x(T_0)) + ... \tag{98}$$

where the overbar indicates that Φ and Ψ are evaluated at $x_0(T_0)$. Similarly, the derivatives $\Phi_x(x(T))$ and $\Psi_x(x(T))$ can be expanded as

$$
\begin{aligned}
\Phi_x(x(T)) &= \bar{\Phi}_x + \bar{\Phi}_{xx}(x(T) - x_0(T_0)) + \\
&\quad \frac{1}{2}(x(T) - x_0(T_0))^T \bar{\Phi}_{xxx}(x(T) - x(T_0)) + \ldots \quad (99) \\
\Psi_x(x(T)) &= \bar{\Psi}_x + \bar{\Psi}_{xx}(x(T) - x_0(T_0)) + \\
&\quad \frac{1}{2}(x(T) - x_0(T_0))^T \bar{\Psi}_{xxx}(x(T) - x(T_0)) + \ldots \quad (100)
\end{aligned}
$$

We now note that the perturbation series expansion (26) for $x(t)$ evaluated at $t = T$ can be expanded in a power series about T_0 such that

$$
x(T) = x_0(T_0) + \epsilon\,(x_1 + \dot{x}_0 T_1) + \epsilon^2 \left(x_2 + \dot{x}_0 T_2 + \dot{x}_1 T_1 + \frac{1}{2}\ddot{x}_0 T_1^2 \right) + \ldots
\tag{101}
$$

Expression (101) can be substituted into (99) and (100) to yield

$$
\begin{aligned}
\Phi_x(x(T)) &= \bar{\Phi}_x + \epsilon\left(\bar{\Phi}_{xx} x_1 + \bar{\Phi}_{xx} \bar{f} T_1 \right) + \\
&\quad \epsilon^2 \left(\bar{\Phi}_{xx} x_2 + \bar{\Phi}_{xx} \bar{f} T_2 + \mathcal{Q}_2 \right) + \ldots \quad (102) \\
\Psi_x(x(T)) &= \bar{\Psi}_x + \epsilon\left(\bar{\Psi}_{xx} x_1 + \bar{\Psi}_{xx} \bar{f} T_1 \right) + \\
&\quad \epsilon^2 \left(\bar{\Psi}_{xx} x_2 + \bar{\Psi}_{xx} \bar{f} T_2 + \mathcal{R}_2 \right) + \ldots \quad (103)
\end{aligned}
$$

where we have used the fact that $\dot{x}_0 = \bar{f}$ from (41). The functions $\mathcal{Q}_2$ and $\mathcal{R}_2$ are functions of the zeroth and first order states, costates, and controls and are given explicitly in Appendix A. Using (96), (102), and (103), the terminal conditions (15) can be written as

$$
\begin{aligned}
p(T) &= \left(\bar{\Phi}_x + \nu_0^T \bar{\Psi}_x \right)^T + \epsilon\left[\left(\bar{\Phi}_{xx} + \nu_0^T \bar{\Psi}_{xx} \right) x_1 + \right. \\
&\quad \left(\bar{\Phi}_{xx} + \nu_0^T \bar{\Psi}_{xx} \right) \bar{f} T_1 + \bar{\Psi}_x^T \nu_1 \Big] + \\
&\quad \epsilon^2 \left[\left(\bar{\Phi}_{xx} + \nu_0^T \bar{\Psi}_{xx} \right) x_2 + \left(\bar{\Phi}_{xx} + \nu_0^T \bar{\Psi}_{xx} \right) \bar{f} T_2 + \right. \\
&\quad \bar{\Psi}_x^T \nu_2 + \left(\mathcal{Q}_2 + \nu_0^T \mathcal{R}_2 \right) \Big] + \ldots \quad (104)
\end{aligned}
$$

But the perturbation series expansion (29) for $p(t)$ evaluated at the final time T can also be expanded in a power series about T_0 such that

$$
\begin{aligned}
p_0(T) + \epsilon p_1(T) + \epsilon^2 p_2(T) &= p_0(T_0) + \epsilon\,(p_1 + \dot{p}_0 T_1) + \\
&\quad \epsilon^2 \left(p_2 + \dot{p}_0 T_2 + \dot{p}_1 T_1 + \frac{1}{2}\ddot{p}_0 T_1^2 \right) \ldots \\
&= p_0 + \epsilon\left(p_1 - \bar{f}_x^T p_0 T_1 \right) + \\
&\quad \epsilon^2 \left(p_2 - \bar{f}_x^T p_0 T_2 + \dot{p}_1 T_1 + \frac{1}{2}\ddot{p}_0 T_1^2 \right) \ldots
\end{aligned}
\tag{105}
$$

Therefore (104) can be rewritten entirely in terms of T_0 as

$$
\begin{aligned}
p_0 + \epsilon p_1 + \epsilon^2 p_2 \dots \; = \; & \left(\bar{\Phi}_x + \nu_0^T \bar{\Psi}_x\right)^T + \epsilon\left[\left(\bar{\Phi}_{xx} + \nu_0^T \bar{\Psi}_{xx}\right) x_1 + \right. \\
& \left(\bar{\Phi}_{xx}\bar{f} + \nu_0^T \bar{\Psi}_{xx}\bar{f} + \bar{f}_x^T p_0\right) T_1 + \bar{\Psi}_x^T \nu_1 \bigg] + \\
& \epsilon^2\left[\left(\bar{\Phi}_{xx} + \nu_0^T \bar{\Psi}_{xx}\right) x_2 + \right. \\
& \left(\bar{\Phi}_{xx}\bar{f} + \nu_0^T \bar{\Psi}_{xx}\bar{f} + \bar{f}_x^T p_0\right) T_2 + \\
& \bar{\Psi}_x^T \nu_2 + \mathcal{S}_2 \bigg] + \dots
\end{aligned}
\tag{106}
$$

where $\mathcal{S}_2$ is a function of the zeroth and first order states, costates, and control and is given explicitly by

$$
\mathcal{S}_2 = \left(\mathcal{Q}_2 + \nu_0^T \mathcal{R}_2\right) - \dot{p}_1 T_1 - \frac{1}{2}\ddot{p}_0 T_1^2
\tag{107}
$$

and all terms in (106) are evaluated at T_0. Equating like powers of ϵ yields the following conditions that must be satisfied

$$
\begin{aligned}
p_0(T_0) \; = \; & \left(\bar{\Phi}_x + \nu_0^T \bar{\Psi}_x\right)^T
\end{aligned}
\tag{108}
$$

$$
\begin{aligned}
p_1(T_0) \; = \; & \left(\bar{\Phi}_{xx} + \nu_0^T \bar{\Psi}_{xx}\right) x_1 + \bar{\Psi}_x^T \nu_1 + \\
& \left(\bar{\Phi}_{xx}\bar{f} + \nu_0^T \bar{\Psi}_{xx}\bar{f} + \bar{f}_x^T \left(\bar{\Phi}_x + \nu_0^T \bar{\Psi}_x\right)^T\right) T_1
\end{aligned}
\tag{109}
$$

$$
\begin{aligned}
p_2(T_0) \; = \; & \left(\bar{\Phi}_{xx} + \nu_0^T \bar{\Psi}_{xx}\right) x_2 + \bar{\Psi}_x^T \nu_2 + \\
& \left(\bar{\Phi}_{xx}\bar{f} + \nu_0^T \bar{\Psi}_{xx}\bar{f} + \bar{f}_x^T \left(\bar{\Phi}_x + \nu_0^T \bar{\Psi}_x\right)^T\right) T_2 + \mathcal{S}_2
\end{aligned}
\tag{110}
$$

$$\vdots$$

For the terminal constraints (103) to vanish to each order in ϵ the following conditions must also hold

$$
\bar{\Psi} = 0
\tag{111}
$$

$$
\bar{\Psi}_x x_1 + \bar{\Psi}_x \bar{f} T_1 = 0
\tag{112}
$$

$$
\bar{\Psi}_x x_2 + \bar{\Psi}_x \bar{f} T_2 + \mathcal{R}_2 = 0
\tag{113}
$$

The terminal condition on the Hamiltonian is given by expression (17). Noting that x and p are functions of time, the Hamiltonian can be expanded around $x_0(T_0)$ and $p_0(T_0)$ to yield

$$
\begin{aligned}
\mathcal{H} \; = \; & \bar{L} + \epsilon\left(\bar{L}_u u_1 + \bar{L}_w w_1\right) + \\
& \epsilon^2\left(\bar{L}_u u_2 + \bar{L}_w w_2 + \frac{1}{2}u_1^T \bar{L}_{uu} u_1 + \frac{1}{2}w_1^T \bar{L}_{ww} w_1\right) \dots + \\
& \left(p_0 + \epsilon\left[p_1 - \bar{f}_x^T p_0 T_1\right] + \right.
\end{aligned}
$$

$$\epsilon^2 \left[p_2 - \bar{f}_x^T p_0 T_2 + \dot{p}_1 T_1 + \frac{1}{2} \ddot{p}_1 T_1^2 \right] + ... \Big)^T \cdot$$
$$\left(\bar{f} + \epsilon \left[\bar{f}_x x_1 + \bar{f}_x \bar{f} T_1 + \bar{f}_u u_1 + \bar{f}_w w_1 + \bar{g} \right] + \right.$$
$$\left. \epsilon^2 \left[\bar{f}_x x_2 + \bar{f}_x \bar{f} T_2 + \bar{f}_u u_2 + \bar{f}_w w_2 + \mathcal{G}_2 \right] + ... \right) \tag{114}$$

where $\mathcal{G}_2$ is a function of the zeroth and first order states and controls and is given explicitly in Appendix A. Rearranging (114) by powers of ϵ yields

$$\begin{aligned}
\mathcal{H} &= \bar{L} + p_0^T \bar{f} + \epsilon \left\{ \left[\bar{L}_u u_1 + \bar{L}_w w_1 + p_0^T \left(\bar{f}_u u_1 + \bar{f}_w w_1 \right) \right] \right. \\
&\quad + p_0^T \left(\bar{f}_x x_1 + \bar{f}_x \bar{f} T_1 + g \right) + p_1^T \bar{f} - p_0^T \bar{f}_x \bar{f} T_1 \Big\} + \\
&\quad \epsilon^2 \left\{ \left[\bar{L}_u u_2 + \bar{L}_w w_2 + p_0^T \left(\bar{f}_u u_2 + \bar{f}_w w_2 \right) \right] \right. \\
&\quad + p_0^T \left(\bar{f}_x x_2 + \bar{f}_x \bar{f} T_2 + \mathcal{G}_2 \right) + p_2^T \bar{f} - p_0^T \bar{f}_x \bar{f} T_2 + \mathcal{F}_2 \Big\} + ... \tag{115}
\end{aligned}$$

where $\mathcal{F}_2$ is a function of the zeroth and first order states, costates, and controls and is given explicitly in Appendix A. Using the optimality conditions (64)-(65), expression (115) can be simplified as

$$\begin{aligned}
\mathcal{H} &= \bar{L} + p_0^T \bar{f} + \epsilon \left[p_0^T \left(\bar{f}_x x_1 + \bar{g} \right) + p_1^T \bar{f} \right] + \\
&\quad \epsilon^2 \left[p_0^T \left(\bar{f}_x x_2 + \mathcal{G}_2 \right) + p_2^T \bar{f} + \mathcal{F}_2 \right] + ... \tag{116}
\end{aligned}$$

For the Hamiltonian to vanish to each order in ϵ, the following conditions must hold

$$\bar{L} + p_0^T \bar{f} = 0 \tag{117}$$
$$p_0^T \left(\bar{f}_x x_1 + \bar{g} \right) + p_1^T \bar{f} = 0 \tag{118}$$
$$p_0^T \left(\bar{f}_x x_2 + \mathcal{G}_2 \right) + p_2^T \bar{f} + \mathcal{F}_2 = 0 \tag{119}$$

Since p_1, p_2, and $\bar{f}$ are all column vectors, $p_1^T \bar{f} = \bar{f}^T p_1$ and $p_2^T \bar{f} = \bar{f}^T p_2$ and (118)-(119) can be written in the more convenient form

$$p_0^T \bar{f}_x x_1 + \bar{f}^T p_1 + p_0^T \bar{g} = 0 \tag{120}$$
$$p_0^T \bar{f}_x x_2 + \bar{f}^T p_2 + p_0^T \mathcal{G}_2 + \mathcal{F}_2 = 0 \tag{121}$$

Using (108)-(109) in (117) and (120) yields the following conditions

$$\bar{L} + \left(\bar{\Phi}_x + \nu_0^T \bar{\Psi}_x \right) \bar{f} = 0 \tag{122}$$

$$\left[\left(\bar{\Phi}_x + \nu_0^T \bar{\Psi}_x \right) \bar{f}_x + \bar{f}^T \left(\bar{\Phi}_{xx} + \nu_0^T \bar{\Psi}_{xx} \right) \right] x_1 + \bar{f}^T \bar{\Psi}_x^T \nu_1 +$$
$$\bar{f}^T \left(\bar{\Phi}_{xx} \bar{f} + \nu_0^T \bar{\Psi}_{xx} \bar{f} + \bar{f}_x^T \left(\bar{\Phi}_x + \nu_0^T \bar{\Psi}_x \right)^T \right) T_1 +$$
$$\left(\bar{\Phi}_x + \nu_0^T \bar{\Psi}_x \right) \bar{g} = 0 \tag{123}$$

$$\left[\left(\bar{\Phi}_x + \nu_0^T \bar{\Psi}_x \right) \bar{f}_x + \bar{f}^T \left(\bar{\Phi}_{xx} + \nu_0^T \bar{\Psi}_{xx} \right) \right] x_2 + \bar{f}^T \bar{\Psi}_x^T \nu_2 +$$
$$\bar{f}^T \left(\bar{\Phi}_{xx} \bar{f} + \nu_0^T \bar{\Psi}_{xx} \bar{f} + \bar{f}_x^T \left(\bar{\Phi}_x + \nu_0^T \bar{\Psi}_x \right)^T \right) T_2 +$$
$$\left(\bar{\Phi}_x + \nu_0^T \bar{\Psi}_x \right) \mathcal{G}_2 + \bar{f}^T \mathcal{S}_2 + \mathcal{F}_2 = 0 \tag{124}$$

The conditions (108), (111), and (122) are used to obtain the zeroth order quantities p_0, ν_0, and T_0, the conditions (109), (112), and (123) are used to obtain the first order quantities p_1, ν_1, and T_1, and the conditions (110), (113), and (124) are used to obtain the second order quantities p_2, ν_2, and T_2.

For purposes of notational simplicity, it will prove convenient to denote the left hand sides of (122)-(124) by Ω_0, Ω_1, and Ω_2 respectively, such that the conditions (122)-(124) can be written in the compact form

$$\Omega_0 = 0 \tag{125}$$
$$\Omega_1 = 0 \tag{126}$$
$$\Omega_2 = 0 \tag{127}$$

We also define $\bar{\Delta}$ as

$$\bar{\Delta} = \bar{\Phi} + \nu_0^T \bar{\Psi} \tag{128}$$

The expressions (109), (112), and (123) can then be written in the compact form

$$
\begin{vmatrix} p_1(T_0) \\ \Psi_1(T_0) \\ \Omega_1(T_0) \end{vmatrix}
=
\begin{vmatrix} \bar{\Delta}_{xx} & \bar{\Psi}_x^T & \bar{\Delta}_{xx}\bar{f} + \bar{f}_x^T \bar{\Delta}_x^T \\ \bar{\Psi}_x & 0 & \bar{\Psi}_x \bar{f} \\ \bar{\Delta}_x \bar{f}_x + \bar{f}^T \bar{\Delta}_{xx} & \bar{f}^T \bar{\Psi}_x^T & \bar{f}^T \bar{\Delta}_{xx}\bar{f} + \bar{f}^T \bar{f}_x^T \bar{\Delta}_x^T \end{vmatrix}
\cdot
$$
$$
\begin{vmatrix} x_1(T_0) \\ \nu_1 \\ T_1 \end{vmatrix}
+
\begin{vmatrix} 0 \\ 0 \\ \bar{\Delta}_x \bar{g} \end{vmatrix} \tag{129}
$$

where the dot "." indicates matrix multiplication. It is straightforward, though tedious, to show that in general, the ith order boundary conditions can be written in the compact form

$$
\begin{vmatrix} p_i(T_0) \\ \Psi_i(T_0) \\ \Omega_i(T_0) \end{vmatrix}
=
\begin{vmatrix} \bar{\Delta}_{xx} & \bar{\Psi}_x^T & \bar{\Delta}_{xx}\bar{f} + \bar{f}_x^T \bar{\Delta}_x^T \\ \bar{\Psi}_x & 0 & \bar{\Psi}_x \bar{f} \\ \bar{\Delta}_x \bar{f}_x + \bar{f}^T \bar{\Delta}_{xx} & \bar{f}^T \bar{\Psi}_x^T & \bar{f}^T \bar{\Delta}_{xx}\bar{f} + \bar{f}^T \bar{f}_x^T \bar{\Delta}_x^T \end{vmatrix}
\cdot
$$
$$
\begin{vmatrix} x_i(T_0) \\ \nu_i \\ T_i \end{vmatrix}
+
\begin{vmatrix} \mathcal{S}_i \\ \mathcal{R}_i \\ \bar{\Delta}_x \mathcal{G}_i + \bar{f}^T \mathcal{S}_i + \mathcal{F}_i \end{vmatrix} \tag{130}
$$

where $\mathcal{F}_i$, $\mathcal{G}_i$, and $\mathcal{S}_i$ are functions of the zeroth, first, ..., $i-1$ order states, costates, and controls.

The expressions (129)-(130) provide the boundary conditions necessary for solving the perturbation equations (86)-(87), and (91)-(92). In the following section, the transition matrix approach is used to obtain solutions to these perturbation equations using quadrature.

3. Transition Matrix Solution Approach

The transition matrix solution approach proceeds as follows. The homogenous part of (91)-(92) can be solved in terms of the state transition matrix $\mathcal{Z}(t_a, t_b)$ such that

$$\left| \begin{array}{c} x_i(t_a) \\ p_i(t_a) \end{array} \right| = \mathcal{Z}(t_a, t_b) \left| \begin{array}{c} x_i(t_b) \\ p_i(t_b) \end{array} \right| \tag{131}$$

Here t_a and t_b are two arbitrary values of time. The state transition matrix satisfies the equation

$$\frac{d\mathcal{Z}}{dt} = \left| \begin{array}{cc} \bar{A} & -\bar{B} \\ -\bar{C} & -\bar{A}^T \end{array} \right| \mathcal{Z} \tag{132}$$

Now define the augmented state vector $y_i(t)$ by

$$y_i(t) = [x_i(t) \quad p_i(t)]^T \tag{133}$$

and define the augmented vector of inhomogeneous terms $\mathcal{D}_i$ by

$$\mathcal{D}_i(t) = [D_i(t) \quad E_i(t)]^T \tag{134}$$

Then the inhomogeneous equations (91)-(92) can be solved in terms of the transition matrix according to

$$y_i(t_a) = \mathcal{Z}(t_a, t_b) y_i(t_b) + \int_{t_b}^{t_a} \mathcal{Z}(t_a, \tau) \mathcal{D}_i(\tau) \, d\tau \tag{135}$$

Thus if the transition matrix can be found explicitly in terms of arbitrary times t_a and τ the second term on the right hand side of (135) can be evaluated through simple numerical quadrature.

The required expression for the transition matrix can indeed be determined through the following process. Define $\tilde{y}_i(t)$ to be the solution of the homogeneous problem

$$\frac{d\tilde{y}_i}{dt} = \left| \begin{array}{cc} \bar{A} & -\bar{B} \\ -\bar{C} & -\bar{A}^T \end{array} \right| \tilde{y}_i \tag{136}$$

for any order i such that

$$\tilde{y}_i(t_a) = \mathcal{Z}(t_a, t_b) \tilde{y}_i(t_b) \tag{137}$$

Defining $\tilde{y}$ as the perturbation series sum of the $\tilde{y}_i$ the following expression is obtained

$$\tilde{y}(t) = \tilde{y}_0(t) + \sum_{i=1}^{\infty} \epsilon^i \tilde{y}_i \tag{138}$$

Using (137) in (138) yields

$$\tilde{y}(t_a) = \tilde{y}_0(t_a) + Z(t_a, t_b)\left(\tilde{y}(t_b) - \tilde{y}_0(t_b)\right) \tag{139}$$

Expression (139) can be immediately recognized as a first order expansion of $\tilde{y}(t_a)$ in terms of $\tilde{y}(t_b)$ with the transition matrix Z identified as

$$Z = \left. \frac{\partial \tilde{y}(t_a)}{\partial \tilde{y}(t_b)} \right|_{\tilde{y}=\tilde{y}_0} \tag{140}$$

However, the zeroth order homogeneous trajectory $\tilde{y}$ is simply the zeroth order trajectory $y_0 = [x_0 \ p_0]^T$ found from the solution to the zeroth order problem. Thus, Z is simply a matrix of partial derivatives:

$$Z_{i,j} = \frac{\partial y_{0_i}(t_a)}{\partial y_{0_j}(t_b)} \tag{141}$$

where $y_{0_i}(t_a)$ is the ith component of the vector $y_0(t)$ evaluated at time $t = t_a$ and $y_{0_j}(t_b)$ is the jth component of the vector $y_0(t)$ evaluated at time $t = t_b$. These partials are easily obtained from the solution to the zeroth order problem.

It is important to note that it is not necessary to include second and higher order terms in the expansion (139). Such terms correspond to second and higher order derivatives of the primary dynamics, and since these derivatives for equations of any order i are evaluated using the state, costate and control histories of orders only up to $i-1$, these derivatives form part of the inhomogeneous terms in the differential equations of order i. Since $\tilde{y}_i$ is defined as the solution to the homogeneous problem of order i, second and higher order expansions in (139) have already been removed from consideration. Thus the transition matrix defined by (141) is indeed an exact expression.

The form of (135) that is most convenient for obtaining the solutions for $x_i(t)$ and $p_i(t)$ is given by

$$\left| \begin{array}{c} x_i(0) \\ p_i(0) \end{array} \right| = \left| \begin{array}{cc} Z_{11}(0, T_0) & Z_{12}(0, T_0) \\ Z_{21}(0, T_0) & Z_{22}(0, T_0) \end{array} \right| \left| \begin{array}{c} x_i(T_0) \\ p_i(T_0) \end{array} \right| + \int_{T_0}^{0} \left| \begin{array}{cc} Z_{11}(0, \tau) & Z_{12}(0, \tau) \\ Z_{21}(0, \tau) & Z_{22}(0, \tau) \end{array} \right| \left| \begin{array}{c} D_i(\tau) \\ E_i(\tau) \end{array} \right| d\tau \tag{142}$$

Here Z_{11}, Z_{12}, Z_{21}, and Z_{22} are partitions of the state transition matrix and the times $t = 0$ and $t = T_0$ have replaced the arbitrary times $t = t_b$ and $t = t_a$ respectively. In order to make the notation as compact as possible, we define the following

$$\left| \begin{array}{c} \mathcal{X}_i \\ \mathcal{P}_i \end{array} \right| = \int_{T_0}^{0} \left| \begin{array}{cc} Z_{11}(0, \tau) & Z_{12}(0, \tau) \\ Z_{21}(0, \tau) & Z_{22}(0, \tau) \end{array} \right| \left| \begin{array}{c} D_i(\tau) \\ E_i(\tau) \end{array} \right| d\tau \tag{143}$$

such that (142) can be written as

$$
\begin{vmatrix} x_i(0) \\ p_i(0) \end{vmatrix} = \begin{vmatrix} \mathcal{Z}_{11}(0, T_0) & \mathcal{Z}_{12}(0, T_0) \\ \mathcal{Z}_{21}(0, T_0) & \mathcal{Z}_{22}(0, T_0) \end{vmatrix} \begin{vmatrix} x_i(T_0) \\ p_i(T_0) \end{vmatrix} + \begin{vmatrix} \mathcal{X}_i \\ \mathcal{P}_i \end{vmatrix} \quad (144)
$$

Using the expression for $p_i(T_0)$ obtained from the first row partition of the matrix equation (130), the first row partition of (144) can be used to express $x_i(0)$ as

$$
x_i(0) = \left(\mathcal{Z}_{11} + \mathcal{Z}_{12} \bar{\Delta}_{xx} \right) x_i(T_0) + \mathcal{Z}_{12} \bar{\Psi}_x^T \nu_i + \mathcal{Z}_{12} \left(\bar{\Delta}_{xx} \bar{f} + \bar{f}_x^T \bar{\Delta}_x^T \right) T_i +
$$
$$
\mathcal{Z}_{12} \mathcal{S}_i + \mathcal{X}_i \quad (145)
$$

The first row partition of (130) can then be replaced by (145) such that

$$
\begin{vmatrix} x_i(0) \\ \Psi_i(T_0) \\ \Omega_i(T_0) \end{vmatrix} = \begin{vmatrix} \mathcal{Z}_{11} + \mathcal{Z}_{12} \bar{\Delta}_{xx} & \mathcal{Z}_{12} \bar{\Psi}_x^T & \mathcal{Z}_{12} \left(\bar{\Delta}_{xx} \bar{f} + \bar{f}_x^T \bar{\Delta}_x^T \right) \\ \bar{\Psi}_x & 0 & \bar{\Psi}_x \bar{f} \\ \bar{\Delta}_x \bar{f}_x + \bar{f}^T \bar{\Delta}_{xx} & \bar{f}^T \bar{\Psi}_x^T & \bar{f}^T \bar{\Delta}_{xx} \bar{f} + \bar{f}^T \bar{f}_x^T \bar{\Delta}_x^T \end{vmatrix} .
$$
$$
\begin{vmatrix} x_i(T_0) \\ \nu_i \\ T_i \end{vmatrix} + \begin{vmatrix} \mathcal{Z}_{12} \mathcal{S}_i + \mathcal{X}_i \\ \mathcal{R}_i \\ \bar{\Delta}_x \mathcal{G}_i + \bar{f}^T \mathcal{S}_i + \mathcal{F}_i \end{vmatrix} \quad (146)
$$

Now note that the left hand side of (146) is the zero vector. As a result this expression can be solved for $x_i(T_0)$, ν_i, and T_i such that

$$
\begin{vmatrix} x_i(T_0) \\ \nu_i \\ T_i \end{vmatrix} = - \begin{vmatrix} \mathcal{Z}_{11} + \mathcal{Z}_{12} \bar{\Delta}_{xx} & \mathcal{Z}_{12} \bar{\Psi}_x^T & \mathcal{Z}_{12} \left(\bar{\Delta}_{xx} \bar{f} + \bar{f}_x^T \bar{\Delta}_x^T \right) \\ \bar{\Psi}_x & 0 & \bar{\Psi}_x \bar{f} \\ \bar{\Delta}_x \bar{f}_x + \bar{f}^T \bar{\Delta}_{xx} & \bar{f}^T \bar{\Psi}_x^T & \bar{f}^T \bar{\Delta}_{xx} \bar{f} + \bar{f}^T \bar{f}_x^T \bar{\Delta}_x^T \end{vmatrix}^{-1} .
$$
$$
\begin{vmatrix} \mathcal{Z}_{12} \mathcal{S}_i + \mathcal{X}_i \\ \mathcal{R}_i \\ \bar{\Delta}_x \mathcal{G}_i + \bar{f}^T \mathcal{S}_i + \mathcal{F}_i \end{vmatrix} \quad (147)
$$

Since the right hand side of (147) contains only known quantities, (147) can be used to obtain numerical values for $x_i(T_0)$, ν_i, and T_i. Numerical values for $p_i(T_0)$ can also be obtained by substituting the numerical values for $x_i(T_0)$, ν_i, and T_i into the first row partition of (130). Now that values for $x_i(T_0)$ and $p_i(T_0)$ have been obtained, these values can be used to obtain numerical values for $p_i(0)$ from the second row partition of the transition matrix equation (142). The values for $p_i(0)$ are therefore given by

$$
p_i(0) = \left(\mathcal{Z}_{21} + \mathcal{Z}_{22} \bar{\Delta}_{xx} \right) x_i(T_0) + \mathcal{Z}_{22} \bar{\Psi}_x^T \nu_i + \mathcal{Z}_{22} \left(\bar{\Delta}_{xx} \bar{f} + \bar{f}_x^T \bar{\Delta}_x^T \right) T_i +
$$
$$
\mathcal{Z}_{22} \mathcal{S}_i + \mathcal{P}_i \quad (148)
$$

Note that the analysis has been carried out for correction terms of arbitrary order i. For the first order correction terms, comparison of (91)-(92)

to (86)-(87) indicates that

$$D_1 = \bar{g} \tag{149}$$

$$E_1 = -\bar{g}_x^T p_0 \tag{150}$$

so that $\mathcal{X}_1$ and $\mathcal{P}_1$ are given by

$$\left| \begin{array}{c} \mathcal{X}_1 \\ \mathcal{P}_1 \end{array} \right| = \int_{T_0}^0 \left| \begin{array}{cc} \mathcal{Z}_{11}(0,\tau) & \mathcal{Z}_{12}(0,\tau) \\ \mathcal{Z}_{21}(0,\tau) & \mathcal{Z}_{22}(0,\tau) \end{array} \right| \left| \begin{array}{c} \bar{g}(\tau) \\ -\bar{g}_x^T p_0(\tau) \end{array} \right| d\tau \tag{151}$$

Also, comparison of (130) with (129) indicates that $\mathcal{S}_1 = 0$, $\mathcal{R}_1 = 0$, $\mathcal{F}_1 = 0$, and $\mathcal{G}_1 = \bar{g}$. Thus the value for the first order costate term at $t = 0$ is given explicitly by

$$p_1(0) = \left(\mathcal{Z}_{21} + \mathcal{Z}_{22} \bar{\Delta}_{xx} \right) x_1(T_0) + \mathcal{Z}_{22} \bar{\Psi}_x^T \nu_1 + \mathcal{Z}_{22} \left(\bar{\Delta}_{xx} \bar{f} + \bar{f}_x^T \bar{\Delta}_x^T \right) T_1 + \mathcal{P}_1 \tag{152}$$

where x_1, ν_1 and T_1 are given by:

$$\left| \begin{array}{c} x_1(T_0) \\ \nu_1 \\ T_1 \end{array} \right| = - \left| \begin{array}{ccc} \mathcal{Z}_{11} + \mathcal{Z}_{12} \bar{\Delta}_{xx} & \mathcal{Z}_{12} \bar{\Psi}_x^T & \mathcal{Z}_{12} \left(\bar{\Delta}_{xx} \bar{f} + \bar{f}_x^T \bar{\Delta}_x^T \right) \\ \bar{\Psi}_x & 0 & \bar{\Psi}_x \bar{f} \\ \bar{\Delta}_x \bar{f}_x + \bar{f}^T \bar{\Delta}_{xx} & \bar{f}^T \bar{\Psi}_x^T & \bar{f}^T \bar{\Delta}_{xx} \bar{f} + \bar{f}^T \bar{f}_x^T \bar{\Delta}_x^T \end{array} \right|^{-1} \cdot$$

$$\left| \begin{array}{c} \mathcal{X}_1 \\ 0 \\ \bar{\Delta}_x \bar{g} \end{array} \right| \tag{153}$$

The main objective of the solution process is of course the determination of the optimal control vector u^* evaluated at the current time (where we have reintroduced the superscript "*"). The perturbation series expansion for u^* is

$$u^*(0) = u_0^*(0) + \epsilon u_1^*(0) + \epsilon^2 u_2^*(0) + \ldots \tag{154}$$

where $u_0^*(0)$ is the zeroth order optimal control at $t = 0$ found from the analytical zeroth order solution, $u_1^*(0)$ is the first order correction term (84), and $u_2^*(0)$ is the second order correction term. The zeroth order control is obtained from the simultaneous solution of (51),(59), (64), (65), (70), (71), (108), (111), (122). The first order control is found directly from (84), which expresses $u_1^*(0)$ in terms of the known quantities $x_1(0)$ and $p_1(0)$. Higher order corrections to the optimal control vector can be found by continuing this process up to the desired order. It should be noted that the control actually used at the current time can be obtained from the truncated perturbation series (154) or by using the expansion coefficients $p_i(0)$ directly in the optimality condition (20).

At long last, we have obtained all the expressions required for implementing guidance laws accurate to any order desired. A summary of the steps required to implement each of these algorithms is presented in the following section.

C. Summary of Algorithm

The guidance laws just presented are implemented by performing the following steps at each guidance law update time:

1. The current vehicle state is determined from the vehicle's navigation subsystem. The desired terminal constraints (if any) are determined from the vehicle's targeting subsystem.

2. The zeroth order control u_0^* is found by solving the zeroth order problem defined by (51),(59), (64), (65), (70), (71), (108), (111), and (122). The zeroth order final time T_0 is identified as part of this process. Note that the current time is assumed to be $t = 0$.

3. If only the zeroth order guidance law is being used, the control vector u_0^* is the control applied at the curent time. In this case, execution proceeds to step 1 for the next guidance update cycle. If the first order corrected guidance law is being used, steps 4 through 8 are executed.

4. Analytical expressions for the partitions of the state transition matrix $\mathcal{Z}(t, T)$ are obtained from (141). Note that the partials are of quantities at time T with respect to quantities at time $t \leq T$.

5. Numerical values for the terms $\mathcal{X}_1$ and $\mathcal{P}_1$ are obtained from (143). The integration can be carried out by any suitable quadrature technique (e.g. Gaussian quadrature).

6. The expression (153) is used to find numerical values for $x_1(T)$, ν_1, and T_1.

7. These values are substituted into (152), which is then used to obtain numerical values for $p_1(0)$.

8. The expression (84) is used to find the first order optimal control correction term $u_1^*(0)$. This control is multiplied by ϵ and added to the zeroth order control vector to obtain the optimal control vector at the current time, accurate to first order in ϵ. If only a first order guidance law is being used, execution return to step 1. Otherwise, step 9 is executed.

9. The first order state and costate equations are integrated forward from $t = 0$ to $t = T$ and stored in memory.

10. The second order correction terms are found by executing steps similar to steps 4 through 8. If higher order corrections are desired, say up to some order i, step 9 must also be executed for each order up to $i - 1$. Otherwise, execution returns to step 1.

The time between guidance law updates is chosen on the basis of the limitations of the on-board computer in terms of processing speed. In general, the shorter the update time the better the guidance law will perform. However, a finite number of calculations must be performed at each update step, and computation delays can degrade performance if this update time is too short. While the computational burden posed by the zeroth and first order corrected guidance laws depends on the specific application, numerical results for the aeroassisted plane change problem indicate that these calculation can be easily performed several times per second, which is more than adequate for near-optimal performance [17]. Furthermore, these guidance laws are orders of magnitude faster to compute than are numerical solutions of the corresponding nonlinear two point boundary value problems.

III. The Aeroassisted Plane Change Problem

The objective of the aeroassisted plane change problem is to find a feedback guidance law that allows a hypersonic reentry vehicle to use aerodynamic forces to change the plane of its orbit by a specified amount while maximizing the vehicle velocity at atmospheric exit. This problem was recently studied in [7] under the assumption that the atmospheric density was known perfectly as a function of altitude. In the present study, the atmospheric density is allowed to vary under the control of Nature, who is assumed to be an intelligent adversary. In this formulation, the vehicle guidance law must maximize the vehicle exit speed in the presence of the "worst case" densities chosen by Nature.

Before this optimization problem can be posed in greater detail, the vehicle equations of motion must be specified. Furthermore, these equations must be transformed such that the resulting equations can be solved analytically when the perturbation parameter ϵ is set to zero.

A. Equations of Motion

The equations of motion for a hypersonic reentry vehicle specify the translational dynamics of the vehicle with respect to the planet. In reality the vehicle attitude also evolves in time, and since the vehicle lift and drag forces depend to some extent on the vehicle orientation, there is some degree of coupling between the translational dynamics and the attitude dynamics. However, the vehicle attitude dynamics usually evolve over a much faster time scale than the translational dynamics, and therefore the equations of

motion are usually assumed to be the translational equations of motion
with instantaneous attitude dynamics.

The translational equations of motion for a hypersonic reentry vehicle
about a spherical nonrotating planet under the assumption of instantaneous
attitude dynamics are given by

$$\frac{dr}{dt} = V \sin \gamma \tag{155}$$

$$\frac{dV}{dt} = -\frac{\rho V^2 S}{2m} C_D - g \sin \gamma \tag{156}$$

$$\frac{d\gamma}{dt} = \frac{\rho V S}{2m} C_L \cos \beta - \left(\frac{g}{V} - \frac{V}{r} \right) \cos \gamma \tag{157}$$

$$\frac{d\psi}{dt} = \frac{\rho V S}{2m \cos \gamma} C_L \sin \beta - \frac{V}{r} \cos \gamma \cos \psi \tan \phi \tag{158}$$

$$\frac{d\phi}{dt} = \frac{V \cos \gamma \sin \psi}{r} \tag{159}$$

$$\frac{d\theta}{dt} = \frac{V \cos \gamma \cos \psi}{r \cos \phi} \tag{160}$$

Here r is the distance from the center of the planet to the vehicle, V is the
velocity, γ is the flight path angle, ψ is the heading angle, ϕ is the crossrange
angle, θ is the downrange angle, t is the time, m is the vehicle mass, S is
the aerodynamic reference area, C_D and C_L are the coefficients of drag and
lift, β is the vehicle bank angle, g is the local gravitational acceleration,
and ρ is the local atmospheric density. The gravitational acceleration g can
be expressed in terms of the distance r as

$$g = \frac{\mu}{r^2} \tag{161}$$

where μ is the gravitational constant of the planet. The density ρ can be
expressed as

$$\rho = (1 + \kappa)\rho_0 \exp \left(\frac{-h}{h_s} \right) \tag{162}$$

where ρ_0 is a reference density, h is the altitude of the vehicle, h_s is the density scale height, and κ is a factor representing the uncertainty in density.
The altitude h is related to the planet radius R by the simple relationship

$$h = r - R \tag{163}$$

While it would be straightforward to include the effects of planet rotation in the above equations of motion, the additional terms add considerably
to the algebra required and therefore obscure the methodology. Furthermore, the effect of these terms on the accuracy of the solution is fairly small

for the problem considered in this section. The nonrotating planet assumption has also been used successfully in many previous studies for similar problems [19][20][21].

The vehicle has two control mechanisms available to guide itself along its trajectory - the lift coefficient C_L and the bank angle β. The lift coefficient is controlled indirectly through control of the angle of attack or through the use of aerodynamic control surfaces. For purposes of this study, it does not matter which method (angle of attack control or aerodynamic surface control) is used to vary the lift coefficient. It is simply assumed that the lift coefficient is directly available as a mechanism for trajectory control. For varying lift coefficient, the drag coefficient C_D is assumed to follow a parabolic drag polar relationship of the form

$$C_D = C_{D_0} + KC_L^2 \qquad (164)$$

where C_{D_0} is the drag coefficient at zero lift and K is the parabolic drag polar proportionality constant. The maximum lift-to-drag ratio E^* will prove to be an important constant in the transformation of the equations of motion and is easily calculted from the definition of lift to drag ratio E

$$E = \frac{C_L}{C_D} \qquad (165)$$

Substituting (164) into (165) and maximizing with respect to C_L yields

$$C_L^* = \sqrt{\frac{C_{D_0}}{K}} \qquad (166)$$

$$C_D^* = 2C_{D_0} \qquad (167)$$

$$E^* = \frac{C_L^*}{C_D^*} \qquad (168)$$

The value of E^* determines the amount of aerodynamic trajectory control the vehicle can exert by virtue of its aerodynamic configuration and/or orientation. Note that the value of E^* is a property of the vehicle configuration. The aerodynamic trajectory controllability of the vehicle also depends on the uncertainty factor κ. In the differential game formulation, κ represents Nature's "control" with which to degrade vehicle performance as much as possible. The allowable range for κ is chosen based on uncertainty bounds for planetary atmospheric models.

B. Transformation of the Equations of Motion

The transformation of the equations of motion (155)-(160) through the introduction of a new independent variable and two new state variables was first suggested by Speyer and Crues[7]. The new dimensionless altitude variable ω is defined as

$$\omega = \frac{C_L^* \rho_0 e^{-\frac{h}{h_s}} S h_s}{2m} \tag{169}$$

and the new dimensionless velocity variable v is defined as

$$v = \ln\left(\frac{V^2}{gr}\right) \tag{170}$$

where g is given by (161). The new independent variable z is defined by

$$\frac{dz}{dt} = \frac{\omega V}{h_s} \tag{171}$$

Note that all quantities on the right hand side of (171) are positive at all times, so the variable z monotonically increases with time. This fact allows the variable z to be used as the new independent variable with much greater ease than the flight path angle γ, which was used by Busemann, Vinh, and Kelly[19] and by Speyer and Womble[20]. It is also useful to define the following quantities

$$\lambda = \frac{C_L}{C_L^*} \tag{172}$$

$$u_L = \lambda \cos\beta \tag{173}$$

$$u_S = \lambda \sin\beta \tag{174}$$

$$\epsilon = \frac{h_s}{R} \tag{175}$$

Here λ is the magnitude of the allowable aerodynamic control, u_L and u_S are the lifting and side force controls, and ϵ is the small parameter chosen as the expansion parameter for the regular perturbation technique. Finally, it is assumed that the flight path angle γ remains small during the entire atmospheric maneuver. This is a valid assumption for the aeroassisted plane change maneuvers considered in this study. This assumption results in the approximations $\cos\gamma \approx 1$ and $\sin\gamma \approx \gamma$.

With these transformations and approximations, the equations of motion for entry about a nonrotating planet become

$$\frac{d\omega}{dz} = -\gamma \tag{176}$$

$$\frac{dv}{dz} = -\frac{\left(1 + u_L^2 + u_S^2\right)}{E^*}(1+\kappa) - \epsilon\frac{R}{r\omega}\left[\left(2e^{-v} - 1\right)\gamma\right] \tag{177}$$

$$\frac{d\gamma}{dz} = u_L(1+\kappa) + \epsilon\frac{R}{r\omega}\left[\left(1 - e^{-v}\right)\right] \tag{178}$$

$$\frac{d\psi}{dz} = u_S(1+\kappa) - \epsilon \frac{R}{r\omega} [\cos\psi \tan\phi] \tag{179}$$

$$\frac{d\phi}{dz} = \epsilon \left[\frac{R\sin\psi}{r\omega}\right] \tag{180}$$

$$\frac{d\theta}{dz} = \epsilon \left[\frac{R\cos\psi}{r\omega\cos\phi}\right] \tag{181}$$

Note that these equations can be written in the compact form

$$\frac{d\boldsymbol{x}}{dz} = f(\boldsymbol{x}, u, \kappa) + \epsilon g(\boldsymbol{x}) \tag{182}$$

where $\boldsymbol{x} = [\omega \ v \ \gamma \ \psi \ \phi \ \theta]^T$ is the state vector, $u = [u_L \ u_S]^T$ is the control vector, κ is the disturbance vector, $f(\boldsymbol{x}, u, \kappa)$ is a linear function of the single state variable γ, and $g(\boldsymbol{x})$ is a nonlinear function of $\boldsymbol{x}$. Also note that the function $f(\boldsymbol{x}, u, \kappa)$ can be written in terms of separate functions $a(\boldsymbol{x})$, $b(\kappa)$, and $c(u)$ as

$$f(\boldsymbol{x}, u, \kappa) = a(\boldsymbol{x}) + [1 + b(\kappa)]c(u) \tag{183}$$

and therefore the state equations can be written as

$$\frac{d\boldsymbol{x}}{dz} = a(\boldsymbol{x}) + [1 + b(\kappa)]c(u) + \epsilon g(\boldsymbol{x}) \tag{184}$$

The function $b(\kappa)$ represents the uncertainty in the coefficient $[1 + b(\kappa)]$ multiplying the control function $c(u)$ (for zero uncertainty, this coefficient is simply $= 1$). This uncertainty can be most effectively handled through the concept of a ficticious internal feedback loop[11][22][23]. Define the vector w as

$$w = \left[\frac{1 + u_L^2 + u_S^2}{E^*}\kappa, \ u_L\kappa, \ u_S\kappa,\right]^T \equiv [w_D \ w_L \ w_S]^T \tag{185}$$

In terms of the new disturbance vector w, the equations of motion become

$$\frac{d\omega}{dz} = -\gamma \tag{186}$$

$$\frac{dv}{dz} = -\frac{\left(1 + u_L^2 + u_S^2\right)}{E^*} - w_D - \epsilon\frac{R}{r\omega} \left[\left(2e^{-v} - 1\right)\gamma\right] \tag{187}$$

$$\frac{d\gamma}{dz} = u_L + w_L + \epsilon\frac{R}{r\omega} \left[\left(1 - e^{-v}\right)\right] \tag{188}$$

$$\frac{d\psi}{dz} = u_S + w_S - \epsilon\frac{R}{r\omega} [\cos\psi \tan\phi] \tag{189}$$

$$\frac{d\phi}{dz} = \epsilon \left[\frac{R\sin\psi}{r\omega}\right] \tag{190}$$

$$\frac{d\theta}{dz} = \epsilon \left[\frac{R\cos\psi}{r\omega\cos\phi}\right] \tag{191}$$

The advantage of modifying the equations of motion in this manner is that the Hamiltonian function in the differential game formulation is separable in u and w, and therefore a solution is much easier to obtain. The specifics of the differential game formulation are now described.

C. The Differential Game Formulation

The aeroassisted plane change problem can be formulated as a differential game between the guidance law and Nature. The objective of the guidance law is to minimize a cost function of the form

$$J = \max_{w \in \mathcal{W}} \left[\int_0^T L(u, w)\, dt + \Phi(x, T) \right] \tag{192}$$

subject to the problem dynamics and to the terminal constraints

$$\Psi(x, T) = 0 \tag{193}$$

Here it is assumed that the vector of uncertainties w is controlled by Nature, who is assumed to be an intelligent adversary.

The magnitude of the control vector u will be automatically limited by the fact that increasing these forces also increases the drag force, thereby depleting velocity. On the other hand, the state equations (186)-(191) are linear in w, so there is no mechanism within the equations of motion that serves to bound the magnitude of Nature's control vector w. Therefore, w must be constrained directly by specifying bounds on the allowable control space $\mathcal{W}$ or indirectly by penalizing large values for w in the cost function. In order to facilitate the derivation of an analytical solution to the zeroth order problem, the second approach is taken here. Noting that the independent variable for the aeroassisted plane change problem is z rather than time, the cost function for this problem is explicitly chosen as

$$J = \max_{w \in \mathcal{W}} \left[-\frac{1}{2} \int_0^{z_f} w^T Q w\, dz - u(z_f) \right] \tag{194}$$

where z_f is the free final value for z. Here Q is a 3×3 positive definite weighting matrix. Generally, Q is chosen such that the disturbance vector w resulting from the differential game solution roughly corresponds to worst case conditions expected to occur in real time along the flight trajectory. Note that Q may be chosen to be a function of z, although for the present study Q will be assumed constant. To further simplify the subsequent analysis, Q will also be assumed diagonal. The terminal constraints are

$$\omega(z_f) = \omega_f \tag{195}$$

$$\gamma(z_f) = \gamma_f \tag{196}$$

$$\psi(z_f) = \psi_f \tag{197}$$

where ω_f, γ_f, ψ_f are specified terminal values.

Using the system dynamics (186)-(191), the Hamiltonian function of the system is formed as

$$\mathcal{H}(x, u, w) = \frac{1}{2}\left(-w^T Q w\right) - p_\omega \gamma$$

$$-p_v \left(\frac{(1 + u_L^2 + u_S^2)}{E^*} + w_D + \epsilon \frac{R}{r\omega}\left[\left(2e^{-v} - 1\right)\gamma\right]\right)$$

$$+p_\gamma \left(u_L + w_L + \epsilon \frac{R}{r\omega}\left[\left(1 - e^{-v}\right)\right]\right)$$

$$+p_\psi \left(u_S + w_S - \epsilon \frac{R}{r\omega}\left[\cos \psi \tan \phi\right]\right)$$

$$+p_\phi \left(\frac{\epsilon R \sin \psi}{r\omega}\right) + p_\theta \left(\frac{\epsilon R \cos \psi}{r\omega \cos \phi}\right) \qquad (198)$$

Here the p_ω, p_v, etc. are the costates associated with the specified states variable. If there are no explicitly stated bounds on the allowable magnitudes of u and w, these vectors are determined from the conditions

$$\frac{\partial H}{\partial u} = 0 \qquad (199)$$

$$\frac{\partial H}{\partial w} = 0 \qquad (200)$$

$$\frac{\partial^2 H}{\partial u^2} \geq 0 \qquad (201)$$

$$\frac{\partial^2 H}{\partial w^2} \leq 0 \qquad (202)$$

Solving (199)-(202) for u and w yields

$$u_L = \frac{E^* p_\gamma}{2 p_v} \qquad (203)$$

$$u_S = \frac{E^* p_\psi}{2 p_v} \qquad (204)$$

$$w_D = -\frac{p_v}{Q_{11}} \qquad (205)$$

$$w_L = \frac{p_\gamma}{Q_{22}} \qquad (206)$$

$$w_S = \frac{p_\psi}{Q_{33}} \qquad (207)$$

The expressions (203)-(207) determine the optimal control and disturbance vectors as functions of the costate vector $p_x = [p_\omega \; p_v \; p_\gamma \; p_\psi \; p_\phi \; p_\theta]^T$. Actually only the costates p_v, p_γ, and p_ψ are present in the control relationships (203)-(207) so the optimal control vectors u^* and w^* at any given

$z \in [0, z_f]$ are completely specified by the values of the state x and the costate elements p_v, p_γ, and p_ψ all evaluated at the current z (assumed without loss of generality to be $z = 0$).

The costates are specified by the set of differential equations

$$\frac{dp}{dz} = -\left(\frac{\partial \mathcal{H}}{\partial x}\right)^T \tag{208}$$

Using the definition of the Hamiltonian (198), the equations (208) become

$$\begin{aligned}
\frac{dp_\omega}{dz} &= -\epsilon R \left(\frac{h_s - r}{r^2 \omega^2}\right)\left[- p_v \left(2e^{-v} - 1\right)\gamma \right.\\
&\quad + p_\gamma \left(1 - e^{-v}\right) - p_\psi \left(\cos\psi \tan\phi\right)\\
&\quad \left. + p_\phi \sin\psi + p_\theta \frac{\cos\psi}{\cos\phi}\right]
\end{aligned} \tag{209}$$

$$\frac{dp_v}{dz} = -\epsilon\left(\frac{R}{r\omega}\right)\left[2p_v e^{-v}\gamma + p_\gamma e^{-v}\right] \tag{210}$$

$$\frac{dp_\gamma}{dz} = p_\omega + \epsilon\left(\frac{R}{r\omega}\right)p_v \left[2e^{-v} - 1\right] \tag{211}$$

$$\frac{dp_\psi}{dz} = \epsilon\left(\frac{R}{r\omega}\right)\left[-p_\psi \sin\psi \tan\phi - p_\phi \cos\psi + p_\theta \frac{\sin\psi}{\cos\phi}\right] \tag{212}$$

$$\frac{dp_\phi}{dz} = -\epsilon\left(\frac{R}{r\omega}\right)\left[-p_\psi \frac{\cos\psi}{\cos^2\phi} + p_\theta \frac{\cos\psi \sin\phi}{\cos^2\phi}\right] \tag{213}$$

$$\frac{dp_\theta}{dz} = 0 \tag{214}$$

The boundary conditions for the costate differential equations (209)-(214) are given at $z = z_f$ as

$$p(z_f) = \left(\Phi_x(x_f) + \nu^T \Psi_x(x_f)\right)^T \tag{215}$$

where the terminal cost $\Phi(x_f)$ is given by

$$\Phi(x_f) = -u(z_f) \tag{216}$$

and ν is a Lagrange multiplier vector determined such that the constraint $\Psi = 0$ holds. The subscripts x on the right hand side of (215) indicate partial differentiation with respect to the state vector. In terms of the terminal cost (216) and constraint equations (195)-(197), expression (215) yields

$$p_\omega(z_f) = \nu_\omega \tag{217}$$
$$p_v(z_f) = -1 \tag{218}$$

$$p_\gamma(z_f) \;=\; \nu_\gamma \tag{219}$$

$$p_\psi(z_f) \;=\; \nu_\psi \tag{220}$$

$$p_\phi(z_f) \;=\; 0 \tag{221}$$

$$p_\theta(z_f) \;=\; 0 \tag{222}$$

In the following section, approximate solutions for the state, costate, and control vectors are obtained as functions of z. By neglecting state equation terms proportional to the small parameter ϵ, an approximate analytical solution (the zeroth order solution) can be obtained. This approximation, when applied to the problem of this study, is equivalent to the assumption that the aerodynamic terms dominate the gravitational terms. A first order corrected solution can also be obtained through the methods presented in Section II. The derivation of each of these solutions is obtained in the sections that follow.

D. The Zeroth Order Solution

The zeroth order solution is an approximate solution to the equations of motion (186)-(191) and the costate equations (209)-(214). The solution is obtained by setting $\epsilon = 0$ in the equations of motion. Before discussing the details of this solution, it is necessary to briefly comment on the notation to be used in the subsequent analysis. In order to be completely consistent with the notation used in Section II, it would be necessary to write the zeroth order state vector x_0 as $x_0 = [\omega_0 \; v_0 \; \gamma_0 \; \psi_0 \; \phi_0 \; \theta_0]^T$. Unfortunately, this notation results in an excessive number of subscripts being attached to a number of variables, thereby increasing the chance of confusion on the part of the reader. We choose instead to denote the zeroth order state by an overbar such that $x_0 \equiv \bar{x}$ and $\bar{x} = [\bar{\omega} \; \bar{v} \; \bar{\gamma} \; \bar{\psi} \; \bar{\phi} \; \bar{\theta}]^T$. As in Section II, a bar over a function such as $\bar{f}$ or $\bar{\mathcal{H}}$ indicates that the function is to be evaluated along the zeroth order trajectory.

Using this notation, the zeroth order equations of motion are

$$\frac{d\bar{\omega}}{dz} \;=\; -\bar{\gamma} \tag{223}$$

$$\frac{d\bar{v}}{dz} \;=\; -\frac{\left(1 + \bar{u}_L^2 + \bar{u}_S^2\right)}{E^*} - \bar{w}_D \tag{224}$$

$$\frac{d\bar{\gamma}}{dz} \;=\; \bar{u}_L + \bar{w}_L \tag{225}$$

$$\frac{d\bar{\psi}}{dz} \;=\; \bar{u}_S + \bar{w}_S \tag{226}$$

$$\frac{d\bar{\phi}}{dz} \;=\; 0 \tag{227}$$

$$\frac{d\bar{\theta}}{dz} = 0 \tag{228}$$

The equations for $\bar{\phi}$ and $\bar{\theta}$ can be integrated immediately to obtain

$$\bar{\phi} = \bar{\phi}(z=0) = \bar{\phi}_i \tag{229}$$

$$\bar{\theta} = \bar{\theta}(z=0) = \bar{\theta}_i \tag{230}$$

The remaining 4 equations depend on the zeroth order optimal control relationships. These are obtained from the zeroth order costate equations

$$\frac{d\bar{p}_\omega}{dz} = 0 \tag{231}$$

$$\frac{d\bar{p}_v}{dz} = 0 \tag{232}$$

$$\frac{d\bar{p}_\gamma}{dz} = \bar{p}_\omega \tag{233}$$

$$\frac{d\bar{p}_\psi}{dz} = 0 \tag{234}$$

$$\frac{d\bar{p}_\phi}{dz} = 0 \tag{235}$$

$$\frac{d\bar{p}_\theta}{dz} = 0 \tag{236}$$

Remembering that the boundary conditions for the costate equations are given at z_f, these equations can be integrated to yield

$$\bar{p}_\omega = \bar{p}_{\omega_f} = \bar{\nu}_\omega \tag{237}$$

$$\bar{p}_v = \bar{p}_{v_f} = -1 \tag{238}$$

$$\bar{p}_\gamma = \bar{p}_{\omega_f} z + C \tag{239}$$

$$\bar{p}_\psi = \bar{p}_{\psi_f} = \bar{\nu}_\psi \tag{240}$$

$$\bar{p}_\phi = \bar{p}_{\phi_f} = 0 \tag{241}$$

$$\bar{p}_\theta = \bar{p}_{\theta_f} = 0 \tag{242}$$

Thus the zeroth order costates are either constants or linear functions of z and depend only on the three unknown constants $\bar{p}_\omega$, C, and $\bar{p}_\psi$. Furthermore only the costates $\bar{p}_v$, $\bar{p}_\gamma$, and $\bar{p}_\psi$ appear in the optimal control relationships (203)-(207), and therefore the optimal control vectors $\bar{u}^*(z)$ and $\bar{w}^*(z)$ depend on the three unknown constants $\bar{p}_\omega$, C, and $\bar{p}_\psi$.

The zeroth order costate relationships (237)-(242), the optimal control relationships (203)-(207), and the $\bar{p}_v$ transversality condition (218) can be substituted into the equations of motion (223)-(226) to give

$$\frac{d\bar{\omega}}{dz} = -\bar{\gamma} \tag{243}$$

$$\frac{d\bar{v}}{dz} = -\frac{1}{E^*} - \frac{E^*}{4}\left(\bar{p}_\omega^2 z^2 + 2\bar{p}_\omega Cz + C^2 + \bar{p}_\psi^2\right) + \frac{\bar{p}_v}{Q_{11}} \qquad (244)$$

$$\frac{d\bar{\gamma}}{dz} = \left(-\frac{E^*}{2} + \frac{1}{Q_{22}}\right)(\bar{p}_\omega z + C) \qquad (245)$$

$$\frac{d\bar{\psi}}{dz} = \left(-\frac{E^*}{2} + \frac{1}{Q_{33}}\right)\bar{p}_\psi \qquad (246)$$

The right hand sides of (243)-(246) can be easily integrated with respect to z yielding

$$\bar{\omega}(z) = \bar{\omega}_i - \bar{\gamma}_i z - \left(-\frac{E^*}{2} + \frac{1}{Q_{22}}\right)\left(\bar{p}_\omega \frac{z^3}{6} + C\frac{z^2}{2}\right) \qquad (247)$$

$$\bar{v}(z) = \bar{v}_i - \frac{z}{E^*} - \frac{E^*}{4}\left(\bar{p}_\omega^2 \frac{z^3}{3} + \bar{p}_\omega C\frac{z^2}{2} + C^2 z + \bar{p}_\psi^2 z\right) - $$

$$\frac{z}{Q_{11}} \qquad (248)$$

$$\bar{\gamma}(z) = \bar{\gamma}_i + \left(-\frac{E^*}{2} + \frac{1}{Q_{22}}\right)\left(\bar{p}_\omega \frac{z^2}{2} + Cz\right) \qquad (249)$$

$$\bar{\psi}(z) = \bar{\psi}_i + \left(-\frac{E^*}{2} + \frac{1}{Q_{33}}\right)\bar{p}_\psi z \qquad (250)$$

The expressions (247)-(250) represent four equations in five unknowns: the final state $\bar{v}(\bar{z}_f)$, the constants $\bar{p}_\omega$, C, $\bar{p}_\psi$, and the zeroth order terminal value of the independent variable $\bar{z}_f$. The additional equation required to completely determine the unknown constants is found from the fact that for free $\bar{z}_f$ the Hamiltonian must vanish at $\bar{z}_f$

$$\mathcal{H}(\bar{x}, \bar{u}, \bar{w}, \bar{p}, \bar{z}_f) = 0 \qquad (251)$$

Written at the final state $\bar{z}_f$ this expression becomes:

$$-\frac{1}{2}\bar{w}^T Q\bar{w} - \bar{p}_\omega \bar{\gamma} + \left(\frac{(1 + \bar{u}_L^2 + \bar{u}_S^2)}{E^*} + \bar{w}_D\right)$$

$$+ (\bar{p}_\omega z + C)(\bar{u}_L + \bar{w}_L) + \bar{p}_\psi(\bar{u}_S + \bar{w}_S) = 0 \qquad (252)$$

Solutions for the five unknowns are obtained as follows. The expressions (247) and (249) for $\bar{\omega}(\bar{z}_f)$ and $\bar{\gamma}(\bar{z}_f)$ can be used to solve for $\bar{p}_\omega$ and C in terms of $\bar{z}_f$, yielding

$$\bar{p}_\omega = \frac{6\left((\bar{\gamma}_i + \bar{\gamma}_f)\bar{z}_f + 2\Delta\bar{\omega}\right)}{k_{22}\bar{z}_f^3} \qquad (253)$$

$$C = \frac{6\Delta\bar{\omega} + 2(\bar{\gamma}_f + 2\bar{\gamma}_i)\bar{z}_f}{k_{22}\bar{z}_f^2} \qquad (254)$$

where $\Delta\bar{\omega}$ and k_{22} are defined as

$$\Delta\bar{\omega} \;=\; \bar{\omega}_f - \bar{\omega}_i \tag{255}$$

$$k_{22} \;=\; \left(\frac{1}{Q_{22}} - \frac{E^*}{2}\right) \tag{256}$$

The expression (250) can be used to solve for $\bar{p}_\psi$ in terms of $\bar{z}_f$ yielding

$$\bar{p}_\psi = \frac{\Delta\bar{\psi}}{k_{33}\bar{z}_f} \tag{257}$$

where $\Delta\bar{\psi}$ and k_{33} are defined as

$$\Delta\bar{\psi} \;=\; \bar{\psi}_f - \bar{\psi}_i \tag{258}$$

$$k_{33} \;=\; \left(\frac{1}{Q_{33}} - \frac{E^*}{2}\right) \tag{259}$$

Having obtained (253), (254), and (257), these expressions can be substituted into the Hamiltonian condition (252), which becomes a function of the single unknown $\bar{z}_f$. After some algebraic manipulations, this expression is seen to be a fourth order polynomial in $\bar{z}_f$ of the form

$$a_4\bar{z}_f^4 + a_2\bar{z}_f^2 + a_1\bar{z}_f + a_0 = 0 \tag{260}$$

Therefore, a solution for $\bar{z}_f$ can be obtained analytically[24]. The coefficients a_i are found to be

$$a_4 \;=\; \frac{1}{E^*} + \frac{1}{2Q_{11}} \tag{261}$$

$$a_2 \;=\; \frac{4k_{33}\left(\bar{\gamma}_i + \bar{\gamma}_f\right)^2 - 4k_{33}\bar{\gamma}_i\bar{\gamma}_f + k_{22}\Delta\bar{\psi}^2}{2k_{22}k_{33}} \tag{262}$$

$$a_1 \;=\; \frac{12\left(\bar{\gamma}_i + \bar{\gamma}_f\right)\Delta\bar{\omega}}{k_{22}} \tag{263}$$

$$a_0 \;=\; \frac{18\Delta\bar{\omega}^2}{k_{22}} \tag{264}$$

The smallest positive real root to (260) should be chosen as the terminal value for $\bar{z}_f$. Once this value is obtained, numerical values for $\bar{p}_\omega$, C, and $\bar{p}_\psi$ can be obtained from (253), (254), and (257). These values can then be substituted into the zeroth order optimal control relationships

$$\bar{u}_L \;=\; -\frac{E^*}{2}\left(\bar{p}_\omega z + C\right) \tag{265}$$

$$\bar{u}_S \;=\; -\frac{E^*\bar{p}_\psi}{2} \tag{266}$$

which are derived from (203)-(204) using (218) and (239). Expressions (265) and (266) can be used to evaluate the optimal control at any value $z \in [0, \bar{z}_f]$. Since at each guidance calculation step the current value of z is $z = 0$, the optimal control to be applied at the current step is calulated from (265)-(266) evaluated at $z = 0$.

To complete the zeroth order solution, the zeroth order terminal constraint Lagrange multipliers $\bar{\nu}_\omega$, $\bar{\nu}_\gamma$, and $\bar{\nu}_\psi$ must be specified. Using (237) and (240) in (253) and (257), $\bar{\nu}_\omega$ and $\bar{\nu}_\psi$ are given by

$$\bar{\nu}_\omega = \frac{6\left((\bar{\gamma}_i + \bar{\gamma}_f)\,\bar{z}_f + 2\Delta\bar{\omega}\right)}{k_{22}\bar{z}_f^3} \tag{267}$$

$$\bar{\nu}_\psi = \frac{\Delta\bar{\psi}}{k_{33}\bar{z}_f} \tag{268}$$

Finally, $\bar{\nu}_\gamma$ is found from

$$\bar{\nu}_\gamma = \bar{p}_\omega \bar{z}_f + C \tag{269}$$

using the values for $\bar{p}_\omega$, $\bar{z}_f$ and C obtained from (253), (260), and (254).

The calculations required in the above procedure are quite straightforward and easily implemented in real time. At each guidance update interval the above procedure is used to calculate the new guidance commands to be applied at the current time. The guidance commands are applied from the current time t until the next guidance update time $t + \Delta t$, at which time a new set of guidance commands are calculated. In the limit as $\Delta t \to 0$, this guidance implementation becomes the optimal feedback strategy for the zeroth order differential game.

E. The First Order Corrected Solution

The zeroth order solution presented in the previous section can be used to obtain a first order corrected solution by reintroducing the dynamics that were ignored in the zeroth order solution. These dynamics are now assumed to be solely dependent upon the zeroth order state trajectory and are therefore treated as driving terms for a set of linear differential equations specifying the first order dynamics. The details of the first order solution methodology are presented in Section II. The present section presents the application of this method to the aeroassisted plane change problem.

The first step in the solution process consists of obtaining the state transition matrix $\mathcal{Z}(0, z)$ for $z \in [0, z_f]$. As shown in Section II.B.3 the elements of the matrix $\mathcal{Z}$ are simply partial derivatives of the form

$$\mathcal{Z}_{i,j} = \frac{\partial y_0(0)}{\partial y_0(z)} \tag{270}$$

where $y_0(z) = [x_0(z) \quad p_0(z)]^T \equiv [\bar{x}(z) \quad \bar{p}(z)]^T$. Taking the derivatives required by (270) yields the transition matrix elements given explicitly in Appendix B.

The next step involved the determination of the particular solutions $\mathcal{X}_1$ and $\mathcal{P}_1$. These solutions are obtained through the quadratures required from (151) using z as the independent variable. The function $\bar{g}(z)$ and its partial derivatives are easily obtained and are presented in Appendix C.1. While these functions are already easy to calculate, it is possible to introduce some approximations to simplify them further. Simulation results indicate that the cross range angle ϕ remains quite small over the entire trajectory so $\bar{g}_4 \cong 0$ over the entire trajectory. Also, $R \cong r$ for the entire trajectory. These approximations result in the expressions for $\bar{g}$ and partial derivatives $\bar{g}_x$ listed in Appendix C.2. Simulation results indicate that essentially no difference in performance results from using either set of equations. Since the approximate set in Appendix C.2 required fewer calculations with no degradation in performance, this set was chosen for detailed numerical calculations. Note that when using this set of equations, $\bar{g}$ becomes a 4×1 vector and $\bar{g}_x$ becomes a 4×4 matrix. In order for the matrix operations in (151) to be compatible, the transition matrix must be reduced to an 8×8 matrix by removing the fifth and tenth rows and columns, i.e., all rows and columns corresponding to ϕ and p_ϕ.

The quadrature required in expression (151) can be obtained through any standard numerical quadrature technique. For this study an eighth order Gaussian quadrature technique was used.

Once the quadratures have been performed, numerical values for $x_1(\bar{z}_f)$, ν_1, and z_{f_1} need to be obtained from (153). For this purpose we need the following:

$$
\begin{aligned}
\bar{\Delta} &= \bar{\Phi} + \nu^T \bar{\Psi} \\
&= -\bar{v}(\bar{z}_f) + \bar{\nu}_\omega(\bar{\omega}(\bar{z}_f) - \omega_f) + \bar{\nu}_\gamma(\bar{\gamma}(\bar{z}_f) - \gamma_f) + \\
&\quad \bar{\nu}_\psi(\bar{\psi}(\bar{z}_f) - \psi_f) \tag{271} \\
\bar{\Delta}_\omega &= \bar{\nu}_\omega \tag{272} \\
\bar{\Delta}_v &= -1 \tag{273} \\
\bar{\Delta}_\gamma &= \bar{\nu}_\gamma \tag{274} \\
\bar{\Delta}_\psi &= \bar{\nu}_\psi \tag{275}
\end{aligned}
$$

and $\bar{\Psi}$ is a 3×4 matrix whose only nonzero elements are

$$
\bar{\Psi}_{1\omega} = \bar{\Psi}_{2\gamma} = \bar{\Psi}_{3\psi} = 1 \tag{276}
$$

All elements of $\bar{\Delta}_{xx}$ are zero. These expressions are substituted into (153) and the matrix inversion is performed numerically. Alternatively, a linear equation solving technique can be used to solve the set of equations (146) directly.

Quantity	Symbol	Value
Vehicle mass	m	2276 kg
Aerodynamic Reference Area	S	16.4 m^2
Zero Lift Coefficient of Drag	C_{D_0}	0.032
Drag Polar Lift Constant	K	1.4
Maximum Lift-to-Drag Ratio	E^*	2.36228

Table 1: Vehicle Physical and Aerodynamic Properties

Once $x_1(z_f)$, ν_1, and z_{f_1} have been obtained, p_1 is found from (152). Finally, (84) is used to obtain the first order control vector u_1, using

$$\bar{\mathcal{H}}_{u_L u_L} = \frac{2}{E^*} \tag{277}$$

$$\bar{\mathcal{H}}_{u_S u_S} = \frac{2}{E^*} \tag{278}$$

Also $\bar{\mathcal{H}}_{ux}$ is a zero matrix and the only nonzero elements of matrix $\bar{f}_u$ are given by

$$\bar{f}_{2_{u_L}} = -\frac{2\bar{u}_L}{E^*} \tag{279}$$

$$\bar{f}_{2_{u_S}} = -\frac{2\bar{u}_S}{E^*} \tag{280}$$

$$\bar{f}_{3_{u_L}} = 1 \tag{281}$$

$$\bar{f}_{4_{u_S}} = 1 \tag{282}$$

Note that the control is assumed to be unconstrained so that β, defined by (82), is simply an identity matrix of the appropriate dimensions.

F. Numerical Results

In order to evaluate the performance of these algorithms, a set of representative aeroassisted plane change missions was selected. For each case the vehicle physical and aerodynamic properties were those presented in Table 1. This hypothetical vehicle was chosen to be similar to the vehicle used in [7]. The initial conditions for all cases were $h_i = 60960$ m (200,000 ft), $\gamma_i = $ -1.0 deg, $V_i = 7980$ m/s (25945 ft/s), and $\psi_i = \phi_i = \theta_i = 0.0$. The specified terminal conditions were $h_f = 60960$ m, $\gamma_f = 1.0$ deg, and $\psi_f = 10, 20, 30$, and 40 deg. Finally, the physical and atmospheric properties of Earth assumed in the simulation are those presented in Table 2.

Guidance law performance was evaluated for two distinct scenarios. In the first scenario, no atmospheric uncertainties were present and it was assumed that the guidance model of the atmospheric properties was perfect.

Quantity	Symbol	Value
Earth radius	R	6378.14 km
Earth Gravitational Constant	μ	$3.986005 \cdot 10^5 \text{ km}^3/\text{s}^2$
Atmospheric Density Constant	ρ_0	1.225 kg/m^3
Density Scale Height	h_s	6.477 km

Table 2: Gravitational and Atmospheric Constants of the Earth

Coefficient	Robust 1 Value	Robust 2 Value
Q_{11}	130.0	60.0
Q_{22}	10.0	4.0
Q_{33}	10.0	4.0

Table 3: Disturbance Weighting Coefficients

In this case, the worst case disturbance terms involving Nature's control vector w were set to zero (achieved in practice by setting the disturbance weighting factors Q_{ii} to some suitably large number such that $1/Q_{ii} \cong 0$). This scenario was chosen in order to allow guidance law performance to be compared with numerically generated optimal solutions. The optimal solutions were generated using the multiple shooting code POPTART developed by the first author [25]. For the second scenario, near-worst-case density profiles were selected for each case. For approximately the first half of the time of flight for each case, the density was a specified percentage greater than nominal, and for the remainder of the time of flight the density was a specified percentage less than nominal. The magnitude of these offsets was varied from 0 to 30 percent. The vehicle guidance system was allowed no knowledge of these density perturbations. Two versions of the robust guidance law were examined. For the first version, referred to as Robust 1, the disturbance weighting factors Q_{ii} were chosen through an iterative process that consisted of guessing values for the Q_{ii}, evaluating guidance law performance via simulation for density dispersions of 10 percent, and changing the Q_{ii} to improve the performance in the presence of these dispersions. For the second version, referred to as Robust 2, a similar process was carried out for density dispersions of 30 percent. This process yielded the values for Q_{ii} listed in Table 3. In the present study, the adjustment of the Q_{ii} was done somewhat heuristically, although for a detailed design it would be straightforward to use a numerical parameter optimization package to numerically optimize the performance as a function of these weighting matrices.

Case	10 deg	20 deg	30 deg	40 deg
Optimal (Multiple Shooting)	7316.5	6781.6	6284.6	5824.1
Zeroth Order - Open Loop	7334.1	6816.7	6332.7	5882.4
First Order - Open Loop	7323.0	6799.0	6309.7	5854.5

Table 4: Comparison of Open Loop Final Velocities (m/s)

1. Performance in a Disturbance Free Environment

Performance was analyzed for required heading angle changes of 10, 20, 30, and 40 degrees. For each case, the performance of the zeroth and first order corrected guidance laws was compared with the numerically generated optimal solution. The parameters examined in the comparison were the states h and γ, the controls u_L and u_S and the final values for velocity V_f. Comparisons were made for both the open loop solutions generated at the beginning of the trajectory and the closed loop solutions found as a result of implementing the guidance laws as feedback algorithms. The open loop solution for each guidance law gives an indication of how accurately the guidance law can predict the optimal solution, while the closed loop solution is the ultimate test of guidance law accuracy.

The results of the open loop simulations are presented in Figures 1-8 and Table 4. The Figures present the state and control histories for 20 and 40 degree heading changes, while Table 4 presents the final velocity for all four heading changes. Note that the first order state and control histories are significantly closer to optimal than the zeroth order histories are. In particular, the flight path angle history for the first order solution approximates the optimal history much better than does the zeroth order solution. Note that both solutions achieve the specified terminal conditions. On the other hand, Table 4 indicates that both the zeroth and first order open loop solutions are somewhat optimistic in terms of their final velocities in that these final velocities are larger than those of the corresponding optimal trajectories, although the first order solutions more accurately predict the optimal final velocities.

In order to examine closed loop performance, the guidance algorithms were implemented as feedback laws in which the optimal controls were recalculated every Δt second. Figures 9-16 present the closed loop state and control histories for 20 and 40 degree heading changes, while Tables 5 and 6 present the final velocity and heading angle for all four heading changes. A guidance update time $\Delta t = 0.5$ seconds was used in all simulation runs. Note that the zeroth order guidance law was unable to meet the specified exit conditions for plane changes greater than 20 degrees. Furthermore, Table 5 indicates that the use of this guidance law resulted in significantly less

Case	10 deg	20 deg	30 deg	40 deg
Optimal (Multiple Shooting)	7316.5	6781.6	6284.6	5824.1
Zeroth Order - Closed Loop	7308.0	6721.7	-	-
First Order - Closed Loop	7316.1	6779.8	6281.9	5820.3

Table 5: Comparison of Closed Loop Final Velocities (m/s)

Case	10 deg	20 deg	30 deg	40 deg
Zeroth Order - Closed Loop	9.999	19.996	-	-
First Order - Closed Loop	9.999	19.999	29.999	40.000

Table 6: Comparison of Closed Loop Final Heading Angles (deg)

than optimal performance even for heading changes less than 20 degrees. On the other hand, the first order guidance law met the exit conditions for all four required heading changes and yielded final velocities within 4 m/s of the optimal solution.

A parameter study was also made to determine the effect on performance of varying the guidance update time Δt. Values of Δt from 0.1 - 10.0 seconds were examined. Table 7 presents the final velocity achieved for the first order guidance law as a function of Δt for all four required heading changes. Note that performance degrades only minimally for $\Delta t \leq$ 1.0 seconds, but degrades significantly as Δt increases to 10.0 seconds. This study indicates that Δt should be kept ≤ 1.0 seconds for an operational system. It was observed during the parameter study that even for a Δt of 0.1 seconds, each second of simulation time took no longer than 0.5 second of real time to run on a Sun SPARCstation 1+ workstation, the recommended range for Δt should pose no difficulty even for present day processors of moderate capability.

2. Performance With Density Dispersions

Performance was also analyzed in the presence of a density wave of the form indicated in Figure 17. The magnitude of the deviation from nominal

Heading Change	0.1 sec	0.5 sec	1.0 sec	5.0 sec	10.0 sec
10 deg	7316.4	7316.2	7315.8	7313.4	7309.7
20 deg	6780.0	6779.8	6779.5	6777.3	6774.6
30 deg	6281.9	6281.9	6281.7	6278.5	6276.8
40 deg	5820.6	5820.3	5820.3	5818.5	5814.5

Table 7: Final Velocities (m/s) Versus Guidance Update Time

density (shown as 10 percent in Figure 17) was varied from 0 percent to 30 percent of nominal. The performance of each version of the robust guidance law (using suitably adjusted values for Q_{ii}) was compared with the performance of the dispersion-free approximate optimal guidance law (using large values of Q_{ii} such that $1/Q_{ii} \cong 0$, effectively eliminating the effects of w on the solution).

Figure 18 presents the final velocity achieved by each guidance law as a function of dispersion magnitude for the 40 degree heading change case. The results for 10, 20, and 30 degree heading changes are qualitatively similar to those presented for a 40 degree heading change. Figure 18 indicates that for small dispersion magnitudes, the approximate optimal guidance law performs only slightly better than the Robust 1 guidance law but noticeably better (by 22 m/s) than the Robust 2 guidance law. However, for large dispersion magnitudes, both robust guidance laws perform significantly better than the approximate optimal guidance law. These results are to be expected, since the Q_{ii} for the robust guidance laws were chosen to optimize the performance in the presence of significant density dispersions. Figure 18 also indicates that guidance law Robust 2 performance is virtually insensitive to density dispersions between 0 and 30 percent. Guidance law Robust 1 performance is somewhat more sensitive than guidance law Robust 2 performance though still less sensitive than the approximate optimal guidance law performance. Thus a tradeoff exists between robustness and dispersion free performance, but significant robustness can be achieved through a judicious choice for the Q_{ii} at the expense of a relatively small loss in dispersion free performance.

Figures 19 and 20 present the first order corrected lift and side force controls for each guidance law (approximate optimal, Robust 1, and Robust 2) for the case of zero dispersions. These figures indicate that the robust guidance laws command larger lift and side forces than the approximate optimal guidance law for most of the trajectory. The reason for this is that at each guidance update step the robust guidance laws anticipate subsequent nonzero density dispersions and try to correct for these in advance. At the very end of the trajectory, the robust guidance laws command lower lift and side force controls than the approximate optimal guidance law since the anticipated density dispersions were not actually encountered. Similar test cases with nonzero density dispersions indicate that, in general, the robust guidance laws command larger forces at the beginning of the trajectory than the approximate optimal guidance law but command smaller forces at the end of the trajectory.

IV. Conclusions

A robust regular perturbation game theoretic guidance algorithm has been derived, and its performance has been demonstrated for the aeroassisted plane change problem. An important feature of this algorithm is that it reduces to a disturbance-free approximate optimal guidance law in the case where no dispersions are expected, since the magnitude of disturbances allowed for in the guidance law can be set arbitrarily low. It has been demonstrated that the dispersion-free approximate optimal guidance law performs extremely close to the optimal performance achievable, while the use of the robust approximate optimal guidance law minimizes the loss in performance that results from encountering unexpected atmospheric density dispersions. Finally, both guidance laws require only a finite set of function evaluations and a small set of numerical quadratures, all easily performed on board.

Future work in this area should concentrate on a number of issue not addressed in this paper. First, the inclusion of control inequality constraints presents little problem in the derivation but could present a problem for the analytical zeroth order solution, since the sequence of constrained versus unconstrained arcs must be guessed *a priori*. Furthermore, the handling of state constraints results in discontinuous costate functions, further complicating the computation of the zeroth order solution. Finally, methods for handling situations in which the perturbation dynamics are of similar or greater magnitude than the primary dynamics need to be explored.

Acknowledgements

This study was supported in part through funding provided by The Aerospace Corporation Work-Study Ph.D. Fellowship Program. The first author would like to dedicate this contribution to the memory of Lia Catherine Ilgen, November 25 1962 - October 29 1989, a sister and a friend who is dearly missed.

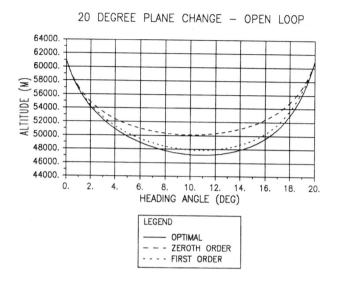

Figure 1. Altitude versus Heading Angle, 20 Degree Plane Change, Open loop

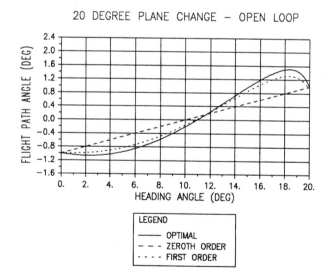

Figure 2. Flight Path Angle versus Heading Angle, 20 Degree Plane Change, Open loop

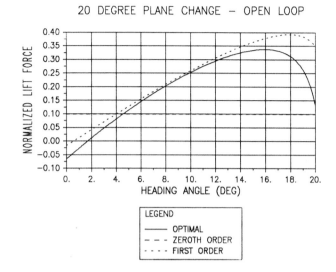

**Figure 3. Normalized Lift Force versus Heading Angle,
20 Degree Plane Change, Open loop**

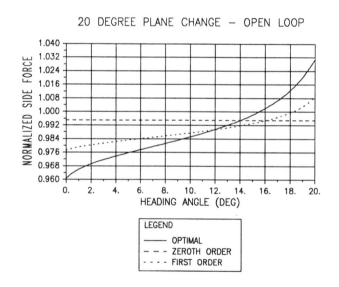

**Figure 4. Normalized Side Force versus Heading Angle,
20 Degree Plane Change, Open loop**

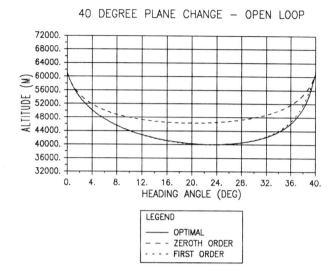

Figure 5. Altitude versus Heading Angle, 40 Degree Plane Change, Open loop

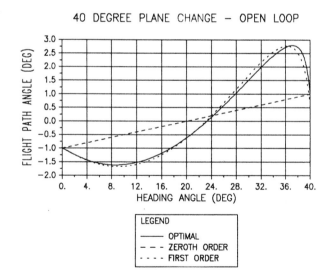

Figure 6. Flight Path Angle versus Heading Angle, 40 Degree Plane Change, Open loop

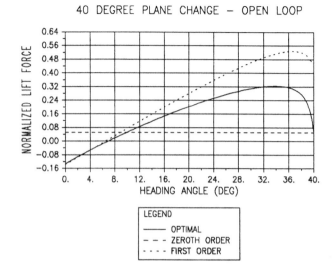

**Figure 7. Normalized Lift Force versus Heading Angle,
40 Degree Plane Change, Open loop**

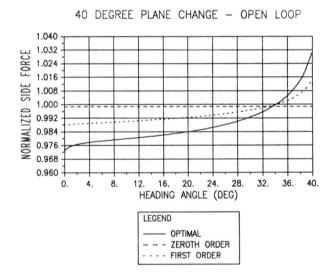

**Figure 8. Normalized Side Force versus Heading Angle,
40 Degree Plane Change, Open loop**

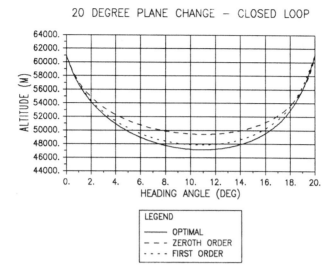

Figure 9. Altitude versus Heading Angle, 20 Degree Plane Change, Closed loop

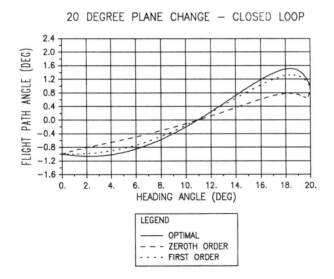

Figure 10. Flight Path Angle versus Heading Angle, 20 Degree Plane Change, Closed loop

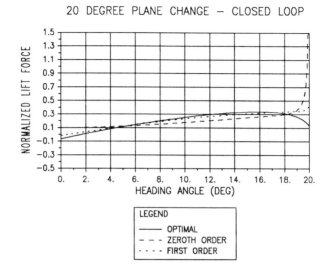

Figure 11. Normalized Lift Force versus Heading Angle,
20 Degree Plane Change, Closed loop

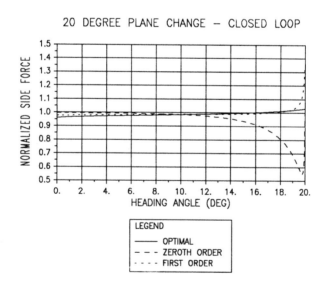

Figure 12. Normalized Side Force versus Heading Angle,
20 Degree Plane Change, Closed loop

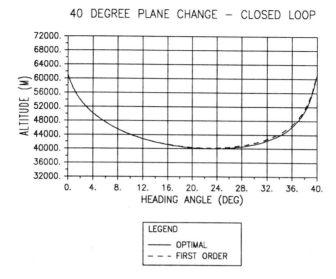

Figure 13. Altitude versus Heading Angle, 40 Degree Plane Change, Closed loop

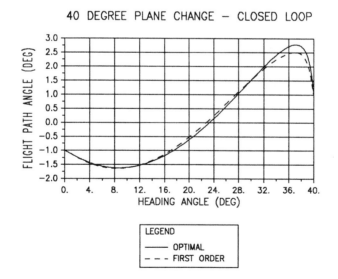

Figure 14. Flight Path Angle versus Heading Angle, 40 Degree Plane Change, Closed loop

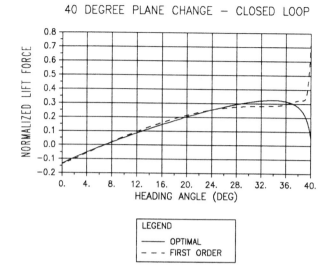

**Figure 15. Normalized Lift Force versus Heading Angle,
40 Degree Plane Change, Closed loop**

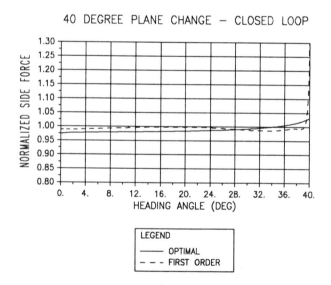

**Figure 16. Normalized Side Force versus Heading Angle,
40 Degree Plane Change, Closed loop**

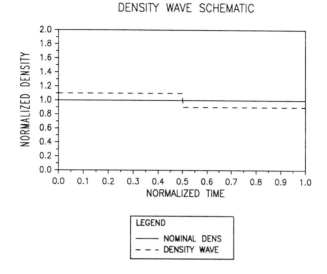

Figure 17. Deviations in Density versus Normalized Time of Flight

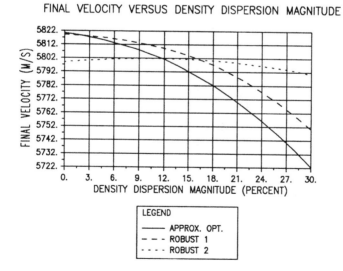

Figure 18. Final Velocity versus Magnitude of Density Dispersions

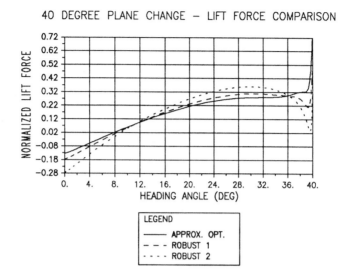

Figure 19. Comparison of Normalized Lift Force Controls For Zero Density Dispersions

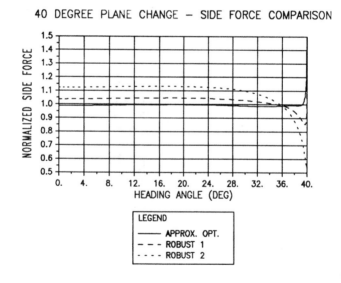

Figure 20. Comparison of Normalized Side Force Controls For Zero Density Dispersions

Appendix A. Expressions for Second Order Terms

This appendix contains expressions for the second order perturbation series terms $\mathcal{Q}_2$, $\mathcal{R}_2$, $\mathcal{G}_2$, and $\mathcal{F}_2$. These terms are given explicitly by

$$
\begin{aligned}
\mathcal{Q}_2 =\ & \bar{\Phi}_{xx}\left(\bar{f}_x x_1 + \bar{f}_u u_1 + \bar{f}_w w_1 + \bar{g}\right) T_1 + \frac{1}{2}\bar{\Phi}_{xx}\ddot{x}_0 T_1^2 + \\
& \frac{1}{2}\left(x_1 + \bar{f}T_1\right)^T \bar{\Phi}_{xxx}\left(x_1 + \bar{f}T_1\right)
\end{aligned}
\tag{283}
$$

$$
\begin{aligned}
\mathcal{R}_2 =\ & \bar{\Psi}_{xx}\left(\bar{f}_x x_1 + \bar{f}_u u_1 + \bar{f}_w w_1 + \bar{g}\right) T_1 + \frac{1}{2}\bar{\Psi}_{xx}\ddot{x}_0 T_1^2 + \\
& \frac{1}{2}\left(x_1 + \bar{f}T_1\right)^T \bar{\Psi}_{xxx}\left(x_1 + \bar{f}T_1\right)
\end{aligned}
\tag{284}
$$

$$
\begin{aligned}
\mathcal{G}_2 =\ & \bar{f}_x\left(\bar{f}_x x_1 + \bar{f}_u u_1 + \bar{f}_w w_1\right) T_1 + \bar{f}_x \dot{\bar{f}} T_1^2 + \\
& \frac{1}{2}x_1^T \bar{f}_{xx} x_1 + x_1^T \bar{f}_{xu} u_1 + x_1^T \bar{f}_{xw} w_1 + \\
& \frac{1}{2}u_1^T \bar{f}_{uu} u_1 + \frac{1}{2}w_1^T \bar{f}_{ww} w_1 + \bar{g}_x x_1
\end{aligned}
\tag{285}
$$

$$
\begin{aligned}
\mathcal{F}_2 =\ & \frac{1}{2}u_1^T \bar{L}_{uu} u_1 + \frac{1}{2}w_1^T \bar{L}_{ww} w_1 + \dot{p}_1^T \bar{f} T_1 + \frac{1}{2}\ddot{p}_0^T \bar{f} T_1^2 + \\
& p_1^T\left(\bar{f}_x x_1 + \bar{f}_x \bar{f} T_1 + \bar{f}_u u_1 + \bar{f}_w w_1 + \bar{g}\right)
\end{aligned}
\tag{286}
$$

Appendix B. Transition Matrix Partial Derivatives

This appendix contains the expressions required to evaluate the transition matrix $\mathcal{Z}(0, z)$ for $z \in [0, z_f]$. This matrix is a 10×10 matrix that can be partitioned as

$$
\mathcal{Z} = \begin{vmatrix} \mathcal{Z}_{11} & \mathcal{Z}_{12} \\ \mathcal{Z}_{21} & \mathcal{Z}_{22} \end{vmatrix}
\tag{287}
$$

where the $\mathcal{Z}_{ij}$ are all 5×5 submatrices. Let $\mathcal{Z}_{ij_{kl}}$ denote the element in the kth row and lth column of $\mathcal{Z}_{ij}$. Then these elements are found from the relations

$$
\mathcal{Z}_{11_{kl}} = \frac{\partial x_k(0)}{\partial x_l(z)}
\tag{288}
$$

$$
\mathcal{Z}_{12_{kl}} = \frac{\partial x_k(0)}{\partial p_l(z)}
\tag{289}
$$

$$\mathcal{Z}_{21_{kl}} = \frac{\partial p_k(0)}{\partial x_l(z)} \tag{290}$$

$$\mathcal{Z}_{22_{kl}} = \frac{\partial p_k(0)}{\partial p_l(z)} \tag{291}$$

Using the state and costate equations (247)-(250) and (237)-(242), the nonzero elements of $\mathcal{Z}$ are given explicitly by

$$\mathcal{Z}_{11_{kk}} = 1 \quad (k = 1, 2, 3, 4, 5) \tag{292}$$

$$\mathcal{Z}_{11_{13}} = z \tag{293}$$

$$\mathcal{Z}_{12_{11}} = \left(\frac{1}{Q_{22}} + \frac{E^*}{2\bar{p}_v} \right) \frac{z^3}{6} \tag{294}$$

$$\mathcal{Z}_{12_{12}} = \frac{E^*}{2\bar{p}_v^2} \left(\bar{p}_\gamma \frac{z^2}{2} - \bar{p}_\omega \frac{z^3}{6} \right) \tag{295}$$

$$\mathcal{Z}_{12_{13}} = -\left(\frac{1}{Q_{22}} + \frac{E^*}{2\bar{p}_v} \right) \frac{z^2}{2} \tag{296}$$

$$\mathcal{Z}_{12_{21}} = \frac{E^*}{4\bar{p}_{v^2}} \left(\frac{2}{3} \bar{p}_\omega z^3 - \bar{p}_\gamma z^2 \right) \tag{297}$$

$$\mathcal{Z}_{12_{22}} = -\frac{E^*}{2\bar{p}_{v^3}} \left(\bar{p}_\gamma^2 z - \bar{p}_\omega \bar{p}_\gamma z^2 + \bar{p}_\omega^2 \frac{z^3}{3} + \bar{p}_\psi^2 z \right) - \frac{z}{Q_{11}} \tag{298}$$

$$\mathcal{Z}_{12_{23}} = \frac{E^*}{4\bar{p}_{v^2}} \left(2\bar{p}_\gamma z - \bar{p}_\omega z^2 \right) \tag{299}$$

$$\mathcal{Z}_{12_{24}} = \frac{E^*}{2\bar{p}_{v^2}} \bar{p}_\psi z \tag{300}$$

$$\mathcal{Z}_{12_{31}} = \left(\frac{1}{Q_{22}} + \frac{E^*}{2\bar{p}_v} \right) \frac{z^2}{2} \tag{301}$$

$$\mathcal{Z}_{12_{32}} = \frac{E^*}{2\bar{p}_{v^2}} \left(\bar{p}_\gamma z - \bar{p}_\omega \frac{z^2}{2} \right) \tag{302}$$

$$\mathcal{Z}_{12_{33}} = -\left(\frac{1}{Q_{22}} + \frac{E^*}{2\bar{p}_v} \right) z \tag{303}$$

$$\mathcal{Z}_{12_{42}} = \frac{E^*}{2\bar{p}_{v^2}} \bar{p}_\psi z \tag{304}$$

$$\mathcal{Z}_{12_{44}} = -\left(\frac{1}{Q_{33}} + \frac{E^*}{2\bar{p}_v} \right) z \tag{305}$$

$$\mathcal{Z}_{22_{kk}} = 1 \quad (k = 1, 2, 3, 4, 5) \tag{306}$$

$$\mathcal{Z}_{22_{31}} = -z \tag{307}$$

Appendix C. Expressions for Perturbation Dynamics and Derivatives

This appendix contains the expressions for $\bar{g}$ and $\bar{g}_x$ required for calculating the particular solutions $\mathcal{X}_1(0)$ and $\mathcal{P}_1(0)$ from (151). Appendix C.1 presents the expressions with no approximations beyond those assumed in obtaining the state equations (186)-(191), while Appendix C.2 presents the expressions obtained by using the approximations discussed in Section 3.5.

Appendix C.1. Exact Expressions for Perturbation Dynamics and Derivatives

The perturbation dynamics vector $\bar{g}$ is a vector of 5 elements. The elements are given explicitly by

$$\bar{g}_1 = 0 \tag{308}$$

$$\bar{g}_2 = -\frac{R}{\bar{r}\bar{\omega}}\left(2e^{-\bar{v}} - 1\right)\bar{\gamma} \tag{309}$$

$$\bar{g}_3 = \frac{R}{\bar{r}\bar{\omega}}\left(1 - e^{-\bar{v}}\right) \tag{310}$$

$$\bar{g}_4 = -\frac{R}{\bar{r}\bar{\omega}}\left(\cos\bar{\psi}\tan\bar{\phi}\right) \tag{311}$$

$$\bar{g}_5 = \frac{R}{\bar{r}\bar{\omega}}\sin\bar{\psi} \tag{312}$$

where $\bar{r}$ is the zeroth order radius found from the zeroth order state $\bar{\omega}$.

The derivatives $\bar{g}_x$ of the perturbation vector $\bar{g}$ with respect to the state vector x is represented by a 5×5 matrix. The elements $(\bar{g}_x)_{ij}$ are found from

$$(\bar{g}_x)_{ij} = \frac{\partial \bar{g}_i}{\partial x_j} \tag{313}$$

The nonzero elements of this matrix are therfore given explicitly by

$$(\bar{g}_x)_{21} = -R\left(\frac{h_s - \bar{r}}{\bar{r}^2\bar{\omega}^2}\right)\left(2e^{-\bar{v}} - 1\right)\bar{\gamma} \tag{314}$$

$$(\bar{g}_x)_{22} = \frac{2R}{\bar{r}\bar{\omega}}e^{-\bar{v}}\bar{\gamma} \tag{315}$$

$$(\bar{g}_x)_{23} = -\frac{R}{\bar{r}\bar{\omega}}\left(2e^{-\bar{v}} - 1\right) \tag{316}$$

$$(\bar{g}_x)_{31} = R\left(\frac{h_s - \bar{r}}{\bar{r}^2\bar{\omega}^2}\right)\left(1 - e^{-\bar{v}}\right) \tag{317}$$

$$(\bar{g}_x)_{32} \;=\; \frac{R}{\bar{r}\bar{\omega}} e^{-\bar{v}} \tag{318}$$

$$(\bar{g}_x)_{41} \;=\; -R\left(\frac{h_s - \bar{r}}{\bar{r}^2\bar{\omega}^2}\right)\left(\cos\bar{\psi}\tan\bar{\phi}\right) \tag{319}$$

$$(\bar{g}_x)_{44} \;=\; \frac{R}{\bar{r}\bar{\omega}}\left(\sin\bar{\psi}\tan\bar{\phi}\right) \tag{320}$$

$$(\bar{g}_x)_{45} \;=\; -\frac{R}{\bar{r}\bar{\omega}}\left(\frac{\cos\bar{\psi}}{\cos^2\bar{\phi}}\right) \tag{321}$$

$$(\bar{g}_x)_{51} \;=\; R\left(\frac{h_s - \bar{r}}{\bar{r}^2\bar{\omega}^2}\right)\sin\bar{\psi} \tag{322}$$

$$(\bar{g}_x)_{54} \;=\; \frac{R}{\bar{r}\bar{\omega}}\cos\bar{\psi} \tag{323}$$

Appendix C.2. Approximate Expressions for Perturbation Dynamics and Derivatives

The expressions in Appendix C.1 can be simplified by introducing the approximations $\phi \cong 0$ and $R/r \cong 1$. The use of these approximations results in the following expressions for $\bar{g}$.

$$\bar{g}_1 \;=\; 0 \tag{324}$$

$$\bar{g}_2 \;=\; -\frac{1}{\bar{\omega}}\left(2e^{-\bar{v}} - 1\right)\bar{\gamma} \tag{325}$$

$$\bar{g}_3 \;=\; \frac{1}{\bar{\omega}}\left(1 - e^{-\bar{v}}\right) \tag{326}$$

$$\bar{g}_4 \;=\; 0 \tag{327}$$

$$\bar{g}_5 \;=\; 0 \tag{328}$$

The nonzero elements of $\bar{g}_x$ are given by

$$(\bar{g}_x)_{21} \;=\; \frac{\left(2e^{-\bar{v}} - 1\right)\bar{\gamma}}{\bar{\omega}^2} \tag{329}$$

$$(\bar{g}_x)_{22} \;=\; \frac{2e^{-\bar{v}}\bar{\gamma}}{\bar{\omega}} \tag{330}$$

$$(\bar{g}_x)_{23} \;=\; -\frac{\left(2e^{-\bar{v}} - 1\right)}{\bar{\omega}} \tag{331}$$

$$(\bar{g}_x)_{31} \;=\; -\frac{\left(1 - e^{-\bar{v}}\right)}{\bar{\omega}^2} \tag{332}$$

$$(\bar{g}_x)_{32} \;=\; \frac{e^{-\bar{v}}}{\bar{\omega}} \tag{333}$$

References

[1] W. L. Garrard, N. H. McClamroch, L. G. Clark, "An Approach to Sub-optimal Feedback Control of Nonlinear Systems", International Journal of Control, 5, 425-435 (1967).

[2] J. F. Baldwin, J. H. Sims Williams, "The Use of Perturbation in the Synthesis of Closed-loop Optimal Control Laws for Nonlinear Systems", Automatica, 5, 357-367, (1969).

[3] W. L. Garrard, "Suboptimal Feedback Control of Nonlinear Systems", Automatica, 8, 219-221 (1972).

[4] W. L. Garrard, D. F. Enns, A. Snell, "Nonlinear Longitudinal Control of a Supermaneuverable Aircraft", Proceedings of the ACC, 142-145, (1989).

[5] M. S. Leung and A. J. Calise, "An Approach to Optimal Guidance of an Advanced Launch Vehicle Concept", Proceedings of the ACC, 1824-1828, (1990).

[6] A. J. Calise, D. H. Hodges, M. S. Leung, R. R. Bless, "Optimal Guidance Law Development for an Advanced Launch System", NASA Contractor Report NASA-CR-187652, 1990.

[7] J. L. Speyer and E. Z. Crues, "Approximate Optimal Atmospheric Guidance Law for Aeroassisted Plane-Change Maneuvers," Journal of Guidance, Control, and Dynamics, 13, (5), (1990).

[8] J. L. Speyer, T. Feeley, D. G. Hull, "Real-time Approximate Optimal Guidance Laws for the Advanced Launch System", Proceedings of the ACC, 2032-2036, (1989).

[9] D. Mishne and J. L. Speyer, "A Guidance Law for the Aeroassisted Plane Change Maneuver in the Presence of Atmospheric Uncertainties", Proceedings of the 25th Conference on Decision and Control, 677-682, (1986).

[10] T. Basar, G. J. Olsder, Dynamic Noncooperative Game Theory, Academic Press, London, 1982.

[11] M. Tahk and J. L. Speyer, "Modelling of Parameter Variations and Asymptotic LQG Synthesis," IEEE Transactions on Automatic Control, Vol. AC-32, (9), (1987).

[12] N. S. Gupta, "An Overview of Differential Games", in Control and Dynamic Systems, Vol. 17 (C. T. Leondes, ed.), Academic Press, New York, 1981.

[13] C. R. Hargraves and S. W. Paris, "Direct Trajectory Optimization Using Nonlinear Programming and Collocation", Journal of Guidance, Control, and Dynamics, **10** (4), 338-342, (1987).

[14] U. M. Ascher, R. M. M. Matheij, R. D. Russel, *Numerical Solution of Boundary Value Problems for Ordinary Differential Equations*, Prentice-Hall, N.J. 1988.

[15] A. Miele, A. Mangiavacchi, A. K. Aggrawal, "Modified Quasilinearization Algorithm for Optimal Control Problems with Nondifferential Constraints", Journal of Optimization Theory and Applications, **14** (5), 529-556, (1974).

[16] D. H. Jacobson and D. Q. Mayne, *Differential Dynamics Programming*, American Elsevier, New York, 1970.

[17] M. R. Ilgen, *Robust Approximate Optimal Guidance Strategies for Aeroassisted Orbital Transfer Missions*, Ph.D. dissertation, University of California, Los Angeles, 1992.

[18] A. E. Bryson and Y.C. Ho, *Applied Optimal Control*, Hemisphere Publishing, Washington D.C., 1975.

[19] A. Busemann, N. X. Vinh, and G. F. Kelly, "Optimal Maneuvers of a Skip Vehicle with Bounded Lift Constraints," Journal of Optimization Theory and Applications, **3** (4), (1969).

[20] J. L. Speyer and M. E. Womble, "Approximate Optimal Atmospheric Entry Trajectories," Journal of Spacecraft, **8** (11), (1971).

[21] D. Mishne and J. L. Speyer, "Optimal Control of Aeroassisted Plane-Change Maneuver Using Feedback Expansions," *Proceedings of the AIAA Atmospheric Flight Mechanics Conference*, 253-258, (1986).

[22] I. Rhee and J. L. Speyer, "A Game Theoretic Controller and its Relationship to H_∞ and Linear-Exponential-Gaussian Synthesis," *Proceedings of the 28th Conference on Decision and Control*, 909-915, (1989).

[23] I. Rhee and J. L. Speyer, "A Game Theoretic Approach to a Finite-Time Disturbance Attenuation Problem," IEEE Transactions on Automatic Control, Vol. **AC-36**, (9), 1021-1032, 1991.

[24] *CRC Standard Mathematical Tables*, W. H. Beyer, Editor, CRC Press, Boca Raton, 1987.

[25] M. R. Ilgen, "POPTART: A General Purpose Multiple Shooting Trajectory Optimization Program", Aerospace Corporation TOR-92(2530)-4, 31 January, 1992.

Application of Multiple Model Adaptive Algorithms to Reconfigurable Flight Control

Peter S. Maybeck

Department of Electrical Engineering
Air Force Institute of Technology / ENG
Wright-Patterson AFB, Ohio 45433-6583

ABSTRACT

A multiple model adaptive controller (MMAC) that provides for reconfiguration in response to sensor and/or actuator failures is developed for the Short Take-Off and Landing (STOL) F-15 aircraft. Each elemental controller within the multiple model controller is based on a Command Generator Tracker / Proportional plus Integral / Kalman Filter (CGT/PI/KF) design employing reduced order models, and each assumes a particular system status: no failures or a single failed surface or sensor (or any second such failure, once a first failure is declared). The entire multiple model adaptive controller is evaluated against a higher order "truth model" with a selected failure, and then repeating the process for all failure modes of interest. This controller is shown to provide effective reconfigurability when subjected to single and double failures of sensors and/or actuators. Its performance is enhanced by an alternate computation of the MMAC hypothesis probabilities, use of MAP versus Bayesian form of the MMAC (or a modified combination of both), and reduction of identification ambiguities through scalar residual monitoring for the case of sensor failures.

CONTROL AND DYNAMIC SYSTEMS, VOL. 52

I. INTRODUCTION

For many applications, it is highly desirable to develop an aircraft flight control system with reconfigurable capabilities: able to detect and isolate failures of sensors and/or actuators and then to employ a controller algorithm that has been specifically designed for the current failure mode status. One means of accomplishing this, in a manner that is ideally suited to distributed computation, is multiple model adaptive estimation (MMAE) [1-4] and control (MMAC) [5-7].

Assume that the aircraft system is adequately represented by a linear perturbation stochastic state model, with a (failure status) uncertain parameter vector affecting the matrices defining the structure of the model or depicting the statistics of the noises entering it. Further assume that the parameters can take on only discrete values; either this is reasonable physically (as for many failure detection formulations), or representative discrete values are chosen throughout the continuous range of possible values. Then a Kalman filter is designed for each choice of parameter value, resulting in a bank of K separate "elemental" filters. Based upon the observed characteristics of the residuals in these K filters, the conditional probabilities of each discrete parameter value being "correct", given the measurement history to that time, are evaluated iteratively. A separate set of controller gains is associated with each elemental filter in the bank. The control value of each elemental controller is weighted by its corresponding probability, and the adaptive control is produced as the probability-weighted average of the elemental controller outputs. As one alternative (using maximum a posteriori, or MAP, rather than minimum mean square error, or MMSE, criteria for optimality), the control value from the single elemental controller associated with the highest conditional probability can be selected as the output of the adaptive controller.

Initial development and investigations of multiple model algorithms assumed uncertain but constant parameters, and some useful convergence results have been obtained for this class of problems [8-10]. For the case of time-varying parameters, one ad hoc approach has been to use an algorithm designed under the assumption of constant parameters, but to provide a lower bound for the computed probabilities to prevent the algorithm from "locking onto" a single parameter value [2,4]. Another approach has been to match each elemental filter to a time history of parameter values rather than just one constant value [4,11]. This would require K^i elemental filters at sample time t_i, which would be impractical for actual implementation. Various approaches to reducing the computational burden of the algorithm have been taken, including the use of Markov models for parameter variation [4,11,12], "pruning" and "merging" of branches in a "tree" of possible parameter time histories [13,14], hierarchical structuring [15], dynamic coarse-to-finer rediscretization [16], and moving-bank multiple model concepts [17-20].

Multiple model adaptation has been successfully applied to a number of practical problems. It has exhibited promising results in the tracking of maneuvering targets [21-29], multiple hypothesis testing [6,13,30], detection of incidents on freeways [31], adaptive deconvolution of seismic signals [32], and problems in which initial uncertainties are so large that nonadaptive extended Kalman filters diverge [33,34].

Maintaining fewer than the maximum specifiable number of elemental filters and/or controllers in the bank enhances the feasibility of multiple model algorithms, but it could aggravate the behavior observed earlier [6] of making hasty decisions when the "true model" is not included in the filter's model set. Some research has been directed at the information theoretic problem associated with this condition [35-38]. Thus, it is essential to demonstrate that any proposed algorithm yields effective performance under all realistic conditions.

Recent research has applied a multiple model adaptive control algorithm with four elemental controllers to sensor or actuator failure detection and control reconfiguration in a STOL F-15 aircraft [39,40]. Each elemental controller was designed for a healthy aircraft, failed pitch rate sensor, failed stabilator, or failed "pseudo-surface" - a combination of canards, ailerons, and trailing edge flaps. This initial feasibility study showed that the elemental filters must be carefully tuned to avoid masking of "good" versus "bad" models, and this specifically argues against Loop Transmission Recovery (LTR) tuning [41-43]. The purpose of the current research [44,45] is to improve the behavior of the multiple model algorithm, to extend its applicability to a wider range of failure conditions (including soft as well as hard failures, and multiple failures), and to reduce the ambiguity of failure identification as much as possible.

II. MULTIPLE MODEL ADAPTIVE CONTROL

Let **a** denote the vector of uncertain parameters in a given linear stochastic state model for a dynamic system, in this case depicting the failure status of sensors and actuators of the aircraft. These parameters can affect the matrices defining the structure of the model or depicting the statistics of the noises entering it. In order to make simultaneous estimation of states and parameters tractable, it is assumed that a can take on only one of K discrete representative values. If we define the hypothesis conditional probability $p_k(t_i)$ as the probability that a assumes the value $\mathbf{a}_k$ (for $k = 1,2,...,K$), conditioned on the observed measurement history to time t_i:

$$p_k(t_i) = \text{Prob}\{\mathbf{a} = \mathbf{a}_k \mid \mathbf{Z}(t_i) = \mathbf{Z}_i\} \qquad (1)$$

then it can be shown [1-4] that $p_k(t_i)$ can be evaluated recursively for all k via the iteration:

$$p_k(t_i) = \frac{f_{\mathbf{z}(t_i)|\mathbf{a},\mathbf{Z}(t_{i-1})}(\mathbf{z}_i \mid \mathbf{a}_k, \mathbf{Z}_{i-1}) \cdot p_k(t_{i-1})}{\sum_{j=1}^{K} f_{\mathbf{z}(t_i)|\mathbf{a},\mathbf{Z}(t_{i-1})}(\mathbf{z}_i \mid \mathbf{a}_j, \mathbf{Z}_{i-1}) \cdot p_j(t_{i-1})} \qquad (2)$$

in terms of the previous values of $p_1(t_{i-1})$, ... , $p_K(t_{i-1})$, and conditional probability densities for the current measurement $\mathbf{z}(t_i)$ to be defined explicitly in Equation (12). Notationally, the measurement history random vector $\mathbf{Z}(t_i)$ is made up of partitions $\mathbf{z}(t_1),...,\mathbf{z}(t_i)$ that are the measurement vectors available at the sample times $t_1,...,t_i$; similarly, the realization $\mathbf{Z}_i$ of the measurement history vector has partitions $\mathbf{z}_1,...,\mathbf{z}_i$. Furthermore, the Bayesian multiple model adaptive controller output is the probability-weighted average [5-7]:

$$\mathbf{u}_{\text{MMAC}}(t_i) = \sum_{k=1}^{K} \mathbf{u}_k[\hat{\mathbf{x}}_k(t_i^+),t_i] \cdot p_k(t_i) \qquad (3)$$

Here $\mathbf{u}_k[\mathbf{x}(t_i), t_i]$ is a deterministic optimal full-state feedback control law based on the assumption that the parameter vector equals $\mathbf{a}_k$, and $\hat{\mathbf{x}}_k(t_i^+)$ is the state estimate generated by a Kalman filter similarly based on the assumption that $\mathbf{a} = \mathbf{a}_k$. If the parameter were in fact equal to $\mathbf{a}_k$, then certainty equivalence [5] would allow the LQG (Linear system, Quadratic cost, and Gaussian noise models) optimal stochastic control to be generated as one of the $\mathbf{u}_k[\hat{\mathbf{x}}_k(t_i^+),t_i]$ terms in the summation of Eq. (3).

More explicitly, let the model corresponding to $\mathbf{a}_k$ be described by an "equivalent discrete-time model" [4,5,11] for a continuous-time system with sampled data measurements:

$$\mathbf{x}_k(t_{i+1}) = \mathbf{\Phi}_k(t_{i+1},t_i)\mathbf{x}_k(t_i) + \mathbf{B}_k(t_i)\mathbf{u}(t_i) + \mathbf{G}_k(t_i)\mathbf{w}_k(t_i) \qquad (4)$$

$$\mathbf{z}(t_i) = \mathbf{H}_k(t_i)\mathbf{x}_k(t_i) + \mathbf{v}_k(t_i) \qquad (5)$$

where $\mathbf{x}_k$ is the state, $\mathbf{u}$ is a control input, $\mathbf{w}_k$ is discrete-time zero-mean white Gaussian dynamics noise of covariance $\mathbf{Q}_k(t_i)$ at each t_i, $\mathbf{z}$ is the measurement vector, and $\mathbf{v}_k$ is discrete-time zero-mean white Gaussian measurement noise of covariance $\mathbf{R}_k(t_i)$ at t_i, assumed independent of $\mathbf{w}_k$; the initial state $\mathbf{x}(t_0)$ is modeled as Gaussian, with mean $\hat{\mathbf{x}}_{k0}$ and covariance $\mathbf{P}_{k0}$ and is assumed independent of $\mathbf{w}_k$ and $\mathbf{v}_k$. Based on this model, the Kalman filter [11] is specified by the measurement update:

$$\mathbf{A}_k(t_i) = \mathbf{H}_k(t_i)\mathbf{P}_k(t_i^-)\mathbf{H}_k^T(t_i) + \mathbf{R}_k(t_i) \qquad (6)$$

$$\mathbf{K}_k(t_i) = \mathbf{P}_k(t_i^-)\mathbf{H}_k^T(t_i)\mathbf{A}_k^{-1}(t_i) \qquad (7)$$

$$\hat{\mathbf{x}}_k(t_i^+) = \hat{\mathbf{x}}_k(t_i^-) + \mathbf{K}_k(t_i)[\mathbf{z}_i - \mathbf{H}_k(t_i)\hat{\mathbf{x}}_k(t_i^-)] \qquad (8)$$

$$\mathbf{P}_k(t_i^+) = \mathbf{P}_k(t_i^-) - \mathbf{K}_k(t_i)\mathbf{H}_k(t_i)\mathbf{P}_k(t_i^-) \qquad (9)$$

and the propagation relation:

$$\hat{\mathbf{x}}_k(t_{i+1}^-) = \mathbf{\Phi}_k(t_{i+1},t_i)\hat{\mathbf{x}}_k(t_i^+) + \mathbf{B}_k(t_i)\mathbf{u}(t_i) \qquad (10)$$

$$\mathbf{P}_k(t_{i+1}^-) = \mathbf{\Phi}_k(t_{i+1},t_i)\mathbf{P}_k(t_i^+)\mathbf{\Phi}_k^T(t_{i+1},t_i)$$
$$+ \mathbf{G}_k(t_i)\mathbf{Q}_k(t_i)\mathbf{G}_k^T(t_i) \qquad (11)$$

Thus, the multiple model adaptive control (MMAC) algorithm is composed of a bank of K separate Kalman filters with associated controllers, each based on a particular value $\mathbf{a}_1,...,\mathbf{a}_K$ of the parameter vector, as depicted in Fig. 1.

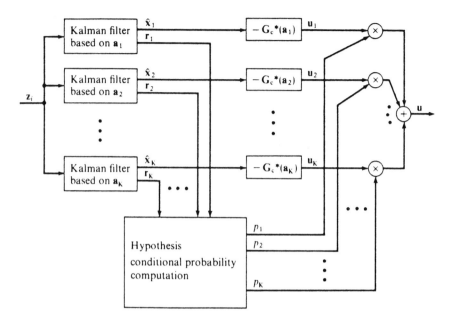

Fig. 1. Multiple Model Adaptive Controller

Actually, this figure portrays the simplest form of MMAC in which each elemental controller is merely a regulator with constant gain $\mathbf{G}_C^*(\mathbf{a}_k)$, such that each summation term in (3) is of the form

$$\mathbf{u}_k[\hat{\mathbf{x}}_k(t_i^+), t_i] = -\mathbf{G}_C^*(\mathbf{a}_k)\hat{\mathbf{x}}_k(t_i^+)$$

For the control law under investigation [39,40,44,45], this regulator form is replaced with a more complex structure, to be described in the next section. When the measurement $\mathbf{z}_i$ becomes available at t_i, the residuals $\mathbf{r}_1(t_i),...,\mathbf{r}_K(t_i)$ are generated in the K filters as the bracketed term in Eq. (8), and used to compute $p_1(t_i),..., p_K(t_i)$ via Eq. (2). Each numerator density function in (2) is given by the Gaussian form:

$$f_{\mathbf{z}(t_i)|\mathbf{a},\mathbf{Z}(t_{i-1})}(\mathbf{z}_i \mid \mathbf{a}_k, \mathbf{Z}_{i-1}) = \frac{1}{(2\pi)^{m/2}|\mathbf{A}_k(t_i)|^{1/2}} \exp\{\cdot\}$$

$$\{\cdot\} = \left\{-\tfrac{1}{2}\mathbf{r}_k^T(t_i)\mathbf{A}_k^{-1}(t_i)\mathbf{r}_k(t_i)\right\}$$

(12)

where m is the measurement dimension and $\mathbf{A}_k(t_i)$ is calculated in the k-th Kalman filter as in Eq. (6). The denominator in Eq. (2) is simply the sum of all the computed numerator terms and thus is the scale factor required to ensure that the $p_k(t_i)$'s sum to one.

One expects the residuals of the Kalman filter based upon the "best" model to have mean squared value most in consonance with its own computed $\mathbf{A}_k(t_i)$, while "mismatched" filters will have larger residuals than anticipated through $\mathbf{A}_k(t_i)$. Therefore, Eqs. (2), (3), and (6) - (12) will most heavily weight the filter based upon the most correct assumed parameter value. However, the performance of the algorithm depends on there being significant differences in the characteristics of residuals in "correct" vs. "mismatched" filters. Each filter should be tuned for best performance when the "true" values of the uncertain parameters are identical to its assumed value for these parameters. One should specifically avoid the "conservative" philosophy of adding considerable dynamics pseudonoise, often used to open the bandwidth of a single Kalman filter to guard against divergence, since this tends to mask the differences between good and bad models. Specifically for this reason, Loop Transmission Recovery (LTR) tuning [41-43] was not employed for robustness enhancement of each elemental controller within the MMAC algorithm.

III. ELEMENTAL CONTROLLER DESIGN

A Command Generator Tracker / Proportional plus Integral / Kalman Filter (CGT/PI/KF) form of controller [5,39,40,44,45,47-50] was selected for each of the elemental controllers within the MMAC algorithm, and each was designed to provide desirable vehicle behavior for a particular failure status of sensors and actuators. LQG synthesis was used to design each multiple-input / multiple-output elemental controller in a systematic manner. The result of this elemental controller design process is as depicted in Fig. 2.

The CGT portion of such a controller is a specific form of explicit model follower that forces the plant to respond desirably to command inputs while rejecting modeled disturbances, so that the system states maintain desired trajectories. In this effort, the CGT is used to specify the preferred response model to mimic, in order to incorporate desired handling qualities [51,52] into

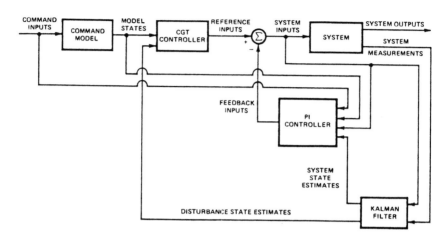

Fig. 2. CGT/PI/KF Elemental Controller

the vehicle. Feedforward gains on the model states produce a precompensator structure in which an explicit simulation of the model dynamics is required within the online controller.

This precompensator is combined with a PI feedback controller rather than a simple regulator, in order to achieve "type-1" properties: able to track a nonzero step input with zero steady-state error, despite unmodeled constant disturbances. In this application, it is important to reject the effects of unmodeled constant disturbances, as particularly due to the aircraft being at a different operating point than used to generate the linear perturbation model upon which its controller is based. Implicit model following [48,49,53] is embedded into the quadratic cost used in the LQG synthesis of the feedback gains to penalize deviations in achieved transient response from the desired, robust characteristics of the implicit design model. By so doing, the robustness, loop shapes, and other closed loop characteristics of the full-state feedback PI controller are enhanced.

Realistically, full-state feedback is not available, and so a Kalman Filter is inserted into the loop to accept noise-corrupted sensor signals and provide estimates of plant states (and disturbance states if desired, as for wind buffet rejection) needed by the CGT/PI law. The filter also generates the residuals required eventually by the MMAC adaptation mechanism for elemental controller selection. In order not to incapacitate this adaptation, LTR tuning is not used for further robustness enhancement, as it might well be employed if a multiple model structure were not envisioned.

As seen in Fig. 2, the overall controller accepts command inputs, as from the pilot's stick, and generates a feedforward control through the command generator explicit model and the CGT compensator. The actual system is then driven to follow the CGT-generated reference inputs by the PI feedback controller, using state estimates from the Kalman Filter.

IV. ENHANCING THE ALGORITHM CHARACTERISTICS

A. Additional Hypothesized Failures

As described in Section I, an initial feasibility study considered a multiple model adaptive algorithm based upon four hypothesized failure conditions for the longitudinal channel of a STOL F-15 aircraft: a healthy aircraft, failed pitch rate sensor, failed stabilator, or failed "pseudo-surface" combination of canards, ailerons, and trailing edge flaps. However, these comprise only a subset of the appropriate failure status conditions for this application. Three actuators are assumed to be available: the "pseudo-surface", the stabilator, and the reverser vanes (conceivable as a fast-response throttle for thrust). Similarly, three sensors are used to provide data: the velocity sensor, the pitch rate sensor, and a flight path angle sensor. Thus, seven failure conditions (fully functional aircraft, any one failed sensor, or any one failed actuator) are the natural basis for a multiple model failure detection and control reconfiguration algorithm, rather than the four used earlier. This was the first extension made to the algorithm. Hard failures of actuators are represented by zeroing out appropriate columns of the control input matrix **B** and hard sensor failures via zeroing out cor-responding rows of the measurement matrix **H**.

Soft failures were also considered in both the simulation of the real-world aircraft and in the construction of the multiple model adaptive algorithm. For actuators, "soft" failures were represented by a certain percentage of actuator power being lost (as due to loss of part of a control surface rather than the whole surface), by multiplying the appropriate column of the control input matrix by a number between zero and one instead of just allowing the two extreme values. For sensors, either biases were introduced into the sensor outputs or the variance of the noise corrupting the sensor was increased. The original MMAC algorithm with only hard failures hypothesized was used under these simulated soft failure conditions, to see if it was capable of handling the situation by "blending" the outputs of the "healthy aircraft" elemental controller with the corresponding "hard failure" elemental controller. If not, a minimum number of "soft failure" elemental controllers could be added to the MMAC structure to allow for stable and adequate control of the vehicle under all conditions. (In fact, such "soft failure" elemental controllers were not required.) Conceptually, this required that the stability robustness region in parameter space for each elemental controller be larger than the region of correct identification of failure status; if the "correct" failure status were not identified (due to misidentification or inability to "blend" two models with the "proper" calculation of the probability weighting coefficients, $p_k(t_i)$ of Eq. (2)), the failure identification was considered faulty but the control action was considered acceptable if stability and good response characteristics were preserved.

B. MAP Versus Bayesian Form of MMAC

Section II described the Bayesian form of the MMAC algorithm that produces the final control as the probability-weighted average of Eq. (3). In practice, a lower bound for the computed probabilities of Eq. (2) is often imposed in order to prevent the algorithm from "locking out" any single parameter value: note that if any $p_k(t_{i-1})$ in Eq. (2) were computed as zero, then that recursion would force $p_k(t_i)$ and all future p_k values to zero for that k. Similarly, a very small computed p_k value would require numerous sample periods in order to be increased to a substantial fraction by Eq. (2). Although such lower bounding enhances identifiability of a changing set of system failure conditions, it forces the nonzero weighting of totally inappropriate controller outputs in the construction of the MMAC control of Eq. (3). For this reason, one might consider using a maximum a posteriori (MAP) approach of selecting the one $\mathbf{u}_k$ control corresponding to the highest probability p_k, rather than forming the probability-weighted average of Eq. (3). Such a technique would, however, preclude the desirable "blending" properties discussed in the preceding paragraph, and so the amount of "robustness region" overlap for elemental controllers would have to be greater in an MAP version than a Bayesian version of the MMAC. An intermediate form of MMAC would include in the averaging of Eq. (3) only those $\mathbf{u}_k$'s that correspond to p_k values that exceed some threshold. Either the MAP or intermediate form has the capability of removing the potentially destabilizing effect of elemental controllers that are designed for conditions that clearly do not pertain to the current system operation.

C. Alternate Computation of Probabilities

Whether a Bayesian or MAP form of algorithm is used, the p_k probabilities are computed according to Eq. (2), with the first numerator term given by Eq. (12). However, it has frequently been noted [2,4,6,44,45] that the leading coefficient preceding the exponential in Eq. (12) has nothing to do with the identification of the "correct" parameter value (failure status in this case), but that all useful information pertaining to "correctness" of parameter value is confined to the quadratic within the exponential, denoted as the likelihood quotient,

$$L_k(t_i) = \mathbf{r}_k^T(t_i)\mathbf{A}_k^{-1}(t_i)\mathbf{r}_k(t_i) \tag{13}$$

as discussed at the end of Section II. However, if it should occur that the likelihood quotients were essentially the same for all k, then the probability calculations of Eq. (2) would be driven so as to assign the highest probabilities to those elemental controllers associated with the $\mathbf{A}_k(t_i)$ matrices (see Eq. (6)) with smallest determinants. This is an artificial and incorrect bias; since a sensor failure is modeled by zeroing out a row of the measurement matrix $\mathbf{H}_k(t_i)$, this might well cause an improper bias towards identifying such sensor failures.

One ad hoc proposal for remedying this situation is to remove the term preceding the exponential in Eq. (12). The result would no longer be a proper density function, since the area under it would no longer be unity. However, because of the scaling effect of the denominator of Eq. (2), the computed $p_k(t_i)$ values would still sum to one. Removing the artificial predisposition to declaring sensor failures may well justify such an ad hoc change to the probability calculations.

D. Reducing Identification Ambiguities Through Scalar Residual Monitoring

In early studies [39,40,44,45], a number of misidentifications or ambivalent identifications were noted, particularly those associated with incorrect declaration of some sensors having failed. This might be fixed in part by the technique of the previous paragraph. Nevertheless, another enhancement to help resolve ambiguities is also possible. Inspection of Eqs. (2), (12) and (13) reveals that the probability calculations are dependent on the magnitude of the entire quadratic form given by Eq. (13), i.e., by the sum of many scalar terms that Eq. (13) represents. However, if the sensor corresponding to row j of the measurement matrix $\mathbf{H}$ were to fail, the predominant indicator of that failure ought to be a large value of the single scalar term in that sum associated with the j-th scalar residual:

$$L_{k_{jj}}(t_i) = r_{k_j}(t_i)^2 / A_{k_{jj}}(t_i) \qquad (14)$$

in any of the elemental filters except for the one specifically designed to expect such a failure (as, in the one that presumes a fully functional system). This additional indicator may be used as an "additional voter" to enhance the identification that sensor j has or has not failed, above and beyond what is possible with straightforward MMAC probability calculations. In fact, it might even replace MMAC techniques for identifying sensor failures if it is less ambiguous than those MMAC methods.

E. Multiple Failures and Hierarchical Modeling

If a multiple model algorithm were based upon all possible single and double failures of K sensors and actuators, it would require one elemental controller for the fully functional status, K single-failure elemental controllers, and $K!/[(K-2)!2!]$ double-failure controllers. This impractical burden can be avoided through the proper design of a hierarchical structure that would require at most only $(K+1)$ elemental controllers to be on-line at any given time: the same number used when only single failures are modeled. Fig. 3 illustrates such a hierarchical structure. At "Level Zero", there are K elemental controllers specifically designed for one of the single-failure conditions and one configured for the fully functional system (denoted as $\mathbf{a}_0$ in the figure). Upon confirmation

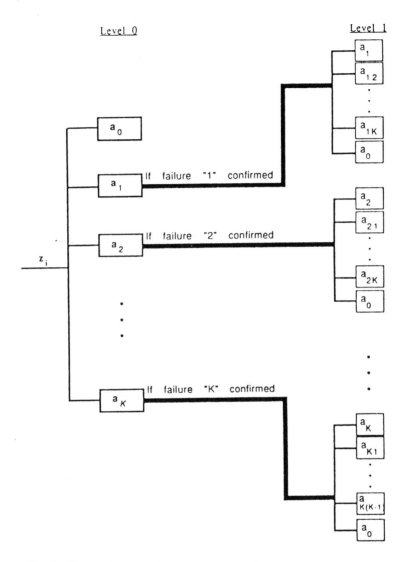

Fig. 3. Hierarchical Modeling - Level 0 and Level 1 MMAC Banks

that failure k has occurred, a new MMAC bank is brought on-line from memory at "Level One" and replaces the original "Level-Zero" MMAC. It would consist of $K+1$ elemental controllers: one designed for the k-th single-failure condition (denoted as $\mathbf{a}_k$), $K-1$ configured for the double-failure condition of the known k-th failure plus one of the remaining possible failures (denoted as $\mathbf{a}_{kl}$), and one designed for the fully functional ($\mathbf{a}_0$) system to allow for using future measurements to change the decision that the first failure had, in fact, occurred. The "bank-switching algorithm" used for this investigation was simple: if the average probability of one of the elemental controllers within the "Level-Zero" MMAC exceeded 0.9 for ten sequential sample periods, then the associated "Level-One" bank was brought on-line. Initialization of the constant-gain elemental filter/controllers within the "Level-One" bank was accomplished by using the state estimate of the identified "Level-Zero" filter to start each "Level-One" filter, and by setting all "Level-One" p_k values to the lower bound except for the one associated with the single identified failure, and setting that p_k to one minus the summed lower bounds. Other, more sophisticated, switching logics could also be considered.

V. PERFORMANCE EVALUATION

A multiple model adaptive controller was developed for the STOL F-15 aircraft in landing phase, flying at 200 ft/sec at sea level and with a nominal weight of 33,576 lbs, using four state variables: velocity, angle of attack, pitch and pitch rate [39,40,44,45]. An earlier design effort [49] had produced good results for a vehicle with no failures, and its CGT explicit model (commanding first order response for velocity and pitch rate, and second order response to commanded flight path angle, in accordance with handling qualities specifications), PI controller implicit model and LQG quadratic cost weighting matrices, and Kalman filter tuning (prior to LTR retuning) were used to produce elemental controllers for the cases of a healthy aircraft, any failed sensor and any failed actuator. In all cases, the plant model was time invariant, and only steady state constant-gain filter and PI controller gains were used, in order to enhance online applicability. Failed actuators were simulated by zeroing out the appropriate column of the control input matrix, and sensor failures were analogously represented through zeroing a row of the measurement matrix. Each design was applied to a "truth model" representation of the aircraft, using higher order actuator models (the design model assumed zero-order actuators), an approximated Dryden wind buffet model, and actuator position and servo rate limits. Fig. 4 indicates a representative time response for the healthy aircraft responding to a commanded negative 5 degree (-0.087 radian) flight path angle while being commanded to maintain zero change in pitch rate and velocity.

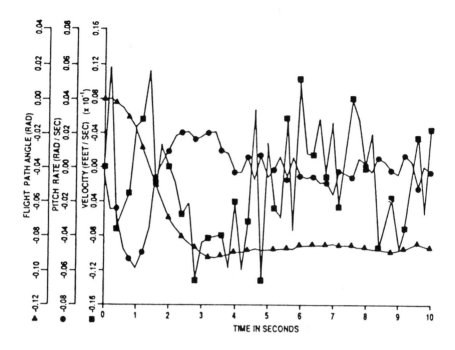

Fig. 4. Controlled Variables (Flight Path Angle, Pitch Rate, Velocity) for Healthy Aircraft and Correct Elemental Controller

Very similar results were produced for the other elemental controllers designed with the correct assumption about the failure status of the aircraft.

Thus, a CGT/PI/KF elemental controller was designed with constant steady-state gains via LQG synthesis for the fully functional aircraft and for a single failure of any of the three sensors or three actuators, as described in the beginning of Section IV. Each of these seven elemental controllers was applied to a "truth model" representation of the aircraft that exhibited any of the seven possible failure conditions. Table I displays the result of this robustness evaluation, indicating whether the result was stable or not and whether desirable control performance (achieving a commanded negative 5 degree change in flight path angle with well-behaved transient, while maintaining zero change in pitch rate and velocity) was attained or not. The robustness regions of the controllers do not overlap in every case, and no single controller can provide stable and

Table I

Robustness of Elemental Controllers

	Truth Model						
Controller	F	B1	B2	B3	H1	H2	H3
F	S&D	S&D	S&N	U	U	U	U
B1	S&D	S&D	U	U	U	U	U
B2	S&D	U	S&D	U	U	U	U
B3	S&D	U	U	S&D	U	U	U
H1	S&N	S&N	U	S&N	S&D	U	U
H2	S&D	U	U	U	U	S&D	S&N
H3	S&D	U	U	U	U	U	S&D

```
                    F = Fully Functional Aircraft
B1 = Failed Pseudo-Surface    H1 = Failed Velocity Sensor
B2 = Failed Stabilator        H2 = Failed Pitch Rate Sensor
B3 = Failed Reverser Vanes    H3 = Failed Flt Path Angle Sensor
```

```
S = Stable Control Obtained     D = Desired Control Obtained
U = Unstable Contol Obtained    N = Desired Control Not Obtained
```

desired control for all possible hard-failure conditions. Although the controller for the fully functional aircraft can provide good control of the aircraft with a failed pseudo-surface, for instance, it is still desirable to identify that failure condition in order to tailor the best control to that condition and to allow for proper identification and reconfiguration with multiple failures subsequently. Notice the (F, B1, B2, B3, H1, H2, H3) nomenclature that is explained in this table for both elemental controllers and real-world simulations; it will be used throughout this section.

For the MMAC implementation, constant precomputed values were employed for the filter and PI controller gains, and also for the A_k matrices of Eq. (6). The conditional probabilities, p_k of Eq. (2), were artificially bounded below by .001 as discussed in Section 2, and these values were initialized at .85 for the no-failure condition and .025 for each of the failed conditions.

Table II lists the mean and standard deviation of the elemental controller $p_k(t_i)$ values on each of the seven elemental controllers, averaged over a ten-second simulation, for the MMAC controller subjected to the various hard

Table II

Time-Averaged p_k Statistics for MMAC with Hard Failures

Fully Functional Aircraft		
p_k	Mean	Std Dev
F	[0.901	0.2507]
B1	0.001	0.0013
B2	0.001	0.0013
B3	0.001	0.0023
H1	0.012	0.0244
H2	0.001	0.0016
H3	0.082	0.2512

Actuator Failures

p_k	B1		B2		B3	
	Mean	Std Dev	Mean	Std Dev	Mean	Std Dev
F	0.005	0.0464	0.004	0.0463	0.004	0.0469
B1	[0.968	0.0925]	0.001	0.0013	0.001	0.0013
B2	0.001	0.0013	[0.978	0.0785]	0.001	0.0013
B3	0.001	0.0013	0.001	0.0013	[0.981	0.1019]
H1	0.007	0.0178	0.005	0.0157	0.002	0.0145
H2	0.001	0.0016	0.002	0.0060	0.001	0.0015
H3	0.017	0.0631	0.009	0.0371	0.009	0.0720

Sensor Failures

p_k	H1		H2		H3	
	Mean	Std Dev	Mean	Std Dev	Mean	Std Dev
F	0.004	0.0463	0.004	0.0463	0.004	0.0468
B1	0.001	0.0013	0.001	0.0015	0.001	0.0013
B2	0.001	0.0013	0.001	0.0021	0.001	0.0013
B3	0.001	0.0013	0.001	0.0013	0.001	0.0013
H1	[0.987	0.0637]	0.002	0.0145	0.002	0.0145
H2	0.001	0.0015	[0.985	0.0746]	0.001	0.0015
H3	0.004	0.0261	0.005	0.0318	[0.989	0.0604]

failure conditions. It demonstrates the MMAC's ability to identify the failed
component correctly (the "correct" identification is bracketted in the table),
reconfigure the control law rapidly, and provide stable and desired control in
each of the modeled hard-failure cases. The "correct" probability weighting is
even more pronounced than implied by the table entries since the statistics are
averaged over the entire 10 sec. simulation time, and not just after the initial
transient has occurred (often lasting only 3 sample periods and usually less than
0.2 sec. for sensor failures and 1.0 sec. for actuator failures); this also caused a
greater reduction of the mean of the correct probability for those cases in which
the initial transients lasted longer.

The time histories that led to this tabulated data typically displayed faster
transients and smaller steady state standard deviations for failed sensors than for
failed actuators. This might be due to the fact that sensor failures exhibit
themselves more directly in single residuals than do actuator failures. However,
as seen in Table II (particularly for the Fully Functional Aircraft), the small
growth of probability values for the controllers designed for a failed velocity
sensor (H1) or a failed flight path angle sensor (H3) when the aircraft is fully
functional or when an actuator fails, indicates a problem caused potentially by
the artificial bias towards sensor failures discussed in Section IV-C. When the
term preceding the exponential in Eq. (12) was removed, the $p_k(t_i)$ time histories
had significantly faster transients and smaller steady-state standard deviations
for the failed actuator cases, rivaling the characteristics associated with failed
sensor cases. Fig. 5 displays this improvement for the representative case of a
failed stabilator: note that the inappropriate tendency to weight the H1 and H3
elemental controllers (indicated by the "+" and "x" symbols in the figure) is
greatly reduced by the alternative p_k computations of Section IV-C. The impact
of misidentified $p_k(t_i)$ values (as well as .001 lower bound values) on controller
performance could also be minimized by use of the MAP form of the MMAC
instead of the Bayesian form, as discussed in Section IV-B; recall from Table I
that neither the H1 nor H3 elemental controller could provide adequate control
over the aircraft with actuator failures.

Simulations of soft actuator failures accentuated the desirability of the
alternate computation of probabilities of Section IV-C. As Table I shows, any of
the hard-actuator-failure elemental controllers can provide stable and desired
control of the fully functional aircraft, implying that each is robust enough to
provide adequate control by itself for any percentage loss of that corresponding

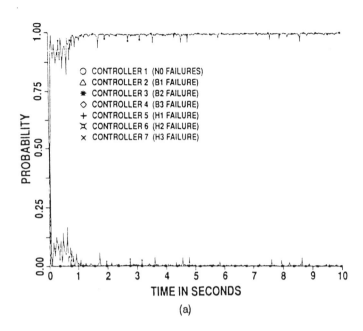

(a)

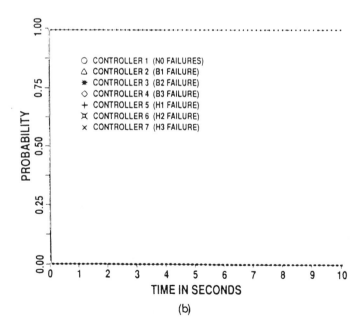

(b)

Fig. 5. p_k Values for Aircraft with Failed Stabilator:
(a) Normal p_k Computations; (b) Alternate Form

actuator. However, the MMAC did not yield adequate (or even stable) control throughout the range of possible soft failures. Additional elemental controllers were developed for a small number of percentages of actuator loss (three for soft pseudo-surface or reverser vane failures, and six for stabilator failures), but resulting MMAC performance was marred by improper identification of sensor failures with non-negligible $p_k(t_i)$ values, especially for the case of stabilator failures, and consequent instability of the closed loop system. In contrast, when the alternate p_k calculations of Section IV-C were used, stable and desirable MMAC control was provided for the entire range of soft failures with the use of fewer or no supporting soft-actuator-failure elemental controllers.

Because of the sensor failure false alarms (when the alternate p_k calculations were not used), it was very desirable to provide an additional voter that would help declare that a sensor had not failed if that were the case. Therefore, scalar residual monitoring was investigated, as described in Section IV-D. Consider a test statistic of the sum of the most recent N values ($N > 1$ for enhanced confidence) of the scalar term in Eq. (14) for the case of $j = 1$ and $k = $ H1, i.e., for the first scalar residual (corresponding to the velocity sensor) in the elemental filter that assumes the velocity sensor has failed. When the velocity sensor has in fact failed, the expected value of each of the N terms is one, and so the expected value of the sum is N. However, if the observed value is significantly greater than N, one can discount the hypothesis that the velocity sensor has failed. Empirically, for $N = 10$, the average observed value was 9.65 and its standard deviation s was 1.86, under the conditions of the velocity sensor actually being failed. Thus, if a conservative threshold of the average plus 3 standard deviations, or 15.23, was exceeded by the test statistic, the velocity sensor was declared not to have failed. Similarly, thresholds were set at 17.16 for $k = $ H2 and $j = 2$, and 17.62 for $k = $ H3 and $j = 3$. These simple tests proved to yield unequivocally correct votes that sensors had not actually failed, allowing the associated elemental controllers to be removed from the MMAC and thereby resolving the identification ambiguity and ensuing stability problem entirely.

Analogous hypothesis testing on the most recent N terms from Eq. (14) for the case of $k = $ F, i.e., scalar residual monitoring in the elemental filter that assumes no failures have occurred, can provide an additional vote that the j-th sensor has actually failed. Corroborating votes could also be obtained for the failure of the j-th sensor from any of the elemental filters except the one that explicitly assumes such a failure has occurred. Moreover, the elemental filter designed for the j-th sensor having failed will have a large value of the test statistic from Eq. (14) when the aircraft is actually fully functional, and a threshold can be established to test for significant diversions from that expected large value when a failure does occur. Rapid and correct decisions were consistently made through these techniques in declaring either that a certain sensor had or had not failed. In fact, this suggests that we might want to exclude failed-sensor hypotheses from the $p_k(t_i)$ computations altogether, and to use the independent "additional" voting to determine sensor failure status. The utility of "additional" voting for handling soft sensor failures of increased measurement noise or unmodeled biases was consistent with the results seen with hard failures.

Double failures were investigated with the hierarchical form of MMAC from Section IV-E. The first failure was simulated at the beginning of the simulation, and the second was simulated 7 sec. later, 0.5 sec. later, or simultaneously. Fig. 6 is typical: in less than 0.3 sec., the level-one bank for a failed pseudo-surface is correctly brought on-line, and the figure portrays the p_k values within that bank properly identifying the second failure, of the flight path angle sensor, at 7 sec. into the simulation. (Note that the probability time histories for the level-zero bank are not shown.)

Table III summarizes the results. The first column identifies by number the controller of the second column; the latter indicates the actuator (**B** column) and/or sensor (**H** row) that has failed. Under "Identified Controller" are numbers that indicate which controller the hierarchical MMAC identified as the proper controller for the stated failure condition for each of the three time lags between successive failures. For those instances when it occurs, "H3#" in the last column specifies that the decision algorithm selected the "H3" level-one bank erroneously, and that instability resulted. (Note that the erroneous level-one bank selection can be eliminated by using the alternate p_k computations described previously in Section IV-C.)   Asterisks in that column relate that this simultaneous failure is equivalent to a preceding entry in the table. Finally, lower case letters correspond to specific notes at the end of the table.

The ability of the hierarchical MMAC to identify and control single and multiple failures is seen to be very satisfactory. The few cases in which

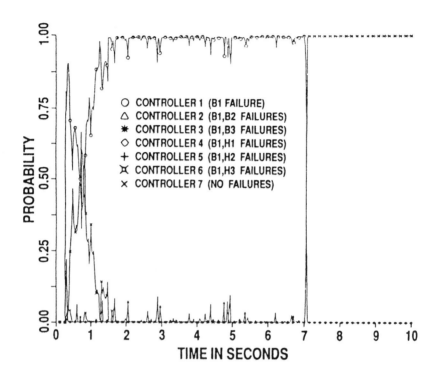

*Fig. 6. Level 1 MMAC p_k Values for Failed Pseudo-Surface (B1)
Followed by Failed Flight Path Angle Sensor (B1H3)*

adequate performance was not obtained can be dismissed as being (1) due to
known and readily countered phenomena, as with alternate p_k computations or
additional voting, or (2) caused by the lack of adequate control authority of the
remaining unfailed components.

Table III

Hierarchical MMAC Identification of Multiple Failures

		FIRST FAILED SYSTEM	SECOND FAILED SYSTEM	TIME LAG BETWEEN FAILURES (Seconds)		
				7.0	0.5	0.0

(a)

				Identified	*Controller*	
1	B1B2	Pseudo-Surface	Stabilator	1 a	1 a	H3#
2	B1B3		Reverser Vanes	2	2	2 b
3	B1H1		Velocity Sensor	3	3	1 6
4	B1H2		Pitch Rate Sensor	4	4	2 1
5	B1H3		Flight Path Angle Sensor	5	5	5

(b)

				Identified	*Controller*	
6	B2B1	Stabilator	Pseudo-Surface	6	6 c	•
7	B2B3		Reverser Vanes	7	7	H3#
8	B2H1		Velocity Sensor	8	8	H3#
9	B2H2		Pitch Rate Sensor	9	9	H3#
10	B2H3		Flight Path Angle Sensor	1 0	1 0	1 0

(c)

				Identified	*Controller*	
11	B3B1	Reverser Vanes	Pseudo-Surface	1 1	1 1	•
12	B3B2		Stabilator	1 2 d	1 2 d	•
13	B3H1		Velocity Sensor	1 3	1 3	1 3
14	B3H2		Pitch Rate Sensor	1 4	1 4	1 4 e
15	B3H3		Flight Path Angle Sensor	1 5	1 5	1 5 e

(d)

				Identified	*Controller*	
16	H1B1	Velocity Sensor	Pseudo-Surface	1 6	1 6	•
17	H1B2		Stabilator	1 7 f	1 7	•
18	H1B3		Reverser Vanes	1 8	1 8	•
19	H1H2		Pitch Rate Sensor	1 9	1 9	1 9
20	H1H3		Flight Path Angle Sensor	2 0	2 0	2 0

(e)

				Identified	*Controller*	
21	H2B1	Pitch Rate Sensor	Pseudo-Surface	2 1	2 1	•
22	H2B2		Stabilator	2 2 g	2 2 h	•
23	H2B3		Reverser Vanes	2 3 g	2 3	•
24	H2H1		Velocity Sensor	2 4 g	2 4	•
25	H2H3		Flight Path Angle Sensor	2 5	2 5	2 5

(f)

				Identified	*Controller*	
26	H3B1	Flight Path Angle Sensor	Pseudo-Surface	2 6	2 6	•
27	H3B2		Stabilator	2 7	2 7	•
28	H3B3		Reverser Vanes	2 8	2 8	•
29	H3H1		Velocity Sensor	2 9	2 9	•
30	H3H2		Pitch Rate Sensor	3 0	3 0	•

Notes for Table 3

a. Control authority started to be lost when the second failure occurred. However, stable control was still exercised throughout the 10-second simulation.

b. For this case, the mean probability of controller B1B3 equalled .80. The mean probability of controller B1H2 equalled approximately .145, which induced instability. This is a good candidate for additional voting. Furthermore, had the alternate p_k computation been used, it is unlikely the instability would have resulted.

c. Here, controller B2H1, with a mean probability of .08, induces instability. This is a good candidate for additional voting. Furthermore, had the alternate p_k computation been used, it is unlikely the instability would have resulted.

d. Correct identification. Goes unstable in some Monte Carlo iterations. This is a control authority problem unrelated to MMAC performance.

e. Although the correct (B3) hierarchy bank was entered and the correct elemental controller was brought on-line, the computer could not solve the differential equation.

f. Controller H1B3 is erroneously, but stably, controlling the aircraft up until the failure of the stabilator. Controller H1B1 should be controlling it until the stabilator fails.

g. Controller H2B3 is erroneously, but stably, controlling the aircraft up until the second failure. Controller H1B1 should be controlling it until the second failure.

h. Here, the mean of the probability of the correct controller, H2B2, is .80; however, a probability mean of .20 on controller H2H3 induces instability. This is a good candidate for additional voting. Furthermore, had the alternate p_k computation been used, it is unlikely the instability would have resulted.

VI. SUMMARY

A multiple model adaptive control (MMAC) algorithm with seven elemental CGT/PI/KF controllers (designed for a healthy aircraft or for one of three failed sensors or one of three failed actuators in the longitudinal control channel) demonstrates consistently effective reconfiguration capabilities when subjected to hard and soft failures of sensors or actuators. Performance can be enhanced considerably by use of MAP versus Bayesian form of the MMAC (or a modified combination of both), alternate computation of the MMAC hypothesis probabilities (particularly to remove the tendency to generate false alarms about sensor failures), and reduction of identification ambiguities through scalar residual monitoring. This latter "additional voting" technique provided unequivocal declarations that a particular sensor has or has not failed, and it may even be used to supplant the MMAC methodology for sensor failures. Since consistently correct identification and control for multiple failures can be readily achieved through the simple hierarchical MMAC structure with just the use of the proposed alternate probability calculations, this is deemed to be a practical and powerful technique of reconfigurable controller design that warrants further investigation. Some preliminary results [54-56] for the case of controlling both longitudinal and lateral-directional axes support these conclusions. They also indicate the importance of purposeful dither signals in the channel (or channels) not receiving a maneuver command, in order to excite the response modes of the aircraft and thereby to enhance unambiguous identifiability of all possible sensor and/or actuator failures.

ACKNOWLEDGMENTS

Fig. 4 is from [40]; Figs 3, 5 and 6, and the tables are from [45]. These are reproduced with permission from the IEEE.

REFERENCES

1. D.T. Magill, "Optimal Adaptive Estimation of Sampled Stochastic Processes," *IEEE Trans. Automat. Contr.* **AC-10**, pp. 434-439, Oct. 1965.

2. M. Athans and C.B. Chang, *Adaptive Estimation and Parameter Identification Using Multiple Model Estimation Algorithm*, Technical Note 1976-28, ESD-TR-76-184, Lincoln Laboratory, Lexington, Mass., June 1976.

3. D.G. Lainiotis, "Partitioning: A Unifying Framework for Adaptive Systems, I: Estimation," *Proc. IEEE* **64**, pp. 1126-1143, Aug. 1976.

4. P.S. Maybeck, *Stochastic Models, Estimation and Control*, Vol. 2, Academic Press, New York, 1982.

5. P.S. Maybeck, *Stochastic Models, Estimation and Control*, Vol. 3, Academic Press, New York, 1982.

6. M. Athans, *et. al.*, "The Stochastic Control of the F-8C Aircraft Using a Multiple Model Adaptive Control (MMAC) Method - Part 1: Equilibrium Flight," *IEEE Trans. Automat. Contr.* **AC-22**, pp. 768-780, Oct. 1977.

7. C.S. Greene and A.S. Willsky, "An Analysis of the Multiple Model Adaptive Control Algorithm," *Proc. IEEE Conf. Dec. and Contr.*, Albuquerque, New Mexico, pp. 1142-1145, Dec. 1980.

8. R.M. Hawkes and J.B. Moore, "Performance Bounds for Adaptive Estimation," *Proc. IEEE* **64**, pp. 1143-1150, Aug. 1976.

9. J.K. Tugnait, "Convergence Analysis of Partitioned Adaptive Estimators Under Continuous Parameter Uncertainty," *IEEE Trans. Automat. Contr.* **AC-25**, pp. 569-573, June 1980.

10. S. Dasgupta and L.C. Westphal, "Convergence of Partitioned Adaptive Filters for Systems with Unknown Biases," *IEEE Trans. Automat. Contr.* **AC-28**, pp. 614-615, May 1983.

11. C.B. Chang and M. Athans, "State Estimation for Discrete Systems with Switching Parameters," *IEEE Trans. Aerosp. Electr. Sys.* **AES-14**, pp.418-424, May 1978.

12. R.L. Moose and P.P. Wang, "An Adaptive Estimator with Learning for a Plant Containing Semi-Markov Switching Parameters," *IEEE Trans. Sys., Man, Cyber.* **SMC-3**, pp. 277-281, May 1973.

13. P.S. Maybeck and W.L. Zicker, "MMAE-Based Control with Space-Time Point Process Observations," *IEEE Trans. Aerosp. Electr. Sys.* **AES-21**, pp. 292-300, May 1985.

14. J.L. Weiss, T.N. Upadhyay and R.R. Tenney, "Finite Computable Filters for Linear Systems Subject to Time Varying Model Uncertainty," *Proc. IEEE Nat. Aerospace & Elect. Conf.*, Dayton, Ohio, pp. 349-355, May 1983.

15. C.M. Fry and A.P. Sage, "On Hierarchical Structure Adaptation and Systems Identification," *Int. Jour. Cont* **20**, pp. 433-452, 1974.

16. P.R. Lamb and L.C. Westphal, "Simplex-Directed Partitioned Adaptive Filters," *Int. Jour. Cont.* **30**, pp. 617-627, 1979.

17. P.S. Maybeck and K.P. Hentz, "Investigation of Moving-Bank Multiple Model Adaptive Alorithms," *AIAA Journ. of Guidance, Contr., and Dyn.* **10**, pp. 90-96, Jan-Feb 1987.

18. R.W. Lashlee, Jr. and P.S. Maybeck, "Spacestructure Control Using Moving Bank Multiple Model Adaptive Estimation," *Proc. IEEE Conf. Dec. and Contr.*, San Antonio, Texas, pp. 712-717, Dec. 1988.

19. P.S. Maybeck, "Moving-Bank Multiple Model Adaptive Estimation and Control Algorithms: An Evaluation," in *Control and Dynamic Systems: Advances in Theory and Applications,* Vol. 31 (C. T. Leondes, ed.), Academic Press, pp. 1-31, San Diego, 1989.

20. P.S. Maybeck and M.R. Schore, "Robustness of a Moving-Bank Multiple Model Algorithm for Control of a Flexible Spacestructure," *Proceedings of the IEEE Nat. Aerosp. Electr. Conf.*, Dayton, Ohio, pp. 368-374, May 1990.

21. J.S. Thorp, "Optimal Tracking of Maneuvering Targets," *IEEE Trans. Aerosp. Electr. Sys.* **AES-9**, pp. 512-519, July 1973.

22. R.L. Moose, "An Adaptive State Estimation Solution to the Maneuvering Target Problem," *IEEE Trans. Automat. Contr.* **AC-20**, pp 359-362, June 1975.

23. R.R. Tenney, R.S. Hebbert and N.R. Sandell, Jr., "A Tracking Filter for Maneuvering Sources," *IEEE Trans. Automat. Contr.* **AC-22**, pp. 246-261, Mar. 1977.

24. N.H. Gholson and R.L. Moose, "Maneuvering Target Tracking Using Adaptive State Estimation," *IEEE Trans. Aerosp. Electr. Sys.* **AES-13**, pp. 310-317, May 1977.

25. R.L. Moose, H.F. Van Landingham and D.H. McCabe, "Modeling and Estimation for Tracking Maneuvering Targets," *IEEE Trans. Aerosp. Electr. Sys.* **AES-15**, pp. 448-456, May 1979.

26. J. Korn and L. Beean, *Application of Multiple Model Adaptive Estimation Algorithms to Maneuver Detection and Estimation*, Tech. Rept. TR-152, Alphatech, Inc., Burlington, Mass., June 1983.

27. C.B. Chang and J.A. Tabaczynski, "Application of State Estimation to Target Tracking," *IEEE Trans. Automat. Contr.* **AC-29**, pp 98-109, Feb. 1984.

28. P.S. Maybeck and R.I. Suizu, "Adaptive Tracker Field-of-View Variation Via Multiple Model Filtering," *IEEE Trans. Aerosp. Electr. Sys.* **AES-21**, pp. 529-539, July 1985.

29. D.M. Tobin and P.S. Maybeck, "Substantial Enhancements to a Multiple Model Adaptive Estimator for Target Image Tracking," *Proc. IEEE Conf. Dec. and Contr.*, Los Angeles, Cal., pp. 2002- 2011, Dec. 1987.

30. R.G. Brown, "A New Look at the Magill Adaptive Estimator as a Practical Means of Multiple Hypothesis Testing," *IEEE Trans. Circuits & Sys.* **CAS-30**, pp. 765-768, Oct. 1983.

31. A.S. Willsky, *et. al.*, "Dynamic Model-Based Techniques for the Detection of Incidents on Freeways," *IEEE Trans. Automat. Contr.* **AC-25**, pp. 347-359, June 1980.

32. C.S. Sims and M.R. D'Mello, "Adaptive Deconvolution of Seismic Signals," *IEEE Trans. Geoscience Electronics* **GE-16**, pp. 99-103, April 1978.

33. L.D. Hostetler and R.D. Andreas, "Nonlinear Kalman Filtering Techniques for Terrain-Aided Navigation," *IEEE Trans. Automat. Contr.* **AC-28**, pp. 315-323, March 1983.

34. G.L. Mealy and W. Tang, "Application of Multiple Model Estimation to a Recursive Terrain Height Correlation System," *IEEE Trans. Automat. Contr.* **AC-28**, pp. 323-331, March 1983.

35. Y. Baram, *Information, Consistent Estimation and Dynamic System Identification*, Rep. ESL-R-718, Electronic Systems Laboratory, Department of Electrical Engineering, MIT, Cambridge, Massachusetts, Nov. 1976.

36. Y. Baram and N. R. Sandell, Jr., "An Information Theoretic Approach to Dynamic System Modeling and Identification," *IEEE Trans. Automat. Contr.* **AC-23**, pp. 61-66, Jan. 1978.

37. Y. Baram and N. R. Sandell, Jr., "Consistent Estimation of Finite Parameter Sets with Application to Linear Systems Identification," *IEEE Trans. Automat. Contr.* **AC-23**, pp. 451- 454, June 1978.

38. K.I. Yared, *On Maximum Likelihood Identification of Linear State Space Models*, Ph.D. dissertation, Rep. LIDS-TH-920, MIT Laboratory for Information and Decision Systems, Cambridge, Massachusetts, July 1979.

39. D.L. Pogoda, *Multiple Model Adaptive Controller for the STOL F-15 with Sensor/Actuator Failures*, M.S. thesis, A.F. Inst. of Tech., Wright-Patterson AFB, Ohio, Dec. 1988.

40. P.S. Maybeck and D.L. Pogoda, "Multiple Model Adaptive Controller for the STOL F-15 with Sensor/Actuator Failures," *Proc. IEEE Conf. Dec. and Contr.*, Tampa, Florida, pp. 1566-1572, Dec. 1989.

41. J.C. Doyle and G. Stein, "Multivariable Feedback Design: Concepts for a Classical/Modern Synthesis," *IEEE Trans. Automat. Contr.* **AC-26**, pp. 4-16, Feb. 1981.

42. G. Stein and M. Athans, "The LQG/LTR Procedure for Multivariable Feedback Control Design," *IEEE Trans. Automat. Contr.* **AC-32**, pp. 105-114, Feb. 1987.

43. C.L. Matson and P.S. Maybeck, "On an Assumed Convergence Result in the LQG/LTR Technique," *IEEE Trans. Automat. Contr.* **AC-36**, pp. 123-125, Jan. 1991.

44. R.D. Stevens, *Characterization of a Reconfigurable Multiple Model Adaptive Controller Using a STOL F-15 Model*, M.S.E.E. thesis, A.F. Inst. of Tech., Wright-Patterson AFB, Ohio, Dec. 1989.

45. P.S. Maybeck and R.D. Stevens, "Reconfigurable Flight Control Via Multiple Model Adaptive Control Methods," *IEEE Trans. Aerosp. Electr. Sys.* **AES-27**, pp. 470-480, May 1991.

46. P.S. Maybeck, *Stochastic Models, Estimation and Control*, Vol. 1, Academic Press, New York, 1979.

47. P.S. Maybeck, R.M. Floyd, and A. Moseley, "Synthesis and Performance Evaluation Tools for CGT/PI Advanced Digital Flight Control Systems," *Proc. IEEE Nat. Aerospace & Elect. Conf.*, Dayton, Ohio, pp. 1259-1266, May 1983.

48. P.S. Maybeck, W.G. Miller, and J.M. Howey, "Robustness Enhancement for LQG Digital Flight Controller Design," *Proc. IEEE Nat. Aerospace & Elect. Conf.*, Dayton, Ohio, pp. 518- 525, May 1984.

49. G.L. Gross, *LQG/LTR Design of a Robust Flight Controller for the STOL F-15*, M.S. thesis, A.F. Inst. of Tech., Wright- Paterson AFB, Ohio, Dec. 1985.

50. J.R. Broussard, *Command Generator Tracking*, Tech. Rep. TIM-612-3, The Analytical Sciences Corp., Reading, Mass., March 1978.

51. *Flying Qualities of Piloted Airplanes*, Military Specification MIL-F-8785C, ASD/ENESS, Wright-Patterson AFB, Ohio, Nov. 1980.

52. *Flying Qualities of Piloted Aircraft*, Military Standard MIL-STD-1797A, Government Printing Office, Washington, D.C., 30 January 1990.

53. J.R. Broussard and P.W. Berry, "The Relationship Between Implicit Model Following and Eigenvalue-Eigenvector Placement," *IEEE Trans. Automat. Contr.* **AC-25**, pp. 591-594, June 1980.

54. R.M. Martin, *LQG Synthesis of Elemental Controllers for AFTI/F-16 Adaptive Flight Control*, M.S.E.E. thesis, A.F. Inst. of Tech., Wright-Patterson AFB, Ohio, Dec. 1990.

55. G.L. Stratton, *Actuator and Sensor Failure Detection Using a Multiple Model Adaptive Technique for the VISTA/F-16*, M.S.E.E. thesis, A.F. Inst. of Tech., Wright-Patterson AFB, Ohio, Dec. 1991.

56. T.E. Menke, *Multiple Model Adaptive Estimation Applied to the VISTA F-16 with Actuator and Sensor Failures*, M.S. thesis, A.F. Inst. of Tech., Wright-Patterson AFB, Ohio, Mar. 1992.

Techniques for On-Board Automatic Aid and Advisory for Pilots of Control-Impaired Aircraft

Elaine A. Wagner

General Dynamics
Fort Worth, Texas 76101

I. INTRODUCTION

Control failures on aircraft are not uncommon. A survey of recent civil aircraft accident reports yielded 25 cases involving failures of controls other than engines [1]. In all but five, most or all persons on board the aircraft perished. In more than half of the catastrophic cases, the flight could have ended safely if the pilot had acted in a correct and timely manner. Reference [2] describes a fascinating complete recovery of a control-impaired aircraft.

Aircraft are increasingly dependent on control for stabilization, maneuvering, and load moderation. However, most of the potential functional redundancy in controls has not yet been exploited. The problem of control reconfiguration and aircraft recovery after actuation failures is gaining increasing high-level attention [3,4].

Generally, when researchers refer to the issue of recovery from control failures, they refer to basic failure-robustness of the automatic control--of which most aircraft have some--or to the problem of reconfiguration of that automatic control [4]. ("Reconfiguration" as used in this chapter encompasses minor control re-assignment, more significant automatic control "restructuring," and real-time onboard automatic control redesign.)   Most research on the problem of control failures has been done in the areas of control loop robustness and reconfiguration.   Motivating this have been the considerations that the aircraft must be dynamically stable or stabilized after the failure to have any possibility for recovery, and that the capabilities of the aircraft should be restored to the maximum possible extent.

The importance of changing the automatic control law after a control failure is evident, particularly for higher-performance aircraft. But automatic control is limited in some ways. Depending solely on robust or reconfigured control in the usual sense will generally not be sufficient to allow a control-impaired aircraft to be recovered. Consider the following:

1) It is probable that neither the pilot nor the traditional automatic control will take into account all of the alternate control capabilities of the vehicle.   Automatic control is usually not designed to drive all controls effective in a given control axis.   For example, longitudinal control may modulate elevator but not thrust.   However, even the use of landing gear, spoilers, leading edge slats, flaps, and reverse thrust when on the ground can all impact recovery in significant ways.

2) Failures often induce significant new constraints on the controllable operation of the aircraft and on the performance that it can achieve. Traditional types of automatic control will not "know" about these constraints and cannot take them effectively into account.

3) A successful recovery control strategy for strenuous failures can be a very complicated multi-goal process involving carefully coordinated changes in controls in multiple axes and, in some cases, unusual or even counter-intuitive actions.

4) The authority regarding important aspects of controlling the aircraft's flight can be expected to continue to rest with the pilot. The pilot's perception

of the remaining capabilities of the control-handicapped aircraft can be crucial in determining whether the flight will ultimately end safely, as was apparent in accident cases studied. Given this, certain advice and warnings should be provided to the pilot during post-failure flight.

Existing approaches for recovering aircraft after control failures are unsatisfactory. This chapter reflects consideration of the aircraft control failure problem from a broader viewpoint. The next section of this chapter, Section II, presents a categorization of the post-failure constraints on operating state and performance that should be taken into account in flying a control-impaired aircraft. In Section III, there is a discussion of the role of explicit determination of appropriate operating points for the impaired aircraft. Next, Section IV presents a rule-based expert system developed to find successful emergency control in the initial post-failure period after certain failures on a simulated C-130 aircraft. As a general means of augmenting traditional control reconfiguration, this type of approach seems to be a way of directing use of any remaining control capability, or use of the unusual or counter-intuitive ideas that are sometimes required in recovery. There is, in Section V, a description of an integrated onboard recovery aid and advisory system, including a brief examination of how advisory information could be made available and of pilot-system interface issues.

The work reported here was based on discussions with pilots, reported accident cases, and work with a simulation of a STOL C-130 aircraft built in the late 1970's. It will be assumed that the failure is a jammed control surface failure, although the considerations can apply whether the failure is a jam, bias, or floating surface failure, or part of the surface is lost, or whether there has been a failure in the propulsion system.

II. CATEGORIZATION OF POST-FAILURE CONSTRAINTS ON OPERATING STATE AND PERFORMANCE

In research on the problem of control failures, there has been little discussion of the changes a failure may induce in safe and feasible operating points and on the performance an aircraft can achieve. This information seems to be very important, however, in fully recovering an aircraft after a failure. As will be discussed, this information may be needed in formulating emergency control strategies and in advising pilots flying control-impaired aircraft.

A. POST-FAILURE OPERATING CONSTRAINTS

The term "controllable airspeed" is already familiar as the minimum indicated airspeed at which rudder can neutralize yaw induced by an asymmetric engine failure. This terminology can be used in a more general way to refer to airspeed-related limitations of the functioning controls to counterbalance effects of any type of control failure.

An example of controllability airspeed constraints for a relatively common but, as accident cases show, still dangerous control failure mode-- jammed asymmetric flap failure--will support this idea. Figure 1 shows a matrix of discretized airspeeds and flap asymmetries for the C-130 aircraft used in this study. Trim points for steady straight-and-level flight were sought at 1000 ft altitude for zero sideslip. As Fig. 1 shows, there may be failure-induced limitations on both minimum and maximum airspeed. The ailerons have limited ability to control the failure-induced rolling when the airspeed is low, and there is limited thrust available to counteract the drag added by the jammed flap at high speeds.

Equilibration by aerodynamic controls achieved at a certain indicated airspeed does not imply that equilibration could be achieved at another airspeed. Jammed extension of a surface may cause effects that vary quite differently with indicated airspeed compared to the effects of the potentially counterbalancing surfaces. There will be situations in which the side effect from usage of alternate controls will itself constrain the airspeeds for which a failure is controllable.

Stall airspeed can change significantly as a result of a control failure, for example, when a leading edge slat fails extended, disrupting flow over the

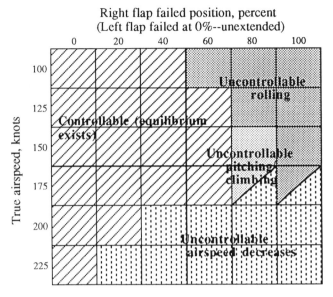

Fig. 1. Effects of Asymmetric Flap Failures
on the C-130 Aircraft
(Looking for trim points at 1000 ft altitude)

wing, or when a lift-augmenting surface fails retracted. When stall speed changes, the corner velocity--the lowest velocity at which limit load can be obtained--will change. The buffet boundary--airspeeds at which high-speed flow separation occurs--can also change with certain control failures. Gust penetration airspeed is the maximum airspeed at which expected gust loadings cannot result in the aircraft limit load being exceeded. When stall speed changes, so will the gust penetration airspeed.

Control reversal airspeed is the airspeed at which aircraft flight can be sustained with minimum power or thrust required. Failures of aerodynamic surfaces can lead to changes in control reversal airspeed either directly or indirectly through controls used to compensate for the failure. Control reversal airspeed is very important in landing an aircraft. Its value would increase with certain types of control failures, making landing at normal speeds quite dangerous. Even if control reversal airspeed does not change with a failure, the nominal value may be of explicit importance during a recovery. In a

certain DC-3 case in which primary aerodynamic lateral and directional control
was lost, very careful use of asymmetric thrust would have been needed for
control in these axes. Any such attempt to control the aircraft, however,
would have decreased total power available for changing airspeed on approach.
Operating below the control reversal airspeed would then have been much
more dangerous than usual.

There are other types of post-failure restrictions on aircraft operating
state. Figure 2 comes directly from a reported accident case. It shows the
variation with angle of attack and Mach number of the difference between the
rolling moment induced by the single failed-extended leading edge slat and that

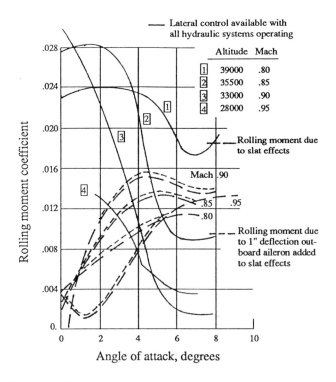

Fig. 2. Rolling Moments from Failed Extended No. 7
Leading Edge Slat on Boeing 727 Aircraft

available from the remaining lateral control resources. The aircraft could not be recovered after roll was allowed to exceed a certain level because Mach number and angle of attack became too large. Potentially, any operating state dependencies (in the functional sense) of aircraft forces and moments can be constrained after a failure if the remaining control resources cannot counterbalance these forces and moments. Note that operating limitations may be expressed more usefully in terms of certain parameters rather than others, such as bank angle rather than Mach number or angle of attack in the example just mentioned.

B. POST-FAILURE PERFORMANCE CONSTRAINTS

Any aspect of aircraft performance can suffer greatly when there has been a control failure. The high drag associated with highly deflected jammed surfaces or, secondarily, with the compensating controls, can bring about significant degradation of such basic types of performance as range, endurance, climb angle and rate, and maximum airspeed and altitude. Failure of a wing surface such as a slat or spoiler, by changing the basic aerodynamics of the aircraft, can also lead to significant changes in power required for flight. Engine failures will bring about degradation of all of these aspects of performance. These types of performance can change after a failure, and so can the vehicle operating state and control configuration at which maximum performance of a certain type is achieved. Misjudging aircraft performance after failures can lead to disastrous errors in deciding whether a certain destination can be reached, as some accident cases have demonstrated. Maximum performance and how it could be achieved with an impaired aircraft would change over the course of its flight, due to changes in altitude and vehicle configuration and weight. In the most strenuous cases, these variations would have to be accounted for along the way if the aircraft were eventually to be landed safely.

An accident case in which post-failure performance limitations played a role was one in which the aircraft's leading edge slats failed to extend on takeoff. The pilot was probably trained to deal with this type of failure, but the aircraft was soon flying at such low speed that available thrust was insufficient to meet the requirements for climb. Two knots of airspeed would have made a difference between the aircraft being able to climb, and the gradual increase in drag, loss of height, and the ground impact (and fire) that actually occurred.

Performance constraints induced by a failure can be very significant, even if the failure seems small. Consider a C-130 case involving an elevator jammed symmetrically 5° off-nominal pitch down (jammed at 8.05°). After the failure, an opposing pitch-up moment--normally effected through elevator deflection changes--was generated as effectively as possible by other vehicle controls (more on this reconfiguration later). The impaired aircraft was carefully flown to 10,000 ft and stabilized. Figure 3 shows the marked contrast in power required for steady straight-and-level flight at altitude with and without the failure. Points on the new power-required curve were obtained

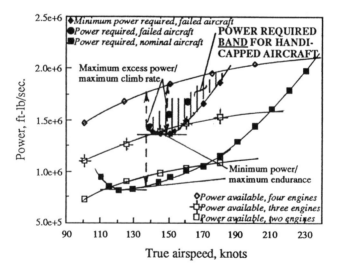

Fig. 3. Power Available/ Power Required Curves,
C-130 with Elevator Jammed at 8.05°;
Steady Straight-and-Level Flight at 10,000 ft

by using quadratic programming, with vehicle dynamics linearized at each successive iteration. State and control settings for the cruise equilibria converged fairly slowly to the exact values for equilibrium at various cruise speeds. It should be noted that reducing the state rates from 10^{-3} to 10^{-6} or 10^{-8} could often result in surprisingly large changes in the solved-for state and control settings, and a not-fully-converged solution would often imply very different post-failure capability than was actually available.

Keeping the C-130 flying level with this jammed elevator failure required considerable leading edge flap extension for its pitch-up effects, and the deployment of full pitch-up collective aileron (the aircraft simulation had been modified so that the ailerons could be deployed symmetrically) and some elevator tab. Deployment of these surfaces, particularly the flaps, resulted in considerable additional drag. The power required for level cruise ("minimum power, failed aircraft" points in Fig. 3) is considerably different from the nominal value. The airspeed range available for steady level flight with all four engines operating was approximately halved by the failure. The steady maximum climb rate and climb angle have been considerably reduced. In a real failure situation, this decrease in capability could have been extremely important. A landing site could not be reached, for example, if this required much intermediate climbing to clear an obstacle. With this elevator failure and compensation, the maximum endurance speed has changed by about 30 knots true airspeed (KTAS), and the maximum range airspeed by about 10 KTAS. The airspeeds for best climb rate and angle have also changed. Failure of even one of the four engines now could restrict cruise operations considerably, as the three-engine power-available curve of Fig. 3 shows.

III. EXPLICIT DETERMINATION OF POST-FAILURE OPERATING POINTS

Would explicit retrim have a useful role in recovery of a control-impaired aircraft? Suppose that an aircraft is flying with state x_0, control setting u_0, and with state rates $\dot{x} = f(x_0, u_0)$ prior to a failure, and that control i

jams Δn off-nominal. Explicit retrim to regain and maintain the pre-failure trajectory would involve trying to achieve a new operating point $x_0 + \Delta x$ with the unfailed controls at a new setting $u_{f0} + \Delta u_f$ such that

$$f(x_0 + \Delta x, u_{f0} + \Delta u_f, u_i + \Delta n) = f(x_0, u_0) \qquad (1)$$

or, in a linear approximation,

$$f(x_0, u_0) + \partial f(x_0, u_0)/\partial x \cdot \Delta x + \partial f(x_0, u_0)/\partial u_f \cdot \Delta u_f + \partial f(x_0, u_0)/\partial u_i \cdot \Delta n$$
$$= f(x_0, u_0) \qquad (2)$$

or

$$A \ \Delta x + B_f \ \Delta u_f = - b_i \ \Delta n \qquad (3)$$

where A and B are the usual linear model matrices: $\partial f(x_0, u_0)/\partial x$ and $\partial f(x_0, u_0)/\partial u$, respectively, B_f is the matrix of columns of B associated with the unfailed controls, and b_i the column of B associated with the failed control. Note that controllable airspeed or other post-failure operating constraints would be involved when determining whether a solution to these equations is possible.

Re-establishing the pre-failure trajectory may not be best. For safety, climbing up or decreasing angle of attack might be preferred. For such cases, retrim might be to a new condition where

$$\dot{x} = f(x_0, u_0) + \Delta r \qquad (4)$$

and the state and control setting changes accordingly satisfy

$$A \ \Delta x + B_f \ \Delta u_f = - b_i \ \Delta n + \Delta r \qquad (5)$$

After multiple or large failures, there would be pronounced need for explicit information about operating regions in which stabilization or some required value of performance could be achieved. This researcher's experience with recovering aircraft with single jammed controls indicated, however, that explicit retrim alone was usually not a very useful idea in early periods of flight after failure manifestation. "Oppose the disturbance" (typically a large one) was a much more powerful general idea. Moreover, just having a single retrim point--which a single solution to these linear equations yields--said nothing about its basic reachability, nor, if guaranteed reachable, how to reach it. These could be extremely difficult issues unless the transition were simulated outright. Just to take a simple example, can a certain angle of attack, even if explicit retrim has shown it to be a useful condition, be achieved after a failure? With an elevator failure, for example, it may not be achievable, since basic control authority might be lacking. Flying the C-130 aircraft to a given state and given control setting was very difficult. If there is one solution, there will be many, perhaps widely spaced solutions [1] to a retrim condition, such as Eq. (3), raising questions about choosing among them.

Explicit information about retrim would probably be most useful and important in periods of relatively quiescent flight with the new operating point clearly reachable. As an illustration of the possible utility of explicit retrim under these circumstances, consider again the C-130 case where the elevator jammed 5° trailing edge down relative to its nominal position, This failure resulted in a very significant decrease in achievable performance, as was discussed in Section II, B. A few additional operating points for steady straight-and-level flight at 10,000 ft were computed for the control-impaired aircraft. These have been superimposed as the higher "power required, failed aircraft" points in Fig. 3. There is a band of power-required values at each airspeed, depending on how the failure compensation is distributed among the various viable controls. For example, two separate equilibria were established for the failed aircraft at 150 KTAS, one with 62% leading edge flaps and angle of attack of -17° (an equilibrium point unintentionally found during a recovery), and the actual minimum-thrust point, with 51% flaps, angle of attack = -2.25°. Thrust setting for the first equilibrium was approximately 8% higher than the minimum thrust to sustain the same cruise airspeed. Achieving the minimum-power operating point would allow three-engine operation, as well as reducing flap deployment from a level near its structurally limited value. Additional flap deployment could then be available for pitch-up maneuvering if needed.

The retrim-related idea of control effectiveness has been crucial in some reported accident cases. However, there were very few cases where flight after the failure continued past the phase where straightforward disturbance opposition would have enabled the aircraft to be restabilized. However, the following could be considered important later retrimming-type goals: 1) Off-load the burden of compensation from controls needed for other purposes, such as maneuvering; 2) Move away from dangerous state constraints; 3) Obtain better performance. These may, of course, be conflicting goals in some situations.

It should be stressed again that transitioning between given operating points might be very difficult. This would especially be the case if only unconventional or degraded controls were available--likely after a failure. It may be difficult to decide how difficult or dangerous any given transition between two operating points would be, even where retrim has identified them as being in themselves valid operating points. Deciding what looks like a feasible, safe transition on the basis of simplified reasoning may be possible in some cases. Instructions could then be provided to the pilot to make the transition.

Reaching a new operating point might involve at least temporary losses in desirable operating quantities. Consider a transition to the maximum-range operating point in Fig. 3 from another, lower-airspeed cruise point. Thrust increase on the C-130 generated a counterproductive pitch-up moment, and airspeed could be gained only through decreasing pitch by decreasing thrust. Altitude, heuristically a very desirable quantity in emergency piloting, would be lost in the transition and might be dangerous or impossible to regain afterwards.

Many extremely interesting issues related to retrim arose during this study. Reference [1] describes the few accessible mathematical properties of the constant-rate regions of systems of general nonlinear equations, such as those governing aircraft dynamics.

IV. POST-FAILURE EMERGENCY CONTROL

Let us consider a different aspect of the problem of control failures. An important part of the aid envisioned for flying control-impaired aircraft is emergency control in the initial period after the failure has manifested itself. According to the pilots interviewed, the most important aspect of control failure recovery would be immediate and correct response to failures, particularly in high-speed or ground-proximity operations. Essentially all of the recoverable accident cases studied were vivid demonstrations of the need for immediate emergency control. The time available for required response was generally 4-5 s, but up to 25 s were available for some of the cases studied. Even more familiar types of failures seem not to have been identified by the pilot, even though the aircraft were usually not particularly high performance aircraft. Pilots interviewed wanted full-authority automatic response after control failures.

A. EXPERIENCE WITH
CONTROL LOOP RECONFIGURATION

The most common solution advanced to the problem of emergency post-failure control is to provide failure-robust nominal control or to reconfigure the control after the failure. In working with the C-130 to try to recover from jammed elevator failures, at first the most conventional reconfigurable control idea was tried: ask that the forces and moments normally generated by the failed control be generated now by the remaining unfailed controls u_f, or, in terms of the linear model, at each time t,

$$B_f \, \Delta u_f = B \, \Delta u \qquad (6)$$

where Δu represents the commanded control setting changes if all controls were working. Typically one solves for Δu_f as

$$\Delta u_f = B_f^\dagger \, B \, \Delta u \qquad (7)$$

where $B_f^\dagger$ is the least-squares, Moore-Penrose pseudo-inverse of B_f.

This approach to reconfiguration is not particularly attractive from a control performance standpoint. Vehicle linear system stability with the control loop reconfigured in this way cannot be guaranteed for all initial conditions [1], unless there is full control redundancy--rank B_f = rank B. This reconfiguration is easy where it does guarantee stability and has been proposed by several researchers. One caution: nominal automatic control for aircraft is often low-gain, for safety or other reasons, and thus might have insufficient authority to oppose failure-induced disturbances, which are usually large.

Reconfiguration via Eq. (7) was unsuccessful (to take one example) in preventing the C-130 from diving to the ground after a 5° off-nominal pitch-down elevator jam failure occurring when the vehicle was flying straight and level at 197 knots indicated airspeed (KIAS) at 1000 ft above the ground. Whether Eq. (6) above can be solved exactly or not, this type of reconfiguration can ask for very large deployments of certain controls, especially if they are particularly or solely effective in effecting changes in certain state rates. This can result in rate and position saturation of the controls (not to mention violating limitations of the linear model), as was clearly demonstrated with the C-130.

The C-130 aircraft was ultimately successfully recovered after this 5° off-nominal pitch-down elevator failure when the control reconfiguration took into account rate and position saturation of the remaining functioning controls. More quickly deploying controls served as a stopgap until slower but more effective surfaces could deploy. This successful emergency control was the solution to the following quadratic programming problem, solving for changes in the compensating controls, Δu_f, given nominal elevator command Δu_i:

$$\min \ [B_f \ \Delta u_f - b_i \ \Delta u_i)^{\mathrm{T}} \ Q \ (B_f \ \Delta u_f - b_i \ \Delta u_i) + \Delta u_f^{\mathrm{T}} \ R \ \Delta u_f] \qquad (9)$$

subject to

$$\dot{u}_{f\min} < \dot{u}_f < \dot{u}_{f\max} \qquad\qquad u_{f\min} < u_f < u_{f\max} \qquad (10)$$

where b_i is the column of B corresponding to the elevator. First attempts at recovering the aircraft via this reconfiguration showed that the intended elevator's effects on velocity, angle of attack, and pitch rate could not all be duplicated with the other controls. By insisting on equal weighting on each of these quantities (i.e., Q = identity matrix), the aircraft was lost. For the successful recovery, Q was a weighting on pitch rate only. This reconfiguration was then used to fly the aircraft with this pitch-down elevator jam to stabilization at cruise at 10,000 ft and then to pitch-stabilized slow descent that would have allowed the aircraft to be flown safely onto the ground in a no-flare landing. The same method of reconfiguration was also successfully used after a certain pitch-up elevator failure.

One choice of diagonal Q that was investigated for use in Eq. (9) reflected the relative nominal effect of the elevator on the various state rates:

$$Q = \textbf{\textit{Diag}} \ (b_1{}^2, b_2{}^2, ...) \qquad (11)$$

where b_x is the value in the xth row of the column of B associated with the elevator's effects. This choice of weighting did not allow recovery after the 5° off-nominal pitch-down elevator failure. It simply diverted too many control resources from opposition of the failure-induced nose-down pitch moment.

The extended pseudo-inverse type of reconfiguration of Eq. (9)-(10) was sometimes successful, but success seemed to be very dependent on choice of Q and R, raising questions about how these should be chosen to cover wide ranges of failures. Most importantly, however, this reconfiguration was not able to help recover the aircraft in certain failure cases where other techniques were in fact successful (more on this later). This type of reconfiguration might be expected to be more useful after the initial disturbance-opposition phase of the recovery.

Numerous automatic control reconfiguration ideas were studied. None proved flexible enough to do everything needed to recover an aircraft after control failures of significant extent.

B. MANUAL RECOVERIES

The studies of standard-type control reconfiguration techniques gave disappointing results. To gain more experience, attempts were made to recover the C-130 aircraft after elevator failures using only manual control inputs. Finding successful emergency control after C-130 elevator failures was usually not immediate and often involved several iterations of piloted simulation. Sometimes the strategy that was finally successful involved rather counter-intuitive use of controls, as will be seen, not opposing the effects of the failure but enhancing them temporarily.   Much more was involved than simply knowing, for example, which controls might be useful in opposing a failure-induced disturbance.   Multiple controls had to be used in combination and deployed very quickly in many cases if recovery was to be possible at all. However, finding a successful strategy was not too difficult, given the possibility of making a few attempts. The reasoning needed to devise effective emergency control strategies was not deep.

Experience with the C-130 showed clearly that the only way to be certain of an emergency post-failure control strategy was to simulate it with a high-fidelity model.   Just 1° of control deployment available in some cases made all the difference between recovery and catastrophic loss of the aircraft. In addition, the side effects from usage of alternate controls ("artifact") could be devastating and difficult to foresee. An aircraft is a complicated nonlinear dynamic system and is very sensitive to changes in controls.   These characteristics made some recoveries difficult, but made close investigation of all possibilities to get a recovering control strategy very worthwhile.

C. RECOVERY PILOTING AS EXPERT BEHAVIOR

An expert, in artificial intelligence (AI) terminology, has wide breadth and depth of knowledge in a given area, and an expert's problem-solving ability degrades gracefully at its boundaries. An expert can apply knowledge to solve problems effectively and efficiently using shortcuts to eliminate useless or unnecessary calculations [5]. This focusing depends on heuristics built up over long experience working in a given domain. Heuristics are the high-level guidelines that direct what to try in solving a problem. The expert's heuristic approach to solving a given problem is what he or she considers the best approach to try, and it often turns out to be the correct one.   The heuristic may turn out to be inappropriate in a given case, and an expert backtracks to try something else.   Heuristic information often seems more qualitative than quantitative.

One of the heuristics developed through the work with control reconfiguration and manually flying recoveries after elevator jam failures on the C-130 was that pitch rate was the most important parameter to control. Failure-induced disturbance opposition was almost always a very useful heuristic, although, as will be seen later, there were exceptions.   Experience soon made clear that heuristic reasoning and very identifiable human problem-solving ideas (e.g., "means-end" problem-solving of AI theory [6]) were sufficient to find a correct strategy.   These techniques all fitted nicely under the heading of expert-type behavior as defined by AI, and *this became the unifying viewpoint for all aspects of piloting control-impaired aircraft*. Piloting by experienced pilots is an almost classical expert behavior.   The long recovery described in Ref. [2] greatly helped confirm this viewpoint.

There were only five reported accident cases among the 25 studied in which a successful landing of the aircraft was eventually made.   In all of these, flight after the failure could be divided into five discrete phases: 1) Regain control of the aircraft; 2) Achieve a safe altitude, on the order of 10,000 ft, or maintain altitude if control was regained with the aircraft already higher; 3) Stabilize at altitude, determine landing capabilities, and decide where to land; 4) Approach landing site; 5) Make final approach and landing.   These became subgoals in short-time-horizon planning, as Fig. 4 shows.   Achieving

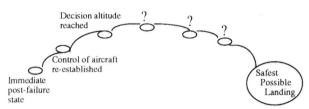

Fig. 4. Near-Horizon Planning in
Post-Control Failure Flight

these flight goals reflects the "planning islands" idea, a very powerful human heuristic. Driving toward islands greatly simplifies the calculations involved in the overall strategy. The ramifications or the identity of the failure would probably be better known in later phases of post-failure flight, anyway.

Flight manual emergency procedures for dealing with control failures were found to be surprisingly non-specific, as the excerpt below [7] illustrates. This information would be of very limited usefulness if an actual control failure were to occur. Note, however, that the planning islands idea is clearly embodied in these procedures:

[T]hree basic rules are established which apply to most emergencies occurring while airborne.
1. MAINTAIN AIRCRAFT CONTROL.
2. Analyze the situation and take proper action.
3. Land as soon as conditions permit.

Normally, ejection is the best course of action in the event both engines flame out...or positive control of the aircraft cannot be maintained.

If structural damage occurs in flight, the pilot must decide whether to leave the aircraft or attempt a landing. If aircraft is controllable, proceed as follows:

WARNING
• In no case allow airspeed to decrease below 90 KIAS.
• Do not reset wing flaps if significant structural damage is located in the wings.

[1. Communicate intentions to the ground.]
2. Climb to 10,000 feet above terrain (if practical) at a controllable airspeed.
3. Simulate a landing approach and determine airspeed at which aircraft becomes difficult to control (minimum controllable airspeed).

Note
If aircraft becomes difficult to control or approaches a stall, lower the nose and increase power for recovery.

4. If aircraft becomes difficult to control above 105 KIAS (full flap), fly a no flap landing approach. Abandon the aircraft if it becomes difficult to control above 130 KIAS (no flaps).
5. Maintain 20 KIAS above minimum controllable airspeed or 110 KIAS, whichever is higher, during descent and landing approach.
6. Fly a flat power-on, straight-in approach requiring minimum flare and plan to touch down at no less than minimum controllable airspeed. Do not begin to reduce final approach speed until the aircraft has crossed the runway threshold and is very close to the runway. Maximum recommended airspeed for touchdown is 105 KIAS (full flaps), 130 KIAS (no flaps).

#

It became clear that a rule-based expert system could be written to find emergency control after C-130 elevator jam failures. Fortuitously, such systems could clearly also facilitate some of the other piloting activities involved in full recovery of a control-handicapped aircraft.

D. AN EXPERT SYSTEM FOR POST-FAILURE RECOVERY CONTROL

An expert system is a computer program performing within a specific task domain at the level of a human expert in that domain. Expert systems are typically written using languages that specifically facilitate including problem-solving information in identifiable, discrete packets. This can be very appropriate for modeling knowledge, which occurs naturally in rule-type (IF-THEN) form. These languages also allow expert systems to be easily built up and modified, and, incidentally, are appropriate for modular-type preliminary development of systems in which strong sequencing might eventually develop. We will proceed now to detail how the expert system for emergency control after C-130 elevator jam failures was developed, and describe some of the information and heuristics included in the system.

The elevator on the C-130 aircraft is a large, highly effective surface, and thus failures of 2°-3° off-nominal out of a 55° total deployment range could result in devastating disturbances. With no loss of generality for the system developed (as will be discussed), the assumption was made that the failure was fully known, and, in order to allow some nominal amount of time for failure identification, emergency control was imposed only after a 3 s post-failure delay. Control dynamics, including actual surface deployment rates and position limits, were included in the simulation model.

When the elevator was failed in the C-130 simulation, the nominal pitch stability augmentation system was automatically completely inactivated. The C-130 could stabilize in pitch on its own when a disturbance was small. However, its longitudinal motion was lightly damped without this elevator loop. Flying the handicapped aircraft to landings was complicated whenever any quick transitions, particularly at low altitudes, were attempted. Some reconfiguration of the pitch damping loop to use other controls would be recommended to decrease the amplitude of the oscillations and reduce the time to stabilize in a new operating condition. Not doing so here, however, does not change the findings of this study.

The development of the expert system began with manual recoveries to gain some initial level of expertise, which was codified in the expert system. With the aircraft initially in each of four different initial states--two straight-and-level flight conditions, and a climb and a descent--the elevator was failed in 1° off-nominal increments throughout its entire range, and the expert system was used to try to find a successful strategy for each case. The recovery strategy was considered successful when the aircraft was flown to stabilization in a climb, heuristically a good goal, although sometimes stabilized descent was the best that could be done [1].

The expert system was built up incrementally using information from successive recovery attempts. The type of programming computations involved easily facilitated this type of incremental development. System rules were modified or new rules added as cases were encountered for which the system could not find the successful recovery. Only enough detail was added as was necessary. After some number of recovery cases, no additional rules were needed. Although the rules were initially expected to be somewhat complicated, what eventually emerged was a system having relatively few simple-looking rules. Much heuristic reasoning was embedded in the rules, however, as will be partly described.

To increase the control redundancy of the C-130, the simulation model was modified so that elevator tab was available for deployment independent of the jammed elevator (thus assuming that the tab would not bend the jammed elevator, changing the basic vehicle aerodynamic and stability derivatives). The ailerons were rendered so that they could be deployed symmetrically ("collective" aileron). Five alternate longitudinal controls were then available--elevator tab, collective aileron, symmetric flaps, thrust, and landing gear. The simplification of a strict hierarchy of control usage in the recoveries was natural to use and worked well when flying manual recoveries. This was part of the heuristic reasoning involved and was carried over to the expert system. The intuitive approach was to try hard-over deflection of successively more controls as needed (added in the order [1] elevator tab, ailerons, symmetric flaps, and thrust) and to examine the response after the addition of each control. The practical effect was that the successful control could be bracketed with few tries between too little and too much.

Another heuristic validated by making recoveries and embodied in the expert system was that, in the initial stages of post-failure emergency control, control changes were "optimally" made as quickly as deployment rates allowed, and that changes in more than one control were "optimally" done simultaneously. Certain recoveries required that control deployments be reversed later in the recovery sequence. Even then the aircraft could be recovered successfully if controls were commanded to move as quickly as possible to their new settings.

Using this scheme of applying separate controls additively, the successful recovering control fell along a discrete spectrum of strategies, according to the amount of off-nominal elevator deflection associated with the failure. Figure 5 illustrates the spectrum for failures occurring while the aircraft was flying straight and level at 147 KIAS. The successful recovery strategy varied from no compensation to partial or hard-over deployment of all of the available longitudinal controls. In no case was more than one later control redeployment necessary. The control change times were successfully chosen heuristically. The expert system also used straightforward interpolation of control deployments in formulating the recovery strategy, the interpolation strategy being successive midpointing between obvious too much and too little deployment of a control.

The rules of the recovery strategy-finding system were codified in a very commonly used rule-based system language [8] and implemented on a personal computer. The expert system computations were quick. The expert

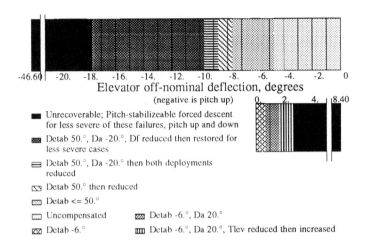

Fig. 5. Recovery Spectrum--C-130 Elevator
Jam Failures During Cruise at 147 KIAS

system was written to ask the user about the vehicle response to the recovery strategy it recommended last. Answers to questions chosen and presented by the expert system were used by it to modify the recommended strategy, and the strategy was applied by the user to the simulation. All of the queries about the response were specifically designed to require information about objective features of the response only, and thus the entire process of finding a successful strategy could have been automated. This should help further the idea of a system that could automatically sweep a wide range of failure cases and make generalizations about successful recovery strategies or about inherent control redundancy of the aircraft. It was possible to accumulate empirical guidelines concerning when the results of using a trial strategy were objectively counter-indicative early and terminate the simulation early accordingly. In trying to recover the C-130 after elevator failures, a minute of aircraft response time was more than sufficient to see pitch stabilization in progress if it was to occur at all.

Ultimately the expert system used a set of rules to decide one of three things: the aircraft stabilized successfully, the failure-induced disturbance was under-opposed, or the failure-induced disturbance was over-opposed. The following system rule is illustrative:

> IF failure was pitch down
>   and pitch rate crosses zero
>   and later decreases below its first minimum
> THEN the failure was under-compensated

The following rule might then come into play:

> IF failure was pitch down
>   and the failure was under-compensated
>   and the emergency strategy simulated does not
>   include elevator tab usage
> THEN try hardover elevator tab deflection to -6°
>   [its maximum pitch-up setting]

Reference [1] contains a complete listing of the expert system program.

E. EXAMPLE FROM USE OF EXPERT SYSTEM

Typical interface between this expert system and the user is shown by an example in the Appendix. This has come directly from actual system usage. The user-supplied answers to questions asked by the expert system are shown in italics. The failure was a -9° off-nominal (pitch-up) elevator jam occurring when the aircraft was flying straight and level at 1000 ft and 147 KIAS. Six expert system-directed attempts (more than usual) were required in order to find a successful recovery from scratch in this case. The expert system used general but objective features of the aircraft response to check its latest trial recovery strategy and suggest corrections to it. These features included, in this case, state zero-crossings and the aircraft pitch angle remaining below a level associated empirically with looping and, ultimately, loss of the aircraft. Experience with the manual recovery cases had shown what features of the response constituted successful stall recovery, and this had also been embodied in rules. These were used by the expert system to find a successful recovery strategy in this pitch-up failure case.

In this example, recovery could not occur unless some kind of compensation was applied. Figure 6a shows the result of hard-over pitch-down elevator tab deployment after the failure. After reaching a high value, angle of attack did decrease through an empirically-based safe value of 25°. In successful cases, pitch rate began a trend toward pitch up within 5 s of this. This did not happen here. A better pitch rate response resulted after full

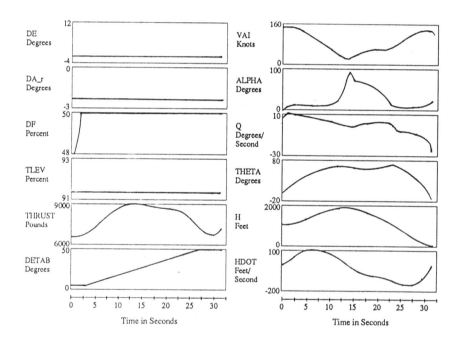

Fig. 6a. C-130 Aircraft Response to -9° Off-Nominal (Pitch Up) Elevator Jam, with Expert System-Directed Compensation; Strategy 1

(Flap setting originally 50%, flap extension airspeed-constrained; DE-elevator, DA_r-right aileron, DF-flap, TLEV-thrust lever, DETAB-elevator tab, VAI-indicated airspeed, ALPHA-angle of attack, Q-body axis pitch rate, THETA-body axis pitch angle, H-height above ground, HDOT-altitude rate)

pitch-down collective aileron was added, as Fig. 6b shows. Next, to get flight path angle to increase to a positive value and thus for the aircraft to climb, aileron was backed off at a later time (completely) as was elevator tab (to an intermediate value). There is a highlighted exchange in the transcript pointing to the surmise that some pitch-down compensation must be relieved after pitch rate recovery. Three adjustments were required to get acceptable final aileron and elevator tab settings. Figure 6c shows the final successful control strategy and the resulting vehicle response.

Only elevator tab and collective aileron deployments were needed to control the disturbance created by this particular elevator jam failure. However, to find a successful strategy in more strenuous cases, the possibilities of also changing flap and throttle settings during the initial part of the

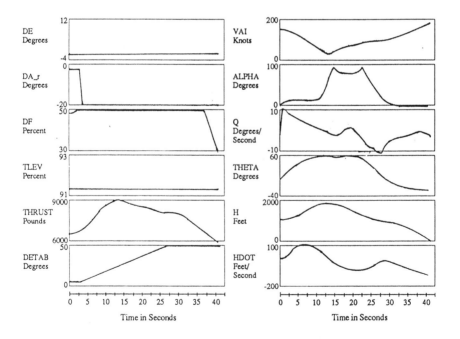

Fig. 6b. C-130 Aircraft Response to -9° Off-Nominal (Pitch Up) Elevator Jam, with Expert System-Directed Compensation; Strategy 2

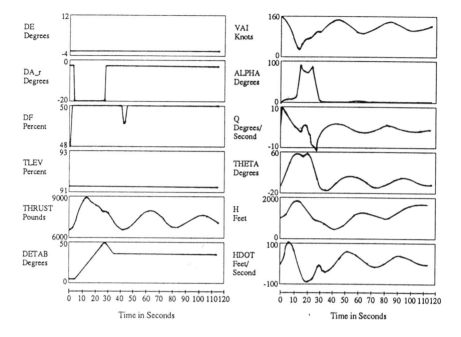

Fig. 6c. C-130 Aircraft Response to -9° Off-Nominal (Pitch Up) Elevator Jam, with Expert System-Directed Compensation; Strategy 6; Successful Recovery from Failure

recovery, and later reversal of these changes, had to be incorporated into the expert system. In cases where the aircraft stabilized in pitch, but in a descent, the expert system could first recommend initial thrust increase but could backtrack if this prevented stabilization in pitch. Then, using heuristic-based information, it could recommend times and amount of delayed thrust change to get transition to climb. Flap deployments in the simulation were limited structurally by airspeed. Expert system rules were written to decrease thrust or extend landing gear to keep airspeed down so that flaps could fully deploy, if necessary. From a problem-solving viewpoint, keeping airspeed up was a subgoal to the goal of pitch-stabilizing the aircraft. Landing gear, if extended, could be raised to help in gaining altitude during the recovery. By the end of the study, the expert system gave successful emergency control, when it existed, for all ranges of elevator jam failure and for all of the varied initial conditions tested.

F. EXTENSIONS AND USE OF THE EXPERT-TYPE RECOVERY-FINDING SYSTEM

It seems very likely that an expert system similar to the one presented could be developed to find recoveries after failures of other types of controls and perhaps after multiple control failures. This type of system might be able to find the control strategy for minimum altitude loss, which might be crucial in recovery, through incorporation of (probably much more elaborate) bracketing of control strategy [1]. It might be possible to use this type of system to achieve other goals at the end of the recovery, for example, optimum climb speed. Through certain additions, the recovery strategy need not be started from scratch, thus decreasing the number of attempts required. Other types of extensions might involve including rules to refine a workable strategy. Then one could reduce deployments of a certain control, redistributing its part of the failure compensation, in order to hedge against future control needs or future additional failures. Similarly, one might be able to include rules to simplify a strategy with numerous control change points, as might be expected in dealing with higher-performance or reduced-stability aircraft. Systems of this type might be taught to find recoveries where coupling between control of different axes is involved, for example, where temporary rolling to let the aircraft nose fall through might be required to recover from large pitch-up longitudinal control failures. If some near-optimum or difficult recovery strategy were being sought, the iterations to find a successful post-failure control strategy would be tedious at best for a human pilot. An automated system could be very sensitive to improvement in the recovery.

The recovery-finding system developed was insensitive to specifics about initial condition or delay for failure identification. It changed the strategy using only information about the vehicle response to it. Relaxing the assumption that the failure is known might greatly enhance the viability of the expert system approach for finding successful recovering control. It may be effective to initiate recovery control on the basis of vehicle response information only, without or prior to the failure being identified. Rational ways of acting in uncertainty could be embodied in the system knowledge, and this is fortunate, since some control failures may not be fully identifiable in the time available before response is required. There are interesting issues to be explored in the focussed qualitative/ quantitative trajectory projection that some pilots [2] can do to determine that a response to a developing situation is needed, and what likely useful responses might be. It should be noted that automatic control can mask the early effects of a failure if the failure detection mechanism (whether an algorithm or the pilot) does not account for it.

The expert-type recovery-finding system could easily be used in conjunction with (possibly reconfigured) automatic control. Figure 7 suggests this. If a relatively low-authority autopilot loop were still engaged, the recovery-finding system could work independently of what control changes were commanded by the autopilot, effectively augmenting or overriding its commands, as necessary. Experience with the C-130 [1] showed that part of finding a workable recovery strategy could naturally involve determining

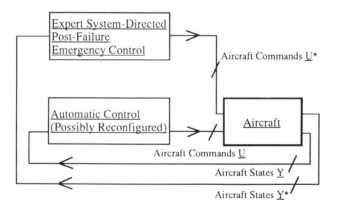

Fig. 7. Expert System to Find Emergency Control
Used in Conjunction with
(Reconfigurable) Automatic Control

autopilot usage. Sometimes disengaging the autopilot in one axis was very beneficial in helping the aircraft recover. However, this would be more helpful than necessary if the expert system itself had high authority to command control changes.

This type of expert system might be useful in giving some rough idea of the basic control redundancy of an aircraft configuration alone. If no automatic control were modeled, the expert system might look for control strategies that yielded rate and state zero-crossings but without stabilization being asked for. It is extremely difficult to establish true control redundancy without some type of outright simulation of the vehicle response to different failures occurring with the vehicle in various initial conditions.

An expert-type system could incorporate many different types of information needed to formulate a recovery strategy. The need to incorporate post-failure constraint information, as least implicitly, should be illustrated. In addition to working with elevator failure cases, many recoveries after C-130 asymmetric jammed flap failures were made in this study. In severe flap failure cases, highest priority efforts had to be made to keep the airspeed above the calculated controllability airspeed, so the ailerons would have sufficient authority to oppose the rolling induced by the failure. Increasing thrust alone was not sufficient to keep the airspeed up in these cases. Instead, temporary forceful pitch down of the aircraft using the elevator, and thrust increase during the resulting dive to enhance the acceleration, were absolutely necessary for ultimate recovery. According to pilots interviewed, this would have been a counter-intuitive strategy--certainly not the first strategy they would have tried. The advantage of the expert system approach is that any counter-intuitive recoveries known to be successful could also become part of the knowledge embedded in rules in the system. In a similar way, calculating post-failure performance-type constraints could also become important in developing a recovery strategy. As one reported accident case demonstrated, part of a successful recovery from a jammed extended surface might involve deliberately attempting to exceed structural limitations on surface deployment, so that it could be broken off. If there were no choice, temporary moderate relaxation of some vehicle constraints might be undertaken. All of these possible aspects of a successful recovery could be embedded in an expert system. Force-moment mapping reconfiguration or other types of post-failure loop reconfiguration could not be expected to produce some of these successful recovery control strategies.

In-flight use of an expert system of the type developed might be very feasible, but it might also be used for finding recoveries from wide ranges of control failures before an aircraft is ever flown. Although it might not be possible to simplify to this extent, the final result of a broad simulation study might be a failure recovery system with processing consisting of straight-through paths from information about the failure to the successful recovery strategy:

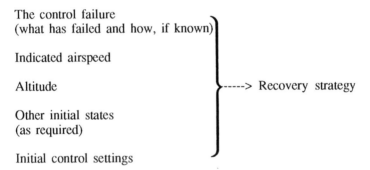

The control failure
(what has failed and how, if known)

Indicated airspeed

Altitude   -----> Recovery strategy

Other initial states
(as required)

Initial control settings

The viewpoint that resulted in this expert-type system for finding emergency post-failure control was quite different from that taken in most failure-accommodating control research. However, it is not at all incompatible with it. The advantages are numerous. Systems like the one developed here can be written to call for use of unusual controls in unusual ways. They can direct the perhaps counter-intuitive strategies that are sometimes required. They can accommodate saturation of controls in a situation in which it can be expected and is very important. Expert-type systems can include the possibilities of calculating and using information about post-failure operating and performance constraints. This approach is an effective blending of natural qualitative- and quantitative-type approaches to emergency control.

V. INTEGRATED RECOVERY AND ADVISORY SYSTEM

Finally, let us consider a complete, integrated onboard aid and advisory system. The most desirable system for automated recovery from control failures would have the capability of making an immediate correct response to the failure. The emergency control strategy could be formulated by an expert system. The pilot would be informed of and could override all automatic control actions. An explanation would be available on demand for advice given by such an expert system (this would be consistent with traditional AI doctrine). A fully automatic emergency control system would probably be disengaged to the extent possible once the aircraft was stabilized--the pilot's good problem-solving skills should be maximally utilized in recovering the aircraft. There would likely follow phases of relatively quiescent flight, and the transitions between flight phases would generally be slowly and carefully done. This was evident in the few successful reported failure cases and is the result of the pilot's natural inclination to reduce demands on a handicapped aircraft. Based on the considerations already established, a system should be provided to support the pilot with advisory information for the rest of the flight. The ideal pilot advisory system interface would have the most important information displayed continuously. Other information about each general flight phase would be kept updated and available to the pilot on demand.

A post-failure advisory system must be able to decide which types of information might have changed significantly after the failure. The goal should be selective substitution in the pilot's knowledge. Piloting is an expert behavior and has evolved naturally to be very efficient from an information standpoint. It makes sense to evaluate and present types of information that pilots would naturally choose, and to try to use and extend their heuristic assessments of what information needs to be recalculated. When faced with a significant failure, a good pilot would know when to evaluate for more precise information, but on the basis of a more qualitative assessment of the situation. The knowledge involved in supporting the advisory would probably be more broad than deep, and probably not extensive. The overall aid/advisory system would probably be a hybrid blending of qualitative rule-based processing directing quantitative computation. This again suggests use of an expert system approach to implement the advisory system. Most languages used for expert systems have a mechanism for calling functions in a standard programming language as part of a rule's THEN actions.

Pilots suggested the following questions about residual control capability as those they would ideally want answered: 1) How much roll capability remains? 2) How much control do I have over vertical acceleration, angle of attack, airspeed, and sink rate? 3) How much sideslip can I use? 4) Am I "committed to land," or can I make a go-around? It turns out that answers to these questions can be impossible to determine or even convey. Any strong notion of control capability must be a function of the aircraft operating state. Even at a given state, it is a function of the available range and allowable rate of deployment of the viable controls, the structural limitations on their deployment, and their "artifact." Furthermore, use of a control may be limited by operating constraints induced by the failure. These types of considerations apply in nominal aircraft operation, but then available control capability need not be assessed precisely, because what is feasible is generally "known" by the pilot from training and experience.

Fortunately, when pressed, pilots wanted less to be apprised of new values of quantitative maneuvering-type figures-of-merit as to know whether or not certain few capabilities were significantly degraded and the vehicle configuration and state at which they were now maximized. Some general sorts of reminders, such as "avoid (adverse) sideslip" after asymmetric engine failure, were also wanted. Pilots want to be able to use standard nominal or standard emergency procedures (which have been practiced and are more automatic) as much as possible. An advisory system should be able to reference standard flight manual information and checklists, although, as seen earlier in this chapter, this sort of advice should generally be augmented with quantitative advice assembled from more fundamental information.

Pilots are accustomed to watching indicated airspeed closely. Most flying is done according to airspeed guidelines, and changes judged large by the advisory system (according to some measure) must be put forward very clearly. Certain background calculations anticipating possible additional failures should also be done. Reference [9] suggests that important pilot advisory information (actually, a subset of what is being recommended in this chapter) be superimposed on a head-up display when possible, and also describes possible display formats.

Reference [1] lists suggested advisory information for each of the four (see Section IV, C) generic-type flight phases after control of the aircraft has been regained. It includes information on how the need to assemble some advisory information might be established and programmed. One of the most important considerations is that the failure of a given control results not only in the loss of at least some of its own controlling potential but, possibly very significantly, in the degradation of that of now failure-compensating controls or changes in state (such as decreased angle of attack for pitch-down effect). Calculations to support post-failure advising need to be keyed to both failed and compensating controls, particularly compensating primary controls, and compensating changes in state. The advisory system should contain enough rules to be able to judge when to make the inference that the "off-nominal-ness" of control or state is such that a given aspect of aircraft performance, for example, must be explicitly evaluated.

As was discussed in Section III of this chapter, explicit retrim during relatively quiescent periods of post-failure flight may be extremely useful. Retrimming might greatly increase vehicle performance or maneuvering ability. The onboard aid and advisory system should probably be able to infer opportunity for retrim on the basis of current apparent steady-state flight. In some cases, upcoming needs might be inferred, and retrim calculations proceed on that basis. The possibility of doing some rational type of continual automatic background retrim should be considered.

Being able to implement the proposed recovery aid and advisory system would probably not require unrealistic computational and display capability. Its goals and features would mesh extremely well with the aircraft installations being developed in current programs to design cockpit aids for fighter and transport aircraft [10].

VI. CONCLUSIONS

Analysis of aircraft accident cases, discussions with pilots, and experience flying simulated recoveries have shown that existing research on the problem of control failures has not yielded entirely adequate answers. Familiar failure-robust or reconfigurable control ideas have definite limitations in finding failure recoveries even when they exist. Failure-induced changes in operating and performance constraints cannot be explicitly taken into account. These approaches cannot utilize all remaining control resources in the complicated, unusual, or even counter-intuitive ways that were shown here to be sometimes required. After considerable experimentation with a wide variety of traditional and other types of solution ideas, the expert system approach was recognized to be of natural and highly effective use. Piloting is an almost classical expert behavior. Expert systems became the backbone for a proposed automatic onboard aid and advisory system.

Types of failure-induced changes in constraints have been discussed. These constraints, although rarely considered in other research, can become crucial in formulating emergency control strategies and advising pilots flying control-impaired aircraft. Elements of the proposed automatic emergency control system have been discussed. A rule-based system to find successful control after elevator jam failures on the C-130 aircraft was developed and has been considered here. Systems of this type seem to be very effective, and extensions to this approach have been presented. Such systems could conceivably be installed on aircraft, and, as was presented, could be important resources on the ground. As was discussed, this type of system can and, in general, should be used in conjunction with more familiar failure-robust or reconfigurable automatic control.

The advisory function of the onboard aid and advisory system is seen to follow usage of emergency high-authority post-failure automatic control. There has been a treatment of what types of information about continued flight should be calculated. The rule-based system approach can provide a way of determining useful qualitative advice about flying a control-impaired aircraft and deciding which types of more quantitative information should be calculated. There was also a discussion of post-failure retrim and some demonstrations of the impact of this that are believed to be novel. Numerous interesting and substantiating examples for all of these points have been included. The automatic aid and advisory system proposed here, including rule-based systems for finding emergency control and directing advisory calculations, seems to promise a good and viable solution to the problem of aircraft control failures.

VII. REFERENCES

1. E. Wagner, "On-board Automatic Aid and Advisory for Pilots of Control-Impaired Aircraft," Ph.D. Dissertation, Dept. of Aeronautics and Astronautics, Massachusetts Institute of Technology, Cambridge MA (1987).
2. J. McMahan, "Flight 1080," *Air Line Pilot* **47**(7), pp. 6-10 (1978).
3. R. Montoya, ed., *Restructurable Controls*, NASA CP-2277 (1983).
4. P. Chandler, "Self-Repairing Flight Control System Reliability and Maintainability Program Executive Overview," *Proceedings of the National Aerospace and Electronics Conference*, Institute of Electrical and Electronics Engineers, New York NY, pp. 586-590 (1984).
5. D. Waterman, *A Guide to Expert Systems*, Addison-Wesley, Reading MA (1986).
6. P. Cohen and E. Feigenbaum, eds., *Handbook of Artificial Intelligence*, William Kaufmann, Los Altos CA (1982).

7. *Flight Manual, USAF Series T-37B Aircraft*, T.O. 1T-37B-1, Secretary of the Air Force, Washington DC (1982).

8. L. Brownston, R. Farrell, E. Kant, and N. Martin, *Programming Expert Systems in OPS5: An Introduction to Rule-Based Programming*, Addison-Wesley, Reading MA (1985).

9. W. Weinstein, "Control Reconfigurable Combat Aircraft Development, Phase 1--R&D Design Evaluation," AFWAL-TR-87-3011, Flight Dynamics Laboratory, Wright-Patterson Air Force Base OH (1987).

10. P. Kinnucan, "Building a Better Cockpit," *High Technology* 6(1), pp. 49-54 (1986).

VIII. APPENDIX

Transcript: Interaction with Expert System, -9° Off-Nominal Elevator Jam, Aircraft Flying Originally at 147 KIAS. (**Emphasis** added later.)

```
;
;The advisory is beginning.
;A simulation may be terminated when...
;The aircraft pitch angle starts to exceed 111. deg.
;with a pitch-up failure or
;Ground impact is imminent or
;Stable oscillations in all states are apparent
;and you can determine the approximate
;steady climb rate of stabilized flight.
;Answer all questions below with yes or no.
;Please be careful with your answers: there is
;no explicit checking for inconsistencies.
;
;Try no compensating control to see if the aircraft
;can recover on its own.
;Did pitch rate ever cross zero?
yes
;
;Was the aircraft stabilizing by our definition
;at the end of the sim?
no
;
;Did pitch angle remain below 111. deg.-and-if it did
;so but crossed 30. deg. did it decrease and recross
;this level later?
no
;
;Try the addition of immediate hardover elevator tab
;deflection to 50. deg.
;Did pitch rate ever cross zero?
yes
;
;Was the aircraft stabilizing by our definition
;at the end of the sim?
no
;
```

;Did pitch angle remain below 111. deg.-and-if it did
;so but crossed 30. deg. did it decrease and recross
;this level later?
yes

;Did angle of attack remain below 25. deg. originally
;-or-if it did cross this level did it always later
;decrease through it at least before rising above it
;again?
yes

;Did angle of attack remain below 25. deg.-or-
;if angle of attack ever exceeded this level did
;pitch rate reach a minimum before the end of the
;simulation and within 5. seconds after angle of
;attack last decreased through 25. deg.?
no

;Add immediate hardover collective aileron deflection
;to -20. deg.
;Did pitch rate ever cross zero?
yes

;Was the aircraft stabilizing by our definition
;at the-end of the sim?
no

;Did pitch angle remain below 111. deg.-and-if it did
;so but crossed 30. deg. did it decrease and recross
;this level later?
yes

;Did angle of attack remain below 25. deg. originally
;-or-if it did cross this level did it always later
;decrease through it at least before rising above it
;again?
yes

;Did angle of attack remain below 25. deg.-or-
;if angle of attack ever exceeded this level did
;pitch rate reach a minimum before the end of the
;simulation and within 5. seconds after angle of
;attack last decreased through 25. deg.?
yes

;Did pitch rate cross back from negative to positive
;if angle-of-attack remained below 25. deg. or after
;angle-of-attack last decreased through 25. deg.?
yes

;Did flight path angle remain positive in the initial
;stall recovery-or-if it was negative at some point
;did it later cross from negative to positive?
no

;Backing off on the last pitch-down input later
;should be tried. In the last simulation
;if pitch rate achieved a
;minimum after angle of atttack decreased to 25. deg.
;state the time in seconds that this minimum
;occurred. Otherwise state the time at which angle
;of attack decreased through 25. deg. If angle of
;attack never exceeded 25. deg. state the time at
;which pitch rate was minimized for the entire run.
28.

;Back off collective aileron hardover to 0. deg. at
;28. sec.
;Was the aircraft stabilizing by our definition
;at the end of the sim?
no

```
;
;Did pitch angle remain below 111. deg.-and-if it did
;so but crossed 30. deg. did it decrease and recross
;this level later?
yes
;
;Did angle of attack remain below 25. deg. originally
;-or-if it did cross this level did it always later
;decrease through it at least before rising above it
;again?
yes
;
;Did flight path angle remain positive in the initial
;stall recovery-or-if it was negative at some point
;did it later cross from negative to positive?
no
;
;Back off elevator tab hardover to 3.65 deg. at
; 28. sec.
;Was the aircraft stabilizing by our definition
;at the end of the sim?
no
;
;Did pitch angle remain below 111. deg.-and-if it did
;so but crossed 30. deg. did it decrease and recross
;this level later?
no
;
;Back off elevator tab hardover to 26.825 deg. at
;28. sec.
;Was the aircraft stabilizing by our definition
;at the end of the sim?
no
;
;Did pitch angle remain below 111. deg.-and-if it did
;so but crossed 30. deg. did it decrease and recross
;this level later?
no
;
;Back off elevator tab hardover to 38.4125 deg. at
;28. sec.
;Was the aircraft stabilizing by our definition
;at the end of the sim?
yes
;
;Was the aircraft settling into an apparent descent?
no
;
;A successful recovery strategy has been found.
;End -- no production true
;(64 productions (560 // 1560 nodes))
;(286 firings (987 RHS actions))
;(10. Mean working memory size (18 maximum))
;(1. mean conflict set size (8 maximum))
;(36. mean token memory size (207 maximum))
;(36. "mean token memory size" (207 "maximum"))
```

PLACEMENT OF SENSORS AND ACTUATORS IN STRUCTURAL CONTROL

Haim Baruh

Department of Mechanical and Aerospace Engineering
Rutgers University
New Brunswick, New Jersey 08903

I. INTRODUCTION

Two of the most important issues when designing a control system to suppress the vibration or to maneuver a flexible structure are

i) How many sensors and actuators to use to implement the control action, and
ii) Where to place the sensors, actuators and their backups

On a flexible structure sensors are used to monitor the overall behavior, the motion amplitudes, as well as the structural integrity of the structure. The control system uses the output of the sensors as feedback. Once the controller decides what the control input should be, this message is transmitted to the actuators, which impart the desired forces or moments to the structure.

The answer to the two questions raised above cannot be separated from the other aspects of the control design. Some general guidelines, however, can be developed. In this article, we outline some general procedures, review the existing research in this field and discuss our own results.

Recent work in determining the number and location of control system components in distributed-parameter systems include [1-20], where a variety of criteria have been considered. References 1-3 use an optimal control cost minimization criterion. Minimization of the control energy is considered in [4], and minimization of the expected value of a performance index is sought in [5]. Reliability issues are utilized in [6-7]. In [6], mission life and in [7] possible actuator failures and controllability after failure are considered. The degree of controllability is also used as a criterion in [8]. Failures of actuators and sensors are investigated in [9] and [10], respectively, where criteria are proposed to locate the actuators and sensors in a way to facilitate the failure detection process. The results of [4], [9], and [10] indicate that an even distribution of the control components generally yields satisfactory results. General reliability and replacement of control components is considered in [11-12]. In [13] the accuracy with which the modal coordinates are extracted from the sensors output is used as a criterion to place the sensors. Minimization of power is used as a criterion in [14] to locate both the sensors and actuators.

Reference 15 presents a literature survey on placement of sensors and actuators. In [16] a set of possible candidate locations of sensors is sequentially reduced to find the optimal number and location of the sensors. Reference [17] uses several measures of controllability to locate the actuators. It also considers placement of torque actuators as well. References [18-19] consider the effects of noise when selecting the locations of the sensors and actuators. In [20] a distributed model is considered.

Spatially continuously distributed sensing and actuation mechanisms are considered in [21-27]. Distributed controllers can be in the form of piecewise-continuous elements [21] or piezoelectric layers on beams [23-27].

II. AN INITIAL LOOK AT THE PROBLEM

The motion of flexible structures is described by coupled sets of partial differential equations. Because of the complexity of these equations and the difficulty in finding closed-form solutions one is almost always forced to use an approximate method of solution, such as the Finite-Element method [28]. In essence, all approximate methods convert the differential eigenvalue problem, which is of infinite order, into an algebraic one of finite order. The equations of motion are in discretized form. This discretized set of equations is used when designing the control law.

Another aspect of the control system design that also is in discretized form are the sensors and actuators. Ideally, one would like to have spatially continuously distributed sensors and actuators, so that one can measure the deformation of the structure at every point and impart control forces and torques wherever desired. We only have either discrete sensors and actuators (acting on a point) or small piecewise continuous sensors and actuators [21]. The end result is that we have to design a control law using a discretized set of equations together with discrete sensors and actuators. Some inroads have been made with distributed sensing and actuation, such as the development of piezoelectric materials [23-27], but research on this subject is still at a preliminary stage. The application of distributed actuation and sensing using piezoelectric layers requires a variable voltage field on the sensor or actuator.

When viewing the selection of the number and locations of the sensors and actuators one can think of the discretization issues above and conclude that our goal should be to approximate as closely as possible the ideal situation of spatially continuously distributed sensing and actuation. To accomplish this

• We should use as many sensors and actuators as we can get a hold of, and
• We should place our sensors and actuators as evenly as possible so as to simulate a continuous distribution. If we can have near distributed sensing and actuation, such as piezoelectric layers, we should cover the entire structure with such layers.

While the general results of our own research has been along the lines given above, one cannot just say that the placement of sensors and actuators is such a simple issue or even a nonproblem. Consider, for example, the following disadvantages of having many more sensors and actuators than necessary:

- The cost involved with acquiring these components,
- The added weight to the structure due to the sensors, actuators and peripheral hardware associated with them,
- The increase in the computational effort when processing the outputs of the sensors, when designing the control law, and when calculating the actuator inputs,
- The possible increase in control effort, measured in fuel and energy,
- The increase in the number of sensor and actuator malfunctions due to the larger number of components used.

In addition, one should also consider that while the actual model of a flexible structure is continuous, an infinite number of modes is really not necessary to describe the motion accurately. The contribution of modes beyond a certain number is insignificant. Also, the internal damping in the structure annihilates the amplitudes of certain modes almost immediately. The implication is that a discretized model of an appropriate order is sufficient to describe the evolution of a flexible structure. The number of sensors and actuators required should then be based on the selected model order.

Considering the above discussion, we need to determine some criteria for selecting the number of sensors and actuators that are necessary for monitoring and controlling a flexible structure. In the remainder of this article, we will first derive the discretized model and then discuss strategies for selecting the number of control system components.

III. EQUATIONS OF MOTION

We begin with a partial differential equation of motion for a structure as

$$Lu(x,y,t) + m(x,y)\ddot{u}(x,y,t) + c(x,y)\dot{u}(x,y,t) = f(x,y,t) \qquad (1)$$

where $u(x,y,t)$ is the deformation at spatial coordinate (x,y), L is a stiffness operator, $m(x,y)$ is the mass per unit area, and $c(x,y)$ contains the damping effects. For discretization purposes, consider the undamped system and adopt a procedure such as the Finite Element method [28] and obtain the discretized equations of motion

$$M\ddot{\underline{a}}(t) + K\underline{a}(t) = \underline{A}(t) \qquad (2)$$

where M and K are the mass and stiffness matrices of order $N \times N$, $\underline{a}(t)$ is the generalized coordinate vector of order N, and $\underline{A}(t)$ is the external excitation. $\underline{a}(t)$ is related to the expansion functions by $\underline{a}(t) = \underline{b}^T\underline{\psi}(x,y)$, where $\underline{\psi}(x,y)$ denote a vector of trial functions $[\underline{\psi}(x,y) = \psi_1(x,y) \ \psi_2(x,y) \ ... \ \psi_N(x,y)]^T$ and $\underline{b}(t)$ are unknown displacements. In the Finite Element method $\underline{a}(t)$ correspond to physical displacements. For complex structures, the order of N can be in the hundreds of thousands. Solving the associated eigenvalue problem we obtain the eigenvalues λ_r and associated eigenvectors $\underline{u}_r$ ($r=1,2,...,N$). The eigenvectors are used to approximate the system eigenfunctions as

$$\phi_r(x,y) = \underline{u}_r^T \underline{\psi}(x,y), \quad r=1, 2, ..., N \tag{3}$$

Using the expansion $\underline{a}(t) = \sum \underline{u}_r \eta_r(t)$, where $\eta_r(t)$ are modal coordinates we arrive at the modal equations associated with the discretized system as

$$\ddot{\eta}_r(t) + \omega_r^2 \eta_r(t) = H_r(t), \quad r = 1, 2, ..., N \tag{4}$$

in which $H_r(t) = \underline{u}_r^T \underline{A}(t)$ are modal forces. The physical displacements can be obtained using

$$u(x,y) = \sum_{r=1}^{N} \phi_r(x,y)\eta_r(t) = \sum_{r=1}^{N} \underline{u}_r^T \underline{\psi}(x,y)\,\eta_r(t) \tag{5}$$

As stated earlier, for a structure with a complicated geometry the order N of the mathematical model can be in the hundreds of thousands. Dealing with this number is both impractical and not necessary. We therefore truncate the number of modal equations to n, where n<<N. We think of our system as a continuous system whose equation of motion is given by Eq. (1), which has n eigenvalues ω_r^2 and n eigenfunctions $\phi_r(x,y)$ (r=1,2,...,n) defined in Eq. (3) and n modes, whose equations of motion are given by Eq. (4).

It should be noted that the selection of the number n is controversial and it depends on the requirements of the structure itself. However, once n is established, we have the advantage of dealing with a continuous system and considering a limited number of modes which are known almost exactly, due to the accuracy of the Finite Element method. For all practical purposes, we can say that we have generated a closed-form solution of the eigenvalue problem.

IV. SELECTION OF THE NUMBER OF ACTUATORS AND SENSORS

The optimal number of actuators and sensors can be defined as the *minimum number of sensors and actuators that can perform the monitoring and control action as required by the mission objectives*. Obviously, having a larger number of control system components will do equally well or better, but they will lead to increased costs, more failures, added weight and possibly larger computational effort and control energy. The objectives of the control action are the main factors to be considered.

Let us, for example, consider vibration suppression. One can group control strategies for vibration suppression into two categories: a) Modal control laws, and b) control laws that do not use modes but calculate the feedback quantities directly from the system output. An example to methods in the second category is decentralized control.

When considering modal control, one has to first determine how many modes need to be controlled. That is, how many of the n modes that we decided to retain in the mathematical model in the previous section need control. One way to determine this is to look at the motion amplitudes. The response of a certain mode can be expressed as

$$\eta_r(t) = \eta_r(0)\cos\omega_r t + \dot{\eta}_r(0)\sin\omega_r t/\omega_r + \frac{1}{\omega_r}\int_0^t H_r(t-\tau)\sin\omega_r\tau d\tau, \quad r=1,2,...,n \tag{6}$$

The case when all the modes are excited the most is when an impulse acts on the structure. Considering zero initial conditions and an impulse of magnitude F_0 applied at (x_0, y_0), the modal response is

$$\eta_r(t) = F_0\phi_r(x_0,y_0)\sin\omega_r t/\omega_r, \quad r=1, 2, ..., n \tag{7}$$

with the response of the structure being

$$u(x,y,t) = \sum_{r=1}^n \phi_r(x,y)\eta_r(t) = \sum_{r=1}^n \phi_r(x,y)F_0\phi_r(x_0,y_0)\sin\omega_r t/\omega_r \tag{8}$$

We denote the number of modes to be controlled by m. If we set a criterion that the response $u(x,y,t)$ to a force F_0 should not exceed a maximum of δ at any point on the structure, we can determine m by the relation

$$\delta/F_0 = \frac{1}{\omega_m} \phi_m^2(x,y)\big|_{max} \tag{9}$$

Another criterion to determine m can be the ratio of amplitudes, such as

$$R_m/R_1 < \varepsilon, \qquad R_i = \frac{1}{\omega_i} \phi_i^2(x,y)\big|_{max}, \quad i=1,2,...,n \tag{10}$$

The number of actuators to use would then depend on the control law and m, the number of controlled modes. Another factor to be considered when selecting the number of actuators is their capacity to generate a desired level of force and torque, or their saturation properties. In general, as more actuators are used lower levels of forces and torques are required of each actuator.

For decentralized control laws all of the n modes retained in the mathematical model need to be considered. Actually, because in that case the number of actuators and sensors is generally the same, analysis of decentralized laws have been conducted within the context of control design [29].

As can be seen from the above discussion, the guidelines that exist for the determination of the number of actuators are vague. This is because there is so far no extensive study conducted for determining the number of required actuators independently of the control law. Because most of the on-line work done for flexible structure control has been carried out in laboratories, for the most time experimenters have had to live with the hardware that could be purchased with the available funds. Also, different structures will have different constraints with regards to the control design.

Selection of the optimal number of sensors, independent of the control law or the way the sensors output is processed, has not been investigated at length, either. The work of Kammer [16] is one of the first that sequentially reduces a candidate set for the sensors. We conclude our discussion with regards to the optimal number of sensors and actuators here and go into the subject of determining the optimal locations of the sensors and actuators. We will investigate the issue of given a certain number of actuators and sensors, where on the structure is the best place to put them.

V.   PLACEMENT OF SENSORS

Placement of sensors on a structure is closely related to how the sensors output is processed. Here, one basically has two options: a) To feed the sensors output directly into the control law, such as in a decentralized controller, or b) To calculate an intermediate quantity, which is used as feedback. The intermediate quantities, for the most time, are modal coordinates or velocities.

In the first case, such as decentralized control, selection of the sensors depends more on the number of actuators necessary to achieve the control objectives. We will discuss this case in more detail when discussing the placement of actuators. In the second case, when an intermediate quantity such as modal coordinates are calculated, the number and location of the sensors are dictated by the accuracy with which the intermediate quantities are calculated.

When extracting modal coordinates from the system output, there are two basic ways: One is by the use of modal filters [13, 30, 31] and the other is by observers [31 - 33]. Observers can be both full-order and reduced order. Full order observers estimate the entire system state and reduced order observers estimate a subset of the system states. We describe both modal filters and observers below.

In modal filtering, use is made of the expansion theorem (Eq. 5) to extract the modal coordinates from the system output. This requires distributed measurements. Implementation using discrete measurements requires generation of an approximate distributed profile by interpolation or extrapolation of the sensors measurements as

$$\hat{w}(x,y,t) = \sum_{j=1}^{l} u(x_j,y_j,t)G(x,y,x_j,y_j) \tag{11}$$

where $\hat{w}(x,t)$ is the approximated profile, x_j and y_j denote the location of the sensors $(j=1,2,...,l)$ and $G(x,y,x_j,y_j)$ are interpolation or extrapolation functions, in which the time and space dependency are separate.   Among common interpolation functions are finite-element functions, splines, and eigenfunction expansions [13]. Our earlier research has shown that splines are very desirable to use when implementing modal filters [13].

Introducing Eq. (11) into the expansion theorem, we obtain the extracted modal coordinates, defined by $q_r(t)$ as

$$q_r(t) = (\hat{w}(x,y,t),m(x,y)\phi_r(x,y)) = \sum_{j=1}^{l} g_{rj}\, u(x_j,y_j,t), \quad r=1,2,... \tag{12}$$

where $g_{rj} = (G(x,y,x_j,y_j),m(x,y)\phi_r(x,y))$ $(j=1,2,...,l; r=1,2,...)$. In matrix form, $\underline{q}_M(t) = G\underline{y}(t)$.

We consider the m of modes of interest (referred to as monitored modes) and partition the modal coordinates into monitored and residual components $\underline{\eta}(t) = [\,\eta_1(t)\ \eta_2(t)\ ...]^T = [\underline{\eta}_M^T(t)\,|\,\underline{\eta}_R^T(t)\,]^T$. We introduce the vector $\underline{q}_M(t)$, where $\underline{q}_M(t) = [\,q_1(t)\ q_2(t)\ ...\ q_m(t)\,]^T$ and express the sensors measurements as $y_j(t) = u(x_j,t) + n_j(t)$, $(j=1,2,...,l)$, where $n_j(t)$ $(j=1,2,...,l)$ denotes noise. The extracted modes are related to the actual modal coordinates by

$$\underline{q}_M(t) = GH_M\underline{\eta}_M(t) + GH_R\underline{\eta}_R(t) + G\underline{n}(t) \tag{13}$$

where $H_M(i,j) = \phi_j(x_i)$ $(i=1,2,...,l; j=1,2,...,m)$ and $H_R(i,j) = \phi_{m+j}(x_i)$ $(i=1,2,...,l; j=1,2,...)$. The objective is to select the number and location of the sensors, the interpolation functions, and the number of monitored modes such that GH_M approaches an identity matrix and GH_R approaches a null matrix.

Note that the design and implementation of modal filters are independent of the number and location of the system actuators. The approach can easily be extended to cases where the measurements are piecewise-continuous or they are by piezoelectric devices.

To optimize the number and location of sensors one can conduct studies based on the error associated with the accuracy of the modal coordinate extraction. The error in modal filtering can be defined as

$$\underline{e}_M(t) = \underline{\eta}_M(t) - \underline{q}_M(t) = [I - GH_M]\underline{\eta}_M(t) - GH_R\underline{\eta}_R(t) - G\underline{n}(t) \tag{14}$$

One performance functional $J = J(x_1, x_2, ..., x_l)$ that has been used is [30]

$$\min\ J = \sum_{i=1}^{m} [\ \sum_{j=1}^{m} (GH_M - I)_{ij}^2/\omega_i\omega_j + \sum_{j=1}^{n-m} (GH_R)_{ij}^2/\omega_i\omega_{m+j}\ ] \tag{15}$$

s.t. $0 < x_i \le L$, $i=1,2,...,l$; $x_{i-1} < x_i < x_{i+1}$, $i=2,3,...,l-1$

The elements of GH_M and GH_R are weighed depending on the natural frequencies of the modes they affect. Equation (15) gives more weighting to minimizing the error in the lower modes.

Next, we consider observers. For brevity, we will only consider full-order observers. To implement observers we need to express the equations of motion for the reduced-order model (m modes) in state form as

$$\dot{\underline{x}}(t) = A\underline{x}(t) + B\underline{F}(t), \qquad \underline{y}_A(t) = C\underline{x}(t) + \underline{h}_S(t) \tag{16}$$

where $\underline{x}(t)$ is the 2n-dimensional state vector, in the form $\underline{x}(t) = [\ \underline{\eta}_M(t)^T \mid \dot{\underline{\eta}}_M(t)^T\ ]^T$ and A and B are state and control influence matrices of orders 2m*2m and 2m*k, respectively. C is the k*2m observation matrix. The observer is defined as

$$\dot{\underline{z}}(t) = A\underline{z}(t) + B\underline{F}(t) + P[\underline{y}(t) - \underline{y}'(t)], \qquad \underline{y}'(t) = C\underline{z}(t) \tag{17}$$

where $\underline{z}(t)$ denotes estimated quantities and P is the observer gain matrix. Defining an error vector $\underline{e}(t) = \underline{x}(t) - \underline{z}(t)$, and a control law in the form $\underline{F}(t) = K\underline{z}(t)$, one can arrive at the well-known observer equations, which, in the absence of actuator and sensor failures and noise, have the form

$$\begin{bmatrix} \dot{\underline{x}}(t) \\ \dot{\underline{x}}_R(t) \\ \dot{\underline{e}}(t) \end{bmatrix} = \begin{bmatrix} A_M + B_M K & 0 & -B_M K \\ B_R K & A_R & -B_R K \\ 0 & PC_R & A_M - PC \end{bmatrix} \begin{bmatrix} \underline{x}(t) \\ \underline{x}_R(t) \\ \underline{e}(t) \end{bmatrix} \tag{18}$$

in which P is chosen such that the observer poles are stable and C_R corresponds to the residual parts of the observation matrix C. Note that the deterministic separation principle is valid when the residual dynamics is ignored (when we cross out the middle row and column).

One implementation problem, of course, is the design of P, especially for high-order systems. Added to this are problems encountered because the state vector used is a finite-dimensional reduced-order vector, and because the residual dynamics contaminates the results, a phenomenon known as observation spillover.

The placement of the sensors would then be done with the following objectives in mind:

• Maximize stability of the observer and its robustness with respect to parameter errors and incorrect model order

• Minimize observation spillover

• Design the observer gains with as little computational effort as possible

• Design the observer gains such that the control effort is minimized

As can be seen from the above, when an observer is used, the control task cannot be separated from the state estimation part. One can say that the gain matrix P can be designed independently of the control law, but this approach may have adverse effects on the stability of the closed-loop system. This statement is true of other types of observers, such as reduced order, as well. By contrast, when modal filters are used the estimation does not depend on the control action. In that sense, modal filters are more modular and they do not adversely influence stability and the control effort. An in-depth analysis of the number of sensors that would be required to control a system of a given order has not been conducted.

VI. PLACEMENT OF ACTUATORS

When considering the placement of actuators, one has to first consider the types of actuation mechanisms that are available. Spatially continuously distributed measurements and controls are not within the state of the art. Piezoelectric actuators, which can be called near-distributed, currently need further refinement for applying distributed voltages, so that they resemble distributed actuation. We will limit ourselves here to four types of discrete actuators: point force actuators, piecewise-continuous force actuators, point torquers and piecewise-continuous torquers. For point force actuators (Fig. 1) we express the force profile as

$$f(x,y,t) = \sum_{i=1}^{k} F_i(t)\delta(x - x_{ai})\delta(y - y_{ai}) \tag{19}$$

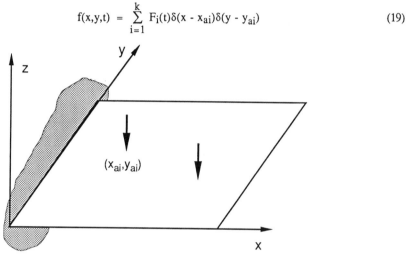

Figure 1. Point actuators.

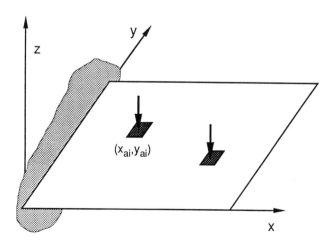

Figure 2. Piecewise-continuous actuators.

in which (x_{ai}, y_{ai}) are the actuator locations and k is the number of actuators. The modal forces associated with these forces become

$$f_r(t) \;=\; \sum_{i=1}^{k} \int\int F_i(t)\delta(x - x_{ai})\delta(y - y_{ai})\phi_r(x,y)dxdy \;=\; \sum_{i=1}^{k} B_{ri}F_i(t), \quad r=1,2,... \tag{20}$$

where $B_{ri} = \phi_r(x_{ai}, y_{ai})$ $(r=1,2,...; i=1,2,...,k)$ are the entries of the actuator influence matrix B.

We next consider control forces that are piecewise-continuous, as shown in Fig. 2. For convenience, we assume that each actuator is in the form of a square, with each side of length $2\varepsilon_i$, for a contact area of $4\varepsilon_i^2$. The midpoint of each actuator is located at (x_{ai}, y_{ai}) $(i=1,2,...,k)$. Each actuator imparts a total force of $F_i(t)$ $(i=1,2,...,k)$. The advantage of a piecewise continuous force actuator over a point force actuator is that stress levels are reduced. We assume that the applied force has the same intensity over the contact area and can be expressed as

$$f(x,y,t) \;=\; \sum_{i=1}^{k} \frac{F_i(t)}{4\varepsilon_i^2} [u(x-x_{ai}+\varepsilon_i - u(x-x_{ai}-\varepsilon_i)][u(y-y_{ai}+\varepsilon_i) - u(y-y_{ai}-\varepsilon_i)] \tag{21}$$

where u is the unit step function. Note that $f(x,t)$ is now a piecewise-continuous function and $F_i(t)/4\varepsilon_i^2$ denotes the force density of the i-th actuator. It follows that

$$f_r(t) \;=\; \sum_{i=1}^{k} \int\int \frac{F_i(t)}{4\varepsilon_i^2} [u(x-x_{ai}+\varepsilon_i - u(x-x_{ai}-\varepsilon_i)][u(y-y_{ai}+\varepsilon_i) - u(y-y_{ai}-\varepsilon_i)]\phi_r(x,y)dxdy$$

$$= \sum_{i=1}^{k} B_{ri}F_i(t), \quad r = 1,2,... \tag{22}$$

where

$$B_{ri} \;=\; \frac{1}{4\varepsilon_i^2} \int_{x_{ai}-\varepsilon_i}^{x_{ai}+\varepsilon_i} \int_{y_{ai}-\varepsilon_i}^{y_{ai}+\varepsilon_i} \phi_r(x,y)dydx \tag{23}$$

For point torquers located at (x_{ti}, y_{ti}) $(i=1,2,...,k)$, one has to indicate whether the torque is in the x-direction or in the y-direction. For torquers in the x-direction one can express the external excitation as [17]

$$f(x,y,t) \;=\; -\partial \overline{m}_x(x,y,t)/\partial x \;=\; \sum_{i=1}^{k} M_i(t)\delta'(x - x_{ti})\delta(y - y_{ti}) \tag{24}$$

in which $\overline{m}_x(x,y,t)$ is the spatial torque distribution in the x-direction, $M_i(t)$ denote the amplitudes of the torque inputs of actuators located at (x_{ti}, y_{ti}) $(i=1,2,...,k)$. Substitution of Eq. (10) into the expansion theorem yields

$$f_r(t) = \sum_{i=1}^{k} \iint -M_i(t)\delta'(x-x_{ti})\delta(y - y_{ti})\phi_r(x,y)dxdy = \sum_{i=1}^{k} B_{ri}M_i(t), \quad r=1,2,... \qquad (25)$$

where

$$B_{ri} = \iint -\delta'(x - x_{ti})\delta(y - y_{ti})\phi_r(x,y)\ dxdy$$

$$= \phi_r'(x_{ti},y_{ti}), \quad r=1,2,...,n;\ i=1,2,...,k \qquad (26)$$

In a similar fashion, one can obtain the entries for B for piecewise-continuous torquers.

The question then may be asked as to which kind of these actuators are more desirable to use. Naturally, because they reduce stress levels, piecewise-continuous actuators seem to be more desirable. However, one then is faced with the question of selecting the size of the contact area of the piecewise-continuous actuator. We will show an example with regards to this later.

The next question that one would ask with regards to which actuator to select is whether there is a difference between force and torque actuators for implementation purposes and whether selecting one or the other will affect the residual dynamics differently. To this end, we examine the orders of magnitudes of the elements of the actuator influence matrix. Because this matrix also affects the unmodeled and uncontrolled modes, it is of interest to us to know these orders of magnitude. It is shown in [21] that the elements of the actuator influence matrix B are of the largest order for point torquers and smallest for piecewise-continuous force actuators. For example, considering one-dimensional systems, for point force actuators the entries of the actuator influence matrix B_{ri} are of order $O(\phi_r(x))$ $(r=1,2,...)$. For point torque actuators $B_{ri} = O(\phi_r'(x)) = O(r\phi_r(x))$, $(r=1,2,...)$. This implies that torque actuators excite the elastic motion more than force actuators, especially for the higher modes. Also, piecewise-continuous actuators excite the elastic motion to a lesser degree than point actuators.

Given all of the above concerns, the best choice for an actuator initially appears to be a piecewise-continuous force actuator, provided that the contact area is selected properly. There are however, other considerations, such as whether a certain actuator is more desirable than the others from a practical perspective. For example, torquers are preferred in many applications because they act as energy storing devices and they may require less energy to implement. Also, the precision of a certain type of actuator may be better than the other. Since actuator technology is rapidly evolving, one cannot make generalizations.

VII. PERFORMANCE MEASURES

In many cases, the performance of a sensing mechanism, of a control law, or of a certain configuration of the system hardware and software needs to be evaluated. The evaluation has to be done using performance measures. We can separate performance measures into two categories: i) quantitative measures, such as energy consumed, fuel usage, elapsed time, time/performance ratio, e.t.c, and ii) qualitative performance measures, such as eigenvalues, and properties of feedback matrices, e.g., norms, largest elements, traces, eigenvalues.

Qualitative performance measures are attractive, because one can often compare the suitability of a control law or a certain combination of actuators and sensors without obtaining the actual system response or without solving for the eigensolution. However, this reason for their attractiveness is also their drawback, because a qualitative measure may make sense in theory and give incompatible results in practice. Also, qualitative measures are indicative more of the transient behavior of a system, and do not give much indication about the steady state problem.

Quantitative measures, on the other hand, are more difficult to evaluate, because for the most part they require the explicit system response. They are, however, much more realistic and they let the analyst compare actual quantities, such as fuel and energy. There are cases where one uses a quantitative performance measure and come up with qualitative results, such as time minimization and fuel minimization problems for simple models.

We consider here quantitative performance measures associated with the control effort. The first measure is the work done by the actuators on the structure, and is defined for distributed force actuators as

$$W = \int_0^T \int \int f(x,y,t)\dot{u}(x,t)dxdy\,dt \qquad (27)$$

where T is the final time. We will refer to this expression as the physical work. We next define the actual work (or absolute work) as

$$W_A = \int_0^T \int \int |f(x,y,t)\dot{u}(x,y,t)|dxdy\,dt \qquad (28)$$

where the absolute value signs are introduced to account for both positive and negative work. This expression indicates the actual total work done by the actuators whereas W gives the difference between the initial and final energy levels. Ideally, for vibration suppression one would like to design a control law that does only negative work. However, depending on the control method, the sign of the velocities at the actuators' locations can cause positive work to be done. Positive work in vibration suppression implies wasted energy and excitation of undesirable motion.

For point forces, the actual work becomes [17]

$$W_A = \sum_{j=1}^k \int_0^T |F_j(t)\dot{u}(x_{aj},y_{aj},t)|dt \qquad (29)$$

and for piecewise-continuous actuators

$$W_A = \sum_{i=1}^{k} \int_0^T \int_{x_{ai}-\varepsilon_i}^{x_{ai}+\varepsilon_i} \int_{y_{ai}-\varepsilon_i}^{y_{ai}+\varepsilon_i} \left| \frac{F_i(t)}{4\varepsilon_i^2} \; \dot{u}(x,y,t) \right| dy dx \, dt \tag{30}$$

which is based on the assumption that the entire area of the actuator is in contact with the structure at all times. Similar expressions can be developed for point torquers and piecewise-continuous torquers [17].

Next, we define modal work, denoted by W_r, describing the work done by the modal forces on the modal coordinates. This expression is not a physical quantity. However, it gives a measure of how each mode is controlled, and whether there is energy transfer from one mode to another. Energy transferred from one mode to another increases the time it takes for the control to take effect and it also increases fuel consumption. For the r-th mode, the modal work has the form

$$W_r = \int_0^T |f_r(t)\dot{u}_r(t)| \, dt, \quad r=1,2,... \tag{31}$$

where, again, absolute value signs are used to add the contributions of the positive and negative work. The total modal work is denoted by W_M and defined by $W_M = \sum_{r=1}^{\infty} W_r$.

For the general case of control the total modal work is not necessarily equal to the actual work, $W_A \neq W_M$.

The modal energy, or Hamiltonian, for each mode is defined as $H_r = [\dot{u}_r^2 + \omega_r^2 u_r^2]/2$ (r=1,2,...). The total modal energy H, which is the same as the physical energy, is $H = \sum_{r=1}^{\infty} H_r$.

The fuel, or impulse, is defined for discrete force actuators as

$$F = \int_0^T \int \int |f(x,y,t)| dx dy \, dt = \sum_{j=1}^{m} \int_0^T |F_j(t)| dt \tag{32}$$

For discrete torques the fuel, which becomes a measure of the angular impulse, is defined as

$$F = \int_0^T \int \int |m(x,y,t)| dx dy \, dt = \sum_{j=1}^{m} \int_0^T |M_j(t)| dt \tag{33}$$

We introduce a new performance measure, namely the work to fuel ratio, denoted by W/F [17]. This ratio is measure of the effectiveness of the control action and it compares the amount of fuel required to do a certain amount of work. A higher value of this ratio indicates a more effective control. For force actuators the dimension of the work to fuel ratio is the unit of speed.

VIII.   OPTIMAL PLACEMENT OF SENSORS

In this section, we summarize our previous results with regards to optimal sensor placement when modal filters are used. The reader is referred to [13] for a more detailed analysis. Here, we quantitatively analyze the performance of modal filters and the accuracy of the modal coordinate extraction.

We consider two mathematical models, bending vibration of a pinned-pinned beam, and axial vibration of a tapered bar fixed at one end and free at the other. These two models are chosen because they both possess closed-form eigensolutions, such that the accuracy of the results can be monitored. Also, the models have different characteristics, with the tapered bar having closely-spaced natural frequencies which increase with almost arithmetic progression, and the beam having frequencies increasing in geometric progression. The asymptotic behavior of the eigenvalues λ_r, as r -> ∞, is of order $O(r^2)$ for the tapered bar and $O(r^4)$ for the beam problem. In general, for a boundary-value problem of order 2p, the asymptotic behavior of the eigenvalues is of order $O(r^{2p})$ as r -> ∞ [34].

For the beam problem the equation of motion has the form

$$\mu(x)\ddot{u}(x,t) + \partial^2[EI(x)\,\partial^2 u(x,t)/\partial x^2]/\partial x^2 = f(x,t),\ 0<x<L \tag{34}$$

$$u(0,t) = 0,\ EI(0)u''(0,t) = 0,\ u(L,t) = 0,\ EI(L)u''(L,t) = 0$$

where $u(x,t)$ is the transverse deformation at point x, $\mu(x)$ is the mass distribution in the form $\mu(x) = \mu$, $EI(x)$ is the stiffness as $EI(x) = EI$, and $f(x,t)$ is the external excitation. This model admits a closed-form eigensolution in the form

$$\phi_{1r}(x) = \sin r\pi x/L,\ r=1,2,... \tag{35}$$

where the subscript 1 denotes that it is the first model used.

For the axial vibration problem, the equation of motion is

$$\rho(x)\ddot{u}(x,t) = \partial[EA(x)\,\partial u(x,t)/\partial x]/\partial x + f(x,t),\ 0<x<L \tag{36}$$

$$u(0,t) = 0,\ EA(L)u'(L,t) = 0$$

where $u(x,t)$ is the axial deformation at point x, $\rho(x)$ is the mass distribution in the form $\rho(x) = 2\rho(1 - x/L)$, $EA(x)$ is the stiffness as $EA(x) = 2EA(1 - x/L)$, and $f(x,t)$ is the external excitation, including controls. The eigensolution can be shown to be in the form

$$\phi_{2r}(x) = J_0[\beta_r L(1 - x/L)],\ r=1,2,... \tag{37}$$

where J_0 is the Bessel function of order zero, and β_r are roots of the characteristic equation $J_0(\beta_r L) = 0$, from which the natural frequencies are obtained. For both the bar and beam, the length is taken as $L = 10$. Also, $\mu=\rho=1$, $EI = 1$, and $EA = 1$.

The following parameters were used for the optimization. For the pinned-pinned beam, the number of monitored modes was taken as m=4, the number of residual modes was taken as n-m = 4, and the number of sensors was selected as l = 5. For the axial vibration problem, the parameters selected were m = 4, n = 8, and l = 6. For the tapered bar one of the sensors was placed at the tip of the bar, i.e., $x_l = L$, and its location was not varied throughout the optimization.

The golden section search method [35], combined with a first-order gradient technique, is used for finding the minimum values of J, defined in Eq. (15). Tables 1-2 compare the results of the optimization for three sets of interpolation functions. We use interpolation functions from the Finite-Element Method, Rayleigh Ritz method and splines (cubic for the beam, quadratic for the rod). We observe that the three interpolation approaches work with comparable accuracy, with Rayleigh-Ritz type filters giving slightly better results for the tapered bar. The optimal sensor locations obtained from all three analyses are very similar to each other, which is to be expected. Comparing the initial and final values of objective function, we observe that there is not too much change, so that a relatively even spreading of the sensors yields satisfactory results. For the tapered bar, the optimal locations tend to move towards the fixed end, which has a larger mass distribution, an expected behavior. Table 3 shows the GH matrices for the optimal sensor locations for the pinned-pinned beam, using cubic splines as interpolation functions.

When the optimization process is repeated with taking failures into consideration, the optimal sensors locations are almost the same as the ones obtained without considering any malfunctions [13]. The objective function is selected so that the effect of failures is included

$$J^* = \sum_{k=1}^{l} J_k w(k) \tag{38}$$

where

$$J_k = \sum_{i=1}^{m} [\sum_{j=1}^{m} (GS_k H_M - I)_{ij}^2 / \omega_i \omega_j + \sum_{j=1}^{n-m} (GS_k H_R)_{ij}^2 / \omega_i \omega_{m+j}], \quad k=1,2,...,l \tag{39}$$

denotes the value of the objective function calculated with the sensors of initial locations as given in Tables 1-2 and S_k is a diagonal matrix denoting the level of failure in the k-th sensor.

When we investigate the number of backups, the issues to be considered are the number of backup components needed and their locations. As is well known, in simple control designs which use a low amount of sensors there is one or more backups for every sensor. For example, all sensors in the Space Shuttle are triply redundant. However, with the large number of sensors expected to be used in future structures for vibration monitoring, it will not be feasible to provide a backup for every operational component.

We consider the case where we have 11 operational sensors, l=11, and consider 12 candidate backup locations, at $z_i = (x_i + x_{i+1})/2$ (i=0,1,...,l), with $x_0 = 0$ and $x_{l+1} = L$. Due to hardware or geometry restrictions the sensors cannot always be placed at their optimally calculated locations. The operational sensor locations are therefore selected using the relation $x_i = il/(l+1) + R$ (i=1,2,...,l), where R is a random variable with a uniform distribution of [-0.1, 0.1]. The results of the optimization are given in Table 4 for all three interpolation functions. The quantity $J_{T\ min}$ corresponds to the minimum value of the objective function J* when a backup is brought on line. The results indicate that having five to six backups are sufficient to give reliable performance in the event of failure. Our other analyses yielded a similar result of the needed number of backup sensors being slightly less than half the number of operational sensors. This ratio of needed number of backups/number of operational sensors goes down as more sensors are used.

We also observe from Table 4 that splines perform considerably better than Rayleigh-Ritz filters. Finite-Element type filters do the worst. The reason for this is related to the contribution from the residual dynamics. One can then raise the question as to how the results of the optimization would vary if the objective function were changed to one which weighs the residual dynamics even less. To investigate this, we define the following objective function

$$J = \sum_{i=1}^{m} [\sum_{j=1}^{m} |GH_M - I|_{ij}/(\omega_i\omega_j)^{3/2} + \sum_{j=1}^{n-m} |GH_R|_{ij}/(\omega_i\omega_{m+j})^{3/2}] \qquad (40)$$

Table 5 shows the values of J_{Tmin} for the above objective function. We observe that the results for Rayleigh-Ritz filters have improved substantially and are slightly better than the results for cubic splines. However, the counterpart of Tables 4-5 for this case (which are not given here for brevity) still show that the off-diagonal elements are very high for Rayleigh-Ritz filters [13].

The above results indicate that the outcome of the optimization analysis and choice of the interpolation function are very much dependent on the amplitudes involved in the residual dynamics. If the system is highly damped, so that the modes that are not monitored have negligible amplitudes, the Rayleigh-Ritz type filters do a better job. If, on the other hand, the residual dynamics has some significance, and failure of more than one sensor is considered, or if the number of backups is limited, splines do an overall better job. The decision as to which type interpolation function to use should be taken considering the above factors, as well as general convergence characteristics. It is for that reason that we conclude this section by stating that in general spline functions perform better when dealing with modal filtering and that a relatively even distribution of the sensors as well as their backups yields satisfactory results. One would have to consider the actual application for more specific results.

One can then ask what number of sensors is a cutoff number so that any sensors beyond that number become unnecessary. This problem has not yet been addressed in detail, except [16]. Determination of this number would involve addition to J a cost factor based on the number of sensors, such as

$$J' = J_{min}(l) + lF_C + F_{fail} \qquad (41)$$

where $J_{min}(l)$ is the minimum value of the objective function J for l sensors and F_C is the cost factor. F_{fail} is a cost factor that takes into consideration the failure of the sensors and depends on the probability of failure. The augmented objective function J' would then be tabulated and compared for different numbers of sensors. Another mode of comparison would be to compare the actual response and the performance measured outlined in section VII, such as fuel, energy and minimum time, which would then be weighted with the cost of having too many sensors. The problem with both types of analyses is that the determination of the cost factor is very subjective. We will be developing guidelines for determining the cost factor and optimal number of sensors in a future publication.

IX. OPTIMAL ACTUATOR PLACEMENT

In this section, we summarize our results from optimizing actuator locations. The interested reader is referred to Ref. 17 for more details. We initially consider a variety of objective functions based on the entries of the actuator influence matrix B. The objective functions are independent of time, thus giving general measures of controllability. To differentiate between these objective functions and the ones used for sensor placement, we will be using subscripts.

The first objective function, denoted by J_1, is selected to measure the general controllability of modal control without considering a particular control method and taking into account that the contribution of the higher modes to the system output is less than the lower modes. It has the form

$$J_1 = - \sum_{r=1}^{m} \sum_{i=1}^{k} B_{ri}^2 - \sum_{r=m+1}^{n} \sum_{i=1}^{k} \frac{B_{ri}^2}{m+1} \qquad (42)$$

The minus sign is present, because the optimization method used is a minimization procedure. The second objective function maximizes the elements of B corresponding to the controlled modes (B_M) and minimizes the elements associated with the residual modes. This objective function insures that each targeted mode is controlled. It is selected as

$$J_2 = \sum_{r=1}^{m} \frac{1}{\sum_{i=1}^{k} |B_{ri}|} + \sum_{r=m+1}^{n} \frac{\sum_{i=1}^{k} |B_{ri}|}{m+1} \qquad (43)$$

The two objective functions above can be used in conjunction with any control law. We next develop an objective function considering decentralized colocated control. It can be shown that the coupling among the modes is given by the matrix BKB^T, where K is the control gain matrix. The objective function is selected to minimize the energy transfer from one mode onto another by diagonalizing BKB^T and has the form

$$J_3 = \sum_{i=1}^{n} \sum_{j=1}^{n} \frac{(BKB^T)_{ij}(1-\delta_{ij})}{(BKB^T)_{ii}} \qquad (44)$$

The next objective function considers modal control and, for illustrative purposes, considers Independent Modal-Space Control (IMSC) [36]. The relation between the modal forces and actual forces (or torques) is $f_M(t) = B_M E(t)$, which, when inverted, yields the actual control inputs as $E(t) = B_M^{-1} f_M(t)$. This constitutes the basis for IMSC.

The modal work W_r (r=1,2,...,m) corresponding to the controlled modes do not change when IMSC is applied. However, as in other modal control laws, the modal work for the residual modes is no longer zero, indicating wasted energy. The expression for the modal forces associated with the residual modes becomes

$$f_R(t) = B_R E(t) = B_R B_M^{-1} f_M(t) \tag{45}$$

One suitable objective in modal control is to minimize the excitation going into the residual modes. We then select the following objective function

$$J_4 = \sum_{r=1}^{n-m} \sum_{i=1}^{m} |(B_R B_M^{-1})_{ri}| \tag{46}$$

The objective functions described above are not functions of time, so that they do not give an indication as to how the work and fuel consumption will be for a given set of actuator locations. In order to get quantitative measures, after the optimal locations are selected, one should calculate and compare the work, fuel, and work energy ratio for the different actuator locations. We carry out this analysis next.

As a numerical example, we consider the same pinned-pinned beam used in the sensor optimization and suppress its elastic motion using point force actuators, point torque actuators, and piecewise-continuous force actuators.

i) Point force actuators. We first plot in Figs. 3-6 the objective functions using two actuators and four modes in the mathematical model. From these figures we observe the following:

• Actuator locations near the boundaries yield larger values for the objective functions, which is to be expected.

• In all plots there exist several local minima.

• for J_1 and J_2 the objective functions are symmetric about the $x_1 = x_2$ line

• The objective function J_3 is very sensitive to the variation in the actuator locations. Also, the amplitudes of the objective function are higher than the others. Note that the z-axis is labeled -log J_3.

• From the plots of J_3 and J_4 it is observed that the two actuators should not be very close to each other. When $x_1 = x_2$ we essentially have a single actuator. The objective functions J_1 and J_2 do not penalize closely-spaced actuators.

The actuator locations that minimize each of the objective functions are used to

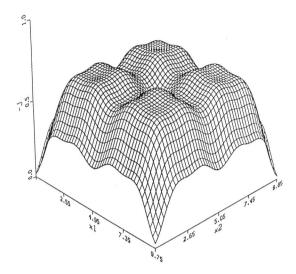

Figure 3. J_1 for force actuators.

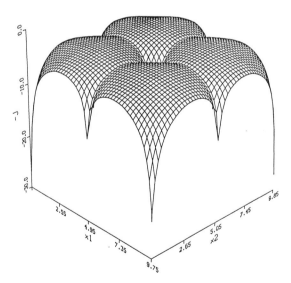

Figure 4. J_2 for force actuators.

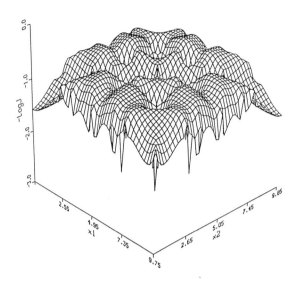

Figure 5. J_3 for force actuators.

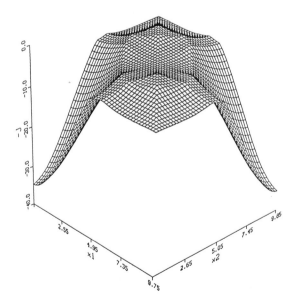

Figure 6. J_4 for force actuators.

compare the work, fuel and energy in Tables 6-9. We consider two control laws: colocation, as illustrative of a decentralized control law and independent modal-space control, as illustrative of a modal control law. The control gains are selected as $f_r(t) = -0.2$ $\dot{u}_r(t)$ (r=1,2,...,n) for IMSC and $F_j(t) = -0.2\dot{u}(x_j,t)$ (j=1,2,...,k) for colocation.

The initial conditions are chosen such that the initial modal velocities have magnitudes of the same order; $\dot{q}(t) = [\ 1.0\ \ -1.0\ \ -1.0\ \ 1.0\ ]^T$. The initial displacements are zero. Table 6 gives the work and fuel used for the IMSC method. Table 7 lists the energy levels. The second set of locations leads to the best fuel efficiency and largest amount of work done on the system. The third set gives the worst results. The locations that minimize J_1, J_2 and J_4 give comparable results. These actuator locations are the most evenly distributed.

Tables 8 and 9 display the work, fuel and energy levels at the end of the control for the colocation control law. We observe that the third set of locations gives the best work performance. The control performance for the different actuator locations is not as different as when IMSC is used, indicating that colocation is less sensitive to the actuators locations. When a similar analysis is performed where the higher modes have lower initial amplitudes. the effects of spillover are found to be less drastic.

We next increase the number of actuators to five and optimize the actuators' locations. The golden section search method combined with a first-order gradient technique is used again. We include ten modes in the model with the lowest five being controlled by five actuators. With this larger number of actuators considered, each objective function has several local minima, and it becomes difficult to determine whether the global minimum is reached. To investigate the general behavior of each objective function, we choose four initial actuator location sets and carry out the optimization. The corresponding local minima are given in Table 10. As in the case of two actuators, when the actuator locations are relatively evenly distributed, magnitudes of the objective functions are comparable. Also, the objective functions yield similar optimal actuator locations.

We conclude that as the number of actuators is increased, their placement becomes less of a problem, a result which is intuitive as well. For systems of high order and having a large number of actuators the optimization procedure will become even more complicated, with several more local minima. We propose to treat such cases by quantifying the number of possible actuator locations and using a search procedure that selects the optimal distribution from the set of possible locations.

   ii) Point torque actuators. We now conduct for point torque actuators the same analysis as force actuators. Based on the results of [21], we expect torque actuators to fare more poorly.

We first plot in Figs. 7-10 the four objective functions when two torque actuators are used with four modes in the mathematical model. The plots, when compared with Figs. 3-6, look like their inverses. They have many more local minima and actuator locations near the boundaries yield smaller values for the objective functions. The amplitudes of the objective functions have larger variations than for force actuators, an indication that the objective functions are more sensitive to the variation of actuator locations. As in the force

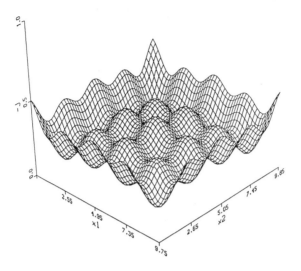

Figure 7. J_1 for torque actuators.

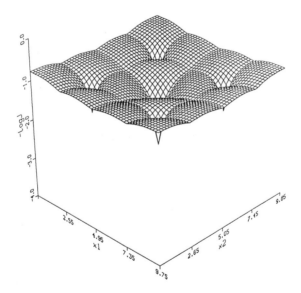

Figure 8. J_2 for torque actuators.

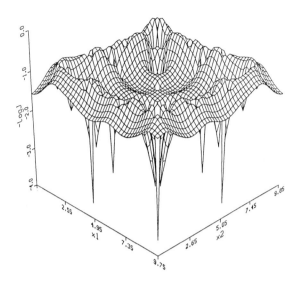

Figure 9. J_3 for torque actuators.

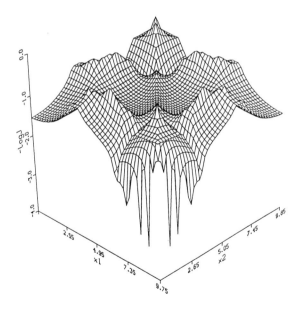

Figure 10. J_4 for torque actuators.

actuator case, having two actuators close to each other is not desirable. The above observations, together with the results of [21], indicate that placement of torque actuators is more critical than placement of force actuators.

As in the point force actuator case, the actuator location pairs that minimize each of the objective functions are used to compare the control performance. The results, given in [17], illustrate that all indicators of performance, such as the work done, fuel used, and energy left in system are higher when torque actuators are used. In addition, there is substantial difference in performance for the three different actuator locations.

When the number of actuators is increased to five, and find the minimum values of the objective functions are sought for a ten mode model, we obtain results similar to the point force actuator case. However, the optimization does not converge for some of the initial locations [17]. We conclude that for torque actuators, similar to the force actuator case, placement becomes less critical as the number of actuators is increased. The actuator placement is more difficult than for force actuators. Also, as shown earlier, torquers excite the higher modes more and use more energy and more fuel, and leave the system with more internal energy at the end of the control cycle. These disadvantages should be compared with the advantages of using torque actuators, such as their being energy storage devices and that they do not saturate easily.

     iii) Piecewise-Continuous Force Actuators.

We consider the four mode model with two controlled modes and the two control laws, colocation and IMSC, used in the previous examples. Tables 11 and 12 compare the work and fuel for different actuator lengths. Note that $\varepsilon = 1$ corresponds to an actuator of length 20% of the length of the beam.

From Tables 11 and 12 we observe that increasing the contact length of the actuators results in more fuel use and decreases the work fuel ratio. For both types of control, the variations are small. The increase in actual work is due to the force density of the actuator being the same throughout the contact length [17]. If there is a sign change in the velocity of the beam within the contact length, the actuator performs both positive and negative work.

When the contact length is small, Tables 11 and 12 indicate that the difference in performance is almost negligible, so that piecewise-continuous actuators present desirable alternative to point actuators. On the other hand, increasing the contact length too much reduces the efficiency of the control. One should compare the reduction in stress levels and the deterioration in the control performance when deciding on the contact length to use.

X. CONCLUDING REMARKS

In this article, we have outlined our thoughts and recent research with regards to determining the number and location of sensors and actuators to be placed on a structure. We first tried to tackle this problem by considering the placement issue separately from other aspects of the control design. This approach was not very fruitful, with the possible exception when modal filters were used. Our first conclusion, therefore, was that it is difficult and possibly not very useful to consider the sensor and actuator placement issue separately from the rest of the control action except when modal filters are used.

If we now say that we are going to optimize the sensor and actuator locations within the context of the control action, then it becomes very difficult to compare results from one control law to another, and we end up comparing control laws. So we ask ourselves if there are some objective measures that can be applied to all approaches, which sort of brings us back to where we started. One possible answer is to look at quantitative performance measures, and especially at the work to fuel ratio. This ratio is useful because it gives an idea of how much work is done with the fuel used.

We compared the performance of sensors using qualitative measures and the performance of actuators using both qualitative and quantitative measures. In all cases, we obtained the following results:

• If the sensors and actuators are evenly distributed along the structure their performance will be satisfactory.

• Small deviations from an even distribution do not change the performance of the control system, so that there are several sensor and actuator distributions that are acceptable.

• If possible, both qualitative and quantitative measures should be used when evaluating the performance of a certain sensor or actuator configuration. Quantitative measures are much more realistic. For example, if Figs. 3-10 are examined, we see that there are several sudden changes in the performance index. However, the performance of both of the control laws used does not change too much when we go from one actuator distribution to another.

• Determination of the optimal number of sensors and actuators is a very subjective issue, depending on the accuracy required, the cost of these components, and the probability of failure. Such an analysis should best be performed separately for each specific application.

• When using actuators, it is more desirable to use force actuators over torquers when the residual dynamics, fuel, and energy are considered. However, torquers have advantages over force actuators, such as being energy storing devices.

Looking at the above results, we basically see generalizations. At first, this may seem as our failure to generate meaningful results, but upon more careful examination it is not. The problem is not with the answers that we obtained, it is with the questions that were asked. Is there really only one optimal number for the sensors and actuators, and one set of actuator locations that give the best performance? What do we really mean by good performance? Maybe, the question that should be asked is: what is an adequate range for the number of sensors and actuators, and at what general locations should these components be placed?

Another set of questions that should be asked is with regards to the control law and the processing of the sensors output. Is the performance of the control very sensitive to the locations of the actuators? Is the processing of the sensors output very much dependent on the locations of the sensors? Is the control action as well as the calculation of feedback quantities substantially affected in the presence of measurement or actuator noise? If the answer to these questions is yes then the problem is not with the number and location of the sensors and actuators. Rather, the problem is more with the control law used and with the way the feedback quantities are extracted from the system output.

XI. REFERENCES

1. W.H. Chen and J.H. Seinfeld, "Optimal Location of Process Measurements," *International Journal of Control*, 21, 1003-1014 (1975).

2. J.E. Martin, "Optimal Allocation of Actuators for Distributed Systems," *Journal of Dynamic Systems, Measurement and Control*, 100, 227- 228 (1978).

3. S.E. Aidarous, M.R. Gevers and M.J. Installe, "Optimal Pointwise Discrete Control and Controllers," *International Journal of Control*, 24, 493-508 (1976).

4. H. Baruh and L. Meirovitch, "On the Placement of Actuators in the Control of Distributed-Parameter Systems," *Proceedings of the 1981 AIAA Dynamics Specialists Conference*, April 9-10, 1981, 611-620 (1981).

5. J.N. Juang and G. Rodriguez, "Formulation and Application of Large Structure Sensor and Actuator Placement," *Proceedings of the 2nd VPI&SU/AIAA Symposium on Dynamics and Control of Large Flexible Spacecraft*, 247-262 (1979).

6. R.C. Montgomery and W.E. VanderVelde, "Reliability Considerations in the Placement of Control System Components," *Journal of Guidance, Control, and Dynamics*, 8, 411-413 (1985).

7. W.E. VanderVelde and C.R. Carignan, "Number and Placement of Control System Components Considering Possible Failures," *Journal of Guidance, Control, and Dynamics*, 7, 703-709 (1984).

8. C.N. Viswanathan, R.W. Longman and P.W. Likins, "A Definition of the Degree of Observability - A Criterion for Actuator Placement," *Journal of Guidance, Control, and Dynamics*, 7, 215-221 (1984).

9. H. Baruh, "Actuator Failure Detection in the Control of Distributed Systems," *Journal of Guidance, Control, and Dynamics*, 9, 181- 189 (1986).

10. H. Baruh and K. Choe, "Sensor Failure Detection Method for Flexible Structures," *Journal of Guidance, Control, and Dynamics*, 10, 474-482 (1987).

11. F.E. Erdle, I.A. Figenbaum and J.W. Talcott, Jr., "Reliability Programs for Commercial Communication Satellites," *IEEE Transactions on Reliability*, R-32, 3, 236-

239 (1983).

12. T. Nakagowa, "Optimal Number of Failures Before Replacement Time," *IEEE Transactions of Reliability*, R-32, 115-116 (1983).

13. H. Baruh and K. Choe, "Sensor Placement in Structural Control," *Journal of Guidance, Control, and Dynamics*, 13, 524-533 (1990).

14. M.L. DeLorenzo, "Sensor and Actuator Selection for Large Space Structure Control," *Journal of Guidance, Control, and Dynamics*, 13, 249-257 (1990).

15. C.S. Kubrusly and H. Melabranche, "Sensors and Controllers Location in Distributed Systems - A Survey," *Automatica*, 1, 117-128 (1985).

16. D.C. Kammer, "Sensor Placement for On-Orbit Modal Identification and Correlation of Large Space Structures," *Journal of Guidance, Control, and Dynamics*, 14, 2, 251-259 (1991).

17. K. Choe and H. Baruh, "Actuator Placement in Structural Control," *Journal of Guidance, Control and Dynamics, to appear*. Also, *Proceedings of the 1990 AIAA Guidance, Control and Navigation Conference*, August 20-22, 1990, Portland, Oregon, 1340-1351 (1990).

18. G. A. Norris and R.E. Skelton, "Selection of Dynamic Sensors and Actuators in the Control of Linear Systems," *Journal of Dynamic Systems, Measurement and Control*, 34, 7, 711-720 (1989).

19. D. Ghosh and C. Knapp, "Measurement Selection for Linear Multivariable Control Systems," *Automatica*, 25, 55-63 (1989).

20. A. Ichikawa and E.P. Ryan, "Sensor and Controller Locations Problems for Distributed Parameter Systems," *Automatica*, 15, 347-352 (1979).

21. H. Baruh and S.S.K. Tadikonda, "Gibbs Phenomenon in Structural Control," *Journal of Guidance, Control, and Dynamics*, 14, 51-58 (1991).

22. D.C. Zimmerman, G.C. Horner and D.J. Inman, "Microprocessor Controlled Force Actuator," *Proceedings of the 27th AIAA SDM Conference*, 573-577 (1986).

23. E.F. Crawley and J. de Luis, "Use of Piezoelectric Actuators as Elements of Intelligent Structures," *AIAA Journal*, 25, 10, 1373-1385 (1987).

24. S.E. Burke and J.E. Hubbard, "Active Control of a Simply Supported Beam Using a Spatially Distributed Actuator," *IEEE Control Systems Magazine*, 25-30 (1987).

25. T. Bailey and J.E. Hubbard, "Distributed Piezoelectric Polymer Active Vibration Control of a Cantilever Beam," *Journal of Guidance, Control and Dynamics*, 8, 5, 605-611 (1985).

26. M.W. Obal and S. Hanagud, "Identification of Dynamic Coupling Coefficients in a Structure with Piezoceramic Sensors and Actuators," *Proceedings of the 29th AIAA SDM Conference*, 1611-1620, Williamsburg, Virginia (1989).

27. H.-S. Tzou, "Active Vibration Control of Flexible Structures via Converse Piezoelectricity," *Developments in Mechanics*, 14, 1201-1206 (1987).

28. G. Strang, and G.J. Fix, *An Analysis of the Finite-Element Method*, Prentice-Hall (1973).

29. L.M. Silverberg, "Uniform Damping Control of Spacecraft," *Journal of Guidance, Control, and Dynamics*, 9, 221-227 (1986).

30. L. Meirovitch and H. Baruh, "The Implementation of Modal Filters for Control of Structures," *Journal of Guidance, Control, and Dynamics*, 8, 707-716 (1985).

31. H. Baruh, and K. Choe, "Reliability Issues in Structural Control," <u>Advances in Aerospace Systems Dynamics and Control Systems, Academic Press Series on Control and Dynamic Systems,</u> C.T. Leondes, Editor, 32, Part 2, 135-162 (1990).

32. L. Meirovitch and H. Baruh, "Effect of Damping on Observation Spillover Instability, *Journal of Optimization Theory and Applications*, 35, No. 1, 31-44 (1981).

33. T. Kailath, *Linear Systems*, Prentice-Hall (1980).

34. R. Courant and D. Hilbert, *Methods of Mathematical Physics*, Vol. 1, Wiley-Interscience (1961).

35. S.L.S. Jacoby, J.S. Kowalik and J.T. Pizzo, *Iterative Methods for Nonlinear Optimization Problems*, Prentice Hall (1972).

36. L. Meirovitch, H. Baruh and H. Oz, "A Comparison of Control Techniques for Large Flexible Systems," *Journal of Guidance, Control, and Dynamics*, 6, No. 4, 302-310 (1983).

	Sensor	Locs				J	Initial J
Initial	1.667	3.333	5.000	6.667	8.333		
Finite-Element	1.677	3.383	5.000	6.618	8.323	0.717	0.727
Rayleigh-Ritz	1.657	3.353	5.000	6.646	8.343	0.097	0.100
Cubic Splines	1.656	3.354	5.000	6.646	8.344	0.087	0.089

Table 1. Optimal sensor locations for pinned-pinned beam.

	Sensor	Locs	Sixth	at 10.0		J	Initial J
Initial	1.667	3.333	5.000	6.667	8.333		
Finite-Element	1.601	3.352	4.966	6.476	7.881	0.582	0.708
Rayleigh-Ritz	1.605	3.210	4.816	6.425	8.048	0.000	0.105
Quadr. Splines	1.592	3.200	4.803	6.403	8.009	0.010	0.253

Table 2. Optimal sensor locations for tapered bar.

GH_M $\begin{vmatrix} 0.999889 & 0.000000 & -0.000584 & 0.000002 \\ 0.000000 & 0.997756 & 0.000000 & -0.000337 \\ -0.000007 & 0.000000 & 0.985518 & -0.000002 \\ 0.000000 & -0.000021 & 0.000000 & 0.939055 \end{vmatrix}$

GH_R $\begin{vmatrix} 0.006552 & -0.000014 & 0.027274 & 0.000027 \\ -0.000001 & 0.033839 & 0.000001 & -0.010428 \\ 0.007790 & 0.000014 & 0.015275 & -0.000025 \\ 0.000003 & -0.009790 & -0.000001 & -0.907108 \end{vmatrix}$

Table 3. GH_M and GH_R matrices for pinned-pinned beam. Cubic Splines used as interpolation functions

No.of backups	Finite Element	Rayleigh Ritz	Cubic Splines
1	6.608	129.492	3.966
2	5.368	13.491	2.814
3	4.523	7.274	1.975
4	3.870	4.423	1.318
5	3.767	2.342	1.076
6	3.731	1.467	0.983
7	3.723	1.324	0.955
8	3.717	1.265	0.955
9	3.717	1.256	0.955
10	3.717	1.256	0.955
11	3.717	1.256	0.955
12	3.717	1.256	0.955

Table 4. Minimum values of J_T, using objective function given by Eq. (15).

No. of backups	Finite Element	Rayleigh Ritz	Cubic Splines
1	46.606	23.901	19.063
2	38.475	9.325	15.241
3	31.031	6.955	12.340
4	26.479	5.173	9.539
5	23.718	3.841	7.877
6	22.198	3.358	7.086
7	21.922	3.268	6.847
8	21.647	3.191	6.742
9	21.647	3.191	6.724
10	21.647	3.191	6.724
11	21.647	3.191	6.724
12	21.647	3.191	6.724

Table 5. Minimum values of J_T, using objective function given by Eq. (40).

Minimizing	(x_1, x_2)	H(20)	W	W_A	W_M	F	W/F
J_1	3.45, 6.55	1.042	-0.962	1.283	1.779	3.498	0.275
J_2	3.05, 6.95	1.077	-0.925	1.008	1.599	3.399	0.272
J_3	1.95, 4.05	1.585	-0.417	2.042	5.093	8.253	0.050
J_4	2.55, 7.45	1.151	-0.849	1.093	1.580	3.580	0.237

Table 6. Work and fuel for IMSC using force actuators. $\underline{u}(0) = [1, -1, -1, 1]^T$

(x_1, x_2)	H	H_1	H_2	H_3	H_4
3.45, 6.55	1.0423	0.0455	0.0093	0.4910	0.4964
3.05, 6.95	1.0777	0.0455	0.0093	0.5277	0.4951
1.95, 4.05	1.5852	0.0455	0.0093	0.8123	0.7180
2.55, 7.45	1.1516	0.0455	0.0093	0.5976	0.4991
at t=0	2.0000	0.5000	0.5000	0.5000	0.5000

Table 7. Modal energy at t=20 sec. IMSC with force Actuators. $\underline{u}(0) = [1, -1, -1, 1]^T$

(x_1, x_2)	H(20)	W	W_A	W_M	F	W/F
3.45, 6.55	0.985	-1.016	1.017	1.115	2.259	0.450
3.05, 6.95	1.075	-0.927	0.927	1.044	2.200	0.420
1.95, 4.05	0.769	-1.231	1.231	1.413	2.636	0.467
2.55, 7.45	1.135	-0.865	0.865	0.951	2.227	0.388

Table 8. Work and fuel for colocation using force actuators. $\underline{u}(0) = [1, -1, -1, 1]^T$

(x_1, x_2)	H	H_1	H_2	H_3	H_4
3.45, 6.55	0.9851	0.1972	0.1725	0.4878	0.1275
3.05, 6.95	1.0748	0.2302	0.1263	0.4553	0.2628
1.95, 4.05	0.7695	0.2110	0.1769	0.1921	0.1892
2.55, 7.45	1.1353	0.2773	0.1034	0.2574	0.4970
at t=0	2.0000	0.5000	0.5000	0.5000	0.5000

Table 9. Modal energy at t=20 sec. Colocation with force actuators. $\dot{u}(0) = [1, -1, -1, 1]^T$.

J_1						
	x_1	x_2	x_3	x_4	x_5	J_1
i*	1.209	3.179	5.000	6.820	8.785	-3.337
ii	1.215	3.185	5.000	6.815	8.785	-3.337
iii	3.185	4.006	5.000	5.994	6.815	-3.058
iv	1.212	3.183	4.987	5.000	5.013	-3.252

J_2						
	x_1	x_2	x_3	x_4	x_5	J_2
i	1.429	3.222	5.000	6.584	8.571	3.629
ii*	1.429	2.954	5.000	7.046	8.571	3.597
iii	2.859	3.750	5.000	6.250	7.141	3.953
iv	1.386	2.857	3.711	5.000	6.289	3.756

J_3						
	x_1	x_2	x_3	x_4	x_5	J_3
i*	1.072	2.177	3.308	4.429	7.750	4.969
ii	1.000	3.000	5.000	7.000	9.000	6.000
iii	2.851	3.996	5.000	6.004	7.149	6.701
iv	1.686	2.833	4.014	5.211	6.392	5.114

J_4						
	x_1	x_2	x_3	x_4	x_5	J_4
i*	1.243	3.7523	4.992	6.253	8.743	2.611
ii	1.111	2.970	5.014	7.031	8.952	3.751
iii	1.293	3.732	5.044	7.470	8.789	2.696
iv	1.111	2.261	3.883	5.153	6.617	6.950

*: minimum J among actuator location sets

Table 10. Local minima for five force actuators using different objective functions.

ε	H(20)	W	W_A	W_M	F	W/F
0.00	0.1494	-0.9434	0.9634	1.1978	3.4989	0.269
0.01	0.1494	-0.9434	0.9638	1.1977	3.4987	0.269
0.10	0.1494	-0.9434	0.9644	1.1989	3.5003	0.269
0.50	0.1486	-0.9440	0.9712	1.1859	3.5417	0.266
1.00	0.1466	-0.9453	0.9842	1.1477	3.6788	0.256

Table 11. Work and fuel for different actuator lengths. IMSC, $(x_1, x_2) = (3.45, 6.55)$

ε	H(20)	W	W_A	W_M	F	W/F
0.00	0.9852	-1.0168	1.0168	1.1151	2.2596	0.450
0.01	0.9852	-1.0168	1.0168	1.1151	2.2596	0.450
0.10	0.9858	-1.0162	1.0162	1.1164	2.2605	0.450
0.50	1.0010	-1.0003	1.0084	1.0999	2.2821	0.438
1.00	1.0520	-0.9475	0.9963	1.0463	2.3488	0.403

Table 12. Work and fuel for different actuator lengths. Colocation, $(x_1, x_2) = (3.45, 6.55)$

Minimum-Exposure Near-Terrain Flight Trajectories for Rotorcraft

P. K. A. Menon
Optimal Synthesis
Palo Alto, California

V. H. L. Cheng
NASA Ames Research Center
Moffett Field, California

Abstract

Aircraft operating in unfriendly environments use the terrain to mask their presence from detection devices in order to maximize the tactical advantage and mission-success probability. In the past, such trajectory problems were driven by the needs of fixed-wing tactical aircraft and cruise missile operations. The current research initiative to automate nap-of-the-earth (NOE) helicopter flight regime has revived the interest in this trajectory synthesis problem.

This chapter discusses a few recently developed methodologies for constructing optimal trajectories for helicopters executing NOE flight over known terrain. Kinematic vehicle models are employed in conjunction with optimal control theory for developing numerical algorithms. These algorithms can be implemented using numerical integration and one-dimensional search schemes. Second-order necessary conditions for these problems are examined. Primary emphasis of this treatise will be on formulating the trajectory synthesis as conventional one-sided optimization problems, although a differential-game version of the problem will also be discussed.

The present trajectory synthesis problems bear a striking resemblance to the classical Zermelo's problem in the Calculus of Variations. In addition to being useful for helicopter NOE flight guidance, the proposed methods are of interest in several other contexts such as robotic vehicle guidance and terrain-following guidance for cruise missiles and aircraft.

I Introduction

Flight in close proximity to the terrain is an important operational regime for high-performance combat aircraft. For instance, terrain-following/terrain-avoidance guidance (TF/TA) of cruise missiles and deep penetration aircraft has long since been recognized as an important aspect of tactical flight operations [1, 2, 3, 4, 5, 6]. Recently, the near-terrain flight guidance problem has received fresh research attention, largely motivated by the need to automate various components of nap-of-the-earth (NOE) helicopter flight regime. Rotorcraft pilots find the NOE flight regime extremely taxing because of the high work load involved in flying the aircraft close to the ground under poor visibility conditions while attending to various threat management functions. The NOE automation research is driven by a need to decrease the pilot work load to acceptable levels. Technology requirements for achieving this objective include not only the synthesis of guidance and control laws, but also the development of various sensors for gathering information about the terrain and obstacles.

The NOE flight guidance system development separates the guidance tasks into three regimes [7]: far-field, mid-field, and near-field. The far-field trajectory planning task selects and prioritizes the set of objectives that a given mission should accomplish. The mid-field guidance scheme synthesizes flyable trajectories satisfying the specified boundary conditions based on a priori known nature of the terrain and threats. The near-field guidance task involves reacting to the obstacles and threats that are not known at the outset, while staying as close as possible to the trajectory synthesized by the mid-field guidance law. Several of these issues have been addressed in Reference [7]. The block diagram in Figure 1 illustrates the NOE flight guidance concept. Research on passive sensors to enable automatic NOE flight is discussed in several recent papers. Specifically, the development of image-based ranging systems for obstacle and terrain detection have been discussed in References [8] and [9]. The near-field guidance problem has received some attention in the literature. For instance, a heuristic guidance law for near-field flight path selection in the presence of obstacles is outlined in Reference [10], and its implementation is described in [11]. An optimal guidance law that uses the image-derived range data has also been discussed for this problem [12]. An approach for far-field mission planning is given in Reference [13]

The focus of this chapter will be on the mid-field guidance segment. The guidance task consists of synthesizing optimal trajectories using available information about the terrain and threats. This information may be derived from digitized terrain maps together with threat overlays generated using aerial or satellite reconnaissance. Optimal control theory is employed together with a kinematic vehicle model for trajectory synthesis. The use of two distinct performance indices will be examined in this work. These consist of: (1) a linear combination of flight time and terrain masking, and (2) a linear combination of terrain masking and the deviation from a specified trajectory. A separate form of vehicle model is appropriate for each of these formulations. In a later section, a differential-game

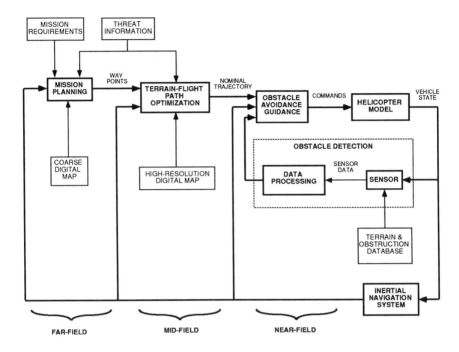

Figure 1: Automatic NOE Flight Guidance Structure

version of the trajectory-planning problem will be given: specifically, the trajectory-planning process will be established for the case where a rotorcraft is being pursued by an unfriendly rotorcraft. This chapter essentially brings together some of the recent research efforts [14, 15, 16, 17, 18] on the near-terrain flight trajectory synthesis problem involving the authors.

Trajectory synthesis methods for similar tasks discussed in the literature [19, 20, 21] invariably resort to discrete dynamic programming or one of its derivatives. Some of these techniques involve gross simplifications based on heuristics, leading to suboptimal solutions. These approaches employ spatial coordinate discretization of the terrain before carrying out a systematic search for the optimal trajectory. As a result, they assume that in a discretized interval, the route consists of straight line segments. On an uneven terrain, this means that a large number of discretization intervals will be necessary to generate sufficiently smooth trajectories. Unfortunately, this increase in the number of discretization intervals is accompanied by an enormous increase in computational complexity. For the discretized dynamic programming problem, the complexity is of the order $[(n+1)^2 - 1]$, where n is the number of discretization intervals in one spatial direction [22]. Trajectory synthesis using control variable parameterization together with multidimensional gradient search has also been reported in the literature [23]. Reference [24] has examined the threat-avoidance trajectory synthesis problem using the method of multiple time scales.

In the present work, alternate formulations of the trajectory planning problem will be advanced. At the terrain resolution levels discussed in previous literature, these methods are capable of rapidly generating optimal solutions. These methods are based on Pontriagin's minimum principle [22]. In general, trajectory synthesis via optimal control theory demands the solution of a two-point boundary value problem which can often be tedious and time consuming. However, for one of the present trajectory synthesis problems, a constant of motion can be invoked to simplify the solution procedure. Moreover, adjoint-control transformations can be used to eliminate the costates in the optimal control problem in favor of physical variables. In the second trajectory-synthesis problem, appropriate redefinition of the independent variable produces a structure that simplifies computations. Unlike the techniques discussed in the literature [19, 20, 21, 23, 24], the optimal trajectory to any desired final condition can be generated simply by selecting the initial value of a specified state and numerically integrating a set of first-order ordinary differential equations. The terrain profile information appears in the coefficients of these differential equations. Known threats are represented as synthetic profiles and are overlayed on the terrain profile to produce a composite profile. Depending upon the chosen performance index, these algorithms require first and second partial derivatives of the surface describing the terrain-threat overlays. These partial derivatives can be estimated using any reasonable numerical scheme. Examples include the use of cubic splines [25] and two-dimensional Fourier transforms [26]. In the present work, these quantities are computed using a cubic-spline parameterization of the digital terrain elevation data.

The trajectory synthesis requires a one-dimensional search routine such as the method of bisections [27], and appears to be implementable in realtime at available terrain resolutions. The emerging trajectories automatically accomplish known threat avoidance. Optimal trajectory construction methods discussed in this paper are closely related to the geodesic problem in the Calculus of Variations [28] and bears a striking resemblance to the classical Zermelo's problem [29].

II   Equations of Motion

Kinematic helicopter models will be employed in the present study. Two different versions of the kinematic model are used in the following formulations. The first of these uses a local tangent plane coordinate system with the local heading angle defined on the tangent plane as the control variable, while the second model uses the heading angle measured with respect to an inertial frame as the control variable. In either case, the complete vehicle dynamics will not be included in the formulation. To a degree, results from the present analysis can be corrected for neglected helicopter dynamics using singular perturbation theory [30, 31, 32, 33, 34, ?, ?].

Let the terrain profile be specified by a function

$$h_t = f(x, y) \tag{1}$$

where h_t is the altitude above a preselected datum at any specified down-range position x and cross-range position y. Both of these variables can be defined once an inertial frame is chosen. It is assumed here that the chosen datum is such that terrain altitude $h_t > 0$ and that continuous first and second partial derivatives may be computed for the terrain profile $f(x, y)$. Since the vehicle position dynamics is of second order, this latter assumption helps to ensure that the trajectories emerging from the present work are implementable. Note that even if the original terrain does not have this property, it is possible to set up interpolation schemes that provide smooth estimates of the derivatives. For instance, a cubic spline terrain profile interpolation scheme will assure the existence of continuous partial derivatives up to second order. On a rough terrain, polynomial or spatial frequency domain smoothing may be employed to ensure adequate accuracy in the computation of partial derivatives.

While executing near-terrain flight, the helicopter altitude is required to follow the terrain profile $f(x, y)$ with a specified altitude clearance h_c. Thus, the helicopter altitude h in terms of down-range x and cross-range y is specified by the algebraic equation

$$h = f(x, y) + h_c \tag{2}$$

The terrain clearance is generally either constant or a specified function of down range and cross range. Known threats and obstacles on the terrain may be incorporated in the trajectory synthesis problem by defining threat envelopes of the form $P(x, y)$ and superimposing them on the given terrain profile. The composite profile can then be used to define the vehicle altitude as

$$h = F(x, y) \tag{3}$$

with

$$F(x, y) = h_c + f(x, y) + P(x, y) \tag{4}$$

The trajectories satisfying the constraint (3) will exhibit automatic threat and terrain avoidance characteristics.

II.A Vehicle Model 1

If the vehicle state variables are chosen as down-range x, cross-range y, and altitude h, the composite profile in Eq. (3) will become an equality constraint on the state variables. State constraints introduce additional necessary conditions and thereby contribute significant complexity in the trajectory-synthesis problem [22]. As an alternative, a coordinate system based on the definition of a local tangent plane can be devised to absorb the composite-profile constraint directly into the equations of motion as follows.

A sample terrain profile with the down-range, cross-range, altitude inertial coordinate system is shown in Figure 2. In this figure, a local co-

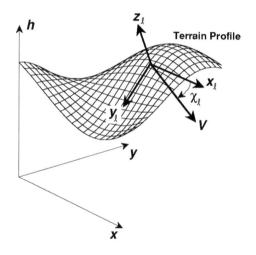

Figure 2: Local Tangent-Plane Coordinate System

ordinate system x_l, y_l, z_l is defined with its origin located on the terrain profile at the current x, y position. The x_l, y_l plane of this coordinate system coincides with the local tangent plane, with z_l defined by the outward normal, x_l defined by the intersection of the local tangent plane with the $x - h$ plane, and y_l completing the orthonormal basis of the local coordinate system. Since the vehicle is constrained to move on the terrain profile given by Eq. (4), its velocity vector lies in the $x_l - y_l$ plane. The local heading angle χ_l is defined on the tangent plane as the angle between the vehicle velocity vector and the x_l direction.

Components of the vehicle velocity vector in the local tangent frame are given by

$$\dot{x}_l = V \cos \chi_l \tag{5}$$

$$\dot{y}_l = V \sin \chi_l \tag{6}$$

The local heading angle χ_l and the airspeed V are treated as the control variables in the first vehicle model. In order to ensure that the controls emerging from this formulation are implementable, the vehicle speed is next bounded as

$$0 < V_{min} \leq V \leq V_{max} \tag{7}$$

Note that the lower bound is essential to ensure the validity of the kinematic model. The velocity components (5) and (6) may next be transformed to the inertial coordinate system defined by down-range, cross-range, and altitude, using the terrain profile gradients F_x, F_y. In all that follows, subscripts on the symbol F denote partial differentiation with respect to that variable.

The outward unit normal vector $\mathbf{n}$ and a unit tangent vector $\mathbf{t}_1$ along the direction x_l on the terrain profile $F(x, y)$ are given by

$$\mathbf{n} = \frac{1}{\sqrt{1 + F_x^2 + F_y^2}} \begin{bmatrix} -F_x \\ -F_y \\ 1 \end{bmatrix}, \quad \mathbf{t}_1 = \frac{1}{\sqrt{1 + F_x^2}} \begin{bmatrix} 1 \\ 0 \\ F_x \end{bmatrix} \tag{8}$$

A unit vector $\mathbf{t}_2$ orthogonal to these vectors along the y_l direction can be obtained by taking the cross product of $\mathbf{t}_1$ and $\mathbf{n}$ as

$$\mathbf{t}_2 = \frac{1}{\sqrt{1 + F_x^2 + F_y^2}\sqrt{1 + F_x^2}} \begin{bmatrix} F_x F_y \\ -(1 + F_x^2) \\ -F_y \end{bmatrix} \tag{9}$$

Next, the unit vectors $\mathbf{t}_1$, $\mathbf{t}_2$, $\mathbf{n}$ in the local tangent plane together with unit vectors $\mathbf{i}$, $\mathbf{j}$, $\mathbf{k}$ in the down-range, cross-range and altitude directions may be used to transform the velocity components in the local tangent plane frame to the inertial frame as:

$$\begin{bmatrix} \dot{x} \\ \dot{y} \\ \dot{h} \end{bmatrix} = \begin{bmatrix} \mathbf{t}_1 \cdot \mathbf{i} & \mathbf{t}_2 \cdot \mathbf{i} & \mathbf{n} \cdot \mathbf{i} \\ \mathbf{t}_1 \cdot \mathbf{j} & \mathbf{t}_2 \cdot \mathbf{j} & \mathbf{n} \cdot \mathbf{j} \\ \mathbf{t}_1 \cdot \mathbf{k} & \mathbf{t}_2 \cdot \mathbf{k} & \mathbf{n} \cdot \mathbf{k} \end{bmatrix} \begin{bmatrix} \dot{x}_l \\ \dot{y}_l \\ 0 \end{bmatrix} \tag{10}$$

Here, the symbol $\cdot$ indicates the inner product operation. This process yields:

$$\dot{x} = \frac{V \cos \chi_l}{\sqrt{1 + F_x^2}} + \frac{V F_x F_y \sin \chi_l}{\sqrt{(1 + F_x^2)(1 + F_x^2 + F_y^2)}} \tag{11}$$

$$\dot{y} = -\frac{\sqrt{1 + F_x{}^2}\ V \sin \chi_l}{\sqrt{1 + F_x{}^2 + F_y{}^2}} \tag{12}$$

The vehicle altitude rate is given by

$$\dot{h} = V \sin \gamma \tag{13}$$

with the vehicle flight path angle γ being given by the equation

$$\gamma = \sin^{-1}\left[\frac{F_x \dot{x} + F_y \dot{y}}{V}\right] \tag{14}$$

Equations (11) - (13) constitute a kinematic model of the vehicle executing near-terrain flight with a specified clearance h_c. If the winds aloft in the down-range and cross-range directions are given by

$$u = Q(x, y), \quad v = R(x, y) \tag{15}$$

these may be added to the right-hand side of (11) and (12) to determine their influence on the synthesized trajectories.

II.B   Vehicle Model 2

During later phases of the present research, it was observed that a simpler vehicle model could be employed with an alternate performance index. This section discusses such a vehicle model.

The helicopter velocity components in the defined inertial reference frame are given by

$$\dot{x} = V \cos \gamma \cos \chi \tag{16}$$

$$\dot{y} = V \cos \gamma \sin \chi \tag{17}$$

$$\dot{h} = V \sin \gamma \tag{18}$$

The heading angle χ is the control variable in the present problem. The flight-path angle γ is completely defined by the terrain profile as in Eq. (14), due to the fact that the helicopter is executing near-terrain flight. The variable V is the helicopter speed, assumed to be a positive quantity in the present formulation. Thus, the kinematic model of the helicopter flight is given by the differential equations (16), (17) and the nonlinear algebraic equation (3).

Next, assume that flight time is not of interest in the trajectory-planning process. Note that in kinematic vehicle models, the time of flight is completely determined by the selected vehicle speed. Moreover, assume that the down-range variable is monotonically increasing with time along all optimal trajectories. The coordinate system can be redefined whenever violation of this assumption seems imminent.

The resulting kinematic model of the vehicle is

$$\frac{dy}{dx} = y' = \tan \chi \tag{19}$$

$$h = F(x, y) \tag{20}$$

The flight path angle γ can be computed a *posteriori* using the trajectory $y(x)$.

An additional model simplification consists of defining the direction joining the initial and final $(x, \, y)$ conditions as the down-range direction. In this case, the variable y can be thought of as the deviation from an intended path.

Sometimes it is desirable to consider a trajectory planning formulation in which the helicopter specific energy is maintained constant. This situation will arise wherever the engine throttle is set to maintain thrust equal to drag while executing the NOE flight. In this case, the airspeed explicitly depends on the terrain profile as

$$V = \sqrt{2g[E - F(x, y)]} \tag{21}$$

In Eq. (21), g is the acceleration due to gravity, and $E = h + V^2/2g$ is the vehicle specific energy. An additional modeling detail includes the definition of vehicle speed as a function of its position. Such a speed variation may be desirable for avoiding air-defense threats. These special cases will not be pursued any further in this chapter.

III   Optimal Trajectory Synthesis

The objective of the trajectory-planning algorithms is to synthesize trajectories that transfer the vehicle from its initial condition to a specified final condition. Since there are innumerable such trajectories, specific performance measures can be used to narrow down the choices.

Systematic optimization procedures [22] can then be used to synthesize trajectories satisfying the specified performance measures. The following discusses the use of vehicle models and performance measures for optimal trajectory construction.

III.A   Minimum-Time Terrain-Masking Trajectories

The trajectory synthesis problem is addressed in this section using the first
vehicle model in conjunction with optimal control theory [22]. The state
variables in this model are down-range x and cross-range y. The local heading angle χ_l and vehicle speed V are the control variables. Note that it is
important to include vehicle speed as a control variable to ensure hodo-
graph convexity required for the existence of optimal controls [37]. The
performance index is defined as a linear combination of flight time and a
terrain masking function. Following the existing literature [19, 20], trajectory masking will be assumed to be accomplished if an integral proportional
to the helicopter altitude above the specified datum is minimized. Admit-
tedly, this masking function is crude since it is based on the premise that
flight at depressed altitude tends to provide better masking. If an improved terrain masking function given as a function of down-range x and
cross-range y is available, it can be included in the following analysis. A
relative weighting factor is next introduced between the flight time and the
terrain masking functions to control the trade-off between these two, often
conflicting requirements. Thus, a composite performance index of the form

$$J = \int_0^{t_f} [(1 - K) + K\ F]dt \qquad (22)$$

with

$$0 \le K \le 1 \qquad (23)$$

will be used in the following. The initial vehicle position $x(0)$, $y(0)$ and
the terminal conditions $x(t_f)$, $y(t_f)$ are specified, while the final time t_f is
free. Note that it is possible to include heading angle and flight path angle
constraints in the present formulation by adding quadratic penalty terms on
these variables in the integrand of (22). Alternately, they can be included as
direct state-control variable constraints in the optimal control formulation.
However, the following analysis will not include these constraints.

The variational Hamiltonian [22] may next be formed by adjoining the
differential constraints (11), (12) to the performance index (22) to yield:

$$
\begin{aligned}
H \;=\; & [(1 - K) + K\ F] + \lambda_x \left[\frac{V \cos \chi_l}{\sqrt{1 + F_x{}^2}} + \frac{V F_x\ F_y \sin \chi_l}{\sqrt{(1 + F_x{}^2)(1 + F_x{}^2 + F_y{}^2)}} \right] \\
& - \lambda_y \left[\frac{\sqrt{1 + F_x{}^2}\ V \sin \chi_l}{\sqrt{1 + F_x{}^2 + F_y{}^2}} \right]
\end{aligned}
\qquad (24)
$$

The Euler-Lagrange equations for this optimal control problem may be obtained from:

$$\dot{\lambda}_x = -\frac{\partial H}{\partial x}, \quad \dot{\lambda}_y = -\frac{\partial H}{\partial y} \tag{25}$$

with the optimality condition $\frac{\partial H}{\partial \chi_l} = 0$ yielding

$$\tan \chi_l = \frac{\lambda_x \, F_x \, F_y - \lambda_y(1 + F_x{}^2)}{\lambda_x \sqrt{1 + F_x{}^2 + F_y{}^2}} \tag{26}$$

Since the initial and final conditions of all the states are specified, the costates λ_x, λ_y are free at the two boundaries. Differential equations (11), (12), (25) together with the condition (26) constitute a nonlinear two-point boundary value problem, which can be solved if the initial conditions or the final conditions on the two costates λ_x and λ_y were known.

The solution procedure may be simplified by noting that this optimal control problem has a constant of motion. Since the variational Hamiltonian is not explicitly dependent on time and the final time is free, it follows that

$$H(t) = 0, \quad 0 \le t \le t_f \tag{27}$$

This constant of motion together with the optimality condition may next be employed to solve for the costates in terms of the control variables as

$$\lambda_x = \frac{-[(1 - K) + K \, F]\sqrt{1 + F_x{}^2} \, \cos \chi_l}{V} \tag{28}$$

$$\lambda_y = \frac{[(1 - K) + K \, F][\sqrt{1 + F_x{}^2 + F_y{}^2} \, \sin \chi_l - F_x \, F_y \cos \chi_l]}{V \sqrt{1 + F_x{}^2}} \tag{29}$$

At this stage, optimal trajectories can be determined if either the control variables χ_l, V or the costates λ_x, λ_y are known. Alternately, all the costates in the problem may be eliminated if the extremals are assumed to be smooth. Smoothness assumption will be invoked in the following analysis. Using second-order necessary conditions it will be shown subsequently that the smoothness assumption is justified.

Expressions (28) or (29) are next differentiated with respect to time and equated to the right-hand sides of Eq. (25). This process yields a differential equation for χ_l as:

$$\dot{\chi}_l = \frac{[(A_1 K + A_2)\cos \chi_l + A_3(A_4 K + A_5)\sin \chi_l]V}{A_6(A_7 K + 1)} \tag{30}$$

where

$$A_1 = B_1 \, A_3 \, F_y, \quad A_2 = F_{xx} \, F_y \, A_3, \quad A_3 = \sqrt{1 + F_x^{\,2} + F_y^{\,2}}$$

$$A_4 = B_1 \, F_x \, F_y^{\,2} + B_2 \, F_{xy} \, F_y - B_3, \quad A_5 = F_x \, F_{xx} \, F_y^{\,2} - (1 + F_x^{\,2}) F_{xy} \, F_y,$$

$$A_6 = [(1 + F_x^{\,2}) \, (1 + F_x^{\,2} + F_y^{\,2})]^{3/2}, \quad A_7 = (F - 1),$$

$$B_1 = (F - 1) \, F_{xx} - (1 + F_x^{\,2}), \quad B_2 = (1 - F) \, (1 + F_x^{\,2}), \quad B_3 = F_x \, (1 + F_x^{\,2})^2$$

Equation (30) was obtained using the *MACSYMA* program [38]. It may be verified that if the terrain gradients were zero, Eq. (30) yields $\dot{\chi}_l = 0 \Rightarrow \chi_l = constant$, which is the familiar solution to the classical *shortest distance on a plane* [28] problem.

Next consider the second control variable in this problem, viz., the helicopter speed. Since this variable appears linearly in the variational Hamiltonian and is bounded, the optimal control is given by the bang-bang control logic [22]

$$V = \begin{cases} V_{max} & S < 0 \\ V_{min} & S > 0 \\ Singular & S \equiv 0 \end{cases} \tag{31}$$

where S is the switching function given by

$$S = \frac{\partial H}{\partial V} = \frac{\left\{ \lambda_x [\sqrt{1 + F_x^{\,2} + F_y^{\,2}} \, \cos \chi_l + F_x \, F_y \sin \chi_l] - \lambda_y (1 + F_x^{\,2}) \sin \chi_l \right\}}{\sqrt{(1 + F_x^{\,2})(1 + F_x^{\,2} + F_y^{\,2})}} \tag{32}$$

Substituting λ_x and λ_y using expressions (28) and (29) in (32), it may be shown that

$$S = \frac{(1 - K) + K \, F}{V} \tag{33}$$

Since this expression is greater than zero by definition, it suggests that the maximum speed setting $V = V_{max}$ is optimal throughout the trajectory.

With the foregoing analysis, the optimal route planning problem has been reduced to that of solving a set of three nonlinear first-order differential equations (11), (12), and (30) with one unknown boundary condition $\chi_l(0)$. Since $x(0)$ and $y(0)$ are known, $\chi_l(0)$ must be selected such that the final values of down range x and cross range y are the specified values $x(t_f)$ and $y(t_f)$.

A simple one-dimensional search procedure such as the method of bisections [27] may be set up to solve this problem. The computational flow chart employing one such iterative technique is illustrated in Figure 3. If a solution for the system (11), (12), and (30) satisfying the given boundary condition exists within the given $\chi_l(0)$ range, then it can be shown that the computation scheme given in Figure 3 will find it in a finite number of iterations [27]. Moreover, since the condition for existence of optimal con-

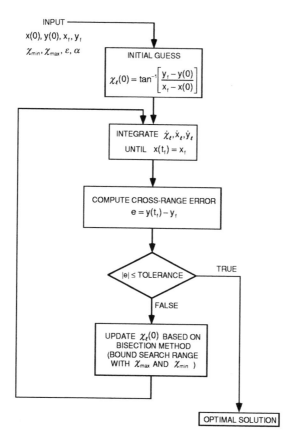

Figure 3: Flow Chart for Minimum-Time Terrain-Masking Trajectory Computation

trols is the convexity of the *extended velocity set* [37], the iterative scheme is guaranteed to find an extremal if one can show that the extended velocity set is convex. In the present problem, the extended velocity set may be found by plotting the variable $\dot{x}$ against the variable $\dot{y}$ for all possible values of the control variables χ_l and V. Note that the extended velocity set is a strong function of the terrain profile gradients F_x, F_y.

If the initial value of the heading angle $\chi_l(0)$ is known, Euler solutions may be generated by numerically integrating the three first-order nonlinear differential equations (11), (12) and (30), starting from arbitrary initial conditions $x(0), y(0)$. A sample terrain data approximating a part of the Nassau Valley area in California is used to illustrate the nature of trajectories emerging from the present analysis. This data was obtained from the U. S. Geological Survey [39]. The terrain data is stored at 1000 ft intervals and interpolated using Cubic Spline Lattices [25]. First and second gradients of the terrain profile required in subsequent calculations are generated by differentiating the spline polynomials analytically and substituting for down-range and cross-range values. Note that any alternate method for partial derivative estimation can be used. The nonlinear differential equations are integrated using a fixed-step fifth-order Kutta-Merson technique and the method of bisections is used to carry out the one-dimensional search. All computations were carried out with double precision arithmetic.

A family of Euler solutions with a large weight on the terrain masking ($K = 1$) is given in Figure 4. These trajectories begin at the point marked O and are obtained by selecting a set of initial values for the heading angle in increments of 30° and integrating the Eqs. (11), (12), (30) forward. The computed trajectories are denoted with arrows, and they superimpose the contour plot of the terrain. Time-optimal trajectories ($K = 0$) with the same initial conditions have also been computed. These extremals appear to be nearly straight lines except in regions of large terrain curvature, and so they are omitted here. When compared with time-optimal trajectories ($K = 0$), the trajectories that emphasize terrain masking ($K = 1$) exhibit a more significant curvature. Figure 5 illustrates the difference between time optimal and maximum terrain masking trajectories joining a specified set of boundary conditions. The corresponding altitude histories are given in Figure 6. Due to the assumption of constant terrain clearance employed in this numerical study, the terrain profiles for these trajectories are simply the altitude histories shifted downwards by a fixed amount. This figure shows that the terrain masking trajectory tends to seek out lower elevations.

In order to illustrate the effect of wind on the Euler solutions, a constant wind field in the down-range direction with a speed 10% that of the vehicle speed is used. The corresponding Euler solutions for the terrain masking criterion ($K = 1$) are given in Figure 7. From this figure it is evident that the trajectories in the direction orthogonal to the wind field are less influenced by the wind than the other trajectories.

An interesting feature of the solution family given in Figures 4 and 7 is that some of the trajectories appear to intersect in certain regions on the

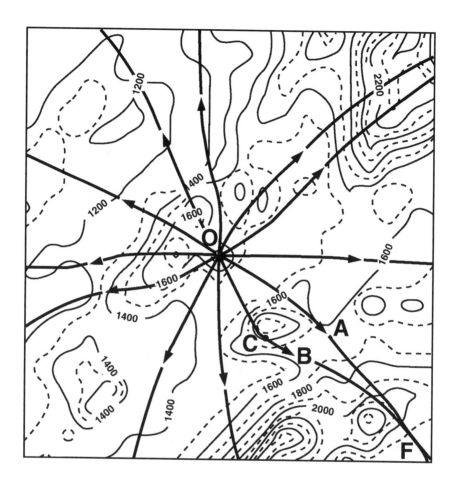

Figure 4: Maximum Terrain-Masking Euler Solutions ($K = 1$)

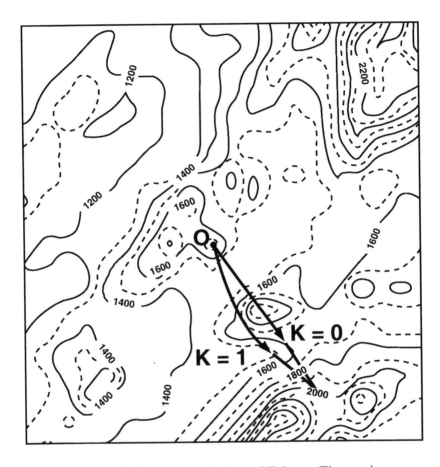

Figure 5: Comparison Between Minimum Time and
Maximum Terrain-Masking Euler Solutions

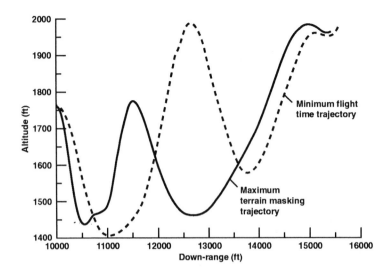

Figure 6: Altitude Profiles along Minimum Time and
Maximum Terrain-Masking Euler Solutions

given terrain. This fact implies the existence of more than one trajectory
satisfying the same set of boundary conditions. Since these trajectories
satisfy first-order necessary conditions, each of them are candidate optimal
solutions. Selection of a particular trajectory out of this set would require
an examination of second-order necessary conditions. Such an analysis will
be presented in Section III.A.2.

III.A.1   Computational Effort

At this point, it is appropriate to examine the computational effort involved
in generating an Euler solution using the methodology developed in this
section. Numerical experiments using a VAX 11/750 computer have shown
that an extremal requiring about 70 integration steps consumes between 1.5
and 2.1 seconds of CPU time. Given the desired initial and final conditions
on down range and cross range, several Euler solutions need to be generated
in order to converge to the one satisfying the desired boundary conditions.
For example, if the terrain gradients F_x and F_y were small such that the
cross-range boundary condition error at the end point, $e_y = y(t_f) - y_f$,
depends in an approximately linear fashion on the initial heading angle
error $\chi_l(0)$, the number of iterations and boundary condition error may be
related as [27]

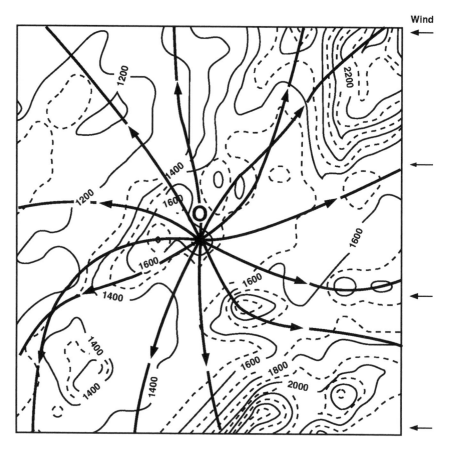

Figure 7: Influence of Wind on Maximum Terrain-Masking Euler Solutions

$$N = \frac{\ln(e_{y_1}/e_{y_N})}{\ln(2)} \tag{34}$$

In Eq. (34), N is the number of iterations, e_{y_1} is the cross-range boundary condition error at the first iteration, and e_{y_N} is the cross-range boundary condition error after N iterations. It is important to stress here that this relationship does not account for the nonlinearities due to terrain profile. Its usefulness is limited to generating a first-order estimate on the number of iterations required to satisfy a specified boundary condition error tolerance.

For the terrain profile used in the present study, about seven iterations were found to be adequate in reducing the boundary condition error by an order of magnitude. However, it needs to be emphasized that the number of iterations required is strongly influenced by the terrain profile under consideration.

III.A.2   Second-Variation Analysis

A sufficient condition for the extremals generated in the foregoing to provide a weak local minimum for the optimal control problem is that the second variation be strongly positive [28, 40, 41]. The second variation will be strongly positive if the Legendre-Clebsch necessary condition is met in the strengthened form and no conjugate points are encountered along an extremal. Each of these conditions will be examined for the present trajectory planning problem in the following.

Legendre-Clebsch Necessary Condition: In an earlier section, it was shown that the optimal value of airspeed is $V = V_{max}$. Since this control variable appears linearly in the Hamiltonian, the Legendre-Clebsch necessary condition for the present problem reduces to the scalar form

$$\frac{\partial^2 H}{\partial \chi_l^2} \geq 0 \tag{35}$$

Carrying out the indicated partial differentiation in Eq. (35), and using the optimality condition $\partial H/\partial \chi_l = 0$ from Eq. (26) and the costates given by the expressions (28) and (29), the second partial derivative of the Hamiltonian with respect to the heading angle turns out to be:

$$\frac{\partial^2 H}{\partial \chi_l^2} = (1 - K) + K\,F \tag{36}$$

The right-hand side of Eq. (36) is strictly positive by definition. Consequently, the Legendre-Clebsch necessary condition is satisfied in the strengthened form at every point on the terrain. Thus, extremals provide a weak local minimum for sufficiently short intervals.

Another implication of satisfying the Legendre-Clebsch necessary condition in the strengthened form is that the extremals emerging from the present formulation are smooth. This observation justifies the assumption made in deriving the heading angle rate equation (30). It may be noted that the smoothness guarantee on the extremals is useful from an implementation point of view because it ensures an acceptable ride quality for the pilot. Furthermore, smoothness of the reduced-order solution is desirable whenever correction for neglected vehicle dynamics is intended using singular perturbation theory [30, 31, 32, 33].

Conjugate Point Test: For extremals of finite length, the task of ensuring that the second variation is nonnegative for admissible variations leads to the *accessory-minimum problem* [28, 40, 41] in the calculus of variations. The accessory-minimum problem attempts to produce a system of admissible variations, not identically zero, which offer the most severe competition in the sense of minimizing the second variation. If a system of nonzero variations making the second variation zero can be found, then a neighboring trajectory is competitive. In this case, the test extremal furnishes at best an improper minimum or at worst a merely stationary value. First value of the independent variable for which such a nontrivial system of variations can be found defines a conjugate point [22, 28, 40, 41].

It has been shown [22] that the accessory-minimum problem leads to an analysis of the nature of solutions to the linearized Euler-Lagrange equations. The conjugate-point test may be constructed using these equations by at least two distinct routes. First of these is to cast the linearized Euler-Lagrange equations in the standard linear-quadratic format using the backward sweep method [22]. This yields a matrix Riccati equation. Nonexistence of a bounded solution to this equation then reveals the existence of conjugate points [22]. The second method for conjugate point testing is based on Theorem 12.3 in Reference [28]. In this approach, a characteristic determinant is constructed using solutions to the linearized Euler-Lagrange equations with a special set of initial conditions. The value of this determinant is then monitored along the nominal trajectory to reveal the existence of conjugate points.

The second method will be employed in this section. For the present trajectory synthesis problem, the solutions required in the characteristic determinant are constructed by perturbing the costates λ_x, λ_y one at a time about their nominal values. These perturbations should satisfy the transversality condition for free final time. The down-range and cross-range initial conditions $x(0), y(0)$ are unchanged. These solutions may also be generated by perturbing the initial value of the heading angle in positive and negative sense about the nominal value corresponding to an Euler solution and integrating the Euler-Lagrange equations forward. The latter procedure is equivalent to perturbing the initial value of costates λ_x, λ_y while enforcing the transversality condition for the free final time problem.

The resulting solutions are then subtracted from the nominal to yield the solutions to the linearized Euler-Lagrange equations. Let these solutions be $\delta x_1(t), \delta y_1(t)$ and $\delta x_2(t), \delta y_2(t)$. Note that these solutions satisfy $\delta x_1(0) = \delta y_1(0) = \delta x_2(0) = \delta y_2(0) = 0$ and must not be identically zero over the time interval $[0, t_f]$. A characteristic determinant $\Delta(t)$ is then formed as:

$$\Delta(t) = \left| \begin{array}{cc} \delta x_1(t) & \delta x_2(t) \\ \delta y_1(t) & \delta y_2(t) \end{array} \right| \tag{37}$$

Since the solutions $\delta x_1(t), \delta y_1(t)$ and $\delta x_2(t), \delta y_2(t)$ are obtained using different initial costate initial conditions and are nontrivial, the determinant (37) will not be identically zero.

Theorem 12.3 of Reference [28] states that if the characteristic determinant (37) after being zero at $t = 0$ subsequently becomes zero at $t = t^*$, with $t^* < t_f$, then the point t^* is conjugate to the point $t = 0$. The reader is directed to Reference [28] for a proof of this theorem.

Therefore, the conjugate point testing procedure consists of monitoring the value of the characteristic determinant (37) along the nominal trajectory. If the determinant is nonzero over the desired interval, the nominal trajectory is optimal. Otherwise, a neighboring trajectory satisfying the desired end points offers a competitive alternative. This numerical conjugate-point test is next applied to the terrain masking ($K = 1$) extremals given in Figure 4. In this figure, the extremals **A** and **B** are of particular interest since these are competing extremals satisfying the boundary condition pair (**O,F**). The characteristic determinant (37) evaluated along extremal **B** is given in Figure 8, which shows that a conjugate point occurs at about 45 sec. Similar computations along extremal **A** shows that the characteristic determinant is monotonically decreasing, indicating the absence of a conjugate point. Thus, the extremal **A** affords a strong local minimum if the desired end conditions were **O** and **F**. On the other hand, trajectory **B** provides merely a stationary value. This fact has been confirmed by computing the performance index along these trajectories.

In view of the observations made in this section, it would be interesting to investigate whether similar phenomena are encountered while computing trajectories using various heuristic methods [21] given in the literature.

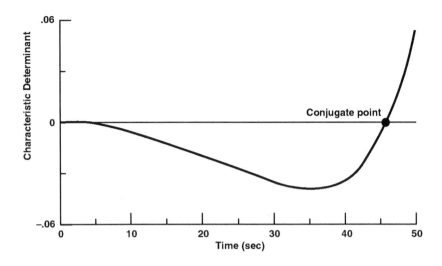

Figure 8: Characteristic Determinant $\Delta(t)$ along
Maximum Terrain-Masking Euler Solution **B**

III.B   Terrain-Masking Minimum-Deviation Trajectories

In the previous section, the optimal trajectory synthesis was carried out using a linear combination of flight time and terrain masking as the performance index. Using an adjoint-control transformation, the optimal control problem was formulated in terms of physical variables. This solution required the use of a one-dimensional search routine such as the method of bisections to obtain the optimal trajectories. That research also examined the second-order necessary conditions and showed that conjugate points may arise for certain sets of boundary conditions. As result, multiple trajectories may be found satisfying the stationarity conditions and the desired boundary conditions. Implementation issues such as convergence rate of the algorithm and execution time were evaluated.

One of the difficulties in the previous approach is that the computational algorithm required the second partial derivatives of the terrain profile. This necessitates the terrain profile to be represented by surfaces that are at least twice differentiable. This is onerous from a computational point of view. In this section, the trajectory synthesis problem is reformulated to enable faster computations. The need for second partial derivatives is eliminated by employing an alternate performance index together with the second vehicle model defined in Section II.B. Although different from that in the previous section, the performance index employed here is a well accepted form used in the development of terrain-following/terrain-avoidance guidance schemes reported in the literature [19]. This performance index is a quadratic form in altitude, deviation in cross-range from a specified trajectory and the heading angle. The first two terms correspond to the standard terrain-following/terrain-avoidance performance index, while the inclusion of the third component is motivated by a desire to constrain helicopter lateral acceleration.

The performance index employed for this study consists of:

$$\frac{1}{2}\int_{x_0}^{x_f}[h^2 + \epsilon\delta y^2 + \alpha\chi^2]dx \tag{38}$$

where δy is the deviation from a specified trajectory $y_c(x)$. This performance index is optimized while satisfying the differential constraint

$$\delta y' = \tan\chi - y_c' \tag{39}$$

where y_c' is the derivative of the desired trajectory.

For mathematical convenience, the χ^2 term in the integrand of the performance index is replaced with $\tan\chi^2$. For moderate values of χ, this change has no noticeable effects on the trajectory optimization problem. An additional simplification will result if the origin of the coordinate system is redefined at the initial point with the abscissa pointing in the direction of the down-range direction. This is consistent with the piecewise-linear trajectory defined in terms of way-points by the far-field mission planner [13]. If this is done, the quantity δy becomes the same as the cross-range variable y. Additionally, since the trajectory lies on the composite terrain profile, the altitude variable h can be replaced by the function $F(x, y)$.

With these modifications, the calculus of variations problem (38) may be reformulated as that of finding a trajectory $y(x)$ that minimizes the performance index, i.e.

$$\min_{y(x)}\frac{1}{2}\int_{x_0}^{x_f}[F^2 + \epsilon y^2 + \alpha y'^2]dx \tag{40}$$

The Euler's necessary condition for this problem can be obtained by setting the first variation to zero [28, 40, 41], yielding:

$$y'' = \frac{1}{\alpha}(\epsilon y + FF_y) \tag{41}$$

The initial condition $y(x_0)$ and the final condition $y(x_f)$ are specified. F_y is the gradient of the composite terrain profile in the cross-range direction. The term FF_y is the source of the nonlinearity in this second-order differential equation. If the terrain were flat, $FF_y = 0$, yielding a linear second-order differential equation. The solution to this differential equation is composed of two exponentials of the form $\exp\left(\pm x\sqrt{\epsilon/\alpha}\right)$, with one component driving the initial deviation to zero and the other diverging. The degenerate case of straight-line trajectory arises if the initial deviation and heading angle were zero. The initial value $\chi(0)$ or $y'(0)$ can be chosen so that the solution satisfies the specified boundary condition at the final range. Whenever the terrain profile has nonzero gradients, a numerical technique must be used to find the solution.

To construct an extremal joining a pair of boundary conditions, one unknown initial condition $y'(0)$ needs to be determined. The method of bisections [27] can be employed to find the solution rapidly and efficiently. Moreover, in order to obtain the solution, the terrain profile can be linearly interpolated since the present method requires just the first partial derivative of the terrain function. A numerical scheme for constructing the extremals is given in Figure 9.

Several Euler solutions were generated using this numerical scheme, some of which are shown in Figure 10 for various initial values of heading angle, with $\alpha = 10^5$, $\epsilon = 0.001$. The effect of increasing α is to produce trajectories that are closer to straight lines, while increasing ϵ permits significant trajectory gyrations. In Figure 11, an Euler solution is compared with a straight line path to illustrate the terrain-masking nature of the optimal trajectories. The weights used for generating the Euler solutions were $\alpha = 10^6$, $\epsilon = 0.01$. Altitude histories corresponding to these trajectories are given in Figure 12. It may be observed that the Euler solution tends to seek out lower altitudes to enhance masking.

III.B.1 Computational Effort

The computational work involved in obtaining numerical solutions is evaluated next. Assuming that the stationarity condition (41) is integrated using the Euler's method, and that a linear interpolation scheme is employed for computing the terrain altitude at various down-range cross-range locations, it is possible to estimate the required number of operations. In the following, it is assumed that multiplication, division, addition, and subtraction each count as one operation. Each integration step is found to require 23 operations. The method of bisections requires two mathematical and one logical operations per iteration. Thus, if there are n discretization intervals in the down-range direction and r bisections iterations, the present method would require approximately

$$m = (23n + 3)r \tag{42}$$

operations. Assuming that it is desired to decrease the interval of uncer-

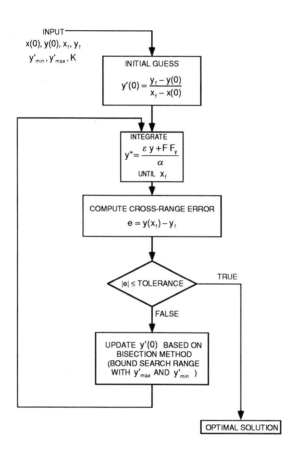

Figure 9: Flow Chart for Terrain-Masking Minimum-Deviation
Trajectory Computation

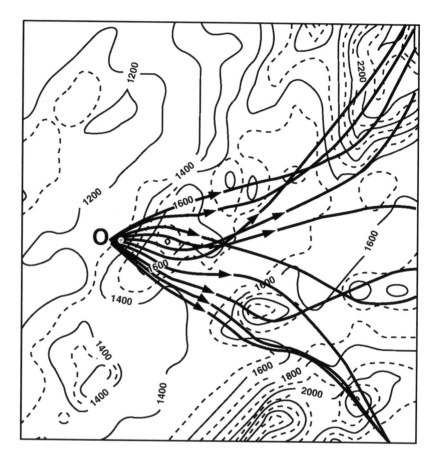

Figure 10: A Family of Terrain-Masking Minimum-Deviation
Euler Solutions

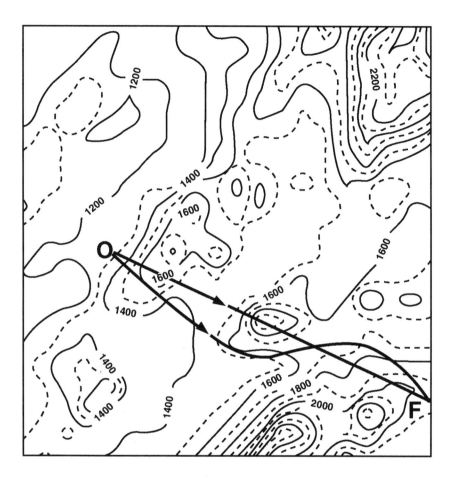

Figure 11: Comparison of a Terrain-Masking Minimum-Deviation
Euler Solution with a Straight-Line Path

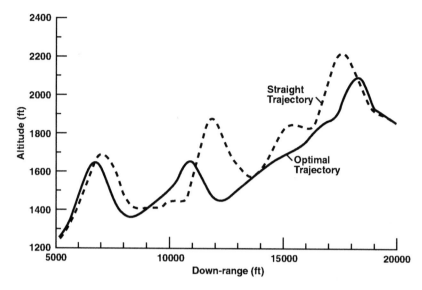

Figure 12: Altitude Profiles along a Terrain-Masking Minimum-Deviation
Euler Solution and a Straight-Line Path

tainty by two orders of magnitude, the method of bisections requires about
7 iterations [27]. Note that it is possible to reduce the interval of uncertainty by eight orders of magnitude by increasing the number of iterations
by about four times.

Next, assuming equal discretization of the down-range and cross-range
directions, the dynamic programming scheme is found to require 23 mathematical operations per node to evaluate the performance index. In a typical
computing scheme [22], this will have to be evaluated at $n^2 - 1$ nodes. After these computations, one has to make $2n - 1$ logical operations. Thus,
the total number of operations required in a full scale discrete dynamic
programming approach is:

$$m = 23n^2 + 2n - 24 \tag{43}$$

operations. Thus, to first order, the two methods are roughly equal in terms
of computational speed if $n = 7$. Whenever the number of discretization
intervals exceeds this figure, the present approach provides a faster solution.
In any case, note that in the present method, computational effort is a linear
function of the number of discretization intervals, while in the dynamic
programming approach, the computational effort is quadratic in the number
of discretization intervals.

On a rough terrain, a large number of discretization intervals are necessary to obtain results with sufficient fidelity. In that case, the advantage of the present approach will be even more significant. While the dynamic programming approach guarantees the optimality of the solution, this has to be verified through second-order necessary conditions in the present approach. The following section discusses this aspect of the trajectory optimization problem.

III.B.2   Second-Order Necessary Conditions

As in Section III.A.2, both Legendre-Clebsch necessary condition and the conjugate-point tests are examined here.

Legendre-Clebsch Necessary Condition: The Legendre-Clebsch necessary condition for this problem is

$$\frac{\partial^2 \omega}{\partial y'^2} \geq 0 \tag{44}$$

where ω is the integrand of the performance index, i.e. $\omega = F + \epsilon y^2 + \alpha y'^2$.
   It can be observed that

$$\frac{\partial^2 \omega}{\partial y'^2} = \alpha > 0 \tag{45}$$

Thus if $\alpha > 0$ the Legendre-Clebsch necessary condition is met with a margin for every extremal produced by the Euler's necessary condition. Note that α is a user-selected quantity. A consequence of this fact is that all extremals emerging from the present computations are smooth.

Conjugate-Point Test: This is an additional second-order necessary condition that must be satisfied by a minimizing extremal. As in Section III.A, an accessory-minimum problem is first defined [28, 40, 41]. The necessary condition for minimizing the second variation yields the Jacobi's differential equation as

$$\eta'' = \left[\frac{\epsilon + F_y^2 + F F_{yy}}{\alpha} \right] \eta \tag{46}$$

where η is the secondary extremal. Equation (46) is a second-order linear differential equation with a varying coefficient. This coefficient should be evaluated along a candidate extremal. The nature of solutions $\eta(x)$ with $\eta(0) = 0$ would determine the existence of conjugate points. After being zero at $x = 0$, if η crosses zero at any point along the candidate extremal, it indicates the existence of a conjugate point. The Jacobi's differential equation can be solved together with the Euler's necessary condition (41) to check for the existence of conjugate points. In the general case, Jacobi's differential equation must be numerically solved.

However, an approximate solution to Jacobi's differential equation can be obtained by invoking the following assumption. If the coefficient $\left(\epsilon + F_y{}^2 + F F_{yy}\right)/\alpha$ is slowly varying over x when compared with η, it can be made a function of a stretched range variable $\tilde{x} = \mu x$, $\mu > 0$. In this case,

$$\eta'' - q(\tilde{x})\eta = 0 \qquad (47)$$

where q defined by

$$q(\tilde{x}) = \frac{1}{\alpha}\left(\epsilon + F_y^2 + F F_{yy}\right) \qquad (48)$$

varies at a much slower rate than η. Approximate solution to this second-order differential equation with a varying coefficient can be obtained using the WKB method [42] as

$$\eta \approx \begin{cases} (-q)^{-\frac{1}{4}}\left\{C_1\cos\left[\int_{x_0}^{x_f}\sqrt{-q(s)}ds\right] + C_2\sin\left[\int_{x_0}^{x_f}\sqrt{-q(s)}ds\right]\right\} & q < 0 \\[2em] (q)^{-\frac{1}{4}}\left\{C_1 e^{\left[\int_{x_0}^{x_f}\sqrt{q(s)}ds\right]} + C_2 e^{-\left[\int_{x_0}^{x_f}\sqrt{q(s)}ds\right]}\right\} & q > 0 \end{cases}$$

$$(49)$$

where the coefficients C_1 and C_2 are determined by applying the initial conditions $\eta(0) = 0$ and some $\eta'(0) \neq 0$. For extremals of sufficiently small length, the accessory variable η, after starting from zero, will not again cross zero. Similarly, if $q > 0$ over the entire extremal, η will not cross zero again after being initially zero. Note that this will be the case if the entire trajectory lies along a saddle or in a valley on the specified terrain profile.

On the other hand, if $q < 0$, implying that the trajectory follows a ridge or goes over a peak, conjugate points will exist for extremals of sufficient length.

The special case of q changing sign along the trajectory is a *turning-point problem* [42], and will not be examined here.

IV   Trajectory Synthesis as a Pursuit Evasion Problem

This section examines the trajectory synthesis process wherein two vehicles with conflicting objectives are involved. The first participant in this process, designated as the evader, is a rotorcraft attempting to reach a specified point on the terrain while avoiding known threats and masking its trajectory. The second participant, designated as the pursuer, has the objective of intercepting the evader before it completes its mission, while masking its trajectory using the available terrain and avoiding threats. The motivation for maximizing terrain masking for both vehicles is to escape detection from each other and also from other ground-based or airborne detection devices. Although the rotorcraft are flying over the same terrain profile, note that the threats perceived by the two aircraft are different. It is assumed here that the evading rotorcraft has no offensive capabilities. Both vehicles may attempt to accomplish their objectives in a time optimal fashion.

This problem is suitable for analysis via the theory of differential games [43, 44]. The present formulation uses a kinematic model with local heading angle as the control variable, as in Section II.A. A formulation of this problem using a point-mass model can be found in Reference [16, 17]. The performance index for the present differential game is a linear combination of flight time and terrain masking.

As in Section II.A, let the composite profile $F(x, y)$ be given by Eq. (4). The composite profiles for the two vehicles may be different, because each of them will perceive air-defense threats differently. The vehicle models for the pursuer and evader moving over this composite profile are the same as the ones given in Eqs. (11) and (12), with the superscripts p and e denoting the pursuer and evader, respectively:

$$\dot{x}^e = \frac{V^e \cos \chi_l^e}{\sqrt{1 + F_x^{e\,2}}} + \frac{V^e F_x^e \, F_y^e \sin \chi_l^e}{\sqrt{(1 + F_x^{e\,2})(1 + F_x^{e\,2} + F_y^{e\,2})}} \tag{50}$$

$$\dot{y}^e = -\frac{\sqrt{1 + F_x^{e\,2}} \; V^e \sin \chi_l^e}{\sqrt{1 + F_x^{e\,2} + F_y^{e\,2}}} \tag{51}$$

$$\dot{x}^p = \frac{V^p \cos \chi_l^p}{\sqrt{1 + F_x^{p\,2}}} + \frac{V^p F_x^p \, F_y^p \sin \chi_l^p}{\sqrt{(1 + F_x^{p\,2})(1 + F_x^{p\,2} + F_y^{p\,2})}} \tag{52}$$

$$\dot{y}^p = -\frac{\sqrt{1 + F_x^{p\,2}} \; V^p \sin \chi_l^p}{\sqrt{1 + F_x^{p\,2} + F_y^{p\,2}}} \tag{53}$$

The vehicle altitude rates are given by the equations:

$$\dot{h}^e = V^e \sin \gamma^e \tag{54}$$

$$\dot{h}^p = V^p \sin \gamma^p \tag{55}$$

The pursuer-evader flight path angles γ^p, γ^e can be computed using the composite terrain profile gradients as

$$\gamma^e = \sin^{-1}\left[\frac{F_x^e \dot{x}^e + F_y^e \dot{y}^e}{V^e}\right] \tag{56}$$

$$\gamma^p = \sin^{-1}\left[\frac{F_x^p \dot{x}^p + F_y^p \dot{y}^p}{V^p}\right] \tag{57}$$

It is assumed that the rotorcraft airspeeds V^p, V^e either remain constant throughout the game duration or is specified as a function of their position on the terrain. Note that as in Section III.A, it is also possible to consider a case in which the rotorcraft airspeeds are included as additional control variables.

The variables $F_x^e, F_y^e, F_x^p, F_y^p$ are the composite terrain profile gradients at the instantaneous evader-pursuer locations. The local heading angles χ_l^p and χ_l^e are the control variables in this problem.

The rotorcraft pursuit-evasion begins at a certain set of initial conditions when the participants first become aware of one another. One of the participants in the game will be identified as the pursuer, while the other participant is assumed to be the evader. Further, it is assumed here that this designation continues unchanged throughout the duration of the encounter. In the present game, the objective of the evader is to reach a specified set of final conditions without being captured by the pursuer. The pursuer, on the other hand, is attempting to capture the evader before it gets to the desired final conditions. The participants in the pursuit-evasion encounter attempt to accomplish their objectives in a time-optimal fashion while providing for terrain masking and known-threat avoidance.

As in Section III.A, it is assumed here that the terrain masking will be accomplished if the participants minimize their altitude above the specified datum. Thus, the performance index employed here is of the form

$$J = \min_{\chi_l^p} \max_{\chi_l^e} \int_{t_0}^{t_f} (1 + W^p \, F^p - W^e \, F^e) \, dt \tag{58}$$

Here, F^p and F^e are the altitudes at the current pursuer-evader locations defined by the composite profile given in Eq. (4). W^p, W^e are weighting factors for the pursuer and evader altitudes. These reflect the participant's concern about the degree of desired terrain masking. The negative sign in the third term explicitly recognizes the fact that the evader is attempting to maximize the performance index. At this stage, the definition of this differential game is incomplete because no criterion has been laid down for the termination of the game. In this section, the pursuit-evasion game is assumed to terminate the first instant the pursuer succeeds in approaching the evader within the firing range of its weapon system. The pursuer's weapon envelope is assumed to be spherical. Note that alternate weapon envelope geometries can also be employed in the present formulation.

It needs to be emphasized that the formulation does not allow for any offensive capabilities for the evader. Additionally, the game is declared a draw if the pursuer-evader trajectories leave a predefined region in the terrain at any instant during the encounter.

For the case of a circular weapon envelope centered at the pursuer, the capture condition can be expressed by requiring that

$$\left[(x^e - x^p)^2 + (y^e - y^p)^2\right]\Bigg|_{t_f} \leq R_w^2 \tag{59}$$

$$\frac{d}{dt}\left[(x^e - x^p)^2 + (y^e - y^p)^2\right]\Bigg|_{t_f} \leq 0 \tag{60}$$

The quantity R_w is a specified capture radius. The condition (60) ensures that sufficient opportunity exists for pursuer weapon usage. The time for capture is then determined as the first time instant when the inequality (59) is met as an equality.

The game termination constraint may be satisfied by augmenting the performance index with Eq. (59) as an equality, i.e.

$$\min_{\chi_l^p} \max_{\chi_l^e} \left[\frac{\nu}{2}\{(x^e - x^p)^2 + (y^e - y^p)^2 - R_w^2\} \right. $$
$$\left. + \int_{t_0}^{t_f} (1 + W^p \, F^p - W^e \, F^e) \, dt \right] \tag{61}$$

The quantity ν is an undetermined multiplier. Given the performance index (61) together with the differential constraints (50) - (53), necessary conditions for optimality can be derived. To this end, define variational Hamiltonian [22] as

$$H = 1 + W^p F^p - W^e F^e + \lambda_1 \dot{x}^e + \lambda_2 \dot{y}^e + \lambda_3 \dot{x}^p + \lambda_4 \dot{y}^p \tag{62}$$

The Euler-Lagrange equations for the evader can then be obtained as

$$\dot{\lambda}_1 = W^e F_x^e - \frac{B_1 \sin \chi_l^e \, \lambda_2 + (B_2 \sin \chi_l^e + B_3 \cos \chi_l^e)\lambda_1}{A_1^3 A_2^3} V^e \tag{63}$$

$$\dot{\lambda}_2 = W^e F_y^e - \frac{B_4 \sin \chi_l^e \, \lambda_2 + (B_5 \sin \chi_l^e + B_6 \cos \chi_l^e)\lambda_1}{A_1{}^3 A_2{}^3} V^e \qquad (64)$$

where

$$A_1 = \sqrt{1 + F_x^{e2}}, \quad A_2 = \sqrt{1 + F_x^{e2} + F_y^{e2}}$$

$$B_1 = \left[-A_2{}^2 F_x^e F_{xx}^e + A_1{}^2 (F_y^e F_{xy}^e + F_x^e F_{xx}^e) \right] A_1{}^2$$

$$B_2 = -\left[A_2{}^2 F_x^e F_{xx}^e + A_1{}^2 (F_y^e F_{xy}^e + F_x^e F_{xx}^e) \right] F_x^e F_y^e + A_1{}^2 A_2{}^2 (F_x^e F_{xy}^e + F_y^e F_{xx}^e)$$

$$B_3 = -A_2{}^3 F_x^e F_{xx}^e$$

$$B_4 = \left[-A_2{}^2 F_x^e F_{xy}^e + A_1{}^2 (F_x^e F_{xy}^e + F_y^e F_{yy}^e) \right] A_1{}^2$$

$$B_5 = -\left[A_2{}^2 F_x^e F_{xy}^e + A_1{}^2 (F_x^e F_{xy}^e + F_y^e F_{yy}^e) \right] F_x^e F_y^e + A_1{}^2 A_2{}^2 (F_y^e F_{xy}^e + F_x^e F_{yy}^e)$$

$$B_6 = -A_2{}^3 F_x^e F_{xy}^e$$

and the optimality condition is:

$$\tan \chi_l^e = \frac{\lambda_1 F_x^e F_y^e - \lambda_2 (1 + F_x^{e2})}{\lambda_1 \sqrt{1 + F_x^{e2} + F_y^{e2}}} \qquad (65)$$

These equations were derived using the symbol manipulation program *MACSYMA* [38]. The Euler-Lagrange equations and the optimality condition for the pursuer has exactly the same form as expressions (63) - (65), and can be written down by inspection. In the interests of conserving space, these will not be given here.

It may be verified that the form of the necessary conditions remain the same regardless of the order of the minimization and maximization. Next, the terminal conditions on the costates can be obtained as

$$\lambda_1(t_f) = -\nu(x^p - x^e), \quad \lambda_2(t_f) = -\nu(y^p - y^e) \qquad (66)$$

$$\lambda_3(t_f) = \nu(x^p - x^e), \ \lambda_4(t_f) = \nu(y^p - y^e) \tag{67}$$

Since the final time is open and the variational Hamiltonian does not explicitly depend on time, this problem has a constant of motion, viz.,

$$H(t) = 0, \ 0 \leq t \leq t_f \tag{68}$$

Using this fact, together with the terminal conditions on the various costates, the undetermined multiplier ν may be computed as

$$\nu = \frac{1 + W^p F^p - W^e F^e}{c_1 - c_2} \tag{69}$$

where

$$c_1 = (x^p - x^e)\dot{x}^e + (y^p - y^e)\dot{y}^e |_{t=t_f} \tag{70}$$

$$c_2 = (x^p - x^e)\dot{x}^p + (y^p - y^e)\dot{y}^p |_{t=t_f} \tag{71}$$

The denominator of this equation is simply the negative of the product of range and range rate at the final time, i.e. the closing rate. It is possible to verify that as in planar pursuit-evasion games [45], the value of this parameter will turn out to be positive if the terrain masking weights were set to zero.

Extremals for the pursuit-evasion problem can be constructed if the initial conditions on the costates or the terminal conditions on the states were known. Since the final condition to be reached by the evader is normally known, in this research, the extremals are obtained by integrating the state-costate system backward in time until the trajectories reach the boundary of the admissible region. Since the last opportunity for the pursuer to catch the evader is at its final position, this represents the upper bound on the duration of the game. The detailed procedure for constructing the trajectories is as follows.

The pursuer's capture set is first superimposed at the evader's desired final position. The terminal condition of the pursuer is selected from this set and the equations are integrated backwards until the trajectories reach the boundary of the admissible region. The relative distance between the two vehicles are continuously monitored along the trajectories. Trajectories are constructed for several conditions in the capture set. From the final time, if the relative distance between the vehicles increase as the trajectories evolve in retrogressive time, it indicates that the pursuer can catch the evader only at the final time. On the other hand, if the relative distance decreases or stays constant while the trajectories are evolving in retro-time, it indicates that capture is possible anywhere along this segment of the trajectories. The results of this exercise can be used to determine the set of initial conditions for the pursuer and the evader that will not result in capture at the specified final conditions. These computations are also useful to delineate the set of initial conditions from which capture is assured. Construction of these sets require extensive numerical computations and will be a future research item.

A sample trajectory will be illustrated in the ensuing. Figure 13 shows the pursuer and evader trajectories in the down-range cross-range plane. A fixed terrain clearance of 50 feet together with unity terrain masking

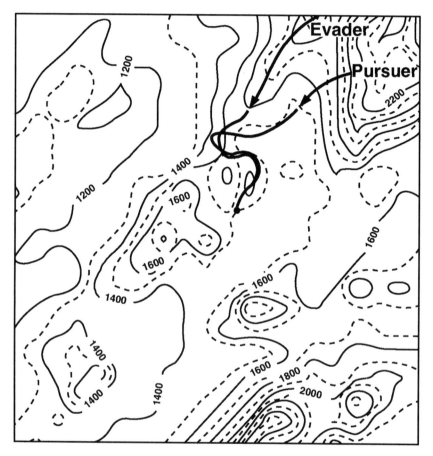

Figure 13: Pursuer and Evader Trajectories
in the Horizontal Plane

weight were used for both the pursuer and the evader in this computation. The value of the parameter ν corresponding to this set of final conditions turned out to be 5.79×10^{-3}. The trajectory duration was approximately 95 seconds. The intricate behavior of the trajectories are apparent from this figure. The corresponding altitude evolution is illustrated in Figure 14. Note that the trajectory in Figure 14 is given in retrogressive time and

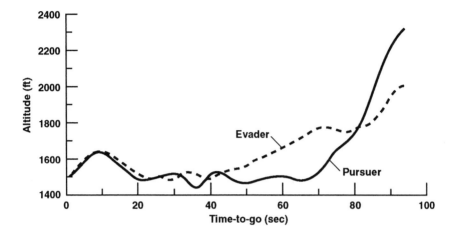

Figure 14: Pursuer and Evader Altitude Profiles

the $t_{go} = 0$ corresponds to the terminal instant. During the course of the present investigation, several such trajectories were generated.

It may be verified that if the terrain gradients were zero, the resulting pursuit-evasion game produces what is called a simple motion [43, 44]. In this case, the trajectories will turn out to be straight lines joining the initial conditions and the intercept point.

From the foregoing discussions, it is clear that the differential game solution is complex even in the case of simple vehicle models. The usefulness of the foregoing analysis is limited to addressing the question of capturability given a terrain profile and threat layout. Generating a large number of trajectories for on-board guidance in real time is not a viable proposition with near-term computer technologies. In practical situations, it is desirable to obtain feedback solutions. It has been shown in Reference [46, 47, 48] that the theory of feedback linearization [49] can be used to solve a class of differential games with high-order nonlinear dynamics and a quadratic payoff. A similar approach for the rotorcraft pursuit-evasion in NOE flight is given in Reference [16, 17]. Details of this study will not be given here.

V Conclusions

The motivation for present research was the need for automating the mid-term guidance segment of the nap-of-the-earth helicopter flight mission for high-performance helicopters. Systematic methodologies for optimal trajectory synthesis were presented. Unlike the techniques given in the literature, the present approaches require only a one-dimensional numerical search for determining optimal trajectories. If optimal solutions exist, it can be shown that the present algorithms will find them in a finite number of iterations. Moreover, in certain situations, the number of iterations required for convergence can be determined before initiating computations. Higher-order vehicle dynamics can be included in the present formulations using singular perturbation theory.

The trajectory synthesis problem was addressed using optimal control theory with performance indices consisting of flight time, terrain masking, and lateral acceleration. Two kinematic vehicle models were used in the analysis. Using adjoint-control transformations and appropriate independent variable choice, optimal control problems were reduced to forms requiring only the search for the initial value of the heading angle. Computational schemes based on the method of bisections and fifth-order Kutta-Merson numerical integration technique were outlined for generating Euler solutions. Families of Euler solutions were presented and compared.

It was shown that the Legendre-Clebsch necessary condition is satisfied in the strengthened form everywhere in the admissible region. Consequently, the trajectories emerging from the present analysis are smooth, facilitating on-board implementation. Further, conjugate points were shown to occur in certain regions of the specified terrain. This test reveals the existence of alternate trajectories joining the initial and final points satisfying the stationarity conditions. In the regions where conjugate points do not occur, the Euler solutions provide a strong local minimum.

Initial research on trajectory-synthesis methods for two vehicles with conflicting objectives was discussed. The first vehicle in this formulation is the evader attempting to reach its objective, while masking its trajectory and avoiding known threats. The second vehicle is a pursuer attempting to intercept the evader before it reaches its objective, while masking its trajectory and avoiding threats. A computational algorithm was given for constructing pursuer-evader trajectories.

Acknowledgment

The authors would like to thank FSN Branch Chief Dr. Dallas Denery and Automated NOE Flight Group Leader Dr. Banavar Sridhar of NASA

Ames Research Center for their continuous encouragement and support of this research.

This research was completed while the first author was an Associate Professor with the School of Aerospace Engineering, Georgia Institute of Technology. NASA Grant NAG2-463 and Cooperative Agreement NCC2-575 from Ames Research Center provided financial support for the first author. During the preparation of this chapter, the first author was supported under IR&D funds from *Optimal Synthesis*.

References

[1] M.J. Wendell, D.R. Katt, and G.D. Young, "Advanced Automatic Terrain Following/Terrain Avoidance Control Concepts Study," *Proceedings of the 1982 IEEE National Aerospace Electronics Conference*, May 18-20, 1982, Dayton, OH, pp. 1366-1372.

[2] R.A. Kupferer, and D.J. Halski, "Tactical Flight Management-Survival Penetration," *Proceedings of the 1984 IEEE National Aerospace Electronics Conference*, May 21-25, 1984, Dayton, OH, pp. 503-509.

[3] R.E. Huss, and J.W. Weber, "Route Finding Using Digital Terrain Data," *1983 IEEE/AIAA Joint Conference Proceedings*, Oct. 31-Nov. 3, 1983, Seattle, WA, pp. 14.4.1-14.4.4.

[4] W. Tang, and G.L. Mealy, "Application of Multiple Model Estimation Techniques to a Recursive Terrain Height Correlation System," *Proceedings of the 1981 IEEE National Aerospace Electronics Conference*, May 19-21, 1981, Dayton, OH, pp. 757-764.

[5] W.K. Lau, S.A. Bernstein, and B.T. Fine, "Integrated Terrain Access/Retrieval System (ITARAS) Robust Demonstration System," *Proceedings of the 1987 IEEE National Aerospace Electronics Conference*, May 19-21, 1987, Dayton, OH, pp. 66-72.

[6] A.C. Woodward, and J.B. Lagrange, "Terrain-Following Radar: Key to Low-Altitude Flight," *Proceedings of the 1979 IEEE National Aerospace Electronics Conference*, May 15-17, 1979, Dayton, OH, pp. 1089-1096.

[7] V.H.L. Cheng, and B. Sridhar, "Considerations for Automated Nap-of-the-Earth Rotorcraft Flight," *Journal of the American Helicopter Society*, Vol. 36, No. 2, April 1991, pp. 61-69; also, *Proceedings of the American Control Conference*, Atlanta, GA, June 15-17, 1988, pp. 967-976.

[8] B. Sridhar, V.H.L. Cheng, and A.V. Phatak, "Kalman Filter Based Range Estimation for Autonomous Navigation Using Imaging Sensors," *XIth IFAC Symposium on Automatic Control in Aerospace*, Ibaraki, Japan, July 17-21, 1989.

[9] P.K.A. Menon, G.B. Chatterji, and B. Sridhar, "Passive Obstacle Location for Rotorcraft Guidance," *Proceedings of AIAA Guidance, Navigation, and Control Conference*, New Orleans, LA, August 12-14, 1991.

[10] V.H.L. Cheng, "Concept Development of Automatic Guidance for Rotorcraft Obstacle Avoidance," *IEEE Transactions on Robotics and Automation*, Vol. 6, No. 2, April 1990, pp. 252-257.

[11] V.H.L. Cheng, and T. Lam, "Automatic Guidance and Control Laws for Helicopter Obstacle Avoidance," *1992 IEEE International Conference on Robotics and Automation*, Nice, France, May 10-15, 1992.

[12] P.K.A. Menon, G.B. Chatterji, and B. Sridhar, "Vision-Based Optimal Obstacle-Avoidance Guidance for Rotorcraft," *Proceedings of AIAA Guidance, Navigation, and Control Conference*, New Orleans, LA, August 12-14, 1991.

[13] O.L. Deutsch, M. Desai, and L.A. McGee, "Far-Field Mission Planning for Nap-of-the-Earth Flight", *Proceedings of the AHS National Specialist's Meeting Flight Control Avionics*, Cherry Hill, NJ, Oct. 13-15, 1987.

[14] P.K.A. Menon, E. Kim, and V.H.L. Cheng, "Helicopter Trajectory Planning Using Optimal Control Theory," *Proceedings of the 1988 American Control Conference*, Atlanta, GA, June 15-17, 1988, pp. 1440-1447.

[15] P.K.A. Menon, E. Kim, and V.H.L. Cheng, "Optimal Terrain Masking Trajectories for Helicopters," *AIAA Guidance, Navigation, and Control Conference*, Minneapolis, MN, August 15-17, 1988.

[16] E. Kim, "Optimal Helicopter Trajectory Planning for Terrain Flight," *Ph.D. Dissertation*, Georgia Institute of Technology, Atlanta, GA, December 1989.

[17] P.K.A. Menon, E. Kim, and V.H.L. Cheng, "Rotorcraft Pursuit-Evasion at Nap-of-the-Earth Altitudes," *Proceedings of AIAA Guidance, Navigation, and Control Conference*, Portland, OR, August 20-22, 1990.

[18] P.K.A. Menon, E. Kim, and V.H.L. Cheng, "Optimal Trajectory Synthesis for Terrain Following Flight," *Journal of Guidance, Control, and Dynamics*, Vol. 14, No. 4, July-August 1991, pp. 807-813.

[19] R.V. Denton, J.E. Jones, and P.L. Froeberg, "A New Technique for Terrain Following/Terrain Avoidance Guidance Command Generation," AGARD Paper No. AGARD-CP-387, 1985.

[20] D.W. Dorr, "Rotary Wing Aircraft Terrain-Following/Terrain Avoidance System Development," *AIAA Guidance, Navigation, and Control Conference*, Williamsburg, VA, August 18-20, 1986, Paper No. AIAA-86-2147.

[21] *The Handbook of Artificial Intelligence* (A. Barr, and E.A. Feigenbaum, ed.), William Kaufman, Inc., Los Altos, CA, 1981.

[22] A.E. Bryson, and Y.C. Ho, *Applied Optimal Control*, Hemisphere, New York, NY, 1975.

[23] S.J. Asseo, "Terrain Following/Terrain Avoidance Path Optimization using the Method of Steepest Descent," *Proceedings of the 1988 IEEE National Aerospace Electronics Conference*, May 23-27, Dayton, OH, pp.1128-1136.

[24] J.L. Vian, and J.R. Moore, "Trajectory Optimization with Risk Minimization for Military Aircraft," AIAA Guidance, Navigation and Control Conference, August 17-19,1987, Monterey, CA, Paper No. AIAA-87-2523.

[25] D.F. Rogers, and J.A. Adams, *Mathematical Elements for Computer Graphics*, McGraw Hill, New York, NY, 1976.

[26] H.J. Nussbaumer, *Fast Fourier Transform and Convolution Algorithms*, Springer-Verlag, New York, NY, 1982.

[27] B. Carnahan, H.A. Luther, and J.O. Wilkes, *Applied Numerical Methods*, John Wiley, New York, NY, 1969.

[28] G.A. Bliss, *Calculus of Variations*, Open Court Publishing Co., LaSalle, IL, 1925.

[29] E. Zermelo, "Untersuchungen zur Variationsrechnung," *Ph.D. Dissertation*, University of Gottingen, 1894.

[30] H.J. Kelley, "Aircraft Maneuver Optimization by Reduced-Order Approximation," *Control and Dynamic Systems* (C.T. Leondes, ed.), Academic Press, New York, NY, 1973, pp. 131-178.

[31] A.J. Calise, "Singular Perturbation Techniques for On-line Flight-Path Control," *Journal of Guidance and Control*, Vol. 4, July-August 1981, pp. 398-405.

[32] R.K. Mehra, R.B. Washburn, S. Sajan, and J.V. Carrol, "A Study of the Application of Singular Perturbation Theory," NASA CR 3167, August 1979.

[33] M.D. Ardema (ed.), *Singular Perturbations in Systems and Control*, CISM No. 280, Springer-Verlag, New York, NY, 1983.

[34] V.H.L. Cheng, and N.K. Gupta, "Advanced Midcourse Guidance for Air-to-Air Missiles," *Journal of Guidance, Control, and Dynamics*, Vol. 9, No. 2, March-April 1986, pp. 135-142.

[35] V.H.L. Cheng, P.K.A. Menon, N.K. Gupta, and M.M. Briggs, "Reduced-Order Pulse-Motor Ignition Control Logic," *Journal of Guidance, Control, and Dynamics*, Vol. 10, No. 4, July-August 1987, pp. 343-350.

[36] P.K.A. Menon, and M.M. Briggs, "Near-Optimal Midcourse Guidance for Air-to-Air Missiles," *Journal of Guidance, Control, and Dynamics*, Vol. 13, No. 4, July-August 1990, pp. 596-602.

[37] E.B. Lee, and L. Marcus, *Foundations of Optimal Control Theory*, John Wiley, New York, NY, 1968.

[38] R. Bogen, et al., *MACSYMA Reference Manual*, The Mathlab Group Laboratory for Computer Science, M.I.T., Cambridge, MA, Version 10, 1983.

[39] *San Andreas, California*, U.S. Geological Survey, N3800-W12030/15, AMS 1860II-Series V795, Denver, CO, 1962.

[40] I.M. Gelfand, and S.V. Fomin, *Calculus of Variations*, Prentice-Hall, Englewood Cliffs, NJ, 1963.

[41] G.M. Ewing, *Calculus of Variations with Applications*, Dover Publications, New York, NY, 1985

[42] J.A. Murdock, *Perturbations: Theory and Methods*, John Wiley, New York, NY, 1991.

[43] R. Isaacs, *Differential Games*, Robert Krieger, New York, NY, 1975.

[44] A. Friedman, *Differential Games*, Wiley-Interscience, New York, NY, 1971.

[45] N. Rajan, and M.D. Ardema, "Barriers and Dispersal Surfaces in Minimum Time Interception," *Journal of Optimization Theory and Applications*, Vol. 42, No. 2, February 1984, pp. 201-228.

[46] P.K.A. Menon, "Short Range Nonlinear Feedback Strategies for Aircraft Pursuit-Evasion," *Journal of Guidance, Control, and Dynamics*, Vol. 12, No. 1, Jan.-Feb. 1989, pp. 27-32.

[47] P.K.A. Menon, A.J. Calise, and S.K.M. Leung, "Guidance Laws for Spacecraft Pursuit-Evasion," *Proceedings of AIAA Guidance, Navigation, and Control Conference*, Minneapolis, Minnesota, August 15-17, 1988.

[48] P.K.A. Menon, and E.L. Duke, "Time-Optimal Aircraft Pursuit-Evasion with A Weapon Envelope Constraint", *Proceedings of the 1990 American Control Conference*, May 23-25, San Diego, CA, pp. 2337-2342.

[49] L.R. Hunt, R. Su, and G. Meyer, "Global Transformations of Nonlinear Systems," *IEEE Transactions on Automatic Control*, Vol. AC-28, No. 1, January 1983, pp. 24-30.

TECHNOLOGY INTEGRATION IN ADVANCED COMMERCIAL AIRCRAFT COCKPITS AND OPERATIONAL SYSTEMS

Jean GROSSIN
AEROSPATIALE
Aircraft Division
31060 Toulouse Cedex 03
(FRANCE)

I. ABSTRACT

Avionics system design has evolved significantly with the advent of electronic technologies. The airborne computer performance improvement brought about by more and more extensive use of digital electronics has made it possible to integrate functions. The most noteworthy applications made by Aerospatiale for the Airbus family concern air data/inertial reference sensors, display systems, fly-by-wire controls and the auto-flight system.

With each new programme, the aircraft manufacturer must make difficult choices, compromising between the benefits due to integration on one hand, and system reliability and availability constraints on the other. New technologies will make it possible to pursue the course of system integration and thus improve performance and reduce the operating costs of future generations of aircraft.

II. INTRODUCTION

The general design of a civil transport aircraft is an iterative process that involves several factors. Optimization of the final product makes it necessary to find a judicious balance between the four main aircraft design activities : Aerodynamics, Structure, Engines and Systems.

The share of systems has greatly increased over the last ten years. Today, it represents almost a third of the cost of an aircraft.

The importance of system design in modern aircraft is thus obvious : through the improvement in systems the aircraft manufacturer attempts to increase the performance and safety of the aircraft as much as he tries to reduce its production cost and the operating cost for the airlines.

Yesterday's aircraft systems were designed independently from one another ; today they are closely interconnected, thanks to improved airborne electronics. The appearance of microprocessors in the seventies made it possible to install a lot of digital equipment, exchanging a large quantity of information via data networks. This event was at the origin of the system integration process in civil aviation, and that of the interdependence of aircraft systems between each other but also, more and moreso, with the structure (progressive implementation of the generalized Active Control Concept).
But integration also involves problems and suitable compromises must be made.
It must be borne in mind that the "last few percent" of an optimization are always the most costly, and that on the other hand, the benefits yielded by system integration are not easy to quantify.
Nevertheless, it must be stressed that over a period of five years, which is the average time between two successive transport aircraft programmes, the volume of electronics remains more or less constant ; computation power, on the other hand, is roughly doubled and functional capabilities increase in the same proportion (see Table 1).

In a general context, the aircraft manufacturer's role is to define integration concepts with the aid of the systems manufacturers, and guide their development efforts so as to draw maximum benefit from these integrations both in terms of performance and operating costs.

To locate the various steps in time, table 1 below summarizes benchmark dates. Furthermore, figure 1 summarizes the main characteristics of the various Airbus models in production for the 1990's.

Table 1

	A300	A310	A320	A340
Volume of electronics (in liters)		745	760	830
Weight (Kg) - Computers - Elec. Bay (*) - Total	470 410 880	455 235 690	380 270 650	460 260 720
Electrical consumption	roughly constant (7,5 to 8 KW for ATA 22, 23, 31 and 34)			
Reliability	Baseline		X4 (per function)	(TBD)
Computation power (Mips)	(Analog)	60	160	250

(*) Racks, wiring and components (relays, ...)

Table 2 : Airbus family :

Airbus Type	Certificate of Airwothiness Date
A300 B2	March 15, 1974
A300 B4	March 26, 1975
A300-FFCC	December, 1982
A310-200	March 11, 1983
A300-600	March 10, 1984
A310-300	December 5, 1985
A320	February 26, 1988
Planned	
A340	December, 1992
A330	November, 1993
A321	December, 1993

Figure 1
The Airbus product line for the 1990s

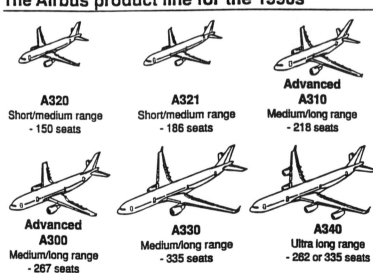

A320
Short/medium range
- 150 seats

A321
Short/medium range
- 186 seats

Advanced A310
Medium/long range
- 218 seats

Advanced A300
Medium/long range
- 267 seats

A330
Medium/long range
- 335 seats

A340
Ultra long range
- 262 or 335 seats

III. AVIONICS SYSTEM INTEGRATION

Avionics system design is a long and delicate task for which several often contradictory objectives must be taken into account. System architecture must, first of all, comply with the safety objectives that are generally imposed by the regulations laid down by the Certification Authorities. System safety is achieved both by hardware and software redundancies.

Although the multiplication of redundant units is a classic technique for meeting high safety objectives for critical systems, application of this concept to software is a novelty, made necessary by the use of systems with large software products.
In addition, reconfiguration processes are being used more and more to achieve "failure tolerant" systems, i.e. systems that continue to fulfil their function after a failure, particularly if the function is critical.

From another point of view, the operators ask for the best possible availability for the aircraft, so that all maintenance operations can be performed only at the airline's main base.

It is generally necessary to increase the number of redundant units to enable an aircraft to take off from each line station, even with a failed unit. The associated disadvantage, is of course, a shorter mean time between system failures and worse overall reliability.

In his many choices, the designer must also take account of the availability of new technologies when the programme is launched.
This concerns not only the latest generation of microprocessors and their memories, but also devices built into sensors or actuators such as laser gyros, electrically signalled servo-controls, liquid crystal screens, optronics, etc...

When the integration of functions or computers is technically possible, the benefits yielded by reducing the number of units are assessed with respect to the system safety and availability objectives, and integration is not always chosen.

The main integrated systems on the latest aircraft of the Airbus family are the primary air data/inertial references, display systems, radio systems, engine control, flight controls and the autoflight system.

The evolution of these systems, which is quite representative of that of all the systems on Airbus family aircraft, is detailed below :

A - Baro-inertial sensing

At the beginning of the 1970's, the Airbus A300 was equipped with 2 ADC's (Air Data Computer) and 3 gyroscopic platforms (HAS : Heading and Attitude Sensor) all of the electro-mechanical type.

The first evolution came in two steps (A300-FFCC, then A310/A300-600) by replacing the analogue ADCs by digital ADCs with almost no mechanical parts. At the same time, AHRS' (Attitude and Heading Reference System) then IRS' (Inertial Reference System) were proposed as an option to replace the HAS.

The second evolution was made by putting the ADC and IRS together in a single piece of equipment. The A320 ADIRS (Air Data and Inertial Reference System) was born, each aircraft being equipped with 3 systems.

The following must be pointed out :

1) Smart probes :

Barometric probes became "Smart" (see note) by putting ADMs (Air Data Module) close to them, eliminating a number of tubes in the forward part of the aircraft.

Note :   we call a piece of equipment, (sensor or actuator) "smart" if it is able to perform electrical signal conditioning by itself.

2) Integration level :

This integration is roughly limited to the fact that the two functions were put side by side in the same LRU (Line Replaceable Unit), each one keeping its own computing devices. The possibility to mix the data (data hybridization) permitted by such grouping was not really used in order to ease the certification process by keeping the independence of the two functions as in a "conventional" architecture.

3) Air data redundancy :

The ADIRS concept, as compared with the previous architectures, provides fewer pieces of equipment (3 computers instead of 5) but increases the redundancy level for the barometric sensing function.

B - Instrument displays

Figure 2 shows the layout of the main instrument panels on the first A300 : the instruments were mainly electro-mechanical.

The evolution of this instrumentation was made in parallel with that of baro-inertial sensing, but with a greater effort to derive maximum benefit from integration, which was needed to introduce new functions (mainly ECAM : Electronic Centralized Aircraft Monitoring) and to ease elimination of the lateral panel (two-man cockpit implying new concepts for the warning system).

As for baro-inertial sensing, there an initial step was to digitize electro-mechanical instruments : these were the hybrid instruments on the A300-FFCC.

Then, CRT's (Cathode Ray Tubes) were used, firstly in 6.25 x 6.25 inch size (A310/A300-600, see figure 3) then in 7.25 x 7.25 inch size (A320/330/340, see figure 4).

The first CRT generation made it possible to group together on one DU (Display Unit), information

A300 main panel

Figure 2

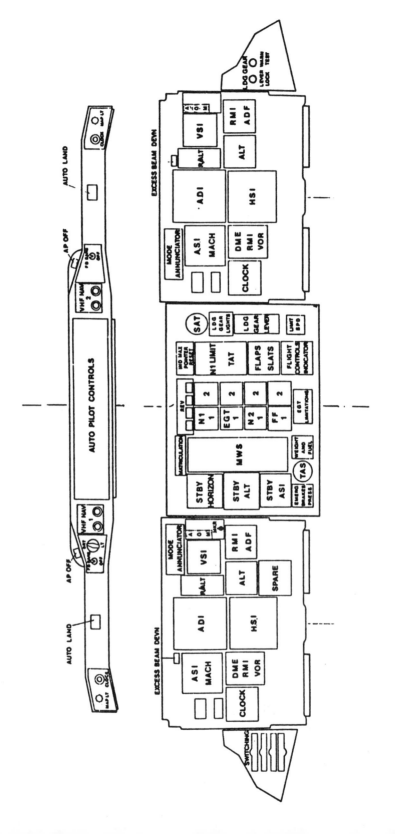

previously provided by several instruments. There are 6 DU's on the main instrument panel to perform the following functions :

- PFD (Primary Flight Display) replacing the previous ADI (Attitude Director Indicator), ASI (Air Speed Indicator), FMA (Flight Mode Annunciator) and radio-altimeter display.

- ND (Navigation Display) replacing the previous HSI (Horizontal Situation Indicator) and the weather radar scope and, at the same time, providing the capability to display the flight plan as computed by the FMS (Flight Management System).

- ECAM which, in addition to all the associated new functions, eliminated a number of indicators such as the FCPI (Flight Control Position Indicators).

Note : this simplification on the instrument panel is linked to the addition of computers in the aircraft electronics bay : the SGU (Symbol Generator Unit) and the SDAC (System Data Acquisition Concentrator) which were needed to perform the added ECAM functions.

The second CRT generation allowed more integration with no additional computers :

- The PFD are now displaying, in addition, heading, altitude and vertical speed : it was then possible to eliminate one RMI (Radio Magnetic Indicator), the altimeter displays and the VSI (Vertical Speed Indicator).

- The two CRT'S previously dedicated to the ECAM function only now display engine parameters (elimination of 10 specific indicators) and flap and slat positions (elimination of the corresponding indicator).

It is useful to recall that, in parallel with the evolution of the CRT's themselves (the visible part of the system), the associated computers were also subject to profound changes since for a smaller volume they had to perform more, with improved performance and greater safety and availability.

A310 main panel

Figure 3

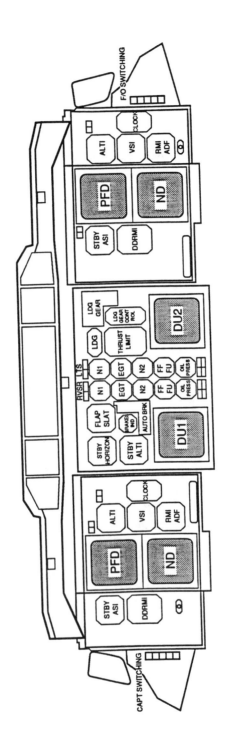

A320 main panel

Figure 4

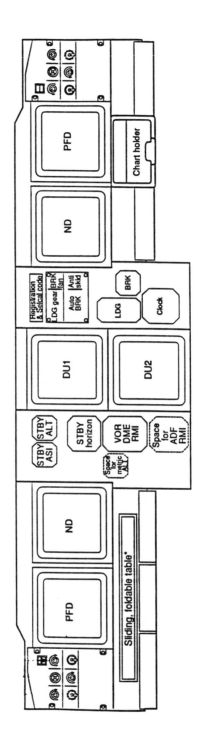

C - Radio frequency management

Traditionally, each radio system had its own control panel in order to manage the corresponding frequencies. For this reason, the first Airbus A300, as all the other aircraft, had an overcrowded pedestal with a lot of control boxes for radio-navigation and radio-communication. The digitization of all these boxes, done with the A300-FCC, did not change this situation significantly.

The A320 provided the solution awaited by the operators by introducing the RMP (Radio Management Panel) concept where, through a single box (duplicated or even triplicated when needed by a specific system configuration), it is possible to manage all the radio-communication functions and provide a back-up to radio-navigation management. In normal operations radio-navigation management is performed automatically by the autotune function of the FMS (Flight Management System) or manually through the MCDU (Multipurpose Control Display Unit), this unit also having a lot of various functions and thus limiting the number of specific screens/keyboards which would otherwise be necessary.

D - Autoflight System

The example of the AFS (Auto Flight System) will make it 'possible to describe the benefit due to integration in this area more precisely.

In the main, the Airbus AFS performs the following functions :

- help for manual flight : yaw damping, pitch trim, thrust limit computation...,

- automatic flight (autopilot, flight director, autothrust) including automatic landing under Cat. 3B weather conditions,

- flight management (FMS) including flight plan managing and its optimization as far as performance and cost are concerned,

- help for the maintenance of this complex system.

In the first generation, installed on the A300, the system (without FMS, but with a PMS (Performance Management System) as an option) comprised 20 computers (12 different types, 8 being fully analogue and 4 already more or less digital).

The first step toward extensive integration to reduce the number of computers involved was to acquire full control of digital techniques. This was done firstly with the A300-FFCC then with the A310 on which, an FMS was installed for the first time. This new AFS generation provided greater availability of the functions and improved operational capabilities. The system using only 10 computers (5 different types, all considerably digitized) was easier to maintain.

Introduction of electrical flight controls (EFCS) and electronic engine control (FADEC) on the A320 induced a new distribution of some functions and, in particular, the AFS is less burdened with the help for manual flight. During the same time, digital technology was improved and highly integrated components became available. It was possible in these conditions to design an AFS within 4 computers (2 types) for the A320 and only 2 computers (1 type) for the A330/340, the system providing new and improved capabilities (significant increase of navigation data base,...). Figure 5 summarizes all these steps.

Airbus AFS history
Automatic flight system (Category III)

Figure 5

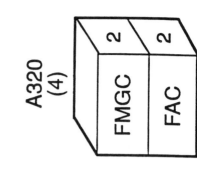

A320
(4)

| FMGC | 2 |
| FAC | 2 |

2nd generation
digital AFS

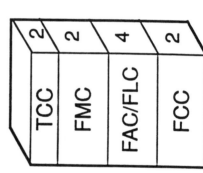

A310 / A300-600
(10)

TCC	2
FMC	2
FAC/FLC	4
FCC	2

1st generation
digital AFS

A300
(19 + 1 optional PMS)

(single ATS)

N1 limit	1
Auto thrt	1
Test computer	2
Pitch trim	4
Yaw damp & lim	4
Logic computer	2
Longitud computer	2
Lateral computer	2

+ 1 FD switching

Analogue AFCS

Integration is not limited to computers only ; it also concerns the control boxes. This is illustrated by the two units of this type used in the automatic flight control system :

1) The auto pilot flight control panel (Flight Control Unit : FCU) has formed the subject of a dual evolution : initially, it was an assembly of electromechanical modules (synchros, push-buttons, lights, indicators) limited to the selection of modes and targets for the auto pilot, flight director and autothrottle. Today, it is fully digitized (optical coding wheels, liquid crystal indicators) with complete redundancy (three segregated processors). It also integrates electronic flight instrument control, and operationally, it makes it possible to define the short term constraints for the flight management computer.

2) The flight management computer control box (Control Display Unit : CDU) which was initially entirely dedicated to this computer is now a multipurpose unit (Multipurpose CDU : MCDU), as it is linked to the airborne maintenance systems. Radio navigation frequency selection and IRS initialization can also be done manually. In its A340 version, it will also be capable of providing a navigation function in the event of complete failure of the flight management computers. A study showed that full integration of the flight management function in the MCDU was then possible but such a solution was not selected for the A340 owing to a concern for commonality with the A320.
The increase in the number of functions of the control boxes has been accompanied by a reduction in their volume (FCU) on the one hand and improved reliability on the other (FCU/MCDU).

IV. PROSPECTS FOR THE FUTURE

The new products of the Airbus range, i.e. the A330 and A340 have taken advantage of all the A320 improvements ; they are part of the same technological family even if they have more sophisticated functions due to their mission (eg : polar flight), and a highly developed airborne maintenance aid system with, in particular, an electronic library which will successfully replace part of the paper documentation.

Beyond this, on future programmes, avionics will form the subject of another evolution with thorough modifications to system architectures. The principles of failure tolerant equipment will be applied and redundant multi-directional centralized data transmission networks will be used (use of modular electronics concepts which form the subject of ARINC 629 and 651).

Considerable integrations, which are possible today as far as electronics are concerned, are not made because of connector limitations. The present computer packaging will thus be given up and will be replaced by a system based on standard cards which will be directly installed in the avionics bay : there will thus be cards dedicated to the interfaces with the external buses near cards containing the processing units and other specific cards making it possible to control actuators for example. The main advantage of such a system is the reduction both in the cost of equipment and its maintenance cost.

The technological evolution of airborne electronics will of course continue thanks to integration processes on a greater and greater scale. These processes will make it possible to increase microprocessor computation power and speed as well as memory capacity. The systems which do not use digital electronics will be exceptions.

Completely new technologies will be applied on airborne electronics. Among the most important of these is optronics which offers considerable advantages such as total immunity from EMI threats and lightning, a broad pass-band and no risk of fire. All these advantages are particularly interesting for flight control systems, thus leading to the concept of optical flight controls or "fly-by-light" controls (electrical flight controls are called fly-by-wire controls).

Man-machine interface performance will be improved by the use of liquid crystal screens possibly equipped with sensitive films providing direct control or the use of voice control and miniaturized or new control devices (eg touch pad).

The performance of fly-by-wire controls will make it possible to generalize active control, such as load alleviation (reduction in the loads applied to the wing) or variable wing camber.

Satellite commnications will greatly extend (Air Traffic Management (ATM) concept, in particular) and it seems obvious that satellites will finally become the major telecommunication means for the various aircraft operators ; this will lead to putting the associated applications into a network (Aeronautical Telecommunication Network (ATN) concept).

In order to be prepared to integrate these new technologies, the aircraft manufacturer must constantly monitor technological evolutions and evaluate promising technologies by conducting research programmes including, of course, laboratory experimentation. Since 1976, Aerospatiale have had a flight simulator specially dedicated to controlled evolutions of innovations in the systems field.

As far as the aircraft is concerned, it must be emphasized that, on the one hand, system integration will continue as far as system interdependence permits, whereas on the other, the aircraft itself, which is relatively isolated at the present time, will in the future, be part of a global system involving all the air transport partners : airlines (operations and maintenance), air traffic control, the met office, airports...

In this perspective, the aircraft manufacturer will continue to play a major part in the general design of systems and system architectures, insofar as he is the only one capable of managing the global integration of the air transport vehicle. However, he will still have to take account of the operator (airline) and equipment manufacturer constraints. The design of avionics systems will be more than ever a subject of team work.

Development of a Pneumatic High-Angle-of-Attack Flush Airdata Sensing (HI-FADS) System

By

Stephen A. Whitmore, PhD
Senior Aerospace Engineer

Timothy R. Moes
Aerospace Engineer

NASA Ames Research Center
Dryden Flight Research Facility
Edwards, California, 93523

and

Cornelius T. Leondes

Professor of Electrical
Engineering/Computer Science
University of California, San Diego
La Jolla, California 92093-0407

I. Introduction

Airmass reference data for flight vehicles-- traditionally referred to as *airdata*--have always been critical measurement parameters for the flight test community. Basically, the airdata parameters define the relative kinematics and dynamics of the local atmosphere with respect to the reference axis of the aircraft. The entire airmass reference

state can be completely defined by a set of
five parameters, traditionally defined in
terms of the parameters--true airspeed, angle-
of-attack, angle-of-sideslip, Mach Number, and
dynamic pressure. Other parameters of interest
such as ambient pressure, density, or
geopotential altitude can be computed directly
from this basic set (Ref. 1).

Historically, airdata measurements were
performed using intrusive booms which extended
beyond the local flow field of the aircraft
and measured airmass velocities by direct
stagnation of the flow through the use of a
pitot tube at the end of the measurement boom.
Flow incidence angles were measured using
mechanical vanes attached to the probe via
short extension stems. Localized aircraft-
induced effects were removed through empirical
calibration. Eventually the National Advisory
Committee for Aeronautics (NACA) standardized
the design and calibration of these
measurement booms (Ref. 1). While excellent at
making steady measurements at low-to-moderate
angles-of-attack, the booms were sensitive to
vibration, alignment error, and often
susceptible to damage, both in-flight and on
the ground.

Traditional uses of airdata have included
gain scheduling for flight control systems,

benchmark comparisons of windtunnel and flight
data, and analyses of data derived from flight
testing programs--especially performance and
flight mechanics evaluations. Recently,
precise airdata measurements have also been
required for accurate benchmarking of
computational fluid dynamics (CFD) codes.
Increasingly, however, advanced flight system
designs for aerospace vehicles require the
availability of airdata for direct flight-
critical feedback values. This application
requires that the airdata values be measured
with accuracy and fidelity.

Unfortunately, the specialized
requirements of these advanced vehicles often
make the use of conventional intrusive airdata
measurement systems highly undesirable. For
example, on the hypersonic National Aerospace
Plane (NASP), where direct feedback of the
angles-of-attack and -sideslip will be
required, the hostility of the hypersonic
environment mandates that alternative
measurement systems be developed. Conventional
intrusive measurement systems would simply not
survive. Further, on low-observable stealth
vehicles such as the B-2, or the YF-22
fighter, where a minimal radar cross-section
is required, it is highly-desirable that
conventional intrusive systems be eliminated.

As a means of circumventing these and
other difficulties with intrusive systems, the
Flush Airdata Sensing (FADS) System concept,
where airdata are inferred from non-intrusive
surface pressure measurements, was developed
at NASA Langley Research Center for the space
shuttle program. The FADS technique was
adapted to aeronautical applications at the
NASA Ames-Dryden Flight Research Facility
(DFRF). Several FADS demonstration programs
have been performed.

The original program, the Shuttle Entry
Airdata Sensing (SEADS) system, was developed
for the space shuttle and demonstrated the
feasibility of the concept (Ref. 2). In this
program a cruciform configuration of pressure
ports was distributed along the normal and
lateral axes of the nosecap. No off-axis port
locations were utilized. Following the SEADS
program, early aeronautical applications
included programs conducted on the KC-135 and
F-14 vehicles (Ref. 3 and Ref. 4). These early
programs also used the cruciform pressure port
configuration.

Early, FADS analyses used only selected
ports, chosen off-line in an ad-hoc manner, as
inputs to curve-fit schemes which related
measured pressure differences to various
airdata parameters. No attempts were made to

reconcile discontinuities between the various curve-fit regions. All of the preliminary programs were intended only to demonstrate the feasibility of the concept and did not attempt to derive algorithms capable of operating on a fully redundant flight system. The emphasis of these flight programs was on measurement and presentation of individual pressure coefficient data and their specific empirical relationships to Mach number, dynamic pressure, and flow incidence angles.

A more advanced program, in which a flush measurement system capable of operating at high angles-of-attack was developed, recently concluded flight-testing during phase I of the F-18 High Alpha Research Vehicle (HARV) program at NASA DFRF. The system, primarily used for research measurements, was required for the high angle-of-attack tests because a noseboom installation would alter the basic flow characteristics in the vicinity of the aircraft nose and would affect aircraft performance at high incidence angles.

The HI-FADS design is an evolution of the earlier non-intrusive systems and emphasized the entire airdata system development, including aerodynamic modeling, algorithms, and system redundancy. For the HI-FADS tests, composite results were expressed as airdata

estimates instead of raw pressure values. The
HI-FADS system provided the opportunity to
research various application techniques for
FADS as vehicle or mission critical flight
systems. The system utilized a matrix of
pressure orifices arranged on the nose of the
F-18 vehicle. For the HI-FADS system, the
cruciform configuration was abandoned in favor
of concentric rings in which measurements were
obtained at locations both on and off the
central meridians. For a given number of
pressure ports, use of these off-meridian
locations increases the measurement
sensitivity of the pressure matrix. Further,
off-axis port locations are less susceptible
to flow separation at high-incidence angles.
The HI-FADS system incorporates an overdetermined algorithm in which *all* surface
pressure observations are used simultaneously
to infer the airdata parameters using nonlinear regression.

   This paper will describe the Hi-FADS
measurement system. It will discuss the basic
measurement hardware, develop the HI-FADS
aerodynamic model, and the basic non-linear
regression algorithm. Algorithm initialization
techniques will be developed and potential
algorithm divergence problems will be
discussed. It will demonstrate how total

system and individual measurement failures can
be identified using $\chi 2$ analysis of the
pressure measurement residuals. Data derived
from HI-FADS flight tests will be used to
demonstrate the system accuracies and to
illustrate the developed concepts and methods.

During the HARV flight tests, excellent
results were achieved for flights conditions
up to an angle of attack of 55 deg. and 1.20
Mach number. Standard errors were empirically
determined to be better than one-half degree
in angle-of-attack and angle-of-sideslip, and
better than 0.004 in Mach Number. Preliminary
results of these flight tests have been
previously reported in references 5, 6, and 7.

II. **Nomenclature**

Symbol	Definition
A	Arbitrary aerodynamic model coefficient (Def. 1)
A	Angle-of-attack triples coefficient (Def.2)
A'	Angle-of-sideslip triples algorithm coefficient
a	Angle-of-sideslip triples algorithm coefficient
B	Arbitrary aerodynamic model coefficient (Def. 1)

B	Angle-of-attack triples coefficient (Def. 2)
B'	Angle-of-sideslip triples algorithm coefficient
b	Angle-of-sideslip triples algorithm coefficient
C	Angle-of-attack triples agorithm coefficient
C'	Angle-of-sideslip triples algorithm coefficient
F	Aerodynamic model functional
f	Initialization algorithm coefficient function
f	Nonlinear model functional
i,j,k	Indices
M	Median HI-FADS residual magnitude
Max[ ]	Maximum value for vector [ ]
N	Number of HI-FADS pressure observations
P	HI-FADS pressure
P_{max}	Maximum allowable pressure for reasonableness test
P_{min}	Minimum allowable pressure for reasonableness test
P_∞	HI-FADS static pressure
Prob( )	Probability of occurrence
Q	Least squares weighting matrix
Q_i	Residual weighting
q	Incompressible dynamic pressure
q_c	HI-FADS compressible dynamic pressure

s	Sample variance
x	Dummy variable of integration
α	Angle-of-attack
β	Angle-of-sideslip
δ	Model perturbation
∇	Gradient matrix
Γ	Gamma function
γ	Probability distribution degrees of freedom
δP	HI-FADS residual
ε	HI-FADS calibration coefficient
θ	Port incidence angle
λ	HI-FADS cone angle
μ	Residual mean
ξ	Number of parameters estimated from HI-FADS data
Σ	Summation operator
$\sigma\alpha$	Standard deviation of HI-FADS residuals
ϕ	HI-FADS clock angle
ν	Pressure measurement noise
χ^2	Random variable distributed as "Chi Square"
$\hat{\chi}^2$	Estimate of Chi-Square variable

III. Test Vehicle Description

The High Alpha Research Vehicle (HARV) is a single-place F-18 aircraft featuring dual engines and a mid-wing with leading and trailing edge flaps. The flight test noseboom has been removed to make way for the HI-FADS installation. The wingtip sidewinder launch racks have been removed and replaced with special camera pods and wingtip airdata booms. For reasons of flight safety during the HARV flight tests the vehicle was limited to 55 degrees angle of attack. The HARV vehicle and the high-angle-of-attack flight test program is described in detail in reference 8.

IV. Data Measurement Systems

The HI-FADS configuration has a simple hardware arrangement with the basic fixture being a fiberglass-reinforced-plastic cap mounted on the nose of the F-18 HARV. A set of 25, 0.046 inch (internal) diameter pressure orifices arranged in four annular rings, were drilled in the nosecap. Flight tests conducted during phase I of the HARV program, indicated that airdata could be satisfactorily measured using a subset of the 25 pressure ports. Test results obtained early in HI-FADS flight tests indicated that satisfactory airdata results can be achieved using as little as 7 pressure measurements. To allow for up to 4 pressure failures at any given data frame, 11 ports were chosen for the HI-FADS analyses; thus quad-redundancy for the pressure measurements could be achieved.

All results presented in this paper use
11-ports symmetrically distributed about the
nosecap. The locations of the nosecap ports
are defined using clock and cone angle
coordinates measured relative to the nosecap
axis of symmetry. The cone angle, λ, is the
total angle the normal to the surface makes
with respect to the nosecap axis of symmetry.
The clock angle, ϕ, is the clockwise angle
looking aft around the axis of symmetry
starting at the bottom of the fuselage. Figure
1 illustrates the definitions of the clock and
cone angles as well as the pressure ports
locations. The coordinate angles of the
various pressure ports used are listed in
Table I.

Table I:

HI-FADS Pressure Port Locations

Port #	Clock Angle (deg.)	Cone Angle (deg.)
1	0.0	0.0
2	0.0	40.0
3	180.0	40.0
4	0.0	55.0
5	90.0	55.0
6	180.0	55.0
7	270.0	55.0
8	45.0	60.0
9	135.0	60.0
10	225.0	60.0
11	315.0	60.0

Pressures at the nosecap were sensed by an electronically scanned pressure (ESP) module, remotely mounted in the aircraft nose cavity. Pressures at the surface were transported to the ESP module using lengths of flexible pneumatic tubing. Analyses performed in reference 7 indicate that the pneumatic tubing did not introduce any significant distortions in the measured pressure values in the bandwith of interest (0-25 Hz). The ESP module, which consists of differential transducers, was referenced to a single, high-accuracy absolute pressure transducer mounted in the aircraft nose cavity. High frequency dynamics in the reference pressure were attenuated by a damping tank also mounted in the aircraft nose. The temperature environments of both the ESP module and the reference transducer were controlled by wrapping the units in heater blankets to maintain a constant operating temperature. All HI-FADS pressure data were digitally encoded onboard using a 10-bit Pulse Code Modulation (PCM) system and telemetered to ground where selected pressures were displayed in real time. All HI-FADS data were recorded at 25 samples per second for post-flight analysis. More detail concerning the HARV flight test program and HI-FADS system hardware may be found in references 5, 6, 7, and 8. A

schematic of the HARV HI-FADS system is
depicted in figure 1.

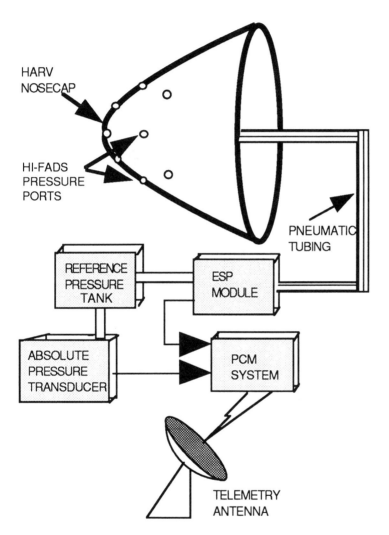

Figure 1: Schematic of HI-FADS System

In addition to the HI-FADS pressure
instrumentation, inertial velocity, aircraft
attitudes, and geometric altitude were
available from the aircraft inertial

navigation system (INS). For the high angle-of-attack flight tests a special research measurement acquisition system was installed. These research measurements included: linear accelerations and angular rates from strapdown acceleration and rate-gyro sensors; and airdata from two calibrated wingtip airdata booms--one on each wingtip.

The right wingtip airdata boom consisted of a pitot-static head with flow direction vanes. The left wingtip airdata boom consisted of a specially constructed swivel-head designed to align with the local air-velocity vector. This swivel design effectively eliminated total pressure loss at high angles of attack. Flow direction sensing vanes were also installed on the left wingtip boom. Prior to the HI-FADS flights, both wingtip booms were calibrated against a standard noseboom-sensor to a steady-state bias accuracy of better than ± 0.005 in Mach number and ± 0.5 deg.in angle-of-attack and -sideslip. Calibration validity range for the wingtip airdata sensors extended up to 40 degrees angle-of-attack. Beyond 40 degrees angle-of-attack the accuracy of the wingtip sensor measurements diminished rapidly due to flow separation at the wingtips. Both wing-tip booms were sensitive to vibration during high-angle-of-attack flight and loaded maneuvering.

All research data were digitally encoded
onboard using Pulse Code Modulation (PCM) and
telemetered to ground where they were
displayed in real time and recorded for post-
flight analysis. As will be described later,
these data, along with radar range data and
weather balloon information were used to
generate reference airdata values via minimum
variance estimation techniques. In this
procedure, high accuracy, high fidelity
reference airdata are generated by merging
complementary information from multiple data,
sources. These reference airdata values will
be used to calibrate the HI-FADS system.

V. __Aerodynamic Model__

This section develops a flow model which
can be used to relate the pressure
measurements to airdata quantities. The model
prescribes measured pressure in terms of four
airdata parameters: dynamic pressure, angle-
of-attack, angle-of-sideslip, and static
pressure. Using these four basic airdata
parameters most airdata quantities of interest
may be directly calculated. For incompressible
potential flow around a sphere, the pressure
coefficient at the surface is given as

$$C_p(\theta) = 1 - 9/4 \sin^2(\theta) = -5/4 + 9/4 \cos^2(\theta),$$

where, θ is the flow incidence angle at the surface. To account for a non-spherical nose shape, compressibility, and afterbody effects, the coefficients are allowed to assume arbitrary values while still retaining the basic *form* of the model, i.e.

$$C_p(\theta) = A + B \cos^2(\theta),$$

The coefficients, A and B are yet to be empirically determined. In order to satisfy conservation of momentum, the stagnation pressure constraint must be enforced (ref. 5), i.e., when $\theta=0$,

$$C_p(\theta=0) = A + B = q_c/q$$

where, q_c is the compressible dynamic pressure, and q is the incompressible dynamic pressure. This constraint may be built into the model by letting

$$A = \varepsilon \, q_c/q \,, \quad \text{and} \quad B = (1-\varepsilon) \, q_c/q \,,$$

where, ε is an aerodynamic calibration parameter yet to be empirically determined. Thus the model may be written as

$$
\begin{aligned}
C_p(\theta) &= q_c/q \, (\, \varepsilon + (1-\varepsilon) \cos^2(\theta) \,) \\
&= q_c/q \, (\, \cos^2(\theta) + \varepsilon \sin^2(\theta) \,)
\end{aligned}
$$

Applying the definition of the pressure coefficient, the model may be written in terms of pressure as

$$P(\phi_i, \lambda_i) = q_c \left[\cos{}^2(\theta_i) + \varepsilon \sin{}^2(\theta_i) \right] + P_\infty \qquad \text{Eqn.1a}$$

where, the coordinates are ϕ_i (clock angle) and λ_i (cone angle) The incidence angle between the surface and the velocity vector, θ_i, is related to the local angle-of-attack and angle-of-sideslip by taking the normalized inner product of the position vector with the free stream velocity vector

$$\text{Cos}(\theta i) = V \cdot R_i \{ ||V|| \ ||R_i|| \}^{-1}$$

to give

$$\cos(\theta_i) = \cos(\alpha)\cos(\beta)\cos(\lambda_i) +$$
$$\sin(\beta)\sin(\phi_i)\sin(\lambda_i) + \sin(\alpha)\cos(\beta)\cos(\phi_i)\sin(\lambda_i) \qquad \text{Eqn.1b}$$

Here angle-of-attack and angle-of-sideslip are not freestream values, but are the local flow angles which are influenced by aircraft induced upwash and sidewash. As with conventional intrusive airdata sensors, the aircraft-induced upwash and sidewash errors, $\delta\alpha$ and $\delta\beta$, must be independently calibrated for. In addition, the aerodynamic calibration parameter, ε, which accounts for non-ideal body shape, energy loss at high angle-of-attack, and compressibility must also be evaluated. Evaluation of the upwash, sidewash, and aerodynamic calibration parameters are described briefly in the Section X.A.

VI. HI-FADS Algorithm

Since the aerodynamic model is non-linear and cannot be directly inverted to give airdata as a function of the measured pressures, the measurements must be used to indirectly infer the airdata state using a non-linear least-squares regression. Within each data frame, the algorithm is linearized about a starting airdata value for each port location

$$P(\phi_i,\lambda_i) - f(\alpha_0,\beta_0,q_{c\infty_0},P_{\infty_0},\varepsilon,\phi_i,\lambda_i) \approx$$

$$\delta P(\phi_i,\lambda_i) = \frac{\partial f}{\partial \alpha}\Big|_0 \delta\alpha + \frac{\partial f}{\partial \beta}\Big|_0 \delta\beta + \frac{\partial f}{\partial q_c}\Big|_0 \delta q_C +$$

$$\frac{\partial f}{\partial P_\infty}\Big|_0 \delta p_\infty, \quad i=1, \ldots N \qquad \text{Eqn.1c}$$

where, $\alpha_0, \beta_0, q_{c\infty_0}, P_{\infty_0}$, are the values about which the algorithm is linearized, and N is the number of pressure observations available. In matrix form, equation 1c may be written as an N x 4 system of the form

$$\delta z = \Delta \ \delta x + v$$

where, δz is the vector of measurement
perturbations, Δ is the gradient matrix, δx is
the vector perturbation about the starting
value, and v is the measurement error. This
overdetermined system of perturbation
equations is solved using weighted least-
squares

$$\delta x = [\Delta^T Q \ \Delta]^{-1} \ \Delta^T Q \ \delta z$$

where Q is the weighting matrix. The resulting
perturbation is added to the starting value
and the system is relinearized about the
resulting update. The iteration cycle is
repeated until algorithm convergence is
reached--typically in 2 to 4 cycles.

At the beginning of each new data frame
the system is re-linearized about the result
of the previous frame, and the iteration is
repeated using new pressure data, thus the
algorithm is time-recursive as well as
iterative. The recursive, iterative, and
overdetermined (more observations than states)
structure makes the algorithm stable and
robust to perturbations in the measured
pressure data. As the Choleski Factorization
techniques used to perform the regression are
fairly standard, the numerical methods used
will not be presented here. Detailed

description of the regression algorithm can be found in ref 5.

VII. Algorithm   Initialization

In order for the regression algorithm to begin computations, a reasonable initial estimate of the airdata parameters must be available. For the HI-FADS algorithm, this initial estimate is provided by strategic manipulation of pressure "triples" which allow the angle-of-attack and angle-of-sideslip to be explicitly solved for. If three pressures along the vertical meridian (ϕ = 0, 180 deg.) are differenced and equation 1a is substituted, then an expression for incidence angle as a function of the measured pressures results

$$\frac{P_i - P_j}{P_j - P_k} = \frac{\cos^2(\theta_i) - \cos^2(\theta_j)}{\cos^2(\theta_j) - \cos^2(\theta_k)} \qquad \text{Eqn.2a}$$

Since the pressure triples lie along the central meridian where, $\sin(\phi)$ =0, β can be eliminated from equation 2a and the result,

$$\frac{P_i - P_j}{P_j - P_k} =$$

$$\frac{[\cos(\alpha)\cos(\lambda_i) + \sin(\alpha)\cos(\phi_i)\sin(\lambda_i)]^2 - [\cos(\alpha)\cos(\lambda_j) + \sin(\alpha)\cos(\phi_j)\sin(\lambda_j)]^2}{[\cos(\alpha)\cos(\lambda_j) + \sin(\alpha)\cos(\phi_j)\sin(\lambda_j)]^2 - [\cos(\alpha)\cos(\lambda_k) + \sin(\alpha)\cos(\phi_k)\sin(\lambda_k)]^2}$$

$$\text{Eqn. 2b}$$

with some manipulation, may be expressed in
terms of an easily solved quadratic equation
in Tan(α),

$$A \, Tan^2(\alpha) + 2BTan(\alpha) + C = 0 \qquad \text{Eqn.2c}$$

where

$$A = P_i\left[\, \sin^2(\lambda_j) - \sin^2(\lambda_k)\right]$$
$$+P_j\left[\, \sin^2(\lambda_k) - \sin^2(\lambda_i)\right]$$
$$+P_k\left[\, \sin^2(\lambda_i) - \sin^2(\lambda_j)\right]$$

$$B = P_i\left[\, \cos(\lambda_j)\cos(\phi_j)\sin(\lambda_j) - \cos(\lambda_k)\cos(\phi_k)\sin(\lambda_k)\right]$$
$$+P_j\left[\, \cos(\lambda_k)\cos(\phi_k)\sin(\lambda_k) - \cos(\lambda_i)\cos(\phi_i)\sin(\lambda_i)\right]$$
$$+P_k\left[\, \cos(\lambda_i)\cos(\phi_i)\sin(\lambda_i) - \cos(\lambda_j)\cos(\phi_j)\sin(\lambda_j)\right]$$

and

$$C = P_i\left[\, \cos^2(\lambda_j) - \cos^2(\lambda_k)\right]$$
$$+P_j\left[\, \cos^2(\lambda_k) - \cos^2(\lambda_i)\right]$$
$$+P_k\left[\, \cos^2(\lambda_i) - \cos^2(\lambda_j)\right]$$

Obviously, equation 2c will give two roots,
however, if one substitutes

$$\cos^2(\lambda) = 1 - \sin^2(\lambda),$$

then clearly, A=-C and the roots (guaranteed
to be real) are given by

$$Tan(\alpha) = -\frac{B}{A} \pm \sqrt{\left(\frac{B}{A}\right)^2 + 1}$$

Further, the product of the roots is always -
1, thus,

$$\text{Tan}(\alpha)_1 \, \text{Tan}(\alpha)_2 = -1$$

and the roots are complementary with
$\alpha_2 = \alpha_1 \pm 90°$ and one root will always lie
between -10 deg. and 80 deg. T root is chosen
as the solution.

A similar expression may be derived for
the angle-of-sideslip, where

$$A' \, \text{Tan}^2(\beta) + 2B' \text{Tan}(\beta) + C' = 0 \qquad \text{Eqn.2d}$$

$$A' = \left(P_i - P_j \right)\left(b_j^2 - b_k^2 \right) + \left(P_j - P_k \right)\left(b_j^2 - b_i^2 \right)$$

$$B' = \left(P_i - P_j \right)\left(a_j b_j - a_k b_k \right) + \left(P_j - P_k \right)\left(a_j b_j - a_i b_i \right)$$

$$C' = \left(P_i - P_j \right)\left(a_j^2 - a_k^2 \right) + \left(P_j - P_k \right)\left(a_j^2 - a_i^2 \right)$$

$$a_{i,j,k} = \cos(\alpha)\cos(\lambda_{i,j,k}) + \sin(\alpha)\sin(\lambda_{i,j,k})\cos(\phi_{i,j,k})$$

and
$$b_{i,j,k} = \sin(\lambda_{i,j,k})\sin(\phi_{i,j,k})$$

In Equation 2d, the pressure triples are not
constrained to lie along any particular plane
of symmetry. Again two roots for Tan(β) will
be obtained, and these roots will be
complementary. The value of β lying between
minus 20 deg. and 20 deg. is chosen as the
answer. In Equation 2d, angle-of-attack is
provided by pre-solving equation 2c. For the
HI-FADS geometry, multiple ports lie along the

vertical meridian and a large number of possible triples are available. The initial angle-of-attack is taken as the median of the values computed from all of the possible angle-of-attack triples. An even greater number of sideslip triples are available. Again the initial angle of sideslip is taken as the median of the values computed from all of the possible angle-of-sideslip triples.

Once the initial values for angle-of-attack and angle-of-sideslip have been estimated, equation 1a can be expressed as a linear equation in terms of q_c and p_∞, and if θ is evaluated using the "triples" values for α and β, then for N total pressure measurements

$$P_i = \left[\begin{pmatrix} \cos^2(\theta_i) + \\ \varepsilon \sin^2(\theta_i) \end{pmatrix} \qquad 1 \right] \begin{bmatrix} q_c \\ P_\infty \end{bmatrix}, \qquad i=1,N \qquad \text{Eqn.3a}$$

and the triples solution for q_c and p_∞ is given by linear least squares in closed form as

$$q_c = \frac{\left[N \sum_1^N (f_i P_i) \right] - \left[\sum_1^N (f_i) \right] \left[\sum_1^N (P_i) \right]}{\left[N \sum_1^N (f_i^2) \right] - \left[\sum_1^N (f_i) \right]^2} \qquad \text{Eqn.3b}$$

and

$$P_\infty = \frac{\left[\displaystyle\sum_1^N \left(f_i^2\right) \sum_1^N (P_i)\right] - \left[\displaystyle\sum_1^N (f_i)\right]\left[\sum_1^N (f_i P_i)\right]}{\left[N\displaystyle\sum_1^N \left(f_i^2\right)\right] - \left[\sum_1^N (f_i)\right]^2}$$

Eqn.3c

where

$$f_i = \cos^2(\theta_i) + \varepsilon \sin^2(\theta_i).$$

The "triples" algorithm tends to be noisy and is not robust to data perturbations; however, it allows a direct computation of the airdata using only measured pressures, and provides a good starting value. The starting airdata parameters are evaluated each time the algorithm is initialized and the HI-FADS regression is iterated to convergence (typically 4-5 iterations). Once initial convergence is reached, the triples algorithm is no longer used and the HI-FADS algorithm is operated in the recursive/iterative mode as discussed earlier.

VIII. Algorithm Stability

Difficulty with the non-linear regression algorithm occurs when a large disturbance such as a data spike or bit-dropout occurs in a measured pressure value. Recall that the HI-FADS algorithm is non-linear, consequently one true minimum and multiple false minima will exist. If a large disturbance is undetected and not weighted out of the regression, the resulting perturbation may dump the algorithm into a node which converges to a false minimum. At this point the algorithm will compute nonsensical results or may diverge altogether. In any case, once a false minimum has been reached, the algorithm will not reliably be able to return to the true minimum without re-initializing the algorithm with a new starting condition.

Figure 2 presents a one-dimensional illustration of the relationship between false minima and algorithm divergence. In figure 2, the marker indicates the value of the least squares cost index (the sum of the squares of the residuals) for a given value of the state estimate. When the marker lies at **1**, the algorithm is non-divergent but still needs additional iterations before convergence is reached. When the marker lies at **2**, the algorithm has reached the global minimum and has converged. If a large pressure deviation were to occur, the algorithm could be dumped into a false node, (marker **3**), and converge to a false minimum which returns a nonsensical answer, (marker at **4**). Since the algorithm is highly-nonlinear, no formal analysis of its stability characteristics has been performed.

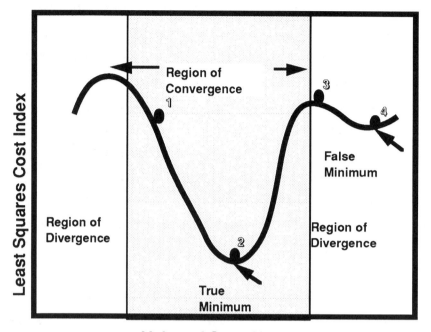

Value of State Variable

Figure 2: 1-Dimensional Illustration of HI-FADS
Algorithm Convergence and Divergence Regions

IX. Failure Detection and Fault Management

Although the multiple port HI-FADS system
is more tolerant to small measurement
disturbances than conventional intrusive
pitot-static airdata systems, as shown above,
under adverse circumstances large undetected
failures in individual pressure ports can
result in algorithm divergence and
catastrophic failure of the entire system.
Thus, development of a reliable failure
detection and fault-management methodology is

essential. This section demonstrates how individual port failures may be detected using $\chi 2$ "goodness-of-fit" analysis. Once identified, the effects of failures are eliminated using variable weights in the least squares algorithm. Background on $\chi 2$ analysis will be presented first. Failure detection and fault management techniques will then be developed from the basic background theory.

A. Background on $\chi 2$ Analysis

If a sample of N independent random data values is taken from a Gaussian distributed population with zero mean and unit variance, then the sum of the squares of those numbers is distributed according to the so-called "chi-squared" distribution (Refs. 9, 10)

$$\text{Prob}(\chi^2) = \int_0^{\chi^2} \frac{\left(\frac{1}{2}x\right)^{\frac{\gamma-2}{2}}}{2^{\gamma/2}\Gamma(\gamma/2)} e^{-\frac{1}{2}x} dx$$

Eqn. 4a

where, $\gamma = N\text{-}1$ degrees-of-freedom (DOF) for the distribution and $\Gamma(\gamma/2)$ is the gamma function evaluated at one-half of the degrees of freedom. In a Gaussian distributed population of random numbers with mean, μ and variance σ^2, if the sample variance, estimated by

$$s^2 = \sum_{1}^{N} \frac{(x-\mu)^2}{N-1}$$

is normalized by multiplying by

$$\frac{(N-1)}{\sigma^2}$$

then resulting ratio

$$\chi^2 \approx \frac{(N-1)}{\sigma^2} s^2$$

is a random number which is approximately distributed according to χ^2. For events selected from a completely independent population, the χ^2 parameter will have N-1 degrees of freedom. If the members of the population are related by ξ parameters which have been estimated from the data, the DOF is reduced by ξ, i.e. $\gamma = N - \xi - 1$.

Thus, if a small subset is taken randomly from a Gaussian-distributed population whose mean and variance are known, and the sample variance is evaluated for that subset; then the odds of randomly selecting that subset are readily evaluated using the "chi-square" distribution. As will be demonstrated in the HI-FADS Failure Detection and Fault Management Techniques section, this feature is particularly useful in least squares-types of problems for evaluating the accuracy of curve-

fits. The $\chi 2$ test is completely reliable and
for small sample populations, statisticians
regard this test as the singularly most
reliable "goodness of fit test" available
(Refs. 9, 10).

B. Application of $\chi 2$ Failure Detection to HI-
FADS System

As mentioned earlier, at the beginning of
each iteration, the HI-FADS algorithm
linearizes the aerodynamic model about the
result from the previous iteration. The first
step of this linearization is the evaluation
of the residuals between the measured pressure
data, and the HI-FADS model predictions for
each port

$$\delta P(\phi_i, \lambda_i) \approx P(\phi_i, \lambda_i) - f(\alpha_0, \beta_0, q_{c_0}, p_{\infty_0}, \varepsilon, \phi_i, \lambda_i)$$

where, i is the port index. For a given data
frame the HI-FADS residuals represent a small
subset of a larger random population whose
statistical properties may be empirically
evaluated using large samples of converged
airdata. If a smoothed histogram of the
residuals (divided by dynamic pressure to
scale the magnitudes) for a large data set is
evaluated, the result is a family of
approximately zero-mean, Gaussian probability

density curves whose variances are
proportional to angle-of-attack.

     For this family of curves the sample
variances, computed empirically using non-
failed HI-FADS flight data, are plotted as a
function of angle-of-attack in figure 3. These
sample variances, evaluated using
approximately one-half million data frames
from multiple flights, are assumed to
represent the true population statistics. Data
in which visual inspection determined that the
airdata computations were not-converged were
excluded from this sample set.

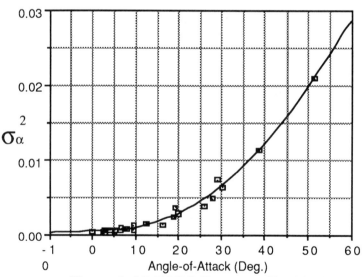

Figure 3: HI-FADS Pressure Residual
Variance as a Function of Angle-of-Attack

If the individual distributions for the
various angle of attack regions are normalized

by the sample-variance values taken from
figure 3, then the distributions reduce to a
single probability density curve that is very
close to the standard zero-mean, unity-
variance Gaussian probability density curve.
This comparison is presented in figure 4.

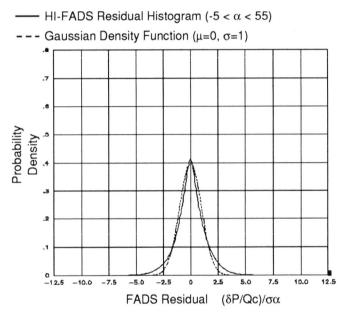

Figure 4: Normalized Probability Density for
HI-FADS Residuals

Since figure 4 gives clear evidence that
the individual residuals are Gaussian
distributed, for a given data frame the sum-
square of the scaled-residuals (divided by the
variance) should be distributed as a χ^2
variable with N-6 degrees of freedom. The DOF
are reduced by 5 because the residuals are
related by five parameters which have been
computed from them. These parameters are the

airdata states, qc, α, β, and P_∞, and the calibration parameter, ϵ. For the case of 11 ports, this would give a distribution with 5 DOF. Indeed the HI-FADs residuals behave according to this distribution. This is verified by evaluating

$$\hat{\chi}^2 = \sum_{i=1}^{N} \frac{\left[\frac{\delta P_i}{q_c}\right]^2}{\sigma_\alpha^2} \qquad \text{Eqn.4b}$$

at the beginning of each iteration, and plotting a histogram of the resulting values. In equation 4b, the variance, σ_α^2, is evaluated using the data of figure 4. The $\hat{\chi}^2$ histogram data are presented in figure 5. The theoretical and empirical density functions are in very close agreement.

Since the residual statistics were evaluated using only converged airdata values, at the beginning of an algorithm iteration, evaluating $\hat{\chi}^2$ allows the hypothesis for airdata failure to be evaluated by comparing the value of $\hat{\chi}^2$ against percentage points of $\chi 2$ distribution evaluated from

$$1 - \text{Prob}(\hat{\chi}^2) = \int_{\hat{\chi}^2}^{\infty} \frac{\left(\frac{1}{2}x\right)^{\frac{\gamma-2}{2}}}{2^{\gamma/2}\Gamma(\gamma/2)} e^{-\frac{1}{2}x} dx \qquad \text{Eqn.4c}$$

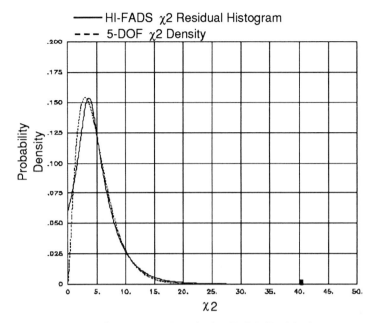

Figure 5: χ2 Density for FADS Residuals

In other words, the probability of a given value of $\widehat{\chi}^2$ occuring without some sort of airdata failure is given by equation 4c. Since $\widehat{\chi}^2$ is a relative probability indicator depending upon the value of $\widehat{\chi}^2$, various failure detection modes can be initiated.

HI-FADS flight data indicates that for a small value of $\widehat{\chi}^2$ the algorithm is near convergence and usually only one additional iteration is necessary. An intermediate value indicates that although the incoming pressure data is of reasonable quality, further iterations are likely required to reach convergence. A large value of $\widehat{\chi}^2$ indicates a high probability that a system failure has occurred and tests on individual pressure data should be performed.

Based on the relative probability properties of the $\chi 2$ distribution, the HI-FADS algorithm is designed to operate in three basic modes, a *nominal mode* in which only one iteration is performed at each data frame, an *iteration mode* in which multiple iterations are required to reach convergence, and a *fault management mode* in which individual pressure failures are detected and weighted out of the regression. Each of the algorithm modes will now be discussed in detail.

C. Nominal Mode

If equation 4c is evaluated for $\hat{\chi}^2$ = 1.61, a (5 DOF) probability of 90% results and indicates a significant likelihood that no airdata failure has occurred. In fact experience with HI-FADs data indicates that for low values of $\hat{\chi}^2$ the algorithm is near convergence and only one iteration per data frame is necessary. This one-iteration-per-data frame is the *nominal mode* for the algorithm and corresponds to the location of marker 2 in figure 2. The nominal mode is the regular operation mode of the algorithm and allows the fastest data throughput. For a 5

DOF system, the nominal mode is implemented as long as $\hat{\chi}^2 < 4.35$, which corresponds to a convergence probability of 50%. As will be illustrated in the Results section, only at high angles of attack, during highly dynamic flight conditions, or when data channel failures occur, does the algorithm drop out of the nominal mode.

D. Iteration Mode

Since a $\hat{\chi}^2$ value of 4.35 corresponds to a probability of approximately 50%, and indicates an equal probability of algorithm convergence or non-convergence. Experience with the HI-FADS data indicates that for intermediate values of $\hat{\chi}^2$, no airdata failure has occurred, however, several iterations may be required to reach the convergence point. In this regard the $\hat{\chi}^2$ value provides a solid convergence criterion. This is the *iteration mode* for the algorithm and corresponds to the location of marker 1 in figure 2. The iteration mode is usually entered at high angles-of-attack or loaded maneuvering and is somewhat slower than the nominal mode. For the 5 DOF system, the iteration mode is implemented when $4.35 \leq \hat{\chi}^2 < 15.1$.

E. Fault Management Mode

A $\hat{\chi}^2$ of 15.1 corresponds to a probability of 1% and indicates a high probability of failure somewhere in the airdata system. In this case some sort of individual channel failure detection and fault management must be implemented in order to keep the algorithm from diverging. This is the *fault management mode* of the algorithm. The fault management mode corresponds to the location of marker 3 in figure 2. Because testing on individual pressure values is required for each failed data frame, the throughput of the fault management mode is reduced considerably. For the 5 DOF system, the fault management mode is implemented when
$$15.1 \leq \hat{\chi}^2$$

The fault management tests which are implemented when the system has failed the χ^2 test (and the fault management mode is entered) will now be defined. The utility of the χ^2 method as an indicator of the overall system health is that it allows a nominal algorithm operation with very little overhead for fault-detection. Failure tests on individual ports need to be performed only when a χ^2 test failure has occurred.

Typically, when a $\chi 2$ failure has occurred, a series of tests, starting from very simple and evolving to very complex and computationally intensive, can be performed. For the HI-FADS algorithm, four tests for individual port failures have been implemented.

The first fault management test is a simple reasonableness check. Upon failure of the $\chi 2$ test ($\hat{\chi}^2$ >15.1 for 5 DOF), the weight of any pressure data value which is less than a specified minimum or greater than a specified maximum is set to zero. Data values which lie between the specified minimum and maximum values are given a weight of 1. The weighted $\hat{\chi}^2$ is re-evaluated using the new weights,

$$\hat{\chi}^2 = \sum_{i=1}^{N} \frac{Q_i \left[\frac{\delta P_i}{q_c}\right]^2}{\sigma_\alpha^2} \qquad \text{Eqn.4d}$$

and the result is compared against the percentage points of $\chi 2$ distribution for

$$\gamma = \sum_{i=1}^{N} Q_i - 6$$

degrees of freedom. If the corresponding probability percentage is greater than or equal to 1% (the probability at which the fault management mode is entered) and $\gamma > 0.0$, the algorithm drops out of the failure testing mode and enters the iteration mode using the newly assigned weights.

If after the reasonableness test has been implemented, $\text{Prob}(\hat{\chi}^2)$ <1% or $\gamma \leq 0.0$, then the next failure detection test, a three-sigma residual test where the weights are re-assigned based on residual magnitudes, is performed. For each of the data channels, if $\delta p_i/q_c < \sigma_\alpha$, then $Q_i = 1.0$. If $\sigma_\alpha < \delta p/q_c < 3\sigma_\alpha$, then the weight for that residual is set to

$$Q_i = -\frac{1}{2} \left\{ \frac{\left[\frac{\delta P_i}{q_c}\right]^2}{\sigma_\alpha^2} \right\} + \frac{3}{2} \, ,$$

For $3\sigma_\alpha < \delta p/q_c$ the weight is set to zero. After re-evaluating the weights, the weighted $\hat{\chi}^2$ value is evaluated again and compared against percentage points of $\chi 2$ distribution for

$$\gamma = \sum_{i=1}^{N} Q_i \, - 6$$

degrees of freedom. If the resulting $\text{Prob}(\hat{\chi}^2)$ $\geq 1\%$ and $\gamma > 0.0$, the algorithm drops out of the failure testing mode and enters the iteration mode using the newly assigned weights. Note that for this tests in which

fractional weights are allowable, non-integer
values for the degrees of freedom are
possible.

If after the 3-σ test has been completed,
Prob($\hat{\chi}^2$) <1% or $\gamma \leq 0.0$, then the next failure
detection test is implemented. The third test,
a measurement consistency test, is more
computationally intensive than are the two
previous tests and is intended as a "catch-
all" test. The term "consistency" refers to
equality of the residual magnitudes. For this
test the weight of the residual whose
magnitude is farthest from the median residual
magnitude is set to zero. All other weights
are set to 1. The weighted value of $\hat{\chi}^2$ is
evaluated and the result is compared against
Prob($\hat{\chi}^2$) for N-7 degrees of freedom. If
Prob($\hat{\chi}^2$) $\geq$ 1% the algorithm drops out of the
failure testing mode and enters the iteration
mode using the newly assigned weights. If
Prob(χ2) <1% , then the weight of the residual
whose magnitude is next farthest from the
median is set to zero. The weighted value of
$\hat{\chi}^2$ is again computed and the results are
compared against Prob($\hat{\chi}^2$) for N-8 degrees of
freedom. Again if Prob($\hat{\chi}^2$) $\geq$ 1%, the
algorithm drops out of the testing loop;

otherwise, the process is repeated again until
or $\gamma \leq 0$.

If $\gamma \leq 0$ at the end of the consistency
test cycle, then either the hold-last-value or
reset sub-modes will be entered. The hold-last
value sub-mode is entered first. In this mode,
the least squares regression is bypassed and
the value of the airdata state remains
unchanged. After skipping the regression, all
of the weights are set to 1.0, the hold index
(which indicates the number of consecutive
holds) is incremented, and the algorithm
returns to the nominal mode for the next data
frame. The hold-last value sub-mode allows
small sections of corrupt input data to be
passed over without triggering algorithm
divergence or nuisance resets.

If the hold-last-value mode has been
entered for a specified number (default 20) of
consecutive data frames, then the algorithm
has likely diverged, and the reset sub-mode is
entered. This condition corresponds to the
location of marker 4 in figure 2. In this case
algorithm must be reinitialized using a new
set of starting values using the triples
algorithm discussed earlier. After re-
linearization, the algorithm is iterated to

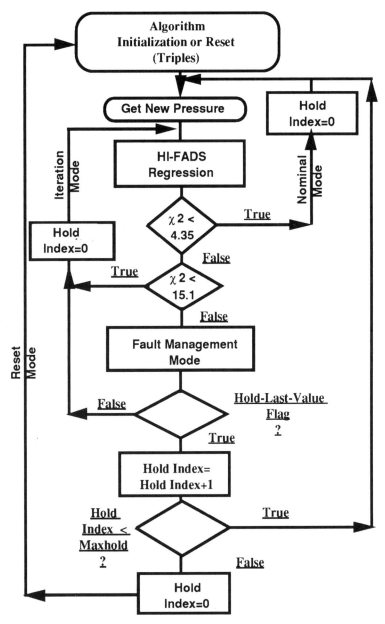

Figure 6 Schematic of HI-FADS
Fault Management Structure

convergence; all of the weights are set to
1.0, the hold index is set to zero, and the
nominal mode is entered. A schematic of the

HI-FADS fault management structure is presented in figure 6.

X. Results

Results of the flight test evaluation of the HI-FADS system will now be presented. First a brief discussion of the aerodynamic calibration will be presented. Next flight data which demonstrates the system performance and accuracy will be presented. Finally, application of the $\chi 2$ failure detection and fault management to prevent divergence of HI-FADS system will be presented.

A. Aerodynamic Calibration Parameters

The calibration parameters were identified using reference airdata values generated from flight data via the Minimum Variance Estimation techniques of references 11, 12, and 13. In this procedure, high accuracy, high fidelity reference airdata are generated by merging complementary information from multiple data sources provided by the research data acquisition system, the INS, and external measurements such as radar tracking and weather balloon data.

All flight maneuvers used to generate the reference trajectories were pre- and post-

ceeded by approximately 20 seconds of
stabilized low angle-of-attack flight. During
this stabilized flight, the wingtip boom
airdata were weighted heavily to give initial
and final estimates of the atmospheric winds.
During the course of the calibration
maneuvers, filter weights were varied to
weight or de-weight the wingboom airdata.

The calibration parameters $\delta\alpha$, $\delta\beta$, and ϵ,
were estimated by substituting the reference
airdata into the aerodynamic model and
comparing the model's pressure predictions to
the pressures which were actually measured.
Residuals between the measured and predicted
pressures were then used to infer the values
of the calibration parameters at each data
frame using a non-linear regression similar to
the HI-FADS algorithm.

Systematic trends in the calibration
parameters were identified by plotting the
estimated calibration parameters as a
function of flight variables and visually
inspecting the results. Once trends were
identified by visual inspection, they were
curve fit and interpolated to generate a
series of tabular breakpoints which were hard-
coded into the HI-FADS algorithm. The
resulting calibration trend are presented in
figures 7a through 7d. Because the HI-FADS

system actually measures local and not
freestream angles-of-attack and -sideslip,
calibration results are presented in terms of
the measured (local) flow angles.

Calibration data for the upwash parameter
$\delta\alpha$ are presented in figure 7a. Plotted on the
ordinate axis is $\delta\alpha$, plotted on the abscissa is
the local angle-of-attack as measured by the
HI-FADS system. The scatter in $\delta\alpha$ grows with
decreasing Mach number, however, $\delta\alpha$ did not
trend with either Mach number or angle-of-
sideslip in a clearly discernable manner.

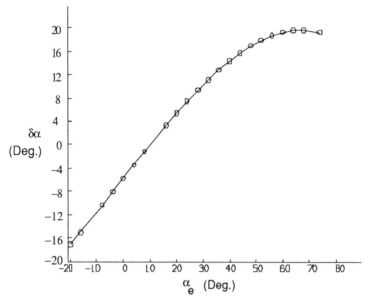

Figure 7a: Calibration Results:
Angle-of-Attack Upwash Parameter

Similar calibration data for the sidewash parameter $\delta\beta$ are presented in figure 7b.

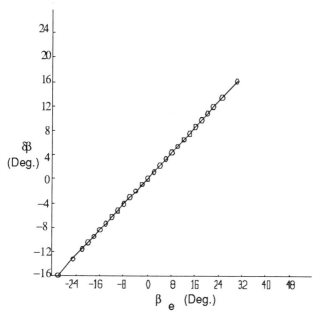

Figure 7b: Calibration Results: Angle-of-Sideslip Sidewash Parameter

Plotted on the ordinate axis is $\delta\beta$, plotted on the abscissa is the local angle-of-sideslip as measured by the HI-FADS system. As with angle of attack, the scatter in $\delta\beta$ increased with decreasing Mach number, and $\delta\beta$ did not trend with either Mach number or angle-of-attack.

Finally, calibration breakpoints for ε are presented in figures 7c and 7d. During the course of the analysis, it was empirically determined that ε may be decomposed into two components: ε_M, which varies as a function of

Mach number, and ε_α, which varies as a function of angle-of-attack, with

$$\varepsilon = \varepsilon_M + \varepsilon_\alpha$$

In figure 7c, ε_M is plotted on the ordinate axis, while Mach number is plotted on the abscissa.

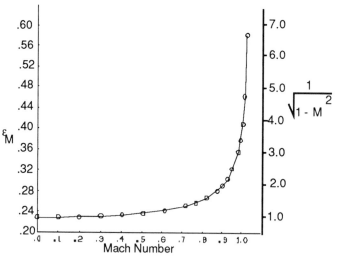

Figure 7c: Calibration Results: ε_M Parameter

Interestingly, the break points of figure 7c closely resemble the curve prescribed by the Prantl-Glauret transformation, an affine transformation where the *incompressible* pressure coefficient is divided by

$$[1 - M_\infty 2]^{(1/2)}$$

to give the *compressible* pressure coefficient. Thus, at least heuristically, ε_M, may be

thought of as a compressibility correction on
the aerodynamic model.

In figure 7d, ε_α is plotted on the
ordinate axis, while angle-of-attack is
plotted on the abscissa. Stagnation pressure
data presented in reference 14 indicate that
ε_α may be considered as an adjustment for the
loss of total flow energy at the HI-FADS
sensing array due to the increasing average
flow angularity over all the pressure ports.

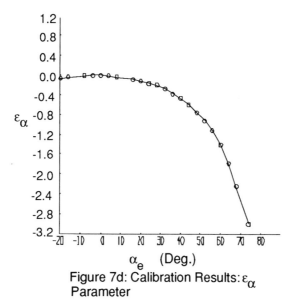

Figure 7d: Calibration Results: ε_α
Parameter

For the moderate angles-of-sideslip
encountered in the HARV HI-FADS tests, no
systematic trend relating angle-of-sideslip to
ε was discernable.

B. Evaluation of HI-FADS System Performance

The performance of the HI-FADS system was empirically evaluated using flight data, where comparisons between various HI-FADS derived airdata estimates and the corresponding reference airdata parameters were performed. The reference airdata were generated using the minimum variance estimation techniques as described previously. During the HARV flight tests, excellent results were achieved for flights conditions up to 55 deg. angle-of-attack and 1.20 Mach number. Standard errors were empirically determined to be approximately one-half degree in angle-of-attack and angle-of-sideslip, and better than 0.004 in Mach Number. These quantitative accuracy levels were obtained by evaluating the sample root mean square (RMS) of the residual between the HI-FADS and reference airdata parameters for a variety of maneuvers. These results are presented in Table II.

Table II:
HI-FADS Airdata Residual RMS Values

Parameter	RMS ($\alpha<20$ deg.)	RMS ($\alpha>20$ deg.)
$\delta\alpha$	0.25 deg.	0.56 deg.
$\delta\beta$	0.25 deg.	0.52 deg.
δM_∞	0.003	0.0040
δV_∞	4.0 ft/sec	10.0 ft/sec
δH_p	11.3 ft.	19.2 ft.

Eight flight maneuvers, obtained from different flights, were used to perform the statistical evaluation, a data base of approximately 45,000 data frames. Over the entire data base, even at high angles-of-attack ($\alpha >$ 20 deg.), the RMS of the HI-FADS residuals is approximately 1/2 degree in angle-of-attack and -sideslip, and 0.004 in Mach Number. At low angles-of-attack ($\alpha \leq$ 20 deg.), the RMS is approximately 1/4 degrees for α and β, and .003 for Mach number. Corresponding airspeed and altitude RMS values are also listed. In interpreting these RMS values, recognize that at least some portion of the residual error is due to the reference trajectories themselves.

As an illustration of typical flight results, data from a moderate rate dutch-roll maneuver will be presented. These HI-FADS results, performed using the 11-port configuration, were not previously used in establishing the calibration tables. Comparisons of HI-FADS and reference angles-of-attack are presented in figure 8. Presented in figure 8a are the actual angle-of-attack time histories. Two curves are presented--the reference angle-of-attack and the HI-FADS angle-of-attack. For the scale used no differences are discernable. Actual differences may be discerned by plotting the

time history of the residual between the HI-
FADS and reference angles-of attack. This
residual time history is presented in figure
8b. Similar comparisons for Mach number are
presented in figures 8c and 8d. With the
exception of minor deviations during the high
rate portions of the maneuver, it is difficult
to identify any differences between the HI-
FADS and reference airdata values.

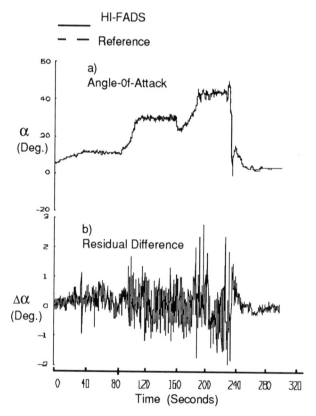

Figure 8: Dutch Roll Maneuver Time
History Comparisons: Angle-of-Attack

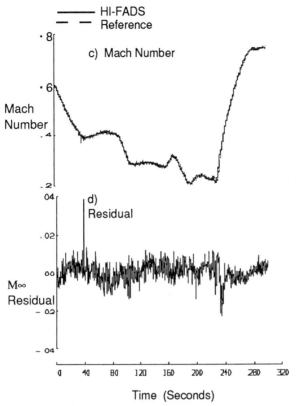

Figure 8 : Dutch Roll Maneuver Time History
Comparison: Mach Number

C. Application of Failure Detection and Fault Management to HI-FADS Flight Data

Applications of the failure detection and fault management techniques are now illustrated using F-18 HARV flight data. In the case to be illustrated, several of the pressure channels experienced large data spikes due to the malfunction of a signal conditioning circuit designed to zero out the DC-level reading of the pressure transducers.

The corrupted pressure data time histories are presented in figure 9a.

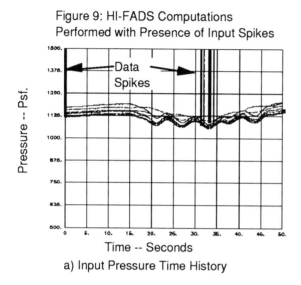

Figure 9: HI-FADS Computations
Performed with Presence of Input Spikes

a) Input Pressure Time History

If the corrupted data are passed to the HI-FADS algorithm unprotected, the algorithm converges to an erroneous solution and the diverged angle of attack time history is presented in figure 9b.

Figure 9: HI-FADS Computations
Performed with Presence of Input Spikes

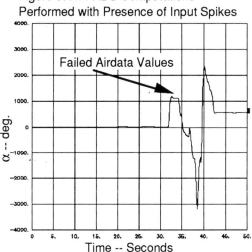

Failed Airdata Values

Time -- Seconds

b) Diverged HI-FADS Angle-of-Attack Time
History (No Divergence Protection)

When the fault management schemes are
implemented and the algorithm is run with full
divergence protection, the resulting angle-of-
attack value is presented in figure 9c. In
this case the algorithm converges and proceeds
in the nominal mode, with the effects of the
data dropout being indistinguishable.

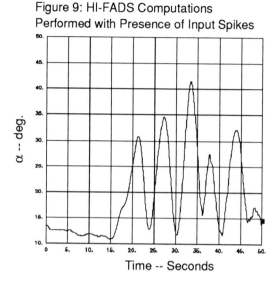

Figure 9: HI-FADS Computations
Performed with Presence of Input Spikes

c) HI-FADS Angle-of-Attack Time
History for Divergence Protected
Algorithm

The computed $\chi 2$ time history is presented in Figure 9d. Only at the large $\chi 2$ values, was the failure testing and fault management mode initiated. The method clearly works as expected. No actual data failures which required the algorithm to enter the consistency tests or trip the hold-last value or reset sub-modes were experienced during the HI-FADS flight tests. These sub-modes were exercised, and verified through extensive simulation. Results of this validation and verification effort will not be presented.

Figure 9: HI-FADS Computations
Performed with Presence of Input Spikes

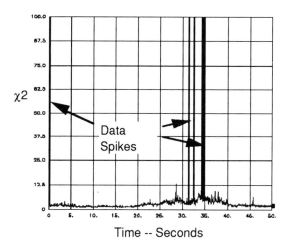

Time -- Seconds

d) $\chi 2$ Time History for
divergence protected algorithm

XI. <u>Summary and Concluding Remarks</u>

A prototype non-intrusive airdata system
was installed and flight tested on the F-18
High Alpha Research Vehicle at NASA Ames
Dryden Flight Research Facility. This system
utilized a matrix of pressure orifices
arranged in concentric circles on the nose of
the vehicle to estimate the airdata
parameters. The HI-FADS system incorporates an
over determined algorithm in which *all* surface
pressure observations are used simultaneously
to infer the airdata parameters using nonlinear regression. The advantage of this
overdetermined method is that the airdata

computations are insensitive to small disturbances in the incoming pressure data.

The HI-FADS system was calibrated using flight maneuvers which covered a large range of Mach number, and angle-of-attack. Reference airdata for the system calibration were generated using a minimum variance estimation technique which blended airdata measurements from two wingtip airdata booms with inertial velocities, aircraft angular rates and attitudes, precision radar tracking, and meteorological analyses.

Standard errors were empirically determined to be better than one-half degree in angle-of-attack and angle-of-sideslip, and better than 0.004 in Mach Number. These quantitative accuracy levels were obtained by evaluating the sample root mean square (RMS) of the residual between the HI-FADS and reference airdata parameters for a variety of maneuvers. Evaluations were performed using data from flights other than those used to perform the calibrations. Excellent results were achieved for flights conditions up 55 deg. angle-of-attack and 1.20 Mach number.

Results presented indicated that if a large disturbance in a measured pressure value is passed undetected into the HI-FADS algorithm, the resulting state perturbation may dump the algorithm into a false minimum and algorithm divergence can result. The need for some sort of algorithm protection was discussed. Failure detection and fault management techniques based on χ^2 analysis and weighted least squares were developed. This paper demonstrates how system failures may be detected using χ^2 analysis. Once identified, the effects of failures are eliminated using weighted least squares. Data obtained from the HARV flight tests are used to demonstrate the techniques.

Use of the developed failure detection and fault management techniques allows a single pressure measurement matrix to be multiply redundant. As illustrated with flight data, the χ^2 method allows several of the pressure measurements to fail simultaneously with little or no degradation of the resulting airdata computations The utility of the χ^2 method as an indicator of the overall system health is that it requires very little overhead for fault-detection. Failure tests on individual ports must be performed only when a χ^2 test failure has occurred and allows the algorithm to operate in a nominal mode with a much greater computational throughput than would be possible if multiple iterations and individual pressure checking were required at each data frame. The increased throughput will be very valuable for feedback systems in which the maximum available airdata rate is desired.

XI. References

1) Gracey, William, *Measurement of Aircraft Speed and Altitude*, NASA Reference Publication 1046, 1980

2)   Siemers, Paul M., III, Wolf, Henry, and Henry, Martin w., *Shuttle Entry Airdata System (SEADS)-Flight Verification of an Advanced Air Data System Concept*, AIAA Paper 88-2104

3)   Larson, Terry J., and Siemers, Paul M., III, *Subsonic Investigation of an All-Flush Orifices Airdata System*, NASA TP-1643, 1980

4)   Larson, Terry J., Whitmore, Stephen A., Ehernberger, L. J., Johnson, J. Blair, and Siemers, Paul M., III, *Qualitative Evaluation of a Flush Airdata System at Transonic Speeds and High Angles of Attack*, NASA TP-12716, 1987

5)   Whitmore, Stephen A., Moes, Timothy R., and Larson, Terry J., *Preliminary Results From a Subsonic High Angle-of-Attack Flush Airdata Sensing (Hi-FADS) System: Design, Calibration, and Flight Test Evaluation*, NASA TM-101713, 1990

6)   Moes, Timothy R., and Whitmore, Stephen A., *Preliminary Results From an Inertial Airdata Enhancement Algorithm with Application to High Angle-of-Attack*, NASA TM-101737, 1991

7)   Whitmore, Stephen A., and Moes, Timothy R., *The Effects of Pressure Sensor Acoustics on Airdata Derived From a High-Angle-of-Attack Flush Airdata Sensing (HI-FADS) System*, AIAA Paper 91-0671, 1991

8)   Schneider, Edward T., and Meyer, Robert R., Jr., *F-18 High Alpha Research Vehicle Description, Results, and Plans,* Society of Experimental Test Pilots (SETP), 1989 Report to the Aerospace Profession, Proceedings, 1989.

9) Bendat, Julius S., and Piersol, Allan G., *Random Data: Analysis and Measurement Procedures,* John Wiley & Sons, Wiley-Interscience, New York, 1971.

10) Freiberger, W. F. , ed., *The International Dictionary of Applied Mathematics,* D. Van Nostrand Co., Inc, Princeton, New Jersey, 1960.

11)   Whitmore, Stephen A., *Reconstruction of the Shuttle Reentry Air Data Parameters Using a Linearized Kalman Filter,* AIAA Paper 83-2097, Aug. 1983.

12) Whitmore, Stephen A., *Formulation and Implementation of A Non-Stationary Adaptive Estimation Algolrithm with Applications to Air-Data Reconstruction,* NASA TM 86727, May, 1985.

13)   Whitmore, Stephen A., Larson, Terry J., and Ehernberger, L. J., *Air Position-Error Calibration Using State Reconstruction Techniques,* NASA TM 86029, September, 1984.

14)   Gracey, William, *Wind-Tunnel Investigation of a Number of Total-Pressure Tubes at High Angles of Attack: Subsonic, Transonic, and Supersonic Speeds,* NACA Technical Report 1303, 1957.

COMMAND, CONTROL AND COMMUNICATIONS: THE HUMAN ROLE IN MILITARY C3 SYSTEMS

G.A. Clapp

Communications Department
Naval Oceans Systems Center
San Diego, CA 92152-5000

D.D. Sworder

Department of AMES
University of California, San Diego
La Jolla, CA 92093-0411

I. INTRODUCTION

To better understand what C^3 entails, a broad definition is useful. One such definition can be obtained by paraphrasing a quotation given in [1].

> Command, control, and communications is the military organizational structure which exercises authority and direction over the available forces in the accomplishment of a specific mission. Battle management functions are performed through an arrangement of equipment, communications, facilities, and subsystem interactions which are employed in directing, coordinating and controlling forces and operations in the accomplishment of the mission.

While vague in some respects, this definition captures the ubiquitous nature of C^3, and focuses attention on the distinction between the all-encompassing system, and its numerous but subordinate parts. In its static state, C^3 assets are aggregates of sensors, weapons, people, computer hardware/software, mobile platforms and communications equipment distributed over wide areas. In a dynamic environment, these assets must be utilized in the presence of uncertain and unknown threats, evolving missions, changing environments, mixed with unreliable communications and possible deception. Events take place over wide geographical regions, and at a mixture of tempos. Under even the best of conditions, C³ systems operate in environments characterized by "noisy" information transfer. Indeed, an epigrammatical definition is that *C³ is the mapping of assets into capabilities.* Actions can, when necessary, follow directly from the capability so generated. When interpreted in this way, it is apparent that the systems aspect of C³ is manifest in the architecture.

The role of the human decisionmaker in C³ does not alter this fundamental view. Many functions can be performed either by a human or by an algorithmic surrogate. Clearly, any task involving the expeditious processing of large quantities of data is of necessity outside the human purview. A judicious aggregation of the data can enable a human to adroitly make those critical decisions upon which the success of the system depends. Changes in rules-of-engagement, demonstration of national will and resolve, and placing the system on alert status are inherently human decisions that must be referred to the National Command Authorities (NCA) acting in a direct management role.

There are C³ concerns which transcend the questions addressed at the subsystem level. This point of view is made clear in the Eastport Study [2] which emphasizes the fact "designing the system first and then writing the software to control it is the wrong approach" for C³. Rather, the performance of subsystem elements must be gauged in terms of quantitative measures of effectiveness (MOE's) related to the ability of the system to accomplish its objectives. It is the current lack of understanding of the explicit behavior of rationally chosen MOE's that prevents the express examination of C³ issues from being universally accepted as a research topic. The need for a broader view is made clear by H.L. Van Trees; "The utility of communications, intelligence, warning, surveillance and reconnaissance cannot be determined without casting these systems in a command and control systems context and understanding ... the dependencies and interrelationships which exist among these contributing subsystems. The ability to evaluate and understand command and control systems which are working properly as designed in situations that are correctly anticipated is not enough. The increasing investment which our adversaries are making in developing countermeasures and in their own command and control systems heightens the need to understand how our systems would operate at diminished levels of capacity and capability and the impact of this reduced performance on our fighting capability".[3]

This chapter describes some recent results in C^3 modeling with an emphasis on the dynamics of human decisionmakers. A comprehensive C^3 model should display: 1) A tractable structure permitting the evaluation of influence functions; 2) Explicit communication dependence; 3) Amenability to aggregation and disaggregation. It would appear that system science would provide a natural paradigm for such a quantitative description. Athans clearly articulates this view in [4], and he observes that C^3 systems "are characterized by a high degree of complexity, a generic distribution of the decision-making process among several decision making 'agents,' the need for reliable operation in the presence of multiple failures, and the inevitable interaction of humans with computer-based decision support systems and decision aids." Without contradicting this point of view, it should be stressed that a C^3 system differs from those commonly discussed in the literature of system theory in at least three primary ways:

1. Military C^3, while supported by an imposing array of sensors, computers, displays communications and weapons is in its essence a human decision making activity. As pointed out in [5] "we need to recognize that the process of military command and control ... is an extension by means of systems of equipment, personnel and procedures of the human decision making process imbedded in a military organization."

2. Any effective C^3 system must have the capacity to evolve over time, and this flexibility must be reflected explicitly in the model. Such systems are frequently established with a limited set of elements. During their lifetime these elements will be modified or replaced, and their roles expanded or constricted as changing demands are placed upon the system. Hence, a flexible description which permits a restructuring of the model on the basis of technological improvements and changing world conditions is an indispensable requirement.

3. In contrast to conventional system design problems, there is no single nominal operating condition about which the system is maintained. Indeed, an important attribute of a C^3 system is its the ability to respond to major changes in condition. Unfortunately, the times of occurrence and the sensory signature of these changes in condition are often ambiguously conveyed by the data received by the command authorities. Furthermore, the system is often used in environments quite different from those envisioned in its design. Hence, the uncertain circumstances within which the decision makers must accomplish their tasks must be properly reflected in the model.

As this cursory review of the issues involved makes clear, a quantitative model of a general C^3 process would be very useful. However, the construction of a flexible model is not without considerable difficulty. In the next sections, some of the basic requisites will be discussed along with observations on the current status of this research activity.

II. ARCHITECTURE, ALGORITHMS, AND COMMUNICATIONS

The study of C^3 leads naturally to an investigation of different architectures, as indeed, the system architecture is the explicit manifestation of a C^3 concept. Architectural forms range from those that are highly centralized to those that are nearly autonomous. The former are vulnerable to countermeasures, and may introduce unacceptable time delays, but they are highly efficient in resource allocation. The latter are more survivable, but are "notoriously" inefficient in their utilization of scarce resources. In any event, communications technology is fundamental to all C^3 functions. Any communications architecture must simultaneously support a sensor architecture, a weapons architecture, a C^2 architecture, and a system adaptation architecture. Ideally, the communication links would be "transparent," i.e., information that is required at any node is assumed to be transmitted to that node unambiguously and with minimal delay. Unfortunately, delayed, omitted, partial, inaccurate or irrelevant (DOPII) information is endemic in geographically distributed communication networks and their supported architectures. Each of the DOPII classes have characteristics have characteristics that are not readily amenable to computer-based algorithmic treatment.

While it is evident that communications by themselves do not convert algorithms into command and control functions, critical battle management issues arise when the communications are not transparent to all users. The decision makers do not operate in a void. They, along with all of the other action nodes in the system, depend upon a sophisticated communication network to provide the information upon which asset allocation is based. Although mentioned peripherally, a detailed examination of the communications issues is frequently not made explicit in current models. This neglect is not replicated in Defense Department purchasing decisions. The investment in communication assets has increased exponentially over the past decade or so, and the gross utilization of these assets has kept pace with their creation.[1] This seems to imply that the demand for data is essentially infinitely elastic, and will not be satisfied by any

---

[1] H.L. Van Trees in a talk at the 1988 Command and Control Research Symposium, Monterey CA, 1988.

reasonable increase in capacity. It has , however, been pointed out that there is no evidence that this increase in transfer rate of data is being matched by a comparable increase in the transfer of useful information. Indeed, anecdotal comments suggest that much of the communication network is now being used for the transfer of data that is of little import. This overloading of the communications network with superfluous transmissions is more than an aesthetic liability. Communications are essential to the proper operation of the C^3 network, but they are vulnerable to interdiction.

It has been suggested that dynamic communications assessment and allocation may "become a critical technology area by the beginning of the next century."[6] A contentious issue in C^3 system design is the allocation of the available communication assets; i.e., what are desirable topological properties of the communications network? When attention is focused on the vexing algorithmic difficulties at the nodes of the system, it is easy to lose sight of the fact that the basic limitation on the effectiveness of the system rests equally and jointly on its ability to guarantee that the requisite quality and quantity of information is available at each node. A shared approach to communication which permits a reallocation of under-utilized channel capacity would improve survivablitiy and flexibility by not requiring critical users to be wholly dependent upon a single communication link.

The possibility of having a dynamic networking control of the communications assets requires considerable attention to the proper identification of the communication state of the system. There are several conventional classes of communications related aberrations:

1. OVERLOAD: More information is being supplied to an operational node than it can handle. This could be a major problem at the corporeal nodes since people can be overwhelmed by superfluous data.

2. ANOMALY: Signals may occur that are outside the range the node is trained or programmed to recognize. Information outside of the recognized domain of discourse can create deviant and wholly inappropriate behavior, though people seem to adapt better to this than do most software algorithms.

3. UNDERLOAD: Algorithms are designed to process a certain flow of input data. When this information does not arrive in a timely fashion, or only arrives in part, or does not arrive at all, the algorithm may again display atypical behavior.

As the above discussion indicates, the response at each node cannot be determined without a careful delineation of the communication network that supplies the node. This in turn depends upon the functional requirements to be met at the nodes, i.e., on the degree of autonomy with which the elements of the system perform their functions. There is, therefore, a need to consider system design in a more extended fashion. The current research effort has led to techniques that help to derive "good" conclusions from marginal communication links. What is needed is the integration of a class of "active" nodes which will clarify anomalous data, and seek missing data by active search. These nodes often contain human decisionmakers who infer the network state, and then choose how to best obtain the requisite data. It has been suggested that roughly half the cost of a complex system accrues to personnel related expenses.[7] To judiciously expend this money, a careful study of the best way in which to utilize the human decision making processes is essential. Similarly, performance descriptions should include the effect of human decisionmakers as an integrated part of the system.

III. THE ROLE OF THE HUMAN DECISION MAKER IN C³

In descriptions of C³ systems the function of human decision makers reappears in various contexts. The specification of precise roles for humans is a controversial theme in discussions of complex systems, both military and civil. Rigorous reasons for this fixation on giving a human an online role are difficult to articulate. One might infer that the justification rests upon simple anthropocentric apologetics. Indeed, in many discussions of complex systems the human is not thought of as an integral part of the system architecture, but is rather given an external position as a "user" of data or an "input" to the rest of the system. This extrinsic view of the human has led some investigators to relegate the human to a very limited position in C³ systems. This circumscribed place of the human is unsatisfactory. The basic issue is how to define and support the role of human decision making, given the characteristics and limitations of the human information processing capabilities. Even an automated system requires a human initiator. Initiation of weapon system on-off switches, a technically simple task, can have catastrophic results if done at an inopportune time. A human, acting as an overseer, must determine whether or not the observations indicate the occurrence of an event requiring a specified action. In any such situation, a set of hypotheses covering the possible operational circumstances is formed; e.g., aircraft detected, high performance aircraft with trajectory of concern detected, missile detection associated with subject aircraft, etc. When some hypotheses subsume others, a set of mutually exclusive

hypotheses on the same event space can be generated which spans the set of acknowl-
edged possibilities. As data is acquired, confidence in a given hypothesis will be
strengthened or weakened. As the encounter evolves, and an old hypothesis is rejected,
all subsequent observations must be reinterpreted in this light. Ultimately, it is the
dynamics of the process of hypothesis formulation and acceptance/rejection that
determines the outcome of the many engagements.

Many techniques and methodologies have been used to better understand the
dynamic performance of C^3 systems. Modeling [8], simulation [9]],[10], war-gaming
[11] are examples of techniques that have been so employed. The status of modeling
the human decisionmaker is less than satisfactory. It is difficult to describe the decisionmaker and the decisionmaking environment in theoretical terms that do not prejudge
either the goals of the techniques of achieving the goals.[12] The human has a
marvelous capacity for coping with uncertain, vague and confusing data; making sense
out of information so incomplete that it would paralyze a computer. The computer has,
in turn, unexcelled capability to process and display vast amounts of data at a rate that
would paralyze a human. A proper marriage of these talented two, humans and
computers, would perform better than either could alone. The proper roles, or more
precisely, the proper sharing of roles between humans and software is difficult to
quantify. Both have ratiocinative capability, but they differ in their ability to process
data and to respond to ambiguity. In network management, for example, their roles
might have the relative importance shown in Figure 1. High speed and large data bases
are within the domain of the computer, while those nodes demanding insight have a
more corporeal flavor.

Within the R&D engineering-based community, there is a technocentric tendency to
"let the computer do all it can do," and depend on humans, aided with video displays
and keyboards, to overcome any perceived performance deficiencies. The Space Defense
System (SDS), for example, is a globally sized collection of sensors and weapons in
which the controlling software is estimated to exceed several hundred thousand lines
of code. With the tight time horizons required, such a system is highly automated. Still,
system control and management during deployment, during long term quiescent
operation, and during brief periods of partial or total engagement will be exercised by
the commander-and-chief and his designated representatives. The system must be such
that this primary human command and control function can be exercised expeditiously
and unambiguously. The system can be expected to perform with speed and precision---

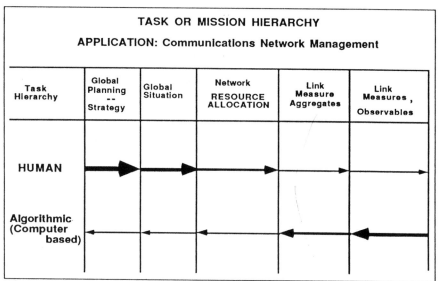

Figure 1: Sample task hierarchy

for precisely defined scenarios. But what will be the performance and outcome for ill-fitted sets of initial and ongoing conditions? A human director is supposed to adapt the system to all extraordinary events. Unfortunately, there is little data upon which to base this confidence. A reliance on "plausible" architectures leads to controversy. At one extreme, it is said in [13] that The SDS introduces an issue "to which technology cannot provide an answer"; to wit, the design of an automatic response algorithm which will cause "the defense to activate itself autonomously, since there would be no more than a minute for human decision." Conversely, current SDS architectures place great importance on human intervention in the initiation of a response to a perceived threat. The variety of potential human roles becomes more apparent when a study of the subsidiary areas of concern are enumerated; e.g., status monitoring, weapon alert, information management, attack characterization, weapon activation, weapon release, target prioritization, target assignment, self-defense coordination and countermeasure management. In order to determine the appropriate procedures for resource allocation, "an appropriate level of human interaction (must) be determined."[14] The question has arisen as to "whether technology may be pushing the fallible humans who operate (these systems) beyond their ability to make wise judgments instantaneously on the basis of what, even with the most sophisticated systems, will often be ambiguous information."[15]

This is not to say that there are no good reasons for the role of the human to remain so ill defined. Superficially, it appears that any precisely defined tasks given to a human could be performed automatically by an algorithm which mimics his input-output relationship. In truth, such algorithmic emulation has proven to be unsatisfactory in many respects.[10] To clearly display the unique contribution that can be played by the human, a clear understanding of his areas of proficiency is essential. Some of the areas of particular human competence are [16];

1. Decision making in semantically rich problem domains

2. Analogical reasoning and problem structuring

3. Information processing and application of heuristics

As this abbreviated list indicates, the human brings a distinctive skill into the operation of a complex system. There are different ways in which human attributes can be phrased. The most promising are models which are based upon the premise that the human decision maker strives to make the best possible decisions, but is constrained by cognitive limitations and to some degree temporal pressures. To be useful in simulation and analysis, the representation chosen must be compatible with the rest of the subsystems models in order that they can be combined to form an all-inclusive system description which includes the human element as a integral element.

This philosophy has been used in references such as [17] in which the Stimulus/Hypothesis evaluation/Options/Response (SHOR) paradigm of human decision making is introduced. The SHOR approach has many attractive features. First, it is applicable to all military echelon levels. Second, it represents the fast dynamics of the system explicitly rather than by implicit relational blocks or physical interconnection of subsystem elements. Finally, there is no pre-bias on whether a function is best performed by a human or by an algorithm.

Organization Level	Time scale of interest	Geographic Extent (km)
Platform	seconds-minutes	10's
Task Force	minutes-hours	100's
Fleet	hours-days	1000's
Theatre	days-weeks	1000's
Service/National	weeks-years	Global

Figure 2: Time scales of an encounter

To create a dynamic model, it is important to identify the times scales of the relevant events. In military engagements, they range from subseconds; e.g., missile point defense operations, to long term development and implementation of global strategy. Decision and control approaches appropriate at one time scale may be inappropriate at another. Because the impact of a pivotal decision will have a long tail, the effect of prior decisions frequently influence current ones. For example, surface Navy echelon levels have the order-of-magnitude time and distance scales shown in Figure 2. At the platform level, the time scale reflects engagement time which may include limited or local tracking. At the Task Force level, the time scale corresponds to tasks such as maneuver, coordinated engagement, and track management.

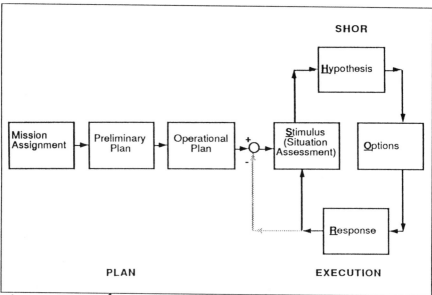

Figure 3: A C³ module

   Any of the indicated organizational levels may have additional planning functions that precede the operational time scales by up to months or years. The planning includes such things as logistics, maintenance, training, and exercises, all of which contribute to forming a more effective system. Figure 3 shows the sequence of events in a typical C³ system. The lighter shaded path is employed when it is necessary to compare status with the current plan. The execution phase is represented in the SHOR paradigm. The speed with which a military organization can circumnavigate the execution loop is one important aspect of performance. The centrality of the loop explains why communications interdiction is an increasingly important operational and technical area. Counter operation need only delay execution of the indicated function in order to be effective.

A. ENCOUNTER DYNAMICS

A decisionmaker views a dynamic encounter as a temporally varying, geographically dispersed system subject to unpredictable events, both continuous and discrete. As
data is transmitted to him through local and extended communications networks, he
decides upon a proper course of action. All of this must be done on a strict time line,
and with the knowledge that a current action will influence subsequent evolution of the
encounter. In studies of a broad class of tactical engagements, the encounter dynamics
have been quantified, and expressed in terms of a set stochastic differential equations.[18] Unfortunately, in any realistic situation the dimension of these equations
must perforce be quite high; there are many interacting objects, each of which has many
dynamic attributes. No one can possibly keep track of all of this detail in real time. A
person responds to this overwhelming complexity by mentally simplifying reality to a
comprehensible level. Studies have suggested that this is done in part by imagining the
actual encounter to be partitioned into a hybrid consisting of separate global and local
parts. It is within such a perceptual context that the decisionmaker frames his response.
For example, just such a procedure is used in the development of the optimal control
model (OCM) studied in [19]. In this model, the macro-environment is assumed to be
known and unchanging, and only the local encounter dynamics need be considered.
Based upon the assumption that an operator reacts rationally to the environment as he
perceives it, the reflexive--short time--response dynamics are shown to have a natural
decomposition into a Kalman filter-based explicator and a linear action block.

When the operational environment is multimodal, the fundamental character of the
human stimulus/hypothesis evaluation functions becomes clearer. The decisionmaker
processes observation stimuli to yield inferences regarding the status of the encounter.
Unfortunately, translating analyses like that of the OCM into this recusant environment
is difficult because the situational dynamics have a very convoluted form. For example,
in a comprehensive study of the structure of battle dynamics, Ingber was led to
investigate a model that is both nonlinear and stochastic (and nongaussian). To be
specific, let $(\Omega, F, \wp; F_t)$ be a probability space, and a filtration which comprehensively
delineates all relevant aspects of the encounter. Ingber's equations have the general form
(see, for example, [8])

$$dx_p = f(x_p, t)dt + g(x_p, t)dw_t \qquad (1)$$

where the state x_p is a vector describing in fine detail the dynamic features of the
encounter, and $\{w_t\}$ is a vector F_t-Brownian motion of intensity W chosen to introduce

uncertainty into the realization of the engagement. Before going further, it is well to note that a model of this specific form has certain inherent deficiencies in this application. First, even with reasonable aggregation, the dimension of x_p must necessarily be quite high. Also, the influence of the decisionmaker's action is not made explicit. Finally, the uncertainty in the sample paths Eq. (1) is generated by a continuous random process $\{w_t\}$.

The model does not have the flexibility required to portray the sudden, large scale variations in circumstances which occur in operations. It is advantageous, therefore, to modify the structure of Ingber's model in such a way as to make explicit its dependence on events of macroscopic scale as well as the decisionmaker's response. To this end, the initial encounter model will be rephrased as:

$$dx_p = f(x_p, u_p, r_t)dt + g(x_p, u_p, r_t)dw_t \qquad (2)$$

where x_p is the "global" system state which delineates the external environment to which the decisionmaker seeks to respond, and the decisionmaker's action variable is u_p. In Eq. (2), $\{w_t\}$ represents only one portion of the primitive randomness in the encounter; that associated with high frequency uncertainty and various wideband disturbances. The supplementary process, $\{r_t\}$, indicates the mode of evolution of the encounter. Transitions in $\{r_t\}$ thus signify major events. These macro-events tend to have more temporal structure than that displayed by $\{w_t\}$, but the times of occurrence are typically unpredictable. Different values of r_t (or alternative "supervariables" [20]) will be identified with different hypotheses delineating the macrostatus of the encounter. It will be supposed that the number of modal hypotheses is finite; i.e., $r_t \in S = \{1, 2, \ldots, s\}$. In what follows, an alternative notation is convenient: if $r_t = i \in S$, let $\phi_t = e_i$.[2] Then $\{\phi_t\}$ evolves on $\mathfrak{R}^s$, and Eq. (2) can be phrased in terms of $\{\phi_t\}$ in an obvious way.

Even with the aggregation of the detailed environmental variables implicit in Eq. (2), the encounter dynamics have a complex form. It would be exceedingly difficult for anyone to interpret the nonlinear behavior described in Eq. (2) in a concurrent manner. Suppose that the decisionmaker mentally converts Eq. (2) into a hybrid form with separate descriptions of the local and global aspects of the engagement. Because of the way in which it is defined, the current value of $\{r_t\}$ gives the macrostatus directly. The determination of the micromodel is somewhat more subtle. Associated with each of the macrohypotheses, it will be supposed that there is a favored operating condition; i.e.,

---

[2] Denote the unit vector in the ith direction in $\mathfrak{R}^s$ by e_i.

if $r_t = i$, the decisionmaker seeks to place x_p in some neighborhood of a nominal state $x_n(i)$. This state is determined by conditions external to Eq. (2), and it could be achieved in the absence of disturbances by some nominal action $u_n(i)$. The decisionmaker is assumed to know what is appropriate for each modal hypothesis---the trained decisionmaker assumption. The collection of these desired macroconditions can be displayed as an indexed set of pairs: $\{x_n(r), u_n(r); r \in S\}$; the nominal state and the nominal action associated with each hypothesis. Even in the presence of the disturbances represented by $\{w_t\}$, if $\{r_t\}$ were constant, the decisionmaker would attempt to maintain the engagement near the associated nominal state. Hence, in a constant macro-environment, it is natural to suppose that the decisionmaker acts in response to a localization of Eq. (2) near the desired operating point.

When the macrohypothesis changes, the decisionmaker faces a much more daunting task. He must move the global states to a location more in keeping with the new macro-environment. Whereas, before the change he was operating incrementally, he must now reinterpret his past observations, and make a large scale reallocation of resources (u_p) to move the encounter state to a more advantageous zone. He sees himself as having to respond to a sudden and large state displacement.

With the indicated global-local devolution, the situational microdynamics are linearizations of Eq. (2) about the operative macrostatus. Because of the way in which the macrostatus is expressed, it is natural to express the actual state of the encounter as the sum of the desired nominal conditions and the deviation from these conditions:

$$x_{pt} = x_n(\phi_t) + x_t \qquad (3)$$
$$u_{pt} = u_n(\phi_t) + u_t$$

The pair $\{x_t, u_t\}$ quantifies the discrepancy between current operation, and that sought for a particular macrocondition. If these variables are small, and if the motion equations are smooth, the perturbation dynamics can be approximated by a set of linear equations

$$dx_t = (A_i x_t + B_i u_t)dt + g_i dw_t \ ; \ \text{if} \ \phi_t \equiv e_i \qquad (4)$$

where (A_i, B_i) are gradients evaluated at the indicated nominal condition $(x_n(\phi_t), u_n(\phi_t), \phi_t)$. Even for a fixed global environment, the local variability of the system will produce fluctuating sample paths in the microstate process $\{x_t\}$. The initial conditions on Eq. (4) will be assumed to be Gaussian, and independent of other exogenous processes. Equation (4) is the orthodox linear model used in most system analyses; e.g, the OCM.

In what follows it will be assumed that $g_i=I$; i.e., local disturbance normalization is achieved in W.

Equation (4) is an exclusively local description of the system, and consists of a family of LGM models, parametrically dependant upon fixed modal conditions. The equation does not capture the variability resulting from unpredictable changes in macroconditions. While Eq. (4) is satisfactory during quiescent conditions, a sudden variation in operating condition changes the appropriate operating point. This in turn creates an immediate and discrete change in the microvariables. If, for example, $\{\phi_t\}$ makes an $i{\rightarrow}j$ transition at time s, the microvariables are referenced to a different nominal state before t=s and immediately thereafter; i.e., $x_s = x_{s-} + \delta(j,i)$ where $\delta(j,i) = x_n(i)-x_n(j)$. The deviation variable before the transition changes suddenly to accommodate the transition in global conditions. It is this volatile environment which exploits---indeed demands---uniquely human capabilities.

These isolated jumps in macrostate can be incorporated into the microdynamics by having $\{x_t\}$ jump at the macrotransition times. Let ρ be a matrix with ith row given by $-x_n(i)'$; i.e., $\rho_{i.}= -x_n(i)'$.[3] An $i{\rightarrow}j$ transition in $\{\phi_t\}$ leads to a jump in $\{x_t\}$; $\Delta x_t = \rho'\phi_t - \rho'\phi_{t-} = \rho'\Delta\phi_t$. This can be integrated with (4) to yield

$$dx_t = (A_ix_t+B_iu_t)dt + dw_t + \rho'd\phi_t; \text{ if } \phi_t =e_i \qquad (5)$$

where ρ links jumps in $\{x_t\}$ to changes $\{\phi_t\}$. A change in macrostate will initiate a microstate transient as the decisionmaker moves $\{x_p\}$ from a neighborhood of the prior operating point toward a region corresponding to the new macrostate. Equation (5) uses linearized dynamics associated with this macrostate for the full transient interval.

Equation (5) gives a complete representation of the micro-environment as abstracted by the decisionmaker. If the sample path of $\{\phi_t\}$ were known *a priori*, $\{x_t\}$ would be a Gaussian random process formed by joining linear Gauss-Markov (LGM) intervals with nonrandom jumps at the transition times of $\{\phi_t\}$. Unfortunately, the timing and sequencing of $\{\phi_t\}$ events are not known to the decisionmaker. He views the macroconditions as being created by external forces. A very simple but natural parameterization of the temporal evolution of $\{\phi_t\}$ suffices to delineate the decisionmaker's perception of the fundamental properties of this exogenous process. His notion of the tempo of the encounter, and his idiosyncratic partitioning of the space of macroconditions are described at a basic level by his sense of the sojourn times in each macrocategory and

---

[3] For any matrix A, let $A_{i.}$ be the ith row and $A_{.j}$ be the jth column.

the likelihood of alternative transitions at the end of a residence in a particular mode. This elementary quantification of the primitive attributes of the encounter can be arrayed as an $s \times s$ matrix $Q=[q_{ij}]$ (s is the number of alternative modes) with diagonal elements, $q_{ii}= -1/($the mean sojourn time in mode i), and off-diagonal elements given by $q_{ij}= -q_{ii}$ times the probability that $i \rightarrow j$ at the end of a residence in i. Then the decision-maker's personal perception of the dynamic structure of the encounter macrostate can be expressed quite simply in probabilistic terms as an F_t-Markov process:

$$\wp(r_{t+\varepsilon}=j \mid r_t=i) = \delta_{ij}+q_{ij}\varepsilon+o(\varepsilon); \ i,j \in S \qquad (6)$$

Alternatively, the macrodynamics can be written as a differential equation for $\{\phi_t\}$ in a form compatible with Eq. (5):

$$d\phi_t = Q'\phi_t dt + dm_t \qquad (7)$$

where $\{m_t\}$ is a purely discontinuous F_t-martingale.

Equations (5) and (7) give the complete environmental model, and it is within this context that the decisionmaker frames his response. He seeks to move the encounter state to a location appropriate to the current macrostatus. Unfortunately, he is never completely sure of his current condition. Before proper action can be determined, the mapping from observation to understanding--explication--must be made explicit, and this in turn depends upon the quality and form of the direct measurements.

B. OBSERVATION STRUCTURE

To portray explicitly the decisionmaker's observation, it will be supposed that his perception is phrased in terms of the hybrid framework proposed in Eqs. (5) and (7). Ideally, both $\{x_t\}$ and $\{\phi_t\}$ would be measured flawlessly. In this event, the decisionmaker would know his current condition, both global and local, and could select an appropriate action policy. Actually, neither constituent of the comprehensive dynamic state is measured without error. Certainly, there is often considerable dispute concerning the implication of data regarding the macrostatus. The appropriateness of the decisionmaker's actions are contingent on his ability to expeditiously infer system conditions. Because of the disjunction of the state categories, this is a hybrid inference problem.

With the environmental model having linked descriptions of the local and global aspects of the encounter, the decisionmaker partitions his observation space in like manner. First consider the measurement of local condition. It will be assumed that the decisionmaker observes the vector process $\{y_t\}$ given by:

$$dy_t = Dx_t dt + dn_x \qquad (8)$$

The noise processes $\{n_x\}$ is independent of $\{w_t\}$ and $\{m_t\}$ as well as the initial conditions on Eqs. (5) and (7), and is an F_t-Brownian motion with intensity $R_x > 0$. Equation (8) is the orthodox description of the observation in linear system analysis. It is based upon the premise that there is a direct measurement of a linear combination of microstates with a wideband noise in the measurement channel. This is quite natural if the components of $\{x_t\}$ represent point-equivalent states of an object; e.g., position, velocity etc. Such models have a long history with the matrix D found from a localization of a nonlinear measurement.

Situational uncertainty is an important part of a tactical environment, and its manner of resolution separates experienced decisionmakers from novices. Proper understanding of the impact of macro-uncertainty on overall system performance is essential if such things as the influence of stress of decisionmaker response is to be integrated into a comprehensive system model. It is in the resolution of global states that human skills--and limitations--are most clearly displayed. At the macrolevel, the decisionmaker's external condition is characterized by three things:

1. The frequency and sequencing of changes in situation.

2. The sensitivity of his observation to changes in situation.

3. The clutter and distortion in the observations.

The decisionmaker interprets external stimuli in a manner characterized by numerous biases. He treats the data sequences in a nonuniform, nonlinear, and individuated manner. These notions can be made more precise if it is supposed that the decision-maker observes a stimulus vector $\{z_t\}$ in which different components represent different attributes of the observed data stream. The primitive stimulus often has a spatio-temporal structure that the decisionmaker subjectively decomposes at a preconscious level into comprehensible aggregates. At this level of abstraction, $\{z_t\}$ is distinct from the raw sensory data. It represents information as combined and categorized by the decisionmaker himself, and has his personal imprint. At the macrolevel, each hypothesis in S is associated with a perceptual signature "h"--or template, or noetic form[21], or schema[22]---by which the situation is identified. The strength and distinctiveness of the signature measures how easily the hypothesis is to identify from the observations. As the decisionmaker groups observations into categories he may subjectively favor a particular hypothesis; e.g., he may imagine h_i to have a neutral shape. In this event, hypothesis i will be "seen" in ambiguous data more commonly than its fellows. Such classes of perceptual bias as conceptual rigidity and tunnel vision can be made explicit by selecting the hypothesis set S appropriately, and by associating suitable h's with favored alternatives.

The signature of the operative macrosituation is blurred in the observation. To represent this, suppose that the decisionmaker observes the macrosignature in a noisy and distorting channel; i.e., instead of $z_t = h_{\phi t}$, the observation is contaminated by a disturbance and

$$z_t = h_t + \text{noise} \; ; \text{if } r_t = i$$

The indicated noise could be a wideband clutter as happens in visual identification of targets or it could be the result of various types of misclassification if the components of z_t are based upon intelligence or status reports. In these latter cases, the DOPII aspect of the problem is prominent, and the decisionmaker weights data according to the perceived fidelity and biases in the source, and the distortion of the transmission medium.

To make this more precise, suppose that the observation $\{z_t\}$ is related to the stimulus $\{h_{\phi t}\}$ by the stochastic differential equation

$$dz_t = h'\phi_t dt + dn_\phi \tag{9}$$

where $\{n_\phi\}$ is an F_t-Brownian motion with intensity $R_\phi > 0$, and independent of all of the primitive random processes introduced earlier. For convenience, it will be assumed that R_ϕ is diagonal which implies that the components of $\{n_\phi\}$ are independent. This modal observation process, $\{z_t\}$, is not commonly found in system models because they are usually based upon the assumption that there is but one modal condition, thus obviating the need for any such measurement. In Eq. (9) on the other hand, $\{z_t\}$ contains the signature of current condition observed in additive noise. In many applications involving human supervisors, the auxiliary observation link has a natural rationale. For example, in visual target recognition the macrohypotheses manifest themselves in the spatial form of the objects within the field-of-view rather than in local motions. In such situations, the measurement architecture is such that the bath based upon the micromeasurement Eq. (8) is augmented with a parallel path incorporating $\{z_t\}$. Often the spatiotemporal nature of the data induces a natural partition into spatial properties related to the macrostatus, and temporal properties more closely related to the microstate. Thus the decisionmaker may receive an undifferentiated data sequence upon which he places the mental partitioning indicated in Eqs. (8)-(9).

The division of the observation $g_t = (y_t, z_t)$ into distinct classes is evocative, but the interpretation of the elements is not exclusive. The micro- and macrostates are coupled in Eq. (5), and thus measurement of either is to some degree a measurement of the other. The observation structure given in Eq. (9) is a natural one when the information flow rate to the decisionmaker is high. The filtration generated by $\{z_t\}$ or $\{y_t\}$ will be called $\{Z_t\}$ or $\{Y_t\}$ respectively with $\{G_t\}=\{Z_t \vee Y_t\}$

Equations (8) and (9) describe the observations received by the decisionmaker. On their basis he must estimate the current values of $\{x_t\}$ and $\{\phi_t\}$. Even if he uses a mean-square error criterion, this is an estimation problem with no known solution. A useful approximation can be deduced if it is assumed that the decisionmaker processes his incoming stimuli with a devolution similar to that found in both the environmental and observational models. To motivate the inferential structure, note that associated with each category of encounter state, there is an exclusive measurement. Thus, $\{y_t\}$ is a measurement of microvariables alone. One element of x_t might represent the position of a threat. The corporeal observation of this threat would be indicated in Eq. (8) by imagining that the true position is observed in a noisy (white) channel. This observation model has been frequently used for describing human "data conditioning" in tracking scenarios. It is a model that is also frequently used in studies of algorithmic trackers.

It is in Eq. (9) that the uniquely human ability to parse data manifests itself. A human has no algorithmic peer in his facility for collecting the panoramic attributes of a cluttered data sequence into meaningful aggregates. This is important because the macrofeatures of the encounter tend to display themselves most clearly in the gestalt of the observation; i.e., in spatial rather than temporal correlations in the observation. Global attributes are inferred from an amalgamation of spatially disjoined aspects of the data. Matching a behavioral, structural, and relational pattern---delineated here by h---to the observation process necessarily requires integrating data of an extended nature. It is, for example, the pattern of the threats which is most important in determining the current mode of evolution of a hostile encounter. The local motions of one of the threats, while important in fire control, provides minimal information bearing on the macrostate. Though it is true that the two observational categories are related at a basic phenomenological level, they are much more closely linked to distinct aspects of the encounter, and their concurrent relationship is weak. Hence, the inference to be drawn from the composite measurement has a devolutionary character in which the contiguous influence of a particular measurement is on the behavior of the affiliated state estimate.

This notion of the primary dependence of a state estimate on a specific observation category has important implications for the estimation architecture. The evolution of the modal state is independent of $\{x_t\}$, and there is a direct and presumably accurate measurement of $\{\phi_t\}$ in $\{z_t\}$. It can, therefore, be assumed that $\{y_t\}$ provides little information regarding $\{\phi_t\}$ that is not implicit in $\{z_t\}$. In this event, the macrostate can be essentially decoupled from Eq. (8), and considered separately from the estimate of the microstate. The relation is not symmetrical, and the estimate of $\{x_t\}$ cannot be isolated because the jumps in the microstate depend upon $\{\Delta\phi_t\}$. Thus in a fundamental sense, macrodata has micro-implications. It is not evident that $\{z_t\}$ has a significant concurrent influence on macro-estimates. For example in tracking a moving target, $\{z_t\}$ gives the comprehensive framework for interpreting the engagement, but $\{y_t\}$ gives the most relevant data upon which to base position estimates. The impact of $\{z_t\}$ on estimates of $\{x_t\}$ tends to have a more remote quality, setting the framework within which estimates of $\{x_t\}$ take place. The estimation architecture has a hierarchical structure, with the self-contained macro-estimate driving the subordinate micro-estimates. The precise form of this interrelation is made clearer in the following sections.

C. A UNIMODAL ALGORITHM

Before investigating the general estimation problem, it is expedient to consider an important special case. Suppose that there is but one macrohypothesis. The index i in Eq. (5) becomes superfluous and $\rho'd\phi_t\equiv0$. The microdynamics sans the adapted action function are given by a reduced version of Eq. (5)

$$dx_t = Ax_tdt + dw_t \qquad (10)$$

with the micro-observation as in Eq. (8):

$$dy_t = Dx_tdt+dn_x \qquad (11)$$

This is the conventional state and observation structure. There is a known solution to the resulting estimation problem which incorporates a Kalman filter as an observation processor. The conditional mean of the local encounter state $(\hat{x}_t=E\{x_t \mid Y_t\})$ is given by the classical algorithm

$$d\hat{x}_t = A\hat{x}_tdt+P_{xx}D'R_x^{-1}dv_x \qquad (12)$$

where $dv_x= dy - D\hat{x}dt$, and P_{xx} is the microstate error covariance matrix. The process $\{v_x\}$ is the micro-innovations.

The appearance of Eq. (12) is common in many applications including those of operator modeling. It has an intuitive interpretation which frequently motivates its use in situations more general than the LGM environment created by Eqs. (10)-(11). In Eq. (12), the increment in $\{\hat{x}_t\}$ is expressed as a sum of a drift and a correction. The increment in the estimate is in the direction of the mean microstate increment

$(E\{d\hat{x}_t \mid Y_t\}=A\hat{x}_t dt)$, and the correction is proportional to the increment in the innovations process $(d\hat{x}_t - E\{d\hat{x}_t \mid Y_t\} = P_{xx}D'R_x^{-1}dv_x)$. The former term has an obvious rationale; i.e., in the absence of new data, extrapolate from the most recent estimate. The latter is more engaging. The innovations gain, $P_{xx}D'R_x^{-1}$, is inversely proportional to the measurement noise intensity (R_x^{-1}), and directly proportional to the signal amplification (D). Both factors are explicit in the parameterization of the observation sequences. The indicated dependence is natural, implying that as communications improve, the estimate becomes more sensitive to new data. The innovations gain is also proportional to the residual uncertainty in the estimate (P_{xx}). It is only this factor that is not given in the model of the observation link, and indeed P_{xx} is determined jointly by the signal dynamics and the observation fidelity.

Note that when P_{xx} is small--little estimation uncertainty--the innovations process is of little note, and the estimate propagates forward along the field of the unexcited system. As the uncertainty in the state estimate increases, new information is accorded increasing value; i.e., as the estimator becomes less sure of the true state, it is more willing to modify its prior estimate in response to new data. It can be shown that $\{P_{xx}\}$ is given by the solution to a matrix stochastic differential equation [23]

$$dP_{xx} = [AP_{xx}+(AP_{xx})'+W-P_{xx}D'R_x^{-1}DP_{xx}]dt + \Sigma_k\pi_{xx}(x_k)(Kdv_x)_k. \qquad (13)$$

The right hand side of Eq. (13) is composed of readily interpreted terms. The microstate error variance is amplified by the system dynamics $((AP_{xx} +P_{xx}A')dt)$, and is reduced by the observation process $(P_{xx}D'R_x^{-1}DP_{xx}dt)$. Again, as the quality of the communication network improves, the error variance decreases. The equation of evolution of the error variance process $\{P_{xx}\}$ is responsive to the influence of the exogenous microstate disturbance as well. As the intensity of this excitation, W, increases, the increment in $\{P_{xx}\}$ is increased proportionately. From Eq. (10), W has another interpretation. It is the intensity of the Y_t-predictable quadratic variation of $\{x_t\}$; i.e.,

$$Wdt = d<x,x>_t. \qquad (14)$$

The final term in Eq. (13) is anomalous and warrants discussion. The error covariance is a random process which responds to the observation through a term containing the third conditional error moment as a factor; $\pi_{xx}(x_k) = E\{\tilde{x}\tilde{x}'\tilde{x}_k \mid Y_t\}$ where $\tilde{x}=x-\hat{x}$ is the estimation error. It is known that $\{\tilde{x}_t\}$ is a Gaussian process, and as a consequence, this central moment is identically zero for all k and for all t; i.e., $\pi_{xx}(x_k)(Kdv_x)_k \equiv 0$ Thus, the last term vanishes in Eq. (13), and the familiar Riccati ordinary differential equation for P_{xx} results; i.e., under the LGM assumption, P_{xx} is not stochastic. This further implies that the observation gain in the microstate estimator is independent of the sample path of the observation. This makes the estimation algorithm "precomputable", an attractive attribute in many applications. It has been found though that this contracted form for the covariance equation must be modified in an appropriate manner if it is to be incorporated into a decisionmaker model. Empirical behaviors appear to be more actively adaptive than would be predicted on the basis of the orthodox Kalman filter.[24]

D. ESTIMATION ALGORITHMS

The preceding section gives the solution to an estimation problem which arises when the environment confronting the decisionmaker is known and constant. Only a single micromodel need be considered since there is no possibility of modal variation. The equation for the microstate is linear, and the innovations gain can be precomputed. The hypothesis evaluation blocks of SHOR are not relevant (see Fig.3). When the more general environmental model Eqs. (5)-(7) is apropos, the situation becomes more complex. In contrast to Eq. (10), the micromodel does not generate continuous Gaussian sample paths. Furthermore, the decisionmaker must address the issue of hypothesis evaluation explicitly.

For reasons outlines earlier, it will be supposed that the inference regarding the macrohypotheses takes place separately. The implications of this assumption can be made more precise as follows. It will be assumed that the primary source of information about the macrostates is contained in the macro-observation.

$$\hat{\phi}_t = E\{\phi_t \mid G_t\} \cong E\{\phi_t \mid Z_t\} \tag{16}$$

That if, there is little loss in fidelity if hypothesis evaluation is based exclusively upon the macro-observation. With this identification and the observation given in (9), the equation for $\{\hat{\phi}_t\}$ can be written directly.[25]

$$d\hat{\phi}_t = Q'\hat{\phi}_t dt + (\text{diag } h - \hat{\phi}_t' h I)\hat{\phi}_t R_\phi^{-1} dv_\phi$$

where I is the identity matrix, and the increment in the modal innovations is $dv_\phi = dz_t - h'\hat{\phi}_t dt$. It is easily shown that

$$P_{\phi\phi} = -\hat{\phi}\hat{\phi}' + \text{diag } \hat{\phi} \tag{17}$$

Consequently the explication algorithm can be written

$$d\hat{\phi}_t = Q'\hat{\phi}_t dt + P_{\phi\phi} h R_\phi^{-1} dv_\phi \tag{18}$$

Because ϕ_t is a unit vector, the solution to Eq. (18) yields everything necessary to compute all of the Z_t-(or G_t) conditional moments of the macrostate. Equation (18) has been referred to as the Stimulus/Hypothesis Evaluation model (SHEM), and has been studied in several references.[26], [27] This general framework can be placed within the SHOR rubric.

The SHEM displays a highly nonlinear response to information in a single set of differential equations, and manifests a range of what appear superficially to be incompatible behaviors. For example, suppose that a decisionmaker acknowledges three possible hypotheses as

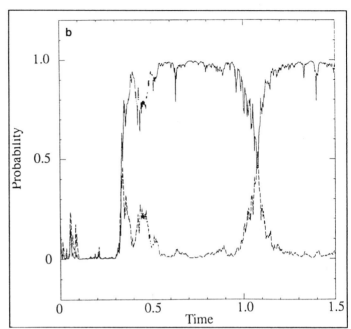

Figure 4: Sample function of the SHEM

exhaustively describing a situation. Let an actual change in situation from that denoted by 3 to that denoted by 1 occur at t=0.3. Based upon his observations, the decisionmaker infers the relative likelihoods of the different hypotheses ($\hat{\phi}_1$, $\hat{\phi}_2$, $\hat{\phi}_3$ respectively). Figure 4 shows the simulated response of $\hat{\phi}_1$ (shown solid) and $\hat{\phi}_2$ (shown dotted) for the indicated scenario. When the decisionmaker is convinced that he has identified the status of a situation (0<t<<0.3), he will tend to under appreciate the value of discordant data; i.e., he "anchors" on prior knowledge. This has the advantage that a brief occurrence of inconsistent information will cause little vacillation. Immediately after a transition 0.3<t<0.5), this model of the human explication is hesitant. After a delay, the decisionmaker recognizes that a transition event may have occurred, and becomes less certain of the true status. This causes his perception of the situation to become more volatile. The occurrence of an anomalous data stream of appreciable length leaves him more open to a modification in his view of the condition of the environment; i.e., he displays "diminished memory." This same behavior pattern reoccurs in the region near t=1.0 (false indication of an event). The quality of diminished memory is made manifest by a high valuation placed upon more recent observations, and this occurs when a person is unsure of his surroundings. As Figure 4 indicates, diminished memory and anchoring are not actually contradictory behavior patterns, but are instead local descriptions of the human response characteristic in different regions of his knowledge space.

In contrast to the SHEM which is independent of $\{y_i\}$, the microstate estimate is contingent upon both data sources. The estimation framework is nongaussian, and this produces nonlinearities in the algorithm for computation of $\{\hat{x}_i\}$. Further, the underlying micro-equations are nonlinear if (A_i, B_i) is a nontrivial function of $i \in S$. This latter situation creates additional complexity in the estimator. The next section gives the general equations for computing $\{\hat{x}_i\}$. The derivation is tedious, and will not be given here. The case in which $[A_i, B_i] \equiv [A, B]$ admits a much simpler estimation algorithm. This is not surprising because the micro-macro linking is linear in this event. The monomorphic model is, of course, a special case, but it is worthy of consideration because of its less convoluted structure.

E. THE MISSION DIRECTED DECISIONMAKER MODEL: MDDM

It is a direct calculation to show that the micro-estimate satisfies:

$$d\hat{x}_t = (A\hat{x}_t + Bu_t + \rho'Q'\hat{\phi}_t)dt + P_{xx}D'R_x^{-1}dv_x + P_{x\phi}hR_\phi^{-1}dv_\phi \qquad (19)$$

Equation (19) is surprisingly simple, and mimics the Kalman filter, Eq. (12). The drift of the estimate is dependent upon the microdynamics, $(A\hat{x}_t + Bu_t)dt$, and on the likelihood of a modal transition, $\rho'Q'\hat{\phi}_t dt$. The latter weights the possible direction of the jumps in state by the conditional probability of the particular jump occurring. This composite term is a natural successor to the first term in Eq. (12).

The last term in Eq. (19) corresponds directly to the second term in Eq. (12). There are two sources of information, and both the micro- and the macro-innovations influence the evolution of $\{\hat{x}_i\}$. The innovations gain contains block elements of the comprehensive error covariance P:

$$P = \begin{bmatrix} P_{\phi\phi} & P_{\phi x} \\ P_{x\phi} & P_{xx} \end{bmatrix}$$

The block $P_{\phi\phi}$ is already known from the SHEM analysis. Once the remaining blocks of this matrix are computed, the complete state estimator can be implemented.

A representation for P_{xx} can be derived using the standard formalism of nonlinear filtering. The most general representation is given by:

$$dP_{xx} = (AP_{xx} + \rho'Q'P_{\phi x} + (AP_{xx} + \rho'Q'P_{\phi x})' + W + \rho'V(\hat{\phi}_t)\rho - P_{xx}D'R_x^{-1}DP_{xx} - P_{x\phi}hR_\phi^{-1}h'P_{\phi x})dt$$

$$+ (\Sigma_{k \in S}\pi_{xx}(\phi_k)(hR_\phi^{-1}dv_\phi)_k + \Sigma_{k \in B}\pi_{xx}(x_k)(D'R_x^{-1}dv_x)_k \qquad (20)$$

where B (respectively S) is the index set denoting the components of the micro- (respectively macro-) states of the encounter, and $V(\hat{\phi}_t)dt = d<m,m>$ is the Z_t-predictable quadratic variation of $\{m_t\}$.

Equation (20) bears obvious similarities to Eq. (13). The mapping

$$AP_{xx} \rightarrow AP_{xx}+\rho'Q'P_{\phi x}$$

$$-P_{xx}D'R_x^{-1}DP_{xx} \rightarrow -P_{xx}D'R_x^{-1}DP_{xx} -P_{x\phi}hR_\phi^{-1}h'P_{\phi x}$$

replaces each term in Eq. (13) with its natural counterpart in Eq. (20). The predictable quadratic variation of the external disturbance in Eq. (5), $d<x_t,x_t>_t = (W + \rho'V(\hat{\phi}_t)\rho)dt$, replaces the corresponding term in Eq. (13). It is interesting to note that applications have been described in which exogenous discontinuities appear, and resort to *ad hoc* approaches has been made in their solution. In the absence of the structure provided by the hybrid framework, the modal variation was viewed as an augmentation to the external influences on the microstates, and analysts were led to consider the combined term $\rho'd\phi_t + dw_t$ as a direct replacement for dw_t in the LGM model. The independence of the disturbances suggests a formal approximation to P_{xx} in which Wt is replaced by the quadratic variance of $\{x_t\}$. This substitution, or something akin to it, has been used in several studies, and is referred to as replacing the discrete disturbance with its "Brownian equivalent." Usually when this is done, the $\{\phi_t\}$ model is such that $d<m,m>$ is deterministic. Equation (20) is more precise in that a correlative term in the error covariance is created. In contrast to the Gaussian environment, the volatility of the ex- ogenous disturbance is partially predictable; i.e., the predictable quadratic variation is a random, Z_t-measurable function. This creates a primitive adaptiveness in the covariance equation in the sense that the evolution of $\{P_{xx}\}$ is responsive to changes in $\{\hat{\phi}_t\}$. Another way to think of this is to say that the external noise intensity is adjusted to suite the macroconditions. If the decisionmaker expects extended periods of smooth operation, $W +\rho'V(\hat{\phi}_t)\rho \rightarrow W$. As the likelihood of modal change increases, $W +\rho'V(\hat{\phi}_t)\rho>>W$. In this way the decisionmaker adjusts the volatility of his micro-estimate to compensate for his sense of environmental variation. Note that the indicated adjust- ment does not depend on the quality of the estimate of the modal state. Rather, it simply averages the likelihoods of exogenous variation over the *a posteriori* probability distribution of the modal variables.

The innovations terms also generalize those found in Eq. (13) in a natural way. In this equation, $\pi_{xx}(x_k)\equiv0$, and consequently

$$d<\textstyle\sum_{k\in B}\pi_{xx}(x_k)(D'R_x^{-1}dv_x)_k,\sum_{k\in B}\pi_{xx}(x_k)(D'R_x^{-1}dv_x)_k> \equiv0$$

as well. If $\{x_t\}$ were Gaussian, the error covariance would not be influenced by the sample path. In the case under study, $\{x_t\}$ is not Gaussian, but it is conditionally Gaussian given $\{\phi_t\}$ in the sense that the continuous part of $\{x_t\}$ is Gaussian. To the degree that $\{\phi_t\}$ can be inferred from $\{z_t\}$ in a timely manner, one would expect $\pi_{xx}(x_k)$ to be small.

The macro-innovations term $(\Sigma_{k \in S}\pi_{xx}(\phi_k)(hR_\phi^{-1}dv_\phi)_k$ warrants careful examination. The micro-error covariance is random because of the macro-uncertainty that exists on the modulation index in the microdynamics. When the decisionmaker is convinced of his macrostatus--$\hat{\phi}_t$-$e_i \Rightarrow \pi_{xx}(\phi_k)$-0--the error variance will settle in a neighborhood near that appropriate to the ostensible condition; i.e., P_{xx} will move to a neighborhood of P_i satisfying

$$dP_i = (AP_i +(AP_i)'+ W +\rho'V(e_i)\rho-P_iD'R_x^{-1}DP_i)dt$$

where the fact that $P_{x\phi}$ is necessarily small has been used to simplify the equation.

When a change in mode occurs, two things happen that influence P_{xx}. The macro-estimate begins to change, thus creating nonnegligible correlation between $\{\phi_t\}$ and $\{x_t\}$ $(\pi_{xx}(\phi_k)\neq0)$, and $\{x_t\}$ is no longer Gaussian $(\pi_{xx}(x_k)\neq0)$. While both effects arise during post transition transients, it will be assumed that the former presages the latter. More precisely, to the degree that either is nonnegligible, it will be supposed that

$$d<\Sigma_{k \in S}\pi_{xx}(\phi_k)(hR_\phi^{-1}dv_\phi)_k, \Sigma_{k \in S}\pi_{xx}(\phi_k)(hR_\phi^{-1}dv_\phi)_k> \quad >>$$
$$d<\Sigma_{k \in B}\pi_{xx}(x_k)(D'R_x^{-1}dv_x)_k, \Sigma_{k \in B}\pi_{xx}(x_k)(D'R_x^{-1}dv_x)_k> \qquad (21)$$

and Eq. (20) can be simplified to yield

$$dP_{xx} = (AP_{xx}+\rho'Q'P_{\phi x} +(AP_{xx}+\rho'Q'P_{\phi x})'+ W +\rho'V(\hat{\phi}_t)\rho-P_{xx}D'R_x^{-1}DP_{xx} -P_{x\phi}hR_\phi^{-1}h'P_{\phi x})dt$$
$$+\Sigma_{k \in S}\pi_{xx}(\phi_k)(hR_\phi^{-1}dv_\phi)_k \qquad (22)$$

Note that is only immediately following a seeming macrotransition that either side of Eq. (21) is important. If $\{\phi_t\}$ moves from $e_i \rightarrow e_j$ at time $t=t_0$, P_{xx} will move after some delay to a neighborhood of P_j given by

$$dP_j = (AP_j +(AP_j)'+ W +\rho'V(e_j)\rho-P_jD'R_x^{-1}DP_j)dt$$

During the reinitialization transient Eq. (21) comes into play. One would expect that P_{xx} would be greater that either P_i or P_j during the post transition interval. There are important implications of this dependence of P_{xx} on $\{v_\phi\}$. The responsiveness of the decisionmaker to micro-innovations is directly proportional to P_{xx} (and $P_{x\phi}$). As P_{xx} increases, past data (old $\{v_x\}$) is forgotten more quickly. Equation (19) indicates that if a modal transition is suspected, the decisionmaker concentrates on his "current" observations to the exclusion of his "past." Heuristically, this makes good sense, but Eq.

(22) quantifies the precise way in which this is done. Following the reasoning leading to Eq. (22), P_{xx} will be assumed to be an essentially Z_t-predictable process, which implies that $\pi_{xx}(\phi_k)$--referred to hereafter as $\pi_{xx}(k)$ in what follows-- is Z_t-predictable as well. With this in mind, it is evident that the complete explication model of the decisionmaker can be displayed as soon as $\pi_{xx}(k)$ is computed.

Under hypothesis (21), the MDDM can be written:

$$d\hat{x}_t = (A\hat{x}_t + Bu_t + \rho'Q'\hat{\phi}_t)dt + P_{xx}D'R_x^{-1}dv_x + P_{x\phi}hR_\phi^{-1}dv_\phi$$

where

$$dP_{xx} = (AP_{xx}+\rho'Q'P_{\phi x} +(AP_{xx}+\rho'Q'P_{\phi x})'+ W +\rho'V(\hat{\phi}_t)\rho \qquad (23)$$
$$-P_{xx}D'R_x^{-1}DP_{xx} -P_{x\phi}hR_\phi^{-1}h'P_{\phi x})dt +\Sigma_{k\in s}\pi_{xx}(\phi_k)(hR_\phi^{-1}dv_\phi)_k$$

and

$$dP_{x\phi} = (\Sigma_i(A_i(\pi_{x\phi}(i)+P_{x\phi}\hat{\phi}_t+\hat{x}_t(P_{\phi\phi})_{.i}')+B_iu_i(P_{\phi\phi})_{.i}')+\rho'Q'P_{\phi\phi}-P_{xx}D'R_x^{-1}DP_{x\phi}$$
$$+P_{x\phi}Q + \rho'V(\hat{\phi}_t) - P_{x\phi}hR_\phi^{-1}h'P_{\phi\phi})dt +\Sigma_{k\in s}\pi_{x\phi}(k)(hR_\phi^{-1}dv_\phi)_k \qquad (24)$$

To complete the MDDM, an equation for $\pi_{xx}(k)$ is required. This is the Z_t-predictable approximation to the mixed third central moment $E\{\tilde{x}_t\tilde{x}_t'\tilde{\phi}_t \mid G_t\}$. It can be shown that [28]

$$d\pi_{xx}(m) = ((A-P_{xx}D'R_x^{-1}D)\pi_{xx}(m)+(\rho'Q'-P_{x\phi}hR_\phi^{-1}h')\pi_{\phi x}(m)$$
$$+[(A-P_{xx}D'R_x^{-1}D)\pi_{xx}(m)+(\rho'Q'-P_{x\phi}hR_\phi^{-1}h')\pi_{\phi x}(m)]'$$
$$+ \rho'V((P_{\phi\phi})_{.m})\rho + \Sigma_j\pi_{xx}(j)((Q'-P_{\phi\phi}hR_\phi^{-1}h')_{jm}$$
$$+ [\rho'U_m(\hat{\phi}_t)\rho+\rho'\Sigma_j(V(e_j))_{.m}(P_{\phi x})_j+((V(e_j))_{.m}(P_{\phi x})_j)']dt$$
$$+\Sigma_k (R_\phi)_k^{-1}[-P_{x\phi}hR_\phi^{-1}e_k(P_{\phi x})_m(R_\phi)_k -(P_{x\phi}hR_\phi^{-1}e_k(P_{\phi x})_m(R_\phi)_k)' -P_{xx}(P_{\phi\phi}h)_{mk}$$
$$+\Sigma_j\Phi_m(j)h_{jk}]dv_k \qquad (25)$$

Equations (19) and (24)-(25) give the detailed structure of the MDDM explicator.

III. CONCLUSIONS:

This chapter presents a discussion of some of the modeling issues which arise in the study of C^3 systems. Such systems have a strongly hierarchical structure, and there are a spectrum of time scales appropriate to each level in the hierarchy. The system is far more than the aggregate of the electro-mechanical equipment found at the individual nodes. The peculiarities of the communication network, and the human decisionmakers underlie the measures of system effectiveness. To be able to predict performance a detailed model of the explicator block of a human decisionmaker operating in a multimodal environment is required. To quantify this, the decisionmaker is assumed to mentally decompose his environment with a hierarchical macro-micro partition, and to infer his current situation within this framework. Since his observations are ambiguous and cluttered, he is never completely sure of his current status, but he can deduce relative likelihoods.

The MDDM has a form that is closely related to those developed by other investigators. It is the higher level portion of the model (the SHEM) which displays peculiar human idiosyncracies. The model is anthropomorphic, and modulates the lower level model (the micromodel) in a novel but broadly interpretable manner. It satisfies the basic requirements for a useful model of a human (operator) model; i.e.,

1. Represents human input-output behavior

2. Is applicable to a wide range of realistic (not artificial) tasks.

3. Is predictive.

4. Presents a common representation for novice through expert skill levels.

5. Has an efficient computer implementation.

Although the fundamental features of the micromodel are intuitive, the detailed structure is not so simply elucidated. The principal characteristics of the conditional moments are hidden by the number and convoluted form of the stochastic differential equations. As this work progresses, the model will be simplified and made more readily interpretable.

REFERENCES

1. A.H. Levis, and M. Athans, "The Quest for a C³ Theory: Dreams and Realities," *1987 Symposium on Command and Control Research*, Aug 1987.

2. *Summer Study 1985*, Eastport Study Group, December 1985.

3. H.L. Van Trees, "Keynote Address," *Proc. for Quantitative Assessment of Utility of Command and Control Systems*, National Defense Univ., Jan. 1980.

4. M. Athans, "Command and Control (C2) Theory: A Challenge to Control Science," *IEEE Trans. on Automatic Control*, Vol AC-32 April 1987, pp. 286-293.

5. J.G. Wohl, "Human Decision Processes in Military Command and Control," *Advances in Man-Machine Systems Research*, Vol. 1, 1984, pp. 261-307.

6. G.A. Clapp, "The Impact of Communications on C3I Technology Investment in the 21st Century Navy," *Proc. of MILCOM 88*, Oct. 1988.

7. *Proc. of the 1987 IST BM/C3 Workshop*, Institute for Defence Analysis, Alexandria VA, November, 1987.

8. L. Ingber, "Mathematic Comparison of Computer-Models to Exercise Data: Comparison of Janus(T) to National Training Center Data," *Proc. of the 1988 Symposium on Command and Control Research*, (Monterey, CA, June 1988), 541-549.

9. J. Callan, et al., "Patterns of Information Use and Performance in Outer-Air Battle Decision Making," *Proc. of the 1990 Symposium on Command and Control Research*, (Monterey, CA, June 1990), 183-187.

10. B. Feher, "A Longitudinal Multi-Method Approach to Command and Decision Making," *Proc. of the 1990 Symposium on Command and Control Research*, (Monterey, CA, June 1990), 124-128.

11. P. Mutcher, DWS- A DARPA Experiment in Distributed Wargaming," *Proc. of the 1990 Symposium on Command and Control Research*, (Monterey, CA, June 1990), 188-193.

12. M.D. Cohen, et al., "Research Needs and the Phenomena of Decisionmaking and Operations," *IEEE Trans. on Systems, Man and Cybernetics*, Vol. SMC-15,6, November 1985, 764-772.

13. A.B Carter, "Directed Energy in Missile Defense," OTA Background Paper, April 1984.

14. *Report to Congress on the Strategic Defense Initiative*, 1985.

15. G.J. Church, "High-Tech Horror," *Time*, July 18,1988,pp 17.

16. J.A. Welch, "State of the Art of C2 Assessment," *Proc. for Quantitative Assessment of Utility of Command and Control Systems*, National Defense Univ., Jan. 1980.

17. J.W. Wohl, "Force Management Requirements for Air Force Tactical Command and Control," *IEEE Trans. on Systems, Man and Cybernetics*, Vol. SMC-11 Sept. 1981, PP 618-639.

18. L. Ingber and D.D. Sworder, "Statistical Mechanics of Combat with Human Factors," *Mathematical Computer Modelling*, 1991 (to appear).

19. S. Baron, "A Control Theoretic Approach to Modelling the Human Supervisory Control of Dynamic Systems," *Advances in Man Machine Systems*, W.B. Rouse, Ed. Vol. 1, 1984.

20. L. Ingber, "Mathematical Comparison of Combat Models to Exercise Data," *Proc. of the 1989 Symposium on Command and Control Research*, (Washington D.C., June 1989),169-182.

21. P.L. Ligomenides, "Real-Time Capture of Experiential Knowledge," *IEEE Trans. on Systems, Man, and Cybernetics*, Vol. SMC-18, July 1988, 542-551.

22. A.P. Sage, "Human Information Processing Principles for Command and Control," *AFCEA Magazine: Principles of Command and Control*, Vol. 6, AFCEA Press, 1987, pp 54-74.

23. R.G. Elliott, *Stochastic Calculus and Applications*, Springer-Verlag, New York, 1982.

24. R. Mallubhatla et al., "A Normative-Descriptive Model for a Team in a Distributed Detection Environment," *Proc. of the 1989 Symposium on Command and Control Research*, (Washington, D.C., June 1989), 255-263.

25. D.D. Sworder and K. S. Haaland, "Algorithms for Design of Teleoperated Systems," in *Control and Dynamic Systems, Advances in Theory and Applications*, Vol. 30, Part 3, Academic Press, Inc., New York, (1989),167-215.

26. D.D. Sworder and K. S. Haaland, "A Hypothesis Evaluation Model for Human Operators," *IEEE Trans. on Systems, Man and Cybernetics*, Vol. SMC-19, 4, September 1989, 1091-1100.

27. D.D. Sworder and K.S. Haaland, "Human Response Models for Interpretive Tasks," in *Control and Dynamic Systems, Advances in Theory and Applications*, Vol. 33, Pt.3,, Academic Press, Inc., New York. (1990), 35-57.

28. D.D. Sworder, *Control Model for an Adaptive Communications Processor*, Final Technical Report to Naval Oceans System Center, D.O. No. 0052, November 1990.

INDEX